MW00572765

8th Edition

A History of Civilization

Volume A: Prehistory to 1300

ROBIN W. WINKS

CRANE BRINTON

JOHN B. CHRISTOPHER

ROBERT LEE WOLFF

Prentice Hall, Englewood Cliffs, New Jersey 07632

Library of Congress Cataloging-in-Publication Data

A History of civilization / Robin H. Winks ... [et al.].—8th ed.
    p.   cm.
    Includes bibliographical references and indexes.
    Contents: v. A. Prehistory to 1300—v. B. 1300–1815—v. C.
1815 to the present.
    ISBN 0-13-393166-8 : —ISBN 0-13-393174-9 : —
ISBN 0-13-393133-1 :
    1. Civilization—History.   I. Winks, Robin W.
CB69.H58   1992
909′.1—dc20   91-25025
                                           CIP

Dedicated to historians
and those who enjoy history everywhere

Acquisitions Editor: *Steve Dalphin*
Editorial/production supervision: *Marina Harrison*
Copyeditor: *Ann Hofstra Grogg*
Designer: *Anne T. Bonanno*
Cover Designer: *Lydia Gershey*
Photo Editor: *Lori Morris-Nantz*
Photo Researcher: *Joelle Burrows*
Cover Photo: *Rodin,* **The Thinker. Photograph from Art Resource, N.Y.**
Page Layout: *Jayne Conte*
Prepress Buyer: *Kelly Behr*
Manufacturing Buyer: *Mary Ann Gloriande*
Supplements Editor: *Sharon Chambliss*
Editorial Assistant: *Caffie Risher*

© 1992, 1988, 1984, 1976, 1971, 1967, 1960, 1955 by Prentice-Hall, Inc.
A Simon & Schuster Company
Englewood Cliffs, New Jersey 07632

All rights reserved. No part of this book may be
reproduced, in any form or by any means,
without permission in writing from the publisher.

Printed in the United States of America

10 9 8 7 6 5 4 3 2 1

ISBN   0-13-393166-8

Prentice-Hall International (UK) Limited, *London*
Prentice-Hall of Australia Pty. Limited, *Sydney*
Prentice-Hall Canada Inc., *Toronto*
Prentice-Hall Hispanoamericana, S.A., *Mexico*
Prentice-Hall of India Private Limited, *New Delhi*
Prentice-Hall of Japan, Inc., *Tokyo*
Simon & Schuster Asia Pte. Ltd., *Singapore*
Editora Prentice-Hall do Brasil, Ltda., *Rio de Janeiro*

Contents

3
The Romans 67

4
Judaism and Christianity 97

5
The Early Middle Ages in Western Europe 124

6
Byzantium and Islam 153

Boxes

Maps

THE NEW YORK TIMES and PRENTICE HALL are sponsoring A CONTEMPORARY VIEW: a program designed to enhance student access to current information of relevance in the classroom.

Through this program, the core subject matter provided in the text is supplemented by a collection of time-sensitive articles from one of the world's most distinguished newspapers, THE NEW YORK TIMES. These articles demonstrate the vital, ongoing connection between what is learned in the classroom and what is happening in the world around us.

To enjoy the wealth of information of THE NEW YORK TIMES daily, a reduced subscription rate is available in deliverable areas. For information, call toll-free: 1-800-631-1222.

PRENTICE HALL and THE NEW YORK TIMES are proud to co-sponsor A CONTEMPORARY VIEW. We hope it will make the reading of both textbooks and newspapers a more dynamic, involving process.

Preface

Each generation will write its own history and will find that the present is best decoded by different approaches to the past. By the end of World War II Americans found that they were expected to be the leaders of "the West"—which was generally taken to mean, of Western civilization—and they extended their study of history to include non-Western societies in Africa and Asia, both because these societies deserved to be studied for their own sake, and also as a simple matter of prudence. Diplomatic history moved into the space often reserved for political or administrative history, and intellectual history (most especially the history of art and of thought) also became both important and popular—which are not the same thing. As a result, a textbook used by thousands of readers in hundreds of schools, colleges, and universities, known familiarly as "Brinton, Christopher, Wolff," went through periodic revision to keep pace with changing expectations.

The 1970s and 1980s saw the most exceptional array of changes in the discipline of history since the nineteenth century—changes both in the way people think about history and in our knowledge of its content. Economic and intellectual history have been transformed, and social history has altered our entire way of looking at ourselves and at our past. Historical scholarship must now embrace statistics, psychohistory, geography, and the arguments usually reserved to political science, sociology, and anthropology. Yet the historian and the student must not forget that the purpose of history is to explain how we came to be as we are: why we find ourselves in our present predicaments, how we achieved our present triumphs, how we have developed across centuries through a *process* to a specific point in time—*our* specific point in time—when a savage light known as the present beats down upon us.

This new edition, now Winks, Brinton, Christopher, and Wolff, is three things at once. It is, first, a body of information, argument, and interpretation that is meant to help the reader understand humanity's long search for security, for meaning, for purpose in life. Second, it is a book by which students may locate themselves in time, decoding in their own way the relevance of the past for the present. And third, it is a document that demonstrates the state of historical learning at the level of broad generalization and for the broadest general need in the early 1990s. Thus, this text is intended to preserve the great strengths in the breadth, depth, and grasp of the original editions of Brinton, Christopher, and Wolff, retaining for these distinguished authors their many loyal readers, while also reflecting the new trends in the study of history.

This, the eighth edition, reflects the continued evolution of historical study. There is substantially more on social history, on how people lived—how they ate, and gave birth, and died; how they worked and dreamed, succeeded and failed—and on what they thought about their lives. Chapters on Greece and Rome, on Byzantium, and on the Middle Ages, have been altered, as has much of the material on relatively recent events. Nineteenth-century imperialism has received added emphasis, the causes of the two World Wars have been reexamined, and material on developments since World War II has been brought up to date in the context of more recent historical interpretations. The world-altering events of 1990 have also been added.

A new feature, outlines at the beginning of the chapter, includes dates in order to provide a simplified overview of a particular historical terrain before elaborating on its detail. But the most obvious change to one familiar with most earlier editions will be two new elements: brief boxed-off sections throughout the text that provide selections from sources and documents contemporary with the events in the text, or that discuss matters of cultural and historiographic interest; and short summaries at the end of each chapter designed to recapitulate major ideas and events.

A particular effort has been made to tie the illustrations closely to the text through captions that explain and put in context the works illustrated as well as identifying them. All maps have been updated and revised with the intention of including every place name mentioned in the text. The Suggested Readings that appear at the end of each volume have been redone so as to include the most recent scholarship and to enable readers to move beyond the text as their interests dictate. In an effort to make the index more useful, the major discussion for each entry has been printed in **boldface** type. The index has been expanded to include concepts as well as events and to provide a pronunciation guide for foreign or difficult names of persons and places.

Much appreciated criticism and guidance was provided by the following reviewers, who saw rough drafts of the manuscript: Elizabeth Carney, Clemson University; Charmarie Blaisdell, Northeastern University; Charles Connell, West Virginia University; Donald Frank, Long Island University; John B. Freed, Illinois State University; Tom Hachey, Marquette University; David Lukowitz, Hamline University; John Nichols, Slippery Rock University; Perry M. Rogers, Ohio State University; and Linda Taber, University of Iowa.

History cannot be told simply in chronological form, for it is necessary at times to carry a particular story forward for purposes of continuity, and then to double back, returning to an earlier time to pick up a different thread. This means that there are occasions, though not many, when a reader may meet a figure briefly in one context, only to encounter that figure again in greater depth later. The index, and in particular the boldface entries in it, have been developed so that the student can quickly find other strands of the same story as needed.

History is a narrative, a story; history is concerned foremost with major themes, even as it recognizes the significance of many fascinating digressions. Because history is largely about how and why people behave as they do, it is also about patterns of thought and belief. Ultimately, history is about what people believe to be true. To this extent, virtually all history is intellectual history, for the perceived meaning of a specific treaty, battle, or scientific discovery lies in what those involved in it and those who came after thought was most significant about it. History makes it clear that we may die, as we may live, as a result of what someone believed to be true in the relatively remote past.

A History of Civilization is about how we, as readers studying the past through the traditions and biases of the West, have come to think about civilization. Neither the title nor the content is meant to imply that there are not equally complex, challenging, and productive civilizations elsewhere. But we must recognize, even as material relating to the Far East, South Asia, or Africa is incorporated into the present edition, that we read history to understand *our own* ancient beginnings (Volume I) or *our* modern heritage (Volume II). Though this is our primary reason for studying Western civilization, we must also recognize that it is impossible to do justice to all civilizations in a single text. If these volumes enable us to understand history as a process, and if they illustrate the methodology of history, then they will surely lead us to appreciate other civilizations as well. The text is, therefore, implicitly and on occasion explicitly comparative. Western civilization may not be

typical, nor need we conclude that our ways are either "right" or "wrong" simply because they are ours and are known to us. They are the views by which we perceive our world; they are the windows on the world that our own historical experience has opened for us. And since Western societies have had so great an impact on the non-Western world in recent centuries, there is a sense in which world history is also quite legitimately viewed through the windows of Western history.

We cannot each be our own historian. In everyday life we may reconstruct our personal past, acting as detectives for our motivations and attitudes. But formal history is a much more rigorous study. History may give us some very small capacity to predict the future. More certainly, it should help us arrange the causes for given events into meaningful patterns. History also should help us be tolerant of the historical views of others, even as it helps to shape our own convictions. History must help us sort out the important from the less important, the relevant from the irrelevant, so that we do not fall prey to those who propose simple-minded solutions to vastly complex human problems. We must not yield to the temptation to blame one group or individual for our problems, and yet we must not fail to defend our convictions with vigor.

To recognize, indeed to celebrate, the equality of all civilizations is essential to the civilized life itself. To understand that we see all civilizations through the prism of our specific historical past—for which we feel affection, in which we feel comfortable and secure, and by which we interpret all else that we encounter—is simply to recognize that we too are the products of history. That is why we must study history and ask our own questions in our own way. For if we ask no questions of our past, there may be no questions to ask of our future.

Robin W. Winks
For the Eighth Edition

The Value of History

History is a series of arguments to be debated, not a body of data to be recorded or a set of facts to be memorized. Thus controversy in historical interpretation—over what an event actually means, over what really happened at an occurrence called "an event," over how best to generalize about the event—is at the heart of its value. Of course history teaches us about ourselves. Of course it teaches us to understand and to entertain a proper respect for our collective past. Of course it transmits to us specific skills—how to ask questions, how to seek out answers, how to think logically, cogently, lucidly, purposefully. Of course it is, or ought to be, a pleasure. But we also discover something fundamental about a people in what they choose to argue over in their past. When a society suppresses portions of its past record, as the Soviet Union did until recently, that society (or its leadership) tells us something about itself. When a society seeks to alter how the record is presented, well-proven facts notwithstanding, we learn how history can be distorted to political ends.

Who controls history, and how it is written, controls the past, and who controls the past controls the present. Those who would close off historical controversy with the argument either that we know all that we need to know about a subject, or that what we know is so irrefutably correct that anyone who attacks the conventional wisdom about the subject must have destructive purposes in mind, is in the end intent upon destroying the very value of history itself—that value being that history teaches us to argue productively with each other.

Obviously, then, history is a social necessity. It gives us our identity. It helps us to find our bearings in an ever more complex present, providing us with a navigator's chart by which we may to some degree orient ourselves. When we ask who we are, and how is it that we are so, we learn skepticism and acquire the beginnings of critical judgment. Along with a sense of narrative, history also provides us with tools for explanation and analysis. It helps us to find the particular example, to see the uniqueness in a past age or past event, while also helping us to see how the particular and the unique contribute to the general. History thus shows us humanity at work and play, in society, changing through time. By letting us experience other lifestyles, history shows us the values of both subjectivity and objectivity—those twin conditions of our individual view of the world in which we live, conditions between which we constantly, and usually almost without knowing it, move. Thus, history is both a form of truth and a matter of opinion, and the close study of history should help us to distinguish between the two. It is important to make

such distinctions, for as Sir Walter Raleigh wrote, "It is not truth but opinion that can travel the world without a passport." Far too often what we read and believe to be truth—in our newspapers, on our television sets, from our friends—is opinion, not fact.

History is an activity. That activity asks specific questions as a means of arriving at general questions. A textbook such as this is concerned overwhelmingly with general questions, even though at times it must ask specific questions or present specific facts as a means of stalking the general. The great philosopher Karl Jaspers once remarked, "Who I am and where I belong, I first learned to know from the mirror of history." It is this mirror which any honest textbook must reflect.

To speak of "civilization" (of which this book is a history) is at once to plunge into controversy, so that our very first words illustrate why some people are so fearful of the study of history. To speak of "Western civilization" is even more restrictive, too limited in the eyes of some historians. Yet if we are to understand history as a process, we must approach it through a sense of place: our continuity, our standards, our process. Still, we must recognize an inherent bias in such a term as "Western civilization," indeed two inherent biases: first, that we know what it means to be "civilized" and have attained that stature; and second, that the West as a whole is a single unitary civilization. This second bias is made plain when we recognize that most scholars and virtually all college courses refer not to "Eastern civilization" but to "the civilizations of the East"—a terminology that suggests that while the West is a unity, the East is not. These are conventional phrases, buried in our Western perception of reality, just as our common geographical references show a Western bias. The Near East or the Far East are, after all, "near" or "far" only in reference to a geographical location focused on western Europe. The Japanese do not refer to London as being in the far West, or Los Angeles as being in the far East, though both references would be correct, if they saw the world as though they stood at its center. Though this text will accept these conventional phrases, precisely because they are traditionally embedded in our Western languages, one of the uses of history—and of the study of a book such as this one—is to alert us to the biases buried in our language, even when necessity requires that we continue to use its conventional forms of shorthand.

But if we are to speak of civilization, we must have, at the outset, some definition of what we mean by "being civilized." Hundreds of books have been written on this subject. The average person often means only that others, the "noncivilized," speak a different language and practice alien customs. The Chinese customarily referred to all foreigners as barbarians, and the ancient Greeks spoke of those who could not communicate in Greek as *bar-bar*—those who do not speak our tongue. Yet today the ability to communicate in more than one language is one hallmark of a "civilized" person. Thus definitions of civilization, at least as used by those who think little about the meaning of their words, obviously change.

For our purposes, however, we must have a somewhat more exacting definition of the term, since it guides and shapes any textbook that attempts to cover the entire sweep of Western history. Anthropologists, sociologists, historians, and others may reasonably differ about the essential ingredients of a civilization. They may also differ as to whether, for example, there is a separate American civilization that stands apart from, say a British or Italian civilization, or whether these civilizations are simply particular variants on one larger entity, with only that larger entity—the West—entitled to be called "a civilization." Such an argument is of no major importance here, although it is instructive that it should occur. Rather, what is needed is a definition sufficiently clear to be used throughout the narrative and analysis to follow. This working definition, therefore, will hold that "civilization" involves the presence of several (though not necessarily all) of the following conditions within a society or group of interdependent societies:

1. There will be some form of government by which people administer to their political needs and responsibilities.

2. There will be some development of urban society, that is, of city life, so that the culture is not nomadic, dispersed, and thus unable to leave significant and surviving physical remnants of its presence.

3. Human beings will have become toolmakers, able through the use of metals to transform, however modestly, their physical environment, and thus their social and economic environment as well.

4. Some degree of specialization of *function* will have begun, usually at the work place, so that pride, place, and purpose work together as cohesive elements in the society.

5. Social classes will have emerged, whether antagonistic to or sustaining of one another.

6. A form of literacy will have developed, so that group may communicate with group, and more important, generation with generation in writing.

7. There will be a concept of leisure time—that life is not solely for the work place, or for the assigned class function or specialization—so that, for example, art may develop beyond (though not excluding) mere decoration and sports beyond mere competition.

8. There will be a concept of a higher being, though not necessarily through organized religion, by which a people may take themselves outside themselves to explain events and find purpose.

9. There will be a concept of time, by which the society links itself to a past and to the presumption of a future.

10. There will have developed a faculty for criticism. This faculty need not be the rationalism of the West, or intuition, or any specific religious or political mechanism, but it must exist, so that the society may contemplate change from within, rather than awaiting attack (and possible destruction) from without.

A common Western bias is to measure "progress" through technological change and to suggest that societies that show (at least until quite recently in historical time) little dramatic technological change are not civilized. In truth, neither a written record nor dramatic technological changes are essential to being civilized, though both are no doubt present in societies we would call civilized. Perhaps, as we study history, we ought to remember all *three* of the elements inherent in historical action as recorded by the English critic John Ruskin: "Great nations write their autobiographies in three manuscripts, the book of their deeds, the book of their words, and the book of their art."

The issue here is not whether we "learn from the past." Most often we do not, at least at the simpleminded level; we do not, as a nation, decide upon a course of action in diplomacy, for example, simply because a somewhat similar course in the past worked. We are wise enough to know that circumstances alter cases and that new knowledge brings new duties. Of course individuals "learn from the past"; the victim of a purse snatching takes precautions in the future. To dignify such an experience as "a lesson of history," however, is to turn mere individual growth from child into adult into history when, at most, such growth is a personal experience in biography.

We also sometimes learn the "wrong lessons" from history. Virtually anyone who wishes to argue passionately for a specific course of future action can find a lesson from the past that will convince the gullible that history repeats itself and therefore that the past is a map to the future. No serious historian argues this, however. General patterns may, and sometimes do, repeat themselves, but specific chains of events do not. Unlike those subjects that operate at the very highest level of generalization (political science, theology, science), history simply does not believe in ironclad laws. But history is not solely a series of unrelated events. There are general patterns, clusters of causes, intermediate levels of generalization that prove true. Thus, history works at a level uncomfortable to many: above the specific, below the absolute.

If complex problems never present themselves twice in the same or even in recognizably similar form—if, to borrow a frequent image from the military world, generals always prepare for the last war instead of the next one—then does the study of history offer society any help in solving its problems? The answer surely is yes—but only in a limited way. History offers a rich collection of clinical reports on human behavior in various situations—individual and collective, political, economic, military, social, cultural—that tell us in detail how the human race has conducted its affairs and that suggest ways of handling similar problems in the present. President Harry S Truman's secretary of state, a former chief of staff, General George Marshall, once remarked that nobody could think about the problems of the 1950s who had not reflected upon the fall of Athens in the fifth century B.C. He was referring to the extraordinary history of the war between Athens and Sparta written just after it was over by Thucydides, an Athenian who fought in the war. There were no nuclear weapons, no telecommunications, no guns or gunpowder in the fifth century B.C.; the logistics of the war were altogether primitive, yet twenty-three hundred years later one of the most distinguished leaders of American military and political affairs found Thucydides indispensable to his thinking.

History, then, can only approximate the range of human behavior, with some indication of its extremes and averages. It can, though not perfectly, show how and within what limits human behavior changes. This last point is especially important for the social scientist, the economist, the sociologist, the executive, the journalist, or the diplomat. History provides materials that even an inspiring leader—a prophet, a reformer, a politician—would do well to master before seeking to lead us into new ways. For it can tell us something about what human material can and cannot stand, just as science and technology can tell engineers what stresses metals can tolerate. History can provide an awareness of the depth of time and space that should check the optimism and the overconfidence of the reformer. For example, we may wish to protect the environment in which we live—to eliminate acid rain, to cleanse our rivers, to protect our wildlife, to preserve our majestic natural scenery. History may show us that most peoples have failed to do so, and may provide us with some guidance on how to avoid the mistakes of the past. But history will also show that there are substantial differences of public and private opinion over how best to protect our environment; or that there are many people who do not believe such protection is necessary; or that there are people who accept the need for protection but are equally convinced that lower levels of protection must be traded off for higher levels of productivity from our natural resources. History can provide the setting by which we may understand differing opinions, but recourse to history will not get the legislation passed, make the angry happy, make the future clean and safe. History will not define river pollution, though it can provide us with statistics from the past for comparative

measurement. The definition will arise from the politics of today and our judgments about tomorrow. History is for the long and at times for the intermediate run, but seldom for the short run.

So, if we are willing to accept a "relevance" that is more difficult to see at first than the immediate applicability of science and more remote than direct action, we will have to admit that history is "relevant." It may not actually build the highway or clear the slum, but it can give enormous help to those who wish to do so. And failure to take it into account may lead to failure in the sphere of action.

But history is also fun, at least for those who enjoy giving their curiosity free rein. Whether it is historical gossip we prefer (How many lovers did Catherine the Great of Russia actually take in a given year, and how much political influence did their activity in the imperial bedroom give them?), or the details of historical investigation (How does it happen that the actual treasures found in a buried Viking ship correspond to those described in an Anglo-Saxon poetic account of a ship-burial?), or more complex questions of cause and effect (How influential have the writings of revolutionary intellectuals been upon the course of actual revolutions?), or the relationships between politics and economics (How far does the rise and decline of Spanish power in modern times depend upon the supply of gold from the New World colonies?), or cultural problems (Why did western Europe choose to revive classical Greek and Roman art and literature instead of turning to some other culture or to some altogether new experiment?), those who enjoy history will read almost greedily to discover what they want to know. Having discovered it, they may want to know how we know what we have learned, and may want to turn to those sources closest in time to the persons and questions concerned—to the original words of the participants. To read about Socrates, Columbus, or Churchill is fun; to read their *own* words, to visit with them as it were, is even more so. To see them in context is important; to see how we have taken their thoughts and woven them to purposes of our own is at least equally important. Readers will find the path across the mine-studded fields of history helped just a little by extracts from these voices—voices of the past but also of the present. They can also be helped by outlines, summaries, bibliographies, pictures, maps—devices through which historians share their sense of fun and immediacy with a reader.

In the end, to know the past *is to know ourselves*—not entirely, not enough, but a little better. History can help us to achieve some grace and elegance of action, some cogency and completion of thought, some harmony and tolerance in human relationships. Most of all, history can give us a sense of excitement, a personal zest for watching and perhaps participating in the events around us which will, one day, be history too.

1

The First Civilizations

Within the lifetime of people now only in their thirties, archaeology, with new tools supplied by other sciences, has revolutionized what we know about the remote past of our earth and the people who live on it. Discoveries continue at a rapid pace. In the 1950s and 1960s no one could have made many of the major statements in this chapter. By the year 2000 our successors will have learned enough that is new to dispute what we say here. Archaeology is, once again, at the cutting edge (as well as the beginning) of what we know about our past.

I BEFORE WRITING

History and Prehistory

It may seem strange that our concepts of the distant past are changing much faster than our concepts of the periods closer to us in time. But when we consider the means by which we know about the past, we can quickly see that this is entirely natural. If we want to know about something that happened, let us say, during the American Revolution, we have the letters of George Washington and his contemporaries, the written records of the British government that tried to suppress the American colonists' rebellion, the proceedings of the Continental Congress, the Declaration of Independence, and literally thousands of other written sources—diaries, memoirs, documents, newspapers, propaganda leaflets—that open to us the minds of the people of that time and enable us to work out for ourselves what most probably happened. When we cannot go directly to these sources for history, we have hundreds of books written since the events of the Revolution by historians who have been interested in it and who have set down their views of what happened for us to accept, challenge, and consider. New sources of information may be discovered and fresh light thrown on some event we thought we understood; we may find out that Paul Revere's teacher at school had been reading radical pamphlets (something that previous students had not known) and that this helped prepare Paul as a youth for his famous ride. But the new sources probably would not force us to reject or even to reconsider all that we had learned before they were discovered.

Most of the sources we would read about the American Revolution would be written in English. If we wanted to find out about the part played by Lafayette and Rochambeau, we would soon find ourselves compelled to read documents in French. If we asked ourselves why a Pole, Tadeusz Kościuszko, joined the American side, we might have to learn Polish and Russian and German to find out. If we were interested in the ideas of Thomas Jefferson, we would have to study several of his favorite classical authors, who wrote in Greek or Latin, and though we could find translations, we might feel it important to read them as Jefferson did, in the original. But whatever the problems of learning languages or of trying to decide which of two contradictory accounts of the same event to accept, we would be dealing with abundant written sources in languages that someone among us knows how to read.

Even for events that took place two thousand years before the American Revolution, or for truly obscure occurrences, or for events that took place in Europe or Asia, we would still usually have written sources in a language of the time and place: Persian, Sanskrit, Greek, Latin, or perhaps Chinese, sometimes fragmentary instead of full, sometimes too biased to be reliable, but written. Where possible we would supplement these sources with other evidence: coins with pictures or inscriptions on them that might tell us of matters we could not find out any other way; statues, paintings, poems, or songs of the age that might reflect the attitudes of artists and their society more surely than a document; indeed, any remnant that we could find from the period and the place to supplement our written sources.

But suppose our written sources are written in a language that no one can read? Or suppose we have no written sources at all? As we move backward in time through human history these problems confront us more and more urgently. Over the last couple of centuries the discovery of texts written in both a known and a previously unknown language has enabled scholars to read the language of the Egyptians and those of the peoples of the ancient Mesopotamian river valleys

Prehistory Chronology	
Years B.C.	
Food-Gathering Peoples	
1,000,000 and before	Australopithicenes
400,000	Homo erectus
110,000	Neanderthal man
35,000	Homo sapiens
28,000	Beginning of cave painting
18,000	Preagricultural revolution
10,000	Retreat of glaciers
Food-Raising Era	
8000	Essentially modern climate
7000	Agricultural villages in Near East Civilization
Just before	Cities of Mesopotamia
3000	Kingdom of Egypt

SOURCE: Chester G. Starr, *Early Man: Prehistory and the Civilizations of the Ancient Near East* (Oxford: Oxford University Press, 1973), p. 4. Copyright © 1973 by Oxford University Press, Inc. Reprinted by permission.

in the Near East. Brilliant use of the techniques of cryptography in the 1950s cracked one of the two scripts commonly used in ancient Crete and on the Greek mainland. Nonetheless an even earlier Cretan script still remains to be convincingly deciphered. Much work must still be done before scholars can confidently read Etruscan—the language, written in Greek letters, of the people who ruled in Italy before the Romans.

People lived on earth for many thousands of years before they learned to write at all. Only their skeletons, the bones of animals, and some of the things they made remain to tell us about the first humans. They are our only sources. Recent developments in science—especially the carbon-14 technique whereby radioactive carbon is used to date ancient objects within a couple of centuries—have helped straighten out chronology. But scholars will continue to find new objects and new ways of dating them that will enable our successors to write with more certainty than we can about our earliest ancestors.

The Old Stone Age

In the seventeenth century Archbishop James Ussher (1581–1656) of the Church of England carefully worked out from data given in the Bible what he believed to be the precise date of the creation of the world by God. It was, he said, 4004 B.C. Adding the sixteen hundred or so years since the birth of Christ, he concluded that the earth was then under six thousand years old. We smile now at the generations that accepted Ussher's views—although nearly everyone did so until the nineteenth century—because we now believe that the earth is billions of years old and that organic life may go back several billion years.

Beginning in 1951, a series of archaeological digs in equatorial east-central Africa in and around Olduvai Gorge turned up fragments of a small creature that lived between 19 and 14 million years ago, for convenience called *Kenyapithecus* (Kenya ape), who seems to have made crude tools. Kenya ape may not be a direct human ancestor, but like us may have branched off from a primate 10 million years older still, and yet more primitive. By about 2 million years ago a creature more like our ideas of humankind had made its appearance *Homo habilis* (the skillful one). A mere quarter of a million years later came *Zinjanthropus*, who was perhaps related to a humanlike animal about the size of a chimpanzee, though with a larger brain, called *Australopithecus*, a term derived from Greek and meaning "southern ape." *Australopithecus* may have been a vegetarian (to judge by its teeth) and seems to have ceased evolving and come to a dead end, while *Homo habilis*, who ate meat, continued to evolve in the direction of the biologically modern human, *Homo sapiens* (the one who knows). All these humanlike animals had larger skulls with more brain than the apes had. In another three-quarters of a million years (approximately a million years ago), *Homo habilis* began to look like a being long

known as Java man, who lived about 700,000 B.C. First found in Java in the late 1880s, *Pithecanthropus erectus* (ape-man that walks erect) is now termed *Homo erectus*. A somewhat later stage is represented by Peking man of about 500,000 B.C., who advanced well beyond *Homo habilis*.

We need to know more about the stages by which *Homo erectus* evolved into *Homo sapiens*, who appeared first in Europe only about thirty-seven thousand years ago. *Homo sapiens* came upon a land of forests and plains that had already been occupied for perhaps a hundred thousand years by another *Homo erectus*, Neanderthal man, named for the Rhineland valley where its remains were first discovered but spread far more widely. Probably far less apelike than the traditional reconstructions of its skull have portrayed, Neanderthal man was apparently capable of thought as we understand the term. We cannot yet locate Neanderthals accurately on a hypothetical family tree, but they probably represent another offshoot from the main trunk.

Neanderthal culture was based on hunting and food gathering. They possessed stone tools and weapons, apparently cooked their meat (their predecessors ate it raw), wore skins, and commemorated their dead through ritual burials. However, what we know remains sophisticated guesswork, based on sixty-eight specific sites. Unless scholars can prevent the destruction of these and other archaeological locations, we may never have satisfactory scientific answers to such questions as: What do we mean by "human" in such a context? Does the size of the brain—customarily used to denote evolution—really tell us much about how humans came to use tools and develop a desire for decoration? There is no point at which "humans appeared" on earth, though for convenience we generally accept *Homo sapiens*—the "wise one," or "one who knows," which implies "one who thinks"—as a convenient point of departure.

We know so little about what was happening during those hundreds of thousands of years that for the historian (as distinguished from the anthropologist) almost all of this time belongs to *prehistory*—that is, history before humanity left written records. During those long, long centuries the advance of the human animal was enormously slow. The first real tools were stones that were used to chip other stones into useful instruments. And it was by those stone weapons and tools that early humans lived for hundreds of thousands of years.

Archaeologists have named the early periods of human culture from the materials used for weapons and tools. During the Old Stone (Paleolithic) Age, roughly before 8000 B.C., give or take a few thousand years according to the region being described, people used chipped stone tools. About 8000 B.C. in some places, perhaps much, much earlier in others—archaeologists now suggest there was a preagricultural revolution by prehistoric hunter-gatherers perhaps twenty thousand years ago—and in others much later, the development of farming and the use of more sophisticated stone implements marked the beginning of the New Stone (Neolithic) Age. Then, about 3000 B.C. the invention of bronze (an alloy of copper and tin) led to the Bronze Age and even greater transitions to new forms of human life and society. Still later, further experiments with metals ushered in the Iron Age.

Paleolithic people left remains scattered widely in Europe and Asia and took refuge in Africa from the glaciers that periodically moved south over the northern continents and made life impossible there. Wherever they went, they hunted to eat, and fought and killed their enemies. They learned how to cook their food, how to take shelter from the cold in caves, and eventually how to specialize their tools. They made bone needles with which to sew animal hides into clothes with animal sinews; they made hatchets, spears, arrowheads, and awls.

They also created art. At Lascaux in southwest France and at Altamira in nearby northern Spain, Paleolithic artists left remarkable paintings in limestone caves, using brilliant colors to depict animals important to them: deer, bison, horses. The Lascaux cave paintings, found in 1940, were closed to the public in 1960 to protect them against the thousands of tourists they attracted. They are the most valuable documentation we have on the life of Cro-Magnon men and women, a type of *Homo sapiens* who apparently stood fully erect.

We can only guess why the Paleolithic artist painted the pictures. Did the artist think that putting animals on the walls would lead to better hunting? Would their pictures give the hunters power over them, and so ensure the supply of food? Were the different animals also totems of different families or clans? Sometimes on the walls of the caves we find paintings of human hands, often with a finger or fingers missing. Were these hands simple testimony of appreciation of one of humanity's most extraordinary physical gifts: the hand, with its op-

posable thumb (not found in apes), which made tool making possible? Were they efforts to ward off evil spirits by holding up the palm or making a ritual gesture? Or were they prayers by hunters and warriors to avert the mutilation of their fingers or to retain their strength despite some mutilation that they had already suffered? We do not know.

Besides the cave paintings and Venuses (small female statuettes) and tools, made with such variety and with such increasing skill of manufacture from about 35,000 B.C. to about 8000 B.C., archaeology has yielded a rich variety of other finds, especially concerning the development of the calendar, by which early people could record a sense of time. Bone tools found in Africa and Europe show markings whose sequence and intervals may record lunar periods. Sometimes only one or two lunar months had been observed, sometimes six, sometimes an entire year. Eventually, the Paleolithic craftsman learned to make the notations more complex, sometimes engraving them in a crosshatched pattern that looks like mere decoration until one learns to read it, sometimes adding extra angled marks at important dates.

Once we realize that late Old Stone Age peoples may well have been keeping a kind of calendar to enable them to predict the regular seasonal changes from year to year, and therefore were presumably regulating their hunting life and their other activities, such as the preparation of skins for clothing, we get a new perspective on the quality of their minds and their perception of the importance of time in their life. The new perspective is so vivid that the "mystery" of their extraordinary skills becomes far less mysterious. Where we find on the same piece of Paleolithic ivory from southwest France a budding flower, sprouting plants, grass, snakes, a salmon, and a seal—which appeared in spring in the local riv-

Ancient cave art, not having been exposed to the weather or to vandalism, has survived over thousands of years. One of the greatest series of cave paintings is at Lascaux, in present-day France. This bull from Lascaux was painted on limestone around 12,000 B.C.
Peter Buckley

The Tower of Babel was meant to represent the origins of diverse languages. A tower was said to have been constructed to heaven in ancient Shinar. Here the Flemish artist Pieter Brueghel the Elder uses the tower as a metaphor; he shows it in a sixteenth-century context, as a honeycomb of tiers on which an army of antlike workers swarm, while a nobleman inspects the project.
Kunsthistorisches Museum, Berlin

ers—we may have an object that symbolically represents the earth's reawakening after winter. When such symbols of spring appear with the lunar calendric notation, we are looking at something very like an illustrated calendar.

In the same way, the stone female images may mark the procession of the seasons, of fertility, conception, and birth. Some representations can be interpreted as sacrifices. Certain animals—reindeer, bison, horses—appear on the artifacts associated with females; others—bears and lions—with males. Late Old Stone Age people apparently had a mythology that involved tales of the hunt, successful and unsuccessful; a ritual that involved killing and sacrifice; and a deep awareness of the passing of time in the world around them and in the bodies of animals and of humans. A nude figure of a woman holding a bison horn that looks like a crescent moon and is marked with thirteen lines (the number of lunar months in a year) may be humanity's first recognizable goddess. She may be the forerunner of the bare-breasted Neolithic moon goddess long known as the Mistress of the Animals, who appears with crescent, fish, flower, plant, bird, tree, and snake, and with a consort who plays sun to her moon and hunts the animals of nature and of myth. Though the people of the Old Stone Age remain dim and remote to us, such research for the first time make them more recognizably human.

The New Stone Age

The advance from the Old Stone Age (Paleolithic) to the New (Neolithic) was marked by certain major changes, found first in the Near East. One of these was the domestication of animals for food. Humans had tamed dogs and used them in the hunt long before. But when they kept goats, pigs, sheep, and the ancestors of our cows in pens, they could eat them when their meat was young and tender, without having to hunt them down when they were fully grown. Parallel with this went the first domestication of plants for food—a kind of wheat and barley. Finally—and this always seems to have been the last step—temporary shelter was replaced by houses with some sense of permanence. By making these changes, humanity made the transition to the New Stone Age.

Accompanying these fundamental steps was the practice of a new technology, the baking of clay vessels—pots, bowls, and storage jars—which were much easier to make than stone ones. It is chiefly by studying the surviving varieties of such clay vessels and their fragments, and the types of glazes and decorations the potters used, that modern scholars have been able to date the sites where ancient people lived before writing was developed. Recent excavations in the Near East have pushed back our previous earliest Neolithic dates. With the boundaries between periods thus in flux, it is probably better here not to try to fix any firm boundaries between late Paleolithic and early Neolithic.

At Jericho, in the Jordan Valley, archaeologists have excavated a town radiocarbon-dated at about 7800 B.C. that had extended over about eight acres and included perhaps three thousand inhabitants. These people lived in round houses with conical roofs—the oldest permanent houses known—and they had a large, columned building in which were found many mud-modeled figurines of animals and modeled statues of a man, a woman, and a male child. It was almost surely a temple of some kind. All this dates from a time when people did not yet know how to make pots, which appear only at a later stage. Evidence now suggests that the site was occupied far earlier and then abandoned for reasons not yet understood, then occupied once again in the eleventh century B.C.

In Çatal Hüyük in southern Turkey, discovered in 1961 and dating to 6500 B.C., the people grew their own grain, kept sheep, and wove the wool into textiles. They also had a wide variety of pottery. A sculpture of a female giving birth to a child, a bull's head, boars' heads with women's breasts running in rows along the lower jaws, and many small statuettes were all found together in what we can be sure was a shrine. A bull and a double ax painted on a wall seem to look forward to the main features of a religion of ancient Crete, as we shall see.

Far to the east, in modern Iraq (ancient Mesopotamia, "between the rivers" Tigris and Euphrates), lay Jarmo,

dated about 4500 B.C., another Neolithic settlement. A thousand years later than Jarmo, about 3550 B.C., and far to the south, at Uruk on the banks of the Euphrates River, farmers were using the plow to scratch the soil before sowing their seeds and were already keeping the business accounts of their temple in simple picture writing. This was the great leap forward that took human beings out of prehistory and into history. Similar advances are also found in Egypt at roughly the same time. But archaeology seems to show that Mesopotamia took the lead, and indeed that it was from Mesopotamia that major cultural contributions—especially the all-important art of writing—penetrated into Egypt.

During the 1960s, still farther to the east in various parts of modern Iran, archaeologists found several of these early Neolithic sites, some of which seem to go back in time as far as Jericho or even before—although no city so large or complex has been found from the

Cradles of Civilization

Areas of earliest civilization

Present-day boundaries in color

△ Pleistocene sites

Present-day national place names in color

PLACE NAMES IN HISTORY

The mention here of Uruk provides an opportunity to discuss a special problem in history, namely that places change their names. In the Bible the city called Uruk, its ancient Sumerian name, was referred to as Erech, one of the cities of Nimrod. Today the same location appears on the map as Warka. Geographically each of the three names designates the same place; historically the names indicate different times, just as present-day Leningrad was once the czarist capital of St. Petersburg and may soon be so again.

Furthermore, the choice of a name may suggest acceptance of one position or another in a controversy, as when the British refer to the Falkland Islands, and the Argentines (taking the name from the French) call the same islands Las Malvinas. Throughout this text the place name appropriate to the time under discussion will be used; for example, Russia and the Soviet Union are *not* synonymous terms. Consult a good atlas if you are not sure of how names convey political values. However, where appropriate or essential, the text will refer to changes of name to avoid the more obvious confusions.

Pronunciation is another problem for historians because the same name takes on different pronunciations as languages change. The currently accepted pronunciation will be supplied in the index where it seems necessary. But the authors will assume that readers can pronounce, or by consulting a good dictionary or encyclopaedia can learn the correct pronunciation of names common to Western culture, such as Dante, Goethe, Freud. Any student of history must, therefore, have at hand a good atlas and a substantial dictionary, for no text can adequately substitute for these tools of civilization.

eighth millennium B.C. The sites are scattered, and many of them are located in the highlands, indicating that the Neolithic revolution was not necessarily confined, as had usually been thought, to river valleys. Many of these Iranian discoveries are still unpublished, and much work remains to be done. But from 6000 B.C. there are several sites in northwest Iran rather like Jarmo, giving plenty of evidence of domesticated animals and grains. And even earlier, perhaps around 7000, in southwest Iran very near the Mesopotamian eastern border, there are mud-brick houses and the same clear evidence of goat and sheep raising and cereal cultivation.

In south-central Iran a fresh site was discovered in 1967 at Tepe Yahya, where the earliest settlement in a large earth mound proved to be a Neolithic village of about 4500 B.C. Here, along with the animal bones and cereal remains, archaeologists found in a mud-brick storage area not only pottery and small sharpened flints set in a bone handle to make a sickle but also an extraordinary figurine sculptured of dark green stone, which in both material and subject is more complex than anything found previously. It appears that Tepe Yahya, a center of soapstone manufacturing, served to link Mesopotomia to the cultures of the Indus Valley.

The Neolithic people of the Near East were not necessarily any more intelligent than those elsewhere. Neolithic remains also have been found in many places around the Mediterranean and far to the north, but the climate in those places was far less favorable. Even when Neolithic people managed to triumph over the environment—as in lake settlements in Switzerland, where they built frame houses on piles over the water—the triumph came later (in this case about 2500 B.C.). It was the inhabitants of the more favored regions who got to the great discoveries first. It was they who learned copper smelting and the other arts of metallurgy and who thus led the Stone Age into the Bronze Age. It was they who first lived in cities.

Writing, metallurgy, and urban life are among the early marks of civilization. Soon after these phenomena appeared in the Tigris-Euphrates valleys, along the Nile, and in Iran, they appeared also in the valley of the Indus, along Chinese rivers, in Southeast Asia, and in South and Central America. In North America, too, recent discoveries—first of Folsom man, who made weapons of flint, and now of the great complexities of the Chaco Canyon culture of present-day New Mexico—have carried our knowledge back twenty thousand years and more.

NEW KNOWLEDGE ON OLD EVENTS

A common mistake is the assumption that the interpretation of history changes most dramatically only for recent times, when new archives and new perspectives cause radical rethinking of the meaning of events. The earliest history also has changed in the last decades, as archaeology literally uncovers new evidence about old civilizations. A dramatic example is the discovery of the great city of Ebla, north of present-day Damascus, in Syria. While Italian archaeologists began to dig at the site of Ebla in 1964, not until a decade later did they realize that the site represented one of the largest habitations of the third millennium B.C. With perhaps 260,000 people, Ebla had a royal palace and the oldest known state archive; it was the center of an extensive trading network; and the people of the city apparently spoke a Semitic language, now called Eblaite, previously unknown to scholars. Some sixteen thousand cuneiform tablets, most in fragments, have enabled scholars to learn much more about Sumerian.

As the Akkadian empire expanded, Ebla waned, and it was destroyed around 2250 B.C. Despite being rebuilt at least twice, it was again destroyed. Until our own time, this early center of civilization remained virtually unknown.

History is aided by many other disciplines. Archaeology is only one such discipline, for an understanding of history requires a knowledge of languages, those of the past as well as modern, and a firm grasp of the findings of economists, political scientists, sociologists, and anthropologists. Thus history is a social science as well as one of the humanities.

II   THE VALLEY PEOPLES AND IRAN

Mesopotamia and Elam

Sumerians   The most recent discoveries have led some scholars to believe that the first Mesopotamian inventors of writing may have been a people the later Babylonians called Subarians. Traditionally they came from the north and moved into Uruk in the south. In any case, by about 3100 B.C. they were apparently subjugated in southern Mesopotamia by the Sumerians, whose name became synonymous with the region immediately north of the Persian Gulf, in the fertile lower valleys of the Tigris and Euphrates. Here the Sumerians were already well established by the year 3000. They had invented bronze, an alloy that could be cast in molds, and they made tools and weapons of it. They lived in cities, and they had begun to accumulate and use capital. They apparently turned the Subarians into slaves, and the word took on precise economic and social connotations. Perhaps most important, the Sumerians adapted writing (probably from the Subarians) into a flexible tool of communication.

We have known about the Sumerians for only a bit more than a hundred years. Archaeologists working at Nineveh in northern Mesopotamia in the midnineteenth century found many inscribed clay tablets. Some they could decipher because the language was a Semitic one (Akkadian), on which scholars had already been working for a generation. But other tablets were inscribed in another language that was not Semitic and previously unknown. Because these inscriptions made reference to the king of Sumer and Akkad, a scholar suggested that the new language be called Sumerian.

But it was not until the 1890s that archaeologists digging in city-states well to the south of Nineveh found many thousands of tablets inscribed in Sumerian only. Because the Akkadians thought of Sumerian as a classical language (as we think of Greek or Latin), they taught it to educated persons and they put vocabularies, translation exercises, and other aids to study on tablets. Working from known Akkadian to previously unknown Sumerian, modern scholars since the 1890s have pretty well learned how to read the Sumerian language. Vast quantities of tablets in Sumerian have been unearthed during the intervening years from numerous excavations.

Over the thousand years between 3000 and 2000 B.C., the Sumerians developed a phonetic alphabet. With a reed pen they impressed little wedge-shaped marks into a wet clay tablet, producing a script that we call cuneiform—a script once lost to us and now recovered—from the Latin *cuneus*, meaning "wedge." The first thousand years of Sumerian history we know from tens of thousands of these tablets, which are mostly economic or administrative records. From the second thousand years (after 2000 B.C.) we have five thousand tablets that provide us with purely literary texts, some short, some very long, some not yet transcribed or translated.

The earliest Sumerians governed themselves through a council of elders, who derived their authority in turn from a general assembly of all adult free males. This assembly, which decided on matters of war and peace, sometimes granted supreme authority to one leader for a limited time. This arrangement—which seems "modern" and even "democratic" to us—apparently did not last long and was replaced by one-man rule in each city. But the human ruler acted only as the representative on earth of the god of the city. In this capacity the ruler built temples to the god to keep him appeased and to obtain divine protection against the torrential floods that swept down the river valleys in the springtime, with disastrous results for the people in their way.

The lives and religion and literature of the people of Mesopotamia were pervaded by terror of these floods; the story of Noah and the ark in Genesis echoes the ancient tradition of the Sumerians that told of a single disastrous flood from which only a remnant of the people was saved, and from which (about 2900 B.C.) all subsequent events were dated. The Sumerians devised an elaborate system of canals to irrigate the fields and to control the force of the floods. Toward the south, near the Persian Gulf, the problem also became one of drainage, to halt the inward flow of salt water that would ruin the fields.

By the toil of many centuries, the Sumerians transformed the bleak marshes of the river valleys into fertile farmland, dotted with prosperous cities, each with its own political bureaucracy and religious institutions. As with all human societies, each passed through occasional oppressions, upheavals, and political overturns, many of which are recorded by surviving inscriptions. (The earliest known inscription recording the ambition of one city ruler to dominate the entire region—to be the first "universal" monarch in history—dates from about 2350 B.C.) The Sumerians also had to fight against infiltrating Semites from the Arabian deserts to the west and the hills to the north. They also campaigned eastward against Elam, the peoples living in what today is western Iran.

About 2300, Sargon, king of Akkad, a Semite from the north, conquered the Sumerian ruler of Uruk. Sargon and his successors called themselves kings of Sumer and Akkad, perhaps indicating that a fusion of the non-

This group of Sumerian statuettes was found near modern Baghdad. They are from the temple to the god Abu, lord of vegetation; their height and dress indicate that they represent gods, priests, and worshipers. These Tel Asmar figures date from around 2600 B.C. This collection presents one problem of studying the ancient past, for while the group shown here was meant to be viewed together, the collection is split between the Oriental Institute in Chicago and the Iraq Museum in Baghdad.
The Oriental Institute. University of Chicago

Gudea was ruler of the city of Lagash around 2050 B.C.
Nearly twenty statues of him, dating from the Sumerian
period, provide both artifactual knowledge—that is,
knowledge derived from the physical nature of the object
itself—and historical information, as derived from the
inscription on Gudea's garments.

The Metropolitan Museum of Art, Harris Brisbane Dick Fund, 1959

Semitic Sumerians and the Semitic Akkadians had
begun. By about 2100, when most scholars date the end
of the early Bronze Age, Sargon's descendants had lost
their power, and for a time there was no force to unify
the tiny states.

Taking the lead against invaders, Gudea, ruler of the
city of Lagash, united the Sumerians about 2050 B.C.
Soon after he died, Ur replaced Lagash as the capital
city, and for a century its rulers played the role of uni-

versal monarch. They again called themselves kings of
Sumer and Akkad. Much of what we know about the
Sumerians comes from the systematic excavation of Ur.
More recently, a portion of a series of statutes promul-
gated by the ruler Ur-Nammu (about 2000 B.C.) has been
discovered, providing fixed punishment for certain
crimes, such as a fine of a quantity of silver for the rape
of a virgin slave girl without her owner's consent. Ur-
Nammu is thus the first known true lawgiver for an
entire people, even though he did not propound a systematic code, since its coverage was erratic and concerned with problems of precedents. Ur enjoyed a century of great prosperity based on farflung trade by sea
in textiles and metals, a carefully recorded systematic
tax system, and a revival of learning. But a decline set
in, in part because Ur had taken on too many responsibilities, and outlying cities began to usurp the power
they saw as overly centralized in Ur.

Sumer was a hydraulic society—that is, one based
on the centralized control of irrigation and flood management by government. When its leaders could no
longer demonstrate this control, the compact, agricul-
turally linked city-states began to fragment (as they also
did later, in China and among the Aztecs). Ur's subject
cities fell away; invading Elamites from the east destroyed it. With Ur's destruction and the end of Sumerian power, the center of political might shifted to the
north.

Besides their city gods, the Sumerians worshiped a
god of the heavens, a god of the region between heaven
and earth (the air, hence storms and winds), and a god
of earth. Another trinity included gods of the sun and
moon and a goddess of the morning star, who was also
associated with fertility. With this female deity was associated a young male god who died and was reborn
as a symbol of the seasons.

Here, in the first religion recorded in sources that
we can read and therefore interpret more fully than
those based on oral tradition, we find elements common to all subsequent human efforts to deal with the
concept of a higher being or beings. For instance, it was
Enki, god of earth and of wisdom, who poured water
into the two great fertilizing rivers, Tigris and Euphrates,
and stocked them with fish; who created grain, filled
the land with cattle, built houses and canals, and set
subgods over each enterprise.

The Sumerian gods were portrayed in human form
and lived recognizably human lives, with rivalries
among themselves. Sumerians also believed in a multitude of demons. From the beginning, they used various arts to foretell the future. The entrails of slaughtered sheep or goats were carefully observed, and
meanings were ascribed to their shapes. Interpreting
dreams was also important, and the stars were observed
ever more scientifically, though always to obtain omens.
Because the temple of the city god (and other gods)
actually owned most of the land, most of the population
worked as serfs of the temple. But the produce of the
land was distributed as pay to them.

The ruins of Nippur, once the leading religious center of Sumer. The excavation of Nippur was of the greatest importance. Excavation began in 1888 and continues to the present time—to the extent that the location, in present-day Iraq, permits continued digging. At Nippur archaeological work emphasized the uncovering of an entire city for the first time, rather than the search for statues and inscriptions. Here the ziggurat was first studied, and here were found perhaps four-fifths of all known Babylonian literary texts, including the ballads of the Gilgamesh cycle.
© *Dr. Georg Gerster*

Life was highly diversified, if not yet truly specialized; blacksmiths, carpenters, and merchants appeared alongside the hunters, farmers, and shepherds of the older days. Fathers had many rights over their children. The society was monogamous, and women held a high position. Punishments seemed mild and specific relative to those found later in the Babylonian society that grew out of the Sumerian; in Sumer they consisted mostly of fines.

In their epic poetry the Sumerians celebrated the brave exploits of Gilgamesh, a mighty hero two-thirds divine and one-third human. He undertook perilous

THE EPIC OF GILGAMESH

Many similarities to the Biblical account of Noah's ark and the great flood are found in the epic of Gilgamesh, the king of Uruk. This epic predates the epics of Homer by 1500 years and is, in the eyes of many scholars, the first major contribution to world literature. Composed about 2000 B.C., the epic tells of the Great Flood in the following words:

For six days and six nights the winds blew, torrent and tempest and flood overwhelmed the world, tempest and flood raged together like warring hosts. When the seventh day dawned the storm from the south subsided, the sea grew calm, the flood was stilled; I looked at the face of the world and there was silence, all mankind was turned to clay. The surface of the sea stretched as flat as a roof-top; I opened a hatch and the light fell on my face. Then I bowed low, I sat down and I wept, the tears streamed down my face, for on every side was the waste of water. I looked for land in vain, but fourteen leagues distant there appeared a mountain, and there the boat grounded; on the mountain of Nisse she held fast and did not budge. A third day, and a fourth day, she held fast on the mountain and did not budge; a fifth day and a sixth day she held fast on the mountain. When the seventh day dawned, I loosed a dove and we let her go. She flew away, but finding no resting-place she returned. Then I loosed a swallow, and she flew away, but finding no resting-place she returned. I loosed a raven, she saw that the water had retreated, she ate, she flew around, she cawed, and she did not come back. Then I threw everything open to the four winds, I made a sacrifice and poured out a libation on the mountain top. Seven and again seven cauldrons I set up on their stands, I heaped on wood and cane and cedar and myrtle. When the gods smelled the sweet savour, they gathered like flies over the sacrifice. Then at last, Ishtar also came.

The Epic of Gilgamesh: An English Version with an Introduction, trans. N. K. Sandars, rev. ed. (New York: Penguin Books, 1972), p. 111. Quoted with permission from N. K. Sandars. Copyright © N. K. Sandars 1960, 1964, 1972. Reprinted by permission of Penguin Books Ltd.

journeys, overcame dreadful monsters, and performed great feats of strength. But even Gilgamesh, strong though he was, had to die; and ultimately a realistic tone, typical of the society, pervades Sumerian literature, its hymns, lamentations, prayers, fables, and even schoolboy compositions. A Sumerian proverb says, "Praise a young man, and he will do whatever you want; throw a crust to a dog, and he will wag his tail before you." In Sumerian literature we are told to glorify god and await the end of life, which may set one free from earthly suffering.

Sumerian art and architecture were largely religious, official in intent, and impersonal in style. They changed very little during more than a thousand years. The Sumerians built their temples of baked brick. The shrine was at first simply an altar against a wall; other rooms and an outer courtyard were added later. The most striking feature of the temple was that the entire structure was set upon a terrace, the first of many terraces, each above and smaller than the last, with a sanctuary at the top, reached by stairs from terrace to terrace. This was the *ziggurat*, the typical Mesopotamian temple, whose construction itself suggests a hierarchical Sumerian social order. It was perhaps a great ziggurat that suggested the tower of Babel to the author of Genesis.

Sumerian tombs were simple chambers, often filled with objects intended for use in the afterlife, which Sumerians envisioned as eternally sad. Their statuary consisted of clothed human figures, solemn and stiff, with large, staring eyes. Gods were represented as larger than kings, and ordinary human beings as smaller, for many were slaves. On monumental slabs (*steles*), on plaques, and especially on seals, the Sumerians showed themselves skillful at carving in relief—clear, informative, stiff, yet human.

A ziggurat at Nippur. Ziggurats were artificial mounds that represented the powers of earth. Each city in Mesopotamia had a single ziggurat, dedicated to the patron diety of that city. Here, at the foot of the temple, archaeologists unearthed some 35,000 tablets, many in Sumerian.
© Dr. Georg Gerster

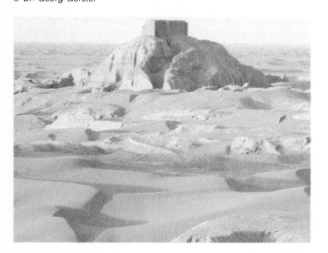

Akkadians: Babylonians and Assyrians

The successors of the Sumerians as rulers of Mesopotamia were Akkadian-speaking Semites to whom belonged first the Babylonians and then their successors, the Assyrians, both originally descended from nomads of the Arabian desert. They owed an enormous debt to Sumer. Power first passed to them with Sargon the Great (2300 B.C.) and returned to them after an interlude (about 2000 B.C.) with the invasion from the west of a people called the Amorites.

Since 1935 excavations at Mari in the middle Euphrates valley have turned up a palace with more than 260 rooms containing many thousands of tablets, mostly from the period between 1750 and 1700 B.C. These tablets were the royal archives, and they include the official letters to the king from his own local officials scattered throughout his territories and from other rulers of local city-states and principalities. Among the correspondents was an Amorite prince named Hammurabi, who from c. 1792 to 1750 B.C., by warfare and diplomacy, made his own Babylonian kingdom supreme in Mesopotamia and reunited it. His descendants retained Babylon and the area around it down to 1530, but had to give up Hammurabi's great conquests.

Hammurabi's code of law was applied from the Persian Gulf to the Mediterranean Sea. Though modeled on its Sumerian predecessors, its punishments were much harsher. Yet its author, the king, boasted less of his warlike deeds than of the peace and prosperity he had brought. Inscribed on a pillar eight feet tall beneath a sculptured relief showing the king standing reverently before the seated sun god, the code reveals a strongly stratified society: a patrician who put out the eye of a patrician would have his own eye put out; a patrician who put out the eye of a plebeian only had to pay a fine. But even the plebeian had rights that, to some degree, protected him against violence from his betters. Polygamy—the taking of more than one wife—and divorce were recognized. One clause says, "If a merchant lends silver to a trader without interest, and if the trader loses on his investment, he need return to the lender only the capital he has borrowed." (The word used for *capital* means "head," just as our word *capital* is itself derived from the Latin *caput*, meaning "head.") The earliest concepts of the profit motive can also be found in Hammurabi's code. It is significant that the scribe used not the Akkadian but the Sumerian word for *silver*, to make the language sound more learned and classical. In its vocabulary as in its concept of the social order, the code reflects the continuing Sumerian impact on the Akkadian-speaking Babylonians.

New nomads, this time from the east (Iran), the Kassites, shattered Babylonian power about 1530 B.C. After four centuries of relatively peaceful Kassite rule, supremacy in Mesopotamia gradually passed to the far more warlike Semitic Assyrians, whose power had been rising, with occasional setbacks, for several centuries in their great northern city of Assur. About 1100 B.C. their ruler Tiglath-pileser reached both the Black Sea

CODE OF HAMMURABI

Set down about 1750 B.C., the Code of Hammurabi incorporated many earlier laws. While the code is, first and foremost, a legal statement about stern justice, it also reveals much about life at the time, since laws are a reflection of society and of the breaches against its decorum that are most feared or may be most common.

1 If a man weave a spell and bring a charge of murder against another man and has not justified himself, the accuser shall be put to death.

2 If a man has put a spell upon another man, and has not justified himself, the one who is charged with sorcery shall go to the holy river, he shall plunge into the holy river, and if the holy river overcomes him, his accuser shall take his estate. If the holy river shows that man to be innocent and has saved him, he who charged him with sorcery shall be put to death and the man who plunged into the river shall take the estate of him who brought the charge against him. . . .

8 If a man has stolen ox or sheep or ass or pig or ship, whether from the temple or from the palace, he shall pay thirtyfold; if he stole from a commoner, he shall render tenfold. If the thief cannot pay, he shall be put to death. . . .

15 If a man has helped a male or female palace slave, or a commoner's male or female slave to escape out of the city gate, he shall be put to death. . . .

21 If a man has broken into a house, he shall be killed before the breach and walled in it. . . .

23 If the robber has not been caught, the man who has been despoiled shall recount before the god what he has lost, and the city and governor in whose territory the robbery took place shall make good to him his loss. . . .

53 If a man has neglected to strengthen the dyke of his canal, and a breach has opened in his dyke, and the waters have ravaged the meadow, the man in whose dyke the breach has been opened shall make good the corn that he caused to be lost. . . .

110 If a nun, a lady of god, who is not living in a convent, has opened the door of a wine shop or entered the wine shop for a drink, that woman shall be burned. . . .

117 If a debt came due against a man, and he has given his wife, his son, his daughter for the money, or handed himself over to work off the debt, for three years they shall work in the house of their buyer or exploiter, in the fourth year they shall be set free. . . .

129 If the wife of a man has been caught lying with another man, they shall bind them and throw them into the waters. . . .

132 If a wife has the finger pointed at her on account of another male but has not been caught lying with another male, for the sake of her husband she shall throw herself into the holy river. . . .

153 If a man's wife has caused her husband to be killed on account of another man, they shall impale that woman on a stake. . . .

195 If a man has struck his father, his hand shall be cut off.

196 If a man has caused the loss of a gentleman's eye, they shall cause him to lose one eye. . . .

200 If a man has made the tooth of a man that is his equal fall out, they shall make his tooth fall out.

201 If he has made the tooth of a commoner fall out, he shall pay one third of a mina of silver.

Code of Hammurabi, in *Western Societies: A Documentary History,* ed. Brian Tierney and Joan Scott (New York: Alfred A. Knopf, 1984), I, 25–27.

and the Mediterranean on a conquering expedition north and west, after which he boasted that he had become "lord of the world." Assyrian militarism was harsh, and the conquerors regularly transported into captivity the entire population of defeated cities. By the eighth century B.C. the Assyrian state was a kind of dual monarchy; Tiglath-pileser III (744–727), their ruler, also took the title of ruler of Babylonia, thus consciously accepting the Babylonian tradition. He added enormous territory to the Neo-Assyrian Empire. But Chaldean tribes resisted Assyrian rule over the whole of Babylonia, and in turn the mighty Assyrian Empire fell to a new power, the Medes (Iranians related to the Persians), who took Nineveh (612 B.C.) with Babylonian and Palestinian help.

For less than a century thereafter (612–538 B.C.) Chaldean Babylonia experienced a rapid, brilliant revival, based in part on slavery, during which King Nebuchadnezzar built temples and palaces, made Babylon a wonder of the world with its famous hanging gardens, overthrew Jerusalem, and took the Hebrews into captivity. But in 539 King Belshazzar, having lost the support of the priesthood, had to surrender all of Babylonia to Cyrus the Great of Persia. The history of the Mesopotamian empires and of the last Akkadian state ended, after 2,500 years.

In religion as in all other aspects of life, the Babylonians and Assyrians took much from the Sumerians. The cosmic gods remained the same, but the local gods were different; under Hammurabi one of them, Marduk, was exalted over all other gods and kept that supremacy thereafter. In Babylonian-Assyrian belief, demons became more numerous and more powerful, and a special class of priests was needed to fight them. Magic practices multiplied. All external events—an encounter with an animal, a sprained wrist, the position and color of the stars at a vital moment—had implications for one's own future that needed to be discovered. Starting with the observation of the stars for such magical purposes, the Babylonians developed substantial knowledge of celestial movement and the mathematics to go with it. They even managed to predict eclipses. They could add, subtract, multiply, divide, and extract roots. They could solve equations and measure both plane areas and solid volumes. But their astronomy and their mathematics remained in the service of astrology and divination. So, too, did jewelry making, goldsmithing, and ivory carving, which reached new and extraordinarily beautiful heights, as shown especially in the archaeological finds at Nimrud.

Egypt

Character of the Society What the Tigris and the Euphrates rivers did for Mesopotamia, the Nile River did for Egypt. Over thousands of years the people along the Nile had slowly learned to take advantage of the annual summer flood by tilling their fields to receive the silt-laden river waters, and by regulating its flow. About 3000 B.C., at approximately the time that the Sumerian civilization emerged in Mesopotamia, the Egyptians had reached a comparable stage of development. Much better known to us than Mesopotamia, Egypt was another ancient valley civilization that made major contributions to our own.

Egypt, though also a hydraulic society based on river-valley agriculture and its resulting slow trend toward centralization, was more dynamic, perhaps more willing—especially as its cities grew—to entertain new ideas than the Mesopotamian states had been. The Egyptians regarded life after death as a happy continuation of life on earth with all its fleshly pleasures, not as a dismal eternal sojourn in the dust. The Mesopotamian rulers—both the early city lords and the later kings who aspired to universal monarchy—were agents of the gods on earth; the Egyptian rulers from the beginning were themselves regarded as gods. The Mesopotamians were conscious of history, the Egyptians less so.

Because Egyptian territory consisted of the long strip along the banks of the Nile, it was always hard to unify. It was, however, rich in agricultural resources and relatively easy to defend, and in time it became the world's first centralized state. At the very beginning (3000 B.C.)

The Great Sphinx and the Pyramids of Giza, in what is today Egypt. The pyramids were royal tombs dating from the Old Kingdom. They represent exceptional mastery of engineering and command of labor. The Great Sphinx, dating from c. 2620 B.C., and the Pyramids at Giza are the best known remnants of the ancient world.
Art Resource

there were two rival kingdoms: Lower and Upper Egypt. Lower Egypt was the Nile Delta (so called because it is shaped like the Greek letter of that name), the triangle of land nearest the Mediterranean where the river splits into several streams and flows into the sea. Upper Egypt was the land along the course of the river for eight hundred miles between the Delta and the First Cataract. Periodically the two regions were unified into one kingdom, but the ruler, who called himself king of Upper and Lower Egypt, by his very title recognized that his realms consisted of two somewhat disparate entities: one looking toward the Mediterranean and outward to other seagirt civilizations; and the other more isolated by its deserts, more self-regarding, more inclined to resist new thoughts, using its isolation as a form of protection. The first unifier, perhaps mythical, was Menes, whose reign (about 2850 B.C.) is taken by scholars as the start of the first standard division of Egyptian history, the Old Kingdom (2700–2160).

Old, Middle, and New Kingdoms When the king is god, his subjects need only listen to his commands to feel sure they know the divine will. As each Egyptian king died, a great sepulchral monument, often in the form of a pyramid, told his subjects that he had gone to join his predecessors in the community of gods. The largest of the pyramids took several generations to build and involved the continual labor of thousands of men— a sign that society accepted and took pride in the divine lineage of its rulers. A highly centralized bureaucracy carried out the commands of the king. A stratified society worked for him. His forces advanced at times westward into the Libyan desert, and at other times—drawn by the pull exerted on every ruler of Egypt from Menes to the present—eastward and northward into Palestine.

The Old Kingdom was first disturbed and eventually shattered by a growing tendency among district governors to pass their offices on to their sons, who in turn tended to regard themselves as hereditary rulers and thus to weaken the central authority. The priests of the sun had also made good their claims to special privileges that helped diminish royal power. After a disorderly interval of perhaps two centuries, a new dynasty (the eleventh of thirty in Egyptian history) restored unity in what is known as the Middle Kingdom (2134–1786), distinguished for its rulers' land-reclamation policies and its victories abroad.

To the south hostile Nubians (from the modern Sudan) were defeated, and their movements were controlled by the building of frontier fortresses. Palestine and Syria came under Egyptian influence. Bureaucracy flourished. Thebes ceased to be the capital, as a new city was founded south of Memphis, from which government could be exercised more effectively. Provincial governorship became hereditary but had to be confirmed by the king, and the king's son at the age of twenty-one became co-ruler with his father. The king himself was less remote and more eager to be regarded as the shepherd of his people.

Secessionist movements and growing internal weakness combined with a foreign invasion and conquest to put an end to the Middle Kingdom. The conquerors were called Hyksos, Asian nomads of uncertain Amorite origin who imported the horse-drawn war chariot and perhaps the bow. The Egyptians hated their rule, which lasted about a century, and eventually rallied behind a new dynasty (the seventeenth) to drive out the invaders. By about 1558 and the eighteenth dynasty the task was accomplished and the New Kingdom (1575–1087) was solidly established.*

The five centuries of the New Kingdom saw extraordinary advances. In foreign affairs, the Egyptians engaged in a struggle for Syria and Palestine, not only with the great powers of Mesopotamia but with the mountain and desert peoples who lived between the two great valley civilizations. The Egyptian ruler (now called pharaoh) Thutmose I reached the Euphrates on the east and marched far south into Nubia. Thutmose III (c. 1469–1436) fought seventeen campaigns in the east, crossing the Euphrates to defeat his Mesopotamian enemies on their own soil. The walls of the great temple of Karnak preserve the carved account of his military achievements and the record of the enormous tribute paid him by his conquered enemies. The Egyptians established their own network of local governors throughout the conquered territories, but ruled mildly, and did not, as the Assyrians were soon to do, deport whole masses of

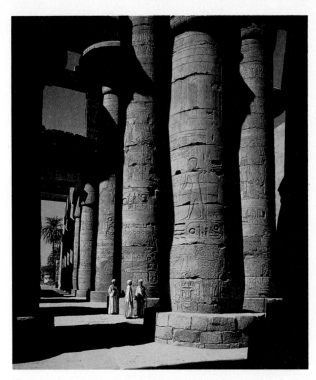

The vast temple at Karnak, now roofless, soars to the sky. This view is from within the sanctuary of Amon.
SuperStock

the population into slavery. Nonetheless, the eighteenth dynasty embarked on a vast building program that depended on a ready supply of forced labor.

It was the pharaoh Amenhotep IV (r. 1364–1350) who caused a major internal upheaval in the successful New Kingdom by challenging the priests of the sun god Amen, who had become a powerful privileged class. Amenhotep urged the substitution for Amen of the sun disk, Aten, and, even more dramatic, commanded that Aten alone be worshiped and that the multitude of other gods be abandoned. Accordingly, Amenhotep changed his name to Akhenaten (Pleasing to Aten) in honor of his only god. Some have seen in this famous episode an effort to impose monotheism on Egypt. To mark the new policy, Akhenaten and his beautiful wife, Nefertiti, ruled from a new capital in Amarna, which gives its name to the "Amarna heretics" who believed in "one true god." Nearby, beginning about A.D. 1880, were found the famous Tell-el-Amarna letters (documents found in a *tell*, or ancient mound, at modern Amarna), a collection of about four hundred tablets including the diplomatic correspondence in many languages of Akhenaten and his father with the rulers of western Asia—an invaluable source for scholars.

Akhenaten's effort to overthrow the entrenched priesthood led to internal dissension and the loss of external strength. His son-in-law, Tutankhamen (r. 1347–1338 B.C.), was eventually sent to rule in Thebes, city of the priests of Amen, with whom (as his name shows) he compromised. With Akhenaten's death, the

---

* Problems of exact dating of the Egyptian kingdoms are extraordinarily difficult; the dates used here are the conventional ones. See Chester G. Starr, *Early Man: Prehistory and the Civilizations of the Ancient Near East* (New York: Oxford University Press, 1973), p. 101. For more detailed, complex, and exacting analysis of dates, consult William W. Hallo and William Kelly Simpson, *The Ancient Near East: A History* (New York: Harcourt Brace Jovanovich, 1971), pp. 299–302.

The pharaoh Akhenaten, shown carrying crossed sceptres and wearing a bracelet bearing Aten's name. This statue from Karnak is a fine example of the new artistic conventions of the time, in showing the pharaoh as emaciated and almost androgenous. It may be that Akhenaten was deformed (scholars continue to debate the point), but it is more likely that the extreme stylization was meant to dramatize the break with the earlier conventions of Egyptian art.

New York Public Library Picture Collection

new religious experiment collapsed, and the pharaohs strove to make up for the interval of weakness by resuming their foreign conquests.

About 1300 B.C. Ramses II (nineteenth dynasty) concluded a treaty with a people from Asia Minor, the Hittites. This treaty, of which we have texts in both Egyptian and Hittite, called for a truce in the struggle for Syria and provided for a dynastic marriage between the pharaoh and a Hittite princess. The interlude was short, however, and soon after 1200 B.C. the New Kingdom in its turn suffered severely as the result of an invasion of its eastern Mediterranean shores by mixed bands of raiders from the sea, sometimes called the Sea Peoples, possibly including ancestors of the later Greeks and Sicilians and others.

Egypt entered into a decline, marked by renewed internal struggles for power between the secular authorities and the priests, and among local and central rulers. Then came the Assyrian conquest of the seventh century, the Persian conquest of 525 B.C., and the conquest by Alexander the Great of Macedonia in 332 B.C..

Religion Religion was the most powerful force animating Egyptian society. If one asked an ancient Egyptian "whether the sky was supported by posts or held up by a god, the Egyptian would answer: 'Yes, it is supported by posts or held up by a god—or it rests on walls, or it is a cow, or it is a goddess whose arms and feet touch the earth.' "* The Egyptian was ready to accept overlapping divinities and to add new ones whenever it seemed appropriate; if a new area was incorporated into the Egyptian state, its gods would be added to those already worshiped.

From the beginning, Egyptian cults included animals (totems perhaps); sheep, bulls, gazelles, and cats are still to be found carefully buried in their own cemeteries. As time passed, the figures of Egyptian gods became human, though often retaining an animal's head or body. Osiris, the Egyptian god who judged the dead, began as a local Nile Delta deity. He taught humans agriculture. Isis was his wife, and animal-headed Seth, his brother and rival. Seth killed Osiris. Isis persuaded the gods to bring him back to life, but thereafter he ruled below (a parallel to the fertility and vegetation-cycle beliefs we have already encountered in Mesopotamia and will encounter again in Greece). Osiris was identified with the life-giving, fertilizing Nile, and Isis with the fertile earth of Egypt. Horus, the god of the sky, defeated the evil Seth after a long struggle.

But Horus was only one kind of sky god. There was also Re, the sun god, later amalgamated with Amen, and still later Aten, as we have seen. The moon god was the baboon-headed Thoth, who was god of wisdom, magic, and numbers. In great temple cities like Heliopolis, priests worked out and wrote down hierarchies of divinities. Out in the villages all the forces of nature were deified and worshiped. One local god was part crocodile, part hippopotamus, and part lion—a touching and clear revelation of what simple farmers along the river banks had to worry about. However numerous the deities, Egyptian religion itself was basically unified. Unlike a Sumerian temple, which was the political center of its city and for which the population toiled, the function of an Egyptian temple was generally focused on religion.

Egyptians were preoccupied with life after death. They believed that after death each human being would appear before Osiris and recount all the evil he or she had not done on earth: "I have not done evil to men. I have not ill-treated animals. I have not blasphemed the gods," and so on, a negative confession to justify admission into the kingdom of the blessed. Osiris would then have the person's heart weighed to test the truth of this self-defense, and the dead person would be admitted or else delivered over to judges for punishment.

Egyptians believed not only in body and soul, but in *ka*, the indestructible vital principle of each person, which left the body at death but could return at times. That is why the Egyptians preserved the body in their elaborate art of mummification—so that the ka, on its

*J. A. Wilson, *The Intellectual Adventure of Ancient Man* (Chicago: University of Chicago Press, 1943), p. 44.

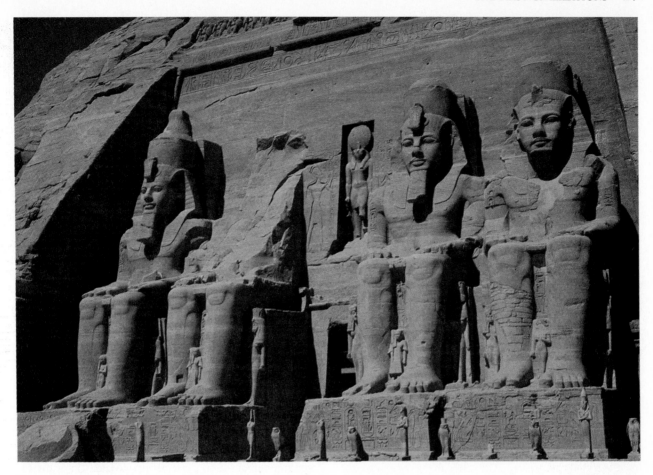

These giant statues of Ramses II at the rock temple of Abu Simbel were reconstructed in the twentieth century to save them from the rising waters of a new dam. Ramses wanted to show his love of the colossal, to tell of his greatness to all who came to view the giant sandstone figures. Graffiti on the smooth surface of the legs in ancient Greek, Phoenician, and Persian show how strong the impulse is for each generation to leave its mark on a previous one. Restoration of the temple was completed in 1970, but the historical graffiti was left intact.
Giraudon/Art Resource

return, would find it not decomposed. And that is why they filled the tombs of the dead with all the objects that the ka might need or take delight in on its return to the body; otherwise it might come back and haunt the living.

Literature We know Egyptian civilization so intimately because of the many inscriptions, which give us the historical materials, and the papyri (fragments of the ancient material the Egyptians wrote on, made of the pith of a water plant), which give us the literary materials. Yet what we have represents a smaller percentage of what once existed and of what may yet be found than does our collection of Mesopotamian literature on its thousands of carefully copied clay tablets.

The Egyptians used a form of picture writing (hieroglyphics, or sacred carvings), which was deciphered in the 1820s. Scholars had possessed the key only since 1799, when a large, inscribed stone was found near the town of Rosetta in the Nile Delta. This piece of black basalt has a long text chiseled into its surface in three scripts: Greek, hieroglyphics, and another (demotic)

Egyptian script developed from hieroglyphics. Although the Greek version was imperfect, it could be read. It proved to be a decree in honor of a pharaoh named Ptolemy V, from 195 B.C., in the period after Alexander the Great's conquest. Even so, it took three decades before a French scholar, Jean-François Champollion, convinced himself that hieroglyphics were intended to be read phonetically, not symbolically, and so got beyond the mere deciphering of the name and title of Ptolemy V. Knowing the language of the Egyptian Christian church of his own day, which was close to ancient Egyptian although written differently, he gradually puzzled out the hieroglyphics on the stone. Since then, scholars have been able to read with certainty the vast number of surviving Egyptian texts. Visitors to the British Museum in London can still see the famous slab that made it possible for the nineteenth and twentieth centuries A.D. to understand ancient Egypt.

The equally famous Egyptian Book of the Dead—actually not a book but a series of papyrus chapters to be read by the living and then placed in tombs to help the dead—brings together stories of the gods with

THE ARROGANCE OF CONQUEST

The Egyptian pharaohs wanted succeeding generations to know of their deeds, and it was the custom to erect columns on which their exploits were shown by illustration and word. At Karnak, for example, Ramses II ordered the following said about himself (which was not, of course, literally true in any sense):

I dashed at them like the god of war; I massacred them, slaughtering them where they stood while one shrieked to the other, "This is no man but a mighty god; these are not the deeds of man; never has one man thus overcome hundreds of thousands!" I slew them all; none escaped me. . . . I caused the field of Kadesh to be white with corpses, so that one did not know where to tread because of the multitude. I fought all alone and overcame the foreigners in their millions.

Quoted in Karl E. Meyer, *The Pleasures of Archaeology: A Visa to Yesterday* (New York: Atheneum, 1971), pp. 75–76.

Wall decoration from the tomb of the son of Ramses II. The medallions at the top provide a caption, to be read from right to left, identifying the reign of Ramses II and events connected with it.
Giraudon Art Resource

hymns and prayers and teaches us much of what we know of Egyptian religion. The Egyptian literature we have includes no epic story of a hero comparable to Gilgamesh, a mortal who cannot quite attain immortality, perhaps because the Egyptians confidently did expect to attain it. But it does include love songs, banquet songs, and what we could call fiction, both historical and fantastic. "If I kiss her," says an Egyptian lover, "and her lips are open, I am happy even without beer"*—a sentiment that seems perfectly up to date. "Enjoy thyself as much as thou canst," says a banquet song, "for a man cannot take his property with him."** The historical romance of Sinuhe (early Middle Kingdom, c. 1980 B.C.) tells the story of an Egyptian noble who was forced by intrigue into exile in Asia, was elected chief of a tribe there, won a magnificent single combat against a local champion, and, at the end, full of longing for Egypt, was happily recalled by the pharaoh and richly dressed, honored, and given a pyramid of his own for his future tomb. Egyptians also had their euphemisms for death—to "go to the West" was to die, and Westerners are "the dead." Thus the famous lines, "How happy is he who hath reached the West when he is safe in the hand of God."

Society The chief social unit was the monogamous family, and thus even a pharaoh, who was entitled to have a harem of wives and concubines, would have a chief wife. Women were not fully subordinate to men: they could own property and, under certain conditions, inherit it; they might also enter into business agreements. Most unusual in ancient societies, women could succeed to the throne, Queen Hatshepsut being one of the best-known examples. Though in theory all of the

* Quoted in A. Erman, *Literature of the Ancient Egyptians*, trans. A. M. Blackman (New York: Blom, 1971).
** Quoted in J. H. Breasted, *The Dawn of Conscience* (New York: Scribner's, 1933), pp. 163–64.

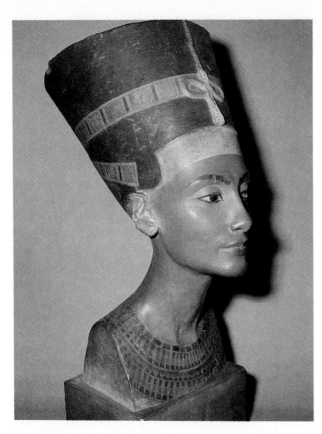

This portrait head of Queen Nefertiti dates from the fourteenth century B.C. Nefertiti was the wife of the pharaoh Akhenaten. Though this is probably the best known work of Egyptian sculpture, it is actually only a model in limestone, discovered in the workshop of the sculptor Thutmose. Nefertiti's name illustrates one of the difficulties in speaking or writing of an ancient culture; the Egyptian language contained no vowels, so her name should be written *Nfrtt.* However, today we would be unable to pronounce such a word, so conventionally vowels are inserted in Egyptian names.
Egyptian Museum/SEF/Art Resource

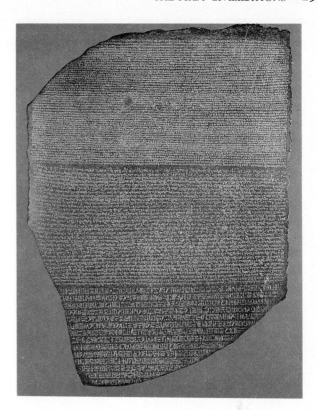

The Rosetta Stone, with its trilingual inscription, was discovered in 1799 and is now in the British Museum.
British Museum/Bridgeman, Art Resource

land was the property of the pharaoh, it was in fact generally held by individuals, male and female.

The upper and lower classes were separated by a great gulf. The wealthy enjoyed meat, fruit, and wine, and they lived in elaborate homes surrounded by well-watered gardens. They treasured gold and silver, and Egyptian craftsmen created much remarkable jewelry. The poor lived in small shedlike structures made of mud-bricks in which a few stools and pottery jars might be found. In the countryside, where agriculture was well developed, the laborer enjoyed a moderately better life, but the cities nonetheless attracted more and more people because small factories made possible the development of some division of labor, which in turn made the worker relatively more valued.

Egyptian society was divided into classes, generally five of them, all distinct. There was the royal family, there were the priests, and there were the nobles, all of whom lived extremely well. There was a growing middle class of well-to-do farmers in the countryside and of merchants, scribes, and artisans in the cities. There were the peasants, by far the largest class. A sixth class—professional soldiers, who came to be ranked directly below the nobles—came into being during the New Kingdom. And as conquest in war led to the acquisition of thousands of slaves, a seventh group, not precisely a class, was identified. The slaves at first worked as forced labor, largely in government-owned quarries or on the estates that grew around the temples. In time, however, they were permitted to join the army and the former slaves achieved a status of their own. Also in time, as Egyptian authority and the area of its domination grew, a number of government functionaries attained the status of nobility, though separate from those who were of the nobility by virtue of birth and inheritance. Thus Egyptian social structure, when viewed over several dynasties, was complex and changing.

III   PEOPLES OUTSIDE THE VALLEYS

For well over a thousand years after their first flourishing, the peoples of the valley civilizations held the stage virtually alone. But the Hyksos invasion of Egypt, the

THE CURSING LITANY

A litany is an incantation. The following litany, intended to quell the enemies of
the sun god, is a striking example of Egyptian religious poetry:

Mayest thou never exist, may thy body never exist.
May thy limbs never exist.
May thy bones never exist.
May thy words of power never exist.
May thy form never exist.
May thy attributes never exist.
May that which springs from thee never exist.
May thy hair never exist.
May thy possessions never exist.
May thy emissions never exist.
May the material of thy body never exist.
May thy place never exist.
May thy tomb never exist.
May thy cavern never exist.
May thy funeral chamber never exist.
May thy paths never exist.
May thy seasons never exist.
May thy words never exist.
May thy enterings in never exist.
May thy journeyings never exist.
May thy advancings never exist.
May thy comings never exist.
May thy sitting down never exist.
May thy increase never exist.
May thy body never exist.
May thy prosperity never exist.
Thou art smitten, O enemy. Thou shalt die, thou shalt
    die.
Thou shalt perish, thou shalt perish, thou shalt perish.

Mayest thou never exist.
Mayest thou never exist.
Mayest thou never exist.
Mayest thou never exist.
Mayest thou never exist.
Mayest thou never exist.
Mayest thou never exist.
Mayest thou never exist.
Mayest thou never exist.
Mayest thou never exist.
Mayest thou never exist.
Mayest thou never exist.
Mayest thou never exist.
Mayest thou never exist.
Mayest thou never exist.
Mayest thou never exist.
Mayest thou never exist.
Mayest thou never exist.
Mayest thou never exist.
Mayest thou never exist.
Mayest thou never exist.
Mayest thou never exist.
Mayest thou never exist.
Mayest thou never exist.
Mayest thou never exist.

From *Egyptian Religious Poetry,* ed. Margaret A. Murray (London: John
Murray, 1949), pp. 64–65.

Kassite invasion of Mesopotamia, and the Hittite attacks
on both warned the river-based societies that the people
of the mountains and deserts had begun to compete
fiercely with the more stable valley societies. By 1500
B.C. the Kassites in southern Mesopotamia, the Hurrians
with their kingdom of Mitanni in northern Mesopotamia, smaller states in southeastern Anatolia (modern
Turkey), and the Hittites in the remainder of Anatolia
had emerged as rivals both to Babylon and to Egypt.

All of them had strong Indo-Aryan ethnic elements,
that is, elements of a strain that would become predominant in Iran and later in the Mediterranean and the
West. All of them were ruled by kings, but their kings
were neither the Mesopotamian agents of god on earth
nor the Egyptian deified monarchs. Rather, they ruled
as the most powerful among a noble class that controlled the instruments of war—horses and chariots—
and shared the fruits of conquest, dividing new land

among themselves. We begin now to find records, not
only of war between these newly emerging peoples and
the settled valley societies, but also of their diplomatic
exchanges and their peace settlements.

For communication everybody used Akkadian, a Semitic tongue often foreign to both parties in a negotiation. The Egyptians, for example, corresponded in Akkadian with the peoples who ruled Syria, who did not
speak it either. Even when they wrote in their own languages, some of them used Akkadian script. This enables
modern scholars to pronounce the words even when
they do not know what they mean, as is still often the
case with Hurrian, written in Akkadian cuneiform but
not related to well-known language groups and still by
no means completely understood.

The Hurrians, in particular, transmitted Babylonian
traditions to Assyria, Palestine, Phoenicia, and remotely
to Greece, and they significantly shaped Hittite culture.

Thus, while a more generalized culture was spread over a wider territory, the valley societies—Mesopotamia and Egypt—did not in fact succumb during the centuries from 1500 to 1200 B.C., when the threat was the greatest.

Hittites

Until the early twentieth century, scholars knew the Hittites chiefly from references in non-Hittite sources. Uriah, for example, whom (the Bible tells us) King David arranged to have killed in battle in order to keep his wife Bathsheba, was a Hittite. And in Egypt a great inscription preserved the text in hieroglyphics of a treaty of 1280 B.C. between Ramses II and a Hittite king. In A.D. 1906–1908, excavations at an ancient Hittite capital, Hattusas, on the plateau of Anatolia, brought to light several thousand tablets, largely in cuneiform script and written in the Indo-European Hittite language and in many others as well. These records revealed that a strong Hittite kingdom emerged about 1700 B.C. Its Indo-European king and his aristocracy controlled a native Anatolian population. Between 1700 and c. 1530, this kingdom made great conquests in Syria and resumed expansion toward Babylon. By 1500 the monarchy had become hereditary. Under Shuppiluliuma (r.c. 1375–1335), a contemporary of Akhenaten, it reached its height, as the Hittites took advantage of Egyptian internal weakness to assert themselves.

Influenced by what he had learned of Akhenaten, Shuppiluliuma began to insist that he be addressed as "My Sun" and to use the solar disk as a symbol. Thenceforth Hittite sovereigns also were deified, though only after death: it is from about this time that the written sources begin to speak of a king as "becoming a god" at death. The onslaught of the Sea Peoples that damaged the Egyptian New Kingdom about 1200 also put an end to the centralized Hittite state, although various smaller "neo-Hittite" principalities continued to exist in Asia Minor in the face of Assyrian expansion down to the late eighth century B.C. They wrote Hittite in hieroglyphics. Much progress was made during the 1930s in deciphering their script, but the first major helpful bilingual text in hieroglyphic Hittite and Phoenician was not found until after World War II.

The Anatolians, the Indo-European Hittite upper class, the Mesopotamians, and the Egyptians all made contributions to Hittite religion. Foreign gods were welcomed and domesticated. No matter where they had originally come from, once part of Hittite religion these gods received homage in forms derived from Mesopotamia. But there were differences here, too. Women played a more prominent role in Hittite religion and society than they did either in Mesopotamia or in Egypt; and alone among the peoples of the ancient Near East, the Hittites cremated their kings.

Though Hittite literature is full of Mesopotamian echoes, the Hittites also wrote sober official histories, which sought to determine and record the motives of rulers for their actions. The treaty, too, as a special literary and diplomatic instrument, was apparently a Hittite invention. Hittite architecture expressed itself in fortresses built on peaks, which became the nuclei of cities. The Hittites' skill at defending themselves, combined with their interest in trade and diplomacy, had given them a dominant position as far as the city of Ugarit which, having one of the best harbors on the eastern Mediterranean, became an emporium for the whole of the region's goods, including the copper so important to Cyprus. Ugarit drew upon Hurrian and Hittite alliances with exceptional skill, enjoying a "golden age" of prosperity and growth between c. 1440 and 1360 B.C.

Hurrians, Canaanites, Philistines, Phoenicians

Far less well known than the Hittites and still posing many unsolved problems are the Hurrians of Mitanni and the upper Chabur River. Their language is still imperfectly read. Like the Hittites, the Hurrians had an Indo-European ruling class and worshiped some Indo-European deities. Their great importance was to act as intermediaries between the civilization of Mesopotamia and the less advanced peoples to the north and west, especially the Hittites.

Like the mountains of Anatolia and northern Mesopotamia, the deserts of Syria (the Biblical land of Canaan) gave rise to a number of Semitic peoples who from time to time invaded the valley societies. Indeed, the Akkadians themselves—both Babylonians and Assyrians—as well as the Amorites had done the same. But there remained behind other Semitic peoples who never penetrated into the valleys and who created societies of their own along the Syrian coast of the Mediterranean and in its hinterland.

At Ugarit on the coast—where the northern portion was called Phoenicia—archaeologists in 1929 found the royal palace of a Canaanite state that flourished between 1400 and 1200 B.C., complete with cuneiform tablets in the northwest Semitic tongue of Ugaritic. They contained the archives of official correspondence, including a treaty with the Hittites written in Akkadian and showing that the Canaanites were under Hittite domination. There were also poems, including an epic about a hero named Kret, who was granted a son by divine favor—as was Abraham in Genesis in the Bible—and who also went to recapture his bride from the fortress of a king who had spirited her away—a leading theme in Homer's *Iliad*. At Ugarit, an eastern Mediterranean culture developed ties with both the Hebrews and the Greeks. Still, Ugarit was only one of many Canaanite city-states, and it went down in the general chaos around 1200 B.C. caused by the Sea Peoples' invasion. Among these invading Sea Peoples were the Indo-European Philistines, who settled to the south of the Canaanites and gave their name to Palestine.

The Canaanites apparently matched their extreme political localism with extreme religious localism. They

INTERPRETING DREAMS

Most cultures have sought to forecast the future by some means of divination. Common means have included the reading of the entrails of animals, scapulimancy (the throwing and reading of bones), and astrology (the belief that the stars influence human lives and can be used to forecast ordained events). The Egyptians developed astrology, as did the Greeks and Romans, who then prohibited its use. In the Middle Ages astrology was compounded with alchemy, or the effort to turn base metals into gold. With the introduction of printing, astrology and dream interpretation spread rapidly, and many people used horoscopes to provide a sense of security and a relationship to their place in the heavens. The Egyptian and Mesopotamian societies felt that dreams provided warnings or omens of events to come. Among accepted interpretations of the meanings of dreams were:

If, in his dreams, he often walks about naked it means: trouble will not touch this man.

If a man flies repeatedly: whatever he owns will be lost.

If he sits on the ground: honors are in store for him.

If he pours his urine into an irrigation-canal: Adad [the Weather-god] will flood his harvest.

If he eats the eye of his friend: his bad luck is straightened out, his property will prosper.

If one gives him wine: his days will be short.

If one gives him a seal of red stone: he will have sons and daughters.

If one gives him a wheel: he will have twins.

From A. Leo Oppenheim, "The Interpretation of Dreams in the Ancient Near East," *Transactions of the American Philosophical Society*, n.s., XLVI (1956), as quoted in Chester G. Starr, *Early Man: Prehistory and the Civilizations of the Ancient Near East* (New York: Oxford University Press, 1973), p. 31.

---

practiced human sacrifice and religious prostitution. The supreme Canaanite god was El, whose name simply means god and about whom little is known. Baal, on the other hand, whose name means lord, was a storm god—like the Sumerian god of the air, the region between heaven and earth. Baal and his wife Astarte—like Osiris and Isis in Egypt and parallel figures in Mesopotamia—symbolized the seasons and cyclical fertility.

After 1300 the Phoenicians (whose name comes from the word for the Tyrian purple dye made from shellfish found along the coast of their capital, Tyre) flourished along the coast south of Ugarit (in what is now Lebanon). They carried on a brisk trade with the western Mediterranean, founding Citium on Cyprus and Carthage (modern Tunis) as colonies. They brought their Semitic tongue (Punic) more than halfway to the Straits of Gibraltar, through which their ships had often sailed.

Perhaps most important, the Phoenicians possessed a genuine alphabet, and they exported it. Unlike cuneiform, which was a collection of signs that stood for entire syllables, the Phoenician alphabet consisted of a system of signs that stood for the sounds of the human voice. This made possible the elimination of syllabic characters and pictographic writing. At some point in the midst of the period of Phoenician growth, which ran from 1000 to 750 B.C., the Greeks began to draw upon this language and in the eighth century developed their own alphabet. From the Greek alphabet would, in time, come the Latin alphabet, which in turn would become the alphabet for most of Western civilization. Phoenician names began to appear among the names the Greeks gave to their gods, place names derived from the Phoenicians began to take root, and the loom of language began its slow process of weaving the words in which this paragraph is written.

Hebrews

History and the Hebrew Bible   The Hebrews were the first people to record their history in a series of books, providing a consecutive story over many centuries. Today, much changed and much debated by biblical scholars, this traditional history is contained in the Bible, especially in Genesis, Exodus, Joshua, Judges, Samuel, and Kings. But one also finds genealogy and ritual law (Numbers, Leviticus, and Deuteronomy), tales (Ruth and Job), proverbs (Proverbs, Ecclesiastes), prophetic utterances (Isaiah, Jeremiah, and the rest), and lyric poems (Psalms, The Song of Songs). For many centuries, these books were held by Jew and Christian alike to express literal and sacred truths; not until relatively recently have scholars begun to apply to them the same tests of authenticity that they apply to other works of history. Nineteenth-century scholars in particular decided that much biblical material was legendary and mythical, and they often questioned its historical accuracy.

But some doubts have been dispelled in our own time by hard archaeological evidence that has piled up in support of the general account that the Bible gives us. The Bible was not written down as the events happened; many of its earliest portions were compiled long after the events. The writings were not arranged in their present form until the second century B.C. Much is folklore. Still, the weight of the growing evidence tends to confirm the biblical story in its broad outlines, so that the Bible must be viewed not only as a work of the finest literature but also as valuable history.

Even the biblical account of the mist-shrouded beginnings of the Hebrews now seems reasonably authentic. They may well have migrated from Ur sometime after 1950 B.C., when that Sumerian center in southern Mesopotamia was destroyed, moving northwest to the prosperous center of Harran. Abraham then may well have migrated westward into Canaan, as Genesis says. The accounts in Genesis of the origins of the universe and the racial origins of the Hebrews, and the stories of Eden, the Flood, and the Tower of Babel, all indicate a northern Mesopotamian residence for the Hebrews before about 1500 B.C., when the westward migration took place. (The Flood has now been localized well north of the once-presumed site, Ur.) Probably a racial mixture including some non-Semitic (Hurrian?) elements from the beginning, the Hebrews may well be a people called Khapiru who are mentioned beginning about 1900 B.C. in cuneiform tablets and in both Hittite and Egyptian sources as raiders, wanderers, and captives. Historians are also convinced that some of the Hebrews lived for several centuries in the Nile Delta during the Hyksos period, before Moses (whose name is Egyptian) became their leader and led them to within sight of their Promised Land about 1300 B.C. Even the miraculous crossing of the Red Sea (actually the shallow Sea of Reeds) in Exodus is not incompatible with the shallow waters, the reedy growth, and the winds of the region at the time.

As outsiders battering their way into Canaan against the entrenched resistance of those already there, the Hebrew confederation of tribes was held together by the new religion that Moses gave them, based on the Ten Commandments, the ark of the covenant, and the many observances that their god prescribed. Gradually, by ruthless conquest, they added to their holdings. The loose confederation became a monarchy about 1020 B.C., when the prophet Samuel chose Saul to be the first king. Saul's son-in-law, rival, and successor, David, known to us by the virtually contemporary account (1000–960 B.C.) in the Book of Samuel, united and strengthened the kingdom. His luxury-loving son Solomon brought the Palestinian kingdom of the Jews to new heights of prosperity at the royal city of Jerusalem, though even then his kingdom was small in size and resources compared to Sumer, Babylon, Assyria, or Egypt.

But at Solomon's death in 933 B.C., the kingdom split in two: the northern kingdom of Israel (933–722 B.C.), stronger but lacking the great center of Jerusalem, and the southern kingdom of Judah (933–586 B.C.), which despite Jerusalem had little real strength. The Assyrians destroyed Israel at Samaria in 722 B.C., and the Babylonians—then, as we have seen, experiencing a brief revival—destroyed Judah under Nebuchadnezzar in 586 and took the Jews into captivity. When the Persians under Cyrus the Great freed the Jews to return to Palestine after 538, the Jews no longer had a state but only a religious community. From then on they were held together by religion alone, and depended politically on three successive empires: the Persian, the Macedonian, and the Roman.

Religion   Had it not been for the extraordinary cohesiveness of their religion, the Hebrews would have been just another people of the ancient Near East, less numerous than most at the time, less talented artistically than any. But of course we would probably not know much about them had it not been for their religion, which gave them and us the books of the Hebrew Bible and an enduring tradition. Many of the most fundamental ideas of the Hebrew religion go back to the days when the Hebrews were still nomads, before they had adopted a settled life. His god's commandments to Moses on Mount Sinai—"Thou shalt have no other gods before me," "Thou shalt not make unto thee any graven image," and "Thou shalt not take the name of the Lord thy God in vain"—determined three fundamental and permanent aspects of Judaism that were new among Near Eastern religions.

Thus, the religion of the Hebrews was monotheistic, recognizing only a single god. Despite the experiment of Akhenaten in Egypt and a few Babylonian texts that try to associate all divine power with Marduk alone, the Jews were the first to insist that their god was the only god and a universal god. Furthermore, the Jews were forbidden to represent this god in sculpture or painting—which stood in contrast to all other religions of the ancient world. More than that, they were forbidden to make any images of living beings, flesh, fish, or fowl—no doubt because their leaders feared that if they did make such images, they would end by worshiping them. And so from these earliest days their art was confined to nonrepresentational subjects. When they deviated from this law, as they often did, it was usually because of the influence upon them of neighbors whose traditions did not forbid animal or human representations in art. Finally, the religion of the Hebrews from the beginning regarded the name of god—Yahweh or Jehovah, meaning "he causes to be," or "the creator"— as literally not to be spoken, a reverence unlike any known in other ancient Near Eastern religions. From the nomadic period of Hebrew life come the feast of Passover, with its offering of a spring lamb and of unleavened bread; the keeping of a sabbath or holy day on the seventh day of the week; an annual day of expiation (Yom Kippur); and other holy days still honored by Jews in our own time.

ISAIAH AND MONOTHEISM

In Chapter 2 of the Book of Isaiah appears the prophet's exhortation to follow one god:

And it shall come to pass in the last days, that the mountain of the Lord's house shall be established in the top of the mountains, and shall be exalted above the hills; and all nations shall flow into it.

And many people shall go and say, Come ye, and let us go up to the mountain of the Lord, to the house of the God of Jacob; and he will teach us of his ways, and we will walk in his paths: for out of Zion shall go forth the law, and the word of the Lord from Jerusalem.

And he shall judge among the nations, and shall rebuke many people: and they shall beat their swords into plowshares, and their spears into pruning hooks: nation shall not lift up sword against nation, neither shall they learn war any more. . . .

The lofty looks of man shall be humbled, and the haughtiness of men shall be bowed down, and the Lord alone shall be exalted in that day.

For the day of the Lord of hosts shall be upon every one that is proud and lofty, and upon every one that is lifted up; and he shall be brought low. . . .

And the loftiness of man shall be bowed down, and the haughtiness of men shall be made low: and the Lord alone shall be exalted in that day.

And the idols he shall utterly abolish.

Isaiah, 2: 2–4, 11, 12, 17, 18.

The Bible teems with episodes in which the Hebrews proved unable to keep the first commandment, broke away from the worship of their one god, tried to propitiate other gods, and were punished. Yet however often they disobeyed, the first commandment remained the central feature of their religion, though there were commandments forbidding murder, adultery, stealing, the bearing of false witness, and covetousness of one's neighbor's property or wife. Jehovah himself, both merciful and righteous, creator of all things, was human in form though not visible to the human eye. Unlike the gods of all other peoples, he did not lead a human life; he had no family; he dwelt, not in a palace, but in heaven. When he wished to speak to the leader of his people, he descended onto a mountaintop (Mount Sinai), or into a burning bush, or into the space he commanded be left for him between golden cherubim set atop a sacred wooden box in which the Ten Commandments, transcribed on two tablets of stone, were to be kept.

This box was the ark of the covenant, built by artisans to the special orders of Moses as relayed to him by his god. The covenant was the special pact between god himself and his chosen people, all the tribes of the Hebrews in confederation, held together by their regard for this most sacred of objects. Kept at first in a very special tent, a portable tabernacle, the ark moved with the Hebrews, first into the hill country of Shiloh, where the coastal Philistines captured it about 1050 B.C., and ultimately into a temple built for it by Solomon in Jerusalem. This was a royal chapel whose decorations incidentally included many that violated the commandment about graven images, since it was built by a Canaanite architect using Phoenician models, showing the increasing influence of non-Israelite peoples on the cult of Jehovah.

There were prophets (men called to prophesy by their god) among the Jews from the beginning; they naturally multiplied during the division of the people into the two kingdoms of Israel and Judah. Summoning the people to return to the original purity of the faith, they sought to avoid the paganism that would threaten if Canaanite influences continued. In ecstasy perhaps brought on by dances, they warned of fearful punishment to come if the people did not heed them. After the punishment, however, the prophets (notably Isaiah) promised that Israel would rise again, and that a descendant of David would appear as a Messiah, a savior, to usher in a new golden age. The punishment came with deportation into Babylonian captivity and the abandonment of Jerusalem. With the prophecies of evil fulfilled, the prophet Ezekiel had a vision of new life being breathed into the dead bones of Israel, and he urged all to prepare for its restoration. While in exile, in the sixth century B.C., the Hebrews selected the sacred writings and arranged them together in a form not unlike the Bible we know. When the captivity was over, the priests became the dominant figures in the restored community, with its rebuilt temple but without a state of its own, and they strove deliberately to return to what they believed to be the practices of their ancestors.

There was much about Hebrew society that recalls what we have already observed about the other peoples of the ancient Near East. The father exercised supreme authority within the family; polygamy and divorce were

THE LANGUAGE OF HISTORY

Unlike most disciplines, history has developed little specialized language. Since history is, in a sense, a story, those who spoke it, write it, or now engage in research in it want to reach as large an audience as possible. Any specialized language cuts off some potential audience. Jargon may prove offensive, technical terms obscure, slang that changes rapidly is generally ineffective in print, vulgarisms may offend and lead one to stop reading or listening. Thus history is written in the vernacular, in formal prose, which though at times difficult nonetheless "goes current"—that is, does not change rapidly and is generally understood at all levels of society— with attention to precision, accuracy, and chronology.

Historians do use some special terminology, however, and such words are used in this book. Students sometimes find puzzling the presence of a lower case c. in front of a date; this stands for *circa* and means "approximately." For monarchs and popes, birth and death dates often are less significant than the dates of a reign, and thus r. is used for regnant, or reigned. Obviously b. is for birth, d. is for death, and—less obviously—fl. is for flourished, which is used when a person's dates are not known to indicate when the person was most active. Of course, the language of history changes as the broad language of the culture of which it is a part changes, so that words once viewed as technical, or vulgar, may come into such common and accepted usage as to become part of the historian's formal prose. Students will note several differences in the way language is used in this text as they move from ancient, through medieval, to modern times, since a text is also an artifact, a document concerning the history of language.

permitted; and, as among the Hittites, a widow married her dead husband's brother. The Hebrews had slaves, but a Hebrew slave could be made to serve no more than six years. A man who had injured his slave was required to set him or her free. Otherwise the law of an eye for an eye, a tooth for a tooth, held sway. Yet the general prescriptions—such as the commandments— and even some specific regulations—not to wrong strangers, not to exact usurious interest for a loan, to help one's enemies as well as one's friends—strike an ethical note as deep as any found in the earlier Mesopotamian Near East, and presage other principles that would eventually emerge from this Hebrew society, which by that time had been greatly influenced by Greek civilization.

IV CRETE AND MYCENAE

Minoans before Mycenae

Among the notable finds in Ugarit was an ivory relief of a bare-breasted goddess, holding ears of wheat in each hand and seated between two goats standing on

their hind legs. She is like nothing from Mesopotamia or Egypt, but she greatly resembles the goddesses frequently found on the large Mediterranean island of Crete, on the westernmost fringe of the Near East. Cretan civilization is often called Minoan, after Minos, the legendary founder of the local dynasty.

Sir Arthur Evans, a British archaeologist whose brilliant work in Crete in the first half of this century enabled modern scholars to appreciate Minoan society at its true worth, divided the culture into three main periods; today these are expressed as Early Minoan (c. 2500–c. 1950 B.C.), Middle Minoan (c. 1950–1550), and Late Minoan (c. 1550–1100). Each of these three periods is further subdivided three times to enable easy discussion of the objects found. Pottery is the key for all such dating; different styles found at different levels of archaeological sites permit scholars to work out a chronological framework. In Crete such dating is of surpassing importance, partly because we have not yet learned how to read the earliest writing, some of it in hieroglyphics and some of it in a script known as Linear A.

Much is now conjectured about Linear A, and some words have been plausibly deciphered, though it cannot yet be read. There is no Rosetta stone for Linear A, which, moreover, is surely not Greek. Professor Cyrus

Middle Minoan culture was sophisticated, complex, and elegant, at least for those who lived at the palace. Court ladies wore embroidered dresses of gold and silver. Great rock gardens, flower beds, and flowing fountains softened the harsh landscape. The Minoans were superb craftsmen, especially in gold, as shown by this delicate pendant of a golden bee, found in the necropolis (burial place) of Malia, and dating from c. 1700 B.C.
Heraklion Museum, Crete

Gordon argued that it is a northwest Semitic dialect related to Phoenician and that the Minoans who wrote it were a Semitic people who came to Crete from the Nile Delta in Middle Minoan times, about 1800 B.C. His views aroused great controversy; other scholars strongly maintained that the Minoans came from Anatolia, from the culture that produced Çatal Hüyük. Since we have only about two hundred Linear A texts, none of which are literary documents, it is probable that, even after scholars have learned to read it confidently, it will add little to what we have long known about the Minoans from purely archaeological evidence.

Such evidence has turned up in abundance in the palace of Minos at Knossos (modern Heraklion), found and partly reconstructed by Evans, and in other palaces and tombs in other parts the island, of which the most recently excavated is at Kato Zakros. Pottery and seals found on Crete show that the Cretans were a busy maritime people whose ships not only plied the Mediterranean but presumably managed to defend the island against invaders, since none of the palaces was fortified. Expanding at the expense of other islanders, the Cretans had garrisons and even colonies abroad—a Bronze Age overseas empire on a small scale exacting tribute from other powers.

The palace of Minos is a Middle Minoan triumph. Resting on earlier foundations, it is characterized by many rooms, a great staircase, strikingly beautiful wall frescoes (recovered from the ruins in fragments), massive columns, many six-foot-tall stone storage jars for

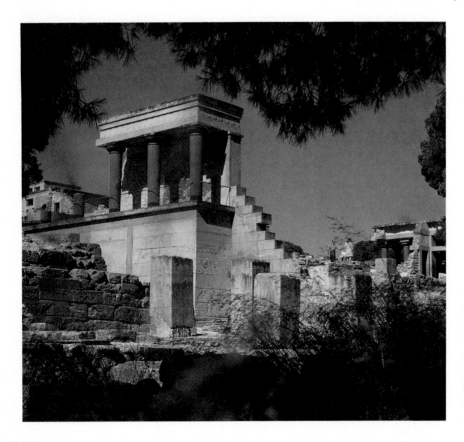

The ruins of the Palace of Minos at Knossos, Crete, from which archaeologists have been able to reconstruct much of Minoan life. By today's standards, archaeologists feel that Sir Arthur Evans, who reconstructed large portions of this palace, went too far, destroying much that might have been learned through a more cautious approach.
© Susan McCartney

olive oil or wine, and an elaborate plumbing system with pipes, running water, and ventilation. So complex was this palace that Evans believed that he had discovered the building that had inspired the ancient Athenian legend of the Labyrinth, a place (most likely a cave) on Crete with a system of rooms and corridors so mazelike that it was impossible to find one's way without a guide or a thread to drop behind, so that one might later retrace one's steps.

Minoan artisans (women achieved a near-egalitarian status and were admitted to the crafts) produced delicate pottery hardly thicker than an eggshell, decorated with birds, flowers, and marine animals. They also made ivory or pottery statuettes of the bare-breasted goddess, who often holds a snake in each hand, and many paintings of bulls, some showing young athletes—girls and boys—leaping over a bull's back, in what was clearly something like a ritual game. Athenian legend held that their ancestors had been forced to send young men and maidens to be sacrificed each year by the Cretans to their Minotaur—half-man, half-bull. Certainly the many pairs of bull horns that have been found in Knossos and elsewhere illustrate the importance of the animal in the Cretan religion, in which a double ax, found in many sizes from full-sized models in bronze to tiny miniatures in gold, also played a role. (The word *labyrinth* means "place of the double ax.")

The reasons for the end of Cretan prosperity are still hotly debated. Was it natural catastrophes (earthquakes, tidal waves, fires) that destroyed the palace of Minos

The small terra cotta snake goddess was found at the Palace of Knossos and dates from 1700–1580 B.C.
The Mansell Collection

The ceremony of the leaping of the bulls, from a fresco taken from Knossos and placed in the Heraklion Museum in Crete.
Nimatallah/Art Resource

around 1645 B.C., again about 1500, and a third time about 1400? Or did invading Hyksos, on their way out of Egypt after their occupation, do the damage? Did mainland Greeks, crossing from the north, cause the destruction of 1500? Nobody can be quite sure about the earlier destructions, which were repaired, but the last disaster may well be attributable to actions of mainland Greeks. Since 1960 the debate has intensified rather than lessened.

Mycenaeans and Minoans

In Greece, too, Bronze Age civilization had taken root. Greece was a largely barren land—mountainous and divided into small valleys and plains separated from each other, with none far from the sea. From earliest times the inhabitants took advantage of the rugged coasts and islands with their many shelters and good harbors to sail from place to place, seldom if ever losing sight of land, profiting by the exchange of olive oil and wine for grain and metal and slaves. Somewhat before 2000 B.C. the village Bronze Age culture of the inhabitants—who were not Indo-European speakers but, like the Cretans, presumably a mixture of Stone Age indigenous peoples and Anatolians who had invaded about 3000 B.C.—was interrupted by the invasion from the north of the first Indo-European speakers. The invaders first destroyed and then settled, no doubt intermarrying with the previous inhabitants, and developed early forms of the Greek language. This society had one of its chief centers at Mycenae, well situated to control land trade near the sea.

The Mycenaeans were led by warrior chieftains, but they also traded with Crete. Minoan objects have been found in the famous royal tombs at Mycenae that perhaps span the century from 1600 to 1500 B.C. In fact, the Minoan influence upon the arts of the mainland was so profound that scholars speak of the "Minoanization" of mainland Greece. The most celebrated objects are great gold masks of warrior princes buried in the tombs and daggers inlaid with various metals that show hunting scenes of astonishing realism and beauty. (When the German archaeologist Heinrich Schliemann found these objects in the 1870s, he thought that he had found the tomb of the Homeric hero Agamemnon. But, as we shall see, Agamemnon actually lived about three hundred years later.) Egypt and Anatolia also shared in the Mycenaean trade, but the chief influences in mainland Greece were Minoan.

Interchange, we now believe, went both ways. Mycenaean Greeks visited Crete as traders or even as tourists; perhaps they observed the absence of physical fortifications that left Knossos vulnerable. Then, it is conjectured, they moved in and seized power, perhaps about 1460 B.C., presumably having first built their own fleet. No longer did they need to send any tribute to Knossos. Indeed, they now controlled the very center of the civilization that had already taught them so much. Military innovations followed in Crete; chariots were

introduced, and arrows stored for large bodies of troops, but the invaders built no fortifications, presumably because they expected no new invasions. In the palace of Minos the Greeks installed a throne room of the type found in their own mainland palaces. Most important, the Minoans showed them how useful it was to keep records; and since Linear A, devised for a Semitic language, would not do, the scribes may have invented a new script—Linear B—in which to write the language of the conquerors: Greek. On the other hand, Linear B may have been developed gradually from Linear A.

Conclusive proof, worked out in 1952 by Michael Ventris, a young English scholar, showed that the language of Linear B is early Greek; it was this discovery that made possible the foregoing tentative reconstruction of events. Evans had found many Linear B tablets at Knossos, but no such tablets were known from mainland Greece until 1939, when an American scholar, Carl Blegen, discovered the first of what proved to be a large collection of them in Pylos, where he was excavating a Mycenaean palace. Since then many more have turned up elsewhere in Greece, including some in Mycenae itself. Acting on the assumption that it was probably Greek (since he now knew that Greeks were keeping records in it on the mainland), Ventris used the wartime techniques of cryptography to show that the script was not an alphabet, but that each symbol represented a syllable, and then he cracked the code. The thousands of Linear B tablets have by no means all been read even now. Nor are all readings certain. The tablets are mostly prosaic inventories of materials stored in the palaces or lists of persons in the royal services—but they are Greek.

This gold Mycenaean death mask is known as the Mask of Agamemnon.
National Museum, Athens/Nimatallah/Art Resource

The disappearance of Linear A in Crete, and the substitution for it about 1460 B.C. of the new Linear B, point clearly to a Mycenaean occupation of the island that lasted almost a century. We cannot be sure how independent of the mainland the new Greek rulers of Knossos were; they may have been subordinate princes. The great palace of Knossos and other major Cretan centers were burned down about 1400, apparently after looting. We do not know who did this. Perhaps the Cretans rose against their Greek masters and burned down their own cities, though it has been plausibly suggested that such an act would have invited fierce reprisals and continued occupation after reconstruction. In any event, there was no reconstruction; rather, there was permanent disruption. So perhaps it was the Mycenaeans themselves who, in revenge against Cretan rebelliousness that may have made the island ungovernable, decided to cut their losses, destroy the Cretan centers, and sail away. Or perhaps the destruction was the result of a volcanic upheaval of the seabed. The rediscovery (1967) and present active excavation of a Minoan city on the volcanic island of Santorin (Thera) to the north of Crete may enable scholars to decide the question one way or another. After the disaster of c. 1405 B.C. Crete remained rich and populous but lost its Mediterranean predominance, which passed to the aggressive mainland peoples.

Mycenae, 1400–1100 B.C.

We still know relatively little about Mycenaean politics and society. We can tell from excavated gold treasures that Mycenae itself was wealthy, which is not surprising considering that it had conquered Crete. But the Mycenaeans seem not to have been overseas empire builders, even in the sense that the Cretans had been; their occupation of Crete may well have been undertaken by an invading captain who retained power for himself in Crete, however much of his revenue he sent back home. The Achaeans or Greeks of whom the Hittite sources speak may well not have been the Greeks of Mycenae at all but Greeks of Rhodes, another island principality. And there were other settlements in the southern Greek mainland (called the Peloponnesus)—Pylos, Tiryns (the latter very close to Mycenae)—which seem to have been extensive, too, and perhaps under local rulers equally powerful if bound in alliance to the Mycenaeans. A loose confederacy among equals seems to fit best with the evidence.

Tombs from the period before 1400 B.C. tell us of the structure of society, for they are of two sharply distinct types: those carefully built to take the bodies of kings and nobles, and simple burial places for the rest of the population. Tombs from the period between 1400 and 1200 show a rise in general wealth; there are more chamber tombs with more gifts to the dead in them. Similarly, at Mycenae, Tiryns, Pylos, Athens, and Thebes there arose great palaces as community centers, with workshops, storage areas, guardrooms, and lesser dwelling houses attached. Good roads and bridges connected the main towns, and good water supply systems provided the towns with security. Artisans attached to the palaces built and repaired chariots, made jars to hold wine and oil, tanned leather, wrought bronze in the forges, made bricks, and sewed garments. Workmen stored goods for preservation, sale, and exchange. A Mycenaean palace was a businesslike and noisy place.

The Linear B tablets preserve records of special royal furniture elaborately inlaid in ivory, glass, and gold; like the Egyptian pharaohs, the Mycenaean rulers obviously valued objects most which they took time and effort to make. Smaller than the great palaces on Crete, those of the Mycenaeans on the mainland nonetheless testify to a vibrant life in a complex society. One of the richest hoards, containing treasures in gold, jewels, and bronze manufactured over five centuries, was found in a private house in Tiryns; it was obviously the booty of a Mycenaean grave robber with a fine taste in antiques.

Mycenaean bureaucrats continually intervened in the life of the ordinary person, keeping elaborate records of how much land and livestock each subject possessed, the cash or commodities owed in taxes, the amounts of bronze issued to each craftsman to make swords and arrowheads, and how much of everything was kept in each storeroom. Such attention to detail was positively Hittite or Ugaritic, and nothing like the Mycenaean bureaucracy ever reappeared in Greece after its destruction. And yet the records do not tell us all that we want to know; although we know that there were slaves, and we know the titles of various officials, we cannot be sure of their duties or gain a clear picture of governmental organization.

Until 1968 no Mycenaean religious shrine had ever been found. Gems discovered in Mycenaean tombs showed Cretan deities and religious scenes. The Linear B tablets from Pylos recorded offerings made to certain gods: Poseidon, god of the sea; Ares, god of war; Artemis, goddess of the moon; and even Zeus and Hera, to later Greeks the supreme ruler of the gods and his consort. The tablets contain the names of other gods who did not survive the Dark Age that lay ahead, and so did not reappear in classical Greece. But in 1968 at Mycenae, in a small storeroom, archaeologists found clay figures that suggest a religious cult—six coiled snakes and sixteen human, mostly female, hollow figures, only one of which is clothed and colored. Next door was a possible "chapel" of the cult, about which so far very little is known.

The most important episode of the three centuries 1400–1100 is the Trojan War, usually dated about 1250 or 1200 B.C., known to every Greek of the classical period from the *Iliad* and the *Odyssey*, epic poems put together about five centuries after the event and known to all the civilized West ever since. The war was a great expedition led by the king of Mycenae, Agamemnon, in command of a fleet and an army contributed by the other towns and islands of Mycenaean Greece, against Troy, allegedly a rich city on the northwest coast of Anatolia (modern Turkey) not far from the mouth of the

The Lion Gate of Mycenae leads into the ancient fortress, the legendary seat of Agamemnon.
New York Public Library Picture Collection

Dardanelles, the straits that lead from the Aegean into the Sea of Marmora. The Trojans were related to the Greeks, though they were less advanced. They did not write, and they seem to have had little contact with their neighbors in the Aegean, the Cretans, or with their neighbors in Anatolia, the Hittites. But many Mycenaean objects found in the ruins of Troy show that the Trojans traded with mainland Greece, perhaps offering in exchange for their goods woolen textiles (a great number of pottery spindles survived in the Trojan ruins) and horses, which the Trojans bred and whose bones are also numerous in the ruins.

The famous Greek expedition to avenge the abduction by the Trojan prince Paris of the beautiful Helen, wife of Agamemnon's brother, Menelaus, prince of Mycenaean Sparta, is simply a romantic tale. The tradition that the siege lasted ten years, involving many ships and men before Agamemnon's forces won and burned Troy, may be romance, too. Excavations show that the city of Troy, destroyed about 1250 or somewhat later, was the seventh city on the site. The first five belonged to an earlier people and had already been destroyed by 1900 B.C., when the Trojans arrived, bringing their horses and a new kind of pottery made also by the Greeks. These newcomers built Troy VI, a magnificent walled citadel enclosing a few houses for the most important people, who ruled over a larger subject population on the slopes of a hillside and in the plain below. Troy VI was ruined about 1300, probably by an earthquake. And then Troy VII, a shriveled, partial restoration of the great Troy VI, was built in and on the ruins.

It is this shrunken city that was destroyed by enemies a few generations later. But its shabbiness is so at variance with the traditions of its splendor remembered in the *Iliad*, and the date of its destruction lies so near the date at which we know that Mycenaean Greece itself collapsed under the blows of new enemies, that a few scholars now believe that there never was a Trojan War at all. Though powerfully argued, this view will probably be slow to win acceptance because the story of Troy is so deeply embedded in our cultural traditions. Scholars who believe in the war gain comfort from the fact that the *Iliad* calls the Greeks Achaeans, and that Achaeans are almost surely mentioned also in Hittite sources as a powerful people who sometimes raided the coasts of Anatolia in the thirteenth century, when Hittite power was waning. Perhaps these "Achaeans" came from nearby Rhodes and were relatives of those who, we have always believed, fought and won the Trojan War. Troy itself, however, went almost without mention in Hittite written sources.

Soon after the fall of Troy VII there began the upheavals in the Mediterranean world in which the so-called Sea Peoples ruined the Hittite state and the Egyptian New Kingdom and left the Philistines as new settlers on the shores of Palestine. These destabilizing changes helped generate a wave of violence that also destroyed Mycenaean Greece. Invaders from the north swept over all of Greece; the palaces and tombs vanished in the disorders, and with them went Mycenaean civilization. Scholars once called these invaders Dorians—Greeks speaking a special dialect that can be identified in later inscriptions—and attributed most of the destruction to them. We now believe that the Dorians did indeed invade about 1100, but that Mycenaean civilization had probably been pretty thoroughly destroyed before they arrived and were able to dominate most of Greece.

The Dark Age: Homer

The three centuries from 1100 to 800 B.C. are known as the Dark Age—dark because we have too little evidence to obtain a clear picture of Greek life, and dark also because civilization took dramatic steps backward. Literacy virtually vanished, and writing stopped. Some argue that Linear B had been too clumsy a script ever to have been useful for any purpose other than keeping records; that in any case only a very small percentage of Mycenaean Greeks (perhaps 5 percent) could ever have been able to read or write it; and that its disappearance was a benefit because when literacy returned, Greek was written in the convenient new alphabet adopted from the Phoenicians. But no one denies that poverty and primitive conditions prevailed in Greece, causing suffering, a loss of skills, a shrinkage of the communities, a great forgetting of the past, and a halt in progress.

After about 1050 B.C., however, iron clearly began to replace bronze as the metal for weapons and utensils. Moreover, we know that there were migrations of Greeks out of Greece to the Aegean coasts of Asia Minor and especially to the central region later called Ionia, which we may date as taking place by 800 B.C. In the hinterland behind these seacoast regions lived the native Anatolian peoples in their own kingdoms. On the mainland, the Athenians escaped the full impact of the Dorian invasions; perhaps their good fortune started them on the way to the leadership of Greece that would be theirs after the Dark Age ended.

The end of the Dark Age is closely tied to the oral composition of two epic poems, the *Iliad* (sixteen thousand lines) and the *Odyssey* (twelve thousand lines). Did the same person compose both? Was it Homer? Did the *Iliad* precede the *Odyssey*? No certain answers can be given to these questions. It does seem probable that both poems took roughly the form in which we know them at some time between 850 and 750 B.C., although some scholars argue for later dates. The *Odyssey* was almost surely composed later than the *Iliad*, though it may be a later work of the same person who composed the *Iliad* in his youth.

This person was really a singer, putting together in these monumental narratives shorter songs about the deeds of heroes. Such singers, accompanying themselves on stringed instruments, sang the shorter separate songs to audiences seated at table in a princely household, or to a gathering of villagers in a public square, or to soldiers around a campfire. The *Iliad* and the *Odyssey* represent only a fraction of the epic material that existed in the Dark Age; there were many other tales of heroes that were less popular or that stood the test of performance less well. The composer of the long poems was selecting favorites that, when assembled, would make a coherent narrative. Such a singer had no written versions of his work; he learned by heart from a predecessor many thousands of lines of poetry. While he sang, he had little time to reflect on what he would sing next, so he had recourse to formulas that would fit the rhythm of the verse and that would be familiar to his hearers. From a huge stock of such formulas, he could choose and blend those that told his story. Works as long as the *Iliad* or *Odyssey* would have taken several days to recite. They may have been put together specifically for some nobleman's prolonged feast or for a religious festival. But it seems more probable that a great singer who knew many of the individual songs was inspired to assemble them "to make a complete and universal Trojan song."

For a long time after their composition, both poems continued to be transmitted orally. At Athens, in the sixth century B.C., two hundred years after the epics had been composed and seven hundred years after the Trojan War itself (always supposing that there was a Trojan War),

the *Iliad* and the *Odyssey* were recited in public every four years at an Athenian festival; the law required that this be done in order and without omissions. By then, presumably, the poems had been written down; but it was not for another three centuries that a stable "scholarly" text was produced in Alexandria, from which the versions that have come down to us ultimately derive.

The *Iliad* deals with a single episode that took place during the siege of Troy—the wrath of the Greek hero Achilles, who stopped fighting and sulked in his tent because the commander, Agamemnon, had taken from him a captive Trojan girl. Agamemnon had allowed himself to be persuaded to restore his own captive girl to her family, and so made up for his loss by taking Achilles' prize away. While Achilles refused to fight, the great combat continued. Eventually, when Hector, a Trojan prince, had killed Achilles' best friend and comrade-in-arms, Patroclus, Achilles returned to the battle and in turn slew Hector. At the very end he returned the body to Hector's sorrowing father, old King Priam, for funeral ceremonies.

The *Odyssey* tells of the ten-year wanderings of another Greek hero, Odysseus, after the siege of Troy was over, and of the extraordinary places and peoples he visited on the way back to his home on the island of Ithaca, where his faithful wife Penelope awaited him despite the attention of many suitors, and whence their son Telemachus had set out to find his father.

Put in this summary form, the two stories seem blunt and commonplace. But a deep humanity pervades both. Despite the continual bloody fighting in the *Iliad*, modern readers—like all before them—are moved by the terror of Hector's baby son, Astyanax, when he sees his father with his fierce plumed war helmet on, until Hector takes it off and shows the child who he really is; feel the truth of the passage in which the old men of Troy admit that Helen—beautiful as a goddess—was well worth all the fuss; share the grief and dignity of Priam as he begs Achilles to return Hector's body for a decent burial; and appreciate Achilles' courteous generosity to an enemy when he reluctantly agrees. The romantic *Odyssey*, with its lotus eaters, sirens, men turned to swine by enchantment, and fierce one-eyed giant, also provides similar moments of high human drama in the homecoming of Odysseus in disguise; in the responses of his favorite dog and his old nurse; and in the sorrow of the beautiful island princess Nausicaa, first seen playing ball on the beach with her maidens, when she finds that Odysseus will not stay and be her lover.

In both poems the gods and goddesses are standard Greek divinities—Zeus, Hera, Apollo (the sun), Artemis (the moon), Ares (war), Poseidon (the sea), Aphrodite (love), Athena (wisdom), and the rest—who play an intimate part in the affairs of mortals, intervening in the fighting to give victory to their favorites, supplying Achilles with an extraordinary shield on which are displayed many instructive scenes in cunning metalwork, saving Odysseus from the perils of his voyage. The immortals on Mount Olympus are only a little larger than the heroes; they live thoroughly human lives, quarreling over the affairs of mortals and having fits of bad temper.

It is possible that there are real links stretching backward from the *Iliad* and the *Odyssey* across the Dark Age, when the singer's art was kept alive in Ionia, to heroic songs composed by Mycenaeans themselves. Many scholars stress such links and believe in a continuous tradition. The long Catalog of the Ships in the *Iliad*, for example, lists the contingents supplied to the Greek armies at Troy by the various Greek settlements, and names their commanders. Many think it a real Bronze Age document that provides genuine, usable evidence about the diverse political organization of Mycenaean society: by city, by the captain the troops followed, and by tribe. So, too, the description of Odysseus's household as including more than fifty slaves is often taken to indicate that slavery was common in Mycenaean times. And some draw conclusions from the poems about the inheritance of royal power or the existence of assemblies of elders.

Most recent scholars, however, prefer to use the poems sparingly for such purposes, or not at all. Still, whether or not we use the poems as history today, the Greeks themselves certainly did so, forming their own conception of their ancestral past from the *Iliad* and the *Odyssey*. Together with the Hebrew Bible, some of which was first being committed to writing at about the same time, the Homeric poems form the greatest literary and cultural legacy of ancient people. Indeed, many modern scholars maintain that both Homeric and Hebrew civilizations grew directly from a common eastern Mediterranean background and point to many parallels in action and attitude. We know so little about these people, their literature, their society. Yet we can recognize so much of ourselves in them—in their search for security, their sense of pleasure, their regard for duty and honor. Clearly, however, distant from us in time, these people and their history are part of our experience.

Summary

The period before humans left written records is called *prehistory*. Our knowledge of this period depends on archaeological findings. Although fossil remains of apelike human ancestors have been found that date back millions of years, the first generally accepted humans appeared in Europe and the Near East about thirty-seven thousand years ago and are called *homo sapiens*, meaning the "one who thinks."

Archaeologists call early human culture the Old Stone (Paleolithic) Age because of the crude stone implements in use at the time. Paleolithic humans have left remarkable cave paintings and carvings. About 8000 B.C. humanity advanced to the New Stone (Neolithic) Age, marked by the domestication of animals and plants and the development of more permanent dwellings.

The decisive step from prehistory to history was the invention of writing by the Neolithic inhabitants of Mesopotamia around 3500 B.C. By 3100 B.C. the Sumerians in southern Mesopotamia had invented bronze and developed *cuneiform* writing into a flexible tool of communication.

Mesopotamia was what historians call a hydraulic society, one based on the centralized control of irrigation and flood management. There were many cities, each with its own bureaucracy and temple. Among the legacies of Mesopotamian culture are the first law codes, the first epic, *Gilgamesh*, and certain religious concepts, such as the story of a primeval flood, that have persisted in Western thought.

The Sumerian city-states gave way to the Babylonian (about 2300 B.C.) and Assyrian (about 1100 B.C.) empires. Eventually, all of Mesopotamia was absorbed by the Persian Empire in the sixth century B.C.

Another Neolithic hydraulic society developed along the Nile River in Egypt, which was first united into a single state around 2850 B.C. Egypt became a highly bureaucratic society ruled by a god-king, the pharaoh. Ancient Egyptian history is divided into three broad areas of unified rule, separated by periods of division and anarchy: the Old Kingdom (2700–2160 B.C.), the Middle Kingdom (2134–1786 B.C.), and the New Kingdom (1575–1087 B.C.). Thereafter, Egypt entered a period of political decline and foreign rule.

Religion was the most powerful force in Egyptian society. The Egyptians had many gods and were preoccupied by life after death. To ensure survival in the next world, they built elaborate tombs and mummified the bodies of the dead. Much of what we know about ancient Egypt comes from what was found in its tombs.

Egyptian writing, called hieroglyphics, was deciphered only in the nineteenth century. Egyptian literature includes love songs and what is perhaps the first fiction.

The Hebrews were nomads who established themselves in Palestine around 1300 B.C. The importance of the Hebrews lies in their religion. They were the first to insist that their god was the only god and a universal god. They were also the first people to record their history in a series of books—the Hebrew Bible.

Cretan civilization is called Minoan after Minos, the legendary founder of the local dynasty. The Cretans ruled a maritime empire from a vast palace at Knossos. Cretan prosperity ended between around 1645 and 1400 B.C., though whether because of natural disaster or foreign conquest is unclear.

Bronze Age civilization in Greece is called Mycenaean because one of its chief centers was at Mycenae in southern Greece. Mycenaean civilization was based on heavily fortified palace centers and was highly bureaucratic. Its most lasting and important legacies are the great epic poems the *Iliad* and the *Odyssey*.

2

The Greeks

*T*he Greeks are the first ancient civilization with which modern society feels an immediate affinity. We like to believe that they thought much as we do—that is, that they were rationalists, intensely curious about their environment, eager to acquire new knowledge and to use it to alter their condition. We recognize them as a reflective people, questioning the human condition, interested in the new, but respectful of the old. Their literature, one of the richest the world has seen, shows a feeling for history. They also believed in their gods with an intensity and good humor that humanized both the gods and the Greeks. They accepted the world of the actual—good or bad—as they understood it, and they consciously strove to understand that world through both science and religion. We trace our political institutions to them.

We think of the Greeks as curious, given to questions: Where does the stranger I see come from? How large is your family? How much money do you make? How can we prove what we believe to be true? Why do people fall ill? How should societies govern themselves? The Greeks felt secure questioning both the specific and the general, and they recognized that people would search for security in the psychological areas that fall between such precise and such general questions. That we recognize elements of ourselves in them—tracing our democracies remotely back to their early city-states, linking our desire for perfection to their heroes, finding in their sense of humor much that we may laugh about today—tells us at least as much about ourselves and our needs as it does about the Greeks. It is this sense of being linked in time that customarily leads modern scholars to begin the history of our concept of Western civilization in the northwest corner of the ancient Near East—on the Greek peninsula, on the islands of the Aegean Sea, and in the Greek-speaking cities on the western coast of Asia Minor.

There is, of course, a special bias at work in this linkage of ourselves to the ancient Greeks. Perhaps they were not more curious about the world than other societies had been; perhaps they simply left better records, by which we can explore their curiosity and see how it relates to our own. They, too, were haunted by superstition, but they had the time and courage to explore their superstitions. They, too, fought endless petty wars with each other, but they produced historians—Herodotus, Thucydides, Xenophon—who explained these wars in ways that make us feel we understand them. They thought deeply and well, but most of their great thinkers belonged to a leisure class that had the time to devote to thought for its own sake—to inquiry without immediate reward—because its members had slaves to assure that daily tasks did not go undone. They were not a wholly admirable people (there are no wholly admirable people, and, in any case, it is not the business of history to make such judgments), but they

are the first people with whom we can identify. We feel that we can actually know the Greeks because we can understand their motivations.

We can also identify with the Greeks because of their art. Of course, civilization is not measured solely or even predominantly by the history of art. One culture is often unable to recognize the art of another culture, but art does provide objects, shapes, indications of how a culture defines beauty, at which we may look, to compare, reject, or accept into our own understanding. Art helps to embody, to objectify, an ideal of perfection—whether of reason, of justice, of balance, or of the human spirit. It attempts to express (as does religion) an ideal. We have inherited such an ideal from the Greeks, in their architecture, in their attempts to define civility, in their awareness of the tension (which they would have called "divine") between the ideal and the actual, as in the structural tension between the upraised arm and the heavier torso in a representative figure of Greek statuary.

To have a sense of civility is to have a sense of permanence. This, in turn, means having an awareness of occupying a place in space and time, knowing that there are other cultures—now, in the past, and in the future—and knowing that the culture of which we are a part must take its place in such a continuum. This is the sense of history which the Greeks developed more acutely than any Western peoples who had preceded them, insofar as the record tells us, and it is that record, which their sense of history led them to retain, upon which we draw today.

Politically we may think of the Greeks as the fathers of democracy—that is, of government by and through the people. They also, at different times and in different places, found the best government to be oligarchy—that is, government by the few, whether those few were a natural-born aristocracy, or the rich, or the "most noble of mind." At other times they accepted tyranny—absolute rule by a single person. They did not "invent" any of these forms of government, for governmental forms evolve and are not the inventions of individuals. But they did use these various forms, for in politics they experienced the tension between the ideal and the actual in terms of competition among groups who felt they alone possessed the right to define society's problems and find society's solutions. In the variety of their political thought, we also perceive ourselves as their kin.

I THE GREEKS BEFORE THE PERSIAN WARS

Modern students have often derived their picture of Greek politics in general from the superb speech that Pericles, the most celebrated of the leaders of Athens,

This figure of a charioteer from Delphi is one of the very few bronze statues to survive from the fifth century B.C.
Scala/Art Resource

Revival after the Dark Age, 850–650 B.C.

For the Greeks the Dark Age began to dissipate about 850 B.C., with the renewal of contact between the mainland and the Near East. Phoenicia, whose trade continued briskly, lay close to the Greek island of Cyprus, where Mycenaean culture had continued after the Dorians had destroyed it on most of the mainland. Objects from Phoenicia began to appear in mainland Greece; the earliest traces of the Phoenician alphabet as adapted to the writing of Greek are now dated about 825 B.C., with new letters added for peculiarly Greek sounds. New styles of pottery also testify to the renewal of communications. Greece proper now received the Homeric poems, first composed in the Ionian Greek settlements of Asia Minor, restoring to the mainland the sense of its glorious past.

In Greece, people looked back through Homer and the poet Hesiod to a time they thought of as far more heroic than their own, and this sense of a heroic past emboldened them to new acts of heroism. Hesiod, in his *Works and Days*, written in the seventh century B.C., set down proper rules for the small farmer and scolded his own brother, who had tried to grab more than his fair share of the family estate. His farm was infertile, the climate bad, and the behavior of people had degenerated, Hesiod felt, since the good old days. Hesiod also wrote a genealogy of the gods (*Theogony*), giving the traditional view of how the universe had come into being; the gods were the children of earth and heaven and had themselves created humankind. Preaching justice, both human and divine, Hesiod's verse reflected the religious ideas of the Greeks in an early phase, perhaps partly under the influence of the oracle at Delphi, a mountain shrine of the sun god Apollo in central Greece, where a divinely inspired prophetess gave advice to all comers. Hesiod's concern for the farmer also reflects the fact that the great majority of ancient populations made their living through farming.

The Polis and Colonization

For the Greeks, the prevailing social and political unit gradually became the *polis* (plural, *poleis*), roughly translated as the "city-state," though many were too small to be cities. The main sense of the term is that of a community of relatives, citizens all descended in theory from a common ancestor. The "kings," or local chieftains, of Mycenaean times had disappeared, and the prominent men—the richer and more noble—in each community had begun to form councils and other variously selected groups to manage public affairs. Usually the community centered upon a fortress built upon a hill, "the high city" or *acropolis*, and also possessed a public square or gathering-place for assemblies, the *agora*.

Our scanty and unclear sources give us a picture of a society in which the rich alone could afford expensive

made in 431 B.C. over the Athenian soldiers killed in the first year of a great war against Sparta—as reported in the history of the war by the historian Thucydides. Praising Athenian democracy, Pericles said that in Athens the law guaranteed equal justice to all, that talent and not wealth was the Athenian qualification for public service, that Athenians expected everyone to participate in public affairs. In fact, his picture corresponded more to an ideal world than to the real Athens, where the courts were often prejudiced, where wealth remained an important qualification for office, and where political ambition burned hotly and was pursued ruthlessly. In the tough world of Athenian politics, we can see strong parallels to human behavior in other, more modern democracies. The Greeks often fell far short of their ideals as expressed by Pericles, but in the expression of these ideals they also defined civility in ways for which society has striven ever since.

Ancient Greece

Athenian Empire, 450 B.C.

■ Battle sites

Black Sea

THRACE

Byzantium

Bosporus

Propontis
(Sea of Marmora)

Amphipolis

Aegospotami

MACEDONIA

Hellespont

Troy

CHALCIDICE

PERSIAN EMPIRE

MT. OLYMPUS

EPIRUS

Dodona

THESSALY

LESBOS

LYDIA

PHRYGIA

ARGINUSAE IS.

Sardis

Thermopylae

ITHACA

Delphi

Thebes

EUBOEA

Aegean Sea

CHIOS

SAMOS

MYCALE

Athens

Miletus

I O n i a n   S e a

Olympia

Corinth

Mycenae

Argos

DELOS

Halicarnassus

PELOPONNESUS

MELOS

COS

Pylos

Sparta

LACONIA

THERA
(SANTORIN)

RHODES

Cretan Sea

0   50   100
Miles

Knossos

CRETE

Mediterranean Sea

MT. PARNASSUS △

Delphi

PHOCIS

Chaeronea

EUBOEA

BOEOTIA

Thebes

Gulf of Corinth

Leuctra

Plataea

Delium

ATTICA

Marathon

Megara

Eleusis

Athens

Saronic

Corinth

Salamis

Piraeus

Gulf

MT. LAURION △

Mycenae

Epidaurus

AEGINA

Argos

Tiryns

Mantinea

25
Miles

Greek Colonial World

Areas of Greek settlement

0   500
Miles

UKRAINE

CRIMEA

ALPS

Danube R.

Black Sea

ILLYRIA

Trebizond

Massilia

PYRENEES

ITALY

Byzantium

ASIA MINOR

IBERI

CORSICA

Paestum

Phocaea

SARDINIA

Croton

Megara

IONIA

Segesta

"MAGNA GRAECIA"

Corinth

Athens

RHODES

SYRIA

Cadiz

Selinus

Agrigento

Syracuse

GREECE

CRETE

CYPRUS

PHOENICIA

Str. of
Gibraltar

Carthage

SICILY

Mediterranean Sea

Cyrene

LIBYA

EGYPT

A F R I C A

36

horses and military equipment and therefore controlled the instruments of coercion. They had organized themselves into an aristocracy of family and wealth, proud of their bloodlines, and they dominated the poor who worked the land. A middle class of well-to-do farmers, merchants, and craftsmen also came into existence and eventually formed the nucleus of the close-order infantry formations, newly developed about 650 B.C., that were more efficient than the traditional cavalry. Social conflict within and among classes was a normal condition of life.

One-man rule became the characteristic form of government within these evolving city-states beginning about 650. To some extent the conflicts were dampened, the power of the aristocracy held in check, and the lower classes protected; but in each case the personal qualities of the tyrant determined the success and decency of his rule. Usually the power of a tyrant did not last more than one or two generations at the most.

Together with the establishment of city-states, there was also large-scale Greek colonial expansion. The city-states of Asia Minor and of mainland Greece sent out naval expeditions to plant new settlements in non-Greek areas where there was no power strong enough to prevent them: around the Black Sea, along the African shore of the Mediterranean (in what we now call Libya), in Sicily and southern Italy (which the Romans later called *Magna Graecia*, "Greater Greece"), and as far west as the coasts of France and Spain. Each new colony became a new city-state—independent of its mother city, though bound to it by historical and economic ties and by similar political and religious practices. Overpopulation and internal strife in the settled cities, together with the wish for trade and adventure, advanced the colonizing movement. Trebizond in Asia Minor, Byzantium (later to become Constantinople and still later Istanbul) at the Black Sea straits, Syracuse in Sicily, Naples in southern Italy, Marseilles in southern France, and Cadiz beyond the Straits of Gibraltar on the Atlantic coast of Spain are among the famous cities that began as Greek colonies.

Combined with the decline of Egypt and the Assyrian conquests in western Asia, such colonization set off a period of Mediterranean trade focusing on Greece. First one Greek city and then another would assume prominence in the busy traffic; the Dorian-founded settlements on Crete, Rhodes, Corinth, and Megara all became powerful and prosperous. By the midseventh century, coins, invented in the Anatolian kingdom of Lydia, had begun to be minted on the island of Aegina in Greece, where silver was the only precious metal available. This convenient system of recording commerce soon spread westward, each city-state making its own coinage. (The coins of Aegina had turtles on them; those of Corinth, foals; those of Athens, the owl of Athena, patron goddess of the city.)

In the area of southern Greece called the Peloponnesus, a fertile, almost landlocked region, the city-state of Sparta developed. (The connotations of the adjective

The owl, sacred to Athena, appeared on Athenian coins beginning in the sixth century B.C. The original coin was struck by Pisistratus, who ruled Athens from 542 to 527 B.C. *New York Public Library Picture Collection*

Spartan are present-day reminders of that unique society.) Later called by the philosopher Aristotle "an association of villages which achieves almost complete self-sufficiency," the Spartan polis was ruled by the descendants of the Dorian conquerers, perhaps 10 percent of the total population and the only citizens, called the *homoioi*, or "equals." Most of the people belonged to the class of *helots*, farm laborers who belonged to the state, which assigned them to work the lands of the citizens. In between was a free class called *perioikoi* (dwellers around), descendants of the pre-Dorian residents of neighboring areas, who lived in the villages under Spartan control and had personal freedom but could not participate in politics or intermarry with the Spartans; they were also subject to Sparta in foreign and military matters. No helots were assigned to the perioikoi, but they could buy slaves abroad if they wished. The ruling Spartans lived in constant fear of revolution; they kept secret agents planted among the helots to report subversive talk, and they barely managed to put down a helot uprising in the late seventh century.

The constitution, which the Spartans attributed to a divinely inspired lawgiver, Lycurgus, provided for two kings, perhaps descendants of two rival Dorian families. Real political power came to reside in five overseers elected annually by an assembly of all Spartan citizens over the age of thirty—excluding all women, helots, and perioikoi. There was also a kind of council of thirty elders representing the more powerful families.

War dominated Spartan thinking. The males lived under military discipline from the age of seven, when a boy was taken from his parents and taught reading, music, running, and fighting. Weak-looking babies were abandoned to die. So that they might bear healthy children, girls were also given strenuous training. Adult males lived in barracks until they were thirty, though they might marry at twenty; they dined in the mess hall until they were sixty. It was a harsh, regimented life, "Spartan" in its merits and in its defects. In battle the Spartan army was excellent, and the citizens were patriotic and willing to bear misfortune. The need to control hostile neighbors and internal dissension led the Spartans to introduce iron bars as money, making ordinary commercial pursuits as unattractive, public, and difficult as possible. It was a barracks state.

Athens, from 632 B.C.

Draco and Solon   Athens—which had never undergone a Dorian occupation—did not become a polis as early as Sparta but lingered as an old-fashioned, aristocratic tribal state, dominating the surrounding hinterland of Attica. It was divided territorially into plains, hills, and coastal land, and politically into four tribes, each of which had brotherhoods (*phratries*) or territorial subdivisions (*trittyes*). Within each phratry a further distinction was drawn between those who owned and worked their farms (the *clans*), and the *guildsmen*, later in origin, who belonged to an association of artisans or merchants. Each mature male was admitted into a phratry either as a clansman or as a guildsman. Land descended in the clan and might not be passed outside it. With the clan went a deep attachment to local religious shrines, whose priests were clansmen. The guildsmen were citizens though not aristocrats; apparently they could sell or transfer their property.

Three *archons* (leaders or chief men)—one of whom managed religious affairs, one military affairs (the *polemarch*), and one civil affairs—were joined in the seventh century by a board of six recording archons (legal officials), making nine in all. Each was elected for a year, at the end of which all nine automatically became members of the Council of Areopagus (from the hill of Ares, god of war, in Athens), the chief judicial and policy-making body. Although a general assembly of all the males directly elected the archons and thus the future members of the Areopagus Council, only clansmen—men of birth and wealth—and not guildsmen could be elected.

These long-standing political arrangements were challenged in 632 by a young noble's plot to seize power, which led to scandal when his followers were massacred even though they had taken sanctuary at the altar of Athena. The noble family held responsible for this sacrilege was banished, and in 621 B.C. a specially appointed official, Draco, allegedly published the first Athenian law code, famous for its severe penalties (hence our term, a *Draconian* measure). The harshest of all Athenian laws were those on debt; a bankrupt clansman could never sell or mortgage his land but was compelled to mortgage its produce to his debtor. Thus he could oblige himself and his heirs to work the land

indefinitely for somebody else, in effect losing his freedom. Bankrupt guildsmen became the property of their creditors as slaves. In time the growing inequity of this system led to internal strife.

In the 590s a reformer, Solon, elected as the sole archon, freed both the clansmen and guildsmen then suffering these penalties for debt, canceled current debts, abolished the harsh system, and published a new constitution, or law code. He tried to improve the general prosperity by emphasizing the need to abandon complete economic dependence on agriculture and to foster a lively new commerce. He even offered citizenship to citizens of other poleis who would come to work in Athens. He opened the most important offices of state to the richest men, whatever their origin. Wealth was measured by the amount of agricultural produce a man's land provided annually; for example, 750 bushels of grain or about 4,400 gallons of olive oil a year put a man into the topmost class and made him eligible for high office. A man whose land produced less than 300 bushels of grain or only about 1,800 gallons of olive oil a year was eligible only for the general assembly.

Solon is also said to have founded a new body, the Council of Four Hundred, consisting of one hundred members from each of the four tribes, all named by Solon himself, to act as an inner circle of the general assembly of the people, preparing materials for discussion and making recommendations for action. The general assembly now could not act without such a recommendation; but it could vote against it, and it still elected the archons. And Solon also made the assembly a kind of court by selecting a panel of its members by lot to review the work of the magistrates.

By introducing these quasi-democratic innovations while retaining aristocratic election of the rich to magistracies and the oligarchic power of the few in the Council of the Areopagus, Solon had introduced a radical set of compromises. In one of his own poems he says of his actions: "I stood holding my stout shield over both parties [the poor and the rich]; I did not allow either party to prevail unjustly." By justice Solon meant what we might call social justice. Though some of his fellow Athenians jeered at him for not taking advantage of his extraordinary powers to make himself rich, he answered (again in a poem) that "money flits from man to man, but honor abides forever." Urging the Athenians to abide by his laws for a hundred years, Solon then withdrew from the scene.

Pisistratus and Cleisthenes   Factional strife soon began again. Athenians seem to have taken sides in accordance with both region and class. The plains people were mostly aristocrats who felt Solon had gone too far, the hill people mostly poor farmers who felt he had not gone far enough, and the coast people mostly artisans who thought he was about right. In 560 B.C. their quarrels delivered Athens into the hands of a *tyrant*, as the Greeks called a dictator, even if benevolent. This was Pisistratus, a noble, who had made himself leader of the hill people. In and out of office for some years, Pisistratus owed his final return in 546 to the vast wealth that he had acquired from the silver mines on his estates in the north and to the mercenary troops from Argos whom he hired with this wealth. Pisistratus and his son, Hippias, dominated Athens until 510 B.C.

Though Solon's constitutional measures had not endured, his economic policy made Athens rich, as Athenian pottery became the best and most-sought-after in Greece. Pisistratus—who collected 10 percent of all revenues for his personal fortune—pushed commercial success still further, partly by shrewd alliances with other poleis. At home, his was the only party. He exiled those aristocrats who refused to support him; he would often keep the son of a noble family as a hostage to ensure the family's loyalty. Having come to power as leader of the poor, he gave them loans, embarked on a lavish program of public works to be sure there were jobs for all, subsidized the arts, and increased the magnificence of state religious celebrations. His sons followed his policies, but the noble families whom Pisistratus had displaced continued in opposition, often from exile. When Hipparchus, one of the sons known as the Tyrant, was murdered in 514 B.C., executions multiplied, the government grew even more tyrannical, and the exiled nobles came back in triumphant alliance with the Spartans in 510 B.C.

By 508 Cleisthenes, one of the exiles who appealed for the support of the guildsmen, came to power on promises of constitutional reform. These he fulfilled by striking at the political influence of the clans in elections, and by giving the guildsmen equal weight. Using as a basic new political unit an old territorial division called a *deme*—a small area something like a ward in a modern city—Cleisthenes ordered all citizens to be registered as voters within their demes, irrespective of their origins, thus giving the guildsmen equal franchise with the clansmen. Whoever was a member of a given deme in 508–507 B.C. remained in it permanently, and so did his descendants, even if they moved away.

Cleisthenes also rezoned Attica into three new regions that did not coincide with the former coast, hill, and plain. He regrouped the demes into trittyes that, unlike the twelve older trittyes, were in general not compact and adjacent, but chosen from all three territorial subgroupings. Finally, by drawing lots he put every three trittyes together into a political "tribe." Instead of the four old racial (or genuinely tribal) groups, there were ten of these new political tribes; their membership cut across the old family, regional, and class lines. Each of these new, artificial tribes had members from each of the three new territorial divisions. Thus the former influence of the noble families had been effectively cut down. Cleisthenes had invented a fundamental tool of democracy—the gerrymander.

Each deme annually elected a number of its members (proportionate to its population) as its representatives, and from them the ten new tribes selected by lot fifty each to be members of the new Council of Five Hundred, replacing Solon's Council of Four Hundred. Solon had given Athenians equality before the law;

Cleisthenes gave them equality at the ballot box. The four old racial tribes, the old brotherhoods, and the clans continued to play a major part in religious and social life, but their political role was virtually over.

The ten groups of fifty tribal members of which the Council of Five Hundred was made up each governed in continual session for a tenth of the year (roughly thirty-six days), and the chairman of the committee of fifty that was sitting at any given time was selected afresh by lot every day. During each continual thirty-six-day session the committee members lived in a special state building and were fed at public expense. They could summon the remaining councilors to a full session whenever they wished. No citizen between the ages of thirty and sixty could be a member of the council more than twice, or chairman of a day's session more than once. Thus, with swiftly changing large groups of citizens receiving responsibilities for short times, almost any citizen could hope to enjoy the experience of participating in government at some time during his life (citizens were still males only). Fortified by their new constitution giving all citizens a stake in the community, the Athenians were prepared for their historic confrontation with the Persian Empire.

Still, Greek society and the growing economy depended upon the systematic exploitation of slaves. Dependent labor is important to any state that must be able to ensure productivity, unless that ability can be generated through other incentives. Public works, manufacture, agriculture, even trade and war production required dependent labor. Thus, in the eyes of the law, slaves were property. Like all ancient peoples, Greeks took slavery for granted, as their law code and their literature show. Free men who could afford slaves, if only as personal servants, did so, and slave women performed household chores. These slaves were outside the political system both as slaves and because most

One may learn much about everyday life in ancient Greece from the art found on *kraters* such as this one, from the third century A.D., in the museum of Cefalù, Sicily. Represented here is the fish market.
Scala/Art Resource

A vase in typical red and black ware showing dogs being trained, from the Archaeological Museum in Florence, Italy
Scala/Art Resource

were foreigners. Thus Athenians were not kept as slaves in Athens, though they might be in Corinth. In time *slave* and *barbarian*, or non-Greek, came to be nearly synonymous for some Greek commentators, and *barbaros* came to cover all non-Greeks. The term did not imply savagery, however, but simply being "they" (outsiders) rather than "we."

We know little about the life of the slaves, for they were not in a position to leave records, and because we do not know how slavery functioned we cannot say how basic to society it was. Their voice is best heard through what we can learn of their actions as revealed in the records of the dominant elements in society. Obviously, some Greeks owned no slaves and may have disapproved of slavery; some owners treated slaves as fellow workers; other owners reduced the life of the slave to a cycle of toil, punishment, and sustenance. Moreover, slaves were of different significance at different times and in different cities. At best we must recognize slavery as an institution basic to Greek society, and in particular to agriculture, but we cannot determine, from our present knowledge, how basic.

We know somewhat more about the role of family life in ancient Greece, though again not enough. Certainly women enjoyed political and legal rights that placed them above slaves; equally clearly, they had no political rights and few legal ones, and the personal freedom most women enjoyed depended on the social position of their husbands. Women in Athens appear to

The ruins of the temple of Apollo at Corinth. Dorian in style, the temple dates from about 630 B.C.
SEF/Art Resource

have had less significance than in Minoan society, for they were likely to be confined to their homes. There, however, they had much, though not absolute, authority over the running of the household. In Sparta alone, where young girls took part in the physical training enjoined upon all by the state, did women play roles outside the home or beyond the religious festival.

The role of women tended to be defined by social class. Among the poor, wives might well work as stall-keepers in the market. Aristophanes refers to "business-women," and still others were courtesans. But the major badge of identity was the key to storeroom or cellar that a wife carried with her. If she was reasonably well-to-do, she would preside over slave girls and a substantial household to which the husband paid little attention. Nonetheless, the household would remain his. And a daughter who inherited property because there was no male heir was required to marry her father's closest relative.

The seclusion of women was intensified by the facts that marriages were social or economic alliances and that men entertained one another in the Agora, the Assembly, or in their homes. Male homosexuality was accepted, especially between an older man and a boy, and though these relations were at times nonphysical, the presumption was that men spent their time outside the home and with each other. Even so, the role of the family was very important, for it was through the family that property was inherited, that citizenship—which was inherited through the legitimate line—continued from generation to generation, and that the moral code was transmitted.

II PERSIA AND THE GREEKS, TO 478 B.C.

The Persian Empire

We have already encountered the Medes, an Indo-European people of the Near East, who in 612 B.C. cooperated with the briefly recovering Babylonians to destroy Nineveh and bring down the hated Assyrian Empire. We have also seen the Medes' southern relatives, the Persians, conquer Babylon (538) and allow the captive Hebrews to return to Jerusalem. It was under Cyrus (r.c. 559–530), who attacked the Medes and took their capital (Ecbatana, south of the Caspian Sea), that the Persians began a meteoric rise toward universal rule, the last and greatest empire in the ancient Near East. Official inscriptions of this Persian Empire—carved in three languages (Old Persian, Elamite, Babylonian), all written in cuneiform script—gave scholars in the early nineteenth century their first chance to learn how to read cuneiform. This led to the gradual deciphering of Babylonian (Akkadian), which in turn made possible all of the discoveries about ancient Mesopotamia discussed in Chapter 1. Inscriptions of the sixth century B.C., when deciphered, opened up more than two thousand years of history that, had it not been for the continued use of cuneiform, might still be unknown. In this way, history is reconstructed backwards on the basis of languages that have, through the consolidation of states or the diffusion of cultures, acquired widespread if not yet universal application.

Uniting his territory with that of the Medes and initially bypassing Babylon, Cyrus moved westward into Anatolia, absorbed the Lydian kingdom of the rich king Croesus, and conquered the Greek cities of Ionia along the Aegean coast. Next he moved east all the way to the borders of India, annexing as he went, though imposing no such tyranny as had the Assyrians. Instead of deporting whole populations, Cyrus allowed them to worship as they pleased and to govern themselves in their own way under his representatives. The fall of Babylon led to the Persian conquest of Syria. Cyrus's son Cambyses (r. 529–521 B.C.) conquered Egypt and died, probably by suicide, on his way home to put down a revolution, which his usurping brother-in-law Darius (521–486 B.C.) succeeded in quelling.

It was Darius who subdivided the empire into twenty provinces (*satrapies*), each with a political governor, military governor, and tax collector, and each allowed to maintain its religion and local customs. Royal agents crisscrossed the vast area from the Aegean to the Indus, collecting information for the king. Darius adopted the Lydian practice of coining money and introduced it into all his dominions. His highway system was superb, a great network whose largest thread was the royal road that ran more than sixteen hundred miles from Susa, Darius's capital, to Sardis, the chief city of Lydia. It is likely that Darius personally introduced Zoroastrianism, the religion of Zarathustra, a Persian prophet who had died a generation earlier. In any case, he accepted the religion and honored its single god without repudiating other gods.

Zoroastrianism began as a monotheistic faith, proclaiming the one god Ahuramazda, whose identifying quality was his wisdom. (He is the only abstractly intellectual deity so far encountered.) The other divinities around him were not gods and godesses but abstract qualities such as Justice and Integrity, which he had created. It was the existence of evil in the universe that led Zarathustra to imagine that life was a constant struggle between a good spirit and an evil spirit, both subordinate to Ahuramazda. A wise person will ponder and then choose the good way; a foolish one will choose the evil way; the supreme spirit will reward the wise and punish the foolish.

Intellectual and abstract, lacking ritual and priesthood, early Zoroastrianism was perhaps too impersonal and rarefied for a popular faith, and it was modified after its founder's death. By identifying Ahuramazda with the good spirit, the generations after Darius in effect demoted the supreme god from being the ruler over the evil spirit (Ahriman) to being a contender with him. The religion became dualistic, giving comparable

Present-day ruins of the great city of Persepolis, ancient capital of Persia, built by Darius and destroyed by Alexander in the third century B.C.
Robin W. Winks

power to good and evil, and revived elements of earlier polytheism, as old deities and ceremonies reappeared and a powerful priesthood asserted itself.

The Ionian Cities, the Threat to Greece, Marathon

The new Persian rulers would not allow their subjects political freedom, which was what the now-captive Ionian Greek cities most valued. Their prosperity declined, as the Persians drew away from Ionia the wealth from the trade routes that had formerly so enriched Aegean towns. By 513 B.C. the Persians had crossed the Bosporus, sailed up the Danube, and moved north across modern Romania into the Ukraine in a campaign against a nomadic people called Scythians. Though tentative, the new advance into Europe alarmed the Greeks, who were now receiving overtures for an alliance from the Scythians; it looked as if Darius would move south against European Greece from his new base in the northern Balkans.

Some of the Greek poleis—Sparta and its allies— were hostile to the Persians, but there were others that had pro-Persian rulers. Pisistratus's son Hippias had taken refuge at the Persian court, awaiting his return to Athens, but the Athenians refused to accept him and helped the captive Ionian cities to resist Persian rule. The Ionians rebelled in 499; with Athenian assistance, they burned down Sardis, the former Lydian capital that was now the Persian headquarters in Asia Minor. Many other Greek cities then joined the rebellion.

The Persians struck back with fury and by 495 B.C. had defeated the Ionian fleet. They burned the most

Zarathustra walks at Persepolis.
Robin W. Winks

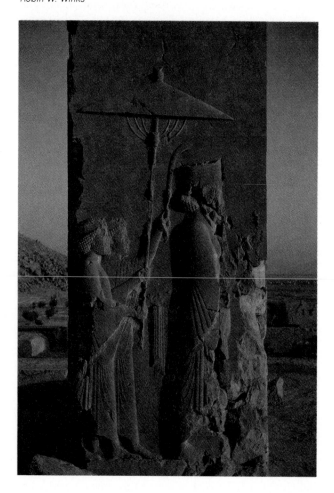

important Ionian city, Miletus, massacred many of its men, and deported its women and children into slavery. By 493 B.C. the Ionian revolt was over, and in the next two years the Persians extended their authority along the northern coasts of Greece proper, directly threatening Athens. It was probably Hippias who advised the Persian commanders to land at Marathon in a region once loyal to his father, Pisistratus, about twenty-five miles north of Athens. There a far smaller Athenian force, decisively led by Miltiades, a professional soldier who had served the Persians and angered Darius, defeated his former colleagues in 490 and for ten years ended the Persian threat to Greece. Because the Spartans had been celebrating a religious festival during which military operations were forbidden, they had been unable to participate in the fighting; only the much smaller polis of Plataea had sent a thousand men to join the ten thousand Athenians. The credit for driving off the Persians therefore went primarily to Athens. Darius now planned a much greater invasion, but an Egyptian uprising and then his death prevented it. His successor, Xerxes (r. 486–465), having subdued the Egyptians, resumed the elaborate preparations for war in 481.

The Persian Wars

By the time Xerxes was ready to attack, Miltiades was dead. A leader of the nobles, he had been brought down by a rival faction. One means of keeping factionalism under control had been introduced by Cleisthenes and, about 487, was revived: ostracism. The word comes from *ostrakon*, a fragment of a clay pot on which citizens scratched the name of any politician they wished to exile from the city for ten years. Apparently a majority of a meeting of 6,000 citizens (3,001 votes) was needed to ostracize. The 480s—the decade of preparation for Xerxes' expected attacks—was a period of frequent ostracism. (Many hundreds of clay potsherds still exist with the names of prominent politicians written on them, a sort of negative ballot.) In the process a leader named Themistocles emerged as the popular choice to lead the resistance to the anticipated Persian invasion.

After 487 the nine archons were no longer elected by the people but selected by lot from a preliminary list, drawn up by the demes, of five hundred candidates drawn from the richer citizens. This change further limited the influence of the aristocratic clans and gradually reduced the influence of the Council of the Areopagus, since more and more of its members were men chosen in the new way. Because the generals were still elected, the old political rivalry for the archonship now shifted to the office of general, and factional struggle continued.

When new supplies of silver were discovered in 483, Themistocles persuaded the Athenians to use the money to build a new fleet instead of passing it out among the citizens. This decision probably determined the outcome of the Persians' new effort, and incidentally suited

the poor, who built and rowed the ships and whose fortunes were associated with the navy. As the leading military power of Greece, Sparta took over the leadership of the anti-Persian Greek poleis, which together formed an anti-Persian league with a congress of delegates from the individual cities and a unified command. Knowing that its forces would be greatly outnumbered, the league abandoned the northern cities, where the wide plains allowed the Persian calvary to operate freely.

In 480 B.C. Xerxes' huge army, its supply lines greatly overextended and its speed slowed down by its numbers, crossed into Europe and swung south into Greece, while a fleet, possibly of three thousand ships of various sizes, sailed along the coast. At the pass of Thermopylae in central Greece, a Greek traitor showed the Persians how to outflank the defenders, but a small army, primarily of three hundred Spartans, defended the pass to the last man, taking a deadly toll of the Persian infantry. A storm, a battle, and a second storm cut the Persian fleet in half. The historian Herodotus (c. 490–425 B.C.) tells us that the Delphic oracle had mysteriously prophesied that Athens would be destroyed and had advised the Athenians to put their trust in their "wooden walls." Themistocles persuaded the Athenians that the message meant they should abandon the city to its patron goddess Athena and rely upon their fleet—their wooden ships—for their defense.

Athens was accordingly evacuated, except for the defenders of the Acropolis, whom Xerxes' men killed as they burned the city. In the narrow waters of the Strait of Salamis, near Athens, the Greek fleet awaited the Persian attack, for an engagement in the open sea would favor the larger Persian fleet. Themistocles sent a misleading message to the Persians pretending that he would betray the Greeks, and so convinced them that it was safe to attack. The Greek fleet—helped by deserters from the Persians who revealed Xerxes' battle plans—won a smashing victory, as Xerxes himself watched from a great throne set upon the shore. Xerxes had to withdraw from Greece; in 479 at Plataea united Greek forces numbering more than a hundred thousand men defeated the Persian troops once again.

Although the maintenance of Greek unity was precarious because of thousands of personal and municipal rivalries among the Greeks, members of the league had kept the oath, "I shall fight to the death, I shall put freedom before life, I shall not desert colonel or captain alive or dead, I shall carry out the generals' commands, and I shall bury my comrades-in-arms where they fall and leave none unburied." An intensely individualistic people had shown, for a time at least, that they could put the general interest ahead of all else. Soon afterward at Mycale (478 B.C.) the Greeks scored another victory on land and sea. The Persians, as it turned out, had been stopped, although peace was not formally made until 449 and many times during those three decades the Greeks were threatened with renewed invasion.

III THE ATHENIAN EMPIRE, 478–404 B.C.

Postwar Reorganization

When the Athenians began to rebuild and refortify Athens, the Spartans advised them to stop, arguing that the new walls might be useful to the Persians if they ever again invaded Greece; but Themistocles, as ambassador to Sparta, played for time until the walls were completed. The episode serves as a symbol of Athens's unwillingness to let Sparta, the strongest military power, take the lead in planning for the future defense against Persia. It was indeed Athens, after 478 the strongest naval power, that organized the new Greek alliance, designed to liberate the Ionian cities still subject to Persia and to maintain the defenses. Athens contributed most of the ships, while the other cities were assessed contributions in both ships and money. Since the treasury of the alliance was on the island of Delos, the alliance is called the Delian League. Under Cimon it scored a major victory over the Persians in Asia Minor in 469 B.C.

About 470 Themistocles was ostracized; while in exile he was charged with corruption. In c. 465 he fled to the Persians, was given rich revenues, and died in the service of Xerxes' son and successor. Themistocles accurately foresaw the great danger that lay ahead for Athens—the long-range threat from Sparta. Like Miltiades, he had lost the confidence of the Athenians after he had done them invaluable service.

In 462 a new reform further democratized Athenian government: The aristocratic Areopagus Council lost most of its powers to the Council of Five Hundred, the assembly, and the popular courts instituted by Solon. The reform was partly inspired by a brilliant young aristocrat named Pericles. By about 457 the patriotic and incorruptible Pericles had become the leading Athenian politician, responsible for the many military and naval operations conducted simultaneously against the Persians in Egypt (an expensive failure), against the Spartans, and against certain members of the Athenian alliance itself who resented Athens's dominating ways.

At home Pericles pressed for democracy, inaugurating a system of state pay, first for jurymen (drawn from a panel six thousand strong, six hundred from each tribe), and later for those rendering other services to the state. State service was thus transformed from an activity that the poor could not afford into one that they welcomed. To limit the number of those eligible for such payment, Pericles also limited Athenian citizenship to those whose parents were both Athenian. He also saw to it that the money to pay all these people would come only from Athens's allies.

From Alliance to Empire

In fact, Pericles was gradually turning the Athenian alliance into an empire, with subject members providing the money for Athens, which would defend them all and would be able to challenge Sparta. In 454 the treasury of the alliance was moved from Delos to Athens and became in effect a major Athenian resource. Since 470 no ally had been allowed to secede. During a truce in the first Peloponnesian War with the Spartans (460–445), the Athenians, operating in the Aegean, increased the number of their allies (about 170 cities at the peak), and in 449 made peace with Persia, liberating the Ionian cities and binding the Persians not to come within three days' journey of the coast.

Athenian settlements were founded on the territories of some allied states, and Athenian coinage became standard throughout the alliance. Resentment against Athens was naturally widespread among the allies. But in 445 a thirty years' treaty with Sparta provided that neither side would commit aggression against the other. Both had lost the goodwill of the other Greek poleis: Athens was now ruling an empire by force, and its protection against the Persians seemed less high minded; Sparta had suffered defeats, and its military reputation was dimmed.

As it turned out, the peace lasted for only fifteen years (445–431). It was a prosperous period during which Pericles continued to dominate the affairs of state, being democratically elected general every year. He had at his disposal the large surpluses in the imperial treasury, which mounted in those years of peace and which with Athens's other revenues were much more than enough to pay the ten thousand rowers of the warships, the seven hundred officials, the five hundred councilors, the six thousand jurors, and many others. Pericles embarked upon a great program of public works, of which the two most famous buildings were the celebrated Parthenon (originally the temple of Athena Parthenos, the virgin, and destroyed by the Persians in 480) and Propylaea (monumental gateway), both on the Acropolis. After one had mounted the steps that led up to the Propylaea and passed through it, one saw at the top of the hill a giant bronze statue of Athena sculpted by Phidias, a personal friend of Pericles; behind it and to the right rose the entrance portico of the magnificent new temple and inside was another statue of Athena by Phidias, in gold and ivory.

There were plenty of jobs available because of the building program, and slaves as well as freemen participated and were paid. There were money and opportunity for nearly everyone: for the *metics* (resident aliens), who had to pay a special tax and were not allowed to own land or participate in politics but who engaged in commerce and contributed to the city's and their own good fortune; for the 80,000 slaves, whose lot was somewhat easier than it was elsewhere and who were at times set free; and most of all for the 168,000 Athenian citizens (4,000 upper class, 100,000 middle class, and 64,000 lower class, as one rough estimate suggests). Counting children, the total population of Attica was perhaps half a million.

Relatively speaking, Athens was a democracy—the word *demokratia* having been coined around the first half of the fifth century B.C.—though we would not consider it one today. But the Greeks often turned to demagogues who, though personally honest, manipulated the *demos* (common people) to their own ends. However, what were these ends, since the function of a leader is to lead? The Greeks believed men to be unequal, not only in economic and social status but also in moral worth, so they justified a narrow base for citizenship. They believed that because communities tend to divide into factions, a well-run state must find a means to control these factions, lest they ultimately destroy the overriding sense of a higher community.

Athens was a direct democracy, not a representative one, which meant that all forty-five thousand male citizens eligible for the assembly in the time of Pericles were entitled to attend; yet we think that in general perhaps not more than six thousand took the trouble to do so. Given the problems of travel and the need for peasants to remain on their land, this group would be, on the whole, well-to-do and dominated by the aged because the young were away at war.

In its Golden Age under Pericles, Athens was a remarkable society, more complex than others among the Greek states. But we must not conclude that the Athenians had a fully articulated democratic theory or that the irrational did not continue to play a significant role in their lives.

The Second Peloponnesian War

The First Fifteen Years, 431–416 B.C. The complex civilization of Athens in the fifth century depended upon the continued exercise of complete control over the subject poleis in the empire. A growing number of incidents in which Athenians ruthlessly asserted their power alarmed the Spartans in particular; if they did not fight soon, they feared, they might not be able to win. They tried to force the Athenians to make concessions, but Pericles, with the support of the assembly, said only that Athens would consent to have all disputed questions arbitrated.

In 431 began the ruinous Second Peloponnesian War (431–404 B.C.). The Spartans invaded Attica to force a military decision. Pericles countered by withdrawing the entire population within Athens's city walls, which had been extended to include the suburbs and to give access to the sea. He intended to avoid pitched battles with the superior Spartan troops on land and to go on the offensive at sea, launching seaborne raids against enemy territory and inviting naval battles.

Though these tactics worked well in the first year of the war, in 430 plague broke out in Athens, where the population of Attica was cooped up with little sanitation. Pericles died of it in 429, leaving Athens without a trusted leader who could make unpopular but necessary policies acceptable. The plague raged until the end of 426 and cost Athens about a third of its population, including its best troops. It did not deter the Athenians from continuing the war under Cleon, however, with general though costly success at sea and even, contrary to Pericles' policies, on land.

By 424 Athens could probably have ended the war on favorable terms, and the upper and the middle classes, which had suffered most from it, were eager for peace. It was their lands in Attica that the Spartans ravaged and their members who made up most of the land forces that did the heavy fighting. But the working classes, who identified with the fleet, which was still in excellent condition, hoped for even greater gains and wanted to continue the war. Since they now dominated the city's politics, the war went on.

Not until 421 could the peace party negotiate the Peace of Nicias (so called after its leader) and terminate this phase of the Peloponnesian War, which was in fact not a single war but a series of wars conventionally linked because of the title Thucydides gave to his history. The treaty provided that each side restore captured places and prisoners and remain at peace with the other for fifty years. This was soon supplemented by an actual Spartan-Athenian alliance, also concluded for fifty years but intended chiefly to give each power a chance to put its own alliance in order while secure from an attack by the other. The war had been marked by numerous acts of brutality on both sides; prisoners had been slaughtered or enslaved, and agreements broken in a way that contemporaries felt to be shameful.

Alcibiades and Failure The peace officially lasted only five years (421–416 B.C.), years that saw the gradual rise to eminence in Athenian politics of Pericles' cousin, Alcibiades, a brilliant, ambitious, dissolute, and unstable youth, who initially succeeded the demagogic Cleon as leader of the lower-class war party against the restrained and unglamorous Nicias. Athenian intrigues to support Argos against Sparta only ended in the defeat of Argos and the strengthening of Spartan prestige. By killing all the adult males of the island of Melos and enslaving the women and children as a punishment for Melos's insistence on staying neutral in the war (416), Athens underlined its ruthlessness. By deciding, against Nicias's advice, to send off a large naval expedition to Sicily to attack the great Greek city of Syracuse, the Athenian assembly once again followed Alcibiades' lead. He had said there would be great glory in it and that all Sicily and then Greater Greece would become subject to Athens.

Yet the project bore no real relation to the politics of mainland Greece, and the Athenians had little sound military intelligence about Sicily. Just before the expedition sailed, a religious scandal broke out in Athens, and Alcibiades—who was known to have committed sacrileges when in a wild and dissipated mood—was suspected of having mutilated sacred statues. He went off to Sicily as co-commander, with the unwilling Nicias, of the greatest naval expedition ever sent out by a Greek polis. But before the fleet reached Syracuse, Alcibiades was recalled to stand trial and fled to Sparta.

The siege of Syracuse was long, drawn out (414–413), enormously expensive, and a total failure. Nicias and other leaders were captured and killed, and the Athenians lost two hundred ships. Meanwhile Sparta, now advised by Alcibiades, renewed the war at home and sent troops to help the Syracusans. The Spartans also

THUCYDIDES' ACCOUNT OF PERICLES' ORATION

From the hand of Thucydides, the historian of the Peloponnesian War, we have an account of Pericles' famous speech, delivered in the winter of 431 B.C., exhorting the Athenians to greater efforts by describing the ideal of an imperial democracy:

Our constitution does not copy the laws of neighbouring states; we are rather a pattern to others than imitators ourselves. Its administration favours the many instead of the few; this is why it is called a democracy. If we look to the laws, they afford equal justice to all in their private differences; if to social standing, advancement in public life falls to reputation for capacity, class considerations not being allowed to interfere with merit; nor again does poverty bar the way, if a man is able to serve the state, he is not hindered by the obscurity of his condition. The freedom which we enjoy in our government extends also to our ordinary life. There, far from exercising a jealous surveillance over each other, we do not feel called upon to be angry with our neighbour for doing what he likes, or even to indulge in those injurious looks which cannot fail to be offensive, although they inflict no positive penalty. But all this ease in our private relations does not make us lawless as citizens. . . .

Our public men have, besides politics, their private affairs to attend to, and our ordinary citizens, though occupied with the pursuits of industry, are still fair judges of public matters; for, unlike any other nation, regarding him who takes no part in these duties not as unambitious but as useless, we Athenians are able to judge at all events if we cannot originate, and instead of looking on discussion as a stumbling-block in the way of action, we think it an indispensable preliminary to any wise action at all. . . .

In short I say that as a city we are the school of Hellas [Greece], while I doubt if the world can produce a man, who where he has only himself to depend upon, is equal to so many emergencies, and graced by so happy a versatility as the Athenian.

Thucydides, *The Complete Writings of Thucydides: The Peloponnesian War,* trans. Richard Crowley (New York: Everyman Edition, 1951), pp. 104–6. Reprinted by permission of J.M. Dent & Sons Ltd.

stirred up the Ionian cities to revolt against Athens. The Persian satraps in Asia Minor, hoping to regain seacoast towns lost so long before, joined with the Spartans, and Alcibiades, who had worn out his welcome in Sparta, turned to the Persians.

Ironically enough, the balance of power between the two great Greek poleis that in 490 and 480–479 had so successfully expelled the Persians from Greece was now, in 412, held by the very same Persians. Alcibiades tried to blackmail the Athenians by telling them that if they would install an oligarchic government he would return and exercise his influence with the Persians on their behalf; meanwhile the Spartans promised the Persians that, in exchange for paying for their fleet, they would permit the cities of Ionia to fall into Persian hands once more.

Civil strife (at times accompanied by assassinations of those who opposed a change in the constitution) created a turbulent atmosphere in Athens. A group of conspirators prevailed on the assembly to appoint a team to draft a new, though still oligarchic, constitution, and then persuaded a rump session to accept the recommendation that the existing officials be dismissed. A group consisting of five presidents appointed one

hundred associates, who in turn drew in three hundred more, and this became a new Council of State, which ousted the former Council of Five Hundred in an armed but bloodless coup d'état. The new Four Hundred could summon at will a new Five Thousand, ostensibly to replace the traditional assembly of all the citizens. The democratic forces, however, still controlled the fleet.

The leading oligarchs would now have liked to proceed at once to peace with Sparta, and probably intended that the more moderate Five Thousand should never be summoned. From exile, Alcibiades, however, indicated his preference for their summoning. Frightened and angered by a naval defeat, the citizens deposed the Four Hundred and elected the Five Thousand—all from the upper class—which governed the city from 411 to 410, when, after some Athenian successes at sea, democracy was restored.

Returning from exile in 407, Alcibiades commanded Athenian naval forces until the Spartan fleet defeated him in 405. He then retired to his estates along the Hellespont (the modern Dardanelles), where he was murdered by Spartan and Persian agents. His career vividly illustrates the vulnerability of the Athenian democracy to a plausible, charming, talented scoundrel and to

MAKING A LIVING

Greek history was not all war, and neither Athens nor Sparta were always garrison states. Of course, war and politics were means of acquiring goods, for the victors could dispose of the defeated and their goods as they wished. War was a primary source of supply for the slave trade, for booty, and for new lands. But the economic order was not necessarily organized around war, even if the different classes tended to have differing attitudes toward the value of warfare itself. Manual workers and those engaged in trade went about their tasks as best they could, and the true hero of Greek life was, in a sense, the artisan who made the statue of Athena, or helped build the Parthenon, or developed the techniques of metal working.

There was a hierarchy to occupations, as there was to politics. In Athens, slaves, metics, and citizens might do the same work, though only citizens could speak in the assembly. Even in the organization of space, Athens showed this ambivalence; there were separate quarters for specific economic functions, divided by the craft to be performed, but neither metics nor slaves were segregated into separate residential sections. Spartan warriors were contemptuous of artisans, and the retail trades were near (though not beneath) contempt on the ground that those practicing them commonly cheated.

This hierarchy in occupation, in methods of acquisition of property and goods, and in political authority gave structure to that portion of society not made up of children or slaves, shaped the social meanings given to how people made their living, and helped in time to distinguish the professions from artisanship. Movement between levels was difficult though possible, creating a stable value system that nonetheless was capable of gradual change.

restless factionalism and narrow competitiveness. Another weakness—the temptation to yield to impulse—was displayed soon afterward, when the Athenians had defeated the Spartan fleet at Arginusae but had suffered heavy casualties, and the Council of State was intimidated by the mourning families of the drowned soldiers into ordering the collective executions of six generals for not rescuing the troops in the water.

In the final naval action of the war, the Spartans captured most of the Athenian fleet, deserted on a beach in the Hellespont while the sailors were hunting food on shore at Aegospotami in 405. The Spartan infantry rounded up thousands of Athenian prisoners, of whom three thousand were executed as direct reprisal for recent Athenian atrocities. Starving, without money, blockaded by land and sea, its alliance in ruins as the allies had revolted or joined the Spartans, Athens had to surrender unconditionally to the Spartan leader Lysander. Some of the Spartan allies wanted to punish the Athenians as the Athenians had punished the Melians, but the Spartans refused. Instead, the Athenians demolished their long walls, abandoned their empire, surrendered their fleet, and agreed to follow Sparta's lead in foreign policy.

IV THE FOURTH CENTURY B.C. AND THE HELLENISTIC AGE

Spartan Domination

As victors, the Spartans found themselves dominant in a Greece where polis was suspicious of polis and where, within each polis, faction disputed with faction. From Ionia, which the Spartans had sold back to Persia as the price of their assistance, the Persians loomed once more as a threat to the whole Greek world. By midcentury, the new state of Macedonia in the north menaced the Greeks. Perhaps wiser or more vigorous leaders would have been able to create some sort of federation among the individual poleis that could have withstood the Persians and the Macedonians, and, still later, the Romans. But since this did not happen, it seems more likely that the polis as an institution was no longer thought to be the appropriate way for the Greek world to be organized. Perhaps it was too small, too provincial, too "old-fashioned" to keep the peace and provide scope for economic advancement and intellectual growth.

Sparta proved as unable as Athens to manage Greece. The Spartan government, suitable for a state that had no central function but war, was largely in the hands of the elders, usually too conservative to meet new challenges. Gold and silver had found their way into the simple agricultural economy whose founders had preferred to use bars of iron as exchange. Many Spartans now, for the first time, found themselves disenfranchised for debt and thus relegated to the status of "inferiors." They joined the helots and perioikoi as part of a discontented majority just when Sparta needed more "equals"—full, enfranchised, fighting citizens. Away from home Lysander could neither free the cities of the former Athenian Empire, in which from 404 he had installed oligarchic governments, nor rule them satisfactorily.

At Athens, for example, at the instigation of the extremist Critias, an oligarchy known as the Thirty Tyrants instituted a reign of terror not only against democrats associated with past regimes but also against moderate oligarchs. In 403 an invading force of exiled democrats killed Critias and touched off a brief civil war. At Athens they restored democracy, but the Thirty Tyrants and their sympathizers were set up as a Spartan puppet government nearby at Eleusis, and no one was allowed to move between the two separate Athenian states. In 401 the Athenians, by treachery, killed the generals of the Eleusid armies, and the two states were reunited. It would be the government of this insecurely reestablished Athens that would sentence the philosopher Socrates to death in 399 B.C.

The Spartans could not pose as the leaders of Greece and keep their bargain with the Persians to sell Ionia back to them; yet if they went back on this bargain, the Persians would start a new war. So in 401 B.C., when the younger brother of Artaxerxes II, king of Persia—Cyrus the Younger, governor of Asia Minor—rebelled against Artaxerxes and asked for Spartan aid, Sparta gave it to him. Cyrus was soon killed in a battle deep in Mesopotamia, and his Greek mercenary army was stranded in the heart of Persia. (Their disciplined march north to the Greek city of Trebizond on the shores of the Black Sea forms the substance of a book called the *Anabasis*, "The March Back," by the Athenian Xenophon, who became one of their officers.) The episode left the Spartans at war with Persia.

The Spartans failed to unite their land and sea commands, giving the Persians time to build a fleet, which they put under an Athenian admiral. The Persians also bribed Thebes, Argos, Corinth, and Athens to stir up so much trouble against Sparta that Spartan troops had to be recalled from Persia to fight a new war in Greece proper. This Corinthian War lasted eight years (to 387), saw the self-assertion of Thebes, seemed to produce the threat of a renewed Athenian Empire, and ended in stalemate, as the Persians and Spartans finally got together and imposed "The King's Peace" in 386 B.C., by which the Persians resumed control of all Greek states in Asia and the rest became autonomous.

Thebes Rises to Leadership

Raising money from their allies and hiring mercenaries to intimidate all resistance, the Spartans systematically disciplined and punished the cities that dared resist, seizing Thebes in 382 B.C. and breaking their promise to respect the autonomy of the Greek cities. A group of Theban democratic exiles conspired to overthrow the pro-Spartan regime there, and when the Spartans tried to punish them, a new war broke out in which Athens participated as the leading power in a new anti-Spartan league of many Greek cities.

By 371 the beleaguered Spartans were ready for peace, willing to guarantee independence to all Greek states and seeking disarmament. But the wording of the treaty gave Persia and Athens the leading roles as guarantors, and Epaminondas, the chief Theban delegate, refused to sign. Soon afterward he defeated the Spartans at the battle of Leuctra. Cities subject to Sparta began to oust their oligarchic governments and install democracies. Epaminondas followed up his successes with two invasions of the Peloponnesus, helped form a league of Arcadian cities, and assisted the freed helots in founding a city of their own. This destroyed Spartan power in its own homeland.

Warfare continued despite the effort of the Persians to dictate a general peace, as the Athenians returned to their former imperialist practices and installed colonies of Athenian settlers on the soil of conquered cities. The Thebans fought in the Peloponnesus, in the north, against Athens at sea, and finally in the Peloponnesus again, where an alliance of Sparta, Athens, and other poleis met them in battle at Mantinea in 362, at which Epaminondas was killed. All hope that Thebes could put an end to the interminable fighting among Greeks died with him.

Though a new Peloponnesian league of city-states was formed in 362 B.C. to end the war and to enable the Greeks as a whole to determine their foreign policy, Athens continued to act as the rival of Thebes and to play the traditional political game of alliance building within the league. Though ineffective, the league was an important effort to create something like a united states of Greece. Without its restraints, Thebes was defeated in a war against the city of Phocis, whose general had seized the shrine of Delphi and used the accumulated funds there to create a large army of mercenaries in 354. Athens strove to reconstruct its old Aegean empire, but in 357 many of its most important outposts rebelled, and Athens was forced to grant them freedom in 355. Athens was exhausted, broke, and weak.

Ironically enough, the inability of the Greek cities to give up fighting was almost surely due in part to general prosperity. Whereas during the fifth century only Athens and Sparta had been able to afford large armies and navies, during the fourth century many other cities grew rich enough to support such forces. Brisk Mediterranean commerce brought wealth to the distant Greek

THE MORAL DECLINE OF ATHENS

In the fifth century B.C. the Greek historian Thucydides, convinced that the Peloponnesian War had led to the moral decline of Athens by brutalizing its citizens, wrote of what he regarded as the loss of will in Athenian society by which power had passed into the hands of Sparta:

Love of power, operating through greed and through personal ambition, was the cause of all these evils. To this must be added the violent fanaticism which came into play once the struggle had broken out. Leaders of parties ... in professing to serve the public interest ... were seeking to win prizes for themselves. In their struggle for ascendancy nothing was barred; terrible indeed were the actions to which they committed themselves, and in taking revenge they went further still. Here they were deterred neither by the claims of justice nor by the interests of the state.... Thus neither side had any use for conscientious motives; more interest was shown in those who could produce attractive arguments to justify some disgraceful action. As for the citizens who held moderate views, they were destroyed by both the extreme parties.

Thucydides, *The Complete Writings of Thucydides: The Peloponnesian War*, trans. Richard Crowley (New York: Everyman Edition, 1951), p. 210. Reprinted by permission of J.M. Dent & Sons Ltd.

settlements from the Crimea to Spain; not only goods flowed, but also slaves and mercenary troops. Shortly after midcentury the Persians alone had perhaps fifty thousand Greek troops fighting in their armies.

Many devices of modern commerce to make international trade easier first made their appearance in Greece: banking and credit, insurance, trade treaties, and special diplomatic and other privileges. Private wealth grew rapidly and was more widely distributed. Slaves increased in number—Nicias appears to have owned more than a thousand of them. By 338 B.C. there may have been as many as one hundred fifty thousand in Attica, working in the mines and at other more skilled occupations. All this prosperity meant that states quickly recovered from defeat in war and could afford to try again. Patriotism became increasingly a matter of cutting up real or anticipated profits. However, the poor who were not slaves grew poorer; unwilling to degrade themselves by engaging in the manual labor that was increasingly the work of slaves, they often became vagrants or mercenary soldiers. A rigid class society was increasingly confining, and the middle class was losing its sense of security between the increasingly rich and the increasingly enslaved poor.

Macedon

North of Thessaly and extending inland into what is today Yugoslavia and Albania lay the kingdom of Macedon, with a considerable coastline along the Aegean. The Macedonians were a mixture of peoples including some of Greek origin; they were organized into tribes, worshiped some of the Greek gods, and spoke a Greek dialect that other Greeks could not understand. Their kings claimed Greek descent, and the king spoke Greek as well as the native language, had title to most of the land, and ruled absolutely, though he might be deposed by the people for treason. There being no written law, he was advised by councilors who were selected from among the nobles of each tribe and felt themselves to be his social equals.

Although the Greeks had planted some poleis along the Macedonian shore, and although Greek cultural influence and Greek trade had penetrated deeply into the country by the fourth century, Macedon did not copy Greek political institutions, keeping its own, which were more like those of Mycenae. The Macedonians traditionally relied on cavalry in war, but in the fourth century they added foot soldiers to fight their neighbors from the west and north, the Illyrians (probably ancestors of the Albanians of today). From the south, both Athens and Sparta persistently interfered in internal Macedonian affairs.

The Achievements of Philip II In 359 B.C., a prince of the ruling house, Philip, became regent for his infant nephew. Having lived for three years as a hostage in Thebes, where he knew Epaminondas, Philip understood Greek affairs. He applied Theban military principles to his army (emphasizing infantry tactics) and led it in person. After defeating the Illyrians and other rivals for power within Macedon, Philip was made king in his own right. To get money, he exploited the rich gold and silver mines in his kingdom, minting his own coinage.

Some Athenian politicians favored Philip's advance.

Others opposed him. It was not until he had won still more territory and begun to use a fleet successfully that the most famous Athenian orator, Demosthenes, began to warn against the threat from Macedon. But Philip had broken Athenian influence in Thessaly and Thrace (modern Bulgaria) and had annexed the peninsula of Chalcidice, which had been ruled by Athenian aristocrats. He also detached the large island of Euboea, close to Attica itself, from its Athenian loyalties.

At that point he suggested peace and an alliance with Athens. In 346 B.C. this was accomplished with the approval even of Demosthenes. Philip meanwhile had secured control over the Delphic oracle. He was moving south and consolidating his power. He made a temporary alliance with Thebes to defeat Phocis. By 342 the Athenians had acquired new allies in the Peloponnesus. In retaliation Philip moved into Thrace to cut off the Athenian grain supplies coming from the Black Sea and to avert a new Persian-Athenian alliance. Once again Demosthenes pressed for war, and Athens took military action in Euboea. By late 339 Philip was only two days' march from Attica. Demosthenes now arranged an eleventh-hour alliance with Thebes. Philip, however, totally defeated the Athenian-Theban alliance at Chaeronea in 338 with the decisive aid of a precisely timed cavalry charge led by his eighteen-year-old son, Alexander. Though Philip occupied Thebes, he spared Athens on condition that the city ally with Macedon. His leniency proved that he had never intended to destroy Athens, as Demosthenes had feared.

Philip's victories aroused in many the old hope of a unified Greece. Isocrates, an Athenian philosopher, had thought Demosthenes wrong in urging resistance to Philip, for he feared a resurgent Persia far more. At Corinth in 338 B.C., all the poleis except Sparta met to organize a league that called itself "The Greeks." Its members bound themselves to stop fighting and intervening in each other's affairs. This body immediately allied itself with Macedon and then joined with Philip in declaring war on Persia to revenge Xerxes' invasion of 143 years earlier. Philip was to command the expedition. By 336 B.C. the advance forces of this army were already liberating Ionian cities from Persia. But Philip, aged only forty-six, was now mysteriously assassinated.

Philip's accomplishments greatly impressed his contemporaries. No such powerful consolidated state as his Macedon had ever existed west of Asia. Instead of allowing the resources of Macedon to be dissipated in flashy conquests, he organized the people he conquered, both in the Balkan area from the Adriatic to the Black Sea and in Greece. He kept morale high in the army and had the contingents from the various regions competing to see who would do the best job. He divided his troops into specialized units for diverse tasks in war, and he personally commanded whichever unit had the most difficult assignment. He could appreciate the strengths of his Greek opponents, and when he had defeated them, he utilized their skills and made sure of their loyalty by decent treatment. In his final effort to unify them against their traditional Persian enemy, he associated himself with the ancient patriotic cause that, despite frequent disappointment, still had great appeal for them. Though he felt himself to be part of the Greek civilization of his own time, he centered his confederacy on Corinth, symbolic of an earlier Greek resistance to the Persians. Somehow he seemed a kind of Homeric hero in the flesh almost a thousand years after the siege of Troy.

The Achievements of Alexander Philip's son, Alexander III, or the Great, belongs to legend as much as to history. Only twenty when he came to the throne, he loved war, politics, athletics, alcohol, poetry, medicine, and science. Within a dozen years he led his armies on a series of triumphant marches that won for Macedon the largest empire yet created in the ancient world. He began by crushing a Greek revolt led by Thebes, whose entire population he sold into slavery, not massacring the males, as the Spartans and Athenians often did. Next he crossed into Asia Minor to continue the war of the Greek League against Persia and to recapture the Ionian cities. He defeated the Persians at the river Granicus in 334 B.C. and took over the coastal cities of Ionia to deny them to the Persian fleet, so that the strategy thereafter would turn upon the contending land armies. In Ionia he established democracies in the poleis. In territories belonging to the Persians, he took title to all land. He thus replaced the Persian king, Darius III, whom he defeated again at Issus and so opened up Syria. He reduced Tyre by siege and refused Darius's offer of his daughter and all territory west of the Euphrates.

Next, Egypt fell easily. Here he founded the great port of Alexandria in the Nile Delta (332), a Greek city from the beginning. Alexander led a daring expedition into the desert to consult the oracle of Zeus Ammon, where he was greeted as "son of Ammon," which encouraged his followers to suggest that Alexander had divine status. Thereby encouraged, he marched east and defeated Darius again in Mesopotamia at Guagamela, near Nineveh, in 331 B.C. The Persian Empire was smashed. Alexander sacrificed to Marduk in Babylon and ordered that the temple the Persians had destroyed be restored. Vast mopping-up operations continued in Persia proper (330–327 B.C.), as Alexander's armies seized the chief cities and all the royal treasure at the Persian capital of Persepolis, which he burned. Still, he treated the Persian royal family with great courtesy and acted toward his new subjects just as a king of Persia would have done. The Persian nobles came to acknowledge him as king by the grace of Ahuramazda. Alexander now was king of Persia, pharaoh of Egypt, king of Babylon, king of Macedon, and commander of the Greek League.

In central Asia, near Samarkand, Alexander fell in love with and married the daughter of a local chieftain, who joined forces with the conqueror in 327 B.C. While this marriage enhanced the loyalty of the Persians to him, it further strained the loyalty of his own Macedonian nobles, who disliked Alexander's occasional adoption of Persian dress and customs to please his new

Alexander the Great is here shown in a detailed mosaic made of hundreds of pieces of tiny inlaid stone. Originally at Pompeii, this mosaic from the National Museum in Naples (from which this is a detail) shows Alexander defeating the armies of Darius at Issus in 333 B.C. Alexander, once idealized, has been the subject of intensive, often negative, revaluation by historians in recent years.
Scala/Art Resource

subjects. Though enjoying his role as "Great King" and claiming divine parentage, Alexander thought of himself as a Greek; he paid his respects to his ancestor Achilles at Troy before he began his Eastern campaigns, and his favorite reading was the *Iliad*. But tensions increased. Alexander, having executed a plotter against his life, said he was forced by Macedonian custom to execute the plotter's father also; unfortunately, the father was the most influential of the Macedonian nobles. Later, in a drunken fury, Alexander killed another of his own Macedonian generals for having taunted him for his Persian ways. There was much truth in the charge, and Alexander continued to purge Macedonians who resisted his orientalization.

The tensions of the conquest did not diminish its efficiency. New levies of troops came from Europe or were raised in Asia; new roads were built; and new towns sprang up, many named after Alexander. Believing that India was the last region in Asia, that it was small, and that beyond India lay the Ocean, via which it was possible to return to Europe by sea, Alexander next set out to conquer modern-day Pakistan from a base in what is now Afghanistan. He found himself fighting hill tribes and princes of Kashmir and Punjab. At first the Indian war elephants terrified Alexander's cavalry, but soon the Macedonians learned how to defeat them and won new victories. Alexander moved east; but India was not small, as he had thought, and his weary troops eventually mutinied. In 326 B.C. Alexander had to give in and call off any further advances; he led his troops on riverboats down the Indus toward the Indian Ocean, fighting all the way, and sacrificing a gold cup to the Greek god of the sea, Poseidon, when he reached the shore. Several new Alexandrias were founded, including the city that is now Karachi (in Pakistan), before he led his forces westward across the southern Persian deserts back to Susa in 324 B.C.

Here he conducted a purge of those he suspected of treason, and dramatically pursued his plan to combine the best features of the Macedonian and the Persian nobilities by staging a mass marriage between eighty Macedonian officers and Persian noblewomen. He himself took a new Persian wife and blessed the union of ten thousand Macedonian troops with Persian women. Those Macedonians who wished to return home were sent off well rewarded; but Alexander kept their wives in Persia and planned to use their children as the nucleus of a future army of mixed blood troops who would owe their lives to him. A great double naval expedition from the mouths of the Tigris-Euphrates, eastward along the shore of the Persian Gulf to India and westward around Arabia (not yet circumnavigated) to Egypt, was in preparation at Babylon, where Alexander had built great dockyards. From the Greeks, who had enjoyed the longest period of internal peace for over a century, Alexander asked for divine honors; apparently he wanted to become a god. No god, in June 323 B.C., at Babylon, he caught a fever and died at the age of thirty-three.

Ever since, scholars have speculated about what Alexander might have accomplished had he lived; he might well have made Greece the center of his empire and would surely have been able to conquer the two states in the western Mediterranean already looming on the horizon as powers there: Carthage and Rome. He respected all races and religions, yet he was ruthless in pursuit of his own power and the stability of his state. Each of his new cities he settled with Greeks, to be centers for the diffusion of Greek culture. A superb general, a clever governor of subject peoples, a believer in the Greek gods, a passionate man with a streak of megalomania, Alexander astonished his contemporaries. It is little wonder that he became to later generations the hero of romances that circulated in every country, in every language, and among every people, down to our own day. Some saw in him only a drunken despot and a murderer. But to more students of his life then and now, Alexander was the first great leader to seek the security of all peoples in a single world state.

A Hellenized Civilization

The Hellenistic period is usually said to be the three hundred years between the reign of Alexander the Great, who died in 323 B.C., and of Augustus, the first Roman emperor, who ruled from 31 B.C. until A.D. 14. The outer reaches of the world as it was known to the Greeks had been Hellenized as far as modern-day Afghanistan. Civic life was transformed throughout the Hellenic lands, as the kings and their officials contended against the entrenched traditions of the cities Alexander had conquered. Cultural diffusion, cultural exchange, and the transformation both of traditional societies and of the encroaching society showed all of the characteristics that would later be associated with the expansion of one society at the expense of another—whether Rome, or the great European empires of the eighteenth and nineteenth centuries, or the processes of Americanization associated with the impact of the United States abroad in the twentieth century.

As soon as the news of Alexander's death became known, his generals began a fierce scramble for portions of his empire, for his Bactrian wife, Roxane, was expecting a child, and his brother was both illegitimate and simpleminded. The generals combined against each other in various shifting alliances and arranged many intermarriages and murders in a confusing period of political and military change. By c. 280–279 B.C. three dynasties had emerged as supreme, each descended from one of Alexander's generals, each in a different portion of the empire: the Ptolemies in Egypt, the Seleucids in Syria and Mesopotamia, and the Antigonids in Macedon and Asia Minor. Fighting continued almost without interruption until the rising power of Rome began to destroy them one by one.

In Egypt the Ptolemies followed the ancient pattern of government, turning themselves into successors of the pharaohs. They became gods; they sometimes married their sisters; they exploited the agricultural wealth of the country to the limit. The Ptolemies claimed title to all land, some of which was farmed by peasants directly for their own benefit and some let out to temples or to military settlers and officials. The Ptolemies' own land gave them all its produce, except what was needed to feed the farm workers; land let to others paid the Ptolemies a percentage in wheat. Oil, flax, and papyrus were royal monopolies. No tree in Egypt could be cut down without royal permission. The Ptolemies governed largely through Greek officials, who poured into Egypt for several generations after Alexander's death. Even the armies of the first three Ptolemies were wholly Greek. It was not until 217 B.C. that Egyptian troops participated in the wars of the dynasty, which were directed chiefly against the Seleucids of Asis for the possession of Palestine and against the Antigonids for the Aegean islands and the Anatolian coasts.

Alexandria, the capital, was the largest city of the ancient world, until Rome eventually overtook it. The city had harbors both on the Mediterranean and on a great lake, which was connected by canals to the Nile, and by the Nile to the Red Sea. Its towering white stone lighthouse, four hundred feet high, was one of the wonders of the ancient world. The city had broad streets, luxurious palaces, and a famous library of approximately a million volumes. In its "museum," scholars, freed from all duties by state subsidies, conducted their researches ("fat fowls in a coop," a skeptical poet called them). Though Alexandria was far too large to be a polis, its Greek population had its own political organization. At Alexandria also were the Ptolemies' warehouses in which all the royal grain was stored after it had come down the Nile.

The Egyptian population lived under its own law and was judged in its own courts. Those who were discontented with the system that exploited them so thoroughly—and there were many—had no escape except to take sanctuary in a temple; accordingly, the government tried to reduce the number of temples that had the right to provide sanctuary. For a long time the Greek population—with its own language, law courts, culture, and customs—did not mingle with the Egyptians, remaining a large collection of foreigners who were getting rich as fast as they could. But by the early second century, Greek immigration had tapered off, Greek-Egyptian intermarriages had begun, and the army became more Egyptian. Rome began to intervene, disorganization set in, and by 118 B.C. Ptolemy VII had to issue a series of decrees calling for reform to reunite his empire and restore public order.

Seleucus I was also one of Alexander's generals. He began as governor of Babylon and eventually won control over all of Alexander's Asian lands except northern and western Asia Minor and the Indian regions in the east, which had to be given up by 303 B.C. Seleucid territorial holdings fluctuated a good deal, however. The Seleucids' Ionian territories centered on the former Lydian capital of Sardis, their Syrian territories on the new city of Antioch-on-Orontes in northern Syria, and their Mesopotamian territories on the new city of Seleucia not far from Babylon. As the heirs of the ancient Near Eastern empires, the Seleucids used the former Assyrian and Persian administrative forms and revived Babylonian religion and literature, which was still written in cuneiform. Some scholars believe that, by deliberately sponsoring a Babylonian religious revival, the Seleucids were seeking a counterweight to Zoroastrianism, the Persian faith. It does appear that the Seleucids failed to achieve what Alexander had so well begun—the securing of Persian cooperation in managing the huge Asian territories.

The Seleucids could not count on deification, like the Ptolemies, nor could they create in Asia anything like the extremely centralized Ptolemaic system of exploitation. Unlike Egypt, the Asian territories were too vast to be governed; there were too many varied traditions of authority, too many local governors to be considered. Instead, the Seleucids founded Greek cities and sponsored their development. To do this they gave up

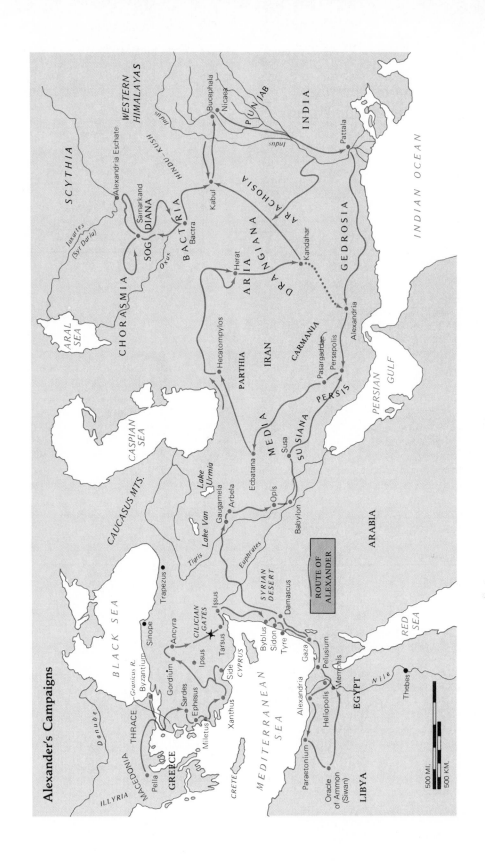

Alexander's Campaigns

ROUTE OF ALEXANDER

Alexander's Empire and the Hellenistic World

Macedonia Alexander's Empire Satellites

→— Route of Alexander, 334-325 B.C.

0   500

Miles

Alexander's Successor States 200 B.C.

MACEDONIA

Pergamum

GREECE   Sardis   SELEUCID EMPIRE

RHODES   Antioch

KINGDOM OF THE PTOLEMIES   Alexandria   Seleucia

Danube R.

ITALY   THRACE   Black Sea

MACEDONIA   Byzantium

EPIRUS   Aegean Sea   Aral Sea

GREECE   Athens   PHRYGIA   Granicus R.   ARMENIA   Caspian Sea   Oxus R.   Alexandria Eschate

IONIA   ASIA   MINOR   Samarkand

CRETE   Issus   Antioch   M E D I A   Alexandria Margiana   BACTRIA   KASHMIR

RHODES   Nineveh   Alexandria

Mediterranean Sea   CYPRUS   Orontes R.   ASSYRIA   Euphrates R.   PARTHIA   Alexandria Ariorum   Alexandria

CYRENAICA   PHOENICIA   SYRIA   Ecbatana   Alexandria Arachosiorum   PUNJAB

Alexandria   PALESTINE   Tyre   Babylon   Susa   Alexandria Opiana

Jerusalem   Tigris R.   Persepolis   Alexandria Sogdiana

EGYPT   PERSIA

Nile R.   Persian Gulf

Red Sea   ARABIA   Indian Ocean

Furthest Extent of the Persian Empire

0   500   1000

Miles

Furthest Extent of the Roman Empire

54

FOOD AND CIVILIZATION

History has been profoundly influenced by shifts in diets, in the migration of foods from one part of the world to another, and by discoveries concerning nutrition. Greek civilization rested to an important extent on the olive. During its height the dry Mediterranean landscape of Greece was well forested and far more green than now, since the goats that have done so much to denude the Greek coasts and mountains were not yet prevalent. By the fifth century the olive grove, interspersed among the forests on lower elevations, was providing the Greeks with a staple to their economy, an important food, and a valuable source of nutrition.

Athena and Poseidon are said to have been in competition for the loyalty of a small Greek settlement in a particularly rocky area. A jury of gods agreed to decide which would provide the inhabitants the best life. Poseidon at once struck a salt spring from the rock, to show that the fruits of the sea would belong to the villagers. Athena caused an olive tree to grow from the rocky soil, and the gods awarded the village to her. Eventually, though history does not record how, the process of soaking olives in a lye of water and wood ash, and then in brine, was learned, (olives cannot be eaten as they come from the tree). By the fifth century olives were being widely cultivated, preserved, and shipped throughout the Mediterranean world, together with grapes, figs, and wheat. Olives were also pressed to make oil, which in time made yet other foods, to which the oil was added, possible. Today the landscape of Greece is utterly different from that of the fifth century, except for the exceptional longevity of the olive orchards and the continuity of use of the fruit of the olive tree.

large areas that were their own royal land, and they also transferred the land of powerful landowners to the cities. The lot of the peasants improved, as they ceased to be private property and gained their freedom.

These Greek cities were military colonies, given both money and land by the king. Their settlement, housing, financial, and other questions were delegated to a military governor. The settlers were required to serve in the army in exchange for the land they received. This founding of Greek cities, however, failed to solve the problem of military security, partly because there were not enough Greeks available to populate the cities and man the armies, and partly because the Seleucids did not learn how to command the loyalty of the Persian population.

In Macedon and Greece, the Antigonids, descendants of Alexander's governor of the western Anatolian province of Phrygia, had won in the struggle for succession. Even so, it was not until almost half a century after Alexander's death that Antigonus Gonatas, son of the first Antigonus, was accepted as king of Macedon. In 277 B.C. he successfully protected Greece from the raids of the Gauls, a migrating branch of Indo-European Celts, who had spread from the region north of the Alps into what is now France and Spain, and across to Britain. Herodotus mentions them only once, for they were still re-

mote in his day. Now they were moving eastward along the Danube, raiding southward into Italy and Greece. Antigonus shunted them on to Asia Minor, where they were given a kingdom of their own, called Galatia, in a region from which their remote Neolithic ancestors may have originally come several thousand years earlier.

Though the Greek cities were now grouped together into two leagues, the Aetolian and the Achaean—larger in membership and more representative in their joint rule than the Athenian and Spartan alliances of earlier times—they fought against each other and against the Antigonid kings of Macedon with customary Greek vigor. By the 220s the Greeks were largely independent of Macedon once again. Athens usually stayed out of the perpetual feuding of other cities. But Sparta, true to its traditions, tried to take over the Achaean League; it would have succeeded had not the Macedonians been brought back into Greece in 222, to defeat the Spartans finally. By the 220s, however, Rome had begun to intervene in the Greek world.

Alexander's heirs had begun their rule in prosperity and unity; they ended it in division, defeat, and economic decline. At first commerce had grown throughout the Hellenized world, for Greek products were widely sought. But as prosperity increased, the division between the well-to-do and the peasants grew; the cities came to be identified with wealth, the rural areas with poverty. Wars, rising inflation, and Persian gold threw the economies into disarray. Both urban laborers and peasants discovered the power they could exert over the middle class if they refused to work. Frequent debates over redistribution of land, demands for the abolition of debt, and civil wars further weakened Alexander's inheritance, so that the Hellenized states were ripe for conquest.

V RELIGION, WRITING, AND THOUGHT

The Gods of the Greeks

To the Greeks, religion was so embedded within society that it influenced every aspect of daily life. Families worshiped together at a single shrine; the great sanctuaries were society's gathering places; the Olympic games, though concerned with athletic endeavor, were equally a celebration for the gods. Religion was practical: it helped people in birth, at puberty, through marriage, and at death. It was also democractic, as aristocratic cults came to shape public calendars.

Nearly all Greeks expected of their gods two great boons: prophetic advice and healing. To obtain advice one visited the shrine of an oracle or consulted with seers; for healing one decorated the shrines of the appropriate gods, quite often bringing an image, made of clay, of the bodily organ that required healing. One also sought healing by passing a night in the temple of the god, hoping that the god would appear in a dream and effect a cure. Healing was especially important, since the present life counted so heavily. Unlike later developments in the Christian church, for example, in which an afterlife was believed to far outweigh the significance of the present life, Greek religious thought held that after death the individual disappeared into an underworld where existence was without meaning. Some people believed there might be rewards and punishments in an afterlife, but most apparently did not.

The Olympian gods continued to reign. The citizens of a polis had special devotion for the divinity who had founded it—Athens for Athena, Sparta for Zeus—though they worshiped the other gods as well, and all worshiped the goddess of the hearth, Hestia, the protectress of home and fireside. Poleis therefore grouped together in special devotion to regional shrines—the temples of Apollo at Delphi and of Zeus at Olympia and at Dodona. The Olympic games—traditionally said to have begun in 776 B.C. though in fact almost certainly much earlier—specifically honored Zeus; they were followed by others held in honor of Apollo at Delphi and of Poseidon, the sea god, on the Isthmus of Corinth.

Still, two Greek cults of particular importance began outside the ordinary worship of the Olympian gods: that of Demeter at Eleusis near Athens, and that of Dionysus. Demeter (the name means literally "earth mother") was the goddess of fertility and of the harvests. Her daughter by Zeus, Persephone, was snatched away by Hades, the god of the underworld, and had to spend a third of the year with him—the months of barrenness, late autumn and winter. Every spring she returned, and the fields became fertile again. Thus, like the Sumerians and the Egyptians, the Greeks invented a story to account for the miracle of rebirth every spring.

Dionysus, the god of vegetation, fertility, and wine, originated in Boeotia, in north-central Greece, and stood for seasonal fertility in its more openly sexual aspects; his celebrants originally carried phalluses in his procession, and were often dressed as goats. In its original form the cult inspired its followers with a wild dancing frenzy in which they ate the flesh of living animals and so acted out the eating of the god himself. The cult was tamer in Athens, where phallic songs were written for the festival, held every two years.

Tragedy

From these and other songs Athens developed the art of tragedy. (The word means "goat song" and shows the original connection with Dionysus.) At first largely sung as choral hymns, the tragedies later began to deal with human problems, and individual actors' roles became

This fifth-century bronze statue, properly called the Striding God of Artemiseion, is generally considered to be an ideal effort to represent Zeus hurling a thunderbolt; however, other scholars believe it to be Poseidon with a trident. It is now displayed in the National Museum in Athens.
Scala/Art Resource

more important. The first competition to choose the best tragedy was sponsored by Pisistratus in 534 B.C., and annual contests were held thereafter. Many hundreds of tragedies were written; comparatively few have survived in full—probably the best—but we have fragments of others. Aristotle (384–322) believed that it was the purpose of tragedy to arouse pity and terror in the spectators and to purge or purify them by causing them to reflect on the fearful punishments that highly placed men and women brought upon themselves by their own sins, the worst of which was *hubris*, or "arrogance."

The first, and some would say the greatest, of the three chief tragedians whose works we have was Aeschylus (c. 525–456 B.C.), of whose seventy-odd tragedies seven survive.

In the trilogy the *Oresteia*, Aeschylus dealt with tragedies in the family of Agamemnon, who sacrificed his daughter Iphigenia to get a favorable wind to go to Troy, was murdered by his unfaithful wife Clytemnestra on his return, and was avenged by his son Orestes, who killed his mother on the order of Apollo. Orestes suffered torments by the Furies and was acquitted by a court presided over by Athena; but only Zeus succeeded in transforming the Furies into more kindly creatures. Crime and punishment, remorse and release, a benevolent and secure god over all—these Aeschylus portrayed in lofty, moving verse.

Sophocles (c. 496–406 B.C.), the second of the three great tragedians, wrote many tragedies, of which only ten survive. He believed deeply in Athenian institutions and in the religion of his fellow Greeks, and he took an active part in the public life of Periclean Athens. In his *Antigone*, the niece of Creon, tyrant of Thebes, defied her uncle's harsh decision that the body of her brother, killed while leading a rebellion, must be left exposed to be devoured by beasts of prey. Proclaiming

that divine law required decent burial, she disobeyed Creon and caused the proper ceremonial earth to be sprinkled on the body. Knowing she would die for her defiance, she acted in obedience to her conscience and resisted the dictator. *Antigone* has carried its message of the sanctity of the individual conscience down through the centuries, proclaiming the superiority of what is eternally right and decent to any mere dictator's brutal whim.

Sophocles, who lived to be ninety, saw the ruin brought by the Peloponnesian War. His last tragedy, *Oedipus at Colonus*, produced after his death, dealt with the old age of the famous Theban king who in ignorance had killed his father and married his mother, and who had torn out his own eyes in horror when he discovered what he had done. A blind beggar, an outcast, Oedipus now knew that he could not have avoided the pollution of his unwitting crimes and that his self-mutilation, too, was justified. Tempered by years of suffering, he sought sanctuary to die, and received it from Theseus, king of Athens. Oedipus's tomb would forever protect the Athenians against Thebes. Reflecting upon the terrible story of Oedipus and on the trials of all human life, Sophocles' chorus sang that it is best never to be born, for all humans are but phantoms, shadows whose actions inevitably bring tragedy upon them.

Nineteen plays remain of the many written by the third and last of the great Attic tragedians, Euripides (c. 480–406 B.C.), who focused upon human psychology, with less emphasis on divine majesty. More realistic in their introduction of children, slaves, and other characters upon the scene, his plays were also more human in their exploration of the far reaches of the obsessed mind. The *Hippolytus* showed the uncontrollable sexual passion of a decent woman, Phaedra, for her ascetic stepson Hippolytus, who rejected it as he would all passion. Ashamed of her lust, she accused Hippolytus of

The ruined theater at Epidaurus, constructed about 330 B.C., still provides a superb example of theater construction from which there has been relatively little change since.
Hans Namuth/Photo Researchers, Inc.

ARISTOPHANES ON "WORTHY THEMES"

Aristophanes maintained that literature best expressed mankind's concerns and that poetry was the most expressive form of literature:

These are the only themes
worthy of poetry, these high themes. Think: from the first
it has been the poets who have served men best.
Orpheus: he taught us to understand the Mysteries and to hate murder; Musaios: the arts of healing and divination; Hesiod: sowing and reaping; and godlike

Homer in his deathless chant: did he not teach us the glory of bearing arms, the black joy of battle?

Aristophanes, *The Frogs: An English Version* by Dudley Fitts. Copyright © 1955 by Harcourt Brace Jovanovich, Inc., renewed 1983 by Cornel Fitts, David Fitts, and Deborah W. Fitts. Reprinted by permission of the publishers.

having attacked her; he was executed, and she committed suicide. The *Medea* showed a woman so far gone in agony brought about by rejection of her love that she killed her children in a fit of madness. The *Alcestis* depicted a husband so selfish that he gladly accepted the offer of his devoted wife to die for him so that he might prolong his life. *The Trojan Women* presented the sufferings of the women of Troy at the hands of the Greeks. Staged in the same year as the Athenian atrocity at Melos, it must have caused the audience many uncomfortable moments of self-questioning. And *The Bacchae* explored the excesses of religious ecstasy, showing a frenzied queen who tore her son to bits, thinking he was a lion. Was Euripides saying that men under the impulse of strong emotion were beasts, or that the old religion had too much that was savage in it, or only that the young king had defied the god and his hubris had brought him a fate that he well deserved? The enduring beauty of all these plays is that we can discuss their meanings in the context of each succeeding century.

Comedy

Comedy, like tragedy, also began at the festivals of Dionysus. (The word may mean "revel" or "village songs.") Aristophanes (c. 450–c. 385 B.C.) has left eleven complete plays and parts of a twelfth. By making his audience laugh, he hoped to teach them a lesson. A thoroughgoing conservative, he was suspicious of all innovation. In *The Frogs*, for instance, he brought onto the stage actors playing the parts of the two tragedians, Aeschylus (then dead) and Euripides (still alive). The god Dionysus himself solemnly weighed verses from their plays on a giant pair of scales; the solemn, didactic, and old-fashioned Aeschylus outweighed the innovating, skeptical, volatile, modern Euripides every time. A tragedian's duty, Aristophanes thought, was to teach the old truths.

In *The Clouds* Aristophanes ridiculed the philoso-

pher Socrates, whom he showed in his "think shop," dangling from the ceiling in a basket so that he could "voyage in air and contemplate the sun." Aristophanes meant to call attention to the dangers offered to Athenian youth by the Sophists. Socrates thought the play very unfair; but, like the others, Socrates taught young men to question the existing order, and he was therefore fair game.

Aristophanes opposed the Peloponnesian War, not because he was a pacifist but because he thought it unnecessary. In *Lysistrata* the women sexually denied themselves to their husbands until the men made peace, and in other plays Aristophanes denounced the Athenian politicians, including Pericles himself, for going to war. In *The Birds* the leading characters set off to found a Birdville (Cloud-cuckoo-land) to get away from war. In one of his later plays, the women took over the state and proposed to share all the men among them, putting prostitutes out of business; in another, Poverty and Wealth appeared in person and argued their cases. These later plays provided a transition to the New Comedy of the fourth century—gentler, more domestic, more respectable, conventionalized. We have portions of several New Comedies by the Hellenic Menander (c. 342–281 B.C.) and one full text, *Misanthrope*, published for the first time only in 1958.

Drama was, of course, only one form that Greek poetic genius took. From the earliest days, the Greeks were also the masters of lyric poetry. Among the most celebrated are poems of love by the poetess Sappho (fl c. 610–c. 580), of war by Spartan poets in the very early days, and of triumph in the Olympic games by Pindar (c. 522 to 438).

History

Much of what we know about the Greeks before and during the Persian Wars we owe to the industry and intelligence of Herodotus (c. 484–425 B.C.), who began to write his history as an account of the origins and course of the struggle between Greeks and Persians, and expanded it into an inquiry into the peoples of the whole world known to the Greeks. Born on the Ionian coast of Asia Minor, Herodotus was a great traveler who visited Egypt, Italy, Mesopotamia, and the coast of the Black Sea, collecting information and listening to whatever stories people would tell him about their own past and their present customs. Although he loved a good story, he was both experienced and sensible. He often alerted the reader about a story that he himself did not believe but had set down only to fill out the record.

Some have tended to scoff a little, especially at Herodotus's tales of a past that was remote even when he was doing his research; but these doubters have often been silenced by archaeological finds. For instance, Herodotus said that the founder of Thebes, the semimythical Cadmus, was a Phoenician who had brought Phoenician letters with him to Greece, about 1350 B.C., some nine hundred years before Herodotus's own day. Herodotus added that Cadmus's dynasty was ousted about 1200 B.C. This was often disbelieved, but in A.D. 1964 archaeologists at Thebes found in the palace of Cadmus a collection of cuneiform seals, one of which was datable to 1367–1346 B.C., demonstrating the high probability of Herodotus's account of Cadmus. Even the date of the ouster was verified, since the seals were in a layer of material that had been burned about 1200 B.C. and had survived because they were already baked clay. Herodotus wrote so well and so beguilingly that we would still read him with delight even if he were less reliable. Nor was he a mere collector and organizer of material. Though he wandered far, he never lost sight of his main theme—the conflict between east and west, which he interpreted as a conflict between despotism and freedom.

For his methods, his curiosity, and his sense of style, he is known as "the father of history." One definition of civilization requires that a civilized people have a sense of history—meaning that the past counts in the present. The Greeks showed this sense not only in their respect for their chroniclers, but in having a muse—one of nine daughters of Zeus who were patron goddesses of the arts—for history alone: Clio.

The equally intelligent, very different historian Thucydides (c. 460–c. 400), wrote of the Peloponnesian Wars. The difference between the two arose partly from their subject matter. Herodotus was dealing with events that had happened largely before his own time, and he had to accept hearsay accounts. Thucydides was dealing mainly with events in which he himself had been a participant. He was an unsuccessful Athenian general who had been punished for his defeat; but he remained impartial, scientific, and serious—collecting and weighing his information with the greatest care. Though he followed Herodotus's custom of putting into the mouths of his leading characters words that represented what they might have said rather than what he could prove they said, he told his readers that he was doing this; the actual words were not available, but the arguments on

both sides of any issue could be revived and reconstructed in the form of speeches. Pericles' funeral oration, with its praise of Athenian democracy, is perhaps the most famous example (see p. 46); but Thucydides also wrote for the Melians, about to suffer terrible slaughter and enslavement at Athenian hands, all the moving arguments appropriate to those who realize they are to be massacred.

As deep a student of human psychology as any tragedian, Thucydides found the cause of war in people and nations; he knew as much about war and human behavior as anybody since has been able to learn. He wrote from the perspective of a loser, but not as a mere loser in a sporting event, where time and perhaps a return match will assuage the hurt. Thucydides had seen his own Athens, so admirable in its best qualities, brought down by the Spartan militarists. He hoped that in the future human intelligence would realize how risky war was and what damage it did to the highest human values; but he knew that human nature would always respond to certain challenges by force, and that the lessons of the past were hard to learn. He wrote in pain and in fierce detachment. His narrative of the great military events, such as the siege of Syracuse, moves with great speed and well-concealed artistry. The much less talented and more pedestrian Xenophon, author of the *Anabasis*, wrote in the *Hellenica* a continuation of Thucydides' work down to 362 B.C. And the still less talented Arrian, basing his work largely on the now lost account by Ptolemy I himself, has left us an account of Alexander's campaigns.

For the century or so that followed the death of Alexander we have no historical work comparable to these. Therefore, we know the period less intimately than any since the Dark Age. It is only with the decade of the 220s that we once again encounter a narrative history, and then its author and his purpose symbolize the change that had taken place. He was Polybius, who wrote in Greek but who had spent much time in Rome, where he had become an admirer and agent of the Romans, and the subject of his book was the rise of Roman power.

Science and Philosophy

Possessed of inquiring, speculative minds, and interested in their environment, the Greeks were keenly interested in science. Stimulated by their acquaintance with Egypt, the Ionians and later the European Greeks, though they lacked instruments to check and refine their results, correctly attributed many of the workings of nature to natural rather than supernatural causes. They knew that the Nile flooded because annual spring rains caused its source in Ethiopia to overflow. They decided that the straits between Sicily and Italy and between Africa and Spain were the result of earthquakes, not the work of gods. They understood what caused eclipses and knew that the moon shone by light reflected from the sun. Hippocrates of Cos (c. 460–c. 377) founded a school of medicine from which there survive the Hippocratic oath, with its high concept of medical ethics, and detailed clinical accounts of the symptoms and progress of diseases so accurate that modern doctors have been able to identify cases of epilepsy, diphtheria, and typhoid fever. Of the first, a supposedly divine disease, a practitioner wrote. "It seems to me that the disease is no more divine than any other. It has a natural cause, just as other diseases have. Men think it divine merely because they do not understand it. But if they called everything divine which they do not understand, there would be no end of divine things."

The mathematician Pythagoras (c. 580–500) seems to have begun as a musician interested in the mathematical differences in the length of lyre strings needed to produce various notes. The theorem that in a right triangle the square of the hypotenuse is equal to the sum of the squares of the other two sides we owe to the followers of Pythagoras. They made the concept of numbers into a guide to the problems of life, elevating mathematics almost to a religious cult, perhaps the earliest effort to explain the universe in abstract mathematical language. Pythagoras is said to have been the first to use the word *cosmos*—"harmonious and beautiful order"—for the universe. Earlier Greeks had found the key to the universe in some single primal substance: water, fire, earth, or air. Democritus (c. 460–370) decided that all matter consisted of minute, invisible atoms.

When Alexandria became the center of scientific research, the astronomer Aristarchus, in the midthird century B.C., concluded that the earth revolves around the sun—a concept not generally accepted till almost two thousand years later. His younger contemporary, Eratosthenes, believed that the earth was round and estimated its circumference quite accurately. Euclid, the great geometrical systematizer, had his own school at Alexandria in the third century B.C. His pupil Archimedes won a lasting reputation in both theoretical and applied physics, devising machines for removing water from mines and irrigation ditches and demonstrating the power of pulleys and levers by single-handedly drawing ashore a heavily laden ship. Hence his celebrated boast: "Give me a lever long enough and a place to stand on, and I will move the world." In the second century, Hipparchus calculated the length of the solar year to within a few minutes.

Rhetoric also became an important study, as the Greeks reflected on the construction of their own language and developed high standards of self-expression and style. The subject began with political oratory, as politicians wished to make more effective speeches—particularly in wartime, when the population was excited and each leader strove to be more eloquent than the last. But to speak effectively, one must have something to say, and a body of professional teachers, who wrote on physics, astronomy, mathematics, logic, and music, traveled about, receiving pay. These multipurpose scholars who in the fifth and fourth centuries B.C. taught people how to talk and write and think on all subjects were called Sophists (wisdom men). Sophists generally tended to be highly skeptical of accepted standards of behavior and morality, questioning the traditional ways of doing things. They tended to focus on the tension between nature and law.

How could anybody really be sure of anything, they would ask? And some would answer that we cannot know anything we cannot experience through one of our five senses. How could one be sure that the gods existed if no one could see, hear, smell, taste, or touch them? If there were no gods and therefore no divine laws, how should we behave? Should we trust laws made by others like ourselves? And what sort of men were making the laws, and in whose interest? Perhaps all existing laws were simply a trick invented by powerful people to protect their position. Maybe the general belief in the gods was simply encouraged and expanded by clever people in whose interest it was to have the general public docile. Not all Sophists went this far, but in Athens during the Peloponnesian War many young people, troubled by the war or by the sufferings of the plague, were ready to listen to suggestions that the state should not make such severe demands upon them. Many citizens, gods fearing and law abiding, saw the Sophists as corrupters of youth.

It is only against this background that we can understand the career and fate of Socrates (469–399 B.C.), whose method (though not affiliation) was that of the Sophists—to question everything, all current assumptions about religion, politics, and behavior—but who retained unwavering to the end his own deep inner loyalties to Athens. Though Socrates wrote no books, we know him well from contemporary reports, chiefly those of his pupil Plato (c. 427–347). Socrates was a stonemason who spent his life arguing in the assembly, in public places, and in the homes of his friends in Athens. He thought of himself as a gadfly, challenging everything anybody said to him and urging people not to take their preconceptions and prejudices as truths. Only never-ending debate, a process of question and answer—the celebrated Socratic method—could lead human beings to truth. Reasoning led Socrates to conclude that human beings were more than animals; they had a mind, and, above all, they had a true self, a kind of soul or spirit. Their proper business on earth was to fulfill this true soul and cultivate the virtues that were proper to it: temperance, justice, courage, nobility, truth. Socrates would pursue the inquiries that led to these virtues even against the wishes of the state.

At about age seventy, Socrates was brought to trial on charges of disrespect to the gods and corrupting the young men of Athens. He argued that he had followed the prescribed religious observances and that he only wanted to make the young men better citizens; he defended his gadfly tactics as necessary to stir a sluggish state into life. But by a narrow margin, a court of 501 jurors voted the death penalty. Socrates could have escaped by suggesting that he be punished in some other way. Instead, he ironically asked for a tiny fine and, to show his respect for the law, forced the court to choose between that and death. Socrates drank the poison cup of hemlock and waited for death, serenely optimistic. He was "of good cheer about his soul." Many contemporaries and most commentators have agreed that he was the victim of hysteria following a dreadful war.

Thereafter, it was Plato who carried on his work. Plato founded a school in Athens, the Academy, and wrote several notable dialogues, intellectual conversations in which Socrates and others were shown discussing problems of life and the human spirit. Much influenced by the Pythagoreans, Plato retained a deep reverence for mathematics, but he found cosmic reality in Ideas rather than in numbers. As each person has a "true self" within and superior to the body, so the world we experience with our bodily senses has within and superior to itself a "true world"—an invisible universe or cosmos. In *The Republic*, Plato has Socrates compare the relationship between the world of the senses and the world of Ideas with that between the shadows of persons and objects as they would be cast by firelight on the wall of a cave, and the same real persons and objects as they would appear in the direct light of day. People see objects—chairs, tables, trees—of the world as real, whereas they are only reflections of the true realities—the universals—the Ideas of the perfect chair, table, or tree. So human virtues are reflections of ideal virtues, of which the highest is the Idea of the Good. Human beings can, and should, strive to know the ultimate Ideas, especially the Idea of the Good.

Plato's theory of Ideas has proved to be one of the great wellsprings of Western thought and has formed the starting point for much later philosophical discussion. Moreover, in teaching that the Idea of the Good was the supreme excellence and the final goal of life, Plato (through Socrates) was advancing a kind of monotheism and laying a foundation on which both pagan and Christian theologians would build.

Politically, Athenian democracy did much to disillusion Plato: he had seen its courts condemn his master. On his travels he had formed a high opinion of the tyrants ruling the Greek cities of Sicily and Italy. So when Plato came to sketch the ideal state in *The Republic*, his system resembled that of the Spartans. He recommended that power be entrusted to the Guardians, a small intellectual elite, specially bred and trained to understand Ideas, governing under the wisest man of all, the Philosopher-King. The masses would simply do their jobs as workers or soldiers and obey their superiors. Democracy, he concluded, by relying on amateurs, was condemned to failure through the fatal flaws in the character of those who would govern.

Plato's most celebrated pupil was Aristotle (384–322 B.C.), called the "master of those who know." Son of a physician at the court of Philip of Macedon and tutor to Alexander the Great, Aristotle was interested in everything. He wrote on biology, logic, ethics, literary criticism, political theory. His work survives largely in the form of notes on his lectures taken by his students. Though he wrote 158 studies of the constitutions of Greek cities, only the study of Athens survives. Despite their lack of polish, these writings have had enormous influence.

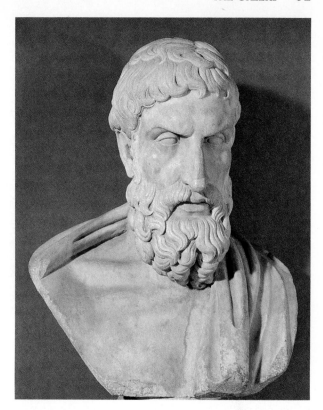

A bust of Epicurus, from the Capitolino Museum in Rome.
SEF/Art Resource

Aristotle concerned himself chiefly with matters as they are. The first to use scientific methods, he classified living organisms into groups, much as modern biologists do, and extended the system to other fields—government, for example. He maintained that governments were of three forms—rule by one man, rule by a few men, or rule by many men—and that there were good and bad types of each, respectively monarchy and tyranny, aristocracy and oligarchy, polity and mob rule. Everywhere—in his *Logic, Poetics*, and *Politics*—he laid foundations for later inquiry. Though he believed that people should strive and aspire, he did not push them on to Socrates' goal of self-knowledge or Plato's lofty ascent to the Idea of the Good. He urged instead the cultivation of the Golden Mean, the avoidance of excess on either side—courage, not foolhardiness or cowardice; temperance, not overindulgence or abstinence; liberality in giving, not prodigality or meanness.

Later, in the period after Alexander, two other schools of Hellenic philosophy developed, the Epicurean and the Stoic. Epicurus (341–271) counseled temperance and reason, carrying further the principle of the Golden Mean. Though he defined pleasure as the key to human happiness, he ranked spiritual joys above those of the body, which he recommended should be satisfied in moderation. Although the gods existed, he taught that they did not interest themselves in human affairs. This last argument led many to think that the Epicureans were atheists bent on attacking religion,

This dramatic view of the Athenian Acropolis is taken from across the valley near the Pnyx. The large temple is the Parthenon. The Acropolis was the civic and religious center of Athens, completed by Pericles and those who succeeded him during the second half of the fifth century.
Robin W. Winks

though they regarded it as simply irrelevant. The Stoics, founded by Zeno (c. 333–262) got their name from the columned porch (*Stoa*) in the Athens agora from which he first taught. They preferred to repress the physical desires altogether. Since only the inward divine reason counted, the Stoics preached total disregard for social, physical, or economic differences. They became the champions of slaves and other social outcasts, anticipating to some degree one of the moral teachings of Christianity. They were often apolitical, for political debate did not help people, and thus they were thought to be fatalistic, even apathetic, in their focus on the inward life.

The Arts

The incalculably rich legacy left by the Greeks in literature was well matched by their achievements in the public arts. In architecture their characteristic public building was a rectangle, with a roof supported by fluted columns. Over the centuries, the Greeks developed three principal types or orders of columns, still used today in "classical" buildings: the Doric, the Ionic, and the Corinthian. Fluting gave an impression of greater height than the simple cylindrical Egyptian columns.

No matter what the order of the columns, a Greek temple strikes the beholder as dignified and simple. On the Acropolis of Athens, the Parthenon, greatest of all Doric temples, rose between 447 and 432 B.C. as the crowning achievement of Pericles' rebuilding program. By means of subtle devices—slightly inclining the columns inward so that they look more stable, giving each column a slight bulge in the center of the shaft so that it does not look concave—the building gives the illusion of perfection. In the triangular gable-ends that

crowned its front and back colonnades (pediments) and on the marble slabs (*metopes*) between the beam ends above the columns, stood a splendid series of sculptured battle scenes, most of whose remains (the so-called Elgin Marbles) are now in the British Museum. Originally, the Parthenon and its statues were brightly

A superb Greek dish dating from c. 530 B.C. depicting Dionysus, the wine god, on a sea voyage.
New York Public Library Picture Collection

This Attic *amphora* (two-handled vase used for storage) of terra cotta shows Achilles and Ajax playing either chess or dice; it dates from c. 540 B.C.
Vatican Museums

painted. (The building survived almost undamaged for two thousand years, until 1697, when a Venetian shell exploded a Turkish powder magazine inside.)

The achievement of Phidias and the other sculptors of the Periclean Age had gradually developed from styles created a century or more earlier, usually of young men rather rigidly posed, with their arms hanging at their sides and a uniformly serene smile on their lips.

Probably influenced by Egyptian models, these statues have great charm for moderns, who sometimes find the realism of the finished classical work rather tiresome. Phidias's great gold and ivory statues of Athena and the Olympian Zeus long ago fell to looters, though the Parthenon frieze survived. Most of the Greeks' sculpture in bronze also was destroyed, but every so often a great bronze statue is fished out of the sea or is found beneath a modern street.

Though Greek painting as such has almost disappeared, we know from written texts that public buildings were adorned with paintings of Greek victories and portraits of political and military leaders. Moreover, the thousands of pottery vases, plates, cups, and bowls that have been discovered preserve on their surfaces—in black on red or in red on black—paintings of extraordinary beauty and of great variety. They show mythological scenes, illustrations of the *Iliad* and *Odyssey*, and the daily round of human activity—an athlete, a fisherman, a shoemaker, a miner, even a drunk vomiting while a sympathetic girl holds his head.

In the Hellenistic age sculpture became more emotional and theatrical; compare the Laocoön group, with writhing serpents crushing their victims, to a statue of the Periclean period. The Venus de Milo and the Winged Victory of Samothrace are two of the most heralded Hellenistic works of art, but there were a good many imitative and exaggerated efforts that today are regarded as comparative failures. In literature, too, beginning with Menander, vigor and originality ebbed, while sophistication and self-consciousness took over.

The Greeks continue to fascinate us for many reasons. They are the first people to have left a record sufficiently intact that we can trace in some detail how their customs changed over time. Their sense of the dramatic and the human, their speculation about the universe and about individual psychology, and the divine tension they felt between the ideal and daily reality all appeal to us, for we find reflections of our own preoccupations in them. Their philosophers phrased the questions we still ask, their politicians used the techniques, both noble and ignoble, our politicians still use,

The Elgin Marbles are the major portion of a frieze, by Phidias or one of his pupils, from the Parthenon in Athens. They were brought to England by the Earl of Elgin in 1806, were sold to the British government ten years later, and are now on display in the British Museum in London. The marbles have become a symbol of that period of European imperialism in which the art treasures of many cultures were removed from their country of origin to the great galleries and museums of western Europe and the United States. In the 1980s the Elgin Marbles became a subject of dispute between Britain and Greece, which demanded their return.
British Museum

From left to right: Doric, Ionic, and Corinthian columns.
New York Public Library Picture Collection

and their artists strove for the sense of human perfection we want to believe attainable. The Greeks are the first people to whom modern men and women can relate, emotionally as well as intellectually.

Women continued to have significant, though clearly subordinate, roles in Greek and Hellenic society, as Aristophanes' *Lysistrata* had clearly demonstrated. The Greek family remained monogamous and, as we say today, nuclear: that is, it consisted of husband, wife, and their children. The family was also an economic unit, and dependent relatives and slaves were often included within the Greek definition of family. Spouses were chosen from within a narrow circle of relatives, in good part in order to protect family property through a closed circle of inheritance. The family thus served to protect women. Women were citizens, though they did not have independent status: they could not trade except in small ways, and they were required to have a guardian—their husband, if they were married, their father or another close male relative if they were unmarried. In Sparta women could inherit land, and by the third century two-fifths of the land was held by women. In Athens, however, women remained without property (except for their own slaves, their clothing, and their jewelry).

Athenian philosophers and writers portrayed women as more prone to extreme emotions and violent acts than men. Women, Athenian leaders argued, needed to be protected both from the outside world and from

Two of the best known works of Hellenistic Greek art are the Laocoön group and the Winged Victory of Samothrace. The Laocoön statue, a study in terror, was done by three sculptors in the first century B.C. The family is caught in a death grip by serpents whom the gods had sent to punish Laocoön because he had urged the Trojans not to touch the wooden horse that had been brought into their midst. In contrast to this horror is the figure of Victory erected on the island of Samothrace about 200 B.C., probably to commemorate a naval victory by the Greeks over those who sought to enslave them.
Vatican Museums and Scala/Art Resource

themselves. Thus a stranger could not enter an Athenian house where there were women unless invited in by the master; quarters for women were segregated away from the street, so that they might not be seen by casual passersby; and women generally did not leave the house unless accompanied by a male. The position of women in Greek civilization was similar to that of women who live under Islam today, though there were and are exceptions—Sparta, for example, or some of the modern Islamicized nations of the twentieth century, such as Indonesia, Pakistan, and Egypt.

Still, unless archaeology and history together produce new evidence, we are likely to see the Greeks as the ancient people to whom Western civilization feels closest. They worried about our worries: What does it mean to be civilized? To lead the good life? To serve the people? To retain one's own identity? How best may we attain a sense of security in a world in which chance exists? By fatalistically accepting that which is? By attempting to change the future? The present? Our environment? Our past?

They asked whether god or gods exist, and, for the most part, having decided that they did, they debated how best to worship, celebrate, or propitiate those gods, individually and in groups. They asked nearly all of what we call The Big Questions, and while we have evolved many different answers to those questions (or conceived of new ways in which to state the same answers),

and while our circumstances are different so that no direct parallels can be drawn from a society so far removed in time from our own, we continue to recognize in the Greeks something of ourselves.

Much of what we know about the Greeks comes from research and discoveries in the nineteenth century. The Greeks seemed to provide answers to many questions with which nineteenth-century society was concerned, and there was a tendency, especially in western Europe, to idealize Greek civilization. Only recently have new techniques and concerns among historians—especially with quantitative methods and in comparative and social history—led us to realize that there was much in Greek society which today we find deplorable. Slavery was essential to the leisure the philosophers enjoyed. Women were systematically and casually kept in subordinate positions. War was used to resolve problems of population and pride as well as for territorial gain. The toilers in the fields, vineyards, and in the expanding ancient city often had no voice, in war or peace. Though professing the rational life, the Greeks could be swept up into the irrational, allowing their rituals to bring on mass hysteria.

In sum, the Greeks—despite nineteenth-century romanticizing and twentieth-century skepticism—were human beings subject to the ambiguities and contradictions shown by every human society. It is this very humanness which strengthens our perception that Greek origins are so relevant to our own.

Summary

The Greeks are the first ancient society with which modern society feels an immediate affinity. We can identify with Greek art, Greek politics, Greek curiosity, and the Greek sense of history. The polis, roughly translated as the city-state, was the prevailing social and political unit of ancient Greece. Athens and Sparta were the two most significant poleis.

Sparta was a conservative military oligarchy ruled jointly by two kings and a council of elders. It had an excellent army, but its society was highly regimented. Sparta produced little of artistic or cultural importance.

Athens progressed from an old-fashioned, aristocratic tribal state in the eighth century B.C. to a tyranny and then to a democracy by the fifth century B.C. Among the most important leaders of this transition from a state based on ties of kinship to one based on political citizenship were the lawgivers Draco and Solon, the tyrant Pisistratus, and the reformer Cleisthenes.

Athens depended, as did all Greek states, upon the systematic exploitation of slaves. Although influential in the home, women were also a subject group. Fathers and husbands determined the extent of their personal freedom.

By the fifth century B.C., the Persian Empire, which had subjugated all of the Near East, including the Greek cities of Asia Minor (Ionia), was extending its rule into northern Greece. Two Persian invasions of Greece were defeated: by the Athenians at Marathon (490 B.C.) and by united Greek forces at the battles of Salamis (480) and Plataea (479).

After the defeat of Persia, Athens and Sparta were rivals for the leadership of Greece. The Athenian Empire that emerged from the Persian defeat was brought to its zenith by Pericles, who beautified Athens and advanced the democratization of its constitution.

Rivalry between Athens and Sparta led to the Peloponnesian Wars (460–445, 431–404 B.C.), in which Athens was eventually defeated after a plague ravaged the city and a great expedition to Sicily met with disaster.

Thereafter, neither Sparta, nor Thebes, nor a revived Athens, could successfully lead Greece. In the 330s Greek disunity led to domination by Philip, king of Macedon, a semi-Greek kingdom to the north.

Philip's son Alexander, the Great, invaded and conquered the Persian Empire in 334–327 B.C. Alexander's conquests spread Greek colonists and culture from Egypt to the borders of India.

After Alexander's death in 323 three main successor dynasties emerged, each founded by one of his generals: the Ptolemies in Egypt, the Seleucids in Syria and Mesopotamia, and the Antigonids in Macedon and Asia Minor. All of these states were eventually absorbed by Rome.

Greek religion was centered upon the worship of the Olympian gods. Greek drama developed out of a festival at Athens in honor of the god Dionysus. The chief Greek playwrights who have survived are the tragedians Aeschylus, Sophocles, and Euripides and the comic writers Aristophanes and Menander. The principal Greek historians whose work has come down to us are Herodotus, who wrote about the Persian Wars; Thucydides, the historian of the Peloponnesian Wars; and Polybius, whose subject was the rise of Roman power.

The Greeks attributed many of the workings of nature to natural rather than to supernatural causes. In medicine, geography, geometry, physics, and astronomy their achievements still command respect.

Greek philosophy had its roots in natural science and in the tendency of science to question established beliefs and traditions. Socrates taught that the truth could be found only in a never-ending debate, a process of question and answer—the famous "Socratic method." His pupil Plato's theory of Ideas is one of the great wellsprings of Western thought. Plato's pupil Aristotle was the first to use scientific method, classifying living things, beliefs, and systems of government. The Epicurean and Stoic schools of philosophy sought to show people how to live contented lives in a troubled world. The influence of Greek art and architecture on Western civilization is incalculable.

3

The Romans

*T*he Romans cherished the legend that after the fall of Troy, Aeneas, a Trojan prince, half-divine, led his fugitive followers to Italy and founded Rome on the banks of the Tiber. The poet Vergil (70–19 B.C.) immortalized the story in his *Aeneid*, written as Roman imperial glory approached its zenith. As Vergil borrowed from Homer, so Rome borrowed extensively from the older Greek and Near Eastern civilizations. The tale of Aeneas symbolizes the flow into Italy of Greeks and Near Easterners as well as Rome's debt to the Greco-oriental world. Yet Rome did not achieve greatness on borrowed capital alone. The Romans were themselves innovative builders, generals, administrators, and law-givers whose legal concepts and procedures passed into later judicial systems.

Compared with Greece, Italy enjoys certain natural advantages: the plains are larger and more fertile, the mountains less a barrier to communications. The plain of Latium, south of the site of Rome, could be farmed intensively after drainage and irrigation ditches had been dug; the nearby hills provided timber and good pasturage. The city of Rome lay only fifteen miles from the sea and could share in the trade of the Mediterranean; yet its seven hills overlooking the Tiber could be easily fortified and defended. By 600 B.C. Greek colonies to the south dotted the shores of Italy and Sicily; this was *Magna Graecia*. To the north, the dominant power was held by the Etruscans—a people of whom we know little, surely foreigners in Italy, perhaps from Asia Minor (and so the source of the Aeneas legend)—who had invaded the peninsula and conquered the region north of Latium by 700 B.C. They extended their power southward, surrounding Rome, and seized it soon after 600.

Rich Etruscan remains have been discovered during the past century and a half, mostly in tombs; they show that the Etruscans had an enormous admiration for Greek art—pottery, sculpture, and painting—which they bought and imitated. They wrote their language in Greek letters, and most of the ten thousand or so existing inscriptions are very short. Many can be read, since they give, for example, only a proper name and perhaps the age at which the person mentioned died. Until 1964 no key to the Etruscan language like the Rosetta stone had turned up. Then, on the seacoast thirty miles from Rome, archaeologists found three golden tablets dated c. 500 B.C. with inscriptions in both Punic (Carthaginian, or late Phoenician) and Etruscan. Although the total number of words is only about ninety, these tablets are now throwing more light on the language.

Expert farmers, miners, and metalworkers, the Etruscans built huge stone walls around their settlements. They practiced divination, foretelling the future from observing flocks of birds in flight or from examining the entrails of an animal slain in sacrifice. Their tomb decoration seems to show that, like the Egyptians, they believed in an afterlife similar to this one, and that they accorded their women a status higher than was usual in ancient society. They also enjoyed gladiatorial combat as a spectacle—a taste the Romans may have borrowed from them.

I THE REPUBLIC

When the Etruscans took over Rome, the people they conquered were apparently Latins, descendants of prehistoric inhabitants of the peninsula. Under its Etruscan kings, Rome prospered during the sixth century B.C. The Etruscans built new stone structures and drained and paved what eventually became the Forum. But the Roman population resented foreign rule and joined with other Latin tribes in a large-scale rebellion. The traditional date for the expulsion from Rome of the last Etruscan king, Tarquin the Proud, is 509 B.C. What he left behind was an independent Latin city-state, still including some Etruscan nobles, much smaller than Athens or Sparta, sharing Latium with other city-states. Yet in less than 250 years, Rome would dominate the entire Italian peninsula.

We can understand this success best by examining Roman institutions. Once they had ousted Tarquin, the dominant aristocratic forces of Rome set up a republic. Only the well-established landowning families, the *patricians* (Latin *pater*, "father"), perhaps not more than 10 percent of the population, held full citizenship. The remaining 90 percent were *plebeians* (Latin *plebs*, "the multitude"), who included those engaged in trade or labor, the smaller farmers, and all those who were debtors as the result of the economic upheaval that followed the expulsion of the Etruscans. The plebeians had no right to hold office; they could amass as much money as they pleased, however, and wealthy plebeians would eventually lead a campaign to gain political emancipation for their class. Fifth-century urban Rome, then, was not unlike sixth-century Athens before the reforms of Cleisthenes.

The patrician class supplied two consuls, who governed jointly for a term of a year, enjoying full *imperium*, or "supreme political power." Each had the right of veto over the other, so that both had to support a measure before it could be put through. Ordinarily they were commanders of the army, but in wartime this power was often wielded for a period not longer than six months by an elected *dictator*, a commander who had obtained his authority constitutionally and had to surrender it when his term was over.

The consuls usually followed the policies decided on by the Senate, a body consisting of about three hundred members, mostly patricians and all ex-officials. It wielded such prestige that it came first in the Roman political emblem—SPQR, *Senatus Populusque Romanorum*, that is, the Senate and the People of the Romans.

An Etruscan bronze, known as "the Capitoline wolf." Figures of Romulus and Remus were added in the late fifteenth century to validate a popular oral tradition which named Romulus as the founder of Rome. Romulus was said to have been abandoned as a child on the banks of the Tiber, with his twin brother Remus. They were saved by being suckled by a she-wolf. Later Romulus killed his brother in a quarrel. Virtually every society has a "founder legend" and Rome's is one of the most famous in art and story.
Art Resource

The reigning consuls, who were themselves senators, appointed new senators. The Romans had another deliberative body, the Centuriate Assembly, based on the *century*, the smallest unit (one hundred men) of the army. Although plebeians were included, the patricians also dominated the deliberations of this body. It enjoyed a higher legal prerogative but less actual power than the Senate, although it elected the consuls and other officials and approved or rejected laws submitted to it by both the consuls and the Senate.

Before a man could be chosen consul, he had to pass through a succession of lesser posts. The job that led directly to the consulate was that of *praetor* (the one who goes in front). Elected by the Centuriate Assembly for a term of a year, the praetor served as a judge; he also often commanded an army and later governed a province. While at first there was only one praetor, the number later rose to eight. Men seeking election as praetor or consul wore a special robe whitened with chalk, the *toga candida*, from which comes our word *candidate*. From among the ex-consuls, the assembly elected two *censors*, for an eighteen-month term, who took a census to determine which of the population was qualified for army service. They also secured the right to pass on the moral qualifications of men nominated for the Senate, barring those they thought corrupt or too luxury loving (hence the connotation of our words *censor* and *censorship*).

The plebeians naturally resented their exclusion from political authority. As early as the 490s they threatened to withdraw from Rome and to found a new city-state of their own nearby. And when this tactic won them a concession, they continued to use it at various times with great effect during the next two hundred years. In 494 B.C. they gained the right to have officials of their own, the *tribunes* of the people, to protect them from unduly harsh application of the laws; by 457 there were ten such tribunes. In 471 the plebeians also gained their own assembly, the Tribal Assembly (named because of the subdivision of the plebeian population into tribes),

which chose the tribunes and had the right, like the Centuriate Assembly, to pass on new laws. Next they complained that the patrician judges could manipulate the law for their own purposes because it had never been set down for all to read. So in 451 the consuls ordered the extremely severe laws engraved on wooden tablets—the Twelve Tables—beginning the written history of Roman law.

In the early Republic, being in debt meant that a plebeian farmer would lose his land and be forced into slavery. As a result, property steadily accumulated in the hands of the patrician landowners. In a significant advance, the plebeians were able to change the laws affecting their economic relationship with the patricians. They obtained legislation limiting the size of an estate that any one man might accumulate, abolishing the penalty of slavery for debt, and opening newly acquired lands to settlement by landless farmers. Still, the farmer-debtor problem, though eased, continued to plague the Romans even during the fifth and fourth centuries, when the plebeians won the right to hold all the offices of the state, including that of consul (366 B.C.). The plebeians also forced the repeal of the laws that forbade their intermarriage with patricians. The fusion of wealthy plebeians and patricians formed a new class, the *nobiles*, who were to dominate the later Republic as the patricians had done earlier.

Life for women in Rome did not differ greatly from the life of women in the Greek city-states. There was, however, more emphasis on family planning. The upper classes practiced both contraception and abortion. To reduce the size of families, infants (usually girls) were abandoned and died. Poor women often had large families and turned to prostitution to feed them. Roman households included female slaves who acted as midwives, nurses, and kitchen help. Freedwomen were part of the working class, often as independent shopkeepers and artisans, especially in wool. Sex roles were stereotyped, and while there were exceptions, especially after the introduction of Christianity, women were expected to remain at home, bear children, and avoid public life. Women are seldom mentioned in classical sources, and this is the best indication the historian has—the evidence of silence—on their social position.

Roman Expansion, 264–133 B.C.

This regime was well designed to carry on the chief preoccupation of the emerging Roman state—war. The Roman army at first had as its basic unit the *phalanx*—about 8,000 foot soldiers armed with helmet, shield, lance, and sword. But experience led to the substitution of the far more maneuverable *legion*, consisting of 5,000 men in groups of 60 or 120, called *maniples* (handfuls), armed with an additional weapon, an iron-tipped javelin, which could be hurled at the enemy from a distance. Almost all citizens of Rome had to serve. Iron discipline prevailed; punishment for offenses was summary or brutal. But the officers also understood the importance of generous recognition and reward of bravery as an incentive.

In a long series of wars, the Romans established their political dominance over the other Latin towns, the Etruscan cities, and the tribes of central Italy. Early in the third century B.C. they conquered the Greek cities of southern Italy. Meanwhile, in the north, a Celtic people, the Gauls, had crossed the Alps and settled in the Lombard plain. Their expansion was halted in 225 B.C. at the little river Rubicon, which was then the northern frontier of Roman dominion.

In conquered areas the Romans sometimes planted a colony of their own land-hungry plebeians. Usually they did not try to force the resident population into absolute subjection, accepting them as allies and respecting their institutions. The cities of Magna Graecia continued to enjoy home rule. Some of the nearest neighbors of Rome became full citizens of the Republic, but more often they had the protection of Roman law while being unable to participate in the Roman assemblies. So the expansion of Rome in Italy demonstrated imaginative statesmanship as well as military superiority.

The conquest of Magna Graecia made Rome a near neighbor of the Carthaginian state. Carthage (modern Tunis) was originally a Phoenician colony but had long since liberated itself and expanded along the African and Spanish shores of the Mediterranean and into western Sicily. Ruled by a commercial oligarchy, Carthage held a virtual monopoly of western Mediterranean trade. When the Carthaginians began to attack the Greek cities in eastern Sicily, the Sicilian Greeks appealed to Rome. So the Romans launched the First Punic (from the Latin word for Phoenician) War (264–241 B.C.).

The Romans won that war by building their first major fleet and defeating the Carthaginians at sea. They forced Carthage to give up all claim to eastern Sicily and to cede western Sicily as well, thus obtaining their first province beyond the Italian mainland. Sardinia and Corsica followed in 237. Seeking revenge, the Carthaginians used Spain as the base for an overland invasion to Italy in the Second Punic War (218–202). Their commander, Hannibal (247–183), led his forces across southern Gaul and then over the Alps into Italy, losing in the snow many of the elephants he used as pack animals. In northern Italy he recruited many Gauls and, making brilliant use of light infantry, won a string of victories as he marched southward. A notable battle was that at Cannae in 216 B.C., when the Romans suffered the most severe defeat in their history.

Gradually the Romans rebuilt their armies, and in 202 B.C. Hannibal, who had been roaming over Italy almost at will for a decade avoiding only the great walled cities, was summoned home to defend Carthage against a Roman invading force under Scipio, who had captured the Punic centers in Spain. Scipio won the battle at Zama, in Numidia, and the title *Africanus* (Conqueror of Africa) as a reward. The Romans forced the Carthaginians to surrender Spain (where the local population resisted Roman rule for another two centuries), to pay a large levy, and to promise to follow Rome's lead in foreign policy. Hannibal escaped to the court of the Seleucid king Antiochus III.

Though Carthaginian power had been broken, the city quickly recovered its prosperity. This alarmed the war party at Rome. Cato, a censor and senator, ended each of his speeches with the words *Delenda est Carthago* (Carthage must be destroyed). In the Third Punic War (149–146) the Romans leveled the city, sprinkled salt on the earth, and took over all the remaining Carthaginian territory as the province of Africa (modern Tunisia), now one of six overseas provinces.

While the Punic Wars were still going on, Rome had as early as 230 B.C. become embroiled in the Balkans and in Greece, first sending ships and troops to put down pirates who were operating in the Adriatic from bases in Illyria (modern Albania), and then intervening again in 219 to punish an unruly local ally. The Greeks were grateful to Rome and admitted Romans to the Eleusinian mysteries and the Isthmian Games. But Philip V (221–179), Antigonid king of Macedon, viewed with suspicion Roman operations on his side of the Adriatic. He tried to help Hannibal during the Second Punic War, but a Roman fleet prevented him from crossing to Italy. Many of the Greek cities—opponents of Philip, if not yet of Rome—came to Rome's aid in the fighting that ensued, helping to defeat him in the First Macedonian War (215–205).

Not eager as yet to expand on the eastern shores of the Adriatic, Rome contented itself with establishing a series of Illyrian buffer states. But Philip kept intervening in these states, and the Romans feared for their loyalty. In 202 B.C. several Hellenistic powers—Ptolemy V of Egypt; his ally Attalus, king of the powerful independent kingdom of Pergamum in Asia Minor; and Rhodes, head of a new naval league—as well as Athens, appealed to Rome to intervene once more against Philip V. Furthermore, the Romans feared the alliance struck between Philip and Antiochus III, the Seleucid king in Asia, and the Senate may have decided upon a preventive war. In the Second Macedonian War (200–197) Rome defeated Philip's armies on their own soil and forced him to withdraw from Greece altogether and become an ally of Rome. At the Isthmian Games of 196 B.C., a solemn Roman proclamation declared that the Greeks were free. Two years later, after more fighting (chiefly against Sparta), the Roman armies left Greece and its largely disillusioned population, who had learned that, though free, they were not viewed as equals by the Romans but as client states.

Antiochus III had profited by the defeat of Macedon, taking over the Greek cities on the Aegean coast of Asia Minor and crossing into Europe. Hoping to keep Greece as a buffer against him and worried at this advance, the Romans, preoccupied with wars in Spain, kept on negotiating with him. But Antiochus, who had with him the refugee Hannibal, opposed the Romans in Greece, unwisely hoping to win wide local support. The Romans defeated Antiochus and then invaded Asia, forcing him to surrender all the Seleucid holdings in Asia Minor in 188. Hannibal escaped but poisoned himself in 183 as he was about to be surrendered to Rome. Rome had become the predominant power in the Greek world, whether by intent, in reactive self-defense, or in pursuit of a theory of imperium.

For the next forty years the Romans felt obliged to arbitrate the constantly recurring quarrels among the Greek states. Rebellions led to or excused repeated armed intervention. In the Third Macedonian War (172–168), Perseus, Philip V's son and successor, was captured and his forces routed at the decisive battle of Pydna. Rome imposed a ruthless settlement, breaking Macedon up into four republics and exiling many who had sympathized with Perseus. Twenty years later the Romans annexed Macedon, their first province east of the Adriatic. In 146 they defeated a desperate uprising of the Achaean League and marked their victory by a brutal sack of Corinth, in which the men were killed, the women and children sold as slaves, and the city leveled. It was the same year that saw the total destruction of Carthage. The period of relatively gentle rule was over; a new harshness was now applied to allies as well as to opponents.

The Romans henceforth dominated Greece from Macedon, but did not yet annex it as a province. Internal

SLAVERY IN THE ROMAN WORLD

Roman Italy and Sicily became a slave society as the Romans conquered the whole of the Mediterranean world. Scholars argue over how fundamental slavery has been to different cultures. Perhaps half of all societies have owned legal slaves. But if we define a slave society as one in which slaves play a significant role in production and constitute, say, 20 percent of the total population, then there have been only five slave societies in known history: classical Athens, Roman Italy (though not the remainder of the Empire), the West Indies under the British and French, the southern portion of the United States before 1865, and Brazil. This does not, of course, include other forms of forced labor.

Slavery was both fed by, and helped to feed, the expansion of the Roman Empire. The presence of slaves in Roman Italy, chiefly the captives of foreign wars, forced major changes in political and economic organization; slaves may have made up a third of the population—2 million out of 6 million people—by the end of the first century B.C. Slaves were brought back to Rome as booty. As the rich invested in new agricultural land, angry peasants were displaced by slaves and forced into the cities, where they supported political leaders who promised to help them. Roman slaves could acquire professions and skills, however. Many were freed and assimilated as citizens, so that slavery was not fixed by unchanging status, color, religion, or origin. Slaves could purchase their own freedom, and thus emancipation meant that owners gained new sums of money produced by the newly freed slaves themselves with which they could purchase younger replacements. The system thereby became, for a time, self-perpetuating.

fighting in Greece came to an end; there was a religious and economic revival; divisions between rich and poor became more pronounced. Rome's prestige was now so great that in 133 the king of Pergamum, whose family had been helpful allies of the Romans—and much hated elsewhere for that reason—left his flourishing Asia Minor state to Rome in his will. It became the new province of Asia.

II CRISIS OF THE REPUBLIC

As Roman territory increased, signs of trouble multiplied. The Republic allowed a few overseas cities to retain some self-government but usually organized its new territories as provinces under governors appointed by the Senate. Some of the governors proved oppressive and lined their own pockets; as long as they raised recruits for the army and collected taxes, they had a free hand. In Italy pressure mounted from Rome's allies, who demanded full citizenship and a share in the new wealth flowing into the capital.

The great majority of those who lived on the Italian peninsula were farmers. By the time of the Republic, Roman farmers had advanced beyond the simple two-field system of the Greeks, in which one field was under cultivation while the other lay fallow. In the Campania the Romans cultivated the land throughout the year, having learned the merits of heavy over light plows, and the pastoral economy shifted to the production of cereal crops. The Romans had learned to exploit the soil in various ways: by cereal and legume cultivation, by growing trees for timber or fruit, by animal husbandry, and by producing vegetable crops both for sustenance and sale. Such mixed intensive farming gave the farmer increased economic power, made him less dependent on the weather, and limited the tendency toward improverishment of the soil so common in Greece—where mountains that were once covered with forest are today relatively bare. The development of sheep farms and cattle ranches on a large scale led to a division between the peasant and the larger farmer similar to the growing division between the rich and the poor that existed in the cities.

These trends in agriculture affected society as a whole. The army needed grain. When military needs increased and fewer fields were put into grain, Rome had to turn to imports, making the Republic more dependent on outside suppliers. Imported grain from Sardinia, Egypt, and Africa became essential to the growing needs of the army, as well as to those who received free grain from the state. Italian farmers who produced cereal crops, however, could thrive, because their product was regarded as superior and was nearby. The farmers tended to be politically and socially conservative, suspicious of outsiders and of new methods. They continued to sow by scattering the seed by hand (the least effective method), rather than adopting the superior method of seed-drilling (dropping seeds in furrows and covering them up)—a technique known to the ancient Sumerians and regularly practiced in China, whence it eventually came to Europe. Even with a large supply of Sicilian grain brought to Italy, there was still no surplus, for the army and the urban poor consumed the increase. Thus wheat-growing, perhaps interspersed with vines and olives, remained commonplace except in those areas where the *latifundia* began to take over. Latifundia were large mixed farms or cattle ranches worked by slaves. Only large landowners could afford them, and increasingly the small farmers were driven penniless into refuge among the urban poor in Rome.

Proprietors of latifundia, successful generals, governors, merchants, and contractors who had built roads for the state or furnished supplies to the army, combined to form a new class of very rich men. Some of them managed to join the Senate—increasingly influential because it had managed the Punic Wars successfully—but the small inner circle, where policy was made, continued to be dominated by the nobles. Those senators who were content with matters as they were called themselves *optimates* (the best people), while those who found themselves unable to get things done their way sometimes tried to get support from the people at large in the Tribal Assembly, and so were called by their opponents *populares*. Social tensions became acute. An old-fashioned conservative like Cato, for instance, hated the luxurious new ways of life imported from Greece and the East. By the time this new class of the very rich achieved real power in politics, senators were no longer included among them.

Two noble brothers named Gracchus (grandsons of Scipio, hero of the Second Punic War) emerged during the late 130s and the 120s B.C. as the champions of the dispossessed, whom they hoped to get back onto the land or into the army. Tiberius Gracchus, who served as tribune of the people in 133, and Gaius, who held the post from 123 to 121, sought to increase the role of the tribunes and the Tribal Assembly at the expense of the anti-Gracchi senators. The wild beasts, said Tiberius, had their dens, but the Romans had not a clod of earth to call their own.

The brothers wanted to resettle landless farmers either abroad or on state-owned lands in Italy that had been leased to agrarian capitalists; to give the urban poor of Rome relief by allowing them to buy grain from the state at cost; and to build roads and granaries, in part as public relief programs, so that the casually employed—who were perhaps most of the urban population—could afford to purchase bread. Politically, Gaius wanted to give certain judicial posts to the *equites* (wealthy Romans below the rank of senator), to extend Roman citizenship to all Latins, and to raise other Italians to Latin status.

The efforts of the Gracchi were not enough, and when the Senate established martial law in the face of growing public unrest and suspicion of Gaius's intentions, he was hunted down and killed. Three thousand of his followers were then condemned to death by a senatorial court. In the succeeding decades the state had to lower the price of grain, until by 58 B.C. the poor were getting their bread free. Had the dispossessed farmers actually received new allotments, the number in the city needing cheap bread would have fallen off sharply. The agrarian capitalists, after being forced by the Gracchi to give up some of the land they rented from the state, were soon expanding their holdings once more. The latifundia had come to stay. On the political side, the Senate resented the extension of rights to the equites and balked at granting citizenship to other Italian cities until, after an uprising in 91–88 known as the Social War, it had to be done. Politics had turned unconstitutional and violent, and the deadlock between Gracchan reformism and senatorial conservatism moved Rome toward autocracy.

Political leadership now passed to generals who cared less for principle than for power. A general victorious in the chronic provincial warfare would celebrate in Rome with a great *triumph*—a parade of his successful troops and their prisoners and booty that would dazzle the public. The troops, rewarded by their commanders, became loyal to them rather than to the state. The prescription for political success in Rome was to make a record as a successful general. But instability outside Rome was increasing. In the provinces the misrule of the governors provoked uprisings. Along the frontiers, by the end of the second century B.C., Germanic tribes were threatening. In 88 B.C. Mithridates, the king of Pontus (in Asia Minor), seized the Roman province of Asia and between 88 and 85 encouraged the massacre of eighty thousand Romans.

Political Generals: Marius, Sulla, Pompey, Caesar, 107–59 B.C.

The first of the generals to achieve power was Marius, leader of the populares, who had won victories against the Numidians (led by their king, Jugurtha) in what is now eastern Algeria, and against a group of largely Celtic peoples called the Cimbri and Teutones, who had been an even graver threat before he beat them in southern France in 102 B.C. Violating the custom that a consul had to wait ten years before serving a second term, Marius had himself elected five times in succession as the savior of Rome. He began a major reorganization of the army, abolishing the requirement that a Roman citizen must pay for his own equipment—a rule that had automatically excluded the poor. Now that the state furnished the equipment, professional volunteers gradually replaced the former citizen soldiers, who in the past had gone back to their normal peacetime occupations once the fighting was over. These professionals wanted booty and a veteran's bonus, and they supported a leader who could provide them. Thus the contest in the Senate often was between a man like Marius and a contender more likely to placate the military.

When Rome went to war against Mithridates in 88 B.C., Marius emerged from retirement and demanded the command. Instead, the Senate chose Sulla, a younger general who was an optimate, and a bloody civil war broke out between the two factions. Marius died in 86, and after Sulla drove Mithridates from Greece, he returned to assume the office of dictator. On the way to and from the East, Sulla's forces plundered the treasury of Zeus at Olympia and of Apollo at Delphi, and sacked Athens for having sympathized with Mithridates. The Romans brought back Greek sculpture, painting, books, and other loot.

It took Sulla two years of bloody fighting to establish himself in power. He had his opponents killed and tried to move the Senate back into its ancient position as the chief force in political life. He curtailed the powers of the tribunes and the Tribal Assembly and put through laws designed to curb the rise of new, younger politicians. He broke all precedent by prolonging his tenure as dictator beyond the prescribed six months. He finally retired in 80 B.C., but the Senate proved unable to recover from the bad fiscal examples set by his rule.

Within ten years Pompey, a ruthless and arrogant young veteran of Sulla's campaigns, rose to power. Having won victories first in Spain and then at home, where he worked with the millionaire Crassus to suppress a slave rebellion led by the gladiator Spartacus (73–71), in 70 B.C. he became consul before he had reached the minimum legal age. Pompey and Crassus forced the Senate to restore the tribunes and the Tribal Assembly to their previous power. After defeating troublesome pirates in the Mediterranean, Pompey took command of a new war against Mithridates for the kingdom of Bithynia (in Asia Minor) that had been left to Rome by its last king. By 65 B.C. Pompey had driven Mithridates into exile at the court of his son-in-law, Tigranes, king of Armenia. Mithridates committed suicide in 63 B.C., and Pompey, who now had imperium, reorganized Asia Minor and the entire province of Asia and territories beyond it. Syria, where the last effective Seleucid had died in 129 B.C., had largely fallen to Tigranes by 83, and Pompey made it a Roman province as well. In 64 B.C. he took Jerusalem. The western fringe of Asia was now virtually Roman, and much new revenue soon flowed to Rome.

On his campaigns Pompey enjoyed unprecedented special powers, forced through by the tribunes of the people against much senatorial opposition. He commanded huge resources in men and money. Foreseeing a showdown on his return, Crassus tried to build up his own power by vainly calling for the annexation of Egypt.

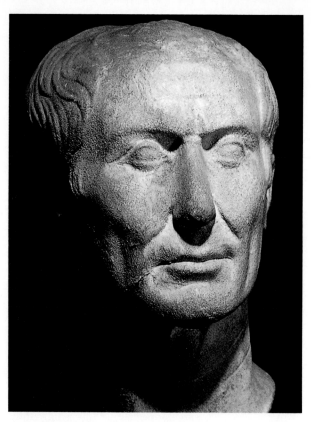

Julius Caesar
Shostal/SuperStock

Pompey the Great
Shostal/SuperStock

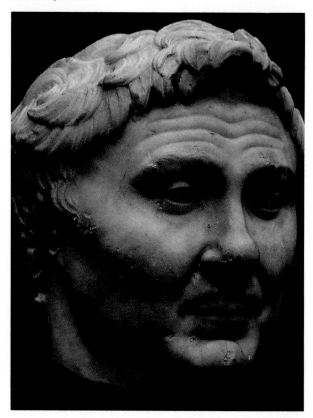

In 63 there came to light a conspiracy, led by Catiline, of a group of discontented and dispossessed nobles who had been the victims of Sulla's purges and who now planned a revolution and a comeback. Cicero, a consul and famous lawyer, discovered the plot and arrested the plotters, some of whom he illegally executed. His speeches in the Senate against Catiline are among the finest surviving examples of the Roman oratorical style. Cicero hoped to cooperate with Pompey in governing Rome and ending the Roman domestic quarrels, but he lacked the family background and personal following necessary to get to the very top in Rome, and Pompey was not responsive.

Having returned to Rome as a private citizen in 62 B.C., Pompey reentered politics because the Senate would not ratify his eastern settlement or give his veterans the usual land grants. He joined in a *triumvirate* (team of three men), with Crassus and Gaius Julius Caesar (102–44 B.C.), a man of enormous energy, talent, and impeccable ancestry. Caesar became consul in 59 B.C.; Pompey married Caesar's daughter; Pompey's soldiers received large land grants to the south, near Naples; and the eastern Mediterranean settlement was confirmed.

The First Triumvirate, 60–43 B.C.

Caesar became governor of the southern strip of Gaul (modern France), which Rome had annexed some sixty years earlier, and other adjacent lands rich in revenue. Between 58 and 50 B.C. he defeated the Celtic Gauls, conquering a huge area corresponding to modern France and Belgium. (These victories spread the Roman language, so that today in France and parts of Belgium and Switzerland, as in Italy, Spain, Portugal, and Romania, the languages have evolved from a Latin background and are called *Romance languages*.) Caesar also crossed the English Channel to punish the Celtic Britons for helping their fellow Celts in Gaul, though he made no effort to conquer Britain permanently.

The Gauls—distant relatives of the Celts—were predominantly a tall, fair-haired, blue-eyed people. Brave, hospitable, clean, loving bright-colored clothes, and enjoying feasts and quarrels, the Gallic tribes were governed either by kings (in the southwest and in the north) or by an aristocracy with appointed chief magistrates (in the central region). To give his achievements against the Gauls maximum publicity in Rome, Caesar wrote his *Commentaries on the Gallic Wars*, our chief written source of information about the Celts.

Caesar found Gallic society divided into three chief classes: the magicians and seers, or *druids*; the nobles, for whom he used the Roman word *equites*; and the common people, or *plebs*. As in Rome, a Gallic noble would have a group of dependents subject to his orders. A Gaul who refused to comply with the order of a magistrate was excluded from the religious sacrifices and from the company of his fellows. Mostly rural elsewhere in Europe, the Celts in Gaul were developing fortresses and urban trading centers.

The Gauls were excellent craftsmen in precious metals, bronze, iron, pottery, and textiles. For centuries they had traded with the Greeks and Etruscans, and they were familiar with Greek painted vases and weapons; they had also had contact with Iranian nomads skilled in metalwork. They expressed their own artistic ideas in mediums adapted from others, and they even struck their own coinage, inspired by Greek, Alexandrian, and Roman models. In Britain they also used as money iron bars of a fixed weight, perhaps unfinished sword blades. They fought from fast, two-wheeled, two-horse war chariots. In earlier times Celtic spear carriers had gone into battle naked as a means of invoking magical protection, and had beheaded their enemies and hung the heads on their saddles. They drank vast quantities of wine and beer and gorged themselves on roast pork; while they feasted bards played and sang to them. These were people living in a heroic age.

Like most peoples in that stage of development, the Celts were obsessed with magic, celebrating seasonal changes with festivals and sacrifice. They had a rich variety of gods and goddesses, some of them animal in form or closely associated with an animal, notably Epona, a goddess-mare and great queen. Some of the gods and goddesses were threefold, and the Celts often depicted them with three heads or three faces, to emphasize their triple power rather than to suggest a trinity. Caesar reported that the Gauls worshiped the chief Roman gods and goddesses. But they seem rather to have given the most suitable Roman name to their own divinities, using "Mars," for example, in inscriptions to their own god of war, who had many attributes of his own. Sacred trees, groves, and forest shrines also played a part in Celtic religion. The Celts sometimes piled their war trophies on the ground and left them exposed to view as a present to the god who had given them the victory, but sometimes they threw the booty into a lake or a stream, and occasionally such a deposit has been found by modern archaeologists.

In Caesar's day the Gauls still performed human sacrifices, a practice the Romans had long since abandoned. Some victims were killed by a sword or spear, and their blood was then smeared on trees; others, chiefly criminals, were burned alive in groups in large wickerwork animal images, or drowned, or hanged. The druids, who were recruited from the children of the fighting nobles, foretold the future while in a frenzy or trance, preserved the secret knowledge of the magic rites, and arbitrated quarrels. Like the singers of the heroic tales of Greece, the druids also transmitted orally from generation to generation the sacred religious and legal wisdom of the tribe, including belief in the immortality of the soul. In fact, the Gauls were famous among the Romans for their eloquence, and the Romans often hired Gallic orators as tutors to their sons.

While Caesar was fighting in Gaul, the German tribes from east of the Rhine often crossed the river and made trouble. Caesar massacred two entire tribes of them, building a bridge across the Rhine for a quick punitive raid into the territory on the east bank and destroying his bridge after his return. He temporarily taught the Germans the lesson that they should stay on their own side of the river. On the Gallic side, his victories meant the spread of Roman language and civilization.

During Caesar's campaigns in Gaul, Crassus had become governor of Syria, where he was drawn into war against the Parthians, a dynasty that had risen in Persia to replace the Seleucids. At Carrhae in Mesopotamia in 53 B.C., however, the Parthians defeated and killed Crassus. The triumvirate had begun to fall apart even before that, when Pompey's wife, Caesar's daughter Julia, died in 54, severing the close personal link between the two men. Pompey, who had been commander in Spain, stayed in Rome as the most powerful politician there and became the first sole consul in Roman history in

52 B.C. A revolt in Gaul kept Caesar busy until 51 B.C. When it was over, Caesar challenged Pompey for supremacy.

In 49 B.C. Caesar defied an order from the Senate to give up his command and stay in Gaul, and he led his loyal troops south across the Rubicon River boundary, beginning a civil war. Within a few weeks Caesar was master of Italy. He then won another war in Spain, and in 48 B.C. he defeated Pompey's troops in Greece, to which most of the Senate had fled with Pompey. Pompey took refuge in Egypt, where he was murdered by troops of King Ptolemy XII. Unaware that Pompey was dead, Caesar traveled to the East and to his famous love affair with Ptolemy's queen and sister, Cleopatra. After new victories over former troops of Pompey in Asia Minor,

JULIUS CAESAR ON THE GAULS: THE PROBLEM OF TRANSLATION

Caesar's commentary on the conquest of Gaul is an early and vigorous account of a systematic military campaign. It has often been translated, and a comparison of two versions of its opening paragraph helps to show how translation itself can serve specific historical and even nationalistic purposes. Clearly certain nationalities, especially in the age of nationalism, would find one translation more to their liking than another:

Gaul comprises three areas, inhabited respectively by the Belgae, the Aquitani, and a people who call themselves Celts, though we call them Gauls. All of these have different languages, customs, and laws. The Celts are separated from the Aquitani by the river Garonne, from the Belgae by the Marne and Seine. The Belgae are the bravest of the three peoples, being farthest removed from the highly developed civilization of the Roman Province, least often visited by merchants with enervating luxuries for sale, and nearest to the Germans across the Rhine, with whom they are continually at war. For the same reason the Helvetii are braver than the rest of the Celts; they are in almost daily conflict with the Germans, either trying to keep them out of Switzerland or themselves invading Germany. The region occupied by the Celts, which has one frontier facing north, is bounded by the Rhone, the Garonne, the Atlantic Ocean, and the country of the Belgae; the part of it inhabited by the Sequani and the Helvetii also touches the Rhine. The Belgic territory, facing north and east, runs from the northern frontier of the Celts to the lower Rhine. Aquitania is bounded by the Garonne, the Pyrenees, and the part of the Atlantic coast nearest Spain; it faces northwest.

The whole of Gaul is divided into three parts; of these one is inhabited by the Belgae, a second by the Aquitani, and the third by a people called Celts in their own language and Gauls in ours. Each differs from the others in language, customs, and laws. The Gauls are separated from the Aquitani by the Garonne, from the Belgae by the Marne and Seine. The most rugged of all are the Belgae, because they are farthest removed from the refinement and civilization of the Province and are less frequently visited by traders introducing wares which serve to slacken virility, and because they are nearest the Germans who live across the Rhine and with whom they are constantly at war. This same factor makes the Helvetii better fighters than other Gauls; they are in virtually daily battle with the Germans, either keeping them out of their own frontiers or carrying war into theirs. The sector occupied by the Gauls, as said above, starts from the Rhone and is bounded by the Garonne, the ocean, and the country of the Belgae; in the direction of the Sequani and Helvetii it touches the Rhine; and its trend is toward the north. The Belgae begin from the farthest frontiers of Gaul and extend to the lower part of the Rhine; they look to the north and east. Aquitania extends from the Garonne to the Pyrenees and the ocean which washes Spain; it looks to the northwest.

The first translation is from Caesar, *The Conquest of Gaul,* trans. S.A. Handford (New York: Penguin Books, 1951), p. 29.

The second translation is from Caesar, *The Gallic War and Other Writings,* trans. Moses Hadas (New York: Modern Library, 1957), pp. 5–6.

Mosaics from the Villa Romana del Casale, depicting life in ancient Rome. The first shows a hunt in progress; the second, three gymnasts at exercise.
Scala/Art Resource

North Africa, and Spain, he returned to Rome in triumph in 45 B.C. Less than a year later, on the Ides of March, 44 B.C., he lay stabbed to death on the floor of the Senate at the foot of Pompey's statue, the victim of sixty senators who thought of themselves as heroic tyrannicides.

During his brief dominance, Caesar had carried the subversion of the institutions of the Republic further than had Marius, Sulla, or Pompey. Unlike Sulla, he could be merciful to conquered enemies. But he was consul five times; he took the title "Liberator," and his dictatorship was twice renewed, on the second occasion for life. As dictator he arrogated to himself many of the powers that usually belonged to the consuls, the tribunes, and the high priest, and he packed the Senate with his own supporters.

Caesar showed a deep interest in the social and economic problems of Rome. He gave his veterans grants of land in outlying provinces; he tried to check the importation of slaves into Rome because they were taking work from free laborers; he made gifts to the citizens from his own private fortune and sharply curtailed the dole of grain that the Gracchi had instituted, forcing the creation of new jobs. He admitted Gallic nobles to the Senate; he issued the first gold coins; he reformed the calendar to bring it into line with the solar year. At his death he was projecting a great public works program: Tiber valley flood control, a trans-Apennine highway, and a canal through the Isthmus of Corinth in Greece.

The Roman populace seems to have regarded Caesar as a benefactor and as the restorer of order and prosperity. His opponents said he was planning to be crowned king, and they may have been right. They also accused him of wishing to be worshiped as a god, and here—so far as Rome was concerned—they were probably wrong. But he was personally autocratic and had ridden roughshod over the Roman constitution.

After Caesar's death, the assassins, to their surprise, found the public hostile. To escape punishment, they were forced to agree to accept the terms of Caesar's will. This document was in the hands of his former aide, the unscrupulous consul Mark Antony, who delivered a fiery funeral oration in Caesar's praise. He goaded the mob to fury against the conspirators, who had to flee from Rome. Antony's control proved only temporary, for Caesar had adopted his grandnephew Octavian and had left him three-quarters of his huge fortune.

Only nineteen years old, Octavian was ready to fight for his inheritance. He was supported by Cicero, who warned the Romans that Antony wanted to be a dictator. To freeze out the murderers of Caesar—Brutus and Cassius—Octavian reached an agreement with Antony and with Lepidus, a former general to Caesar, and the three formally joined in the Second Triumvirate for five years. Antony took most of Gaul; Lepidus, Spain and the rest of Gaul; Octavian, Africa, Sicily, and Sardinia.

The armies of Brutus and Cassius threatened from Macedonia and Asia Minor, and Pompey's son Sextus, another aspirant for power, had a fleet and held Sicily. Reverting to Sulla's policy of widespread proscriptions, executions, and confiscations, the triumvirs raised money by terror. With their new forces, Octavian and Antony defeated Caesar's assassins in Macedonia at Philippi in 42 B.C., whereupon Brutus and Cassius committed suicide. Antony moved to the East, and Octavian took over most of the West. Rivalry between them was postponed when Antony married Octavian's sister in 40 B.C., and in 37 the triumvirate was renewed for another five years. Sextus was defeated, Lepidus was dropped by the other two triumvirs, and Octavian ultimately controlled the entire West. He made his holdings more secure by mopping up the pirates of the Adriatic. Now calling himself Imperator Caesar, he was highly regarded in Italy as the bringer of order and justice.

In the East, meanwhile, Antony had fallen in love with Cleopatra, who bore him three children. After a victory over the Parthians in 34 B.C., Antony made his own bid for empire. He put forward Cleopatra's young son by Julius Caesar as the legitimate heir to Rome, and he assigned Roman provinces to her and to their own three children. Recognizing the threat and capitalizing on Roman distaste for these oriental arrangements, Octavian broke with Antony in 33. He cleverly roused the Romans to a war of the West against the East, which he said Antony now represented. At Actium, off the coast of Greece, Octavian's ships won a critical naval battle in 31 B.C. Antony and Cleopatra fled to Alexandria and committed suicide. Rome thus acquired Egypt, the last of the great Hellenistic states to disappear. Egypt became, not a Roman province, but the personal property of Octavian and his successors, the Roman emperors, administered for them by their agents. At thirty-two Octavian had become master of the entire Roman heritage. The Mediterranean world was now virtually united under one master, and the Republic had come to an end.

III THE ROMAN EMPIRE

Augustus and His Immediate Successors, 27 B.C.–A.D. 68

Octavian was too shrewd, too conscious that he was heir to a long tradition, to startle and alienate the people of Rome by formally breaking with the past and proclaiming an empire. He sought to preserve republican forms, but also to remake the government along the lines suggested by Caesar, so that Rome would have the capacity to manage the huge territories it had acquired. After sixty years of internal strife, the population welcomed a ruler who promised order. Moving gradually, and using his huge personal fortune—now enlarged by the enormous revenues of Egypt—Octavian paid for the pensions of his own troops and settled over one hundred thousand of them on their own lands in Italy and abroad. He was consul, *imperator* (a military-style emperor), and soon governor in his own right of Spain, Gaul, and Syria. He was *princeps* (first) among the senators. In 27 B.C. the Senate gave him the new title of *Augustus* (revered one), by which he was thereafter known to history, although he always said his favorite title was the traditional one of princeps, and his regime is called the *Principate*.

Augustus had far more power than anybody else, but since he called himself the restorer of the Republic, Romans could still feel that they were again living under republican rule. In 23 B.C. the Senate gave him the power of a tribune, larger powers than those held by any other provincial governor—the power to veto and

This figure of Emperor Augustus (27 B.C.–A.D. 14), known as the Augustus of Primaporta, shows him about seven years after he became the first emperor. The figures on the armor are symbolic, telling the story of the emperor's greatness. In the center of the breast plate Tiberius, who would be Augustus's successor, receives a captured Roman army standard.
Vatican Museums

the right to introduce the first measure at any meeting of the Senate. As censor he reduced the membership of the Senate in 29 B.C. from one thousand to eight hundred members, and in 18 B.C. from eight hundred to six hundred. He also created small inner steering commitees in the Senate on which he sat. As senators, he appointed men he thought able, regardless of their birth. He created a civil service where careers were open to talent. Having endowed a veterans' pension department out of his own pocket, he created two new taxes—a sales tax of one-hundredth and an estate tax of one-twentieth—to support it. He initiated the most careful censuses known to that time, both to help in the collecting of taxes and because he simply felt it wise to have as much information about his empire as possible. His social laws made adultery a crime and encouraged larger families.

The Romans were superb architects and engineers. Augustus in particular wished, as he said, to turn Rome from a city of brick to a city of marble. His reign marked an enormous burst of architectural excitement, for the political stability his methods brought, as well as the patronage he and his family extended to artists, made possible long-range planning for the city and the many monuments he was determined to place within that city.

Public monuments, like modern-day historical plaques, are a form of public historiography: the citizenry is taught who it should regard as its heroes, which events are remarkable, what it should take pride in. Centralized control of state funds, a fully mobilized building industry, and the realization that buildings constituted a form of propaganda led to the great age of Roman construction.

Thus Augustus was able to claim that he built or restored eighty-two temples in a single year and that the populace was benefited by unprecedented growth in amphitheaters, baths, basilicas, temples and forums. Architects and engineers produced magnificent, innovative structures, improved roads—in part for the movement of troops—throughout Italy, and developed the first extensive use of concrete. The popularity of marble led to the need for Greek craftsmen, however, and the vocabulary of architectural ornamentation came to be based on classical Greek. Roman taste (and money), wedded to Greek skills and ideas, led to some of the most noted buildings of antiquity. Augustus also gave Rome its first police and fire departments.

Aided by the growing network of new roads, the army—which at one point numbered about 400,000 men—occupied permanent garrison camps on the frontiers. In peacetime the troops worked on public projects such as aqueducts or canals. The legions were made up of Roman citizens who volunteered to serve and who retired after twenty-six years' service with a bonus equal to about fourteen years' salary. Noncitizens in somewhat lesser numbers served as auxiliaries, becoming citizens after thirty years of service. Augustus also created the Praetorian Guard: nine thousand specially privileged and highly paid troops, of whom about one-third were regularly stationed in Rome.

In the East, Augustus reached a settlement with the Parthians and thus probably averted an expensive and dangerous war. In 4 B.C. Herod, the client king of Judea, died, and the Romans henceforth ruled the country through a Roman procurator, who resided outside Jerusalem as a concession to the Jews. Jews retained their freedom of worship, did not have to serve in the Roman armies, and did not have to use coins bearing "graven images"—the portrait of Augustus. Under Augustus most of Spain was pacified, and the Romans successfully administered Gaul. Roman power was extended in what is now Switzerland and Austria and eastward along the Danube into present-day Yugoslavia, Hungary, and Bulgaria, to the Black Sea.

But in A.D. 9* the Roman armies suffered a disaster in Germany. A German chief named Hermann—who had served in the Roman army, became a Roman citizen and had his name translated as Arminius—turned against Rome and ambushed the Roman armies, wiping out three full legions at the battle of the Teutoburger Forest. Now an old man and increasingly distrustful of foreign adventures, Augustus made little effort to avenge the defeat. The Rhine River frontier proved to be the final limit of Roman penetration into north-central Europe. Thus the Germans did not at this time become Romanized.

The Roman provinces were now probably better governed than under the Republic. Certainly, and despite occasional slave uprisings and violence in the countryside, the early Roman Empire was orderly and relatively stable economically. Regular census taking permitted a fair assessment of taxes. In Gaul the tribes served as the underlying basis for government; in the urbanized East the local cities performed that function. Except for occasional episodes, Augustus had done his work so well that the celebrated *Pax Romana* (the Roman Peace) lasted from 27 B.C. until A.D. 180—more than two hundred years. As a second-century writer put it,

* Note here that we have crossed the time line from B.C. to A.D.

This architect's plan of Nero's house makes clear its size and elaborate nature. The ground floor (shown here) provided for a variety of functions: rooms 2 to 5 were most likely bedrooms, with the largest facing onto a courtyard (no. 6). From the dining room (no. 8), one entered a room (no. 9) with a fountain. The wing to the right focussed on a great courtyard (no. 12, viewed from a suite, no. 11). The large octagonal room (no. 16) was set off by a waterfall (no. 15) and was a major architectural achievement. A portico (no. 14) ran the length of the outer wing. Numbers 10 and 13 may have been bedroom suites. A columnar facade (no. 1) ran the length of the building.
Reprinted with permission from Roman Architecture *by Frank Sear, Cornell University Press.*

Growth of Roman Dominions
under the Empire
44 B.C.-A.D. 180

At death of Caesar, 44 B.C.
To death of Augustus, 14 A.D.
To death of Marcus Aurelius, 180 A.D.
■ Battle sites

"Through the Romans the world has peace, and we go wherever we like without fear, walking along the roads or sailing the sea." Whatever may have been Augustus's faults of character, he should be remembered as he wished to be remembered: as one who had maintained the Roman state firmly, had laid long-lasting constitutional foundations for its future, and had developed the basis for bureaucracy.

When Augustus died in A.D. 14, the only possible surviving heir was his stepson, Tiberius, son of his wife Livia by her first husband. Gloomy and bitter, Tiberius reigned until A.D. 37, emulating Augustus during the first nine years but thereafter becoming preoccupied with the efforts of Sejanus, commander of the Praetorian Guard, to secure the succession to the throne. Absent from Rome for long periods and in seclusion on the isle of Capri, Tiberius became extremely unpopular, even though he reduced taxes and made interest-free loans available to debtors. Ultimately, he recognized the threat to his authority posed by Sejanus, whom he had executed in 31. About two years later his procurator in Judea, Pontius Pilate, allowed the execution by crucifixion of Jesus, who called himself "the Anointed" (in Greek, *Christos*), because this Messianic claim was considered seditious. Tiberius's grandnephew and succes-

sor, Caligula (r. 37–41), was perhaps insane and certainly brutish. The number of irrational executions mounted, and the emperor enriched himself with the property of his victims. He made elaborate preparations for invasions of Germany and of England, which failed, and he convulsed Judea by insisting (unsuccessfully) that his own statue be set up in the Temple in Jerusalem. Caligula was assassinated in A.D. 41.

Caligula's uncle Claudius (r. 41–54)—youngest of Tiberius's nephews and the best of the first four emperors to succeed Augustus—was a learned student of history and languages who strove to imitate Augustus by restoring cooperation with the Senate. He added to the size and importance of the bureaucracy by dividing his own personal staff of bureaucrats—mostly freed slaves—into regular departments or bureaus not unlike those in modern governments. As a result, the private imperial civil service made great strides in his reign. Claudius was also generous in granting Roman citizenship to provincials. Abroad, he added to Roman territory in North Africa, the Balkans, and Asia Minor. And in A.D. 43 he invaded Britain, ninety-eight years after Julius Caesar's first invasion. Southeast England became the province of Britain, whose frontiers were pushed outward toward Wales. But the conspiracies of his fourth wife,

AUGUSTUS CAESAR'S *RES GESTAE*

As emperor, Augustus wished to be certain that history remembered him as he thought of himself. He therefore composed his own statement of his achievements (*res gestae*, "deeds"), which was to be engraved on his mausoleum after he died. He listed thirty-five specific accomplishments, of which the following were the last two:

In my sixth and seventh consulships, after I had put an end to the civil wars, having attained supreme power by universal consent, I transferred the state from my own power to the control of the Roman senate and people. For this service of mine I received the title of Augustus by decree of the senate, and the doorposts of my house were publicly decked with laurels, the civic crown was affixed over my doorway, and a golden shield was set up in the Julian senate house, which, as the inscription on this shield testifies, the Roman senate and people gave me in recognition of my valor, clemency, justice, and devotion. After that time I excelled all in authority, but I possessed no more power than the others who were my colleagues in each magistracy.

When I held my thirteenth consulship, the senate, the equestrian order, and the entire Roman people gave me the title of "father of the country" and decreed that this title should be inscribed in the vestibule of my house, in the Julian senate house, and in the Augustan Forum on the pedestal of the chariot which was set up in my honor by decree of the senate. At the time I wrote this document I was in my seventy-sixth year.

Augustus Caesar, *Res Gestae,* trans. Naphtali Lewis and Meyer Reinhold, in *Roman Civilization* (New York: Columbia University Press, 1955), II, 19.

Agrippina, to obtain the succession for Nero her son by an earlier marriage, culminated in her poisoning Claudius in 54. Agrippina herself was murdered by Nero in 59.

Although dissolute, Nero (r. 54–68) did not start the great fire that burned down much of Rome in 64, nor did he fiddle while Rome burned. Indeed, he personally took part in the efforts to put the fire out and did what he could for those who had been left homeless. But the dispossessed did blame him for incompetence, and to find a scapegoat he accused the new sect of Christians, now for the first time attracting attention in Rome. Their secret meetings had led to charges of immorality against them, and Nero persecuted them to distract attention from himself.

There were serious revolts in Britain in 61, led by Queen Boadicea. She was "huge of frame, terrifying of aspect, with a harsh voice. A great mass of bright red hair fell to her knees; she wore a great twisted golden torc [neck ring], and a tunic of many colors, over which was a thick mantle fastened by a brooch. She grasped a spear, and terrified all who saw her," a Roman historian reported.

But the chief threat in the provinces arose in Judea, where Roman rule had alternated between extremes of tolerance and intolerance, and where rival sects had proliferated among the Jews. Only a small upper class supported Roman rule, and the Romans had too few troops to keep order. In 66, after the Jewish high priest refused to sacrifice to Jehovah for the benefit of Nero and a group of Jewish zealots massacred a Roman garrison, there was open warfare. Faced with rebellion in Spain and in Gaul, and unable to control his armies, Nero was displaced by the Senate, and in 68 he committed suicide. The Empire appeared on the verge of disintegration.

Social tension was particularly acute, and racial prejudice was marked at this time. Fearful of the northern "barbarians," the Romans depicted them as utterly without culture, even though there is now ample evidence through their pottery, ironwork, and weaponry that Germania was by no means as backward as Caesar and subsequent commentators said. The Romans were not content to say that they possessed a more complex technology and social structure than the Germans did. Strabo (c. 64 B.C.–A.D. 14), author of one of the earliest geographies, described Asia, Egypt, and Libya in terms that showed all at a disadvantage in comparison to the imperial center. However, he described the Iberians as a "civilized society," for they were within the Empire, while the Lusitanians (inhabitants of today's Portugal) were "strange"; they used butter rather than olive oil, drank beer rather than wine, slept on the ground, and wore their hair very long. Prejudice was overt—whether in persistent jokes and slurs on Celts, or in the massacre of ten thousand Jews at Damascus during the war with Nero's legions.

From Nero to Marcus Aurelius, A.D. 68–180

Augustus's first four successors are called the Julio-Claudian emperors. Each had been a member, though sometimes a distant one, of the family of Julius Caesar and Augustus. But now the line had run out wretchedly in Nero, and the Senate and people of Rome learned that emperors could be found in other families and chosen in other ways. In 68–69, four emperors, each a general supported by his own troops, ruled in rapid succession. The first three died by violence. The fourth was Vespasian, Nero's commander in Palestine, who had left his son Titus in command of the campaign there, in which the Roman troops sacked Jerusalem and destroyed the Temple in 70.

Vespasian (r. 69–79), a professional soldier from the Italian middle class, founded the second Roman imperial dynasty, the Flavian. The throne passed successively to his two sons, Titus (r. 79–81) and Domitian (r. 81–96). Tough and competent, Vespasian added new talent to the Senate by appointing numerous non-Romans, especially Spaniards. He put through financial reforms, subdued the rebellion in Gaul, made gains in Britain, and fought off the potential uprisings of other generals' troops against him by using some soldiers to build public works, stationing others in dangerous areas of the frontier, and keeping too few soldiers in any one place to encourage an ambitious commander to rebel. During the short reign of Titus, Vesuvius, the great volcano overlooking the Bay of Naples, erupted and wiped out the population of the provincial town of Pompeii, burying all that today testifies so eloquently about daily life there. Domitian was a suspicious tyrant, seeing plotters against him everywhere; in 96 he was assassinated in a palace conspiracy.

When an emperor died, the Senate—so subservient during his lifetime—had the power of appointing his successor. In 96 it chose a mild, sixty-five-year-old official named Nerva (r. 96–98), who had no children and therefore could not found a dynasty. Called in retrospect the first of the five Good Emperors, Nerva found a method of providing for the succession: he adopted the great general Trajan (r. 98–117) as his son and successor. When Nerva died, Trajan thus succeeded him peacefully. This was the first of a series of four successive fortunate adoptions that gave the Empire its most prosperous and peaceful years at home, A.D. 98–180. In a series of successful but expensive campaigns, Trajan moved north of the Danube to annex the gold mines of Dacia (part of modern Romania), which became a Roman province. To the east, he campaigned against the Parthians and occupied but failed to retain Mesopotamia. A massive revolt of the Jews confronted Trajan's successor, his nephew and adoptive son Hadrian, when Trajan died in 117.

Hadrian (r. 117–138), a widely experienced soldier and administrator and a highly cultivated man, put down the Jewish uprising. Realizing that Roman communication lines became too extended whenever Roman troops tried to cross the Syrian desert against the Parthians, he abandoned Trajan's war against them and made peace. He made himself generally popular with the upper and middle classes by canceling all private debts to the government, and with the lower classes by furthering charities and putting on great spectacles in the circus. Among his advisers were some able lawyers who helped him adjust taxes and control prices in bad years and improve the legal position of slaves and soldiers. They codified all past decisions of the praetors; for the first time citizens knew when they ought to sue someone and were assured of uniform procedures under Roman law. Thorough censuses were restored, to be taken every fifteen years, as an inventory of the Empire and to determine how many aliens there were within it (and, of course, to facilitate collecting taxes).

Hadrian believed that all the provinces should be equal under Roman imperial benevolence, with himself as the "father of the fatherland." So he caused each of the armies for provincial defense to be recruited within the province itself. And he himself lived much of the time away from Rome touring the provinces. In Britain he built the defensive system of walls and ditches still called Hadrian's Wall, to contain invasions by the Scots and Picts to the north, and in Germania he constructed a wall of wood to link the Rhine and Danube rivers. Everywhere he inspected the troops and defenses, built buildings, and made himself known to the population, and everywhere (except Palestine) he was admired. After a decade abroad, he returned to Rome, where he began to build Hadrian's Villa at nearby Tivoli, with entire areas built in his favorite Greek and Egyptian styles. He built the great Pantheon at Rome, a temple to all the gods originally commissioned by Agrippa in 27–25 B.C., and he used the giant Colosseum, originally built by Vespasian, Titus, and Domitian, for gladiatorial combats and other spectacular entertainments.

Hadrian's successor, Antoninus (r. 138–161), called Pius because he was so loyal an adoptive son to Hadrian, immediately adopted as his future successor his own nephew, Marcus Aurelius (r. 161–180). The forty-two years of their combined reigns won glowing praise as an era of peace and prosperity. The eighteenth-century English scholar Edward Gibbon, whose massive history of *The Decline and Fall of the Roman Empire* influenced modern perceptions about Roman life, remarked that there had never been another period "in which the happiness of a great people was the only object of government." He was echoing Antoninus Pius's contemporary, the Greek orator Aelius Aristides, who wrote:

Neither sea nor land is any bar to citizenship, and Asia is treated exactly the same as Europe. In your empire, every avenue of advancement is open to everyone. No one who deserves office or responsibility remains an alien. A civil world-community has been set up as a free republic, under a single ruler, the best ruler and teacher . . . of order. From Rome, the center, there emanates throughout the world a

PLINY'S DESCRIPTION OF THE DESTRUCTION OF POMPEII

Pliny the Elder (A.D. 23–79) was a Roman naturalist who compiled an encyclopedic *Natural History,* in thirty-seven books. He died of asphyxiation near Mount Vesuvius, having gone personally to investigate the eruption. In a letter to Tacitus, his nephew Pliny the Younger (A.D. c. 62–c. 113), who in 100 became consul, described the eruption:

My uncle, true savant that he was, deemed the phenomenon important and worth a nearer view. He ordered a light vessel to be got ready, and gave me the liberty, if I thought proper, to attend him. I replied I would rather study; and, as it happened, he had himself given me a theme for composition. As he was coming out of the house he received a note from Rectina, the wife of Bassus, who was in the utmost alarm at the imminent danger (his villa stood just below us, and there was no way to escape but by sea); she earnestly entreated him to save her from such deadly peril. He changed his first design and what he began with a philosophical, he pursued with an heroical turn of mind. He ordered large galleys to be launched, and went himself on board one, with the intention of assisting not only Rectina, but many others; for the villas stand extremely thick upon that beautiful coast. . . .

And now cinders, which grew thicker and hotter the nearer he approached, fell into the ships, then pumicestones too, with stones blackened, scorched, and cracked by fire, then the sea ebbed suddenly from under them, while the shore was blocked up by landships from the mountains. . . .

In the meanwhile Mount Vesuvius was blazing in several places with spreading and towering flames, whose refulgent brightness the darkness of the night set in high relief. But my uncle, in order to soothe apprehensions, kept saying that some fires had been left alight by the terrified country people, and what they saw were only deserted villas on fire in the abandoned district. . . .

It was now day everywhere else, but there a deeper darkness prevailed than in the most obscure night; relieved, however, by many torches and divers illuminations. They thought proper to go down upon the shore to observe from close at hand if they could possibly put out to sea, but they found the waves still ran extremely high and contrary. There my uncle having thrown himself down upon a disused sail, repeatedly called for, and drank, a draught of cold water; soon after, flames, and a strong smell of sulphur . . . dispersed the rest of the company in flight. . . . He raised himself up with the assistance of two of his slaves, but instantly fell. . . . When day dawned again . . . his body was found entire and uninjured, and still fully clothed as in life; its posture was that of a sleeping, rather than a dead man.

Pliny, *Letters,* trans. William Melmoth, rev. W.M.L. Hutchinson (Cambridge, Mass.: Harvard University Press, 1931), I, 478–83. Reprinted by permission of the publishers and the Loeb Classical Library.

Thus Pliny the Younger humanized the sudden death of an entire city. The first cloud from Vesuvius, he wrote, looked like "a pine-tree, for it shot up a great height . . . into several branches." The people of Pompeii fell in the streets where gas and molten lava overcame them: "a black and dreadful cloud . . . now and again yawned open to reveal long fantastic flames." Pompeii disappeared under thirty feet of ash.

The eruption of Mount Vesuvius caught the residents of Pompeii as they slept. This man, preserved to the present day by volcanic ash, was either asleep or trying to shield himself from the poisonous gas released by the volcano.
Alinari/Art Resource

This relief of a Roman battle appears on Trajan's Column in Rome, set up in celebration after the conquest of Dacia.

security that rests on a power compared with which the walls of Babylon were mere child's play and women's work. All depends on the legions, who assure the perpetual peace, because Mars, whom you have never slighted, dances his ceaseless dance upon the banks of the outer rivers [Rhine, Danube, Euphrates] and thus averts the shedding of blood.*

As Aristides said, there was little civil strife. Public buildings continued to rise, and those who lived comfortable lives had never been more comfortable. For the less privileged, in Rome itself and more widely throughout Italy, the Antonine monarchy showed great concern and softened the worst pains of poverty. However, Egypt, as always, continued to be ruthlessly exploited, and slavery remained important to the economy. Stability still rested on the legions' ability to assure "perpetual peace" by fighting perpetual local wars along the borders.

Among the less privileged were the women of Rome, though they took a much more active role in affairs than women had in Greece. They were understood to be central to the *familia*, or Roman household, which included relatives dependent on the head of the family

* Adapted and abbreviated from the edition of J. H. Oliver, "The Ruling Power," *Transactions of the American Philosophical Society*, n.s., XLIII (1953), part 4.

and slaves. In general they were in charge of the slaves, and they ran the household while their husbands managed the land. Daughters were sent to school, and at home they learned spinning and weaving, so that in the poorer households they contributed significantly to the domestic economy. Among the rich, women were expected to devote much time to their clothing and to the etiquette of social occasions, particularly dinner parties: the ability of women to engage in amusing conversation at these affairs was prized in the later Empire.

After Augustus, women who had presented their husbands with three to five children could manage their personal property, and many women engaged in business. They did not, apparently, seek to have the law altered so that they could enter politics or administration. The law's intent was to assure that women gave birth to children, preferably to sons, and this was particularly so after Romans began to think of their population as in decline. Under Augustus girls were married at twelve and boys at fourteen, both to cement an economic or political alliance and to assure early childbirth.

As there were fewer females than males in the upper class, Roman women found husbands easily and often remarried; upper-class women were probably less numerous because of deaths through childbearing and the

Hadrian's Wall, which runs across present-day northern England, is the major monument to the Roman occupation of Britain. The wall was built between A.D. 122 and 130 as a defense against the Celts in Scotland. It ran for seventy-three miles, and it was garrisoned until A.D. 383.

Thomas B. Hollyman/Photo Researchers, Inc.

selective infanticide of unwanted female infants. (A father was bound to raise all male children but need nurture only the first-born female.) By now women could easily break across class barriers, since men of the upper classes often had to take a wife from a lower class, and this helped soften class barriers in general. The primary function of women continued to be determined by the state to be biological. Once having fulfilled that function, they often were free to play other and more independent roles.

Antoninus Pius, unlike Hadrian, never left Italy, and the dance of the war god Mars along the banks of the frontier rivers was less vigorous. So Marcus Aurelius—the cultivated Stoic philosopher who found no pleasure at all in his powers as emperor and whose melancholy *Meditations* (written in Greek) serve as a corrective to official optimism—was forced to fight in Dacia and beyond the Euphrates against the Parthians. Although he was victorious, he allowed certain barbarians to settle within the imperial frontiers and to be enrolled in the Roman armies, thus jeopardizing the unity of the traditional defensive system.

During the pivotal reign of Marcus Aurelius the ever-increasing pressure from the Germanic tribes of central Europe began. The more Germans who were allowed to settle inside the frontiers, the greater the pressure from those still outside who wanted to come in. The Empire, with perhaps 60 million people, an army of 300,000, and a small and very rich upper class, could not in the long run adjust to the demands made upon it. There was no modern technology of weaponry or communications to make possible a quick settlement—through peace or war—of the frontier problem, which continued for more than three hundred years. In the end, a declining population could not cover both the farms and the frontiers. Although no one in Marcus Aurelius's entourage could have predicted it, a long downward slide was now beginning; it was signaled for a

century by a catastrophic falling off in the quality of the emperors themselves.

Why did the population of the Empire decline? We do not know, though there is abundant evidence that it did and that the emperors took major steps to stop the decline. Augustus passed laws discouraging divorce and prohibiting abortion. His creation of charities to feed orphan children and provide emergency supplies to the poor so that their children would not die was less for humanitarian reasons than because the state required more and healthier bodies. Large families were encouraged by exempting from certain services fathers who had five or more children; women were urged to have dowries to be more attractive marriage candidates. The incorporation of barbarians into the Empire and the ready acceptance of new immigrants showed both a sense of tolerance and a desire for more peasants from whom a sturdy army could be drawn. Efforts were made to improve crop production and to reduce malaria, which was increasing, by draining swamps. Even soldiers were encouraged to marry and live in cities, where morals were more lax and the birth rate might increase.

Nonetheless, the population declined, in a vicious cycle the state could not control. Barbarian raids caused more violent deaths; malnutrition and higher mortality followed economic decline; cities became more crowded, spreading disease. Debasement of coinage and general inflation led to social unrest, brigandage, and to so sharp a decline in official revenues that the emperors had to create unpopular new taxes or demand services in nonslave labor directly from the people.

Because Rome's widespread trade had created a pool of diseases, epidemics regularly ravaged the crowded cities or the unhealthy countryside. In A.D. 65 and again more devastatingly in 165 (when the plague was carried throughout the Eastern empire by troops returning from Mesopotamia) there was an outbreak of febrile disease that lasted until 189 and took 7–10 million lives.

MENU FOR A ROMAN BANQUET

At its height, the Roman Empire put great emphasis on dining well—at least for the rich. The name of one Roman epicure, Lucullus, has given us the adjective "lucullan" to denote the most luxurious of food. A Roman chef, Apicius, produced the first surviving cookbook. Apicius's menu for one Roman banquet, which would begin in the late evening and run through the night to the accompaniment of musicians, dancers, acrobats, and poets, follows. Allowing for modern substitutions, we can see that there are some similarities to a so-called gourmet meal today:

Appetizers

Jellyfish and eggs
Sow's udders stuffed with salted sea urchins
Patina of brains cooked with milk and eggs

Boiled tree fungi with peppered fish-fat sauce
Sea urchins with spices, honey, oil, and egg sauce

Main Courses

Fallow deer roasted with onion sauce, rue, Jericho dates, raisins, oil, and honey
Boiled ostrich with sweet sauce
Turtle dove boiled in its feathers
Roast parrot

Dormice stuffed with pork and pine kernels
Ham boiled with figs and bay leaves, rubbed with honey, baked in pastry crust
Flamingo boiled with dates

Desserts

Fricassee of roses with pastry
Stoned dates stuffed with nuts and pine kernels, fried in honey

Hot African sweet-wine cakes with honey

From Moses Hadas, *Imperial Rome* (New York: Time Inc., 1965), p. 85.

The meal also tells us something of the extent of Roman trade, for the ostrich and flamingo came from Africa, the dates from Judea, and the spices from throughout the Empire. Apicius's book shows but ten lines devoted to beef and veal, three pages to pork; meat was not a main article of diet, and only pigs were raised to be eaten.

Again in c. 251–266 plague struck Rome, with five thousand dying daily, while the human destruction in the countryside may have been relatively even greater. In the shortage of agricultural labor supply and recruits for the army, Rome faced the most grave demographic problems it had ever known.

We do not know for certain what these diseases that reduced the population were, although they resemble modern measles and smallpox. Malaria certainly played a chronic role (though it is probably not true, as the Romans believed, that malaria came with Hannibal; the Romans associated it with swamps, but not with the mosquitoes that bred there). While both Greeks and Romans studied disease with care, they knew of no ready cures. In any case, extensive trade was likely to introduce new diseases against which immunities were not developed. In the first century A.D. the Romans traded with the

Chinese along the Silk Road (so named for the principal commodity transported from China), and fashionable women of the upper class wore semitransparent silks produced in Antioch. Such trade routes, as well as the organization of complex trading patterns by sea, helped spread diseases in patterns that are still not fully understood today.

The Downward Slide: Commodus to Diocletian, A.D. 180–284

Commodus (r. 180–192), the true son of Marcus Aurelius, ended the line of fortunate adoptions and proved to be a throwback to Caligula, Nero, or Domitian—a tyrant without talent. In the end, his closest advisers

THE MEDITATIONS OF MARCUS AURELIUS

Marcus Aurelius (121–180), nephew and adopted son of Antoninus Pius, became emperor in 161. Much of his life was spent in military campaigns far away from Rome. During these campaigns, especially on the Danubian frontier, he wrote his *Meditations,* by which he sought to express a sense of order for his own life. He did not have publication in mind, and not until the sixteenth century did his thought on the transient nature of life become a classic statement about consolation at death. This passage is from Book IV in which he reflected upon the transient nature of all emperors:

If thou workest at that which is before thee, following right reason seriously, vigorously, calmly, without allowing anything else to distract thee, but keeping thy divine part pure, as if thou shouldst be bound to give it back immediately; if thou holdest to this, expecting nothing, fearing nothing, but satisfied with thy present activity according to nature, and with heroic truth in every word and sound which thou utterest, thou wilt live happy. And there is no man who is able to prevent this. . . .

Consider, for example, the times of Vespasian. Thou wilt see all these things, people marrying, bringing up children, sick, dying, warring, feasting, trafficking, cultivating the ground, flattering, obstinately arrogant, suspecting, plotting, wishing for some to die, grumbling about the present, loving, heaping up treasure, desiring consulship, kingly power. Well, then, that life of these people no longer exists at all. Again, remove to the times of Trajan. Again, all is the same. Their life too is gone. In like manner view also the other epochs of time and of whole nations, and see how many after great efforts soon fell and were resolved into the elements. But chiefly thou shouldst think of those whom thou thyself hast known distracting themselves about idle things, neglecting to do what was in accordance with their proper constitution, and to hold firmly to this and to be content with it. And herein it is necessary to remember that the attention given to everything has its proper value and proportion. For thus thou wilt not be dissatisfied, if thou wilt apply thyself to smaller matters no further than is fit. . . .

Time is like a river made up of the events which happen, and a violent stream; for as soon as a thing has been seen, it is carried away, and another comes in its place, and this will be carried away too.

Marcus Aurelius Antoninus, *Meditations,* in *Man and Man: The Social Philosophers,* ed. Saxe Commins and Robert N. Linscott (New York: Random House, 1947), pp. 296, 304–306.

---

murdered him. After two other emperors had been installed and murdered by the Praetorian Guard within a year, Septimius Severus (r. 193–211), a North African who commanded the Roman troops in what is now Hungary, marched his army into Rome and disbanded the guard, replacing it by a new elite body chosen from his own officers. He emerged successful from the first civil strife Rome had known in more than a century. To reward his armies for their loyalty in a campaign against the Parthians in which Mesopotamia was added as a province, he provided better food, pay, and allowed his legionaries to marry native women. Married legionaries might live off the base and could keep their own flocks and grow their own crops.

Septimius Severus was succeeded by his two sons, one of whom, Caracalla (r. 211–217), extended citizenship in 212 to all freeborn inhabitants of the Empire. This was a natural climax to the earlier acts gradually expanding the circle of Roman citizens, though it also was a money-raising device, since all new citizens would be liable to inheritance taxes from which noncitizens were exempt.

Caracalla's successors were all assassinated in their turn. It was an unedifying parade. Alexander Severus (r. 222–235), soberer and more virtuous than some, tried to revive cooperation with the Senate and to restore the traditional virtues to Roman life, but he was only fourteen on his accession and was dominated by his mother. The Senate was impotent, and the army resented Alexander's neglecting to appease it by the now-traditional bribes. Though his campaign against the new Sassanian dynasty that had replaced the Parthians in Persia was a success (231–233), his military zeal was halfhearted. In Germany on another campaign, he fell victim to another military conspiracy.

During the half-century (235–284) there were twenty-six emperors, of whom twenty-five were murdered. Most of them were chosen by their troops, held power briefly, and were in turn supplanted by another ambitious military commander. But the army had been weakened by Septimius Severus's changes, for soldiers had grown accustomed to being used for nonmilitary purposes as police, tax collectors, judges, and even artisans, and they often were not ready for combat.

Attracted by Roman weakness (indeed urged on at times by the Romans themselves) and pushed from behind by other people on the move, the so-called barbarians crossed the Roman frontiers at many points. The emperor Decius was killed in battle; the emperor Valerian was captured by the Persians and died in captivity. When the plagues raged, whole provinces temporarily escaped from the central authority, population fell off, public order virtually vanished, and the Empire seemed doomed to collapse. The tide turned with the reign of Aurelian (r. 270–275), the "Restorer of the World," and with the accession of Diocletian (r. 284–305). Aurelian, a soldier, drew the best troops back from the frontiers and concentrated on the defense and restoration of Rome. Within the wider empire he turned increasingly to non-Roman mercenaries for protection. Diocletian and his successors, especially Constantine (r. 306–337), put through numerous reforms, although we do not know exactly when some of the new measures were adopted. The result is usually called the New Empire, but what looks new about it often proves to have been, instead, a return to earlier practice. The combination of all the experiments, however, was certainly new.

Under Diocletian there gradually evolved a system that when complete was called the *tetrarchy* (rule by four men). As emperor, Diocletian first appointed a talented officer as Caesar—an action often taken previously—and then was forced by circumstances to promote him to the title of Augustus, or co-emperor, though it was understood that Diocletian, as the senior Augustus, was above the other. Each Augustus in turn appointed a Caesar of his own, whom he also adopted as his son; such adoption was also an old practice. It was understood that the two emperors would eventually abdicate, each to be succeeded by his own Caesar, who upon becoming Augustus would appoint a new Caesar as his son and eventual successor. The scheme was designed to assure a peaceful succession and to end the curse of military seizures of the throne. Thus the Empire, though in practice ruled by four men, still in theory remained a single unit.

This was particularly important, because accompanying the gradual establishment of the tetrarchy was a shift in territorial administration, as each of the four new rulers took primary responsibility for his own large area. Diocletian made his headquarters at Nicomedia in Asia Minor, and from there he governed Asia Minor, Syria, and Egypt, plus Thrace in Europe—the whole becoming the prefecture of the East. From Sirmium in what is now Yugoslavia, his Caesar governed the Balkans, which became the prefecture of Illyricum. From Milano, Diocletian's co-Augustus, the junior emperor Maximian, governed the prefecture of Italy, which included North Africa together with parts of what is now Austria. And from Trier in the Rhineland, his Caesar governed Gaul, Spain, and Britain, which were grouped into the prefecture of Gaul. Note that not even the prefecture of Italy was governed from Rome. The new imperial territorial reorganization exposed as a sham the ancient pretense that the emperor shared power with the Senate.

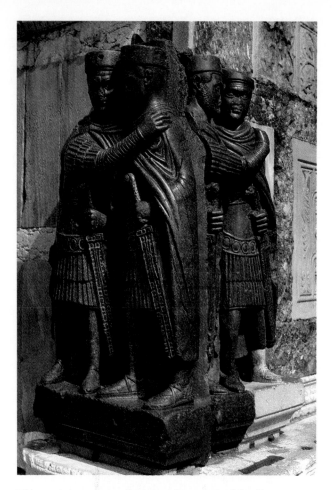

This sculpture shows the tetrarchs, rulers of the Roman Empire: Diocletian, Maximian, Galerius, and Constantius Chlorus. The sculpture is now in the basilica of St. Mark's, in Venice.
Art Resource

A tough Balkan soldier, Diocletian simply walked out on Rome, leaving the citizens with their free bread and circuses. It is of great importance, too, that he moved his own headquarters to the East, for Diocletian now adopted the full trappings of oriental monarchy. He wore silk robes of blue and gold to symbolize the sky and the sun; he sprinkled his hair with gold dust to create a nimbus when light shone upon him; his clothes glittered with jewels; he wore ruby and emerald bracelets, necklaces, and rings; his fingernails were gilded; and his boots—which were to become the new symbol of imperial power—were of purple leather. He entered his throne room carrying a golden scepter topped with a golden ball or orb—the earth—on which was seated a Roman gold eagle with a sapphire in its beak to symbolize the heavens. Servants followed, sprinkling perfume, which fan bearers spread through the air. Every person in the room sank to the floor until Diocletian was seated on his throne, after which the privileged might kiss the hem of his garment. Diocletian was making a deliberate attempt to elevate the prestige of the emperor—a divine and deified emperor—so high that it could not be shaken by the ambitions of a rival. Diocletian chose the additional surname Jovius, thus associating himself with Jupiter (Jove), the ruler of the gods.

Mechanical reorganization and geographical regrouping of forces could not have prevented by themselves the recurrence of military uprisings. Therefore, Diocletian firmly separated the military from the civil power, so that the commanders of local garrisons had no local political authority and his new civil officials had no military authority. Moreover, Diocletian subdivided the old provinces, so that the number of new provinces rose to over one hundred, each much smaller than provinces had formerly been; these in turn were regrouped into twelve so-called dioceses, which constituted the four great prefectures. Accordingly, the bureaucracy grew enormously. The various financial departments, the secret service, the post, and foreign relations each had its own structure, and the top officials became a kind of advisory body, almost a cabinet. While a Roman senator might find a place in such a system, it was independent of the Senate as such, and the Senate as a body continued only as a group of privileged magnates. Diocletian also enlarged the army, which probably reached a new high of about 600,000. He reorganized the forces and improved their pay and promotion system. He adapted military tactics to a new age, introducing a more heavily armed cavalry and developing frontier defenses that allowed troops to move rapidly to any danger point.

The new bureaucratic and military costs required new contributions from most of the population. By using as a unit of land measurement for tax purposes the amount of land that could be cultivated by a single farm laborer, and by trying to force the farm laborer to stay put, work his land, and pay his taxes, the New Empire greatly stimulated the growth of that class of rural resident called the *colonus* (plural, *coloni*), who was attached to the soil. The colonus was not a slave and could not be sold apart from the land he and his family cultivated, but when it was sold, the coloni went with it. (Slave labor was used extensively only in Italy and Spain.) Other men in other walks of life were also bound to their jobs, and sons to their fathers' jobs after them: sons of bakers had to become bakers; sons of goldsmiths, goldsmiths. To stabilize the economic situation, Diocletian also tried to fix prices but was thwarted by black marketing and riots.

The lowest territorial administrative level was the *civitas* (a city and its surrounding countryside). The city senators (*curiales*) had to make up out of their own pockets any difference between the tax payments assessed for the civitas and the amount actually collected. From being an honor, the position of curialis became a burden, and curiales had to be compelled to stay in their posts, to do their duty, and to pass their jobs on to their eldest sons. Society became more rigidly stratified than ever before in Roman history. The combination of this increased social stratification with oriental-style despotism, a huge bureaucracy, and continuing dependence on the military made life extremely bleak for the ordinary person. Corruption, inequity, violence, and despair were frequent. The tax collector became the symbol, not of the stability of the state but of corruption and greed, and the people seem to have been hungry for change.

Diocletian retired in 305 and left his half of the Empire to his Caesar; he forced his fellow Augustus, Maximian, to do the same. Each of the new Augusti in turn named a new Caesar; but the system broke down as the four top officials began to struggle against one another for supreme power. By 324 Constantine, son of the Western Caesar, emerged as sole Augustus, and the Empire was reunited; he ruled until 337. Though the tetrarchy did not survive, the other reforms of Diocletian and Constantine, who carried his work forward, staved off collapse.

Why Did the Empire Decline?

Few subjects have been more debated than the reasons for the long decline of the Roman Empire. The celebrated eighteenth-century historian Edward Gibbon blamed Christianity, charging that it destroyed the civic spirit of the Romans by turning their attention to the afterlife and away from their duties to the state. Michael Rostovtzeff, a Russian scholar who wrote in the 1920s and 1930s, attributed the decline in part to the constant pressure by the underprivileged masses to share in the wealth of their rulers, of which there was not enough to go around anyhow. Gibbon and Rostovtzeff each reflected his own time and experience: Gibbon the anticlerical rationalism of the eighteenth century; Rostovtzeff the bitter lesson of the Bolshevik Revolution in his native Russia. Others have emphasized the influx of Greeks and orientals into Roman society, intimating that the original Roman sense of unity was thus diluted. Still others have pointed to climatic change and disease. Most recently, archaeologists working with chemical analyses of skeletons from A.D. 79 have concluded that a generally healthy people had fallen prey to chronic lead poisoning, for Roman food and wine were apparently heavily contaminated with lead.

Economically, losses in population caused by plagues and civil war crippled an agriculture already hampered by unprogressive methods and increased soil exhaustion. The growing concentration of land in large estates and the absorption of free farmers into the status of coloni diluted Roman prosperity, which suffered from chronically feeble purchasing power and inflation. The urban middle class was declining, while psychologically the masses became alienated from their rulers. The replacement of citizen-soldiers with mercenaries testified to the decline of the old Roman patriotism. Dependence on slavery may have retarded innovation in labor organization and the application of technology. Yet even with all these factors, it would be hard to imagine the Roman decline without terrific pressure from outside forces. It was in the third and fourth centuries that the "barbarian" cultures began to expand, and it was the barbarian threat that most immediately contributed to the collapse of the Roman structure in the West, while permitting its survival in the East in a modified form.

The scholar Henri Pirenne argued that the Mediterranean economy, culture, and society of Rome, greater Italy, Gaul, and Spain were not destroyed by invaders—Visigoths, Ostrogoths, and Franks—since these cultures adapted to the Roman culture. Rather, Rome decayed in the face of the Arabs, who diverted the Carolingians away to the north, after which a long siege weakened Rome economically and politically. The whole of Europe emerged from this siege in the midtenth century, by which time ruling families other than Carolingian (particularly the Ottonians and the house of Wessex) had displaced traditional military and political authority. Goods that the West had imported from the East no longer played a role in politics, trade, or city and artisanal activity when blocked by the caliphs of Damascus, Baghdad, and, in Spain, Cordoba. More recent research argues that this trade was already in decline well before the rise of the caliphs and suggests that overtaxation, plagues, internal migration, and relocation of settlements from the plains to the hilltops were far more disruptive than any Arab activity.

Given all these arguable "causes" for the decline of the Roman Empire, perhaps the best summary is still Gibbon's famous judgment: "The stupendous fabric yielded to the pressure of its own weight." Rather than asking why the Empire fell, he thought, historians ought to ask why it had survived so long.

IV RELIGION, WRITING, AND THOUGHT

Greek Influences

Greece, though conquered, took its conqueror captive. Indeed, Greek influence from Magna Graecia affected the Romans long before they conquered Greece itself. In the arts, the Romans found much of their inspiration in Greek models. In literature, the Greeks supplied the forms and often much of the spirit, though the highest Roman literary achievements could not be mistaken for Greek works; they have a Roman spirit and quality. In science and engineering, the Romans accomplished more than the Greeks, as they did in law and government.

The Greece the Romans gradually conquered was not the Greece of Homer or Pericles, so that the Romans, for example, did not imitate the Greek tragedians of the fifth century B.C. There was no Roman Aeschylus, Sophocles, or Euripides. This was the Greece of the decades after the death of Alexander—of the New Comedy of Menander, not the Old Comedy of Aristophanes. Literature, much of it produced in Alexandria, was more artificial, more charming and graceful, often trivial, less grand, less concerned with the central themes of human existence. The surviving Alexandrian epic, Apollonius Rhodius's *Argonautica*, which tells of the adventures of the mythical hero Jason on his way to find the magic golden fleece, was a scholar's effort to be Homeric long after the heroic age was over. When the Romans first began to imitate the Greeks, the greatest Greek works, though deeply respected, were no longer being written. It was a lesser age.

Religion

Before the first contacts with the Greeks, the Romans had already evolved their own religion—the worship of the household spirits, the *lares* and *penates*, that governed their everyday affairs, along with those spiritual beings that inhabited the local woods, springs, and fields. Like the Greek goddess Hestia, the Roman Vesta presided over the hearth and had in her service specially trained vestal virgins. From the Etruscans the Romans took the belief in omens which they never abandoned. They foretold the future through observing the flight of birds (the *auspices*) and examining the entrails of sacrificed animals (the *auguries*). From Greece there came the entire Olympic collection of gods and goddesses, some of them merging their identities with existing Roman divinities, and most of them changing their

A law student and his wife, from the National Museum in Naples. This fresco tells us much about Neapolitan life, from hair styles to clothing. Some scholars have argued that the male figure is not a lawyer but a baker.
Scala/Art Resource

names; Zeus became Jupiter; Hera, Juno; Poseidon, Neptune; and so on, although Apollo remained Apollo. But the Romans had nothing like the Greek Olympic games or the festivals of Dionysus that had led to the writing of Athenian tragedy and comedy. For the Romans religion was largely social in function.

Julius Caesar, Augustus, and many of their successors were deified after their deaths, and Augustus consented to be worshiped in Gaul at temples set up to "Rome and Augustus." Indeed, from Alexander the Great and earlier, a basis for believing in the divinity of a king, and thereby in the divine right of kings, was persistently, if unevenly, maintained. But except for certain notable social festivals each year, the individual Roman took little part either in the imperial cult or in other religious rites. The official priests performed most rites, headed by their chief priests, the *Pontifex Maximus*—a title and role taken over by the emperors themselves. The state religion early lost its appeal for the Romans. Moreover, there was no reason they could not worship as many other gods as they chose, after rendering due veneration to the ordinary deities, including the emperor. Rome therefore imported cults from other places, chiefly the East, which competed for popularity. (Since Christianity eventually joined and won the competition, we shall postpone discussion of it and its competitors until the next chapter, where we can more easily examine the reasons for the growth of Christianity.)

Literature

One of the great unifying forces of the Roman Empire was its language; Latin slowly became the *lingua franca*, the universal language of the Roman world. Language unites (and, there being different languages, also divides). It does so at a given time, as, for example, when two merchants, unable to speak the same language, communicate in a third, more nearly universal language. And it does so across time, as when scholars of different nationalities attempt in common to reconstruct a past event. Latin became both the most widespread language of its time and the most influential language of all time, for it formed the basis of the great Romance languages of western Europe, Romania, and Latin America, and it was the language of universal scholarship until the nineteenth century. Until displaced by French, it was the language of diplomacy, and until displaced in the twentieth century by English, it was the language of technology.

A people self-consciously interested in their own civilization strive to preserve their language and to use it well. Where they borrow, as the Romans did persistently from the Greeks, they do so not only to imitate elegantly, but also to communicate effectively. To the Romans, as to the Greeks, to speak and write well and to recognize these qualities in others were significant indications of the civilized mind. Their frequent and shared reference to the people beyond their borders as "barbarians" was more a statement about the language those people spoke than about their customs. For the Romans, their literature—in history, poetry, drama, and prose—was an indication of both their unity and their sense of a separate identity (what the nineteenth century would call the "national character"); it also posed for them intriguing questions of translation when they sought to render Greek works into Latin. For us, therefore, Latin literature takes on a dual significance; first it tells us about the Romans themselves and, second, it shows how the Romans used language to incorporate other cultures, chiefly Greek, into their own.

The figure known to us as the "father of Latin poetry," Quintus Ennius (239–169 B.C.), was born and brought up in Magna Graecia and therefore naturally turned to Homer for inspiration when he put into epic form his patriotic account of Roman successes down to his own time. Although only fragments (between six and seven hundred lines) of the *Annales* are preserved, we have enough to appreciate Ennius's admiration for military virtues and to understand his lasting influence on later Roman writers. And as Ennius used Homeric verse to celebrate Roman toughness and resilience, Plautus (254–184 B.C.). and Terence (190–159) took their inspiration from the Greek New Comedy of Menander. Plautus was the more raucous and knockabout. Many of his characters—the two sets of twins, masters and servants, who are always being taken for each other; the rich but stupid young gentleman with an immensely clever and resourceful valet; the money-grubbing miser—recur throughout European literature. Gentler and milder in every sense, Terence remained closer to the Greek originals. He was not a success in his own day, but was a major influence during the Renaissance and later on the French playwright Molière. After Plautus and Terence, various Roman authors tried to write comedies with a native Italian inspiration, but none of their work survives. The Romans also enjoyed crude farces of the kind that had always been staged in the villages.

During the late Republic appeared two of Rome's greatest poets—Lucretius (96–55 B.C.) and Catullus (84–54 B.C.). Lucretius, a disciple of the Greek philosopher Epicurus, wrote a long poem. *De rerum natura* (On the Nature of Things), putting into moving verse his master's beliefs that there is no human survival after death and that the gods, far from governing human affairs, do not intervene at all. He wrote that the universe is made up of atoms, whose motions and behavior are governed by fixed laws, right out to the edges, the "flaming walls of the universe," though human beings control their own actions.

Catullus, looking to certain Alexandrian poets of the emotions, wrote passionate love lyrics recording his feelings for his mistress. Sometimes playful and charming, as in poems addressed to her pet sparrow or celebrating the first days of spring, sometimes bitter and obscene (she was unfaithful and made Catullus miserable), these brief poems seem to some readers the highest achievement of Roman literature.

In Cicero (106–43 B.C.) the late Republic produced its greatest writer of prose, who adjusted the ideas of Greek philosophy to distinctive Roman values. His oratorical skill furthered his career as a successful lawyer and politician; he won his listeners with an occasional injection of wit or irony into an otherwise somber and stately passage. He carefully studied not only what he wanted to say, but also how to choose the most effective—sometimes the most unexpected—words in which to say it, and how to combine them into a rhythmical and pleasing pattern, so that the sound and the sense would combine to make his point irresistibly. As the recognized supreme master of oratory, he wrote treatises on the art. We also have almost a thousand letters that Cicero wrote to his friends (and some of the answers) that reveal his personal joys and sorrows.

Philosophically, Cicero largely agreed with the Stoics, as modified by Greek teachers who had adapted the originally abstract and remote concepts of Stoicism to Roman taste by allowing for the exercise in ordinary life of the Stoic virtues and admitting that one can have some virtues without possessing all knowledge. Cicero helped popularize these ideas in his essays on *Old Age*, on *Friendship*, on *The Nature of the Gods*, and on other political and social subjects; he introduced into the Latin language terms capable of conveying the meanings of the Greek concepts he was discussing.

Cicero tutored his fellow Romans about the concepts of "natural law" that existed independently of all human legislation and a "law of nations" that should regulate the relationships of different people with each other. Practical, perhaps conservative, Cicero believed that law, custom, and tradition led to stability, which was essential to liberty, from which sprang a person's true security. The influence of these Ciceronian works radiated far into human history: the early Christian fathers studied Cicero, as did the humanists of the Italian Renaissance and the men who made the eighteenth-century revolutions in America and France and who wrote the Declaration of Independence and the Constitution of the United States.

Still it was the writers who came after Cicero who gave Rome its literary Golden Age. Augustus himself recruited and subsidized talent, even genius, to proclaim the glories of the new era, the Augustan Age. For example, Vergil (70–19 B.C.), in his *Georgics* and *Ecologues*, which followed the models of Greek pastoral poetry, praised the pleasures and satisfactions of rural life. Written before Augustus reached political supremacy, these poems helped him advance his later program of propaganda to get workers back to the farms. He persuaded Vergil to write the *Aeneid*, the great national epic of Rome's beginnings, in which the poet could "predict" the future glories that Augustus's rule would bring. Though designed in part to please Augustus, these passages nonetheless reveal Vergil's own sincere and intense patriotism. Vergil often reflected upon the sacrifices that necessarily accompany a rise to greatness,

on sorrow, and on death. In the sweep of his interests, Vergil also reflected on the brotherhood of man.

Vergil's fellow poet Horace (65–8 B.C.) showed more humor and expressed a greater range of feelings in a greater variety of meters. He, too, praised the joys of rural life and the virtues of moderation, but in more solemn terms celebrated the Roman qualities of quiet toughness, love of the simple life, the traditional religious attitudes, while glorifying the Augustan order. Ovid (43 B.C.–A.D. 17) gave worldly, often cynical, advice on the art of love. In the *Metamorphoses* he also told of the mythical transformations reported in Greek stories in which various divinities became birds, animals, or plants. Ovid died in exile because of his involvement in a sexual scandal affecting the granddaughter of Augustus.

To match in prose Vergil's epic of Rome's early days and to reemphasize the virtues that had made Rome great, the historian Livy (59 B.C.–A.D. 17) set out to write a prose history of the city from the moment of its founding. Only 35 of the 142 books into which he divided his work have come down to us complete, but we have summaries of the missing portions. Though Livy could use as his sources many Roman writers now lost, for the earliest periods he had to fall back on legend. While he knew the difference between reliable and unreliable accounts, he often used the latter because they were the only sources available. Vividly written, his long work was soon condensed for less ambitious readers.

Insistence on the great Roman virtues reflected the uneasy sense that they were declining. As the government after Augustus became more arbitrary and autocratic, writers began to fear the consequences of expressing themselves too freely, and disillusionment set in. Moreover, admiration for the achievements of the Augustan writers, especially Vergil, became so intense that poets were often content to imitate the authors of the Golden Age and to suppress their own originality.

The greatest Roman historian, Tacitus (c. A.D. 55–c. 115), himself a master of prose style, was convinced that the Romans had degenerated. His *Germania*, an essay ostensibly in praise of the rugged and still primitive German barbarians, was in fact an acid commentary on the Romans' descent into the love of luxury for its own sake. Similar disillusionment pervades his history of the period from Tiberius to Domitian. Brilliant and prejudiced, allowing his personal opinions to color his accounts (sometimes in ways we cannot check), he was the greatest writer of the period between Tiberius and Hadrian, known as the Silver Age.

Silver Age poets included Seneca (c. 5 B.C.–A.D. 65), Nero's tutor, by birth a Spaniard, a Stoic philosopher, and author of nine sensational tragedies imitating Greek originals. Seneca committed suicide at Nero's order. Seneca's nephew, Lucan (39–65), wrote an epic poem (*The Pharsalia*) about the struggle between Caesar and Pompey. Persius ((34–62) and Juvenal (c. 60–c. 140) satirized contemporary society, and as satirists often do,

THE SATYRICON

In 1663 in Dalmatia (in present-day Yugoslavia), portions of an apparently enormously long manuscript known as *The Satyricon* were found. This bawdy satire, which cleverly mixes prose and verse, romance and philosophy, is attributed to Petronius, one of Nero's court officials who, like Lucan, committed suicide in A.D. 66 at Nero's orders. Though undoubtedly exaggerated, the work tells us much about contemporary attitudes and practices among the most wealthy and leisured, illustrating the theme "Eat, drink, and be merry, for tomorrow we die." One of the longest sections of what has sometimes been called "the first novel" is the wildly funny account of a lavish banquet given by the newly rich and ultra-vulgar Trimalchio. Buried amidst the humor, however, is biting commentary on social perceptions:

At long last the tumblers appeared. An extremely insipid clown held up a ladder and ordered a boy to climb up and do a dance on top to the accompaniment of several popular songs. He was then commanded to jump through burning hoops and to pick up a big jug with his teeth. No one much enjoyed this entertainment except Trimalchio. . . . Just at this point the ladder toppled and the boy on top fell down, landing squarely on Trimalchio. The slaves shrieked, the guests screamed. We were not, of course, in the least concerned about the boy, whose neck we would have been delighted to see broken; but we dreaded the thought of possibly having to go into mourning for a man who meant nothing to us at all. Meanwhile, Trimalchio lay there groaning and nursing his arm as though it were broken. Doctors came rushing in. . . . [T]hey began flogging a servant for having bound up his master's wounded arm with white, rather than scarlet, bandages. . . . [I]nstead of having the boy whipped, Trimalchio ordered him to be set free, so that nobody could say that the great Trimalchio had been hurt by a mere slave. We gave this ample gesture our approval and remarked on the uncertainties of human existence.

The Satyricon, trans. William Arrowsmith (New York: New American Library, 1960), pp. 60–61.

The Colosseum in Rome, known to the Romans as the Flavian Amphitheatre. Used for gladiatorial combat, animal hunts, mock sea battles, races, and other popular spectacles, the Colosseum seated 45,000 people; it was dedicated in 80 A.D.
SEF/Art Resource

Detail of a mosaic pavement, c. 300 A.D., showing gladiators in combat. It is now in the Borghese Gallery in Rome.
Scala/Art Resource

they overstated the case. Juvenal enjoyed painting the vulgarities and wretchedness, the cruelties and greed of Rome in the harshest colors.

Law and Science

The legal code published on the Twelve Tables in the fifth century B.C. reflected the needs of a small city-state, not those of a huge empire. As Rome became a world capital, thousands of foreigners flocked to live there, and of course they often got into disagreements with each other or with Romans. But Roman law developed the flexibility to adjust to changing conditions. The enactments of the Senate and assemblies, the decrees of each new emperor, and the decisions of the judges who were often called in as advisers—all contributed to a great body of legal materials.

It was the *praetors* (the chief legal officers) who heard both sides in every case and determined the facts before turning over the matter to the *judex* (a referee) for decision. Gradually, these officials developed a body of rules for deciding cases that were not covered by existing law. As they dealt with foreigners with different languages and customs, they worked out a body of common legal custom—the *jus gentium* (law of the peoples)—to be applied to all of them. Romans also gradually acquired the benefits of the jus gentium. As each new praetor took office for a year, he would announce the laws by which he intended to be bound, usually following his predecessors and adding to the body of law as necessary.

The expert advisers (*jurisconsults*) to both praetor and judex felt an almost religious concern for equity; it was the spirit rather than the letter of the law that counted. This humane view found support in the philosophical writings of the Stoics, who believed that above all human law stood a higher natural law, which was divinely inspired and applied to all people everywhere. In practice, of course, judges were often poorly trained, the emperors brutal or arbitrary; Roman law could be used to exalt the authority of the state over the individual. Yet the law recognized the rights of the citizen, afforded legal redress even to slaves, and gave wide scope to local legal practices. Its clarity and flexibility gave it progressive authority over other legal systems especially in its subtle development of the idea of the unity of mankind and the value of Stoic thought. The law of much of western Europe today goes back to its provisions.

Medicine, too, advanced. Roman surgeons made a variety of ingenious instruments for special operations, including the Caesarean operation—supposed (probably wrongly) to have first been performed at the birth of Julius Caesar—for babies who could not be delivered normally. The Romans developed the first hospitals, both military and civilian. However, much superstition survived in Roman medicine, and it was the Greeks, notably Galen (c. 129–199), who continued to make the major theoretical contributions, compiling medical encyclopedias and diffusing learning.

What Galen did for medicine, a contemporary, Ptolemy of Alexandria (c. 85–161), did for geography. Both remained the chief authorities on their subjects as late as the seventeenth century. Some learned Romans followed the Alexandrian Eratosthenes in believing that the earth was round. Pliny the Elder (23–79) made observations of ships approaching the shore to support this hypothesis; it was the tip of the mast that appeared first to an observer on shore, and the hull last—a proof Pliny felt, that the surface of the earth was curved. Pliny died when he was overcome by carbon monoxide gas while observing the eruption of Vesuvius that destroyed Pompeii (see p. XX).

Architecture, Sculpture, and Painting

Roman architecture used the Greek column, usually Corinthian, and the round arch, originated by the Etruscans; from this developed the *barrel vault*, a continuous series of arches like the top of the tunnel that could be used to roof large areas. The Romans introduced the dome, and a splendid one surmounts the Pantheon at Rome, a structure that well illustrates the conjunction between Roman art and ideas. Here surface ornament and interior space celebrated the planetary gods and their relationship to all of humanity. Roman structures emphasized bigness: the Colosseum seated forty-five thousand spectators; the Baths of the emperor Caracalla accommodated thousands of bathers at a time (the ruins are still used for grand opera); Diocletian's palace at Split in modern Yugoslavia contains most of the modern city within its walls. Amphitheaters, temples, villas, and other monumental remains of Roman domination can be found throughout the Middle East, North Africa, and western Europe.

Roman sculpture, though derived from Greek and Hellenistic models, had a realism of its own, especially in imperial portrait busts. A sculptured frieze running spirally up a monumental column vividly records the victories of the emperor Trajan (see p. 84). Of Roman painting we have chiefly the pretty (sometimes obscene) wall decorations of the villas at Pompeii and the mosaic floors of public and private buildings, in which a favorite subject was a hunting scene along the Nile, with crocodiles and hippopotamuses among papyrus plants. A recently discovered villa at Piazza Armerina in Sicily has a superb series of third-century floors, including a scene of women in a gymnasium tossing a ball from hand to hand. At Ostia Antica, the port for Rome, numerous mosaics tell us of art, daily life, and social customs, including for the first time evidence on the nature of tenant-landlord relations for rented houses. These ruins have only recently been uncovered and have yet to yield all their secrets.

A Final Appraisal

Tacitus was right in thinking that Rome had lost some of its traditional virtues with its conquest of huge territories, its accumulation of wealth, and its assumption of imperial responsibilities. Nevertheless, the first two centuries of the Empire mark the most stable and, for many, the most prosperous era that had yet occurred in human history. No doubt the profits of flourishing commercial life were unevenly distributed, and there were glaring contrasts between rich and poor. But many of the harshest aspects of ancient society elsewhere were softened in Rome. Slaves could obtain their freedom more easily, and once free, they enjoyed the privileges of citizenship, including that of owning slaves themselves. Women had more rights and commanded more respect (we have much evidence of harmonious family life, though there were more divorces perhaps than at any period before our own). Physical comforts were abundant for those who could afford them.

In the city of Rome itself, however, great areas were unsanitary, overcrowded slums; six- and seven-story wooden tenements often burned down or collapsed and were rebuilt, despite building codes and fire departments. Rents were exorbitantly high. Streets were narrow and dark, noisy with cart traffic, full of crime at night, covered with hucksters' wares exposed for sale by day. Perhaps worst of all was the chronic urban unemployment; at the height of the Pax Romana perhaps half the population of the capital received free bread. The inhabitants were given free chariot races and gladiatorial combats, and the poor squandered their few pennies on betting. Bloodshed exerted a morbid fascination. Criminals were crucified and even burned alive on the stage as part of spectacles to entertain the populace; in the last century of Roman life these shows had become so popular that they superseded the theater, despite the protests of the occasional horrified citizen, like Seneca.

As we shall see in the next chapter, the structure of the Roman state did not disappear in the West until the end of the fifth century A.D. This Roman influence gave a permanent shape to western Europe. Italian, French, Spanish, Romanian, and Portuguese were all languages derived from Latin, and English has almost as many Latin as Germanic words. Roman legal concepts provided the foundations of respectability for many a chaotic society. Rome itself became the capital of Christianity and its administrative organization was the model for the structure of the church. Thus transformed into new roles, the metropolis of the Empire continued to exert power, intellectual influence, and multilayered historical fascination for each succeeding century.

Summary

Early Rome was a Latin city influenced by Greek colonies in the south of Italy and by the Etruscans to the north. Rome expelled its Etruscan kings in 509 B.C. and became a republic.

Early Roman society was divided between the dominant aristocratic minority (the patricians) and the plebeians, who formed the mass of the population. The government was led by two elected consuls, who were advised by a Senate of ex-officials. At first most officials were patricians, but by the fourth century B.C. the plebeians had won the right to hold most offices, including consul.

By the third century B.C. Rome had conquered all of Italy and had come into conflict with Carthage, a former Phoenician colony that ruled much of Spain and Sicily. In three wars (264–241, 218–202, 149–146), Rome defeated and destroyed Carthage. During the same period Rome began to expand to the east, conquering Macedon and Greece and dominating Egypt and most of Asia Minor by 133 B.C.

Overseas expansion led to economic, social, and political trouble in Rome. The institutions of a small city-state could not cope with an empire. Small farms were increasingly replaced by large estates (latifundia) owned by rich generals and profiteers and worked by slaves, who made up an increasingly large share of the population. Attempts at reform failed as civil strife ultimately developed into civil war.

In the last years of the Republic, various generals either seized power or dominated the state: Marius, Sulla, Pompey. Finally in 45 B.C. Julius Caesar, who had conquered Gaul, emerged as the master of Rome. Caesar was assassinated in 44 B.C., but his nephew and heir, Octavian Augustus, was able to be defeat his rivals and become the first Roman emperor.

Augustus's rule (27 B.C.–A.D. 14) inaugurated the *Pax Romana*, two centuries of relative peace, stability, and prosperity for the Mediterranean world. His successors developed the bureaucracy, extended Roman citizenship, and carried out a vast program of public works. Although the Romans failed to conquer Germany east of the Rhine River, Britain and Romania were added to the Empire during this period.

Women in late Rome had many more rights and played a much more public role than in Greece, though their position depended in part on the number of children they had borne. The Romans were concerned by their declining population, perhaps the result of plagues against which ancient medicine could do little.

After A.D. 180 civil wars and struggles over the succession disrupted Roman society and weakened the economy. The barbarians began to push across the European frontiers. The reforms of Diocletian and Constantine staved off collapse but imposed new burdens on an overtaxed and demoralized population.

Roman culture was deeply influenced by Greece. Latin literature often imitated Greek forms. Among the greatest Roman writers were Cicero, Vergil, Horace, Ovid, Livy, and Tacitus.

Their system of law was one of the Romans' most enduring achievements. The law of much of western Europe and Latin America today goes back to its provisions.

Roman art was also heavily influenced by Greece, but the Romans also made significant contributions of their own: for example, the barrel vault and the dome in architecture, and the realistic portrayal of individuals in sculpture.

4

Judaism and Christianity

The Romans constructed great buildings, baths, aqueducts, viaducts, and roads; they left behind in the writings of Vitruvius some of the earliest technical accounts from which modern technology, and especially engineering, may be dated. Hero of Alexandria, a Hellenistic inventor and writer of the first century B.C., wrote a treatise, *Pneumatics*, which set out a variety of problems in science and engineering upon which the Romans apparently drew. Between them, Hero and Vitruvius understood the cam (a disk or cylinder that can power an engine by imparting a rocking motion to an adjacent piece), surveying instruments, and how to measure the flow of water. They also had devised an early turbine that used steam to make automatic puppets turn and dance for a miniature theater and had developed a model fire engine. Stonecutting, essential to Greek and Roman architecture, was an application of descriptive geometry. In short, both the theoretical and practical sciences were known to Greece and Rome.

Yet neither the Greeks nor the Romans systematically developed what they knew either into the practical art of engineering or into the critical mass of ideas, inventions, and technicians from which a true industrial age could develop. Hero's inventions were applied to toys rather than to productivity. Throughout the classical world, including ancient China (where trip hammers were used for hulling rice by A.D. 290, on the principle of the cam), there was no evolutionary connection between the gadgetry, the inventions, and the perceptions of education. The great inventions of Chinese technology—gunpowder, the compass, printing—did not produce the first industrial people; nor did the many clever discoveries, essentially unchallenged by the scientific world even today, which the Greeks and Romans made about their environment. Not until medieval times, for example, did the cam actually contribute to industrialization.

Why was this so? Why were there individual scientists, but no scientific community? Why were there engineers, but no profession of engineering? Hero's *Pneumatics*, written in Greek, was translated into Arabic (for the Arabs early developed a more systematic approach to science) and only then into Latin; its principles remained essentially dormant until the twelfth century A.D. Euclid's theorems, his *Elements* dating from the third century B.C., first passed into Arabic and not into Latin, in which language scholars of the Middle Ages could draw upon them most effectively, until the early twelfth century. Though known to some, the theories developed by the classical scholars did not become common knowledge, even among the educated, for well over a thousand years. From Hero's work on steam, seventeen hundred years passed before the steam engine was invented. Why?

I THE IMPORTANCE OF RELIGION IN THE LATER ROMAN WORLD

The Failure of Reason

There are many arguments as to why civilization had to wait so long before scientific knowledge was given a systematic application. Whatever the answers, a tendency to see science as being in opposition to religion was developing. Perhaps the answer lay, in part, in the attitudes of the Roman ruling groups. They considered "idle speculation" beneath them; they also looked down on commerce and industry—two of the incentives for technical inventiveness. The ruling classes who had the money to spend on developing new areas of knowledge spent it instead on warfare, on luxurious living, or increasingly on the growth of the church. While monastic orders always recognized the value of manual labor, church doctrine was developed in a later period that put emphasis on contemplation or disputation.

Science formed no part of Roman education, and scattered statements show that the Romans scorned what we would now call research. They feared new inventions that might put people out of work; the emperor Tiberius is said to have executed a man who had invented a process for making unbreakable glass. The prevalence of slaves and the lack of consumer markets meant that owners did not need to develop methods of mass production, even though the more thoughtful may have realized that slave labor was adaptable to mass production provided a market existed for the increased productivity. Although the earlier advance of science in the Greek and Hellenistic world had given rise to small groups of rationalists who believed in improving their lives by using their reasoning powers, even these minorities seem virtually to have disappeared.

Throughout the Roman Empire pessimism mounted, accompanied by a lack of faith in humanity's ability to work out its own future. The old gods seemed powerless to intervene, and to many life appeared to be a matter of luck. Beginning as early as the third century B.C. and gathering increasing momentum, the cult of the goddess Fortune became immensely popular in the Mediterranean world. Chance governed everything; today's prosperity might vanish tomorrow; the best thing to do was to enjoy good fortune while the goddess smiled upon you. Closely related was the belief in Fate. What happened was inevitable because it had been fated from the beginning; when you were born, the moment of your death was already fixed. Some, like Cicero, protested that people could affect their own fate and so take advantage of fortune. Vergil attributed both fate and fortune to the will of the divine providence, but most

Romans seem to have felt helpless to change their own fates or to influence events. Human beings, it was said, were slaves to two emotions, hope and fear, and sought ways of assuaging both.

Astrology

To escape from alternating between hope and fear, most Romans came to believe that the movements of the heavenly bodies influenced their fortunes and fates and governed their decisions. Thus the science of astronomy became lost in the speculations of astrology. If one could do nothing to change one's destiny, one could at least try to find out what that destiny might be by consulting an expert astrologer. The astrologer would study the seven planets (Saturn, Jupiter, Mars, the Sun, Venus, Mercury, the Moon), each of which had its own will, character, gender, plants, numbers, and attendant animals, and each of which was lord of a sphere. Seven itself became a mystic number: there were seven ages of man, seven wonders of the world. Then, too, there were the twelve Houses of the Sun—constellations of stars through which the sun passed on its way around the earth: these were the signs of the zodiac, itself an imaginary belt of the heavens.

From the position of the heavenly bodies and the signs of the zodiac at the moment of conception or birth, astrologers would draw up a horoscope foretelling a person's fate. The Roman emperors, like most of their subjects, profoundly believed in astrology. Some people continue to believe in it, even to our own day. Especially valuable for the art of prophecy were so-called unnatural events—the appearance of a comet, the birth of a monster. Similarly, people believed in all sorts of magic and tried by its power to force the heavenly bodies to grant their wishes. The *magus*, or "magician," exercised enormous power.

New Cults: Cybele, Isis, Mithra

The state religion of the Olympian gods and of the deified emperors still commanded the loyalty of many Romans, who regarded the proper observance of its rites as the equivalent of patriotism. But by the first century A.D. the old faith no longer allayed the fears of millions who believed in blind fate and inevitable fortune: people increasingly sought a religion that would hold out the hope of an afterlife better than the grim reality on earth. So, along with astrology and magic, mystery religions began to appear in Rome.

These new faiths taught that the human soul could be saved by union with the soul of a savior, who in many cases had experienced death and a form of resurrection. This union was accomplished by a long initiation, marked by purifications, ritual banquets, and other ceremonies designed to overcome human unworthiness. The god would enter the candidate, who would be saved after physical death. The initiate sought a mystical guarantee against death by survival in a hereafter. One could join as many of these cults as one liked and still practice the state religion.

The Greeks had such cults in the rites of Demeter at Eleusis and in the mysteries of Dionysus. The rites of Dionysus, now called Bacchus, became popular in Rome, celebrating as they did carnal pleasures and the abandonment of all restraint. On hundreds of late Roman sarcophagi can be seen the Bacchic procession celebrating the joys of drink and sex. But the cult of Bacchus was too materialistic to satisfy all Romans.

One of its major competitors was the cult of the great mother-goddess Cybele, which came from Asia Minor at the end of the Second Punic War. Cybele's young husband, Attis, died and was reborn annually (like Demeter's daughter Persephone). Attis was thus a symbol of renewed fertility. The rites of Cybele included fasting, frenzied processions, self-flagellation, and self-mutilation by the priests. The first temple to Cybele at Rome dated from 204 B.C., but the zenith of the cult was reached in the second century A.D. By that time the practices included the slaughter of a bull above a pit into which the initiate had descended to be bathed by the blood, with subsequent cleansing by milk and wool in a rite of purification.

Even more popular, mainly with women, was the cult of the Egyptian goddess Isis, whose consort, Osiris, died and was reborn each year. The Isis cult was apparently first spread by sailors. All "feminine" elements—lascivious or chaste—were concentrated in an elaborate ritual of worship for Isis, the loving mother-goddess, who promised her adherents personal immortality. As Apuleius's satire *The Golden Ass* (written in the second century) makes clear, conversion to Isis worship often emphasized her chastity and morality, and the prospect of salvation for her followers, in contrast to the presumed depravity and growing commercialism associated with Cybele.

From Persia about the first century A.D. came the cult of the god Mithra, allied to the supreme powers of good and light, and so connected with the sun. The male initiates passed in succession through seven grades of initiation (corresponding to the seven planets and named after animals), qualifying for each by severe tests. Baptism and communion were also part of the ritual. Unconquered, physically rough, and self-denying, Mithra became a model for the Roman soldier, to whom he held out the hope of salvation. Mithraism had no priests and welcomed the gods of other cults; it tended to absorb other sun-worshiping cults, including that of Apollo, and was often supported by the emperor. Temples of Mithra have been found in every province of the empire.

This dramatic figure represents a *Taurobolium*, or sacrifice of a bull to Cybele, mother of the gods. It is in the Pio-Clementine Museum at the Vatican, in Rome.
Scala/Art Resource

These cults appealed widely to the masses rather than to the educated. But there were trends in mysticism that were popular among intellectuals, too. The older philosophical positions, somewhat altered, continued to be influential. Long before, after the death of Alexander the Great, the philosopher Epicurus had taught that unnecessary fear lay at the root of the troubles of humanity. Whatever gods might exist took no interest in what humans might do; life after death was only untroubled sleep. A quiet life and the cultivation of friendships would bring happiness; if evil came, one could endure it. Both Lucretius and Horace were Epicureans. But as ordinary people could hardly banish fear or pain or desire by following Epicurean formulas, the Epicureans were few in number.

So were the Stoics, who prescribed the suppression of human emotions; people should accept the universe and simply defy evil to do its worst. These ideas won a substantial following among the disillusioned Roman upper classes. But by compromising with astrology and with polytheism, by teaching that the universe was periodically destroyed and reconstituted, by harshly condemning human pity, Stoicism ultimately lost much of its following.

Perhaps halfway between religion and philosophy was the school of the so-called Hermes Trismegistus (Thrice-Great Hermes), which prescribed abstinence, concentration, and study as a preparation for a flash of ecstasy and a spiritual rebirth. Stronger still was Neoplatonism, whose adherents claimed to be disciples of Plato. They taught that each human soul makes a pilgrimage toward an eventual union with the divine spiritual essence—the One, the True, the Good, the last great abstraction. By contemplation, the mystic would gradually become free of material ties and achieve ecstatic vision. Though Neoplatonism soon became identified with far less lofty and rarefied rites like those of the cults, for most believers the divine reason, the *logos* (literally, the word), joined with the divine soul and the ultimate divinity itself as a sort of trinity. Despite its trinitarian overtones, however, it tended, like the other oriental religions, toward monotheism and pantheism—the worship of One, and the identification of that One with the universe.

No single mystery religion or philosophic movement appealed to men and women of all classes in Rome. Mithraism, which perhaps had the most adherents, especially in the army, excluded women and lacked love and tenderness. Neoplatonism had no appeal for the masses. We have already noted the presence of Christians in the Roman world, especially under Nero, who made them the scapegoat for the great fire of A.D. 64. Indeed, Christianity competed with the cults in the Roman world for more than three centuries after the death of its founder; sharing some beliefs in common with them, it also possessed qualities they lacked.

II JUDEA

History, it is said, is written by the victor. Since the Judaeo-Christian ethic came to dominate Western religious beliefs, separating precise, verifiable fact (as used by the historian) from generally held perceptions and beliefs is exceptionally difficult. Indeed, for the true believer of any faith, such an effort is felt to be unnecessary. There is, however, usually a body of material commonly accepted by believer and nonbeliever. Even so, Jewish and Christian sources present problems for the historian, for the earliest account of Jesus (by Mark) comes from about A.D. 70, and the account by John is from the end of the same century. These accounts are *Gospels*, that is, statements about the teachings of Jesus of Nazareth, written so that those teachings would not be lost. They were not written to separate religious doctrine from historical fact and myth.

We know that Jesus was born in Palestine sometime between the years we now call 8 and 4 B.C. and was crucified probably in A.D. 29 or 30 in the reign of Tiberius. He was a Jew all his life and stoutly declared that he had not come to lead a movement of secession from Judaism, but one of reform and fulfillment within it: "Think not that I am come to destroy the law, or the prophets: I am not come to destroy, but to fulfill. For verily I say unto you, Till heaven and earth pass, one jot or one tittle shall in no wise pass from the law, till all be fulfilled" (Matthew 5:17–18). But we cannot understand this apparently straightforward and uncomplicated idea without appreciating the extraordinary complexity of the Roman and Judean society in which Jesus was born, taught, suffered, died, and—as his followers declared—was raised from the dead.

The Roman Conquest

Hellenism and the Hasmoneans   When, after a century of struggle between the Ptolemies and Seleucids for control of Palestine, the Seleucids won a permanent victory about 200 B.C., their monarch issued special tax privileges for the Jewish Temple and the Jews. The high priest of the Temple of Judea represented the Jews in their dealings with their Seleucid overlord and was responsible for collecting the taxes for him. The upper classes among the Jews found themselves greatly attracted by Greek culture—Hellenism—as, to varying degrees, were most inhabitants of the Near East in the wake of Alexander's conquests and the establishment of the successor kingdoms. Some Jews engaged in athletics naked in the Greek fashion; Jews discovered Greek music; Greek artistic motifs and symbols appeared on Jewish monuments and coins. In some of the later books of the Hebrew Bible compiled in this period—notably Jonah—Jewish separateness, the sense of being a chosen people, so notable elsewhere, seems to have disappeared in favor of a concern for all humanity, non-Jew and Jew alike. The Greek language spread widely; many Jews took Greek names. Certain Jewish writings echo Homer, such as Ecclesiasticus (note that this is not the same as Ecclesiastes), written about 185 B.C.

This Hellenization of upper-class Jews in Judea led to conflict with the many Jews who sought to keep the traditions pure. And the poorer population—tenant farmers on the lands of the rich or humble artisans in the cities—hated their fellow Jews who oppressed them in association with the Seleucid monarchy. Party strife and civil war led to the intervention of Antiochus IV in 168 B.C., and to a concerted attempt to destroy Judaism by force. Judaism was declared illegal, and an altar on which pigs were sacrificed to Zeus was superimposed on the altar of the Temple. The Jews rebelled; the Maccabean wars (named after Judah Maccabeus, the Jewish commander) were savage. Seleucid dynastic rivalries added to the political complexity. On December 25, 160 B.C., the Maccabees restored Jewish worship at the defiled Temple in Jerusalem in a feast of dedication (commemorated in the festival of Hanukkah).

In 153 B.C. Judah Maccabeus's brother Jonathan became high priest, and his descendants (called Hasmoneans after a priestly ancestor, Hasmon) held the office for 117 years, until 37 B.C. The Hasmonean state of Judea was virtually independent until 63, when Pompey annexed it to the Roman Empire with the rest of Syria. The Hasmoneans made war on the territories adjoining Judea, forcibly circumcising non-Jewish men (in Greek, Roman, and Arab cultures circumcision was held in contempt) and added greatly to the anti-Jewish feeling already powerful among the gentiles (originally meaning any people not Jewish) of the Mediterranean seacoast and across the Jordan River. To the gentiles' complaints, the Hasmoneans replied that they were reestablishing themselves in the lands of their ancestors.

Yet another party of Jews, highly puritanical, participated in the war against the Seleucids until the Jewish faith was secure but opposed the Hasmonean conquests, for they were content to live under foreign rule so long as the Jewish religion was protected. They expected that the power of the gentiles would in any case pass away, that the "Ancient of Days" would sit upon his eternal throne and grant to a Messiah—"one like the son of man"—an everlasting earthly dominion. To this party—the "pious people" (Hasidim or Assidaeans)—the Hasmoneans were arrogant usurpers.

Under Roman Rule   As the Romans replaced the Seleucids as foreign overlords of the Jewish lands, Pompey liberated the areas the Hasmoneans had conquered and made the areas with Jewish majorities a client state (*civitas stipendiaria*) of Rome. In the midfifties the Roman governor of Syria divided Judea into five subareas (*synhedria*, or "councils") as a step toward later dismemberment.

In 47 B.C. Julius Caesar reversed this trend, reunited Judean territory, and gave the governorship to Antipater, a convert to Judaism from one of the neighboring areas that the Hasmoneans had conquered. Rivalry and civil war between the last of the Hasmoneans and the family of Antipater (one of whose sons was Herod) were complicated by a Parthian invasion and culminated when the Roman Senate made Herod king of Judea. In 37, with the help of troops sent by Mark Antony, Herod was able to take Jerusalem. He survived the collapse of Mark Antony after Actium by serving Augustus obediently.

This illuminated manuscript, from the National Library in Florence, depicts the biblical story of Moses making the water spout.
Scala New York/Florence

Most Jews hated Herod, not so much for being an outsider and a descendant of a convert as for his subservience to the foreign ruler and his ruthlessness in wiping out not only all those who engaged in acts of violence or sabotage but all suspects, including the last of the Hasmoneans. Rome was far more powerful than the Seleucids had ever been, and was equally unacceptable to the Jews as a source of the same Hellenistic influence. Tyrannical though Herod was, he was also a thorough realist; he believed the Jews could survive only by reconciling themselves to living within the Roman Empire. Secret police, prisons, death were for resisters; for others, survival lay through abandoning exclusiveness and adapting to the Greco-Roman world.

Until his death in 4 B.C., Herod built Greek cities in Judea with splendid public buildings; he created a major new seaport at Caesarea, the provincial capital of Judea, patronized Greek artists and writers, and sponsored musical and athletic contests, to which non-Jews were invited as guests. He also began a cult of himself in the non-Jewish areas. Among Jews he represented himself as descended from the line of David and as the restorer of the ancient glory of the kingdom. To that end he rebuilt the Temple on a grander scale than ever before.

Parties among the Jews The Romans put down the rebellion that erupted on Herod's death, and ten years later, at the petition of the Jews, they deposed Herod's son as king of Judea and installed the first Roman prefect. By this time, there were at least three parties distinguishable among the Jews of Judea: the Sadducees, the Pharisees, and the Essenes. The Romans took advantage of this divisiveness to maintain their rule over Palestine until their empire collapsed at the center.

The Sadducees were a small, influential group of aris-

tocrats who had long ancestral associations with the Temple priesthood; they were generally regarded as collaborators with the Romans. What we know of their beliefs is derived from texts written by their enemies, but they apparently did not believe in the resurrection of the dead or in rewards and punishment after death. They also repudiated the belief in good and evil spirits, rejected predestination, and believed in the full responsibility of individuals for their actions.

We know much more about the Pharisees, who survived to become the prevailing force in later Judaism. They apparently originated as an Assidaean faction that, about 160, abandoned the belief that at the last judgment only they would be saved and all other Jews forever damned. The Pharisees nonetheless held themselves strictly apart (the name itself means "the separated ones") from the common people who did not observe every letter of Jewish law. They reconciled themselves to life under Herod and under the Roman prefects. They strove to achieve the Kingdom of God here on earth, and they opposed what they regarded as the unrealistic attitude that all hope must be put off until the final day.

The Pharisees' reverence for Jewish law admitted of argument and differing interpretations with respect to it. They made divorce difficult, but they did not forbid it altogether; they believed in keeping the Sabbath (seventh day) for rest, but they would break it to save a life. So the written law, as laid down in the first five books of the Bible, was supplemented by an oral law of rabbinical interpretations. Pharisees conceded that there were righteous non-Jews. They believed that fate determined some human actions, though not all. Unlike the Sadducees, the Pharisees believed in a last judgment separating the righteous from the sinners.

A third school of thought among the Jews was that of the Essenes, known before 1947 only by a few ancient texts; in that year began a series of discoveries in the caves of Qumran near the Dead Sea of the so-called Dead Sea scrolls. Dating from 200 to 70 B.C., the scrolls are important to our understanding of the history of Christianity and crucial to the history of the Hebrew language. They include fragments of the teachings of the Essenes, who lived in a monastic community nearby. Its buildings were destroyed by the Romans in A.D. 68, but we know that this was not the only Essene settlement, and some Essenes lived in cities or other than monastic communities.

In the Essenes' monastic community, the men lived in celibacy, engaged in ritual baths and meals, and shared communal property. (Some women and children buried nearby were probably relatives of members or wives and children of members not yet fully accepted.) At the Essenes' communal meal, bread and wine were taken but were not thought of as transmuted as in later Christianity, and the meal did not symbolize salvation. They took ritual baths and repeated them often, so the baths were not similar to the single ceremonial baptismal bath performed by John the Baptist for penitents. When the age of wickedness drew to an end, the Essenes believed that they, the "poor in spirit," would prevail.

The scrolls refer to a Teacher of Righteousness, a Suffering Just One, who had been greater than all the prophets. He was not the same as the deliverer, the Messiah, whom they still awaited, and who would be a priest and a descendant of the house of David—the same "Son of Man" who appears in the Book of Daniel, and in whom the Essenes' forerunners, the Assidaeans, had also believed. In one passage in the scrolls, the Teacher of Righteousness referred to himself as the father of a man-child who would have all his own powers. Thus the texts that tell us about the Essenes reveal them as a reforming movement within Judaism that apparently had much in common with the Christianity that was to appear later.

Besides the Sadducees, the Pharisees, and the Essenes, there were also groups of Jews who belonged to a "fourth philosophy" and devoted themselves to resistance against the Romans, like modern guerrillas or partisans. Though they are sometimes called Zealots by modern scholars, they may have called themselves simply Israel, to indicate that they were the only true Jews. As the Roman grip upon Judea loosened in the years immediately before the uprising that began in A.D. 66 and ended with the destruction of the Temple in 70, some of the resisters turned to terrorism and committed many murders, after which they were called "the dagger men" (*sicarii*). Many Jews had indeed been moved by zeal against the Romans, but the true Zealots, as a political party, a grouping of rural peasant groups and urban militants, hostile to both the Jewish upper classes and to the Romans, did not exist before 67–68.

From the Roman point of view, the Jews were par-

Carved onto the side of this fifth-century sarcophagus, or stone coffin, is a distinctly Christian scene—the Apostles of Christ. The sarcophagus is in the Basilica of St. Apollinaris in Classe, south of Ravenna, Italy.
Art Resource

ticularly privileged subjects whose religion was protected by the Roman state. Unlike other Roman subjects, they could become citizens of any city without forfeiting the right to their beliefs. They were exempt from military service, which would have implied for them idolatry and would have required them to break their Sabbath, since armies cannot choose a day on which not to fight. They were excused from participating in the imperial cult for the same reason and said prayers for the emperor in the synagogues instead. Their local copper coinage was struck without the emperor's likeness. Their own judges (*sanhedrin*) acted as local administrators and handled all purely Jewish court cases.

Such privileges contributed to widespread anti-Jewish feeling among non-Jews in the Empire, who resented Jewish freedom from so many of the responsibilities of the Roman state. Non-Jews scoffed at the worship of a god who could not be portrayed and who required abstinence from pork, the most commonly eaten meat in the ancient world. They regarded Jewish abstention from emperor worship as atheism and Jewish separatism as elitism. Despite what appeared to the Romans to be generous treatment, the sense of a Jewish nationality refused to die.

The Teaching of Jesus

It was thus in a troubled and divided land that Jesus came to preach to his fellow Jews. He preached the love of one God for all people. He preached to the poor, the weak, and the simple, rather than to the priests of the Temple. His "Blessed are the poor in spirit" has an Essene echo, though Jesus was not a revolutionary like the Essenes, nor a revivalist, nor an ascetic, since he preached the enjoyment of the good things of this world, an enjoyment freed from rivalry, ostentation, and vulgarity. He was kind but stern—good intentions were not enough: "He that heareth, and doeth not, is like a man that without a foundation built a house upon the earth" (Luke 6:49). Above all, he preached gentleness and love—humility, charity, honesty, toleration: "Judge not, that ye be not judged" (Matthew 7:1). He also warned that "Wide is the gate, and broad is the way that leadeth to destruction" (Matthew 7:13). Though he preached that the abused should turn the other cheek, he also said at another time that he came not to bring peace, but a sword. Plain people understood him and took comfort from his words.

From Jesus' preaching would arise theological conclusions of enormous importance. From the books of his disciples, the Gospels, we learn what Jesus said. He spoke of his Father in heaven, referred to himself as the Son of man, and taught that he was the Messiah whom God had sent to redeem humanity from sin. Those who hearkened and led decent lives on earth would gain eternal bliss in heaven; those who turned a deaf ear and continued in their wicked ways would be eternally damned in hell. Jesus was the Christ, the anointed one. His followers said he was begotten by the Holy Spirit and miraculously born of a virgin mother. He was baptized by John the Baptist in the waters of the Jordan, and therefore his followers were also required to be baptized. He gave bread and wine to his followers at a feast of love and told them that it was his body and his blood, and that they should partake.

Such teaching—though not without parallel in earlier Jewish thought—aroused alarm and hostility among the Jewish authorities. Sadducees and Pharisees mistrusted all reformist efforts, of which Jesus' seemed only one more. When the Roman prefect, Pontius Pilate, asked Jesus, "Are you the king of the Jews?" and Jesus affirmed that he was, he was doomed, both by the sanhedrin and by the Romans. On the cross itself a title was inscribed to show that a leader of the resistance had been executed. In Christian thought the crucifixion became the supreme act of redemption: Jesus died for everyone. His followers declared that he rose from the dead on the third day and would soon return—during their lifetime, they believed—to end this world in a final Day of Judgment, when he would sit at the right hand of the Father.

Even in this bare summary we can see elements of Christian belief that are similar to Judaism and others that were present in the mystery cults. But Jesus' sacrifice of his life for humanity, and the intimacy with God promised in the future eternal life, gave Christianity a simplicity and a popular appeal that no mystery religion could duplicate.

The Early Christians: Judaeo-Christianity

There are no historical sources contemporary with Jesus himself from which to draw an account of his life and teaching. Paul's epistles to the Corinthians were written about A.D. 55, the Acts of the Apostles about 60–62 (though they are a chronological sequel to Luke), and the four Gospels that tell Jesus' story in the years that followed: Mark about 70, Matthew and Luke about 80–85, and John about 100. Late in the second century or early in the third these texts were revised in Alexandria. We have no canonical Christian text written down before this revision was prepared.

Before A.D. 60 a collection of the sayings of Jesus existed, written in Aramaic, the Semitic language that he spoke. This collection is lost. Many other texts also existed that were not regarded as authentic. Among them was a so-called Gospel of Thomas, written in the native Egyptian language (Coptic) in the early second century, of which fragments, including 114 sayings attributed to Jesus, were found in Egypt in 1945 and after.

All New Testament sources, then, belong to a period of at least several decades after the death of Jesus. They were written in Greek for non-Jews and do not reflect the situation immediately after he died, which has only recently begun to be understood by scholars who have studied inscriptions, monuments, and manuscripts that help tell the story. After the crucifixion of Jesus, a little group of his followers stayed together in Jerusalem; these first Christians were Jews who followed, as indeed Jesus himself had followed, the Jewish law. This was the Judaeo-Christian church, or "Church of the Circumcision," which had a succession of fifteen bishops. Because it regarded itself as the only true Israel, it was in conflict with the Pharisees and Sadducees.

But Christian belief had drawing powers that were attractive beyond the Jewish communities. Jesus had told his followers: "There be some standing here, which shall not taste of death, till they see the Son of man coming in his kingdom" (Matthew 16:28). This doctrine of the Second Coming, the immediacy of the emotional tie that Christianity created between the believer and Christ, and the tight bonding among members of the Christian brotherhood, explain why the *evangel*, the "glad tidings" that appealed to many gentiles as well as to Jews, was indeed dramatic and hopeful.

Saul of Tarsus (A.D. c. 3–c. 67), who as a Jew had vigorously persecuted Christians and who had never known Jesus himself, was converted to Christianity by a blinding vision. He took the Roman form of his name, Paul. Apparently it was Paul and a co-worker Barnabas who, laboring together in Antioch, were the first disciples to call themselves Christians and to take the evangel to the gentiles. Problems quickly arose. Must a non-Jewish convert to Christianity be circumcised, a painful and at the time even dangerous operation? Some Judaeo-Christians were willing to exempt pagan converts from circumcision and other Jewish observances; others were not. Even those who made the concession were often reluctant or unwilling to eat in company, or mingle socially, with such converts. Paul himself went further, however, than even the more liberal Judaeo-Christians; he would have freed even former Jews from Jewish ritual requirements. Many Judaeo-Christians, therefore, strongly opposed Paul's views.

WHAT IS A GOSPEL?

The gospels are the teachings of Jesus as revealed in the first four books of the New Testament: Matthew, Mark, Luke, and John. Mark, for example is referred to as The Gospel According to St. Mark in the King James version of the Bible. One of Mark's most powerful statements appears in the first chapter, verses 14 and 15:

Now after that John was put in prison, Jesus came into Galilee,
preaching the gospel of the kingdom of God,
And saying, The time is fulfilled, and the kingdom of God is at hand:
repent ye, and believe the gospel.

These two verses carry a host of meanings. Consider a few. "Preaching" carries a meaning beyond that understood today, for in Greek—the language in which the text was originally written—it was *Kerygma,* which meant that Jesus "proclaimed" the kingdom of God, and in turn that the early Christians "proclaimed" Jesus. Thus preaching was not a sermon but a proclamation of the truth. That which is proclaimed is a *gospel*—that is, "good news." Not all religions have invariably brought good news, for those who preach of damnation exclusively do not bear news that can be considered good. The word here is meant to carry two meanings: that there is "good news of God" in the sense that the good news is *about* God and is *from* God. Furthermore, a gospel requires a response. Inaction nullifies the good news, but belief in the proclamation of the gospel, followed by a change in life, is the affirmative response demanded.

The second verse is similarly charged with meanings. The Greek original for "time," as used here, was *kairos,* which meant "the appropriate time"—that is, the fitness of things makes a specific moment the right time, again requiring a response. Repentance also requires a positive act. Most important, the verse indicates that which is at hand: the kingdom of God. The Jews looked toward a Messianic kingdom of peace and righteousness ruled by the Anointed (Messiah and Christ both mean "Anointed"). But Jesus spoke in Aramaic, in which "kingdom" meant authority. Thus Jesus could also assert that the kingdom was already present, since he had asserted his authority.

Moreover, Jesus is said to have declared "The kingdom of God is within you," on the basis of a saying found on a papyrus in Egypt and incorporated into the Bible. This was not unlike the Greek concept "Know thyself." Generally scholars believe that the meanings collectively argue that the "kingdom" is an authority that is inward and spiritual, thus literally at hand. Other scholars argue that the Aramaic was mistranslated, and that a better reading is "The kingdom of God is in the midst of you"—that is, that Jesus was moving among the people demonstrating in his actions the authority of God.

The above example of how a gospel is read in its components has been derived from John Ferguson. *What Is a Gospel?* (Bletchley, England: Open University Press, 1971), distributed by Harper & Row. The argument however, is by Robin W. Winks.

The last of the Judaeo-Christian bishops of Jerusalem governed the church in the time of Hadrian, when the last of the Jewish rebellions in Judea was crushed (A.D. 132–135). Thereafter Judaeo-Christianity died out in its native habitat, even though it was active in the Aramaic-speaking regions east of Palestine, and traces of it probably survived in the mighty Christian church of Roman North Africa and perhaps in that of Egypt, all areas where Paul did not labor as a missionary. But although the Judaeo-Christians held on in Jerusalem until the reign

This thirteenth-century *psalter,* or illustrated prayer book, was prepared in Denmark. It shows Jesus washing the feet of the disciples. The original is in the Conde Museum in Chantilly, France.
Giraudon/Art Resource

of Hadrian, it was Titus's capture of the city in 70 that ended their influence in the church. Thereafter—Paul himself was already dead—the church of the gentiles triumphed, and Christianity separated from Judaism.

Paul and Gentile Christianity

Between A.D. 48 and 62 Paul traveled to Cyprus, twice to Syria and Asia Minor, twice to Greece, to Macedonia, back to Jerusalem, and eventually to Rome. Everywhere he taught that "there is neither Jew nor Greek" (Galatians 3:28). The Jewish law had been a forerunner, a tutor: "For by one Spirit are we all baptized into one body, whether we be Jews or Gentiles, whether we be bond or free" (1 Corinthians 12:13); and most simply: "For the letter killeth, but the spirit giveth life" (2 Corinthians 3:6). The Christian was to be saved, not by the letter of the Jewish law, but by the spirit of the Jewish faith in a righteous God. Since "there is neither Jew nor

Greek," Christianity must be involved with the Hellenistic world as represented by the Roman Empire.

Paul was from the first a Hellenized Jew. He united in his person a mystic who sought to transcend the world and the flesh, a gifted spiritual adviser of ordinary men and women troubled in their everyday lives, and an able administrator of a growing church. In all Paul's writings there are passages that show him to have been ascetic in his morality and firmly convinced that Christian truth was not a matter of habit or reasoning, but of transcendent faith:

> *Howbeit we speak wisdom among them that are perfect: yet not the wisdom of this world, nor of the princes of this world, that come to nought: But we speak the wisdom of God in a mystery, even the hidden wisdom, which God ordained before the world unto our glory: Which none of the princes of this world knew: for had they known it, they would not have crucified the Lord of glory (*1 Corinthians 2:6–8)**

Paul was no Eastern mystic who preached denial of this world in magical ecstasy. Indeed he expressed clearly a characteristic Christian tension between this world and the next, between the real and the ideal, which firmly marks Western society. Paul's symbol for it was the mystic union of Christ with Christianity in the religious act known as communion. Christians are children of God who are destined, if they are true Christians, to eternal bliss. But on this earth they must live in the constant imperfection of the flesh, not wholly transcending it, always aware that they are at once mortal and immortal.

The Pauline epistles deal frequently with church discipline. Here we see Paul keeping a firm hand over scattered and struggling Christian congregations in the lands to which he traveled. He tried to tame the excesses, to which the emotionally liberating doctrines gave rise, urging the newly emancipated not to take their new wisdom as an opportunity for wild ranting ("speaking in tongues") but to accept the discipline of the church, to lead quiet, faithful, firmly Christian lives.

Paul was not one of the twelve apostles, the actual companions of Christ, who, according to tradition, separated after the crucifixion to preach the faith in the

---

* Most matters touching upon religion are controversial, and summaries therefore involve choices. Readers should be aware, for example, that the version of Paul's teaching given here is from the Authorized (King James) Version of the Bible. It is used because it is the best-known translation in modern times. However, there are other translations, including modernized ones that use present-day equivalents for old terms. The fact that this translation was produced in England means that it is rejected by many Christians, either because it is English, or felt to be Protestant, or for other reasons. Further, we have here referred to Paul by his name, though since the Christian church viewed all of the disciples as being exceptionally holy, today Paul is referred to as St. Paul. Finally, this extract from the New Testament does not show, as some do by using italics, that three words in the quotation were supplied later by scholars through accepted techniques intended to make the meaning clearer. Thus, like Pericles' funeral oration, the final historical document may be, and probably is, very like what Paul said but cannot be expected to be precisely as he wrote in his famous epistles (or letters) to the Christians at Corinth.

ECCLESIASTES ON TRANSIENCE AND HISTORY

Ecclesiastes (The Preacher), is best known for his sense of the vanity of human history:

Chapter 1

1 THE words of the Preacher, the son of David, king in Jerusalem.
2 Vanity of vanities, saith the preacher, vanity of vanities; all is vanity.
3 What profit hath a man of all his labour which he taketh under the sun?
4 One generation passeth away, and *another* generation cometh: but the earth abideth for ever.
5 The sun also ariseth, and the sun goeth down, and hasteth to his place where he arose.
6 The wind goeth toward the south, and turneth about unto the north; it whirleth about continually, and the wind returneth again according to his circuits.
7 All the rivers run into the sea; yet the sea *is* not full: unto the place from whence the rivers come, thither they return again.
8 All things *are* full of labour; man cannot utter *it:* the eye is not satisfied with seeing, nor the ear filled with hearing.
9 The thing that hath been, it *is that* which shall be; and that which is done *is* that which shall be done; and *there is* no new *thing* under the sun.
10 Is there *any* thing whereof it may be said, See, this *is* new? it hath been already of old time, which was before us.

Chapter 3

1 To every *thing there is* a season, and a time to every purpose under the heaven:
2 A time to be born, and a time to die; a time to plant, and a time to pluck up *that which is* planted;
3 A time to kill, and a time to heal; a time to break down, and a time to build up;
4 A time to weep, and a time to laugh; a time to mourn, and a time to dance;
5 A time to cast away stones, and a time to gather stones together; a time to embrace, and a time to refrain from embracing;
6 A time to get, and a time to lose; a time to keep, and a time to cast away;
7 A time to rend, a time to sew; a time to keep silence, and a time to speak;
8 A time to love, and a time to hate; a time of war, and a time of peace. . . .
11 He hath made every *thing* beautiful in his time: also he hath set the world in their heart, so that no man can find out the work that God maketh from the beginning to the end.

The italics of the King James Version of the Bible have been used here. Italics indicate textual problems in translation, not emphases.

four corners of the earth. But he has been accepted as their equal in his apostolate. Of the twelve, tradition holds that Peter (who disagreed with Paul about the purity of gentile food) went to Rome, of which he was the first bishop, and so became the first pope, and was martyred there under Nero on the same day as Paul. Thus the Church of Rome had both Peter and Paul as its founders.

In the imperial Roman capital the first Christians were a despised sect, suspected of incest, infanticide, and ritual murder. They also allowed women to play an important role in the spread of Jesus' word after the crucifixion, just as women had played a vital role in his life. But by the year 100 the new beliefs had penetrated into many of the Eastern territories of the Empire and had established a tenuous foothold in the West.

III CHRISTIANITY IN THE PAGAN WORLD

The Period of Persecution

What to Christians was persecution, to the Roman authorities was simply the performance of their duty as defenders of public order against those who seemed to be traitors to the Empire or irresponsible madmen. The Christians ran afoul of Roman civil law not so much for their positive beliefs and practices as for their refusal to make concessions to paganism. To cultivated Greeks and Romans of these first centuries A.D., Christians

Detail from the side of a tomb of a
Roman governor, depicting
Christians dressed in Roman togas.
Vatican Museums

seemed wild enthusiasts; to the masses they were dis-
turbers, cranks, revolutionaries. "Who prevents you
from worshiping this god of yours also, along with the
natural gods?" a bewildered Roman official of Egypt
asked a Christian who insisted there was but one true
faith.

The Empire was not very deeply concerned with details about the morals and faiths of its hundreds of com-
ponent city-states, tribes, and nations. Scores of gods
and goddesses, innumerable spirits and demons, filled
the minds of the millions under Roman rule, and the
rulers—themselves often Stoics with a philosophic,
though scornful, toleration of mass superstitions—were
willing to tolerate them all as part of the nature of things.

There was, however, a practical limit to this religious
freedom, which after all was not based on any ideal of
religious liberty (for freedom and liberty are different
matters in the law) and certainly not on any concept of
separation of church and state. To hold this motley collection of peoples in a common allegiance and give
them something like the equivalent of a modern national identity, the emperor was deified. Simple rites of
sacrifice to him were added to local religious customs.
One more god did not offend the conscience of those
who believed in the Greco-Roman pantheon, or in Isis
or Cybele, or in any other conventional polytheism. Another pinch of incense on another altar was simple
enough. Those who did not believe in the customary
local gods—and such disbelief was widespread in the
Roman Empire—had no trouble in doing what was expected of them, for they did not take any religion, new
or old, with undue seriousness. The act of public worship was often essentially social, and did not signify a
deeply held conviction.

The Christians, however, would not sacrifice to the

emperor any more than the Jews of old would sacrifice
to Baal. Indeed, they felt that if an emperor pretended
to be a god, he revealed that he was in fact a devil. The
more cautious administrators of the growing Christian
church were anxious to live down their reputation for
disorderliness, and they did not want to antagonize the
civil authorities. These leaders may have been responsible for the familiar statement, "Render therefore unto
Caesar the things which are Caesar's, and unto God the
things that are God's" (Matthew 22:21), which historians
believe is a later addition to the New Testament. But
sacrifice clearly was a "thing of God's"; the dedicated
Christian, then, could not make what to an outsider or
a skeptic was merely a decent gesture of respect to the
beliefs of others. Moreover, if he was a very ardent
Christian, he might feel a sacrifice to Caesar was wicked,
even when performed by non-Christians, and he might
show these feelings in public, or try to prevent the practice because of its inherent wickedness.

The imperial authorities did not consistently seek to
stamp out the Christian religion, and persecutions were
sporadic over the course of three centuries, varying in
severity at different times and different places. The first
systematic persecution was under Nero in 64, who had
some of the Christians torn to pieces by wild beasts and
others set alight as torches in the dark. He opened his
gardens to the public for the entertainments, but even
the Roman mob obviously felt some doubts and compassion.

A generation or so later, in c. 110–111, an imperial
administrator, Pliny the Younger, wrote from his post
in Asia Minor to the emperor Trajan that he was puzzled
about how to treat the Christians, and asked for instructions. Should he make allowance for age, or punish children as severely as adults? Should he pardon a former

Christian who now recanted? Should he punish people simply as Christians, or must he have evidence that they had committed the crimes associated publicly with their name? Up to now Pliny had asked the accused if they were Christians, and if they three times said they were, he had them executed. Pliny had interrogated the alleged Christians partly on the basis of an anonymous document listing their names. He had acquitted all who denied that they were Christians, who offered incense before the emperor's statue, and who cursed Christ, and all who admitted that they had once been Christians but had recanted. As Christians,

the sum total of their offense or error was this: that they were in the habit of meeting on a certain fixed day before sunrise, to sing hymns antiphonally to Christ, as to a god, and to bind themselves by an oath—not for any criminal purpose—but that they would not commit theft, robbery, or adultery, or falsify their word, or deny that they had received a deposit at the moment when they should be called upon to give it back. Then they reassembled and partook of food, a meal taken in unison, but altogether innocent. This they had given up since . . . I forbade meetings. So I felt it necessary to make a further effort to discover the truth by torture from two slave-women, who were called "deaconesses," but I could discover nothing more than superstition, shameless and excessive.

Trajan answered with moderation that Pliny had done right. Trajan left the question of sparing children to Pliny's own judgment. He said that Christians need not be sought out, though any who were denounced and found guilty must be punished, as Pliny had done. Any who denied that they were Christians, even if they had been suspect in the past, should gain pardon by penitent prayer to the Roman gods. As for "any anonymous documents you may receive," they "must be ignored in any prosecution. This sort of thing creates the worst sort of precedent, and is out of keeping with the spirit of our times." Trajan thus established the guidelines by which the Romans dealt with the Christians under the law until the reign of Decius, in 249–251, when vigorous persecution was renewed.

Alone among the emperor's subjects, however, unrepentant Christians might be killed "for the name alone," presumably because their "atheism," as Trajan saw it, threatened to bring down the wrath of the gods on the community that tolerated it. The Jews, equally "atheist" in this sense, could be forgiven because they were continuing to practice their ancestral religion—worthy in itself in Roman eyes—and because Rome had long since officially tolerated the Jewish faith, provided that the Jews did not rebel against the Roman state. A single act of religious conformity brought acquittal.

Not until the third century, when the Roman world felt threatened from within and without, did persecutions become frequent and severe. By then Christians were far more numerous, as the faith had spread rapidly. After an anti-Christian riot in Alexandria, Decius commanded that on a given day everyone in the Empire must sacrifice to the gods and obtain a certificate to prove having done so. The dangers then threatening Rome were real enough—Decius himself would soon be killed by the Goths—and he wanted a single act of conformity from all his subjects to demonstrate that the Empire was united in the face of peril. The pope, the bishops of Antioch and Jerusalem, nineteen Christians of Alexandria, and six at Rome are known to have been executed. No bishop in North Africa died, though there were cases of torture. In Spain two bishops recanted. Many Christians who had not obeyed the edict escaped arrest afterward for failing to have the certificate; some hid until the persecution had died down, and in parts of the Empire the edict was not enforced. In the Latin West others bribed officials to issue them false certificates saying that they had sacrificed; later they were received back into their churches with some protest. In the Greek East, the same bribery probably took place but apparently was not regarded as sinful.

Under Valerian in 257–259, the government for the first time tried to interfere with the assembly of Christians for worship, and the clergy were ordered to sacrifice. After Valerian had been captured by the Persians, however, his successor granted toleration. But the systematic persecution begun in 303 by Diocletian was the most intense of all, especially in the East, where it lasted a full decade, as compared to about two years in the West. Churches were to be destroyed and all sacred books and church property handed over. In Palestine—for which alone we have figures—nearly a hundred Christians were martyred. A good many actively sought martyrdom by violent antipagan acts, although church officials often discouraged such "voluntary martyrdom" lest it provoke mass retaliation.

Persecution as a policy was a failure; it did not eliminate Christianity. Quite the contrary—many influential persons in the Empire had become Christians. Moreover, persecution did not avert disasters, which continued to befall the Roman state whether it persecuted Christians or not. In 311 and 313, respectively, the persecuting emperors Galerius and Maximinus officially abandoned the policy. In 313 the Edict of Milan confirmed that Christians might exist again, own property, and build their own churches, so long as they did nothing against public order. The state was to be neutral in matters of religion.

Christians had often called for universal toleration. "It is a privilege of nature," wrote the North African Christian Tertullian (c. 160–230), "that everyone should worship as he pleases," and almost a century later Lactantius (died c. 325) said that, while Christians believed that their god was the god of all, whether they liked it or not, Christians did not force anyone to worship him and were not angry with those who did not. But once the Christians were free from persecution, it was not long before many forgot this view that religion was a matter of free choice. In the later fourth and in the fifth centuries the pleas for toleration would come from pagans.

TACITUS ON NERO

Tacitus said that the emperor Nero was using the Christians as a scapegoat for the great fire of A.D. 64:

But all human efforts, all the lavish gifts of the emperor, and the propitiations of the gods, did not banish the sinister belief that the conflagration was the result of an order. Consequently, to get rid of the report, Nero fastened the guilt and inflicted the most exquisite tortures on a class hated for their abominations, called Christians by the populace. Christus, from whom the name has its origin, suffered the extreme penalty during the reign of Tiberius at the hands of one of our procurators, Pontius Pilatus, and a most mischievous superstition, thus checked for the moment, again broke out not only in Judaea, the first source of the evil, but even in Rome, where all things hideous and shameful from every part of the world find their centre and become popular. Accordingly, an arrest was first made of all who pleaded guilty; then, upon their information, an immense multitude was convicted, not so much of the crime of firing the city, as of hatred against mankind. Mockery of every sort was added to their deaths. Covered with the skins of beasts, they were torn by dogs and perished, or were nailed to crosses, or were doomed to the flames and burnt, to serve as a nightly illumination, when daylight had expired.

Nero offered his gardens for the spectacle, and was exhibiting a show in the circus, while he mingled with the people in the dress of a charioteer or stood aloft on a car. Hence, even for criminals who deserved extreme and exemplary punishment, there arose a feeling of compassion; for it was not, as it seemed, for the public good, but to glut one man's cruelty, that they were being destroyed.

From *The Complete Works of Tacitus*, trans. A. Church and W. Brodribb. Copyright 1942 and renewed (c) 1970 by Random House, Inc. Reprinted by permission of Random House, Inc.

The Conversion of Constantine

In 312, the year before he associated himself with the edict of toleration, Constantine had a religious experience akin to that of Paul. Just before going into battle against his rival Maxentius, the emperor supposedly saw in the heavens the sign of a cross against the sun and the words, "Conquer in this sign." He put the sign on the battle standards of his army, won the battle, and attributed the victory to the Christian god. Though the story has been challenged, there is little evidence for the counterargument that Constantine acted because he simply foresaw the eventual triumph of Christianity, since few at this time would have predicted such a victory and his army remained predominantly pagan. Though he continued to appease the sun god as well as the god of the Christians, Constantine regarded himself as Christian. Before his death in 337 official policy held that confiscated church lands had to be returned, even if it was necessary to draw upon the state to do so, implying steady transfers of funds from Constantine's private imperial wealth.

One last formal attempt was made to reconstruct the old polytheism of the Empire. The emperor Julian, called "the Apostate" (r. 361–363), a pagan and philosopher much influenced by the Neoplatonists and in particular by Plotinus (205–270), sought to merge the old classical and rational philosophies with the mysticism of Egypt. However, Julian's restoration of paganism died with him, and Christianity quickly regained and extended its position. In 375, Emperor Gratian gave up the title Pontifex Maximus, so dear to Claudius and Domitian, and refused to use the public treasury to support popular pagan festivals. At last Theodosius I (r. 379–395) made Christianity the official religion of the Empire, abolished the pagan calandar, and in 394 he began to persecute pagans. Paganism continued in the countryside, in the army, and among the upper classes and the intellectuals for another century or so, but in the cities it was no longer an organized force.

IV THE ORGANIZATION OF THE CHURCH

To maintain order, the Christian community needed some authority to discipline or even oust those who misbehaved. It had to organize to survive in the midst of an empire originally committed in principle to its suppression. Prophets, or teachers, appeared in the very first churches, the informal groups of Christians organized by the missionaries; soon elders, overseers, and presidents followed.

More and more, an overseer (Greek *episkopos*) ex-

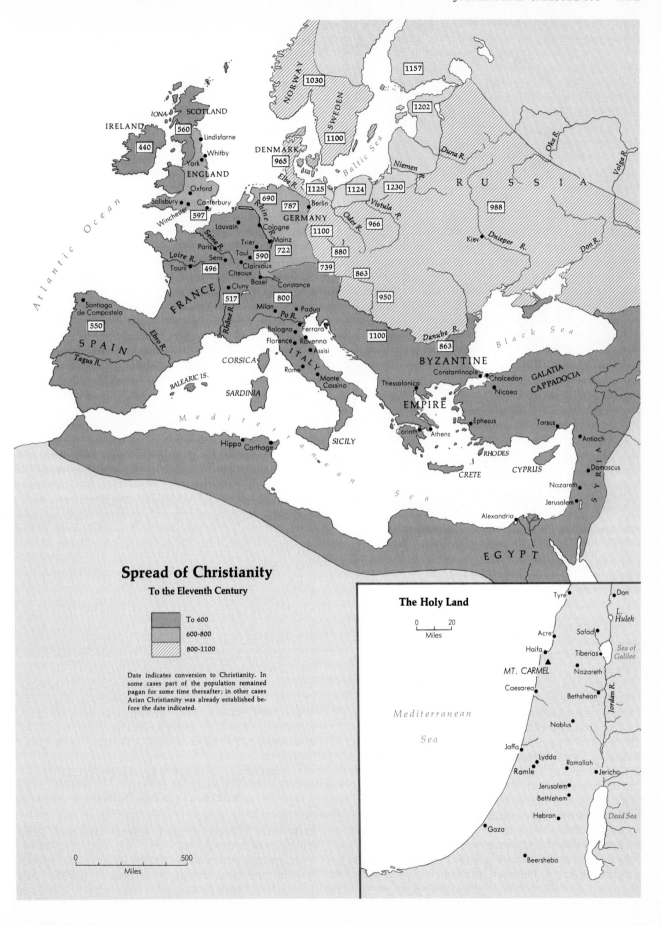

Spread of Christianity

To the Eleventh Century

- To 600
- 600-800
- 800-1100

Date indicates conversion to Christianity. In some cases part of the population remained pagan for some time thereafter; in other cases Arian Christianity was already established before the date indicated.

0   500
Miles

The Holy Land

0   20
Miles

This massive bust of Constantine the Great stresses his strength and brute power. The marble sculpture is from the early fourth century A.D. The head stands over eight feet high; a hand and two feet have also survived from the original statue, which was forty feet high.
Scala/Art Resource

ercised authority over a compact administrative area, his *see*; this was the bishop, who became the key figure in church administration. It was claimed that each see had been founded by one of the original apostles, and its bishop thus held office through apostolic succession. Since it had been Jesus himself who had chosen the apostles, every bishop, in effect, became his direct spiritual heir. Groups of bishoprics or episcopal sees were often gathered together into larger units under an archbishop, or head overseer (*archiepiskopos*). Just as the bishop often had his headquarters in a Roman *civitas* (city-state unit) and exercised authority over the churches in the adjoining countryside, so the archbishop governed the civitates from a mother city, a *metropolis*, usually the capital of a Roman province, and his see was called a *province*.

At the top of the hierarchy stood the bishop of the imperial capital, Rome itself, the father of them all—*papa*, or "pope"—who claimed supreme authority. The prestige of Rome contributed powerfully to his claim. So did the association of Peter and Paul with Rome. Jesus had said to Peter, "Thou art Peter and upon this rock I will build my church"—a celebrated pun, since the Greek word for Peter is *Petros*, and that for rock is *petra*. Because Peter had been martyred in Rome, the bishops of that city could claim that Christ himself had picked Rome as the "rock" upon which to build, a claim that was embodied in the "Petrine theory." The bishops of the great cities of the eastern Mediterranean—Alexandria and Antioch—however, claimed to exercise a paternal rule equal in authority to that of the pope. They called themselves *patriarch* (fatherly governor). Still later, after Constantinople had been made the imperial capital (A.D. 330), its bishop, also a patriarch, would oppose papal claims to supremacy.

With the removal of imperial government from Rome, the popes gradually made themselves more and more responsible for the government of the great city. And as the barbarians began to pour in and Rome itself came under attack, the pope became the surviving symbol of the old Roman sense of order and certainty—a rock indeed. A succession of outstanding men became bishop of Rome, notably Leo the Great, also known as Pope Leo I (r. 440–461). A theologian, splendid administrator, and brave man, he helped save the city from the invading Hun, Attila. By the time of the breakup of the Roman Empire in the fifth century, few in the West would have disputed the claim of papal supremacy. The papacy had emerged as the firmest institution in a new and unstable world.

The government of the church had taken shape gradually, in response to need. The church strengthened its organization by utilizing the existing political machinery of the Roman Empire, placing its major officials in centers that were already administrative capitals. Bishops and archbishops, meeting in council, determined which religious ideas or practices would be accepted and which rejected, which writings were truly Christian and which false. In this way the church selected the twenty-seven canonical books of the New Testament, written in Greek, and the Old Testament writings as preserved in a Greek translation from the Hebrew. In the Greek (or Eastern) church today these orthodox versions are still in use; in the Roman (or Western) church the Latin version, called the Vulgate and made by Jerome after 386, is used. (Many of the writings that the church rejected have survived; though not canonical, they have much interest for the modern historian and theologian.)

Bishops and Their Duties: Church and State

Each bishop presided over several churches. Each church was under the care of a priest (Greek, *presbyteros*, or "elder") who had been qualified by special training and by a ceremony of ordination. The area

The Virgin and saints, from the chapel of the Coptic monastery of St. Apollo in Egypt. From the second cengtury until the Arab conquest in 641, Christian Copts formed the dominant religion in Egypt. Their practices probably remained the closest to the historical origins of any of the early Christian groups. This fresco dates from the sixth century.

served by each church and its priest came to be known as the parish. In the early church the office of deacon, often held by a man who had other occupations besides the service of the church, had much importance. In some of the early churches, the congregation itself elected its officers, and the church was governed by boards of elders (presbyteries), but the system of appointment from above prevailed over that of election, even if the congregation was consulted. Before long, then, a distinction between those who were merely faithful worshipers (the laity) and those who conducted the worship and administered the affairs of the church (the clergy) became well defined. Despite frequent rumbles of protest during the two thousand years of Christianity, and despite differences of degree, most Christian sects maintain some distinction between laity and clergy.

By the seventh century the broad lines of church government in both the East and the West had been established. The organization was hierarchical—that is, there was a regular series of levels from subordinate to superior, from priest to pope or patriarch, somewhat as military lines of command run from lieutenant to general. But at almost every level there were councils made up of officials who met to debate problems and to make decisions. Church government, then, was no simple relation of silent underling to commanding superior; in these early centuries the critical decisions were made by assemblies rather than by individuals.

After the conversion of Constantine, the first Christian emperor, the election of bishops obviously became a matter of particular concern to the state. To retain the initiative, the officials of the church worked to put the election of each new bishop into the hands of the clergy of the cathedral (episcopal church) of the see. Practice remained uneven, however; sometimes the citizens simply gave assent to an accomplished fact by approving elections; at other times the people had real power, as when Roman mobs under the sway of rival political leaders controlled the choices for the papal throne. Since bishops often exercised actual governing power and had their own law courts, lay rulers often insisted on approving or even selecting them. The problem of the degree to which laymen could participate in the choice of the bishops remained acute in the West down to the eleventh century, as the popes strove to have the ulti-

THE RULE OF ST. BENEDICT

The Benedictine rule blended Roman law with the new Christian view to produce the most enduring form of monasticism in Western society. Consider the concepts of authority, rule, and equality contained in the following portions of the rule of St. Benedict:

An abbot who is worthy to preside over a monastery ought always to remember what he is called, and carry out with his deeds the name of a Superior. For he is believed to be Christ's representative, since he is called by His name, the apostle saying, "Ye have received the spirit of adoption of sons, whereby we call Abba, Father." And so the abbot should not—grant that he may not—teach, or decree, or order, any thing apart from the precept of the Lord; but his order or teaching should be sprinkled with the ferment of divine justice in the minds of his disciples. Let the abbot always be mindful that, at the tremendous judgment of God, both things will be weighed in the balance: his teaching and the obedience of his disciples. And let the abbot know that

whatever the father of the family finds of less utility among the sheep is laid to the fault of the shepherd. . . . [The abbot] shall make no distinction of persons in the monastery. One shall not be more cherished than another, unless it be the one whom he finds excelling in good works or in obedience. A free-born man shall not be preferred to one coming from servitude, unless there be some other reasonable cause . . . for whether we be bond or free we are one in Christ; and, under one God, we perform an equal service or subjection; for God is no respecter of persons.

The Rule of St. Benedict, in *Select Historical Documents of the Middle Ages,* trans. E.F. Henderson (London: George Bell, 1982), pp. 176–77.

---

mate say, and this struggle was one of the major causes of debate by which present democratic institutions slowly evolved.

The point becomes clear when we look at the very different history of church and state in the East. In the East, the emperor at Constantinople (today, Istanbul) usually acted as the real head of both church and state. No organized clerical body could tell him where to stop. Although religious disputes regularly broke out in the Eastern empire, no clear-cut moral or legal code set limits to the emperor's rights. The Russian church inherited this Eastern tradition. In the West, however, pope and emperor continually struggled over the issue. Gradually it was accepted that no single person or institution could wield both political and religious power. Such an understanding probably helped pave the way for further acceptance of the rights of smaller groups and of individuals.

Monasticism

Deacons, priests, bishops, archbishops all serve the laity and are called *secular* clergy (*sæcularis*, "temporal"). Early in the history of the church, however, another kind of devotee to Christianity appeared in Syria and Egypt—the monk, a man who felt that he must deny the urges of his own flesh and become an ascetic. The New Testament, in Paul's writings and elsewhere, extolled the merits of abstaining from sexual relations if possible,

and from all other fleshly indulgence. Therefore, monks would leave civilization behind and go into the desert to live in solitude, meditation, and prayer, subsisting on the minimum of food and drink. By the third century there were many of these hermits, who enjoyed reputations for extreme holiness and often competed with each other in torturing themselves or in self-denial. Some lived in trees or in holes in the ground; others on the top of columns, to which they would haul up food supplied by pious followers.

To keep extremists from using the cloak of holiness to cover un-Christian self-assertion, certain leaders, such as the Egyptian hermit Anthony, drew monks to themselves and formed communities, living by a *rule*. The Greek Basil (c. 330–379) wrote the most famous of these rules, which became standard in the Greek church and still regulates Greek monasticism today. Basil prescribed celibacy and poverty but combated the dangers of extreme asceticism and isolation by requiring that the monks work in the fields or elsewhere to make their communities as self-supporting as possible. Because after Basil monks lived by a rule, they are known as the *regular clergy* (Latin *regula*, "rule"), as contrasted with the secular clergy. In Greek monasticism, the monks not only worshiped together but also ate and worked together. Although dedicated to a life outside this wicked world, they were also required to do works of charity, such as setting up orphanages and hospitals.

In the West the perception of a growing materialism was responded to by the rule of St. Benedict of Nursia

(c. 480–c. 543), who founded an abbey at Monte Cassino in southern Italy. His Latin rule, like Basil's Greek rule, prescribed hard work for all and urged the monks to be tolerant of one another's interests and infirmities. In the West particularly, the monks broke new ground around their monasteries, acted as pioneers in opening up the wilderness, performed missionary service among the unconverted heathen tribes, and provided much charitable and medical work among the poor and the sick. In both East and West, scholarship early became one of the recognized occupations for monks. The monastic scribe, who copied the works of the ancients and built up the library of his foundation, helped preserve the literature of the past.

Tensions often arose between secular and regular clergy, each feeling that its own work was more valuable to Christianity as a whole. Constant care and strict government were needed to maintain the high ideals of the monasteries and of the convents for women that soon appeared. This continuing need prompted successive monastic reform movements that played a major role in Christian history. The abbots of the greater monasteries often participated, along with the bishops, in the councils of the church, and thus helped form Christian doctrine and frame the rules of church observance and discipline.

V THE DEVELOPMENT OF CHRISTIAN THOUGHT

The Christian clergy could hardly have attained their great power had they not been essential intermediaries between this visible world of actuality and an invisible other world that, to the devout Christian, is as real as this one. In Christianity certain important ideas about the other world are embodied in ritual acts called *sacraments*. These sacraments, administered by the clergy, are central to an understanding of Christian doctrine.

The central mystery (or rite known only to the initiate) of Christianity was the sacrament of the *Eucharist*, or Holy Communion. It was a mystery made available to simple men and women, as part of ordinary living, by the services of the church. The sacrament stems from Jesus' last supper with his disciples, where he

> took bread, and blessed it, and brake it, and gave it to the disciples, and said, Take, eat; this is my body. And he took the cup, and gave thanks, and gave it to them, saying, Drink ye all of it; For this is my blood of the new testament, which is shed for many for the remission of sins.*

By the third century, the Eucharist had become a ceremony that made the Christian believer feel a personal link with God and experience the wonder of salvation. If the sacrament of *baptism* figuratively washed away the stain of original sin and made a person a Chris-

tian, then the sacrament of the Eucharist enabled one to remain in Christian communion—subject always to good behavior—and to sustain its faith and fellowship. There were to be many grave theological disputes over the doctrine of the Eucharist, notably at the time of the Protestant revolt, but it has remained central to the drama of the Christian faith even when, as for some Protestants, it is simply a commemoration of the Lord's (or the Last) Supper.

Theological explanations were given for this symbolic act of the Mass, or Eucharist. Adam, who began with the chance for a perfect life on earth in the Garden of Eden, disobeyed God, was driven from Eden, and was exposed to death and suffering on earth. This was Adam's "original sin," and all his descendants shared his fate. But the Jews, in spite of individual or group backsliding, kept alive their faith in God; after generations of suffering, God took mercy and sent to earth his only son, Jesus. By suffering on the cross, Jesus atoned for human sins, made redemption to God the Father, and made it possible in the future for faithful Christians to be saved, despite Adam's sin. The faithful would enjoy in the other world after death the immortal happiness they could only anticipate in this one, since this world is no longer the Garden of Eden.

Even so elementary an outline of the doctrine of salvation bristles with the kinds of difficulties Christians have been arguing about for centuries. What was the relation between God the Father and his only begotten son? In this context, what does the term *begotten* actually mean? What was Adam's original sin? How did one attain salvation? Was it enough to belong to the church, or must there be some inward sign? This last question raises what has been for two thousand years perhaps the central point of debate in Christianity—the problem of faith versus good works.

Those who believe that salvation is primarily an inward and emotional matter for the individual Christian—a matter of faith—tend to minimize the importance of outward acts, even of the sacraments. Those who believe that a person must behave in strict accordance with God's directions to be saved put more emphasis upon good works. Either position, carried to its logical extreme, poses great dangers: on the one hand, the withering of the structure of the church and the taking over of the priestly role by the individual believer; on the other, the withering of the individual's role and dictatorship over daily behavior by the clergy.

As time passed the sacraments grew in number to seven: (1) *baptism*, by which a person was washed of the stain of original sin and brought into mystical union with Christ; (2) *confirmation*, by which one was formally brought into the discipline of the church; (3) the *Eucharist*, the central act of Christian observance; (4) *penance*, whereby a confessed and repentant sinner was granted absolution (forgiven) by the priest, having the guilt of sin and eternal punishment lifted subject to a temporal punishment assigned as penance; this temporal punishment might or might not be sufficient to

---

* Matthew 26:26–28.

satisfy God's justice, and hence a given penance itself could not guarantee the penitent's salvation; (5) *extreme unction*, "the last rites of the Church," a ceremony performed by the priest at the dying moments of the Christian in preparation for the life to come; (6) *ordination*, the ceremony by which a candidate was made a priest; and (7) *matrimony*, holy marriage. Baptism and the Eucharist have remained as sacraments in almost all the Protestant groups. Of the other sacraments, the one that has been most heavily attacked and most vigorously rejected by Protestants generally is that of penance.

Heresy: To the Nicene Creed

The early centuries of Christianity saw a series of struggles to define the accepted doctrines of the religion—*orthodoxy*—and to protect them against the challenge of rival or unsound doctrinal ideas—*heresy*. The first heresies appeared almost as soon as the first clergy. In fact, the issue between those who wished to admit gentiles, who were outside the law, and those who wished to confine the Gospel to the Jews foreshadowed the kind of issue that was to confront Christianity in the first few centuries, when heresy followed on heresy. The points at issue sometimes seem unimportant to us today, but we must not regard these religious debates as trivial; people believed that salvation depended upon the proper definition and defense of religious belief and practice. Also, bitter political, economic, and national issues often underlay disputes that took a theological form.

It has always been difficult to understand and explain how evil can exist in a world created by a good God. The *Gnostics* (from the Greek word for "knowledge") affirmed that only the world of the spirit is real and good; the physical world is evil, or an evil illusion. Thus they could not accept the Old Testament, whose god created this world; they regarded him as a fiend or decided that this world had been created by Satan. Nor could they accept Jesus' human life, work, and martyrdom in this world—an essential part of Christian belief. They could not accept baptism, because to them water was matter, or venerate a crucifix, which to them was simply two pieces of wood. Like the Zoroastrians, with their god of good and their god of evil, the Gnostics were dualists. Clearly heretical, the Gnostics focused on Christ's miracles and on other sorts of magic. Among them there arose a sharp distinction between an elite, whose members led especially pure lives, and the ordinary flock, less able to bear self-denial or the mysteries of the faith, who usually worked hard to support the elite.

Closely related to Gnosticism were the ideas of Mani, a third-century Mesopotamian prophet who called himself the Apostle of Jesus. He preached that the god of light and goodness and his emanations were in constant conflict with the god of darkness, evil, and matter and his emanations. These Manichaean dualistic views became immensely popular, especially in North Africa dur-

ing the third and fourth centuries. The Christians combated them and throughout the Middle Ages tended to label all doctrinal opposition by the generic term *Manichaean*. Yet dualist ideas persisted, more or less underground, and cropped up frequently for over a thousand years.

Within Christianity, heresy sometimes involved very practical problems. The emperor Constantine faced the so-called Donatist movement in North Africa. The movement arose because a number of priests yielded to the demands of Roman authorities during the Roman persecutions of the Christians after 303 and handed the sacred books over to them. After the edicts of toleration of 311 and 313, these "handers-over" (*traditores*) had resumed their role as priests. Donatus, bishop of Carthage, and his followers maintained that the sacraments administered by such traditores were invalid. Donatus's wish to punish collaborationist priests was understandable but divisive, because once a believer questioned the validity of the sacraments as received from one priest, he might question it as received from any other. Amid much bitterness and violence Constantine ruled that once a priest had been properly ordained, the sacraments administered at his hands had validity, even if the priest himself had acted badly. The effectiveness of the sacraments derived solely from their performance, not from the moral character of the clergy. But the Donatists persisted in their views, and North Africa was much troubled by the continued rivalry between them and their opponents.

Heresy also arose over essentially philosophical issues. One such was Arianism, named after Arius (c. 280–336), a priest of Alexandria. Early in the fourth century Arius taught that if God the Father had begotten God the Son through God the Holy Ghost, then God the Son, as begotten, could not be exactly of the "same essence" (*homoousios* in Greek) as God the Father, but must be somehow inferior to, or dependent upon, or at the least later in time than his begetter, who was of a "similar essence" (*homoiousios* in Greek), but not the same. It is difficult to refute this position. Far from a quarrel over one letter (*homoousios* or *homoiousios*), Arius's view threatened to diminish the divinity of Christ as God the Son and to separate Christ from the Trinity of Father, Son, and Holy Ghost.

Arius's bitter opponent, Athanasius (c. 293–373), patriarch of Alexandria and "the father of orthodoxy," fought him passionately, disdaining logic and emphasizing mystery. Athanasius and his followers maintained that Christians simply had to accept as a matter of faith that Father and Son are identical in essence, and that the Son is equal to, independent of, and contemporaneous with the Father. Even though the Father begat the Son, it was heresy to say that there was ever a time when the Son did not exist. To Athanasius, the Arian view stood in the way of the doctrine relating to salvation, which he considered central to Christianity. In the Greek East especially, this philosophical argument was fought out not only among churchmen and thinkers,

THE NICENE CREED

The Council of Nicaea created a religious organization to run in parallel to civil administration, and in the Nicene Creed set out a basic statement of what Christians believe.

We believe in one God, the Father all-sovereign, maker
of all things, both visible and invisible:
And in one Lord Jesus Christ,
    the Son of God,
begotten of the Father, and only-begotten,
that is from the essence [*ousia*] of the Father.
    God from God
    Light from light,
    True God from true God,
begotten not made,
being of one essence [*homoousion*] with the Father;
by whom all things were made,
    both things in heaven and things on earth;
who for us men and for our salvation came down
from heaven and
    was made flesh, was made man
    suffered and rose again on the third day,

ascended into heaven,
    cometh to judge quick and dead:
And in the Holy Spirit.

But those who say
    that there was once when he was not
    and before he was begotten he was not
    and he was made of things that were not
Or maintain that the Son of God is of a different
    essence or substance
    or created or subject to moral change or
    alteration—
Them doth the Catholic and Apostolic Church
    anathematize [condemn to damnation].

The Nicene Creed, in *Documents of the Christian Church*, ed. Henry Bettenson, 2nd ed. (London: Oxford University Press, 1963), p. 35.

but in the barbershops and among the longshoremen. A visitor to Constantinople complained, "I ask how much I have to pay; they talk of the born and the unborn. I want to know the price of bread; they answer 'the father is greater than the son.' I ask if my bath is ready; they say 'the son has been made out of nothing.'"

After trying to stay out of the quarrel and urging the bishops to stop discussing it, Constantine realized that for political reasons it would have to be settled. In 325 he summoned the first council of the whole church, a council called *ecumenical* (from the Greek *oikoumene*, "the inhabited world"), at Nicaea (now Iznik) near Constantinople. A large majority of the bishops decided in favor of the Athanasian view, which was then embodied in the Nicene Creed, issued with all the force of an imperial decree by Constantine himself. The emperor had presided over the council, and against his will found himself assuming the role of head of the church, giving legal sanction to a purely doctrinal decision, and so playing the role both of Caesar and of pope. In time this "Caesaropapism" became the tradition of empire and church in the East.

But the decree of Nicaea did not dispose of Arianism. Arians disobeyed; Constantine himself wavered; his immediate successors on the imperial throne were themselves Arians. Between 325 and 381 there were thirteen more councils that discussed the problem, deciding first one way, then another. One pagan historian sardonically commented that one could no longer travel on the roads because they were so cluttered with throngs of bishops riding off to one council or another. Traces of Arianism remained in the Empire for several centuries after Nicaea. Because the missionary Ulfilas (c. 311–c. 383) preached the Arian form of Christianity to the Goths beyond the frontiers of the Empire, the heresy was spread among most of the Germanic peoples then being converted to Christianity, especially through his translation of the Bible into Gothic. Later, when the German tribes took over large parts of the Empire in the West, the Arian heresy would return in force.

The Debate over the Two Natures of Christ

Long before Arianism disappeared, a new and related controversy had shaken the Eastern portion of the Empire to its foundations. Exactly what was the relationship of Christ the god and Christ the man? He was both man and god, but how was this possible? And was the Virgin Mary—a human woman—the mother only of his human aspect, or, if not, how could a human being be the mother of god?

One extreme position separated the human nature of Christ from the divine and so refused to regard the human virgin as the mother of god. This view later became unfairly linked with the name of Nestorius (died c. 451), patriarch of Constantinople in the early fifth century, and its followers were called Nestorians. They took refuge in Asia—Persia, and beyond to China. The other extreme view was that of the *monophysites* (one-nature-ites), who argued that Christ's human and divine natures were totally merged; they carried their thesis so far that they almost forgot Christ's human attributes and tended to make him a god only.

Again the dispute flared into physical violence in the East; again the decision hung in the balance; again the emperor (now Marcian, r. 450–457) called an ecumenical council—at Chalcedon, near Constantinople in 451. Supported by Pope Leo the Great, the council condemned monophysitism and, like the Council of Nicaea, took a mystical rather than a rational position; the true believer must believe in the two natures of Christ, human and divine, coexisting yet not distinct from each other; thus the Virgin is properly called the mother of god. The council also recognized Constantinople as having the same religious status in the East as Rome had in the West.

Like the decision at Nicaea, the decision at Chalcedon did not definitely dispose of the opposition. Monophysites were concentrated in Egypt and Syria, and they apparently expressed in their religious beliefs the resentment of the ancient Mediterranean cities of Alexandria and Antioch against the new domination by the upstart Constantinople, and the Egyptian and Syrian dislike for the Greeks who dominated at the capital. Partly because it was identified with what we would call nationalism, monophysitism did not die out, and the emperors strove to deal with it by one compromise or another. Since there were few monophysites in the West, the Roman church regarded the issue as closed; each time an emperor at Constantinople tried to appease his Egyptian and Syrian monophysite subjects, he was condemned by the pope for heresy.

The disaffection of the monophysite provinces of Syria and Egypt was to facilitate their conquest in the seventh century by the new religion of Islam. To this day there are still monophysite Christian remnants in Egypt, Syria, and Ethiopia, and Nestorian remnants in farther Asia. The continuing quarrel illustrates the lasting political impact that theological disagreement has provided.

VI THOUGHT AND LETTERS IN THE FIRST CHRISTIAN CENTURIES

Though a good deal of dislike and misunderstanding had always characterized the attitudes of most Greeks and Romans toward each other, Roman admiration for

This mosaic from the fifth century shows Christ as a warrior, dressed in the uniform of a Roman legionary. His feet are planted on the heads of a serpent and a lion, and the inscription on the book he holds reads, "I am the Way, the Truth, and the Life." The cross is carried over his shoulder, much as a sword. The mosaic, finished by 519, though begun earlier, is in the Bishop's Palace of Ravenna.
Scala/Art Resource

Greek literature and art deeply influenced the work of Roman writers and artists. The triumph of Christianity tended to contribute new sources of misunderstanding and tension to the relationships between Easterners and Westerners. The political divisions imposed by Diocletian and repeated by many of his successors expressed the geographic distinction between Eastern and Western provinces that corresponded roughly to the old Greece and Rome. As Germanic inroads began increasingly to disrupt communications in the fourth and fifth centuries and to threaten all the established institutions in the West, the opportunities for Westerners to know Greek and embrace the early classical tradition decreased. In the Eastern provinces few except soldiers and professional administrators had ever spoken or read Latin, though it remained the official language of legislation at Constantinople through the fifth century. Despite the growing division, however, the literature of the late Roman and early Christian world may be treated as a whole, often because of subject matter.

The Turn from Pagan to Christian Literature

In the West pagan literature declined and virtually disappeared, while in the East a few passionate devotees of the old gods still made their voices heard. Constantine's nephew Julian the Apostate was taught by a group of anti-Christian pagan scholars. As emperor he wrote satirical and moralistic essays and orations.

Christian writings increasingly took the center of the stage. In the East, writers devoted much energy to polemical statements on the burning doctrinal questions and disputes of the day. In both East and West the best minds among Christians faced the problem of how to treat Greek and Roman literature. At first, a few thinkers, mostly in the West, advised against reading anything but Scripture, for fear of pagan error. Later they acknowledged that one had to read the great pagans of the past to be able to refute pagan philosophical ideas. Still, there was always the danger that in the pleasure of reading a delightful classical author one might forget that the prime concern was to expose his errors and refute his arguments. The Greek Christians worried far less about this problem. In the fourth century three great Cappadocian fathers (so called for the province in Asia Minor where they were born)—Basil, author of the communal monastic rule; his brother, Gregory of Nyssa (died c. 394); and their friend, Gregory of Nazianzos (329–389)—all had excellent classical educations and used the techniques of the pagan philosophers to discuss religious ideas.

One of the most important writers in Latin was Jerome (340–420), who studied with Gregory of Nazianzos and who produced the Latin Bible (the Vulgate) as the climax of a life of devoted scholarship that had made him the master of Hebrew and Greek as well as Latin. Ambrose (c. 340–397), a Roman civil servant who became bishop of Milan, wrote many theological works and commentaries. Christianizing much that he found in the classics, he transformed Cicero's Stoic concept of duty to the state into a Christian concept of duty to God. Ambrose put his own preaching into practice when he publicly humiliated the emperor Theodosius I (r. 379–395) and forced him to do penance for savagely punishing some rioters. The act symbolized the Western church's insistence that, in matters of morals and faith, church would be supreme over the state—an attitude that ran exactly counter to the practice growing up in the East.

Augustine, the Early Church's Most Influential Figure

Early Life We know Augustine (354–430) intimately through his famous autobiography—*The Confessions*—written when he was forty-three and a bishop. He was born in a small market town in what is now Algeria, inland from Carthage, the administrative and cultural center of the African provinces. Here the population still spoke Punic (Phoenician), but the upper classes were Latin speaking, wholly Roman in their outlook, and deeply imbued with the classical traditions of Rome. Prosperous planters lived on their great estates, while peasants toiled in the fields and olive groves. The Africans admired eloquence, disputation at law, and education, which they applied to religion. With a sense of irony, Augustine would reflect upon the society in which he matured, even as he grew away from it.

Of modest means and often at odds with one another, Augustine's father and his devoutly Christian and possessive mother were determined that he should be given a good education, for this was the path to advancement. But all that his teachers did was force him to memorize classical Latin texts and to comment on them in detail. Augustine was so bored that he never did learn Greek, and so was cut off from the classical philosophers and forced to pick up their ideas at secondhand, largely through Cicero. His parents' ambitions for him prevented him from getting married at seventeen, like most of his contemporaries. While at school, which he left for a year for lack of funds, Augustine, barely out of his adolescence, took a concubine, as was the custom, with whom he lived happily for fifteen years and by whom he had a son.

Disappointed with his reading of the Bible, which he found insufficiently polished and too confining, Augustine at nineteen joined the Manichaeans. Rejecting the Old Testament and its stern paternal Jehovah, and considering themselves true radical Christians, the Manichaeans were highly influential in fashionable Carthaginian society. Nonetheless, the sect was regarded by pagans and Christians alike as subversive and had been declared illegal. The "elect" among them fasted and abstained from sexual relations and from labor in the world, while the "hearers" learned Mani's wisdom from their secret books and supported the elite. Gone were Augustine's plans to become a lawyer, as his mother had wished; he determined to learn and teach the Manichaean "wisdom," passively keeping the good side of his nature unsullied by the encroaching baseness of the fleshly side.

When he went back to his birthplace as a teacher, his mother was so angry with him for having become a Manichaean that she would not let him into the house. But the static quality of Manichaean belief, the naiveté of its rituals, and the disappointing intellectual level of its leaders began to disillusion Augustine, and he returned to Carthage to teach rhetoric. Highly placed friends invited him to move to Italy. Steeling himself against his mother's pleas, he sailed off. At twenty-eight he was appointed professor of rhetoric at Milan, the seat of the imperial court. The job required him to compose and deliver the official speeches of praise for the emperor and for the consuls—propaganda for the official programs. He owed his advancement partly to the wishes of influential pagans to balance the orthodox Christian influence at court with that of a Manichaean.

Conversion and The Confessions

But at Milan, Augustine abandoned the Manichaean faith and fell under the spell of Ambrose, the bishop of Milan, who stood staunchly against the pagan and pro-pagan elements in the city and against the Arianism of the Goths, who formed the main force of the imperial garrison. Better educated than Augustine, a superb preacher, indifferent to the demands of the flesh, Ambrose stimulated Augustine to reexamine all his ideas. And Augustine's mother, who had followed him to Milan, eagerly drank in Ambrose's words "as a fountain of water."

Augustine toyed briefly with Stoicism. He liked the Neoplatonist idea that material things of this world were reflections of ideas in the eternal other world, and that there were means—to be painfully achieved—by which one could move away from the external world of the senses and toward the One. Augustine's world widened. Evil, instead of looming at the center of it, took a less terrifyingly prominent place; his god became more distant, more powerful, more mysterious than Mani's god. But in the end Augustine could not accept the Neoplatonist view that a person, unaided, could by reason alone attain to the vision of god; he was therefore ready for conversion to Christianity.

This was a major step, involving not only the abandonment of Augustine's promising worldly career (including his engagement to marry a daughter of a rich and prominent family), but also the rite of baptism, which was then felt to be so great a spiritual ordeal that many Christians preferred to put it off until their deathbeds, as the emperor Constantine had done. At Easter 387, aged thirty-three, he was baptized by Ambrose. Soon afterward—his mother having died—Augustine returned to his native North Africa.

In his hometown he soon found himself in intellectual combat with his former co-religionists, the Manichees, debating them publicly, writing pamphlets against them, arguing that evil—the central problem that worried them—was in large part simply human bad habits; once a person had derived pleasure from an evil act, the memory of the pleasure prompted doing it again. The solution was to allow God to make one take pleasure in good actions, to make one hunger for perfection. Within three years Augustine had been forced into the priesthood by the demands of a local congregation, and in 395 he became bishop of the large town of Hippo (the modern Bône) in Algeria. Here he wrote *The Confessions*, describing his spiritual journey in an effort to lead his reader to God. Augustine's great book—in its selection of individual experiences, its vivid sketches of persons and places, its communication of Augustine's familiar intimacy with God, and its honesty in reporting his past behavior and feelings—was wholly original.

Augustine's gravest practical problem was the Donatists, who regarded themselves as the only true church

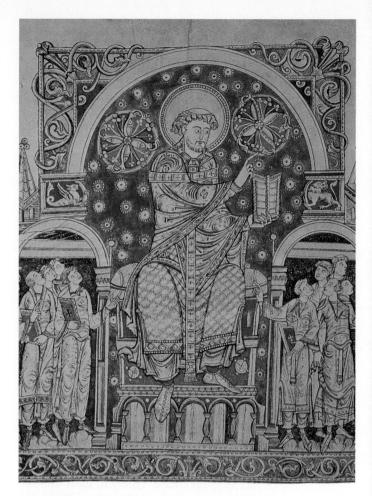

This illuminated page from the Laurenziana library in Florence shows Augustine giving instruction in the Scriptures.
Art Resource

and who outnumbered the Catholics in Hippo. He preached against them, wrote pamphlets against them, turned out a popular set of verses satirizing them. Convinced that there could be no salvation outside the church, Augustine also persecuted the Donatists when the Christian emperors began in 399 to take severe measures to suppress paganism—itself so recently the imperial persecuting faith.

When the Goths sacked Rome in the year 410, refugees poured into North Africa with accounts of the fear that had gripped the inhabitants and the ruthlessness of the barbarians. Though no longer the imperial capital, Rome was still the symbol of the imperial tradition and of all ancient culture. The North African governors, worried about the stability of the province, issued an edict of toleration for the Donatists. Some blamed the sack of Rome on the abandonment of the old gods in favor of Christianity. Augustine protested and contrasted the City of Man, the secular world where evil was commonplace, with the City of God, toward which history was moving humanity spiritually.

The City of God In a new work, *The City of God*, written between 413 and 425, Augustine combated the pagan argument that it was Christianity that had been responsible for the catastrophic sack of Rome. It was easy to show why many pagan empires had fallen in the past, and Augustine quickly moved beyond his original subject. Virtually ignoring the recent mystery religions, he attacked the core of traditional pagan worship and of pagan interpretations of Roman history, systematically demolishing pagan philosophy, in particular the Neoplatonists who had so attracted him in earlier years. All of them were limited to earthly values, to the mere "earthly city." Honest in seeking and generous in spending their wealth, the Romans had been allowed by God to acquire their great empire; but they became too eager for praise and glory. True glory belonged only to the citizens of the City of God, *civitas Dei*. Though apparently mixed together on earth, the community of those who served the devil in the earthly city would be separated in the afterlife from those who served God, the Christians, who even in this world lived in a heavenly community. As the demons took over Rome because the Romans had not submitted to the authority of Christ, so only in that heavenly City of God—when death itself would be defeated—could the Christian achieve the true peace. Augustine thus elaborated a complete Christian philosophy of history

Free Will and Predestination Later in life Augustine found himself engaged in a final philosophical controversy with Pelagius (c. 354–420), a British-born Christian layman who had lived for many years in Rome and who believed that humans not only could, but must, perfect themselves. He denied original sin and believed in free will. Yet such an exaltation of human possibilities, highly attractive at many times in history, is in its essence non-Christian, since it exalts human beings and diminishes God's majesty. Pelagius's ideas instantly affected questions of Christian behavior. For example, if there were no original sin, then newborn infants could not be guilty of it, and infant baptism was unnecessary. The Pelagian message, that one must simply will oneself to obey God's commandments wholly, virtually meant that every Christian must lead a monk's life. In Rome many rich upper-class Christians, who served the imperial regime, used judicial torture on prisoners, and led luxurious lives, regarded Pelagius's views as a summons to reform and purify themselves.

Augustine fought Pelagius's ideas and claims, recognizing that for the first time he had met an intellectual opponent of his own caliber, skilled at disputation. He feared for "the crisis of piety" that the Pelagians could create. On the practical level, he preferred to see zealous, rich, puritanical radicals give their property to the church rather than directly to the poor, to assure its growth and security. On the theological level, he argued that not all sins were committed willfully or could be willfully avoided; some came through ignorance, weakness, or even against the desire of the sinner. It was for these sins that the church existed. Baptism was the only way to salvation. For Pelagius, humans were no longer infants dependent upon a heavenly Father; they were emancipated beings who must choose to be perfect; the idea required true stoicism. For Augustine, human behavior was still dependent upon God, as a nursing infant upon the breast. Human beings were not stoics, not perfect, for they had sinned.

Pelagius had won a considerable following in the Holy Land. In 419 a young and brilliant successor, Julian, bishop of Eclanum, took up the contest with the aging and determined Augustine. Augustine defended the concept of original sin by citing the passage in Genesis in which Adam and Eve instantly cover their genitals after they have eaten of the forbidden fruit—there was the point, Augustine said, at which sin had arisen. All sexual feelings create guilt; only baptism and the Christian life could wipe it out. Julian answered in disgust that this imagery was blasphemous, making the devil into the true creator of humanity, destroying free will, and sullying the innocence of the newborn. Sexual power, he said, was a natural good, a sixth sense.

Both positions were held by devout Christians. Yet to Julian, Augustine's god seemed unjust, a persecutor of infants, and not the loving god who sacrificed his only son for human salvation. Justice—like the fabric of the Roman law—must underlie all society and all religion. For Augustine, God's justice was indisputable and could not be defined by mere human reason. God had said he would visit the sins of the fathers upon the children, and so Adam's sin had been visited upon all humanity. The world of the fifth century was large enough for both points of view to be heard, but it was Augustine's view that would prevail, for Julian was seen as too intellectual, too insistent on a solely rational god, while the clergy preferred a god whose mystery could not be fully grasped.

In his old age Augustine came to believe that God had already chosen those people who would attain salvation—the elect—and that a person's actions were determined beforehand, that is, predestined. Early African views of the true church as a group of saints helped Augustine arrive at his ideas of predestination. The conflict with the Pelagians—in which Augustine had been concerned to minimize free will, while they maximized it—also made an important contribution. In the face of new barbarian onslaughts—this time from the Vandals—on the hitherto safe shores of North Africa itself, predestination was a message with some comfort for those who had persevered in what was believed to be God's work. The elect would survive all earthly disaster; clearly this comforted Augustine as he faced the destruction of his life's work.

When Augustine died, a year before the Vandals devastated Hippo, a disciple listing his writings said that no one could ever hope to read them all; and yet anyone who did would still have missed the greatest experience—knowing Augustine as a human being, or seeing him in the pulpit and listening to him preach. Although the Catholic church turned away from the doctrine of predestination—always insisting that God's grace must be supplemented by good works before a person could be saved—it still considered Augustine the greatest Western father of the church. More than a thousand years later, other non-Catholic Christians would return to his teaching of predestination.

The Christian Triumph as a Historical Problem

Why did Christianity triumph in the fourth century? It began as a despised sect of simple enthusiasts in a rich, well-organized, sophisticated society, yet it took over that society. In general, we might postulate the need for a religion of peace in the savage and insecure world of Rome. Jesus' teachings gave Christianity certain advantages over the mystery cults. The cult of Isis lacked a missionary priesthood, that of Mithra any priesthood at all. Isis was chiefly for women; Mithra, entirely for men. Apuleius, a second-century Latin novelist who followed Isis in the eighth book of his *Golden Ass*, described a troupe of eunuch priests carrying about an image of their "omnipotent and omniparent Syrian goddess" and behaving like a rowdy circus troupe. The complexity of their rites and the lack of a great leader or teacher to make clear the ideas associated with the cult gave it little sustained popular appeal.

So the evangel really was "good news"—with its promise of personal immortality, its admonition to behave with kindness and love toward one's fellow human beings, its goal of an uplifting moral code. The expanding church provided a consoling, beautiful, and dramatic ritual, and the opportunity to become part of the exciting, dangerous, and challenging task of spreading the gospel. The would-be convert could find in it ideas and rites closely related to those of Egyptians, Greeks, and Jews. In the opening of the Gospel of John—"In the beginning was the Word, and the Word was with God, and the Word was God"—the Word was identified with the Greek *logos*, the divine reason, the spark of life, the intellect celebrated by the Neoplatonists. It was at Ephesus, the shrine of the virgin mother-goddess known as Diana of the Ephesians, that quar-

reling Christian theologians of the fifth century would proclaim the Virgin Mary to be the mother of God. In short, the new beliefs were compatible with various already held beliefs, making possible that merging of bodies of ideas that is called *syncretism*.

From its cradle in Jerusalem, Christianity did not penetrate far into the lands of Zoroastrian, Hindu, and other Eastern faiths, nor into Africa south of the Sahara. Instead, it spread westward along the trade routes of the Mediterranean and north into Europe, essentially within the structure of the Roman Empire, for it needed the political and cultural framework of the state.

Christianity succeeded not only because it set itself against the earthly compromises and indecencies of pagan cults and the dryness and sterility of later pagan philosophy, but also because it contained so much of Judaism and of paganism—both religious and philosophical, Hellenistic and oriental. Even more important perhaps is the extent to which Christianity allowed the old uses—the old rites and habits, the unintellectual, practical side of religion—to survive and the extent to which it mastered and tamed pagan habits. Christmas celebrates the birth of Jesus, but it also marks the turning northward at last of the European winter sun, the promise of its returning warmth; and Easter is an echo of thousands of prehistoric years of celebration of the coming of spring, the resurrection of life in nature.

So Christianity appealed to men and women (though it meant a legal setback for women, since Hebraic myths, such as the story of Eve tempting Adam lessened the traditions of Roman law, in which women could own property or be granted a divorce). Christianity offered a new and believable spiritual promise, yet preserved reassuringly familiar elements; it extolled mutual love; it had a capacity for adaptation; it was well led and taught. Moreover, Christianity eventually triumphed within the Roman world because of the organization of the church, something that Jesus had not foreseen, much less planned. The Roman principle of the union of state and church, with the first predominant, was applied in reversed order of importance in the West, the better to give humanity the sense of security it needed in a period of vast and rapid change.

Summary

The Romans relied on religion, not science, to explain their world. The increasing pessimism of the late Roman Empire fostered the growth of astrology, religious cults promising personal salvation, and mystical philosophy.

The Jews under Roman rule were hard to control and divided among various political and religious factions. Many Jews believed in the imminent coming of some sort of deliverer, or Messiah.

Christianity began as a Jewish movement. Paul separated Christianity from Judaism and spread its beliefs throughout much of the Empire.

Roman persecution of Christianity was intermittent. It arose because the Christians' refusal to sacrifice to the emperor threatened the unity of the Empire. Despite persecution, Christianity continued to spread.

Constantine ended the persecution in A.D. 312. The emperor Theodosius made Christianity the official religion of the Empire in 380.

In the West the bishop of Rome (the pope) became the surviving symbol of the old Roman sense of order and authority. He was head of the church and an important political figure. In the East the emperor at Constantinople usually acted as the real head of both church and state.

Monasticism arose out of the desire of some Christian believers to escape the temptations of the world. The rule of St. Benedict became the basis for most monasteries in the West.

The development of a complex Christian theology gave rise to many heresies in the early church, which led to both political and theological controversy.

Augustine of Hippo was the most influential figure in the early church. His writings have continued to influence Christians, and his doctrine of predestination was one of the bases of Protestantism.

Christianity had beliefs in common with its rivals, the other mystical religions and philosophic movements. Christianity succeeded because it set itself against the earthly compromises of paganism and the dryness of later pagan philosophy and because it retained much pagan religious practice and philosophic thought.

5

The Early Middle Ages in Western Europe

*T*he period from the collapse of the Roman Empire in the West down to about A.D. 1000 provides an outstanding example of the breakdown of a whole civilization. Historians used to call the centuries from 500 to 1000 by the name still generally used for the centuries between 1100 and 800 B.C.: *the Dark Ages*. This suggests a gloomy barbarian interruption between a bright classical flowering and a later bright recovery or rebirth (*Renaissance*). But today historians prefer the more neutral term *early Middle Ages*, for they have come to believe that "dark" is a misleading exaggeration. Middle Ages accurately enough suggests a time lying between the ancient and the modern world, and the adjective *medieval*—meaning of the middle age—is in general use. Obviously, these terms—*medieval, modern*—are words we use about ourselves; that is, we naturally perceive historical chronology in relation to our own times. Thus there is much (generally fruitless) debate over when medieval history ends and modern history begins.

I THE BREAKDOWN OF ROMAN CIVILIZATION

Much of Roman civilization was lost in these years, but much, notably Christianity, was retained and developed, and many new ways of life and even new techniques were adopted and discovered. New kinds of social relationships arose, combining Roman and barbarian practices. New inventions, such as deeper plowing and better drainage, the horse collar (a great improvement on the old yoke), and the seaworthy Norse ships (which could face the hazards of Atlantic navigation in a way the old Mediterranean vessels never could), marked technological advances over the ancient ways of farming and sailing. Yet by the standards of classical civilization, the early Middle Ages by and large represented a catastrophic decline into a dark and barbarous age.

Viewed in the long perspective of world history, the so-called barbarian conquest of the Roman Empire is only another instance of a mature, somewhat decadent civilization falling to simpler peoples of a less complex background. Even the centuries of the *Pax Romana* had been filled with Roman combat against the tribes on the far side of the Rhine-Danube line. Tacitus had lectured his fellow Romans on the contrast between their own soft degeneracy and the simple toughness of the Germans. His account of the Germans is the fullest report we have on their tribal life before their first major breakthrough to the Roman side of the frontier, which took place in the fourth century. Despite Tacitus's fears, it was apparently not so much Roman decline that opened the way to the Germans as sheer pressure on the Germans from other tribes further beyond that drove them to try to cross the Roman borders, by force if necessary.

Indo-European in language (like the Greeks, the Romans, and the Celts), the Germans originated along the shores of the Baltic, both on the Continent and in Scandinavia. Very early in ancient times some migrated southward. When the Romans first began to write about them, they were already divided into tribes, though with no overall political unity. One group of Germanic tribes—the Goths—had settled in what we now call Romania, on the north side of the Danube boundary, and in the adjacent plains of what is now the southwestern part of the Soviet Union. In the fourth century, conditions in central Asia about which we still know very little led a fierce Asian people known as the Huns to invade the territory of the Goths.

Living on horseback for days, traveling swiftly, and reveling in warfare, the Huns started a panic among the Goths and other Germanic tribes. The shock waves, beginning in the last half of the fourth century, continued throughout the fifth into the sixth. They shattered the Roman structure in the West and left its fragments in barbarian hands. Since the Eastern territories suffered much less, the imperial tradition continued uninterrupted in Constantinople.

Besides barbarian military raids, penetrations, and conquests, there were slower and more peaceful infiltrations lasting over long periods. German laborers settled and worked on the large Roman estates, especially in Gaul. Before, during, and after the invasions, individual barbarians joined the Roman side, often rising to high positions and defending the old Empire against their fellow tribesmen. The Romanized barbarian became as familiar a figure as the barbarized Roman.

We must remember that the term "barbarian invasions," though frequently used to describe the steady encroachment upon Roman peoples by non-Romans, was also used at various stages of history to attack the origins of essentially Germanic and Asian peoples. Actually *barbarian* merely described any people outside the Roman Empire. To speak of invasions by barbarians is redundant, in that the Empire has been invaded from outside and thus, by definition, by barbarians. Often the absorption of the Roman peoples was peaceful, with the Germanic groups establishing permanent settlements into which the Romans were then assimilated. Although there was much bloodshed and there were numerous genuine invasions of the land of one people by another, in general the process might more properly be thought of as a steady migration of peoples that was achieved sometimes peacefully, sometimes forcefully.

Thanks to chronicles and histories, almost all written in Latin by monks, we know a great deal about the routes of the encroaching bands, about their chiefs, and about the politics of the separate states they set up. These accounts are inferior to the best Greek and Roman historical writings not only in style and in wealth of detail, but in psychological insight and accuracy. Moreover, because these narratives were written by clerics whose ideals and property suffered from the invaders, they almost certainly exaggerate the cruelty and destructiveness of the invasions, making it even more difficult for us to gain any sympathetic understanding of the cultures of the invaders.

As a result, our own knowledge is in a kind of dark age. We do not know how numerous the invaders were in proportion to the invaded population; we do not know to what degree the barbarians replaced peoples who were there before them; we do not know whether the total population of western Europe was greater or less under the barbarians than under the late Roman Empire. Modern research has generally tended to diminish the numerical importance of the German invaders, but we are working with only the most approximate figures. We do know that the Visigoths (or West Goths) were Christianized, but we do not know how thoroughly or to which Christian views. Though nearer to us in time, the "barbarian invasions" involve more guesswork than does the study of earlier Greek and Roman history, in part because of the lack of a retained literary record.

How complete was the breakdown of Roman civilization in the West? The loss can be seen most clearly at the level of large-scale political and economic organization. These early medieval centuries—with the brief but important interlude of Charlemagne's revived empire, just before and after the year A.D. 800—were marked by failure to organize and administer any large territory as an effective state and society. Only the Roman Catholic church consistently asserted its authority beyond the relatively narrow limits of the medieval duchy, county, or other small unit that was coming into existence and maintained an effective organization to which millions of persons adhered. And politically, even the church was subject to grave lapses of discipline and control; its local clergy were caught up in the web of lay rule, and weakness and disorder appeared in its very heart at Rome.

Roads, postal systems, and communications deteriorated from the Roman efficiency that had allowed both persons and goods to travel in freedom and ease. Thousands of little districts came to depend upon themselves for almost everything they used, and thus became relatively *autarkic* (self-sufficient). And these same little districts took to fighting among themselves. Some invading Germanic tribes did exercise loose control over sizable areas, but these areas were much smaller than the old Empire had been, and the control was uncertain and unsophisticated when compared to that made possible by the sophisticated governmental machinery of the Roman state. The network of habits of command and obedience that held a great, complex community together was rudely cut; centuries later it had to be gradually and painfully restored.

The early Middle Ages also lost command over the classical tools of scholarship and science. Spoken Latin gradually broke down into local languages—*vernaculars*—French, Italian, Romanian, Portuguese, and Spanish. Even where it survived as a learned tongue, written as well as spoken, Latin was debased and simplified. The general level of cultivated literature and philosophy fell. Most writers in Latin imitated the already enshrined classics, like the works of Cicero and Vergil. Similarly, traditional skills in the arts underwent a profound change.

But much of ancient civilization did survive the early Middle Ages. People could weave, farm, use horses, and make the necessary implements of peace and war as well in the year 1000 as in the year 100; in some ways and in some places, they could do these things better.

The Oseberg ship, dating from the ninth century, was excavated in 1904 and carefully reconstructed before being set up in the Viking Ship Museum in Oslo. The ship had been buried with a Viking queen, Asa. The detail, a serpent ready for attack, is from the headpost of the ship. The work was done by the queen's carvers, probably specifically for the burial site.
Mittet Foto and University Museum of National Antiquities, Oslo, Norway © Erik Irgens Johnsen

Among churchmen there survived, in the libraries of monastaries, and to some degree in the education of the cleric, an admiration for and some familiarity with the classics. The Germanic chiefs so admired the Rome they were destroying that they retained an almost superstitious reverence for its laws and institutions, even if they understood them only in part. As we shall see, the most striking political and economic event of the early Middle Ages was the revival in the West under Germanic kings of the title and the claims of the Roman Empire.

Thus generalizations about the early Middle Ages are extraordinarily difficult, in part because our knowledge is uneven. For the sixth and seventh centuries we have very few written sources (Gregory of Tours, for example, is almost the only data base for Frankish history in the sixth century), while we have a great many sources, both literate and apparently accurate, for both the fifth and the ninth centuries.

Visigoths, Vandals, Anglo-Saxons, 410–455

When the fourth-century Hunnic push began, one tribe of Goths, the Visigoths, petitioned to be allowed to cross the Danube and settle on the south bank in Roman territory, in present-day Bulgaria. The Roman border guards took cruel advantage of the Visigoths' fear and hunger; soon there were many desperate Goths milling about only a few miles from Constantinople. In the year 378 at Adrianople, the mounted Goths defeated the Roman legions of the Eastern emperor Valens, who was killed in battle. More and more Goths now freely entered the Empire. Unable to take Constantinople or other fortified towns, they proceeded south through the Balkans, under their chieftain Alaric, ravaging Greece (including Athens) and then marching around the Adriatic into Italy. In 410 Alaric and his Goths sacked Rome itself, an event that made a staggering impression on the inhabitants of the Empire. Pagan and Christian blamed each other for the disaster, and as we have seen, it inspired Augustine to write his *City of God.* Alaric died soon afterward, and his successors led the Visigoths across Gaul and into Spain.

Here, in the westernmost reaches of the continental Roman Empire, the Visigoths, after their long wanderings, founded a Spanish kingdom that lasted until the Muslim invasions of the eighth century. In southern Gaul a large area (Aquitaine) was given to them by the Western Roman emperor Honorius (r. 395–423), into whose family their king married; but they would lose this area in less than a century to a rival German tribe, the Franks. Since the Visigoths were Arians, they had some difficulty in ruling the orthodox Christians among their subjects.

Almost simultaneously with the Visigothic migration, another Germanic people, the Vandals, still residing in Germany, crossed the Rhine westward into Gaul and moved southward into southern Spain, where they settled in 411. The southernmost section, Andalusia (from *Vandalusia*), still reflects their name. The Vandals entered North Africa from Spain, moved eastward across modern Morocco and Algeria—partly destroying Augustine's city of Hippo—and established their capital at Carthage in 439. Here they built a fleet and raided Sicily and Italy, finally sacking Rome (455) in a raid that has made the word *vandalism* synonymous to this day with wanton destruction of property. Like the Visigoths, the Vandals were Arians and often persecuted the orthodox. They held on in North Africa until 533, when the emperor Justinian conquered their kingdom.

Under pressure on the Continent, the Romans early in the fifth century began to withdraw their legions from Britain. As they left, Germanic tribes from across the North Sea in what are now northern Germany and Denmark began to filter into Britain. These Angles, Saxons, and Jutes, coming from an area that had undergone little Roman influence, were still heathen. They gradually established their authority over the Celtic Britons, many of whom survived as a subject class. The barbarians soon founded seven Anglo-Saxon kingdoms, of which Northumbria, Mercia, and Wessex successively became the most important. Scotland and Wales remained Celtic, as did Ireland, which was in large measure converted to Christianity in the fifth century by Catholic missionaries coming from Gaul, led by a Briton, Patrick (c. 389–c. 461).

Ireland escaped the first great wave of barbarian invasions, and its Celtic church promoted learning, poetry, and the illustration of manuscripts by paintings. By the end of the sixth century, Catholic Christianity was moving into England from both Celtic Ireland and Rome. Irish monasticism became so strong that many Irish monks and scholars went out from Ireland as missionaries to convert the heathen on the Continent, too; Columban, for example, headed missions from the Low Countries to the Frankish courts.*

Huns, Ostrogoths, 451–526

Not only the Germanic peoples but the central Asian Huns also participated in the onslaught on Roman territories. Early in the fifth century the Huns conquered much of central and eastern Europe. Under their domination lived a large collection of German tribes. The Hunnic rulers also extracted tribute money from the Roman emperors of the East at Constantinople. Under their ruler, Attila, the Huns pressed westward, crossed the Rhine, and were defeated in 451 at Châlons in northeastern France by a Roman general. Attila then invaded

* Historians use the language of the time under discussion, hence they speak of Paul rather than of St. Paul during his life time. Canonization, which occurs after a person's death, is the authoritative declaration that the person was a saint in his or her lifetime, and historians customarily apply the term St. to the name only retrospectively. Often, however, certain figures, such as Patrick, who are the patron saints of an entire national consciousness, are referred to as St. contemporary to the emergence of that consciousness. Often the date of canonization is not known, at least until the tenth century.

Italy, where Pope Leo the Great apparently persuaded him to withdraw without attacking Rome.

Like many nomad empires, that of the Huns in central Europe fell apart after the death of its founder in 453. A plague decimated their ranks, and many withdrew into Asia. But other related Asian peoples—nomads and pagans like the Huns, and like them Mongol in appearance—entered Europe before the age of the barbarian invasions was over: Avars in the sixth century, Bulgars in the sixth and seventh, and Magyars in the ninth. The Magyars eventually set up a state in the Danubian plain, and their descendants still inhabit modern Hungary. As the first distant Asian invaders, the Huns had not only precipitated the invasions of the Germanic tribes but had directly helped to smash Roman influence in central Europe.

Among the German tribes liberated after the collapse of the Hunnic empire, the first to make a major impact were the Ostrogoths (East Goths). They moved into the general disorder left in Italy after the last of the Western emperors, Romulus Augustulus (the little Augustus), was dethroned by his barbarian protector Odovacar in 476—a date often used by historians to mark the "end" of the Roman Empire in the West. Actually, like his immediate predecessors, Romulus Augustulus had been an ineffectual tool of the nearest barbarian general who could command loyal troops. Roman imperial power, however, continued uninterrupted in the East. In fact, it had been the Eastern emperor Zeno, who ruled in Constantinople from 474 to 491, who had hired the Ostrogoths to intervene in Italy on his behalf against Odovacar.

The leader of the Ostrogoths, Theodoric, had been educated in Constantinople and admired both Greek civilization and the Roman Empire. For most of his long rule from Ravenna in northern Italy (r. 493–526), he was content to serve as nominal subordinate to Emperor Zeno's successors in the East, as a kind of governor of Italy. Like many other Christianized German tribes, the Ostrogoths were Arians. To the popes and the Italians, they were therefore heretics as well as German foreigners. Although Theodoric hoped to impose the civilization of the Roman Empire upon his Germanic subjects, he did not have enough time to bring about any real assimilation. Moreover, toward the end of his reign, Theodoric—who had made dynastic marriages with the Vandal and other Germanic ruling houses—became suspicious of the Empire and planned to go to war against Constantinople.

Many other barbarian peoples participated in the breakup of Roman territory and power in the West during the fifth and sixth centuries but failed to found any lasting state. They remain tribal names: Scirae (from whom Odovacar came), Suevi, Alamanni, Gepides. There were two other German tribes, however, whose achievements we do remember—the Burgundians, who moved into the valleys of the Rhine and Saône rivers in Gaul in the 440s and gave their name to a succession of "Burgundies," varying in territory and government; and the Franks, most important of all, from whom France derives its name.

II THE FRANKS: THE BUILDING OF AN EMPIRE

Destined to found the most lasting political entity of any of the Germanic tribes, the Franks appear to us first as dwellers along the lower Rhine. They engaged in no long migrations, expanding gradually west and south from their territory until eventually they were to create an empire that would include most of western Europe except for the Iberian peninsula and the British isles. Clovis (r. 481–511), a descendant of the house of Merevig or Merovech (called Merovingian), was the primary founder of Frankish power. Moving into Gaul, he successively defeated the last Roman governor (486), the Alamanni (496), and the Visigoths of Aquitaine (507). Large areas of modern France, northwest Germany, and the Low Countries were now Frankish.

The most important factor in Clovis's success, aside from his skill as a general, was his conversion in c. 496 to Christianity, not as an Arian heretic but as an orthodox Catholic. This gave him the instant support of the clergy of Gaul, especially of the powerful bishops of Aquitaine, who welcomed the Franks as a relief from the Arian Visigoths. Probably the greatest liability of the Franks was their habit of dividing up their kingdom among the king's sons in every generation. In time Clovis's sons and grandsons gained control of Burgundy and much of present-day Germany. This meant not only a periodic parceling out of territory into petty kingdoms and lordships, but constant secret intrigues and bloody rivalries among brothers and cousins and other relatives who strove to reunite the lands. Indeed, Merovingian history forms one of the most divisive and savage chapters in Western civilization.

According to the sixth-century historian Gregory, bishop of Tours (not an unbiased source), King Childeric, Clovis's grandson, married Fredegund, who stopped at nothing to achieve their ambitions. She sent her husband's son by an earlier marriage into a plague-infested region in the hope of killing him off, and when that failed she stabbed him. Next, she sent an assassin to kill her sister-in-law, Brunnhild, and when the assassin returned unsuccessful, Fredegund had his hands and feet cut off. Brunnhild, nearly eighty, was dragged to her death by wild horses.

By the end of the seventh century, the divisive Merovingian kings became so weak that they became known as *rois fainéants* (do-nothing kings). They delegated real power to their chief officials, the "mayors of the palace," a title showing the close connection between the household service of the monarch and the actual external government. By the eighth century one particular family, the house of Pepin, had made this office hereditary from father to son; these were the Carolingians (named for *Carolus*, Latin for Charles). One of the mayors of the palace, Charles Martel, "the Hammer" (r. 714–741), organized the Frankish nobles into a dependable cavalry and in 732 near Poitiers in western France defeated an Arab advance north from Spain. Because this was the

Germanic Invasion Routes 371-568 A.D.

farthest north in Europe that the Muslims ever came, the battle came to be seen as a landmark in western European history. Charles Martel's son, Pepin III, the Short (r. 751–768), assumed the title of King of the Franks and consolidated the kingdom once again. Pepin's adventurous policy in Italy initiated a new chapter in Western history, for there, in the two centuries preceding, significant new efforts had been made to reconsolidate Rome.

Italy from Theodoric to Pepin, 527–768

Soon after the death of the Arian Theodoric, the great Eastern emperor Justinian (r. 527–565) launched from Constantinople an ambitious effort to reconquer the major areas of the West that had been lost to the bar-

barians. The imperial forces tackled the Vandals in North Africa in 533, and then, before consolidating their successes, invaded Italy from Carthage via Sicily. For almost twenty years savage and destructive warfare ravaged the peninsula, and Rome changed hands several times. The towns and countryside were devastated and the survivors reduced to misery. Justinian's proclamation of an imperial restoration in 554 was short-lived, even though in the same year imperial forces took back part of southern Spain from the Visigoths.

Three years after Justinian's death, a new Germanic tribe, the Lombards, entered Italy from the north. They easily conquered the north Italian plain that still bears their name (Lombardy) and established a kingdom with its capital at Pavia. Further to the south they set up the duchies of Benevento and Spoleto. Ravenna, Rome, and Naples remained free of Lombard rule. Italy lay once again in fragments, even though the emperor at Con-

Germanic Kingdoms
About 526

■ Battle sites

0 ————— 500
Miles

stantinople appointed a governor (called the *exarch*), who had his headquarters at Ravenna and was responsible for the defense of Italy.

Constantinople was far away; danger threatened the emperors from the east, and they often could not afford to pay much attention to Italy's needs or send money and troops to help the exarchs fight the Lombards. In this chaotic situation, the church emerged more and more as the protector of the Catholic population; the bishops often received privileges from the non-Catholic Lombard conquerors that conferred upon them virtual governing rights in the towns if they would keep them peaceful. Among the bishops, the pope took the lead; and among the popes, the most remarkable was Gregory I, the Great (r. 590–604).

Born into a rich and aristocratic Roman family, Gregory abandoned worldly things and became a monk—the first to become pope—and a founder of monasteries. His administrative talents were extraordinary; he served as papal ambassador to the Roman imperial court at Constantinople before becoming pope in 590. Besides his religious duties, he had to take virtually full responsibility for maintaining the fortifications of Rome, for feeding its population, for managing the great financial resources of the church and its lands in Italy, for conducting diplomatic negotiations with the exarchate and Lombards, and even for directing military operations. It was he who sent the mission to Britain under Augustine of Canterbury in 597 that began the papal contribution to the conversion of the Anglo-Saxons there. Gregory had an exalted conception of papal power, and he stoutly defended its supremacy over the Eastern church in his letters to the emperor and to the patriarch at Constantinople.

During the seventh and early eighth centuries, the alienation between the Empire in the East and the pa-

This twelfth century Venetian fresco, from the Chapel of St. Sylvester in the Church of Quattro Coronati, depicts the so-called Donation of Constantine. Frescoes are painted on a moist plaster surface and were especially popular as forms of interior church art.
Scala/Art Resource

pacy was greatly increased by religious disagreements and a related political and economic dispute (see Chapter 6). Simultaneously, the Lombards were gradually consolidating and expanding their power, taking Ravenna and putting an end to the exarchate. Menaced by the Lombards and unable to count on help from Constantinople, Pope Stephen II in 753 paid a visit to Pepin III of the Franks.

Pepin was unsure of his position, being only a descendant of a line of mayors of the palace. In exchange for papal approval of his new title of king, he attacked the Lombards and forced them to abandon Ravenna and other recent conquests. Then, although these lands did not truly belong to him, he gave a portion of them to the pope, as the celebrated Donation of Pepin. Together with Rome and the lands immediately around it, the Donation of Pepin formed the territory over which the pope ruled as temporal sovereign down to 1870. These were the Papal States, and Vatican City is their present-day remnant. Pepin's son, Charles the Great (Charlemagne, 742–814), completed the destruction of the Lombard kingdom in 774.

The new alliance with the Franks marked the end of papal dependence upon the Empire at Constantinople and the beginning of the papacy as a distinct territorial power. The Franks—too busy to take over these Italian lands themselves and no doubt also aware of the pious responsibilities that they had acquired when they became the protectors of the church—did not try to dictate to the popes. Sometime between 750 and 760 the clerks of the papal chancery forged "proof" that Pepin had been confirming a gift of lands to the church made long

ago by the emperor Constantine. For about seven hundred years, until the Italian Renaissance scholar Lorenzo Valla proved it a forgery in 1440, people believed the document on which the "donation" was based was genuine. Constantine had, after all, made many donations to the church, and there were many in the chaos that was Italy who wanted to believe in this additional donation.

Charlemagne and the Revival of Empire, 768–814

Charlemagne (r. 768–814)—so Einhard, his contemporary and his at times misleading biographer tells us—was a vigorous, lusty, intelligent man who loved hunting, women, and war. All his life he wore Frankish costume and thought of himself as a Frankish chieftain. Although he could read and kept pen and ink under his pillow, he could never teach himself how to write; he spoke Latin, however, and understood some Greek. A great conqueror, Charlemagne crossed the Rhine and in campaigns lasting more than thirty years conquered the heathen Saxons, who lived south of Denmark, and converted them at sword's point to Christianity. Monks and priests followed his armies.

Charlemagne also added to his domain the western areas of modern Czechoslovakia (Bohemia), much of Austria, and portions of Hungary and Yugoslavia. The eastern boundaries of his realm reached the Elbe River in the north and the Danube, where it turns sharply south below Vienna. Along these wild eastern frontiers he established provinces (*marks* or *marches*). His advance into eastern Europe also brought him victories over the Asian Avars, successors to the Huns along the lower Danube. Far to the west, Charlemagne challenged Muslim power in Spain and set up a Spanish march in what is today Catalonia. A defeat of his rear guard at the pass of Roncesvalles in the Pyrenees Mountains in 778—though only a skirmish—formed the theme of the heroic epic *Le Chanson de Roland* (The Song of Roland), which in its most accepted surviving form was composed several centuries later.

By the end of the eighth century, Charlemagne had reunited under Frankish rule all of the western Roman provinces except for Britain, most of Spain, southern Italy, Sicily, and North Africa, but had added to his domains central and eastern European areas the Romans had never possessed. On Christmas Day, 800, Pope Leo III crowned Charlemagne emperor in Rome. So mighty was the tradition of the Roman Empire and so great its hold on people's minds that, more than three centuries after the disappearance of Romulus Augustulus, last of the Western emperors, the chief bishop of the Christian church, seeking to honor and recognize his mighty Frankish patron, automatically crowned him "Roman Emperor Carolus Augustus."

It is likely that Charlemagne himself was surprised and not altogether pleased by the coronation; he probably relished the title, but he almost surely disliked the role played by the pope and the implication that the pope had the right to choose and crown emperors. The Roman emperors at Constantinople were horrified at the insolence of the once-barbarian king of the Franks in assuming the sacred title, and considered him a usurper.

Within his territories, Charlemagne now was, by virtue of his consecration, a sacred ruler with spiritual rights and duties as well as temporal ones. His lofty concept of his office and his personal power enabled him to influence the church—even in matters of doctrine—more like Constantine or other Eastern emperors than any other Western monarch. He himself named Louis the Pious, by then his only living son, his successor in 813, and the pope played no part in the ceremonies. Had not all but one of his sons died before him, he would have divided the kingdom in the standard Frankish way.

Charlemagne's government was very simple. His personal household staff were also the government officials: the chamberlain, the count of the stable (constable), and so on. On major decisions the emperor conferred with great nobles of state and church, but he told them what he (and they) were going to do, rather than asking them for advice and permission. Since the Franks, like other Germans, believed that law preexisted and could not be made by humans, even Charlemagne could not, in theory, legislate. But he did issue instructions to his subjects, which usually dealt with special administrative problems. His was a highly personal rule. Einhard says about it:

When he had taken the imperial title he noticed many defects in the legal systems of his people; for the Franks have two legal systems, differing in many points very widely from one another, and he therefore determined to add what was lacking, to reconcile the differences, and to amend anything that was wrong or wrongly expressed. He completed nothing of all his designs beyond adding a few capitularies, and those unfinished. But he gave orders that the laws and rules of all nations comprised within his domains which were not already written out should be collected and committed to writing.

He also wrote out the barbarous and ancient songs, in which the acts of the kings and their wars were sung, and committed them to memory. He also began a grammar of his native language.*

Charlemagne's territories included about three hundred counties, each governed by a count. The counties that lay in former Roman territory each corresponded to the lands of a former Roman civitas. The count had to maintain order, render justice, and recruit and command soldiers. Alongside the count, the bishop of the diocese and the various local magnates might have considerable powers of their own when on their own lands. Only a powerful king could keep the local authorities from taking too much power to themselves. Charlemagne required his counts to appoint teams of judges, whose appointment he would then ratify and who would actually take over much of the counts' role in rendering justice. He also sent out from his own central administrative staff pairs of royal emissaries (the *missi dominici*, literally "the lord's messengers"), usually a layman and a cleric, to investigate local conditions and to correct abuses. As representatives of the emperor, they could overrule the count.

The Carolingian empire depended heavily upon Charlemagne personally—on his energy, on the brilliance that all observers attributed to him, on his administrative talents, and on the happy fact that his succession was not divisive. But he had assembled more territory than could be effectively governed, in view of the deterioration of administrative machinery and communications since Roman days. Under his less talented successors, the Frankish practice of dividing lands and authority among the heirs to the throne continued. Quarrels over the allotment of territory raged among brothers and cousins. Although the title of emperor now descended to a single heir in each generation, it had become an empty honor by the middle of the ninth century.

Thus Charlemagne's achievement was short-lived, if brilliant. Historians have taken differing views of it; some have emphasized its brevity and denied its lasting influence. Others have stressed its brilliance and declared that the mere resurrection of the Roman imperial title in the West helped determine the future direction

---

* Einhard, in *Early Lives of Charlemagne*, ed. A. J. Grant (London: Chatto & Windus, 1922), pp. 44–45. Since Einhard (c. 770–840) tells us that Charlemagne could not write, we know that this passage must mean that Charlemagne did not do this writing himself, but ordered it to be done.

Carolingian Empire

▨ Kingdom of Charlemagne, 768

▨ Acquired by Charlemagne to 814

▨ Areas tributary to Charlemagne's empire

▨ Byzantine Empire

■ Battle sites

of European political action; the next time a new revival began, statesmen instinctively launched it by reviving the Roman Empire once again. These historians add that, as events turned out, this title lured later generations of German rulers over the Alps into Italy in search of an illusory honor, prevented them from forging Germany into early national unity, and so kept Italy and Germany tied together in an unnatural connection that helps explain why neither became a unified nation until the nineteenth century.

Some insist that Charlemagne's revival of the imperial title at least kept alive the ideal of a unified Christian Western society, as opposed to a collection of parochial states devoted to cutthroat competition. Others maintain that, thanks to Charlemagne's act, an ambitious secular power could oppose the temporal claims of a spiritual power, the papacy. Of course, a spiritual power well anchored in Italy could oppose the temporal power. The existence of these two claimants to supreme power—the pope and the emperor—saved the West from the extremes of secular domination of religion on the one hand and religious domination of the state on the other. This rivalry and tension helped promote such typically Western institutions and attitudes as individual rights, the rule of law, the dignity of the individual, and ultimately the separation of church and state.

A mosaic from the Church of St. John Lateran in Rome provides an eighth-century view of how spiritual and temporal authority issued from the same source. Here St. Peter presents a *pallium* (pope's garment) to Leo III, while handing a flag to Charlemagne.
The Granger Collection

All of this lies in the realm of political theory and speculation. Nevertheless, the revival of the old Roman imperial idea is clearly one of the great threads that run through all subsequent European history. With Charlemagne the "Roman" Empire became in fact largely a German one, though the name "Empire" always retained some suggestion of a common, stable, political order within which prolonged instability was somehow "unnatural," not right. In this sense, the medieval empire, reinforced by the concept of Christendom, links Roman unity with all later dreams of a united Europe. And apart from political theorizing, all students of the intellectual and artistic revival in the time of Charlemagne and his successors would agree that the period provided a dazzling flash of light after centuries that had indeed been relatively dark.

In the struggle among Charlemagne's successors, one episode deserves special notice: the Strasbourg Oaths of 842. Two of his grandsons, Charles the Bald, who held the Western regions, and Louis the German, who held the Eastern regions, swore an alliance against their brother, the emperor Lothair, whose lands lay between theirs. Each swore the oath in the language of the other's troops—Louis in a Latin-like language on its way to becoming French that scholars call Romance, and Charles in Germanic. The symbolism was a striking sign of things to come in European history. Charles and Louis could hardly have chosen a more appropriate place than Strasbourg—chief city of Alsace, in the heart of the middle zone, long to be disputed between modern France and Germany—to swear their bilingual oath.

In the ninth century, however, there were as yet no national states in Europe. Indeed, instead of coalescing into large national units, the Frankish dominions were even then breaking up into much smaller ones, despite the formal settlement reached at the Treaty of Verdun in 843. As the power of the central Frankish state was frittered away in family squabbles, smaller entities—duchies or counties—emerged as virtually autonomous units of government, many with names we still recognize as belonging to provinces of modern France or Germany: Brittany, Champagne, Bavaria, Saxony.

III AFTER CHARLEMAGNE: THE NORTHMEN

Charlemagne's conquests in Germany had for the first time brought the home ground of many of the barbarians into Christendom. Still outside lay Scandinavia, from whose shores there began in the ninth century a new wave of invasions that hit Britain and the western parts of the Frankish lands with savage force. The Northmen conducted their raids from small ships that could easily sail up the Thames, the Seine, or the Loire. Their appetite for booty grew with their successes, and soon they organized fleets of several hundred ships, ventured farther abroad, and often wintered along a conquered coast. They ranged as far east as Yaroslavl in northern Russia, as far south as Spain, penetrated into the Mediterranean through the Straits of Gibraltar, and raided Italy. To the west they proceeded far beyond Ireland to reach Iceland and Greenland. About 986 some of them almost certainly sighted Newfoundland (Vinland), Labrador, or even New England, although some scholars still question the validity of the evidence for settlement in the last.

Desire for booty does not by itself account for the Norse expansions. Polygamy was common among the upper classes of the pagan Scandinavians (the lower ones could not afford it), and the younger sons of these Viking chiefs probably had to leave home to seek more wives. Like most migrations, however, the chief motivation most likely was to find new lands to settle in the face of growing overpopulation. Cultivable land became scarce, throwing families onto marginal lands to face

The bronze statuette of Charlemagne from the early ninth century appears to diminish him. Compare it with the magnificent fourteenth-century bust of Charlemagne showing him dressed in his Frankish cloak.
The Granger Collection and Giraudon/Art Resource

the fear of famine in a bad year. In addition, Scandinavian chiefs were imposing more controls, and some families chose to leave rather than submit.

The Norsemen's first captured base was along the lower Seine River, which is still called Normandy after them. In 915 the Frankish king was forced to grant the Norse leader Rolf, or Rollo (c. 860–c. 931) a permanent right of settlement. The Normans became an efficient and powerful ruling class—in fact, the best administrators in the new feudal age. From Normandy soon after the year 1000 younger sons would go off to found a state in the southern Italian and Sicilian territories that belonged to the Eastern Roman Empire and to the Arabs. And from Normandy in 1066, as we shall see, Duke William and his followers would conquer England. Kinsmen of these Norsemen who had settled in Normandy also did great deeds. In the 860s the first wave of Viking invaders crossed the Baltic Sea to what is now the Soviet Union and penetrated deep inland to the south along the river valleys. They conquered the indigenous Slavic tribes and, at Kiev on the middle Dnieper, consolidated the first Russian state.

While the Normans were raiding and developing Normandy, other Scandanivians were paralleling their

Plan of a medieval manor. The solid strips are the lord's demesne.

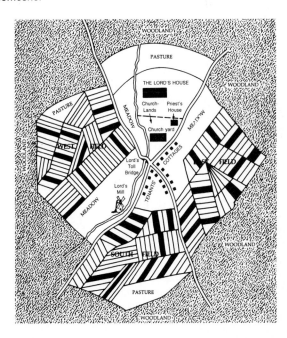

achievements in the British isles. The Northmen were soon firmly established in Ireland, especially in the ports of Dublin, Waterford, and Limerick. But in the interior the Celtic chieftains held on. In 1014, under the leadership of Brian of Munster, these chieftains won the battle of Clontarf against the Northmen and their native allies. Eventually, the Northmen were absorbed into the texture of Irish society. But the two centuries of struggle had disastrously interrupted the brilliant development of Irish civilization, and thereafter tribal warfare was to reign unchecked until the English invasions of the twelfth century.

The Anglo-Saxon Kingdoms and the Danes, 871–1035

In England, savage Danish attacks on the northern and eastern shores soon led to settlement. The chief barrier to the Danes was the Anglo-Saxon kingdom of Wessex under Alfred the Great (r. 871–899). Although Alfred defeated the Danes, he had to concede the whole northeast of England to them, a region thereafter called the Danelaw. By the midtenth century, Alfred's successors had reunited the Danelaw to Wessex, whose royal family ruled over all England.

Soon after the turn of the eleventh century, new waves of Danes scored important successes under the command of Canute, or Knut (b. 994), the king of Denmark. In 1016 Canute was chosen king of England by the Anglo-Saxon *witenagemot*, a "council of wise men." Able ruler of a kind of northern empire (he was also king of Norway), Canute allied himself with the Roman church and brought Scandinavia into the Christian community. His early death (1035) without competent heirs led to the breakup of his holdings, and England reverted to a king of the house of Alfred, Edward the Confessor, who reigned from 1042 until 1066.

Like the Carolingian monarch, the Anglo-Saxon king was crowned and anointed with holy oil and ruled as God's deputy on earth, with responsibility for both church and state. His revenue came in part from an ancient practice, the *feorm*—originally a tax of food levied for the support of the monarch and his household as they moved about England, though by the time of Edward the Confessor it was often paid in money. There was also the *Danegeld*, a war tax on land first levied in 991 to bribe the Danes, which continued to be collected long after its original purpose was unnecessary. The king also had income from his own estates and from fines levied in court cases. His subjects were required to work on the building and repair of bridges and defense works and had to render military service in the *fyrd*, the ancient Germanic army.

The Anglo-Saxon king was the guarantor of law, and serious crimes were considered to be offenses against him as well as against the victims; he was also a lawgiver, like the Carolingian monarch. His council of wise men, made up of important landholders, churchmen, and of-ficials, advised him when asked on major questions of policy—war, taxes, new laws—and sometimes acted as a court to try important cases. The council also played a major role in the election and deposition of kings. In the king's personal household staff, which moved with him and did his business from day to day, lay one of the origins of future specialized governmental departments in England and the many lands ultimately influenced by it. The Anglo-Saxon monarchy resembled the Carolingian, but it flourished while that of the Carolingians declined.

Carolingian Decline: The Saxon Empire, 911–996

By the end of the ninth century, Carolingian power in the German territories had almost disappeared in the face of domestic challenges by ambitious local magnates (great lords) and foreign threats from Norsemen, Slavs, and the Asian Magyars, who poured into the Hungarian plain in the mid-890s. Their predecessors, the Huns and Avars, had vanished, but the Magyars stayed, forming the nucleus of a Hungarian state. The Hungarian language thus remains today the only non-Indo-European tongue in Europe except for Finnish and Basque.

When the last nominal Carolingian ruler, Louis the Child, died in 911, the German magnates elected the duke of Franconia as King Conrad I (r. 911–918). The most important units in Germany were now duchies—Franconia, Saxony, Swabia, and Bavaria—each under an autonomous ruler. Conrad I failed to control either the other dukes or the Magyars, and eventually his strongest enemy, Henry the Fowler, duke of Saxony, succeeded him. Henry's son, Otto I (936–973), checked the rival dukes and defeated the Magyars at the battle of Lechfeld in 955, ending their threat to western Europe.

Master of his German territories, the Saxon Otto next sought to revive Charlemagne's title of Roman Emperor, which had passed from one Carolingian prince to another. Deep in decline after the reign of the great pope Nicholas I (r. 858–867), the papacy had fallen into the hands of rival Roman noble families, usually corrupt and ineffectual. Without strong central administration and under a two-pronged attack from Muslims in the south and Magyars in the north, Italy had become anarchic. Yet Rome, even at its lowest depths in the midtenth century, was an irresistible magnet that attracted all who sought supreme power. Like Charlemagne almost two hundred years before him, Otto therefore went to Italy and had himself crowned emperor by the depraved Pope John XII in 962. Otto then deposed John for murder and installed his own candidate on the papal throne. He forced the Roman aristocracy to promise that imperial consent would hereafter be necessary for papal elections, and he renewed the Donation of Pepin and the subsequent grants of the Carolingians to the papacy. Though the papacy for the next hundred years was

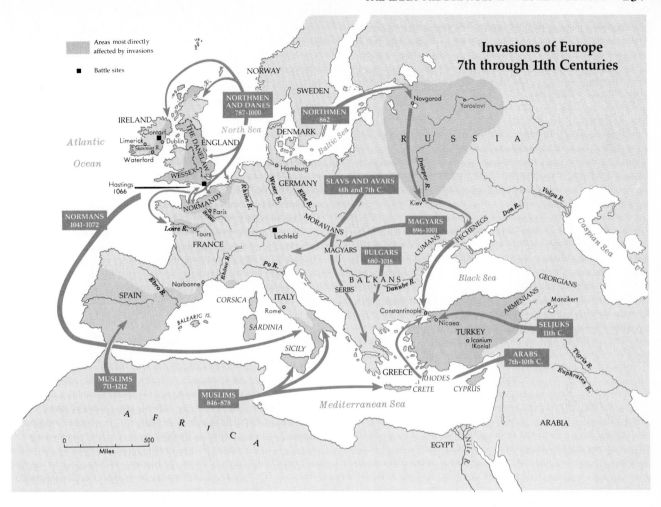

hardly more than an instrument manipulated by his successors, Otto's action eventually ensured the continuity of the papacy as an independent institution; it also tightly linked the political fortunes of Germany and Italy for centuries to come. In practice, relations between emperor and pope were regulated by a pact that assured imperial supremacy.

In the western Carolingian lands, which we now call France, partitioning, strife, and feebleness led to the fragmentation of both territory and power among several ambitious landowners. As early as 887 one faction of these magnates chose a non-Carolingian, Odo, count of Paris, as king, and civil war between him and the Carolingian claimant added to the chaos. For the next century the families of the two rivals alternated in power. Finally, in 987 the magnates elected as king Hugh Capet (r. to 996), a descendant of the early count of Paris. Though several of the nobles who chose Hugh were actually more powerful than he was, he founded the Capetian dynasty that lasted almost to our own time. (When Louis XVI went to the guillotine in 1793 during the French Revolution, his executioners would call him "Citizen Capet.")

Europe about 1000

By about the year 1000 England was a centralized monarchy; France was nominally ruled by an elected king who was feebler than his great supporters; Germany was divided into duchies, one of which, Saxony, had asserted its supremacy and claimed the old imperial title; and Italy still remained anarchic, although the papacy had begun to revive. Out of the debris of the Roman Empire, buffeted by two successive waves of barbarian incursions and held together only by a common Christian faith, these major fragments had begun to take on certain features that we can recognize today. Elsewhere, the Scandinavian kingdoms had imposed order on the turbulent peoples who had carried out the Viking expansion, and the little Christian kingdoms in the north of Spain were beginning to reconquer the peninsula from the Muslims (see Chapter 6).

In the East, the Empire, with its direct descent from Rome and its Greco-oriental character, still stood firm at Constantinople, despite many shocks. It had started its work of Christianizing the Slavic peoples nearest to it—the Bulgarians, the Russians, the Serbs. The western Slavs—Czechs, Poles, Croats, and others—and the Magyars, lying between the Germans and the influences radiating from Constantinople, had received Roman missionaries. By the year 1000 there was already visible a fateful line of demarcation between the Western Catholic world and the Eastern Orthodox world, each with a different alphabet and a different outlook.

IV   FEUDAL EUROPE

If the old Roman ways of governing largely collapsed, as they did, during the centuries that we have called the early Middle Ages, what replaced them? It is all very well to speak of relative anarchy before and after Charlemagne, but what was anarchy like and how were human relations governed? Did everyone just slaughter everyone else indiscriminately? What were the rules that enabled life to go on, however harshly?

In fact, of course, there were mutual arrangements that allowed people to work and fight, to survive if they could, to seek out some way of assuring at least temporary security. In these arrangements we find elements surviving from Roman times, innovations introduced by the barbarians, and changes linked with conversion to Christianity. The settled inhabitants of western Europe and the invaders underwent a long, slow, mutual adjustment, as new and old ways of regulating human affairs competed and often combined with each other.

Feudalism: The Rulers

To these widely varying social and political combinations scholars give the name *feudalism*. Feudal institutions were the arrangements—personal, territorial, and governmental—that made survival possible under the conditions that existed in western Europe during the early Middle Ages. The arrangements were made between important people who were concerned with maintaining order, though the customs that evolved also applied to the masses of population. Because central authority could no longer maintain itself locally, a closer, truly local authority had to be improvised to replace it. But because the processes and their results were anything but systematic, scholars seldom now use the outmoded term "feudal system."

One of the most influential arrangements among the barbarians was the war-band (or *Gefolge*) of the early Germans (or the *comitatus*, as Tacitus called it in Latin). In the war-band the leader commanded the loyalty of his followers, who had put themselves under his direction for fighting and for winning booty. It was one of the most important institutions of the Scandinavian invaders of future Russia, where it acquired the Slavic name *druzhina*. Among the Anglo-Saxons the word for chieftain was *hlaford*, the direct origin of our word *lord*.

Chief and followers consulted together before a raid or before making peace; those who disagreed might go and serve another chief; booty was divided among all the fighters.

In the Roman provinces, too, local landowners often built their own private armies, while in Rome itself the magnates had long maintained their groups of *clients*, to whom they acted as *patron* and gave legal protection. When a humble man wanted to enter the client relationship, he asked for the *patrocinium* of the great man and secured it by performing the act of *commendation*, recommending or entrusting himself to the patron. He remained free, obtaining food and clothing in exchange for his services, whatever they might be. If the man was of the upper classes, he was called *fidelis*, a faithful man. By the Carolingian period, the term *vassus*, originally denoting a man of menial status, had come to mean a man who rendered military service to his patron, or lord. To be a vassus, or vassal, meant no disgrace; it was the new name for status gained by the act of commendation. So a combination of old Germanic and old Roman practices contributed to new relationships described in new terms.

A Roman patron sometimes retained title to a piece of property but granted a client temporary use of it, together with the profits to be derived from it, so long as he held it, often for life. The Romans used the term *precarium* for this kind of tenure, and the Carolingian rulers commonly adopted the old practice—sometimes using the old Roman term, sometimes the newer *beneficium* (benefice), to describe land temporarily held by a vassal in exchange for service. By the year 1000 the act of becoming a vassal usually meant that a man got a benefice; he might even refuse faithful service or loyalty unless he was satisfied with the land he received. The feeble later Carolingians and their rivals outbid each other in giving benefices to their supporters to obtain armed support and service. This was one of the practices that depleted the royal estates.

In the later Carolingian period, the benefice came more often to be called *feudum*, a fief—the term that has given us the words *feudal* and *feudalism*. When the benefice became a fief, it also became hereditary. Though title to the fief remained with the lord who granted it, the fief itself passed, on the death of a vassal, to the vassal's heir, who inherited with it the obligations to serve the lord and his heirs.

The man who received a fief often got with it certain rights to govern the farmers who lived and worked on the lands that made it up. This practice, too, had its precedents. In late Roman times the emperors had often granted an *immunity* to those residing on their own estates—an understanding that imperial tax collectors or other law-enforcing officials would stay away from the inhabitants. Because the immunity exempted the farmers from onerous duties, it was hoped that they would enjoy their privileged status and therefore stay put and supply the emperor with predictable quantities of badly needed produce. The Frankish kings adopted this practice, sometimes extending it to lands of the church and even to those of private proprietors. By the tenth century an immunity meant that the king undertook to keep his officials off the privileged lands and that the holder of the lands would himself perform such governmental functions as collecting taxes, establishing police arrangements, and setting up a court of justice. He might keep the profits from fines or assessments.

From late Roman times, too, came the local offices of duke and count. Originally military commanders, they took over civil authority as the power of the central government relaxed. In Frankish times they were sometimes very powerful rulers, kings in all but name. In the disorders of the Carolingian decline, these offices gradually became hereditary; at the same time the dukes and counts were the vassals of the Carolingians. So the title and office, the duties of the vassal, and the fief (or territory that went with the office) all became hereditary.

Vassals and Lords

Feudalism and feudal practice did not extend uniformly over all of Europe. Northern France and the Low Countries were the most thoroughly feudalized areas, Germany much less so. Some pieces of land never became fiefs but remained the fully owned private property of the owners; these were called *allods*. Feudal practices varied from place to place and developed and altered with the passage of time.

Nonetheless, certain general conceptions were accepted almost everywhere. One of the most significant was that of a *feudal contract*. The lord (or *suzerain*, as he was often called) owed something to the vassal, just as the vassal owed something to the lord. When they entered into their relationship, the vassal rendered formal homage to his lord; that is, he became the lord's "man." He also promised him aid and counsel. *Aid* meant that he would appear when summoned, fully armed, and fight as a knight in the lord's wars, subject perhaps to limits on the number of days' service owed in any one year. *Counsel* meant that he would join with his fellow vassals—his *peers*, or social equals—to form the lord's court of justice, which alone could pass judgment on any one of them. He might also be required at his own expense to entertain his lord for a visit of specific length, and to give him money payments on special occasions—the marriage of the lord's eldest daughter, the knighting of his eldest son, or, later on, his departure on a crusade. The vassal also swore *fealty* (fidelity) to his lord. In his turn, the lord was understood to owe protection and justice to his vassal.

If the vassal broke this contract, the lord would have to get the approval of a court made up of the vassal's peers before he could proceed to a punishment, such as depriving the vassal of his fief (*forfeiture*). If the lord broke the contract, the vassal was expected to withdraw his homage and fealty in a public act of defiance before proceeding to open rebellion. Sometimes the contract

was written; sometimes it was oral; sometimes the ceremony included a formal *investiture* by the lord in which he would give his kneeling vassal a symbol of the fief that was being transferred to him—a twig or a bit of earth. When lord or vassal died, the contract had to be renewed with the successor. The son of a vassal, upon succeeding to his father's fief, often had to pay *relief*, a special and often heavy cash payment similar to a modern inheritance tax. If the vassal died without heirs, the fief would *escheat*, or revert to the lord, who could bestow it on another vassal or not, as he saw fit. If the vassal's heir was still a minor, the lord exercised the right of *wardship*, or guardianship, until the minor came of age; this meant that the lord received the revenues from the fief, and if he was unscrupulous he could milk it dry.

Within a feudal kingdom, the king theoretically occupied the top position in an imaginary pyramid of society. Immediately below him would be his vassals, men who held fiefs directly from the king, called *tenants-in-chief*. They in turn would be feudal lords; that is, they would give out various parts of their own property as fiefs to their own vassals. These men (the king's vassals' vassals) would be the king's *rear vassals*, and so were at the next lower levels of the theoretical pyramid. But they, too, would often have vassals, and so on down for many more levels in a process called *subinfeudation*. But this was only theory.

Practice was more complicated still. A tenant-in-chief might hold only a very small fief directly from the king and not be a very important person at all, while a vassal's vassal's vassal might be rich and powerful. The dukes of Normandy, who were vassals to the king of France, were for some centuries much stronger than the king. A person might receive fiefs from more than one lord, and so owe homage and fealty to both. What was he to do if one of his lords quarreled with the other and went to war? Which of his lords would have a prior right to count on his military help? This happened very often; one Bavarian count had twenty different fiefs held of twenty different lords. Gradually, therefore, there arose a new concept, that of a *liege lord*, the one to whom a vassal owed service ahead of any other. But in practice the difficulties often persisted. Even though feudal law became more subtle and more complex, armed might ultimately counted for more than legality.

Manorialism

These complex arrangements directly involved only the governing class who fought on horseback as mounted knights and whose fiefs consisted of landed property known as manors or estates. Even if we include their dependents, the total would hardly reach 10 percent of the population of Europe. Most of the other 90 percent of the people worked the land. In late Roman times, as we have seen, the large estate, owned by a magnate and worked by tenant farmers, had been called a latifundium. The tenant farmers, or coloni, were often descendants of small landowners who had turned over their holdings to the magnate in exchange for a guarantee of protection and a percentage of the crop. While the coloni were personally free, not slaves, they could not leave the ground they cultivated, nor could their children.

If the coloni lived in groups of houses close together, the latifundium could be described as a villa. Though conditions varied widely, we are not far wrong if we think of the late Roman latifundium becoming the medieval manor, the late Roman villa becoming the medieval village, and the late Roman coloni becoming the medieval serfs. As we shall see, the early German village community also contributed to the new social structure. While the Roman landed estate had often produced its food for sale at a profit in the town and city, the centuries of disorder beginning with the Germanic invasions led to a decline of commerce, of cities, and of agriculture for profit. The medieval manor usually produced only what was needed to feed its own population.

The oldest method of cultivation was the two-field system, alternating crops and fallow so that fertility could be recovered. Later, especially in grain-producing areas, a three-field system was devised—one field for spring planting, one for autumn planning, and the third lying fallow. Elsewhere—in the mountains, in wine-growing areas, in the "Celtic fringes" of Brittany and Wales, and in the new areas of pioneer settlement in Eastern lands—there were many variant agricultural techniques and social arrangements. Here, as so often, there was no "typical" medieval way.

On the manor, oxen had originally pulled the plow, but the invention of the horse collar (so that the horse would not strangle on the old-fashioned strap around his neck) and the use of horseshoes (which allowed horses to plow stony soil that hurt oxen's feet) helped make it possible to substitute horses for oxen. So did the increasing use of tandem harnessing, enabling the horses to work in single file instead of side by side. A heavy-wheeled plow also made its appearance in advanced areas.

The pattern of agricultural settlement varied from region to region. Insofar as a "typical" manor existed, each of its peasant families had holdings, usually scattered long strips of land in the large open fields. In theory this gave each family a bit of the good arable land, a bit of the less good land, a bit of woodland, and so on. The strips might be separated from each other by narrow, unplowed *balks*, but there were no fences, walls, or hedges. The lord of the manor had his own strips, his *demesne* (perhaps a quarter to a third of the land), reserved for the production of the food that he and his household needed. It was understood that the peasants had to work this demesne land for the lord, often three days a week throughout the year, except perhaps in harvest time, when the lord could command their services until his crops were safely in the barns. Of course, the size of the lord's household varied, depending on his importance in the feudal hierarchy. The

more important he was, the more armed men he had to feed, and the more dependents and servants they all had, the more numerous and bigger would be his fiefs, and the more peasants he would need to work the manors that made up those fiefs.

When a serf died, his son made the lord a payment (*heriot*) to inherit his father's right to cultivate the family strips. In exchange for permission to pasture their beasts in the lord's meadows, the serfs might perform other duties. They often had to dig ditches or maintain roads. They paid to have their grain ground at the lord's mill and their bread baked in his oven. They could not marry or allow their daughters to marry outside the manor without the lord's permission and usually the payment of a fine (*merchet*). Serfs, a hereditary caste of farm laborers, were bound to the soil. But they were not slaves; the lord could not sell them; they and their children descended with the land to the lord's heirs.

Undoubtedly the bulk of the hours of labor on the manor went directly into farming, mostly grain farming. But some of the manor's inhabitants were also craftsmen, such as blacksmiths or tanners, and they, too, cultivated their own plots of land. Each manor had at least one church of its own, with its priest. If the lord was a great lord, he might have several priests, including his own chaplain for the household and a village priest for the local church.

The organization of the countryside by manors developed earliest in eastern France and in parts of Italy and Germany. Still, even at its height, it did not include some parts of these and other European countries. In the large areas where manorialism did prevail, the old Roman landlord's economic power over his tenants had fused with the traditional Germanic village chief's political power, and by the eleventh century, with the governing rights that the lord received with his fief. The deep respect for custom often tended to prevent the lord's extorting more work from his serfs or more food than they traditionally owed him. But they had nowhere to appeal when the lord was oppressive. Custom prevailed in the lord's court of justice, where he or his steward sat in judgment on the serf-tenants, enforcing the traditional rules of the village community. Custom regulated the agreements among serfs for the use in common of plows and plow teams, which few could hope to own individually. Even though custom no doubt retarded inventiveness and stifled initiative, it was the main force that gave the serfs some sense that they were protected against unreasonable demands and cruelties.

By no means were all the peasants on every manor serfs, however. Some of them were freemen, called *franklins* in England, who virtually owned the land they worked. And between the freemen and the serfs there were probably always landless laborers who were not tied to the land as serfs, and peasants with dues so light that they were almost freemen.

The manor was not usually completely self-sufficient. Only rarely could the manorial forge have produced all the plowshares and other implements for farming and

LIFE IN THE COUNTRY

Selections from the *Capitulare de Villis* (Laws and Regulations of the Country) help to show what life may have been like in the countryside around the year 800. Scholars do not agree on precisely what these instructions, which were prepared for the guidance of stewards who administered royal properties in France, always meant or which part of present-day France they were applied to, though majority opinion holds that they probably were prepared by the king of Aquitaine, in southwestern France:

1. We wish that our estates which we have instituted to serve our needs discharge their services to us entirely and to no other men.
2. Our people shall be well taken care of and reduced to poverty by no one.
3. Our stewards shall not presume to put our people to their own service, either to force them to work, to cut wood, or to do any other task for them. And they shall accept no gifts from them, either horse, ox, cow, pig, sheep, little pig, lamb, or anything else excepting bottles of wine or other beverage, garden produce, fruits, chickens, and eggs.
4. If any of our people does injury to us either by stealing or by some other offense he shall make good the damage and for the remainder of the legal satisfaction he shall be punished by whipping, with the exception of homicide and arson cases which are punishable by fines. The stewards, for injuries of our men to other men, shall endeavor to secure justice according to the practices which they have, as is the law. Instead of paying fines our people, as we have said, shall be whipped. Freemen who live in our domains or estates shall make good the injuries they do according to their law and the fines which they have incurred shall be paid for our use either in cattle or in equivalent value.
5. When our stewards ought to see that our work is done—the sowing, plowing, harvesting, cutting of hay, or gathering of grapes—let each one at the proper season and in each and every place organize and oversee what is to be done that it may be done well. If a steward shall not be in his district or can not be in some place let him choose a good substitute from our people or another in high repute to direct our affairs that they may be successfully accomplished. And he shall diligently see to it that a trustworthy man is delegated to take care of this work.
6. We wish our stewards to give a tithe of all our products to the churches on our domains and that the tithe not be given to the churches of another except to those entitled to it by ancient usage. And our churches shall not have clerics other than our own, that is, of our people or our palace.

The *Capitulare* also reveal the detail in which life was administered:

40. Each steward shall always have on our estates for the sake of adornment unusual birds, peacocks, pheasants, ducks, pigeons, partridges, and turtledoves.
41. The buildings on our estates and the fences which enclose them shall be well taken care of and the stables and kitchens, bake-houses and presses shall be carefully ordered so that the workers in our service can perform their duties fittingly and very cleanly.
42. Each manor shall have in the store-room counterpanes, bolsters, pillows, bedclothes, table and bench covers, vessels of brass, lead, iron, and wood, andirons, chains, pot-hooks, adzes, axes, augurs, knives, and all sorts of tools so that it will not be necessary to seek them elsewhere or to borrow them....
43. For our women's work-shops the stewards shall provide the materials at the right time as it has been established, that is flax, wool, woad, vermilion dye, madder, wool-combs, teasels, soap, grease, vessels, and the other lesser things which are necessary there....
45. Each steward shall have good workmen in his district—iron-workers, goldsmiths, silversmiths, leatherworkers, turners, carpenters, shieldmakers, fishermen, fowlers or falconers, soap-makers, brewers who know how to make beer, cider, perry or any other beverage fit to drink, bakers who can make bread for our needs, net-makers who are skilled in making nets for hunting as well as fishing or for taking birds, and other workmen whose listing would be a lengthy matter.
46. They shall take good care of our walled game preserves which the people call parks and always repair them in time and on no account delay so that it becomes necessary to rebuild them. They shall do the same for all the buildings....
48. The wine-presses on our estates shall be well taken care of. The stewards shall see to it that no one presumes to press our grapes with his feet but that all is done cleanly and honestly.
49. The women's quarters, that is, their houses, heated rooms, and sitting rooms, shall be well ordered and have good fences around them and strong gates that our work may be done well.
50. Each steward shall see to it that there are as many horses in one stable as ought to be there and as many attendants as should be with them. And those stablemen who are free and hold benefices in that

district shall live off their benefices. Similarly if they are men of the domain who hold *mansi* they shall live off them. Those who do not have such shall receive maintenance from the demesne.

51. Each steward shall see to it that in no manner wicked men conceal our seed under the ground or do otherwise with the result that our harvests are smaller. And likewise, concerning other misdeeds, they shall watch them so that they can do no harm.

52. We wish that our stewards render justice to our *coloni* and serfs and to the *coloni* living on our estates, to the different men fully and entirely such as they are due.

Contemporary Civilization Staff of Columbia College, eds., *Introduction to Contemporary Civilization in the West*, 2nd ed. (New York: Columbia University Press, Courtesy of Columbia University Press.

all the weapons needed for defense, the manorial quarry all the stone, its forests all the lumber needed for building, and its fields and its animals everything necessary to eat or to wear. At least the iron that went into implements had to be bought, and often such luxuries as furs or salt or occasional spices had to be bought also. The manor, then, was only comparatively self-sufficient and unspecialized. It had surpluses and deficiencies that gave it the motivation and the means for trade with outsiders. It provided something above a bare minimum of livelihood, for at least a minority of the men and women who worked upon it.

Slavery also existed. All Germanic law codes prescribed enslavement as a penalty for many *delicts* (violations of laws or rights, hence *delinquents*). Since legal codes are the record of common practice, we have evidence that slavery was relatively commonplace, especially in Spain, Italy, and the eastern Mediterranean. The church recognized that slaves had souls, so it would intervene to some extent to protect slaves; but the church was often a major slaveholder itself and generally resisted movements for emancipation, since this would diminish its resources. However, slaves could be freed, thus adding to the ranks of freemen—as in Visigothic Spain, where they constituted a distinct legal class, indeed two classes of emancipates, or *liberti*. We have no reliable figures on the numbers of slaves or the extent of slavery, though it is believed that slavery declined after the collapse of the Roman Empire and was at its low point in the ninth century.

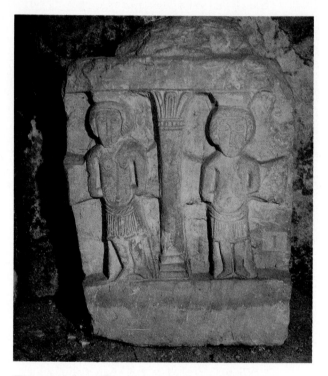

These sculptured figures are from the underground mausoleum at Poitiers of a seventh-century abbot, Mellebaude. Modeled on ancient tomb-chambers, this remarkable Merovingian sculpture shows two thieves who are to be crucified with Christ, each bound to a cross of his own. In Latin on a wall nearby is painted the inscription, "Everything goes from bad to worse, and the end of time is near." This sense of pessimism and the primitive nature of the figures reinforce the later tendency to refer to the early Middle Ages as a dark period of "the barbarians."
Giraudon/Art Resource

V   THE CIVILIZATION OF THE EARLY MIDDLE AGES IN THE WEST

In letters and in the arts, the early medieval centuries saw a severe decline in the skills that had characterized the Roman Empire, even in its latest periods. Judged by comparison with the achievements of Greek, Hellenistic, or Roman civilizations, or by those of the Byzantine and Muslim East, those of western Europe in these centuries may sometimes seem feeble or primitive. But this

is what one would expect in a world where life was often too turbulent to allow much leisure for the exercise of creative skills. The efficient Roman communication system had deteriorated. Cities, historically the homes of culture and of the commerce that makes culture possible and available, were often mere shells of the vibrant centers of communication they had once been. Technical skills were lost, as was command over Latin, the western European language of intellectuals

SLAVERY IN THE EARLY MIDDLE AGES

A Christian prelate, Theodore, drafted a set of rules pertaining to male and female slaves in seventh-century England. The following is from the second penitential book—that is, a book on penances arising from the failure to adhere to discipline— of Theodore at Canterbury, section XIII:

1. If he is compelled by necessity, a father has the power to sell his son of seven years of age into slavery; after that, he had not the right to sell him without his consent.
2. A person of fourteen [years] can make himself a slave.
3. A man may not take away from his slave money which he has acquired by his labor.
4. If the master of a male and a female slave joins them in marriage and the male slave or the female slave is afterward set free, and if the one who is in slavery cannot be redeemed, the one who has been set free may marry a free-born person.
5. If any freeman takes a female slave in marriage, he has not the right to put her away if they were formerly united with the consent of both.
6. If anyone acquires [as a slave] a free woman who is pregnant, the child that is born of her is free.
7. If anyone sets free a pregnant slave woman, the child which she brings forth shall be [in a state] of slavery.

Early Welsh law also speaks of slavery. For example, the so-called Welsh Canons, dating from c. 550–650, include entries such as these:

1. If anyone commits homicide by intention, he shall pay three female slaves and three male slaves and shall receive security....
4. If a slave kills a freeman, and this was through the freeman's fault, and if he was slain with a cudgel or an axe or a hoe or with a knife, that murderer shall be given over to the parents, and they shall have the power to do [with him] what they will.
5. If any master permits his slave to bear arms and he slays a freeman, the master shall be prepared to hand over the slave and another with him....

22. If any freeborn man or slave commits a theft by night and in the act of committing it is struck with a spear and killed, he who slays him shall have no need to make restitution....
38. If any slave kills another's slave, he shall remain alive as the joint property of the masters.

Published by Octagon Books, a division of Hippocrene Books, Inc.

and writers. No one spoke good Latin any more, and few could write it. The slowly developing vernacular languages—Romance-French or German—were written only infrequently, and usually hesitantly.

Yet a large question remains. Can we fairly use classical standards to judge the writing and art of a post-classical age, now evolving in many new directions? Most scholars today would be reluctant to do so, which is why we now reject the term *Dark Ages*. We now know enough about the original barbarian contributions to the culture of this period to dismiss old prejudices against them. Many barbarians loved and admired the Roman world that their fellow barbarians were destroying. They painstakingly kept alive, however crudely, the Roman literary and artistic tradition. Moreover, the widely traveled invading tribes brought with them art forms of their own—poetry, sculpture, and painting— that have only recently been widely appreciated by scholars.

Everywhere in the West, then, the story in general is the same, although it varies greatly in detail. The people of these centuries were gradually moving away from their Roman past, though still cherishing, and often trying with varying degrees of success to imitate, Roman models. They were also creating new and original writings and works of art that reflected their own barbarian past. While the Christian faith that the invaders took from the dwellers in the Roman Empire gave them a more permanent and firmer link with Rome itself and with its traditions than they would otherwise have had, they neither entirely absorbed the Roman heritage nor wholly abandoned their own traditions and practices.

Latin Literature

It was in Italy that the fight against the loss of the classical heritage was waged most vigorously and most successfully. Under the Ostrogothic king Theodoric (r. 493–

526), an admirer of the Greek and Latin cultural traditions, two distinguished intellectuals combated the general decline: Boethius and Cassiodorus.

Boethius (c. 480–524), unlike most of his contemporaries, knew both Greek and Latin. Learned and versatile, he advised Theodoric on many points. He gave detailed directions to the king's brother-in-law, ruler of the Burgundians, for the making of a water clock. A recognized authority on music, he selected the best available harpist to play at the court of Clovis, king of the Franks. He thwarted an effort of Theodoric's military paymaster to cheat the troops by showing that the paymaster had "sweated" the silver from the coins. He held the posts of consul (by then honorary, but still carrying enormous prestige) and of Master of the Offices, something very much like a prime minister and by no means honorary only.

Boethius planned a Latin translation of the works of Plato and Aristotle, and in the small portion that he completed he took care to make his translation as literal as possible. He also made the first efforts to apply to Christian theological writings the logical methods of Aristotle, writing works about the art of argument. These were to inspire scholars and thinkers who lived six hundred and more years after his death. Had Boethius survived to carry out his plans for rendering the greatest Greek philosophers into Latin, western Europe perhaps would not have been denied these materials for another five hundred years, and its intellectual development might have been speeded up. But only two years after making him Master of the Offices, Theodoric imprisoned Boethius on a charge of treason. After a year in jail, Boethius was executed at age forty-four, perhaps because he was sharply opposed to the Arian Christianity practiced by Theodoric and the Ostrogoths.

In jail he wrote his most famous work, *The Consolation of Philosophy*, a dialogue between himself in his cell and the female personification of Philosophy, who appears to him. Written in excellent Latin, the *Consolation* is a moving and noble book in which the prisoner seeks—and is helped by Philosophy to find—answers not only to why he is suffering injustice, but also to the larger questions of human life and death on earth and the relationship between humans and God. Filled with reminiscences of classical authors and so sometimes criticized for its lack of originality, the book dwells on the prevalence of suffering, on the fickleness of fortune—which often unjustly punishes the innocent—and on the transitoriness and relative worthlessness of worldly triumphs. Everything we gain here on earth, even fame, will vanish. Largely owing to this book, Boethius's fame grew, for *The Consolation of Philosophy* became one of the most popular schoolbooks of the Middle Ages.

Cassiodorus (c. 480–575) managed to stay in Theodoric's good graces and, like Boethius, became consul and Master of the Offices. He collected Theodoric's official correspondence. But his great ambition was to found a new Christian seminary in Rome, where the

Also preserved at Poitiers is the carved wooden bookstand owned by the Merovingian queen Radegund at the end of the sixth century. At the center of the carved reading surface is a lamb, representing Christ, and in each corner is the symbol of one of the four apostles: an eagle's head for John, a man's head for Matthew, a bull's head for Luke, and a lion's head for Mark. At the top, between two doves, is the Greek monogram for Christ, while at the bottom, also between two doves, is a cross in a circle. As in all Christian art, each decorative device carries a symbolic meaning that would have been well understood by contemporaries. *Giraudon/Art Resource*

sadly neglected classical subjects could be taught and where a revival of learning and scholarship might take place. The terrible disorders that accompanied Justinian's reconquest of Italy from the Goths between 535 and 554 made this impossible. Instead, Cassiodorus founded a monastery in southern Italy where he tried to keep learning alive in its Christian form. The monks copied by hand not only the Bible but the best pagan Latin authors: Cicero, Vergil, and the rest. Cassiodorus himself wrote books on spelling, to help the monastic scribes with their task; on the Psalms, to provide the biblical text with a classical commentary; and on the soul, following in the footsteps of Cicero and his Greek masters. Some of his monks translated Greek works into Latin, helping turn the monasteries into centers of rote learning. When monks elsewhere encountered Greek passages in texts, they often wrote, "Greek; it can't be read," giving rise to our expression for anything incomprehensible—"It's Greek to me."

Far more typical of the period, however, were the views of Pope Gregory the Great, whom we have already encountered as the talented administrator who kept the church alive and prevented Italy from falling into total chaos in the strife between the Lombards and the Eastern Empire. Practical in every way, Gregory was ready to abandon the classical past if he could bring more order into the barbarian and Christian present. "The same lips," he wrote one of his bishops, "cannot sound the praises of Jupiter and the praises of Christ," and he enjoined him to stop holding conferences where ancient literature was read. In Gregory's own writings, the same practical tendency appears; his *Dialogues* deal in four volumes with the lives and miracles of the Italian church fathers, providing edifying anecdotes to attract Christian readers away from pagan authors and toward the proper contemplation of their own salvation.

But perhaps the most important of Gregory's writings is his surviving correspondence, more than a thousand letters dating from the fourteen years of his papacy. Sent to all corners of the Christian world and dealing with every sort of problem in the management of the church and its relations with secular rulers, these letters reflect Gregory's humanity, commanding nature, enormous sense of the importance of his office, and even, at times, unexpected humor. No other pope of the early Middle Ages has left us so many letters, nor is there anything remotely resembling these documents as a vivid historical source for any other period that is so little known to us, both before and after they were written.

Away from Italy, the center of the Roman world, the survival and cultivation of Latin letters weakens. In Gaul, a highly Romanized province, there remained even during the invasions a cultivated group of Gallo-Roman aristocratic landowners and churchmen who still found it natural to communicate with each other in Latin. There were good poets among them, but perhaps the most distinguished writer of all was chiefly a prose stylist, Sidonius Apollinaris (fl. 455–c. 475).

Born of a family long prominent in imperial affairs and educated at the school of Lyon (still a major Roman provincial center), Sidonius eventually became bishop of Auvergne in south-central France during the invasions of Visigoths and Burgundians, while Huns and Franks were active nearby. Yet in 147 letters, written with an eye to preservation and future publication, Sidonius—essentially an aristocrat in his habits and tastes—writes almost as if nothing very alarming were happening in the outside world, and as if he and his fellow nobles, well born and well educated, still had control of what would happen in the future. With gentlemanly distaste, he refers to the Germanic invaders as underbred and coarse. He had no apprehension that they were bringing with them the doom of Sidonius and all his friends. He sneers at one of his fellow nobles who had learned the language of the barbarians. Still, his letters correct the oversimplified view that the barbarian inroads invariably produced chaotic social upheaval.

By the time of the Frankish triumph in the next generation, the Gallo-Roman culture that Sidonius so proudly represented had virtually died. There was now very little literary activity. We have some moving sixth-century Latin hymns and descriptive poems by a writer known as Fortunatus, who deeply influenced Radegund of Poitiers, one of the first Frankish women to found and rule over a nunnery in France, and a poet in her own right. We have the history in which Gregory, bishop of Tours, chronicles the unedifying behavior of the Merovingian rulers. Gregory's Latin prose would have shocked Sidonius, but there is a vigorous if primitive quality about him, a mixture of credulity, native goodness, and calm acceptance of atrocities that gives the reader deep insight into the Merovingian age.

In Spain, too, farther from Rome than Gaul though still a Romanized province, there was a good deal of writing in Latin, at least into the seventh century, which saw the *Etymologies* of Isidore (c. 570–636), archbishop

Contrasting details from two sculptured tombs in the crypt of Jouarre, in the Abbaye St. Paul, east of Paris. Crypts (underground chapels) were common at the time. On the left is the tomb of Agilbert, of the late seventh century, with a poignant representation of men and women praying at the Last Judgment, their arms upraised. It is believed the artist was an Egyptian Christian who had fled from the Arab Muslim conquest. On the right is the tomb of Theodechilde, of the eighth century, with carved shells and beautifully lettered Latin, in the Roman tradition. Thus an intense, emotional carving could be found side-by-side with the clean composition of classical art. Since Jouarre had close connections with Britain, similar sculptural styles are found in the crosses of northern England and of Ireland.
Giraudon/Art Resource

THE VENERABLE BEDE

Bede tells us how, in 627, when the still-pagan king Edwin of Northumbria had received a letter from the pope, and a Latin missionary was at his court urging him to accept Christianity, he called his *witenagemot* (council of wise men) on the matter. One of Edwin's counselors then said:

Man's life here on earth, O King, seems to me—so far as its uncertainties go—just the same as if, when you were sitting at dinner in the wintertime with your companions in arms and their servants, and a great fire had been kindled in the middle of the hall, and the hall was warm with its heat, but outside all about there raged the storms of winter rain and snow, a sparrow might come to the house, and fly through it swiftly, entering at one window and flying out at another. For the time while the bird is inside the house, it feels no chill from the winter blast, but after this tiny spell of fair weather has passed, that lasts only for a moment, the sparrow quickly passes again from winter to winter, and so is lost to your view. In the same way, this life of men comes into being for a brief moment, but what follows it and what went before it we certainly do not know. So if this new teaching [Christianity] has brought us anything surer to cling to, I think it should be followed.

Bede, *Historia Ecclesiastica Gentis Anglorum,* book II, chap. xiii (London and New York: Loeb Classical Library, 1930), I, 283 ff. Translation ours.

Soon after, Edwin was converted. And the metaphor about human life on earth remains moving and effective more than thirteen centuries later.

of Seville, a sort of encyclopedia. Isidore became perhaps the most influential and certainly the most representative literary figure of his time. His work was known in Ireland by the middle of the seventh century, and because the patristic texts (that is, texts written by eminent theologians called "Fathers of the Church") were often used during the Middle Ages by writers on church liturgy and law, Isidore's listing of the cleric's duties became so well established that it was accorded semiofficial status by the middle of the twelfth century.

Besides works that can be attributed with reasonable accuracy to a specific writer, there were many accounts of the lives of the saints, known as *hagiographies*. Many people read or learned about the saints through these anonymous works. Homely tales about the virtues of the saints as well as rousing exhortations to bravery in the manner of the early Christians created what may be the most influential literary sources of the period. When the church eventually canonized many hundreds of early leaders in the development of Christian theology or administration, this hagiography was heavily drawn upon.

The seventh century, then, saw the rapid decline of literary activity in the classical vein on the Continent. For a different spirit, destined eventually to restore Roman culture to the Continent, one turns to Britain, which had produced no Latin authors before the barbarian invasions. Christianity came to Britain, as we have seen, in three waves: one with the Roman troops, which virtually died out; one from Ireland, where it was of Gallic origin; and the third from Rome, at the end of the sixth century and the beginning of the seventh, in the mission sent by Gregory the Great. In England Christianity produced the first original writing in Latin. The combined influence of the Celtic and the Roman traditions brought such fruitful results that by the end of the eighth century missionaries from Britain stimulated a revival on the Continent—sponsored by Charlemagne himself, who provided the necessary interest and patronage.

Of several cultivated writers, the greatest was Bede (c. 673–735), called the Venerable for his learning. Abbot of his monastery, he could read Hebrew and Greek, knew the Latin writings of the church fathers intimately, and wrote the famous *Ecclesiastical History of the English People*, the story of the spread of Christianity in England from the arrival in 597 of the missions sent by Gregory down to 731, almost to the moment of Bede's death. Written in Latin of astonishing vigor and purity, it tells almost everything we know of the progress of the new religion among the pagan Anglo-Saxons, about the church's relationship with the Anglo-Saxon kings, and about the foundation of the many monastic houses, where monks found a shelter for themselves and their books. Bede's own even-tempered personality shines through the work, which sometimes rises to true poetic greatness.

Churchmen from Britain in particular helped make

possible the great flowering of Latin letters that took place under Charlemagne. Alcuin of York (735–c. 804), who had studied under a pupil of Bede, went to Charlemagne's court in 781 and helped to transform the palace school there into a serious and practical educational institution where men studied the seven liberal arts: grammar, rhetoric, dialectic (the art of argument), arithmetic, geometry, astronomy, and music. Alcuin wrote much prose and verse and took the lead in reviving biblical scholarship and in teaching such practical subjects as legible handwriting to the scribes, who now began to copy manuscripts in monasteries. We owe the survival of much of Latin literature to the efforts of these Carolingian scribes.

The foundations laid by scholars such as Alcuin permitted their successors in the next two generations, after Charlemagne's empire had disintegrated, to write history, poetry, saints' lives, works on theology and ethics, and vast numbers of personal letters in Latin. In new monastic centers the literary work made possible by the British immigrants who had been responsible for the "Carolingian Renaissance" went on, and the continuity of knowledge in Western civilization was assured.

Vernacular Literature: Beowulf

Britain's distance from Rome and its failure to become completely Latinized during antiquity allowed it to profit greatly from the double wave of Latin Christian missionaries—Celtic and papal—and so provide the needed stimulus for the Carolingian Latin literary revival. But the thinness of the Latin veneer probably encouraged the Angles, Saxons, and Jutes to produce a literature in their own language (called Anglo-Saxon or Old English). In contrast, the continental former Roman provinces were too inhibited by the overpowering prestige of Latin and perhaps also delayed by less stable political conditions than prevailed in Britain. Many writers in England did not hesitate to write in their own language. Sometimes they were translators; Boethius's *Consolation of Philosophy* was rendered into Old English, and King Alfred the Great himself translated Bede's *Ecclesiastical History*. Sometimes they were original writers, setting down a group of proverbs, or the life of a saint, or a chronicle, or—in verse—an account of one battle or another.

By far the most remarkable Old English literary survival is *Beowulf*, a poem of almost 3,200 lines, preserved in only a single manuscript in the British Museum, written down about the year 1000. Hundreds of scholars have written thousands of pages about this poem; almost every statement about it might be questioned by some authority.

It is clear that the poem was composed well before the date of the surviving manuscript, perhaps as early as about 680 (it includes historical characters from the 500s), perhaps as late as 800 or even later. Until 1939 some scholars thought it had been composed in Nor-

thumbria, some in Mercia; but in that year a spectacular archaeological discovery at Sutton Hoo in Essex (East Anglia) turned up the ship-tomb of a king of the East Angles dating from the late seventh or early eighth century and containing a harp, jewels, and armor like those described in *Beowulf*, which also includes a description of a ship-funeral. So now some scholars think the poem may be of East Anglian origin. Some argue fiercely that the poem was written by a single author, others that it is a composite; some that it is a pagan poem with Christian interpolations, others that it breathes a wholly Christian spirit; some think that it has two parts, some six, some three. The poem has been described as "a museum for the antiquarian, a source-book for the historian, a treatise for the student of Christian thought, and a gymnasium for the philologist." It is, however, also unmistakably a poem meant for oral recitation.

The Arts

Like literature, the arts also gradually moved away from the standardized Roman forms toward newer achievements that were introduced as the barbarians merged their arts with those of the lands they settled. The early great churches of such important imperial cities as Milan or Trier were still large rectangular structures taken over from the secular architecture of the Romans, but innovations were tried for certain smaller Christian structures, especially baptisteries, which were detached from the main church. Some were square, others many-sided; rich mosaic decoration became common. As soon as a barbarian tribe was firmly established in its new territory, its kings, as a matter of prestige, built churches—often small, and generally imitative of the Roman models. While most of these structures have dis-

Viking jewelry was both precise and ornate. This shawl buckle of bronze and gold shows the complexity and skill of Viking art.
Statens Historiska Museum, Stockholm, Photo by Sóren Hallgren

BEOWULF

Beowulf begins in Denmark, where it tells of the founding of the Danish royal line and the building of a great hall by King Hrothgar. The hall is repeatedly raided by a savage monster, Grendel, who seizes and eats the Danish warriors as they lie asleep after dinner, until from over the sea in southern Sweden comes a hero, Beowulf. He lies in wait for the monster and in single combat so severely grips his hand that Grendel has to flee, leaving his entire arm, ripped out at the socket, in Beowulf's hands. The wound is fatal, but Grendel's mother, more terrifying than her son, tries to avenge him. Beowulf has to slay her at the bottom of a wild and lonely lake. The Danes celebrate in delight. Beowulf returns home, becomes a king, and dies in a victorious combat with a dragon. Though *Beowulf* exalts heroic behavior, it is deeply concerned with the transitoriness of human life. The climax of all Beowulf's heroism, and the end of the poem, is the hero's death and funeral.

Here, in a famous passage, Hrothgar's queen, Wealhtheow, thanks Beowulf for killing Grendel:

To him she carried the cup, and asked in gracious words
if he would care to drink; and to him she presented
twisted gold with courtly ceremonial—
two armlets; a corselet and many rings,
and the most handsome collar in the world.
I have never heard that any hero had a jewel
to equal that.

　　Applause echoed in the hall.
Wealhtheow spoke these words before the company:
"May you, Beowulf, beloved youth, enjoy
with all good fortune this necklace and corselet,
treasures of the people; may you always prosper;
win renown through courage, and be kind in your
　　counsel
to these boys [her sons]; for that, I will reward you
　　further.
You have ensured that men will always sing

your praises, even to the ends of the world,
as far as oceans still surround cliffs,
home of the winds. May you thrive, O prince,
all your life. I hope you will amass
a shining hoard of treasure. O happy Beowulf,
be gracious in dealing with my sons.
Here, each warrior is true to the others,
gentle of mind, loyal to his lord;
the thanes are as one, the people all alert,
the warriors have drunk well. They will do as I ask.

　　Then Wealhtheow retired to her seat
beside her lord. That was the best of banquets.

Beowulf, II, 1190–1196, 1215–1234, trans. Kevin Crossley-Holland. Reprinted by permission of Farrar, Straus & Giroux, Inc., and Macmillan & Co. Ltd. Translation © 1968 by Kevin Crossley-Holland; introductory matter © 1968 by Bruce Mitchell.

appeared, we know from contemporary written accounts and archaeological research that they often had domes and tin or gilded bronze roof tiles that shone in the sun.

To find clear-cut examples of the kind of art the barbarians brought with them, it is easiest to turn to goldsmithing and jewelry. Fleeing before the Huns, the Germans who had settled along the shores of the Black Sea brought with them objects made by local craftsmen working in an Iranian or other Eastern tradition and characterized by brilliant color and the use of gems (often from as far away as India) or colored glass for ornamentation. In the Roman Empire, the tribes, notably the Ostrogoths, continued those arts. The Vikings also produced magnificent jewelry—sword hilts, brooches, pendants—often embellished with gold, silver, and niello, in which silver, copper, lead, and sulfur were combined.

To understand the influences exerted by the Byzantine outpost of the exarchate at Ravenna in particular, we must remember that between 642 and 752 virtually all the popes were of Greek or Syrian origin. These popes surely sponsored imports from the East and fostered the continued popularity of Eastern objects. The presence in the royal funeral-ship at Sutton Hoo of a massive round silver plate made at Byzantium in 491–518 and of two silver spoons with Greek inscriptions emphasizes the continuous contacts between the barbarians and the East.

The influence of the East, greatly stimulated by the influx of barbarians, led to the gradual abandonment of realistic representation of humans and beasts in art. Imported Byzantine silver, ivories, and textiles, as well as Byzantine monuments like those of Ravenna, on Italian soil, helped speed the change in styles. The Carolingian period brought a new flowering of the arts. Surviving

THE EARLY MIDDLE AGES IN WESTERN EUROPE

monuments in Italy gave the artists some of their inspiration, and Charlemagne's ability to attract the best craftsmen from everywhere in Europe enabled them to put their ideas into practice. Paintings and mosaics in Roman churches illustrated for worshipers what could be made of Christian subjects treated in the classical style.

Wall painting and mosaics are fixed monuments, and can be seen only by a traveler; but books are transportable, and it was largely through book illustration—the illumination of manuscripts—that inspirations from one region or one school could intermingle in other regions with influences from other schools. So north Italian books that embodied all these classical and Byzantine influences traveled across the Alps into Gaul and into Britain with Gregory the Great's missionaries. In due course the same influences penetrated into Germany.

Charlemagne himself made five trips to Italy. Lombards from northern Italy joined Anglo-Saxons like Alcuin of York (735–804) at a court that had no permanent residence during the long years of continual campaigning but that settled at last at Aachen in the Rhineland in 794. Here the new royal (soon imperial) residence was built at forced-draft speed. To Aachen came Romans, Lombards, Greeks from southern Italy and probably from Byzantium itself, Syrians, Anglo-Saxons, Irish, Spaniards from the Visigothic parts of Spain, Jews, Arabs, and the inhabitants of Gaul and Germany.

Charlemagne enjoyed receiving foreign travelers, many of them, especially officials, bringing rich gifts—relics, books, textiles, jewels. In 796 arrived a treasure trove captured from the Avars, who had been pillaging for two centuries. It filled sixteen oxcarts. The most sensational present was sent in 802 by the caliph at Baghdad, Harun al Rashid—a white elephant, Abu'l Abbas, who became a general favorite at Aachen and whose bones remained a wonder for many centuries

Eastern influences contributed to the gradual abandonment of the realistic representation of humans and beasts in art. This change is shown by a set of stucco statues in the front of the church of Santa Maria in Valle at Cividale in northern Italy. These saints were carved by sculptors whose exceptional skills would have permitted them to do almost anything they chose. The detail is realistic, which had led scholars to date the statues from about 800 and to ascribe them to Byzantine artists working in Italy. But at the same time, art was more commonly becoming abstract, less concerned with exact detail—both cruder visually and more challenging emotionally. Compare the Cividale figures with the stone *stele*, or tomb slab, from Germany which is perhaps half a century earlier. On one side (not shown) the stele depicted a warrior; on the other, shown here, Christ was also depicted as a warrior. Contrast this with the fifth-century mosaic of Christ as a warrior in Chapter 4. The stele is now in the Rheinisches Landesmuseum in Bonn.
EPA/Art Resource

after he died. Harun also sent Charlemagne a clock of gilded bronze with twelve mounted mechanical knights who, on the stroke of noon, emerged from twelve doors that shut behind them. Perfumes, silken tents, oriental robes abounded. Charlemagne had a good many beautiful daughters, whom the gentle, aging Alcuin nicknamed "the crowned doves that flit about the chambers of the palace" (and against whom he warned his students). The exotic atmosphere of the court remained a vivid memory for many centuries after the glory had departed.

Reflecting upon the Carolingian artistic explosion as well as upon a galaxy of writers that ranges from Boethius and Pope Gregory the Great to Isidore of Seville, the Venerable Bede, and the author of *Beowulf*, no scholar would now seriously maintain that the early Middle Ages in the West were "dark." Troubled, yes; often agonizingly wretched, yes; but certainly not dark.

This superb example of mosaic art shows Constantine IV (r. 668–685). The mosaic, from the seventh century, is in the Basilica of St. Apollinaris in Classe, near Ravenna, Italy.
Scala New York/Florence

Charlemagne's decision to adopt southern building principles revolutionized architecture in northern Europe. Having traveled in Italy, he used Rome and Ravenna as models when he had his Palatine Chapel constructed at Aachen in 792–805. Here Byzantine sophistication was combined with dramatic and blunt geometrical strength. The chapel and Charlemagne's marble throne are still in place today.
Photo Ann Münchow

The Church of San Apollinaris in Classe, near Ravenna, shows how a sixth-century Christian church evolved from the style of the Roman basilica. Between 642 and 752 almost all the popes were of Greek or Syrian origin, and these Eastern popes sponsored many stylistic imports from the East, especially at Ravenna, the Byzantine outpost of the exarchate. The round tower shown here was added in the tenth century.
Art Resource

A CELTIC FLOWERING

Historians once referred to the early Middle Ages as a "Celtic twilight," for little was known about the literature and oral traditions of the time. In more recent years medieval European thought has been extended to include areas once dismissed as the Celtic fringe, which included Brittany. One body of material that has been reevaluated are the eleven stories collectively known as *The Mabinogion,* which were preserved in two Welsh collections, the White Book of Rhydderch and the Red Book of Hergest. Rediscovered in the sixteenth century, these stories were inaccurately edited and translated in the nineteenth century and ultimately made known in a form as near to the original as can be recovered in 1948. The title is modern—a *mabinog* was a literary apprentice, and not all the stories came down through the bards—but the stories show both the influence of other oral traditions, especially the French, and a largely idiomatic Celtic expression similar to the epic romances of the Vikings. The host of circumstantial detail, the sly sense of storytelling, and the emphasis on the gruesome and cruel were typical of tales meant to be recited. The second of the Four Branches of the Mabinogi tells of a war between the Irish and the Welsh, with all the encrustations of legend:

The terms of truce were drawn up, and the house was built big and roomy. But the Irish planned a ruse. The ruse they planned was to fix a peg on either side of every pillar of the hundred pillars that were in the house, and to fix a hide bag on each peg, and an armed man was in every one of them. Efnisien came in ahead of the host of the Island of the Mighty, and scanned the house with fierce, ruthless looks, and he perceived the hide bags along the posts. "What is in this bag?" he said, to one of the Irish. "Flour, friend," said he. He felt about him till he came to his head, and he squeezed his head till he felt his fingers sink into the brain through the bone. And he left that one and put his hand upon another, and asked, "What is here?" "Flour," said the Irishman. He played the same trick on every one of them, until of all the two hundred men he had left alive but one: and he came to him and asked, "What is here?" "Flour, friend," said the Irishman. And he felt about him until he came to his head, and he squeezed that one's head as he had squeezed the heads of the others. He could feel armour on that one's head. He left him not till he had killed him.

The Mabinogion, trans Gwyn Jones and Thomas Jones (London: Everyman's Library, 1968), pp. 35–36. Reproduced by permission of David Campbell Publishers Ltd.

Summary

In the fifth century the structure of Roman government in the West collapsed under the pressure of invasion and migration by Germanic tribes. Much of the Roman heritage, however, was preserved by the church and the barbarians' own reverence for Roman civilization.

The Franks founded the most lasting political entity to arise from the ruins of Roman power. In alliance with the papacy, the Frankish king Charles the Great (Charlemagne) sought to revive the Roman Empire in the West.

In the tenth century Norse invasions severely disrupted Britain, Ireland, and northern France. By the year 1000 those invasions had died down and medieval Europe had begun to take shape.

Feudalism was the system of social and political arrangements that replaced the centralized Roman administration. Basically, it was a means of coping with the absence of strong central government. Local lords ruled over the peasants on their estates. In turn, these lords were the vassals of other lords, meaning that they owed them allegiance and services. Still other lords might be above these. This complex system varied from one part of Europe to another.

Most of Europe was organized into units called manors, owned and ruled by a noble or by the church. Most of the peasants on these manors were serfs, hereditary laborers who could not leave the land they worked. In return for protection given by the lord of the manor, the serfs were required to fulfill various obligations and hand over part of their crops. In time many lords came to prefer cash payments, so that they could purchase goods that the manor could not produce.

Early medieval culture was a blend of barbarian and Roman influences. Most serious writing was in Latin, especially in Italy and Gaul. Latin also enjoyed a revival in eighth-century England. Literary use of the vernacular languages was rare except in England, where the remarkable epic poem *Beowulf* was written in Old English.

The arts of this period combined Roman, German, and Byzantine elements. Under Charlemagne there was a significant artistic revival.

6

Byzantium and Islam

At the far southeastern corner of Europe, on a little tongue of land still defended by a long line of massive walls and towers, there stands a splendid city. Istanbul it is called now, a Turkish form for three Greek words meaning "to the city." After 330, when the first Christian Roman emperor Constantine the Great made it his capital, it was often called Constantinople, the city of Constantine, but it also retained its ancient name— Byzantium. For more than eleven hundred years thereafter it remained the capital of the Eastern Roman Empire, falling to the Ottoman Turks in 1453.

The waters that surround it on three sides are those of the Sea of Marmora, the Bosporus, and the city's own sheltered harbor, the Golden Horn. A few miles to the north, up the narrow, swift-flowing Bosporus, lies the entrance to the Black Sea. To the southwest of the city, the Sea of Marmora narrows into the Dardanelles, a long passage into the Aegean, the island-studded inlet of the Mediterranean. The Dardanelles, the Sea of Marmora, and the Bosporus connect the Black Sea with the Mediterranean and separate Europe from Asia. Together, these are the Straits, perhaps the most important strategic waterway in European diplomatic and military history. The city dominates the Straits. To the Slavs of Russia and the Balkans, who owe to it their religion and much of their culture, this city has always been Tsargrad— city of the emperor. It was the center of a civilization similar in many ways to that of medieval western Europe, yet startlingly different in others.

I BYZANTIUM: THE STATE

The Emperor

After Constantine, Byzantium called itself New Rome. Its emperors ruled in direct succession from Augustus. Its population, predominantly Greek, called itself Rhomaian, Roman. Yet many non-Roman elements—Christian, Greek, Armenian—became increasingly important in Byzantine society. A Roman of the time of Augustus would have been ill at ease in Byzantium. After Constantine had become a Christian, the emperor was no longer a god; but he was ordained of God, and his power remained sacred. As there could be only one god in heaven, so there could be only one emperor on earth. The pagan tradition of the god-emperor was thus modified, not abandoned.

In theory, the will of God manifested itself in the unanimous consent of the people, the Senate, and the army to the choice of each new emperor. A reigning emperor usually followed the Roman practice and chose his heir, often his son, by co-opting him during his own lifetime. When an emperor selected someone not his son, public opinion required that he adopt him formally.

Each new emperor was raised aloft on a shield as a sign of army approval, thus becoming *Imperator* (commander-in-chief). By the midfifth century, he might also be formally crowned by the highest dignitary of the church, the patriarch of Constantinople, and he would swear to defend the Christian faith. In the seventh century the emperor began to call himself *Basileus*, King of Kings, in token of his military victory over the Persians. Later still he added the term *Autocrat*, for the emperor was an absolute ruler. Empresses bore corresponding feminine titles and in general played an important role. Three times in Byzantine history women ruled alone. While Byzantine dynasties sometimes lasted several centuries, politicians and the mob often intervened. They imprisoned and exiled emperors, murdered them, blinded or mutilated them (which made them ineligible to rule again), and then enthroned their own candidates. Revolution was viewed as the proper recourse against imperial tyranny.

An elaborate and rigid code of etiquette governed every movement the emperor made every day of the year. So complex were the rules of imperial life that books were written to describe them. The emperor's subjects remained silent in his presence. The emperor spoke and gave commands through simple, brief, and established formulas. When given gifts, subjects hid their hands beneath their cloaks, a Persian gesture implying that the touch of a mere human hand would soil the emperor. Those admitted to an audience approached with their arms held fast by officials and ceremoniously fell on their faces in homage when they reached the throne. On public occasions the emperor was acclaimed in song, to the sound of silver trumpets.

The "sacred palace," the emperor's residence, was the center of the state, and the officials of the palace were the most important functionaries of the state— administrative, civil, and military. All officials had a title that gave them a post in the palace as well as a rank among the nobility. At Byzantium many of the greatest and most influential officials were eunuchs—or *castrati*—(including Justinian's highly successful general Narses, who recaptured Rome, Naples, and Ravenna). This was an oriental feature of the state that astonished Westerners and made them uneasy. There was never a prime minister as such, though in practice an imperial favorite often controlled policy.

Despite such complex organization, the early emperors were at times threatened by the people of Constantinople. In the Nika revolt of 532 Justinian might have lost his throne had it not been for the coolness and bravery of his celebrated empress, Theodora, who said,

Now, above all other times, is a bad time to flee, even if we get away safely. Once a man has seen the light, he must surely die; but for a man who has been an emperor to become a refugee is intolerable. May I never be separated from the purple [the symbol of imperial rank] and may I no longer live on that day when those who meet me shall not call me mistress. Now if you wish to save yourself, O Emperor, that is easy. For we have much money: there is

These detailed mosaics from the Basilica of San Vitale in Ravenna, both from the sixth century, show the emperor Justinian and his wife, the empress Theodora. Theodora (c. 500–547) played a major role in the long theological debates of the time.
Scala/Art Resource

the sea, here are the boats. But think whether after you have been saved you may not come to feel that you would have preferred to die. As for me, I like a certain old proverb that says: royalty is a good shroud.*

The Law

As the direct agent of God, the emperor was responsible for preserving the tradition of Roman law. Only the emperor could modify the laws already in effect or pro-

---

* Quoted in Procopius, *History of the Wars* (Cambridge, Mass.: Harvard University Press, 1961). I. xxiv, 35–38. Our translation as adapted from H. B. Dewing.

claim new ones. From time to time the emperor ordered the redrafting and recompiling of the statute books; thus he had on hand an immensely powerful instrument for preserving and enhancing power.

Justinian (r. 527–565) between 528 and 533 ordered his lawyers to dispose of obsolete, repetitious, and conflicting enactments, thus codifying existing Roman law. His *Code* included all legislation since Hadrian (r. 117–138). The authoritative opinions of legal experts were collected in the *Digests*, an even bulkier work. The *Institutes*, a handbook for students, served as an introduction to both compilations. All these were set down in the Latin in which they had been issued, though Justinian's own laws, the *Novels*, or newly passed enactments, appeared in Greek. In the eighth century a new collection modified Justinian's work in accordance with Christian attitudes toward the family and with the decreasingly Roman and increasingly Greek and oriental character of the Empire. Under Leo VI, the Wise (r. 886–912), a new collection rejected much that dated from an earlier period, when the absolutism of the emperor had been less developed.

In the Byzantine Empire, justice could be rendered only in the emperor's name. The emperor was the supreme judge, and rendering justice was perhaps his most important function. Subordinate officials handed down decisions only by virtue of the power the emperor delegated to them, and the emperors themselves often rendered judgement in quite ordinary cases brought to them by their subjects.

The emperors of the later ninth century took great care in the systematic appointment of judges and created a kind of legal aid bureau to enable the poor of the provinces to make appeals to the capital. Judges were obliged to render, write out, and sign all decisions. New courts were set up, and new officials were created. Later, even in the provinces, side by side with the martial law administered by the local commanding general, soldiers could be tried in civil courts for civil offenses.

War

As defenders of the faith against hostile invaders, the Byzantine emperors fought one war after another for eleven hundred years. Sometimes the invaders were moving north and west from Asia: Persians in the seventh century; Arabs (adherents of the new Islamic religion) from the seventh century on; and Turks beginning in the eleventh century. The Empire was often shaken by these blows. Syria and Egypt, Roman for more than seven hundred years, were lost forever to the Arabs in the seventh century. But Charles Martel's victory in 732 was a far less significant check on the Muslims than was the victory of the Byzantine emperor Leo III, who had broken a major Arab siege of Constantinople in 717–718, fifteen years earlier.

Byzantium thus absorbed the heaviest shock of Eastern invasions and cushioned the West against them. The Byzantine state was also engaged on all its frontiers in almost constant warfare against a variety of Asian enemies: the Huns of the fifth century, the Avars of the sixth and seventh, the Bulgars of the seventh and succeeding centuries, the Magyars of the ninth and later centuries, and the Pechenegs and Cumans of the eleventh, twelfth, and thirteenth centuries. All these peoples were initially Turkic, Finnish, or Mongol nomads, at home for days at a time on their swift horses.

Sometimes the enemies were native Europeans, like the Slavs, who from the sixth century filtered gradually south into the Empire in a steady flow that eventually covered the entire Balkan peninsula with Slavic settlement. In the northeastern part of the peninsula just south of the Danube, the Slavs were conquered by the Hunnic tribe of the Bulgars but slowly absorbed their conquerors. These Bulgars, and much later the Slavic Serbs, fought exhausting wars against Byzantium.

So did the Russians, (or Varangians), another Slavic people, whose Scandinavian upper class was gradually absorbed into a Slavic lower class. They first assaulted Byzantium by sea in 860, having sailed across the Black Sea; they several times repeated the attack. (The Varangians, actually Vikings who moved through Russia, eventually formed the bodyguard of the Byzantine emperors.) Beginning in the eleventh century, the enemies were western Europeans: Normans from the southern Italian state in Italy and Sicily; crusaders from France, Germany, and Italy; freebooting commercial adventurers from the new Italian cities seeking to extract economic concessions by force or to increase the value of the concessions they already held.

For more than seven hundred years after Constantine, until the late eleventh century, when both Turks and Normans inflicted serious defeats, the Byzantines held their own. Though hostile forces sometimes swarmed to the foot of the walls or threatened from across the Straits, Constantinople itself remained inviolable until 1204. In that year it was taken for the first time by a mixed force of Venetian traders eager for profit, and French, Italian, and German crusaders, who had set out to fight the Muslims in Palestine and had been detoured.

Only a state with phenomenally good armies and navies could have compiled so successful a military record. From all periods of Byzantine history, there survive studies of the art of war, discussing new ways of fighting and new weapons. The Byzantines were adaptable, learning and applying lessons from their enemies. Often commanded by the emperor in person, carefully recruited and thoroughly trained, well armed and equipped, entertained by bands playing martial music, served by medical and ambulance corps, by a signal corps with flashing mirrors, and by intelligence agencies far more competent than those of their rivals, the Byzantine armies, though occasionally defeated, by and large maintained their superiority.

The same is almost as true of the Byzantine navies. The appearance of a Muslim fleet in the eastern Mediterranean in the seventh century forced a naval reorganization by the Byzantines, who by the tenth century had recaptured their former control of these waters. In the eleventh century, like many Byzantine institutions, the navy suffered a decline from which it never recovered. Gradually, the developing Italian merchant cities replaced Byzantium as the great Mediterranean naval power; this was one of the main causes of the Empire's downfall. At its height, however, the Byzantine fleet played a major role in imperial defense. It was equipped with one of the most deadly weapons of the Middle Ages: Greek fire, a chemical compound squirted from tubes or siphons in the shape of lion's heads mounted on the prows of the Byzantine ships, which

THEOPHILUS ON JUSTICE

The emperor Theophilus (r. 829–842) appeared every week on horseback at a given church and handed down judgments so fair and equitable that they have passed into legend:

One day when the Emperor appeared, a poor woman threw herself at his feet in tears, complaining that all light and air had been shut off from her house by a huge and sumptuous new palace which a high official of the police was building next door. Moreover, this official was the brother of the Empress. But the Emperor paid no heed to this. He ordered an instant inquiry, and when he found that the woman had told the truth, he had the guilty man stripped and beaten in the open street, commanded the palace to be torn down, and gave the land on which it stood to the woman. Another time, a woman boldly seized the bridle of the horse which the Emperor was riding, and told him that the horse was hers. As soon as Theophilus got back to the palace, he had her brought in and she tes-

tified that the general of the province where she lived had taken the horse away from her husband by force and had given it to the Emperor as a present to curry favor with him. Then he had sent the rightful owner of the horse into combat with the infantry, where he had been killed. When the general was haled before the Emperor and was confronted by the woman, he finally admitted his guilt. He was dismissed from his post, and part of his property was confiscated and given to the plaintiff.

Quoted in Charles Diehl, "La Légende de Théophile," *Serminarium Kondakovianum* (Belgrade: Institute Imeni N.P., Kondakova, 1931), *Annales* IV, 35, Our translation.

Byzantine Empire

- Territory lost by Byzantine Empire between 565 (death of Justinian) and 1000
- Byzantine territory about 1000
- Battle sites

The Straits

would set enemy vessels aflame, burn even when in contact with water, and strike terror into the hearts of enemy sailors.

Diplomacy

The Byzantines, however, preferred negotiating to fighting, and they brought diplomacy to a high level. The subtlety of the instructions given their envoys has made "Byzantine" a lasting word for complexity and intrigue. First Persia and then to some extent the Muslim caliphate were the only states whose rulers the Byzantine emperors regarded as equals. All others were "barbarians," and when they claimed an imperial title, as in the case of the Franks or the later emperors, the claim was usually ignored in scornful silence or openly disputed.

Yet, although theory proclaimed that the Empire was universal, in their endless effort to protect their frontiers the Byzantine emperors dealt realistically with those "barbarian" peoples whom they could not conquer. They negotiated treaties, obtaining military assistance and allowing the vassal peoples to share in imperial prestige and to enjoy the luxuries that Byzantine money could buy. A kind of "office of barbarian affairs" kept imperial officials supplied with intelligence reports on the internal conditions of each barbarian people, so that a "pro-Byzantine" party might be created among them and any internal stresses and quarrels might be turned to the advantage of the Byzantines.

As in Roman times, when the emperor sent arms to the chieftain of a foreign tribe, it was the equivalent of adoption. The Christian Byzantine emperor could make the paternal relationship even stronger by sponsoring a pagan barbarian ruler at his baptism. The son of such a chief might be invited to be educated at Byzantium, and thus introduced to all the glories of Byzantine civilization. Titles in the hierarchy of the palace, with their rich and valuable insignia, were bestowed on barbarian rulers; even a royal crown might be granted. Marriage was also a most useful instrument. Barbarian leaders were pleased to marry Byzantine women of noble family; and when it was a question of a particularly desirable alliance, the emperor himself might marry a barbarian princess or arrange to give a princess of the imperial house to a foreigner.

The Economy

Good armies and navies and impressive diplomacy always cost money. Byzantium was enormously rich. It was a great center of trade, to which vessels came from every quarter of the compass. From the countries around the Black Sea came furs and hides, grain, salt, wine, and slaves from the Caucasus. From India, Ceylon, Syria, and Arabia came spices, precious stones, and silk; from Africa, slaves and ivory; from the West, especially Italy, came merchants eager to buy the goods sold in Constantinople, including the products of the imperial industries.

The Byzantine emperors were able for centuries to maintain a monopoly of the manufacture and sale of silk textiles, purple dye, and gold embroidery—which were then not merely luxuries but absolute necessities for the dignitaries of church and state in both West and East. Long a closely guarded secret of the Persians, silk manufacture came to Byzantium in the midsixth century, when—so the story goes—two monks explained to the

A fourteenth-century manuscript illumination illustrating the use of Greek fire.
The Granger Collection

DAZZLING THE BARBARIAN

A solemn formal reception at the imperial court usually dazzled a foreign ruler
or envoy, even a sophisticated Western bishop like Liudprand of Cremona (d. 972),
ambassador of the king in Italy, who has left us his account from the year 948:

Before the emperor's seat stood a tree made of
bronze gilded over, whose branches were filled with
birds, also made of gilded bronze, which uttered different cries, each according to its varying species. The
throne itself seemed so marvellously fashioned that at
one moment it seemed a low structure and at another
it rose high into the air. It was of immense size and was
guarded by lions, made either of bronze or of wood
covered over with gold, who beat the ground with their
tails and gave a dreadful roar with open mouth and
quivering tongue. Leaning upon the shoulders of two
eunuchs I was brought into the emperor's presence. At
my approach the lions began to roar and the birds to

cry out, each according to its kind.... After I had three
times made obeisance to the emperor with my face
upon the ground, I lifted my head and behold! The man
whom just before I had seen sitting on a moderately
elevated seat had now changed his raiment and was
sitting on the level of the ceiling. How it was done I
cannot imagine, unless perhaps he was lifted up by
some sort of device as we use for raising the timbers
of a wine-press.

Liudprand, *Antapodosis*, VI, v, in *The Works of Liudprand of Cremona*,
trans. F. A. Wright (London: Routledge & Kegan Paul Ltd., 1930), pp.
207–8.

emperor that the mysterious cloth was the product of
worms. Later, bribed by the promise of a great reward,
they brought back silkworms' eggs hidden in a hollow
cane. They taught the emperor that the worms must be
fed on mulberry leaves. Great plantations of mulberries
were established, especially in Syria, and a mighty enterprise was under way.

The power derived from control over the manufacture and sale of silk has been compared with modern
control over such strategic materials as oil. But it was
not only the imperial treasury that profited. The rich
were able to embellish their persons and their homes;
many middle-class merchants and craftsmen found a
livelihood in the industry; and the flow of revenue into
the imperial treasuries allowed the emperors to tax the
lower classes less than would otherwise have been necessary for national defense and other official expenses.
An elaborate system of control over manufacture (which
was in the hands of carefully regulated guilds) and over
sales (which were permitted only in official salesrooms)
safely secured the monopoly down to the eleventh century.

Besides controlling silk, the emperor forbade the export of gold, to prevent the depletion of reserves. The
nomisma, as the Byzantine gold coin was called, was
standard all over the Mediterranean and even in the East.
Until the mideleventh century it was rarely debased, and
even then only gradually under the impact of a crisis
brought about by civil strife and foreign invasion. For
eight hundred years this money was stable.

Throughout Byzantine history the sources of state
income remained much the same. Money came in from

state property in land—farms, cattle ranches, gold and
silver mines, marble quarries. This money was distinct
from that which came in the emperor's personal estates.
Booty seized in war or fortunes confiscated from rich
men in disgrace provided cash. And of course there was
also revenue from taxation—on land and persons, sales
and profits, imports and exports, and inheritances.

From Diocletian (r. 284–305) the Byzantines inherited the concept that land and labor were taxable together. The territory of the empire was considered to
be divided into units called *yokes*, each of which was
defined as the amount of land that could feed a single
laboring farmer. To be taxable as a unit of land, each
yoke had to have its farmer to work it; to be taxable as
a person, each farmer had to have a yoke to work. The
government thus had to find a person to cultivate every
yoke; otherwise there would have been no revenue.

This concept led to the binding of many peasants to
the soil and to their slow degeneration into serfs. Large
private landowners naturally flourished under such a
system, since it was easier for the state to lease them
large tracts of land and leave it to them to find the supply
of labor. Moreover, inferior land or abandoned or run-
down farms were compulsorily assigned to nearby landowners, who were then responsible for the taxes on
such property as on their more productive acres. Only
a landowner with rich and productive farmland could
pay such taxes on the more marginal farms. So this aspect of the system also contributed to the growth of
large private estates. Yet, though the large estate may
have predominated in the early period, the small private
freeholder seems never to have disappeared. In later

centuries the balance between the two types of holding would swing one way or the other. But whether in large or small units, the economy rested primarily on agriculture, despite the glitter and sophistication of the imperial capital and it emphasis on trade.

The Byzantine *oikos*, or "household," included slaves and, in the upper classes, women who were segregated to apartments of their own, in the manner of the Muslim harem, which may have derived from Constantinople. Daughters were literally kept under lock and key, for an unchaste daughter brought disgrace upon every family member. Women could not consume alcohol before others, even at family dinner. Everyone in the family took part in decisions about marriage, since one of its purposes was social advancement. The delivery of children—which took place either seated or standing up, not reclining, and at which, if the family could afford it, a physician was in attendance—was an important social, and thus economic, function for women within the context of the family.

II   BYZANTINE CHRISTIANITY AND RELATIONS WITH THE WEST

Religion governed Byzantine life from birth to death. The church governed marriage and family relations, filled leisure time, helped determine all critical decisions. Religion also pervaded the life of the mind: the most serious intellectual problems of the age were the theological and were attacked by brains second to none in power and subtlety. Religion dominated the arts and literature, economic life and politics. What the late twentieth century would think of as predominantly private issues, especially in the West, were for the Byzantines political issues. What was the true relationship of the members of the Trinity to one another? What was the true relationship of the human to the divine nature of Christ? Was it proper to worship holy images? Such problems were argued not only in monasteries and universities but also in the streets. A particular faction might riot if the emperor opposed its views. The questions were desperately important. The right answer meant salvation and future bliss; the wrong answer, damnation and eternal punishment.

Foreign policy was also pervaded by religion. When the emperor went to war, he went as the champion of the faith. Most often the enemies were infidels, heretics, or schismatics. The emperor went into battle against them with a sacred picture borne before him—an *icon* (image) of the Virgin, perhaps one of those that legend said had been painted by St. Luke, or one not even made by human hands at all but miraculously sent from heaven itself.

Contrast with the West

Yet much of this was also true in the medieval West. The real contrast is most apparent when we compare the relationship between church and state in the West with that in the East. In the West, the departure of the emperors from Rome permitted local bishops to create a papal monarchy and challenge kings and emperors. In Constantinople, however, the emperor remained in residence, and no papacy developed. Constantine himself summoned the Council of Nicaea in 325; he paid the salaries of the bishops, presided over their deliberations, and as emperor gave to their decrees the force of imperial law. When he legislated as head of the Christian church in matters of Christian dogma, he was doing what no layman in the West would do. In the East the emperor regularly deposed patriarchs and punished clerics. He took the initiative in church reforms. The faith was a principle of civil law; the emperor often helped prepare canon (church) law. Constantine's successors were often theologians themselves; sometimes they even legislated on matters of faith without consulting churchmen. In short, the church often functioned as a department of state, of which the emperor was the effective head, as he was of the other departments. One of his titles was "Equal to the Apostles."

A system in which a single authority plays the role of both emperor and pope is known as *Caesaropapism*, and this term is often, though at best only loosely, applied to Byzantium. Sometimes, for example, a patriarch of Constantinople successfully challenged an emperor. Moreover, absolute though they were, none of the emperors could afford to impose new dogma without church support or risk offending the religious beliefs of the people. The absolutism of the emperor did not apply to the inner, or "esoteric," form of the church, for the sacraments (that is, the mystery) remained the preserve of the clergy. Thus the emperor was more an "imitator of Christ"—the deputy of God on earth—with authority over both church and state.

Constantine had not wanted to intervene in the theological quarrel over Arianism, but he did so because the very structure of the Empire was threatened. The Council of Nicaea failed to impose a settlement, and the quarrel continued for another three-quarters of a century. New battles began over the relationship between the human and divine natures in Christ. Egyptian and Syrian Christians were monophysites—believers in a single, divine nature for Christ—as they are to this day, and they successfully resisted attempts to force them to compromise that were repeatedly made by the emperors, notably Zeno (r. 474–491), Justinian (r. 527–565), and Heraclius (r. 610–641).

The Byzantines assumed, far more than did the western Europeans, that a person had very little chance of salvation. In the East, more than in the West, monasticism became an ideal of the Christian life; to become a monk was to take a direct route to salvation. Worldly men, including many emperors, became monks on their deathbeds to increase their chances of going to heaven. At Byzantium, monks enjoyed enormous popular prestige and often influenced political decisions; they provided the highest ranks of the church hierarchy. Rich and powerful laymen, from the emperor down, founded new monasteries as an act of piety. Often immune from taxation, monasteries acquired vast lands and much treasure. Though some emperors tried to check monastic growth, the monks continued to influence policies because of their hold over the popular imagination.

For the ordinary Christian, the sacraments of the church provided the way to salvation. In the East every religious act took on a sacramental quality. Every image, every relic of a saint, was felt to preserve the essence of the holy person in itself. God was felt to be actually present in the sanctuary; he could be reached only through the proper performance of the ritual. In the East the emphasis fell more on mystery, ritual, and a personal approach to the heavenly saviour than on the ethical teachings of Christianity. Once believers accepted the proper performance of an act as the right way to reach God, they could not contemplate any change in it; for if the old way was wrong, then their parents and grandparents were all damned.

Quarrels and Schism with the West, 1054

A difference in the wording of the liturgy, it is sometimes argued, caused the *schism*, or split between the Eastern and Western churches in 1054. The Greek creed states that the Holy Ghost "proceeds" from the Father; the Latin adds the word *filoque*, meaning "and from the son." But this and other differences might never have received much notice, and would probably not have led to a schism, had it not been for a political question at issue and for increasing divergences between the two civilizations.

More than three hundred years earlier, in the eighth century, a religious controversy arose in the Byzantine Empire over the use of sculptured and painted sacred images (icons) and the nature and amount of reverence that a Christian might properly pay them. Something very like idolatry was widespread, and twice, for long periods (726–787 and 813–842), the emperors adopted the strict Old Testament rule that all images must be banned—*iconoclasm*, or image breaking. The Western popes, who believed that images were educational and might be venerated (though not worshiped), were shocked and condemned iconoclasm.

In the end the emperors restored the images, but as early as the 730s an iconoclastic emperor had punished the pope by removing from papal jurisdiction southern Italy, with its rich church revenues, and Illyricum (the Balkan provinces) and placing them under the patriarch of Constantinople. The papacy was determined to recover its rights and incomes in these territories. Even more decisive than iconoclasm was the papal belief that Byzantium could not, or would not, defend Italy and the papacy against Lombards and Muslims, and the consequent decision of Pope Stephen II to turn for support to the Frankish Pepin and Charlemagne.

Competition in the 860s between papal and Byzantine missionaries to convert the Bulgarians again led to a political quarrel. It was then that the Byzantines "discovered" the Roman "error" in adding *filioque* to the creed. Though this quarrel, too, was eventually settled, an underlying mistrust persisted and was increased by the deep corruption into which the papacy fell during the tenth century. The Byzantines became accustomed to going their own way without reference to the bishops of Rome. When the papacy was eventually reformed in the eleventh century, the Byzantines did not at first understand that they were no longer dealing with the slack and immoral popes they had grown used to.

Under these circumstances the Byzantines were unprepared for a revival of the old papal efforts to recover jurisdiction over southern Italy. Norman adventurers began just after the year 1000 to conquer Byzantine territory in southern Italy and to restore its churches and revenues to the pope. The pope naturally welcomed this, but the Byzantine patriarch was unhappy over his losses. A violent and powerful man, he dug up the old *filioque* controversy, largely as a pretext for pushing his own grievances. In answer to his complaints, the pope in 1054 sent to Byzantium one of his most energetic and unbending cardinals. Patriarch and cardinal thereupon excommunicated each other, and the papal envoy shook the dust of Constantinople from his feet and sailed for home. From this clash we traditionally date the schism—the split between the Roman Catholic and Greek Orthodox churches. Despite numerous efforts at reconciliation since 1054, the mutual excommunications of the individuals involved were lifted only in 1965.

Eastern and Western Christians were also increasingly suspicious of and resistant to each other's cultures. To the visiting Westerner, in part jealous of the high standard of living in Constantinople, the Greeks seemed soft, effeminate, and treacherous. To the Byzantine, the Westerner seemed savage, fickle, and dangerous—a barbarian much like other barbarians. Nowhere is the Western attitude shown better than in the writings of Bishop Liudprand, who had been so impressed by the emperor's movable throne when he first visited Constantinople in 948. On a second official visit in 969 as ambassador from Otto I, he describes his reception by the emperor Nicephorus Phocas:

On the fourth of June we arrived at Constantinople, and after a miserable reception ... we were given the most miserable and disgusting quarters [that] ... neither kept out the cold nor afforded shelter from heat. Armed soldiers were set to guard us and prevent my people from going out and any others from coming in. ... To add to our troubles the Greek wine we found undrinkable because of the mixture *in it of pitch, resin, and plaster. The house itself had no water, and we could not even buy any to quench our thirst.... Nicephorus himself ... is a monstrosity of a man, a dwarf, fatheaded and with tiny mole's eyes; disfigured by a short thick beard half going gray; disgraced by a neck scarcely an inch long; piglike by reason of the big close bristles on his head; in color an Ethiopian, and, as the poet says, "you would not like to meet him in the dark."* *

When Liudprand met the emperor's brother, they "tired [them]selves with a fierce argument over your imperial title. He called you not emperor, which is Basileus in his tongue, but insultingly Rex, which is king in his." As Liudprand left, he scrawled graffiti on the wall of his quarters, beginning

Trust not the Greeks; they live but to betray;
Nor heed their promises, what'er they say.
If lies will serve them, any oath they swear,
And when it's time to break it feel no fear. **

On the other side, the Byzantine reaction to Westerners is illustrated by the famous *Alexiad*, written by the princess Anna Comnena more than a century later, a history of her father, Emperor Alexius I Comnenus (r. 1081–1118). She says that two Normans, Robert Guiscard and his son Bohemond

might rightly be termed "the caterpillar and the locust"; for whatever escaped Robert ... Bohemond took to him and devoured....

For by nature the man was a rogue and ready for anything; in roguery and cunning he was far superior to all the Latins [Westerners].... But in spite of his surpassing them all in superabundant activity in mischief, yet fickleness like some natural appendage attended him too....

He was such a man ... as no one in the Empire had seen before.... for he was a wonderful spectacle ... so tall that he surpassed the tallest man by a cubit [about eighteen inches]; he was slender of waist and flank, broad of shoulder, and fullchested; his whole body was muscular.... very white; his face was mingled white and ruddycolor. His hair was a shade of yellow, and did not fall upon his shoulders like that of other barbarians; the man avoided this foolish practice, and his hair was cut even to his ears. I cannot say whether his beard was red or some other color; his face had been closely shaved and seemed as smooth as chalk.... A certain charm hung about the man but was partly marred by a sense of the terrible. There seemed to be something untamed and inexorable about his whole appearance ... and his laugh was like the roaring of other men.... His mind was manysided, versatile, and provident. His speech was carefully worded and his answers guarded.†

The mutual dislike between Byzantines and Westerners was to grow steadily more intense after the late eleventh century, until it climaxed in tragedy in 1204.

* Liudprand, *The Works of Liudprand of Cremona*, trans. F. A. Wright (London: Routledge & Kegan Paul Ltd., 1930), pp. 235–36.
** Ibid., p. 270.
† *Alexiad* (New York: Barnes & Noble, 1901), pp. 37–38, 266, 347. Translation partly ours, partly from Elizabeth A. S. Dawes.

III   THE FORTUNES OF EMPIRE, 330–1081

When we are dealing with more than eleven hundred years of history, as with Byzantium from its dedication by Constantine in 330 to its capture by the Turks in 1453, subdivisions are useful. The late eleventh century provides the major break in Byzantine history; by then the decline in imperial strength could be plainly seen. We shall here bring the story only to 1081.

The first period runs from Constantine's dedication of his capital in 330 to the accession of the emperor Leo III in 717. Despite their efforts, the emperors at Constantinople could not reconquer the West and thus reconstitute the Roman Empire of Augustus. Indeed, theological controversy, reflecting internal political strain, and combined with Persian and Arab aggression, cost the Empire Syria and Egypt. The internal structure was modified to meet the new situation.

From 717 to 867 the threat of Arab conquest was safely contained, the Bulgarians were converted, the major religious and political struggle over church images was fought and decided, and the large landowners began to emerge as a threat to the financial and military system.

From 867 to 1025 the Byzantine Empire was at its height. The emperors counterattacked the Arabs and regained much territory and prestige; the grim Bulgarian struggle was fought to a bloody conclusion; the Russians were converted; and the emperors made every effort to check the growth of the great landowning aristocracy. But the years 1025–1081 represented a period of decline, slow at first, accelerated as the period drew to a close. External military disaster accompanied and was related to the triumph of the landowners.

Constantine to Leo III, 330–717

The emperors immediately following Constantine were Arians until Theodosius I (r. 379–395), who in 381 proclaimed orthodox Nicene Athanasian Christianity to be the sole permitted state religion. All those who did not accept the Nicene Creed were to be driven from the cities of the Empire. Theodosius's enactment illustrates the close relation of theology to politics and to imperial initiative. The Empire, East and West, was united under Theodosius, but his sons Arcadius (r. 395–408) and Honorius (r. 395–423) divided it, with Arcadius ruling at Constantinople. Although in theory it remained one empire, it was never again fully united in fact.

Until the accession of Justinian in 527, the eastern portion of the Empire successfully used Goths and other barbarians as troops and usually managed to deflect the new blows of invaders further westward. Despite the challenge from Huns and Persians, the East continued to prosper. Only the monophysite controversy warned of internal weakness. The subtleties of theological argument partly revealed the challenge of Alexandria to Constantinople and the dangers of Syrian and Egyptian defection.

Justinian was so controversial an emperor that even his own historian, Procopius, besides several works praising him, wrote a *Secret History*, never published in his own day, that viciously denounced Justinian. We do not have to believe that Justinian was greater than Cyrus the Great or Themistocles, as Procopius says when praising him; neither do we have to believe that he was a demon who walked around the palace at night without his head, as Procopius tells us in the *Secret History*.

In an epic series of wars, Justinian's armies reconquered North Africa from the Vandals, Italy from the Ostrogoths, and southern Spain from the Visigoths. It was a last desperate effort to reunite all of Rome's Mediterranean lands. But the long campaigns and a vast new system of fortifications proved extremely costly. By limiting his wars with the Persians on the eastern frontiers to defensive efforts, Justinian permitted the Persian danger to grow. His immediate successors could not check it, while in Europe Slavs and Avars crossed the Danube line and filtered into the Balkans.

The Empire did not have to pay the full bill for Justinian's policies until the early seventh century. During the reign of Phocas I (r. 602–610), internal bankruptcy and external attacks from the Persians seemed to threaten total destruction. But Heraclius (r. 610–641), the son of the Byzantine governor of Africa, sailed in the nick of time from Carthage to Constantinople and seized the throne. He spent the first years of his reign in military preparations, absorbing heavy losses as the Persians took Antioch, Damascus, Jerusalem, and Alexandria. The Persians threatened Constantinople from the Asian side of the Straits, while the Slavs and Avars were besieging it in Europe; in 626 the Byzantines beat off the double threat. Heraclius defeated the Persians on their own territory and recaptured all the lost provinces.

But only a few years later, the new movement of Islam exploded out of Arabia and overran the very provinces that Heraclius had recaptured from the Persians. In both the Persian and the Muslim victories over Byzantium, the antagonism of the monophysite Syrians and Egyptians played a major part. From Egypt the Muslims pushed westward to Carthage in 698, putting an end to Byzantine North Africa. Muslim ships began to operate from Cyprus and Rhodes. In northern Italy the Lombard kingdom now threatened the imperial possessions. Heraclius's work and that of Justinian were seemingly undone.

Despite the desperate crisis, the emperors completely overhauled the administrative machinery of the state. Gradually they extended the system of government previously introduced into Italy to their remaining territories in Asia Minor and the Balkans. The loss of Syria and Egypt required the transformation of Asia Minor into a reservoir of military manpower; the perpetual raids of Slavs, Avars, and Bulgars into the Balkan

Silver plate showing the emperor Theodosius with his sons Honorius and Arcadius on either side, bestowing the insignia of office on a local official. This Mass dish, made about 390, was found in the nineteenth century in Spain by two peasants, who split it in order to divide the profits, hence the clear broken line that runs across it.
Accademia de la Historia, Madrid/Art Resource

provinces made the emergency more acute and increased still more the dependence on Asia Minor. Eventually the emperors divided Asia Minor and the Balkans into army corps areas, with the local military commanders also exercising civil authority. These new military districts were called *themes*, from a word meaning permanent garrison. In each theme the troops were recruited from the native population; in return for their military services, the independent farmers were granted land, but they were not allowed to dispose of it or to evade their duties as soldiers. Their sons inherited the property along with the obligation to fight. From the start, one of the themes was naval.

Though in theory responsible to the emperor, the commanding generals of the themes often revolted, and in the late seventh and early eighth centuries such rebellious generals seized the imperial throne. The imperial government strove to combat this danger—inevitable when military and civil powers were united in the same hands—by dividing the large original themes into smaller ones. From seven big themes at the end of the seventh century, the number mounted to about thirty smaller ones by the year 900.

This system embodied a change in concepts of taxation. As new immigration and settlement apparently ended the labor shortage of earlier centuries, it was now possible to separate the land tax from the tax on persons. The latter was transformed into a hearth tax, which fell on every peasant household without exception. For purposes of the land tax, each peasant village was considered a single unit. Imperial tax assessors regularly visited each village, calculated its total tax, and assessed each inhabitant a portion of it. The community as a whole was held responsible for the total tax, and often the neighbor of a poor peasant or of one who had abandoned a farm would have to pay the extra amount to make up the total. This obligation was onerous, and when the tax could not be collected the state itself sometimes had to take over the property and resell or rent it. Displaced officials, overburdened landowners, harried peasants, new immigrants who did not in their hearts accept the religious principles emanating from Constantinople—all these weakened the idea of unity for a common purpose. A loyal peasantry became increasingly disillusioned. Nonetheless, the Empire experienced sustained economic growth well into the twelfth century.

Leo III to Basil I, 717–867

In 717–718 Leo III, who had come to the throne as a successful general, defeated the Arabs who were besieging Constantinople. Thereafter the Byzantine struggle against the Muslims gradually became stabilized along a fixed frontier in Asia Minor. But the Muslim capture of Crete and Sicily in the ninth century opened the way for repeated pirate raids against the shores of Byzantine Greece and southern Italy. In northern Italy the Lombards extinguished the exarchate of Ravenna in 751, and Byzantine rule was interrupted by the alliance between the Franks and the papacy. The Byzantine *dux* of Venetia moved his headquarters to the island of the Rialto and thus became the forerunner of the *doges* (chief magistrates) of Venice, which from 810 enjoyed considerable autonomy. And in the Balkans the Bulgarian menace reached a new peak of severity.

Under the iconoclastic emperors, iconoclasm took on in its later phases a violent antimonastic aspect, since the monks of Byzantium were the great defenders of the images, and the monasteries, being free from taxation, were competing centers of wealth. During this phase of the struggle some of the monks challenged the right of emperors to legislate in matters of religion. But the images were twice restored by imperial decree (each time by an empress, in 787 and 843), as they had twice been banned by imperial decree. As a result of the struggle, the Byzantines drew more careful distinctions between superstitious adoration paid to images and proper reverence. When the controversy was resolved, it was tacitly understood that no more religious statues would be carved in the round.

Although the new system of small military holdings and the growth of a free peasantry retarded the development of large estates during the eighth and ninth centuries, large landlords were nevertheless again beginning to accumulate big properties. One cause may have been the ruin of the small farmers in Anatolia as a result of disorders that accompanied a great rebellion under Thomas the Slav. After twice threatening to subvert the throne, this rebellion was put down in 824.

Basil I through the "Time of Troubles," 867–1081

Although intrigue and the violent overthrow of sovereigns remained a feature of Byzantine politics, the people developed a deep loyalty to the new ruling house that was established in 867 by the Armenian Basil I (r. 867–886) and called the Macedonian dynasty because of his birth there. Even usurpers now took pains to legitimize themselves by marrying into the imperial house. As political disintegration began to weaken the opposing Muslim world, the Byzantines counterattacked in the tenth century. They captured Crete in 961 and Antioch and much of northern Syria in 962, after three centuries of Arab domination.

A new Muslim dynasty in Egypt, which also took over in Palestine, stopped the Byzantine advance short of Jerusalem. But like the later crusaders from the West, the Byzantine emperors still hoped to liberate Christ's city from the Muslims. While pushing back the Muslims, the Byzantines allied themselves with the Armenians and gradually annexed Armenia. This was almost surely a mistake. Armenia, which had been a valuable buffer against the Turks of Central Asia who were now beginning to raid eastern Asia Minor, lay open to direct attack. Firmly reestablished in southern Italy in the face of the Muslim threat from Sicily, the Byzantines dominated the neighboring Lombard duchies until after the advent of the Normans in the early eleventh century. From then on the emperors would find themselves under attack on three fronts—in Asia Minor, in southern Italy, and against the Bulgarians.

Under the early emperors of the Macedonian dynasty, the large landowners continued to flourish. Whole dynasties of nobles lived on their great estates. They were "the powerful," who were constantly acquiring more land at the expense of the poor. The more they got, the more they wanted. They bought up the holdings of the poor and made the peasantry once more dependent upon them. The growing might of the local magnates meant that the state was losing both its best taxpayers (the free peasants) and its best soldiers (the military settlers).

During the tenth and eleventh centuries, a great struggle developed between the emperors and the powerful, parallel in some ways to the struggle between the monarchy and the feudal nobility in France though destined to end differently. The powerful thwarted all imperial attempts to check the growth of their economic and military power and eventually seized the throne itself. Laws intended to end the acquisition of land by the local magnates could not be enforced; in times of bad harvest especially, the small free proprietor was forced to sell out to his rich neighbor.

The great emperor Basil II (r. 976–1025) made the most sustained efforts to reverse this process. He confiscated the estates of those who had acquired their estates since the rule of his grandfather. Others could keep their lands on satisfactory proof of prior ownership. As a final blow to the powerful, Basil II ordained that they would have to pay all the tax arrears of the delinquent peasants, thus relieving the village communities of the burden and placing it on the shoulders of the rich.

But a few years after Basil died, this law was repealed under the influence of the magnates, who thenceforth proved "more merciless than famine or plague." As the landlords got more and more of the free military peasants as tenants on their estates, their own military role grew more important and they became virtual commanders of private armies. After Basil, only the civil servants acted as a counterweight to the landowners. To reduce the landlords' power, the civil servants tried to cut down the expenses of the army, in which they were now playing the leading role. Strife between these two parties weakened the imperial defenses.

The Macedonian dynasty died out in 1057, and a "time of troubles" began. The Normans drove the Byzantines from the Italian peninsula by taking the great southern port of Bari in 1071. In the same year, after three decades of raids across the eastern frontier of Asia Minor, the Seljuk Turks defeated the imperial armies at Manzikert in Armenia and captured the emperor Romanos IV. Asia Minor, mainstay of the Empire, now lay open to the Turks, who pushed all the way to the Straits and established their capital in Nicaea. Meanwhile other Turkic tribes—Pechenegs and Magyars—raided southward into the Balkans almost at will. In 1081 one of the powerful magnates of Asia Minor, Alexius I Comnenus, came to the throne and seized Constantinople.

IV BYZANTIUM AND THE SLAVS

Perhaps the major Byzantine cultural achievement was the transmission of their civilization to the Slavs. Much as Rome Christianized large groups of "barbarians" in western Europe, so Constantinople, the new Rome, Christianized in eastern Europe. Some of the problems that beset the West today in its dealings with the Soviet Union arose because the Soviet Union is first and foremost Russia—a country in the Orthodox and not in the Western Christian tradition, a country that still shows the effects of having experienced its conversion from Byzantium rather than from Rome.

Conversion of the Bulgarians

The first Slavic people to fall under Byzantine influence were the Bulgarians, product of a fusion between a Slavic population and a smaller group of Asiatic Bulgar

invaders. From the time these barbarians crossed the Danube in the late seventh century, they engaged in intermittent warfare against the Byzantine Empire. The Bulgars created a powerful state and imported Greek artisans to build the palaces of the native rulers. But the Bulgarian rulers hesitated to accept missionaries from Byzantium, fearing the extension of Byzantine political power.

At the same time, a Slavic people called the Moravians had also established a state of their own in what is now Czechoslovakia. Their rulers associated Christianity with their powerful neighbors, the Germans, and feared both German and papal encroachment, as the Bulgarians feared Byzantium. To avoid German or papal influence, the king of the Moravians in 862 sent to Byzantium and asked for a Greek missionary to teach the Moravian people Christianity in their own Slavic language.

The Byzantine emperor Michael III sent to Moravia two missionaries, Cyril and his brother Methodius, called the Apostles to the Slavs. They knew Slavic and invented an alphabet in which it could be written. That alphabet, still employed by the Russians, the Bulgarians, and the Serbs, is still called *Cyrillic* after its inventor. Almost at once, as a countermove, Boris, ruler of the Bulgarians, asked for Christianity from the Germans. But these efforts by the two Slavic rulers to avoid conversion at the hands of their powerful neighbors and to obtain it instead from a less threatening distant court failed. German pressure and papal dislike for church services conducted in any language but Latin proved too strong. The German clergy and Roman Christianity eventually triumphed in Moravia.

Similarly, despite Boris's long correspondence with the popes, the power of nearby Byzantium was too strong. Boris found that he could not obtain an independent church from the papacy. Byzantium, on the other hand, permitted the Bulgarians virtual ecclesiastical autonomy. Only in the fold of the Eastern church could Boris unify his country and consolidate his own autocratic power. In Bulgaria, then, from the late ninth century on, the language of the church was the native Slavonic tongue preached by followers of Cyril and Methodius.

But the ambitions of the Bulgarian rulers were ultimately too great to permit friendly relations with Byzantium. Under Simeon (r. 893–927), second son of Boris, educated in Constantinople and called "half-Greek," there began a bitter hundred years' war, during which the Bulgarians tried to make themselves emperors by conquering Constantinople itself. In 981 the Bulgarian ruler Samuel defeated Basil II. But in 1014 Basil captured fourteen thousand Bulgarian prisoners and savagely blinded ninety-nine out of every hundred; the hundredth man was allowed to keep the sight of one eye, so that he could lead his comrades home. At the ghastly sight of his blinded warriors, Samuel fell dead of a stroke. Basil II took the appropriate name of "Bulgar slayer," and shortly afterward Byzantine domination over Bulgaria became complete. The country was ruled as a conquered province. But its inhabitants were never deprived of their own church, whose archbishop had as much jurisdiction as in the days of Bulgarian independence.

The great expenditures of money and manpower incurred in the long pursuit of the Bulgarian war played their part in weakening Byzantium for the military disasters that were to come at Manzikert and at Bari in 1071. But the war helped to determine where the line between East and West would be drawn for future history. The Bulgarians are an Orthodox people to this day, and their civilization throughout the Middle Ages directly reflected the overpowering influence of Byzantium. In much the same way, more than three hundred years later, the western neighbors of the Bulgarians, the Serbs, also took their faith from the Greek East after a flirtation with the Latin West.

Conversion of the Russians

To the north and east of the Balkan Bulgarians, between the Baltic and the Black seas, lie the great plains of European Russia. Here movement is easiest by water, along rivers that flow north to the Baltic or south to the Black or Caspian seas. Beginning in the eighth century, the Scandinavians expanded into Russia. First taking control of the Baltic shore, they moved south along the rivers to the Sea of Azov and the northern Caucasus. Their name was *Rus*, which has survived in the modern term *Russian*. Gradually they overcame many of the Slavic, Lithuanian, Finnish, and Magyar peoples who were then living to the steppe. The details of this process are obscure. The story told in the Old Russian *Primary Chronicle*, compiled during the eleventh century, is suggestive of what may have happened among the inhabitants of Russia sometime in the 850s:

> *There was no law among them, but tribe rose against tribe. Discord thus ensued among them, and they began to war one against another. They said to themselves, "Let us seek a prince who may rule over us, and judge according to the law." They accordingly went overseas to the Varangian [i.e., Scandinavian] Russes ... [and] said to the people of Rus, "Our whole land is great and rich, but there is no order in it. Come to rule and reign over us."**

This is known as the "calling of the princes." The *Chronicle* goes on to tell how the Viking Rurik accepted the invitation in 862 and settled in the Slavic trading town of Novgorod. Scandinavian princes then moved south along the Dnieper River. They seized the settlement called Kiev, still today the major city of the Ukraine, and made it the center of a state at first loosely controlled and devoted to trade. In 860, for the first time, a fleet of two hundred of their warships appeared off Constantinople, where they caused panic before they were repulsed. During the next two centuries there were three further attacks as well as other wars, which the Byzantines won.

Fifteenth century Russian icon depicting legendary events in Novgorod's defense against the rival city of Vladimir-Suzdal in 1169. The outnumbered Novgorodsti brandish a miraculous icon of the Virgin of the Sign, who, according to tradition, invoked God's aid to save them.
The Granger Collection

Though a brisk trade developed between the Byzantines and the Rus people, the continuing religious influence that Byzantium exercised upon the Russians was even more important. There is evidence in a trade treaty of 945 that some of the Russian envoys were already Christians, swearing by the Holy Cross to observe the provisions of the treaty. In the 950s Olga, the ruling princess of Kiev, visited the emperor at Constantinople.

> *Olga came before him, and when he saw that she was very fair of countenance and wise as well, the Emperor wondered at her intellect. He conversed with her and remarked that she was worthy to reign with him in his city. When Olga heard his words, she replied that she was still a pagan, and that if he desired to baptize her, he should perform this function himself; otherwise, she was unwilling to accept baptism. The Emperor, with the assistance of the Patriarch, accordingly baptized her. . . . After her baptism, the Emperor summoned Olga and made known to her that he wished her to become his wife. But she replied, "How can you marry me, after yourself baptizing me and calling me your daughter? For among Christians that is unlawful, as you yourself must know." Then the Emperor said, "Olga, you have outwitted me."**

* Samuel H. Cross, *The Russian Primary Chronicle*, in *Harvard Studies and Notes in Philology and Literature* (Cambridge, Mass.: Harvard University Press, 1930), XII, 145. Reprinted by permission.

* Ibid, pp. 168–69.

The Russians were converted as a people during the late 980s during the reign of Vladimir. He felt the inadequacy of the old faith, about which we know little except that the Russians worshiped forest and water spirits and a god of thunder. According to the partly legendary story in the *Chronicle*, Vladimir was visited by representatives of the different faiths, who told him about their beliefs. He discarded the faith of Mohammad because circumcision and abstinence from pork and wine were disagreeable to him. "Drinking," said he, "is the joy of the Russes. We cannot exist without that pleasure." Judaism he rejected because the god of the Jews had not been strong enough to enable them to stay in their native Jerusalem. Roman Christianity he rejected because it required a certain amount of fasting, as of course did the Christianity of the Greeks. But the cautious Vladimir did not accept this fourth possibility, Orthodox Christianity, until after he had sent a commission to visit various countries where all the faiths were practiced and to report back to him. Shortly after he received their report he was baptized and married a Byzantine princess. Returning to Kiev, he threw down all the idols in the city. It is said that in one day he forcibly baptized the entire population in the waters of the Dnieper.

Despite its legendary features, the story of Vladimir reflects the various cultural influences to which the Kievan state was exposed. It had Muslim, Jewish,** and Roman Catholic Christian neighbors, but the most powerful and influential neighbor was the Orthodox and Greek Byzantium. Doubtless the marriage alliance with the Byzantine princess and the resulting gain in prestige played a part in Vladimir's decision. To secure the conversion of the Russians to the Byzantine form of Christianity was also important for the Byzantines, who needed to protect their possessions along the Black Sea and their capital itself against renewed Russian attack.

The church became an important social force in Kievan society, and the Slavic clergy formed a new and influential social class. Although the Byzantines always asserted theoretical sovereignty over the Russian church, and although the first archbishops of Kiev were mostly Greeks appointed from Byzantium, the Russian church early asserted its independence in practical matters. From the first, the church in Russia became an important landowner, and, as in the Byzantine Empire, monasteries multiplied. The clergy came to have legal jurisdiction over all Christians in cases involving morals, family affairs, and religious matters. The concept that crimes should be punished by the state replaced the old concept that punishment was a matter of personal revenge. For the first time formal education was established; the Cyrillic alphabet was adopted, and literature written in Russian began to appear, almost all of it ecclesiastical. Byzantine art forms were imported and imitated; the great Church of Saint Sophia at Kiev is in its way as magnificent as its namesake in Constantinople. However, the pagan faith persisted in the enormous

Early Russia about 1100

rural areas, and the new culture was largely confined to the few cities and to the monasteries.

Many scholars have argued that the short-run gain from conversion by Byzantium was outweighed by a long-run loss. The very use of the native language in the liturgy (so great an advantage to the Byzantines when, as missionaries, they sought to spread their faith without insisting on the use of Greek) meant that the culture of Russia had little contact with Western thought. In the West, every priest and every monk had to learn Latin; as soon as he did so, he had the key to the treasures of Latin classical literature and the works of the Latin church fathers, themselves formed in the schools of pagan rhetoric, philosophy, and literature. The educated person in the West, usually a cleric, had access to Vergil, to Ovid, to Cicero, and to the other Roman authors— some quite unsuitable for clerical reading but all giving the reader a sense of style, a familiarity with ancient taste and thought, and sometimes solid instruction. He had Jerome and Augustine. For those in the West who had the leisure, the talent, the inclination, and the luck to find themselves in a monastery with a good library, the opportunity for learning was open.

The fact that the Byzantines did not insist on the use of Greek in the liturgy meant that the Russian clergy did not automatically learn Greek, as French or English or German or Spanish priests had to learn Latin. And of

---

** The Turkic tribe of the Khazars, settled along the lower Don River, had been converted to Judaism.

course the Latin heritage was not available to the Russians either. A very few Russians did learn Greek, but by and large the great Greek classical heritage of philosophy and literature was closed to the Russians. Byzantine sermons, saints' lives, some chronicles and history, and certain other pieces of Byzantine literature were indeed translated and circulated in Church Slavonic. But these were no substitutes for Plato and Aristotle, Homer and the dramatists. The conversion to Christianity from Byzantium thus had the effect of stunting the intellectual and literary progress of Russia. The Kievan Russians of the tenth century were not ready for Plato and Aristotle, but when the time in their development came that the Russians were ready, they were cut off from access to the treasure house.

Indeed, in the nineteenth century an influential group of Russian thinkers argued that conversion from Byzantium had led Russia into stagnation and intellectual sterility, because it had cut Russia off from Rome, the fountainhead of the intellectual and spiritual life of the West, without providing a substitute. Their opponents argued just as vigorously that it was precisely the Orthodox faith accepted from Byzantium that gave modern Russia its high degree of spirituality, its willingness to bend to the will of God, and indeed all the virtues that they found in the Russian character and the Russian system. This difference of opinion persists, but most students argue that modern Russia has shown a considerable cultural lag in comparison with Western countries, that this cultural lag is partly attributable to the fact that Christianity was accepted from Byzantium, and that the very privilege of using Slavonic in the church services prevented the growth in Russia of a class educated in the wisdom of the ancient world.

It would be a grave mistake, however, to attribute the cultural lag solely to these factors. It was perhaps in even greater measure due to the effect of the Tatar invasions in the thirteenth and fourteenth centuries.

Kievan Russia

Kievan Russia developed a society different in some ways from that in western medieval Europe, despite a common emphasis on property, the law, and security. Scholars have disputed whether agriculture or commerce was economically more important in Kievan Russia; the answer appears to be commerce. In trade, with Byzantium in particular, the Russians sold mostly furs, honey, and wax—products not of agriculture but of hunting and beekeeping. Since the Byzantines paid in cash, Kiev had much more of a money economy than did western Europe. From the economic and social point of view, Kievan Russia in the eleventh century was in some ways more advanced than manorial western Europe, where markets, fairs, and industries were only beginning to develop.

Before the Tatar invasions, which started in the early 1200s, the Kievan state began to have close diplomatic and political relations with the West. Dynastic marriages were arranged between the ruling house of Kiev and the royal families of Sweden and France, and alliances were reached with the states of Germany. Merchants from the West appeared in Russia, especially at Novgorod and at Kiev. Whatever isolation was imposed by Byzantine Christianity might have been overcome had Kiev been allowed to maintain its free lines of communication and its vigorous and valuable exchange from the West. But Russia was denied this opportunity.

The Kievan state had many internal political weaknesses. It failed to make any rules for the succession to the throne, and it followed the practice (similar to that of the Franks) of dividing the land among a prince's sons. The resulting fragmentation of the Kievan state into often mutually hostile provinces weakened it in the face of outside dangers. Beginning in the eleventh century the Turkish tribe of Polovtsy, or Cumans, appeared in southern Russia. The Russian princes warring against one another made a tragic error by hiring bands of Polovtsy to fight for them. Thus when the Mongol Tatars appeared in the early thirteenth century, Kievan Russia had been softened for the blow.

Never entirely centralized politically, the Kievan state nonetheless strove for unity. It bequeathed the ideal of unity, together with a literary language and a single Christian faith, to the future Russian state of Muscovy (Moscow) that was to emerge after more than two centuries of Mongol domination. Moscow would take from the Byzantines not only their religion, already deeply entrenched in the Russia of Kiev, but also their political theory of autocracy.

V BYZANTINE LEARNING AND LITERATURE

Byzantine achievement was varied, distinguished, and of major importance to the West, though scholars came to realize this only in the last century. Byzantine literature may suffer by comparison with the classics, but the appropriate society with which to compare medieval Byzantium is the Europe of the Middle Ages. Both were Christian and both the direct heirs of Rome and Greece. The Byzantines maintained learning on a level much more advanced than did the West, which, indeed, owes a substantial cultural debt to Byzantium.

Early Byzantium as Preserver of the Classics

In the West, the knowledge of Greek had disappeared, and no one had access to works of ancient Greek philosophy, science, and literature. During all this time the Byzantines preserved these masterpieces, copied and recopied them by hand, and studied them constantly. Again in contrast to the West, study was not confined to monasteries, although the monks played a major role.

It was also pursued in secular libraries and schools. The teacher occupied an important position in Byzantine society; books circulated widely among those prominent in public life; many of the emperors were scholars and lovers of literature. Because of its strong pagan tradition, Justinian closed the school of Athens in the sixth century, but the imperial academy at Constantinople supplied a steady stream of learned and cultivated men to the bureaucracy, the church, and the courts. Its curriculum emphasized secular subjects: philosophy, astronomy, geometry, rhetoric, music, grammar, law, medicine, and arithmetic. The School of the Patriarch of Constantinople, also in the capital, provided instruction in theology and other sacred subjects.

Had it not been for Byzantium, it seems certain that Plato and Aristotle, Homer and Sophocles would have been lost to us. We cannot even imagine what such a loss would have meant to Western civilization as we know it, how seriously it would have retarded us in science and speculation, in morals and ethics, how much harder it would have been to deal with the fundamental problems of human relationships. That these living works of the dead past have been preserved to us we owe to Byzantium.

Byzantine Writing: Epic, History, Theology, Hymns

In prose, Byzantium established over the long centuries an almost unbroken line of those who wrote the history of the Empire in a popular style. A great succession of Byzantine historians opens up for us a world as yet little known. As we might expect, however, it is theological writing that forms the most substantial part of prose literature. Early Byzantine theologians hotly debated the controversies that rent the Empire about the true relationship between God the Father and God the Son, or between the divine and human natures of Christ. Too difficult for most people to read or understand, such works nonetheless enormously influenced the lives of everyone. The leaders of the society were directly or indirectly affected by the answers to the problems of human social and economic life in general, or of the life of the human individual in particular, and of a person's prospects for eternal salvation or damnation. The early theologians also drew up appropriate rules for monks, balancing the need for denying the desires of the flesh with the provision of reasonable opportunities

A BLENDING OF LITERATURE AND RELIGION

Unique among the stories of saints' lives is an extraordinary document of the tenth century, a highly polished tale of an Indian king who shuts away his only son, Ioasaph, in a remote palace to protect him from the knowledge of the world, and especially to prevent his being converted to Christianity. But the prince cannot be protected; he sees a sick man, a blind man, and a dead man. And when he is in despair at life's cruelties, a wise monk in disguise, named Barlaam, succeeds in reaching him by pretending to have a precious jewel that he wishes to show. The jewel is the jewel of the Christian faith, and the rest of the long story is an account of the wise Barlaam's conversion of Prince Ioasaph.

During the conversion, Barlaam tells Ioasaph ten moral tales illustrating the Christian life. One of these reappears in Elizabethan literature as the casket story in Shakespeare's *Merchant of Venice*; another is the tale of Everyman, which later became common in all Western literatures; other Barlaam stories were used by hundreds of Western authors and preachers of all nationalities.

What is most extraordinary about this piece of Byzantine literature is that the story originally comes from India. The life of Ioasaph is a Christianized version of the life of Buddha, the great Indian religious leader of the sixth century B.C. His life story passed through Persia via the Arabs to the Caucasian kingdom of Georgia before it was turned into Greek legend and transmitted to the West. And the stories that Barlaam tells to convert Ioasaph are also Indian in origin and are either Buddhist birth-stories (recitals of the Buddha's experiences in earlier incarnations used as comment upon what was going on around him) or Hindu moral-cosmic tales. Indeed the very name *Ioasaph* was once *Bodasaph*, and so is the same as the Indian word *bodhisattva*, which means a person destined to attain Buddhahood. Prince Ioasaph has been canonized a saint of both the Orthodox and the Roman Catholic churches, and thus through this legend Buddha himself became and has remained a Christian saint in the eyes of many commentators.

for work. Later, in the eleventh century, under the influence of the Neoplatonic philosophers, Byzantine theologians developed a mystic strain in which they urged contemplation and purification as stages toward illumination and the final mystic union with God. For the ordinary person, the mysteries of faith were enhanced by the beauties of the church service, where magnificent original hymns were sung, often composed by major poets.

Saints' lives (hagiographies), usually written for the ordinary person, depicted adventure, anxiety, deprivation, violence, and agony of various sorts before the final triumph of virtue and piety. The eyes of the reader were directed upward toward a heavenly reward, since the hero of the story was often martyred here on earth. Exciting, edifying, and immensely popular in their day, these stories supply valuable bits of information about daily life, especially among the humbler classes, and about the attitudes of the people, for which we sometimes have no other source.

The study of saints' lives, by which a saint was taken to embody an abstraction that could best be understood by the study of the life of a person believed to have personified an idealized state, became even more intense in the Latin West. The purpose and result were similar; in both, the contemplation of the saint's lives was a function of education and doctrine. Around each saint arose a cult, and the saint became a patron, protector, even friend and intimate with whom the worshiper could communicate. By projecting the real into the supernatural world—sailors, weavers, specific types of warriors each having a saint charged with their welfare—the Christian societies in the early Middle Ages found a source of authority and security close at hand, when the secular authority of the emperor seemed far away and unable to respond quickly. The rise of the saints was neither an unthinking superstition nor a mass cultural means of preserving polytheism; rather, it was a search for earthly security through the creation of new and immediately accessible heroes.

In the late fourth century, debates in East and West over the growing role of the saints and over the development of sanctuaries devoted to specific patrons reflected the tendency of the wealthy to make religious practice more private and exclusive, as opposed to the common people's desire for access by the total Christian community. The issue was not an arid one, for access to a heavenly patron depended on who was that patron's representative or intermediary on earth. The wealthy could afford to build shrines and sanctuaries to specific saints, as the poor could not. When the bishops—that is, the church—emerged victorious over the wealthy families in place after place, episcopal power became fully entrenched in the West. In the East the powerful families were generally successful in preventing the growth of a truly mass religion, contributing another element to the growing sense of distance and lack of unity between Constantinople and the broader Empire. Efforts in the late twelfth century to require that persons could be canonized only after certification that they had performed miracles became, especially in the West, one effective means of curbing the growth in the number of cults.

The Arts

The Church of Hagia Sophia (Holy Wisdom) in Constantinople, built in the sixth century, was designed to be "a church the like of which has never been seen since Adam nor ever will be." The dome, "a work at once marvelous and terrifying," says a contemporary, "seems rather to hang by a golden chain from heaven than to be supported by solid masonry." Justinian, the emperor who built it, was able to exclaim, "I have outdone thee, O Solomon!" The Turks themselves, who seized the city in 1453, have ever since paid Hagia Sophia the sincerest compliment of imitation; the great mosques that throng present-day Istanbul are all more or less directly copied after the great church of the Byzantines.

Before Hagia Sophia could be built, other cities of the Empire, particularly Alexandria, Antioch, and Ephesus, had produced an architectural synthesis, a fusion of the Hellenistic or Roman basilica with a dome taken from the Persians. This is just one striking example of how Greek and oriental elements were to be blended in Byzantine society. In decoration, the use of brilliantly colored marble, enamel, silk and other fabrics, gold, silver, jewels, and paintings and glowing mosaics on the walls and ceilings reflect the sumptuousness of the orient.

Built centuries later in Venice—first the client, then the equal, and finally the conqueror of Byzantium—the Cathedral of St. Mark's was a true Byzantine church of the eleventh century whose richness and magnificence epitomized perhaps better than any surviving church in Istanbul itself the splendor of later Byzantine architecture. Built to house the remains of the Evangelist Mark (which were said to have been carried away from Alexandria), the structure is both authentically Byzantine and a showpiece of Byzantine-influenced later styles.

Along with the major arts of architecture, painting, and mosaics went the so-called minor arts, whose level the Byzantines raised so high that the term "minor" seems almost absurd. The silks, the ivories, the work of the goldsmiths and silversmiths, the enamel and jeweled bookcovers, the elaborate containers made to hold the relics of a saint, the great Hungarian sacred Crown of Saint Stephen, the superb miniatures of the illuminated manuscripts in many European libraries—all testify to the endless variety and fertility of Byzantine inspiration.

Even in those parts of western Europe where Byzantine political authority had disappeared, the influence of this Byzantine artistic flowering is often apparent. Sometimes actual creations by Byzantine artists were produced in the West or ordered from Constantinople by a connoisseur; these are found in Sicily and southern

Exterior and interior views of Hagia Sophia, Justinian's massive church at Constantinople. In the foreground are remnants of Roman construction. The Church of the Holy Wisdom- the English translation of *Hagia Sophia*- was built in 532 to 537 and represents a triumph of Byzantine architecture. (Minarets, buttresses, and foreground tombs were added to it after the Turkish conquest of Constantinople in 1453.) When finished, it was regarded as the finest church in the Christian world. Hagia Sophia served as a mosque until 1935, when it was made into a secular Turkish national museum.
Robin W. Winks and Art Resource

Italy, in Venice, and in Rome. Sometimes the native artists worked in the Byzantine manner, as in Spain, in Sicily, and in the great Romanesque domed churches of southern France. Often the native product was not purely Byzantine, but rather a fusion of Byzantine with local elements—a new art diverse in its genius, one of whose strands is clearly drawn from Constantinople.

VI ISLAM BEFORE THE CRUSADES

Islam (the Arabic word means "submission to God") is the most recent of the world's great religions. Its adherents (*Muslims*, "those who submit" to God) today inhabit the entire North African coast, much of central and west Africa, part of Yugoslavia, and Albania, Egypt, Turkey, the entire Near and Middle East, Pakistan, parts of India, the Malay peninsula, Indonesia, and the Philippine Islands, as well as Soviet central Asia and portions of China. Through immigration to western Europe and North America, Islam has become a worldwide religion; indeed, Muslims are the second largest practicing religious group in Great Britain today. Relations with the Muslim world have been crucial to Western civilization since Muhammad founded Islam in the early seventh

century. Islamic society rapidly joined the Latin and Greek Christian societies as the third major civilization west of India.

Muhammad, 570–632

What we know of Muhammad is derived from Muslim authors who lived some time after his death. The Arabia into which he was born about A.D. 570 was inhabited largely by nomadic tribes, each under its own chief. These nomads lived on the meat and milk of their animals and on dates from palm trees. They raided each other's flocks of camels and sheep and often feuded among themselves. The religion of the Arabs, a people known by inscriptions from the ninth century B.C., centered upon sacred stones and trees. Their chief center was Mecca, fifty miles inland from the coast of the Red Sea, where there was a sacred building called the *Kaaba* (the Cube), in which the Arab worshipers revered many idols, especially a small black stone "fallen from heaven," perhaps a meteorite. This building seems to have been the object of religious pilgrimages by the pagan Arabs.

In the sixth century Mecca was inhabited by a tribe called the Kuraish, a trading people who lived by caravan commerce with Syria. Muhammad was born into one of the clans of the Kuraish. Orphaned early, he was brought up by relatives and as a young man entered the service of a wealthy widow older than himself, whom he later married, after successfully performing several trading journeys for her. We do not know how he became convinced that he was the bearer of a new revelation, perhaps in visions when he was about forty.

Muhammad was keenly aware of the intense struggle going on between the two superpowers, Byzantium and Persia. News of the shifting fortunes of war reached him, and he apparently sympathized with the Christians, and perhaps even thought of himself as destined to lead a reform movement within Christianity. He could read no language except Arabic, and there were no religious books written in Arabic. His ideas and information on other religions must therefore have been derived from observations on his caravan journeys and from conversations with Christians and Jews.

Muhammad seems to have spent much time in fasting and vigils, perhaps suggested by Christian practice. He became convinced that God was revealing the truth to him and had singled him out to be his messenger; these revelations came to him gradually over the rest of his life, often when some crisis arose. He probably wrote them down himself in a rhythmic, sometimes rhyming Arabic prose, and included entertaining stories from the Old Testament and from popular and current Arabian folklore, such as the legends that had come to surround the memory of Alexander the Great.

The whole body of revelation was not assembled in a book until some little time after Muhammad's death; this book is the *Koran*. The chapters were not arranged in order by subject matter, but mechanically by length, with the longest first, which makes the Koran difficult to follow. Moreover, it is full of allusions to things and persons not called by their right names. Readers are often puzzled by the Koran, and a large body of Muslim writings explaining and debating it has grown up over the centuries. Muhammad regarded his revelation as the confirmation of the Old and the New Testaments. Muslims called Jews and Christians, as they call themselves, "people of the Book." Thus Islam was a universal religion, the perfection of both Judaism and Christianity, the final revelation of God's truth.

Muhammad was a firm monotheist. His god, Allah, is the god of the Jews and Christians, yet Muhammad did not deny that his pagan fellow Arabs also had knowledge of god. He declared that it was idolatry to worship more than one god, and he believed the trinity of the Christians to be three gods and therefore polytheism. (Muslims dislike the term "Mohammadanism," once widely used in Europe, because it might imply worship of the man Muhammad.) If Judaism emphasizes God's legal covenant with the Jews and his justice, and Christianity the mercy that tempers God's wrath, Islam may be said to emphasize his omnipotence—his absolute ability to do anything he may wish to do. Acknowledgment of belief in God and in Muhammad as the ultimate prophet of God and acceptance of a final day of judgment are the basic requirements of the faith. A major innovation for the Arabs was Muhammad's idea of an afterlife, which was to be experienced in the flesh.

The formal demands of Islam were not severe. Five times a day in prayer, facing toward Mecca, the Muslim, having first washed face, hands, and feet, would bear witness that there is no god but Allah and that Muhammad is his prophet. During the sacred month of Ramadan—perhaps suggested by Lent—Muslims may not eat, drink, or have sexual relations between sunrise and sunset. They must give alms to the poor, and, if they can, they should at least once in their lifetime make a pilgrimage (the *haji*) to the sacred city of Mecca. This was, and is, all, except for rules about certain aspects of daily life—for example, prohibitions against strong drink and other rules about food and its preparation, mostly taken from Jewish practice. The rest was social legislation; polygamy was sanctioned, but four wives were the most a man, save the Prophet himself, could have. Divorce was easy for the husband, who needed only to repeat a prescribed formula. Even so, the condition of women and of slaves was markedly improved by the new laws.

Historians of religion note many similarities between Islam, Judaism, and Christianity. All are monotheistic, and all worship the same God, using different language. Muslims worship together but do not require an organized church to attend: individual prayer is at the heart of expressing faith. Jews, too, worship together but require no formal church. Muslims and Christians both believe in the Last Judgment. To Muslims, Jews and Christians were "people of the Book," that is, people who worshiped through a holy scripture. Allah's message also appeared in a text, the Koran or, in Arabic, *Qur'an*, but it did not represent a series of commandments so much as a guide to living in such a way as to achieve salvation. The Qur'an describes the tortures of the damned at the Last Judgment, as did Christian texts and illustrations, but the vision of the rewards of the saved differed: to the Muslim, heaven was a place of running water and green parks and gardens—a vision natural to a people who resided largely in waterless and essentially barren lands—and the saved would retain their riches, dressing handsomely and eating well in the company of physical beauty. One who reads the scriptures of all three religions often is struck by the similarities, especially in the story and advisory elements, rather than by the differences.

At first Muhammad preached this faith only to members of his family; then he preached to the people of Mecca, who repudiated him scornfully. In 622 some pilgrims from a city called Yathrib, two hundred miles north of Mecca, invited Muhammad to come to their city to settle a local war. He accepted the invitation. This move from Mecca is the *Hegira* (flight), from which the Islamic calendar has ever since been dated. Thus the

THE KORAN

The Koran is of greater significance to Islam than the Bible is to Christianity, since it supplies both the canon of the faith and also the ritual and principles of civil law. Nonetheless, the West had little interest in the Koran until the Crusades, when (1143) a Latin version was prepared. No serious effort to study the Koran with the kind of care applied to the Gospels took place until the end of the seventeenth century, however, and the first English translation, the work of George Sale (c. 1697–1736), was published in 1734. In recent years Arabic scholars have criticized the accuracy of this translation, though it remains the one through which the greatest number of Westerners first gained access to the Koran.

The Koran states that God gave revelations not only to Muhammad, but to Moses, Jesus, and other prophets, but Muslims maintain that the later revelations were altered and corrupted over time so that they are no longer genuine. Reference is made to this in the following extract from Chapter II of the Koran:

There is no doubt in this book; it is a direction to the pious, who believe in the mysteries of faith, who observe the appointed times of prayer, and distribute alms out of what we have bestowed on them; and who believe in that revelation, which hath been sent down unto thee, and that which hath been sent down unto the prophets before thee, and have firm assurance in the life to come; these are directed by their Lord, and they shall prosper. As for the unbelievers, it will be equal to them whether thou admonish them, or do not admonish them; they will not believe. God hath sealed up their hearts and their hearing; a dimness covereth their sight, and they shall suffer a grievous punishment. There are some who say, We believe in God and the last day, but are not really believers; they seek to deceive God, and those who do believe, but they deceive themselves only, and are not sensible thereof. There is an infirmity in their hearts, and God hath increased that infirmity; and they shall suffer a most painful punishment because they have disbelieved. When one saith unto them, Act not corruptly in the earth, they reply,

Verily, we are men of integrity. Are not they themselves corrupt doers? but they are not sensible thereof. And when one saith unto them, Believe ye as others believe; they answer, Shall we believe as fools believe? Are not they themselves fools? but they know it not. When they meet those who believe, they say, We do believe: but when they retire privately to their devils, they say, We really hold with you, and only mock at those people: God shall mock at them, and continue them in their impiety; they shall wander in confusion. These are the men who have purchased error at the price of true direction; but their traffic hath not been gainful, neither have they been rightly directed. They are like unto one who kindleth a fire, and when it hath enlightened all around him, God taketh away their light and leaveth them in darkness, they shall not see; they are deaf, dumb, and blind, therefore will they not repent.

The Koran, trans. George Sale (London: Frederick Warne, many editions and dates), pp. 2–3.

Christian year 622 is the Muslim year 1.* Yathrib had its name changed to al-Medina, *the* city. Medina became the center of the new faith, which grew and prospered.

The Jews of Medina, on whose conversion Muhammad had been counting, did not convert. This aroused his hostility. He came to depend more upon the Arabs of the desert, the nomads, and became less universal in his appeal. Allah told him to fight against those who had not been converted. The holy war (*jihad*) is a concept

very like the Christian Crusade; those who die in battle against the infidel die in a holy cause. After Heraclius defeated the Persians (whom Muhammad considered to be pagan), Muhammad returned in triumph to Mecca in 630. Muslim historians believe that he appealed to Heraclius and other rulers to recognize him as a prophet and was disappointed when they did not do so. He cleansed the Kaaba of all idols, retaining only the black stone, and he made it a shrine of his new religion.

Two years later, in 632, Muhammad died. Much of Arabia had by then become Muslim, but it seems clear that many Arabs had not yet heard of the new faith. Yet within a century Charles Martel was battling Muham-

* Throughout, this text employs the Gregorian Christian calendar for dating; the book is thus itself an artifact of a Western point of view on history. Since the Muslim calendar is a lunar one, a year takes 354–355 days; hence one may not simply subtract 622 to arrive at the date as used in the Islamic states today.

A sixteenth-century Persian miniature showing the ascent of Muhammad into Paradise. It is illustrative of the style developed at the Safavid court, where artists at Tabriz and Herat produced many manuscripts and miniature paintings for the shahs. This work was prepared for Shah Tahmasp between 1539 and 1543 by a famous group of court painters directed by Sultan Muhammad.
British Museum

mad's co-religionists in far-off France, the great Byzantine Empire was locked in a struggle with them for its very existence, and Islam had reached India.

Expansion of Islam, 633–725

Scholars used to believe that this startling expansion was due to the religious zeal of the converts to the new faith. Now students of early Islam often argue that overpopulation of the Arabian peninsula set off the explosion of the Arabs into so huge an area. In fact, Arabs had been quietly emigrating for some time to Iraq, Palestine, and Syria. Now they had a new faith to symbolize their new unity. The first stages of their advance took them into lands already infiltrated by fellow Arabs. The movement quickly gathered momentum; Islam was its battle cry, but for many its motives included the age-old ones of conquest for living space and booty. Moreover, the organization of the Arab Muslims into armies dispatched abroad to fight surely prevented the disrup-

tion of hard-won unity inside Arabia itself. These conquering Muslims were generally tolerant toward Christians and Jews, regarding both as fellow monotheists and "people of the Book."

Syria, Palestine, and Persia were conquered almost simultaneously by two armies between 633 and 641. The Syrian province, disaffected from Byzantium by monophysitism, fell easily. And the Persians, because of their weakness after recent defeats at the hands of Heraclius, failed to put up the resistance that might have been expected. By 639 Jerusalem had been captured; in 651 the native Persian dynasty was ended. During 639–642 the Arabs added Egypt, the major Byzantine naval base, which was also monophysite in religion and ripe for conquest. Launching ships, they seized Cyprus and Rhodes and began attacking southern Italy and Sicily. Moving west across North Africa, they took Carthage in 698 and conquered the native Berber tribes, who had resisted Romans, Vandals, and Byzantines. In 711 with a mixed force of Berbers and Arabs under the command of Tariq, a freed slave, they invaded Spain across the Straits of Gibraltar. (The very name *Gibraltar* is a corruption of Arabic words meaning "Rock of Tariq.") By 725 the first Muslims had crossed the Pyrenees, to meet Charles Martel near Poitius seven years later. Meanwhile, they had been spreading east from Persia throughout what is today Soviet Turkestan, and in 724 they had reached the Indus River and the western frontiers of China. They also moved south from Egypt and North Africa into the little-known desert regions of central Africa. These conquests of the first century of Islam were virtually final. Only the Mediterranean islands and Spain were permanently reconquered by Christians.

Disunity in Islam, 634–1055

The unity of this rapidly acquired empire was more apparent than real. The Arabs had overrun a vast collection of diverse peoples with diverse customs. Moreover, internal dissensions among the Arabs themselves prevented the establishment of a permanent unified state to govern the whole of the conquered territory. After Muhammad's death, there was disagreement over the succession. Finally, Muhammad's eldest companion, Abu Bekr, was chosen *khalifa* (caliph, the representative of Muhammad). Abu Bekr died in 634, and the next two caliphs, Omar (r. 634–644) and Othman (r. 644–656), were also chosen from outside Muhammad's family, to the distress of many Muslims. Moreover, many Arabs resented the caliphs' assertion of authority over them and longed for their old freedom as nomads. In 656 Othman was murdered. By then those who favored choosing only a member of Muhammad's own family had grouped themselves around Ali, an early convert and cousin of the Prophet. This party also opposed all reliance on commentaries, or supplemental works, explaining the Koran. Fundamentalists with regard to the holy teachings, they became known as Shi'ites (the sec-

CHINA

INDIA

Arabian Sea

Indian Ocean

A S I A

Aral Sea

TRANSOXIANA 705–715

674

Oxus R.

652

699

KHORASAN 637

PERSIA 637

S A S S A N I D S

714

Indus R.

733 Caspian Sea

GEORGIA 644

ARMENIA 644

Mosul

Baghdad

Tigris R.

Euphrates R.

Persian Gulf

ARABIA

Medina (Yathrib)

Mecca

640

SLAVS

500

Miles

0

Black Sea

Constantinople

EMPIRE

Athens

RHODES

CRETE

CYPRUS 649

Antioch 634

Damascus

Jerusalem

Alexandria

Cairo

Red Sea

Nile R.

E U R O P E

AVARS

Danube R.

Ravenna

LOMBARDS

Rome

SARDINIA

CORSICA

SICILY

BYZANTINE

Mediterranean Sea

Tripoli

642

EGYPT 644

Tunis

Carthage

698

LIBYA

FEZZAN

A R A B I A

S A H A R A   D E S E R T

FRANKS

732 Tours

725 Narbonne

VISIGOTHS

Cordova

711

Str. of Gibraltar

MAGRIB 699

B E R B E R S

A F R I C A

Atlantic Ocean

Muslim Expansion

Conquests to 632 (death of Muhammed)

Conquests under first three Caliphs, 632–656

Conquests under Umayyad Caliphs, 661–750

Dates show when first conquered

Boundary of the Byzantine Empire about 750

Present-day boundaries

175

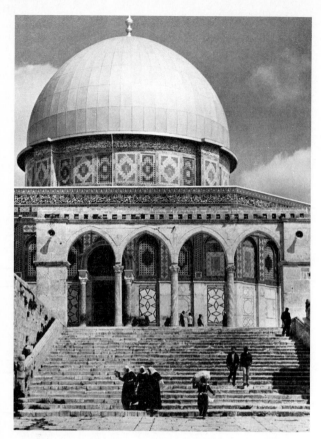

The Dome of the Rock in Jerusalem is a fine early example of monumental Islamic building. Built in the seventh century, it continues to have great significance for two religions. Moslems believe that Muhammad ascended to heaven from this rock, while Jews maintain that Abraham prepared to sacrifice Isaac on this spot.
Rapho/Photo Researchers, Inc.

tarians). Opposed to them was a prominent family, the Umayyads, who backed one of their members, Muawiyah, as caliph.

In 656 Ali was chosen caliph, and civil war broke out. Ali was murdered in 661. His opponent, Muawiyah, had already proclaimed himself caliph in Damascus in 660. Thus began the dynastic Umayyad caliphate (661–750). On the whole, it saw ninety years of prosperity, good government, brisk trade, and cultural achievement along Byzantine lines, of which the Dome of the Rock mosque in Jerusalem (which takes its name from the rock from which Muslims believe Muhammad ascended to heaven) is an outstanding example. The civil service was run by Greeks, and Greek artists worked for the caliph; the Christian population, except for the payment of a head tax, were on the whole unmolested and better off than they had been before.

Shi'ite opposition to the Umayyads, however, remained strong. The enemies of the Shi'ites called themselves Sunnites (traditionalists). There was little difference between the two groups with regard to religious observances and law, but the Shi'ites felt it their duty to curse the first three caliphs who had ruled before

Ali, while the Sunnites deeply revered these three caliphs. The Shi'ites were far more intolerant of the unbeliever, conspired against the government, and celebrated the martyrdom of Ali's son Hussein, who was killed in battle in 680 as the result of treachery. Southern Iraq was the stronghold of Shi'ite strength, although in modern times Persia (Iran) has become the center.

From these Eastern regions came the leadership of the plot in 750 that was responsible for the overthrow and murder of the last of the Umayyad caliphs at Damascus, together with ninety members of his family. The leader of the conspirators was Abu'l Abbas—not a Shi'ite himself, but the great-grandson of a cousin of Muhammad. The caliphate was shortly afterward moved east to Baghdad, capital of present-day Iraq and close to the former capital of the Persian Empire, and was thereafter known as the Abbasid caliphate. The days when Islam was primarily an Arab movement under Byzantine influence were over. At Baghdad the caliphate took on more and more of the color of the Persian Empire, in whose former territory it was situated. Still, its Christian subjects were on the whole well treated.

Other groups appeared in Islam with varying views of how to interpret the Koran. Some were mystics seeking ecstatic union with God—Sufis, for example, who attempted to lose themselves in divine love and whose name was given them from *suf*, wool, for the undyed wool garment they wore, much like Christian ascetics. Politically the rest of the Muslim world fell away from its dependence upon the Abbasids. One of the few Umayyads to escape death in 750, Abd ar-Rahman made his way to Spain and built himself a state centered in the city of Cordova. Rich and strong, his descendants declared themselves caliphs in 929. Separate Muslim states appeared in Morocco, Tunis, and Egypt, where still another dynasty, this time Shi'ite, built Cairo in the tenth century and began to call themselves caliphs, though they were soon displaced by Sunnites. Rival dynasties also appeared in Persia, in Syria, and in the other Eastern provinces. At Baghdad, though the state took much of its character and culture from its Persian past, power fell gradually into the hands of Turkish troops. It was the Seljuk Turks who emerged supreme from the confused struggle for power when they took Baghdad in 1055. Although the caliphate at Baghdad lasted to 1258, during its last two centuries the caliphs were puppets in Turkish hands.

Islamic Civilization

The Arab conquerors were moving into provinces that had an ancient tradition of culture, regions which, until the Arabs appeared, had been parts of the East Roman or Persian empires. The Arabs brought their new religion and their language to the peoples they conquered. The religion often stimulated new artistic and literary development, and by requiring a pilgrimage to Mecca, it fostered mobility among the Muslims and encouraged the exchange of ideas with fellow Muslims from other parts of the Muslim world. Arabic had to be learned by everyone who wished to read the Koran, since it was forbidden for believers to translate "the Book." Since Arabic is an extraordinarily flexible and powerful literary instrument, it became the standard written language of the whole Islamic world. Indeed, Muslims were highly conscious of its merits; they felt that incessant study of it was necessary for comprehension, and they gave the composition of poetry the highest position among intellectual pursuits, rating it even above science.

Spreading their religion, though seldom by force, and clinging to their family and social traditions, the Arabs in the early stages of their expansion founded new cities in the conquered territories that were purely Arabic in population. But as conversions increased, the Arabs absorbed non-Arabs. And in their way of life—houses, clothes, gardens—the Arabs borrowed much from the older urban societies they were now absorbing. So, aside from religion and language, the chief contribution to Muslim culture came from the civilizations of Persia and of the Greco-Roman world. Islamic government learned much from the Persian tradition; Islamic philosophy learned much from the classical tradition; and Islamic literature learned much from both.

Like both Roman and Greek Christianity, Islam was convinced of its superiority to all other religions and ways of life. Like the Byzantine Empire, Islam aspired to dominate the civilized world, which it thought of as divided between those lands already part of Islam and those lands still to be conquered. Like the Byzantine emperor, the caliph was an absolute autocrat, a vicar of God, chosen by election and hereditary principle, who could not be mutilated and still keep the throne.

Christians and Muslims felt themselves to be members of religions that were on the same level of intellectual advancement and parallel in many respects—in their attitudes toward creation, human history, the last judgment, and the instability of everything mortal. When at peace with the Muslims, the Byzantines thought of them as the successors of the Persians and as such the only other civilized nation. As a concession to the Muslim attitude toward women, which viewed all matters relating to them as intensely private, diplomatic protocol prescribed that ambassadors from the caliph were not to be asked the customary questions about the health of the ladies of the caliph's household. And the caliph's ambassadors were given the highest places at the imperial table. Furthermore, each court had the highest respect for the other's attainments in science.

Science

The reign of Mamun the Great (r. 813–833) is often said to mark the high point in the development of Arabic science and letters. In Baghdad he built an observatory, founded a university, and ordered the great works of Greek and Indian scientists and philosophers translated into Arabic. We hear of a young Byzantine geometry student who was taken prisoner by the Muslims and brought to Baghdad as a slave:

> One day his master's conversation turned on the Caliph, and he mentioned Mamun's interest in geometry. "I should like," said the Greek youth, "to hear him and his masters discourse on that subject." ... Mamun ... eagerly summoned him to the palace. He was confronted with the Moslem geometers. They described squares and triangles; they displayed a most accurate acquaintance with the nomenclature of Euclid; but they showed no comprehension of geometrical reasoning. At their request he gave them a demonstration, and they inquired in amazement how many savants of such a quality Constantinople possessed. "Many disciples like myself," was the reply, "but not masters." "Is your master still alive?" they asked. "Yes, but he lives in poverty and obscurity." Then Mamun wrote a letter to the master, Leo, inviting him to come to Baghdad, offering him rich rewards.... The youth was dispatched as ambassador to Leo. Leo discreetly showed the Caliph's letter to an imperial official, who brought the matter to the Emperor's attention. By this means Leo was discovered and his value appreciated. The Emperor gave him a salary and established him as a public teacher.... Mamun is said to have communicated with Leo again, submitting to him a number of geometrical and astronomical problems. The solutions he received made him more anxious than ever to welcome the mathematician at his court, and he wrote to the Emperor begging him to send Leo to Baghdad for a short time, as an act of friendship, and offering in return eternal peace and 2,000 pounds of gold [about a million dollars]. But the Emperor, treating science as if it were a secret to be guarded like the manufacture of Greek fire, and deeming it bad policy to enlighten barbarians, declined.*

Although the charge that the Muslim mathematicians did not understand geometrical reasoning is surely absurd, the story nonetheless reflects a real situation—the immense eagerness of the Muslims to acquire Greek learning, which seems to have stimulated the Byzantines to appreciate their own neglected students of science. In any case, the last portion of the story, showing how jealously guarded were not only the secret weapons of the Byzantines but also what we would call today their basic research in mathematics, has a modern ring indeed.

Aristotle and the other philosophers and scientists of the ancient world were in any case available to the Arabs, whether in the original Greek or in Syrian or Persian translations. Under Harun al-Rashid (r. 785–809), the fifth Abbasid caliph (of *Arabian Nights* fame), schools of translators were set up, and manuscripts were ordered from Constantinople and elsewhere. Even more was done by Mamun.

One of the chief fields of interest was medicine, which the Muslims developed beyond the standard works of the Greek masters. They wrote textbooks, for instance, on diseases of the eye, on smallpox, and on measles, which remained the best authorities on those

---

* Adapted from J. B. Bury, *A History of the Eastern Roman Empire* (London: Macmillan, 1912), pp. 437–38.

THE CALAMITIES OF LOVE

A poetic treatise on the calamities of love describes the kinds of "avoidance" a lover encounters:

The first kind is the avoidance required by circumstances because of a watcher being present, and this is sweeter than union itself. Then there is the avoidance that springs from coquetry, and this is more delicious than many kinds of union. Because of this it happens only when the lovers have complete confidence in each other. Then comes avoidance brought about by some guilty act of the lover. In this there is some severity, but the joy of forgiveness balances it. In the approval of the beloved after anger there is a delight of heart which no other delight can equal. Then comes the avoidance caused by boredom. To get tired of somebody is one of the inborn characteristics of mankind. He who is guilty of it does not deserve that his friends should be true to him. Then comes the avoidance brought about when a lover sees his beloved treat him harshly and show affection for somebody else, so that he sees death and swallows bitter draughts of grief, and breaks off while his heart is cut to pieces. Then comes the avoidance due to hatred; and here all writing becomes confused, and all cunning is exhausted, and trouble becomes great. This makes people lose their heads.

Adapted from *Medieval Islam* by G. E. von Grunebaum. Copyright 1946. Reprinted by permission of The University of Chicago Press.

---

subjects until the eighteenth century. Al-Razi, a Persian, wrote a twenty-volume compendium of all medical knowledge, and the philosopher Avicenna (980–1037) was perhaps even more famous for his systematization of all known medical science and for his work on Aristotle and the Neoplatonists that, when translated into Latin, stimulated renewed European interest in both. As an aspect of physics, al-Kindi (d. 870) wrote more than 250 works on musical, sounds, optics, and the tides.

Muslim scientists adopted Indian numerals (the ones we use today and call "Arabic"). The new numerals included the zero, a concept unknown to the Romans, without which higher mathematical research could not be carried on. The Muslims began analytical geometry and founded plane and spherical trigonometry, and they progressed much further than their predecessors in algebra. (*Algebra* is itself an Arabic word, as are *alcohol, alchemy, cipher, nadir, zenith*, and others that testify to early Muslim scientific achievement.)

Philosophy, Literature, and the Arts

In philosophy, the Muslims eagerly studied Plato, Aristotle, and the Neoplatonists. Like the Byzantines and the western Europeans, they used what they learned to enable them to solve theological problems. These focused on the nature and the power of God and his relationship to the universe, or on the distinctions to be drawn between the apparent (outer) meaning and the true (inner) meaning of the Koran. Al-Ghazali (d. 1111), having written a *Refutation of Philosophy*, became a Sufi mystic for a decade before returning to his desk to write an autobiography and more theological works, all Sunni. The philosophy he sought to refute was that of the Mu'tazila, a body of theologians who had arisen under Mamun and who had carried rationalism so far as virtually to claim that reason had parity with revelation in the search for religious truth.

In opposition to al-Ghazali's dismissal of philosophy and dialectical theology, the great Spanish Muslim Averroës (1126–1198) strove to reconcile philosophy and the Koran. The debate deals with a problem present in every faith. Averroës's commentaries on Aristotle translated from Arabic into Latin were available to the Christian West by the 1240s. Thus the Muslims came to share with the Byzantines the role of preserver and modifier of the classical works of philosophy and science. And eventually, in the twelfth century and later, when the West was eager for ancient learning, it was the Muslims in Sicily and in Spain, as well as the Greeks, who could set it before them.

Indeed, the process had begun even earlier in Spain, where the physical splendor and intellectual eminence of Cordova caused its fame to spread abroad. Cordova was only dimly known to non-Spaniards, but they were deeply aware of its superiority to their own cities. In Spain itself, a Spanish Christian in 854 complained that his fellow Christians were irresistibly attracted by Muslim culture:

My fellow-Christians delight in the poems and romances of the Arabs; they study the works of Moslem theologians and philosophers, not in order to refute them, but to acquire a correct and elegant Arabic style. Where today can a layman be found, who reads the Latin Commentaries on the Holy Scripture? Who is there that studies the Gospels, the Prophets, the Apostles? Alas! The young Christians who are

IBN KHALDUN, PHILOSOPHER OF HISTORY

The great Arab philosopher of history Ibn Khaldun (1332–1406) was the first to work out a substantial methodology for historical knowledge. Though he did not use the terms, he drew upon sociology, economics, geography, and religion. Building on the insights of Avicenna, Averroës, al-Ghazali, and others, he presented the most comprehensive statement of social philosophy in the medieval Muslim world. In the Prolegomena to his work he analyzed the "sources of error in historical writing":

All records, by their very nature, are liable to error—nay, they contain factors which make for error. The first of these is *partisanship* toward a creed or opinion. For when the mind receives in a state of neutrality and moderation any piece of information it gives to that information its due share of investigation and criticism, so as to disengage the truth it contains from the errors; should the mind, however, be biased in favour of an opinion or creed, it at once accepts every favourable piece of information concerning this opinion....

The second factor conducive to error is *overconfidence* in one's sources. Such sources should be accepted only after thorough investigation....

A third factor is the *failure to understand* what is intended. Thus many a chronicler falls into error by failing to grasp the real meaning of what he has seen or heard and by relating the event according to what he thinks or imagines.

A fourth source of error is a *mistaken belief in the truth.* This happens often, generally taking the form of excessive faith in the authority of one's sources.

A fifth factor is the inability rightly to *place an event in its real context,* owing to the obscurity and complexity of the situation. The chronicler contents himself with reporting the event as he saw it, thus distorting its significance.

A sixth factor is the very common desire to *gain the favour* of those of high rank, by praising them, by spreading their fame, by flattering them, by embellishing their doings and by interpreting in the most favourable way all their actions....

The seventh cause of error, and the most important of all, is *the ignorance of the laws* governing the transformations of human society. For every single thing, whether it be an object or an action, is subject to a law governing its nature and any changes that may take place in it.... And it has often happened that historians have accepted and transmitted stories about events which are intrinsically impossible, as did Al-Mas'udi [a historian] when relating the adventures of Alexander the Great. Thus, according to him, Alexander was prevented by sea monsters from building the port of Alexandria. Thereupon he plunged to the bottom of the sea in a glass case enclosed in a wooden sarcophagus, made a picture of the devilish monsters he saw there, cast metal statues in the shape of these beasts, and set them up on the walls of the buildings; no sooner had the monsters emerged from the sea and seen these statues than they fled away, and thus the city was completed. All of this is related in a long tale full of impossible myths....

Another cause of error is *exaggeration.*... The real cause of this error is that men's minds are fond of all that is strange and unusual, and that the tongue easily slips into exaggeration.

Ibn Khaldun, *An Arab Philosophy of History,* trans. and arranged by Charles Issawi (London: John Murray, 1950), pp. 27–29.

---

most conspicuous for their talents have no knowledge of any literature or language save the Arabic; they read and study Arabian books with avidity, they amass whole libraries of them at immense cost, and they everywhere sing the praises of Arabian lore.*

These Arabic poems of which the Spaniard spoke were derived from the pre-Islamic classical Arab tradition, and portrayed life in the desert, with its warfare and hunting, its feasts and drinking bouts. Love was a favorite subject. Composition was governed by a strict code of convention; it was customary, for example, for

the poet to praise himself, but not possible for him freely to portray human character, so that nuance was very important. Still, much understanding of fundamental human experience shines through.

Arabic love poetry, especially as developed in Spain, deeply influenced the poets (called *troubadours*) across the Pyrenees in Provence, in the south of France. Earthly love became an important element of medieval literature. The troubadours' songs spread to Germany, where the *minnesinger* adopted the convention. The troubadour created an interest in the theme of courtly love, or highly mannered and elegantly elaborately formal relations between men and women, and in the fourteenth and fifteenth centuries troubadour literature

* From G. E. von Grunebaum, *Medieval Islam* (Chicago: University of Chicago Press, 1946), pp. 57–58.

helped preserve and, for the aristocracy, elevate chivalric attitudes. Some of the greatest masterpieces of Western love poetry thus find their ancestry in the songs of the Muslims of Spain.

But love was not the only theme of Arabic verse. The famous blind Syrian poet al-Mʾarri (979–1057) lamented human helplessness in the face of the vicissitudes of life, sometimes in verses of a haunting beauty:

> *My friend, our own tombs fill so much space around us,*
> *imagine the space occupied by tombs of long ago.*
> *Walk slowly over the dust of this earth;*
> *its crust is nothing but the bones of men.**

Besides poetry there is much interesting autobiography and excellent history in Arabic. Fiction is of a limited sort only—sad misfortunes of a pair of lovers; exciting incidents of urban life in the capital, with the caliph and his chief minister, the vizier, participating; the adventures of a rogue. These stories were collected in the celebrated *Arabian Nights* between 900 and 1500. Stories of Persian, Indian, and Jewish origin are included, as well as some that derive from Greek and Hellenistic works. Thus Sinbad the Sailor's famous roc with its enormous egg came from the Greek romance

of Alexander, and the *Odyssey* supplied the adventure with the blinded giant.

Deeply appreciative of secular music and dancing, the Arabs in the early Islamic period seem to have preferred the role of spectators to that of performers, most of whom were slaves or former slaves. Stringed instruments like lutes, as well as whistles, flutes, and drums, were popular in the Islamic world, whose music can be rendered only by instruments that can produce quarter tones. Many musical words we take for granted derive from Arabic. The Morris dance, for instance, is simply a *Moorish* dance, a dance derived from the Moors of black North Africa. *Lute, tambourine, guitar,* and *fanfare* are all words of Arabic origin.

From the Muslims of Spain across the Pyrenees into France and thence to the entire western European world came not only the poetry of courtly love but the instruments the singer played as he sang of his beloved. Through Sicily and Spain came Greco-Roman and Muslim science, philosophy, and art. Understandably, however, the vast body of Muslim theological disputation and treatises on the development of dogma remained unabsorbed into European thought, even though Muslims and Christians debated many of the same religious issues. When considering the contributions of the Byzantines and the Muslims to the culture of Western society, historians are altogether justified in saying that much light came from the East.

* From Wilson B. Bishai, *Humanities in the Arabic-Islamic World* (Dubuque, Iowa: Wm. C. Brown Company, 1973), p. 94. Slightly modified.

Summary

The Byzantine Empire survived in the East with its capital at Constantinople until 1453. The emperors were absolute rulers chosen in theory by God and were responsible for preserving the traditions of Roman justice.

Byzantium was the buffer that cushioned Europe against frequent invasions from the north and east. The Byzantine armies and navies were well organized and led. The Byzantines also developed great diplomatic skill.

Byzantine strength was based on a rich economy. Trade and a monopoly of silk and luxury goods were important, but agriculture was the mainstay of both the economy and society. The Byzantines faced constant problems caused by the absorption of small farms into large estates.

Religion dominated Byzantine life. The emperor was also the effective head of the church, a system known as *Caesaropapism*. Religious controversies such as the iconoclast heresy were also political issues.

Differences between Latin Western Christianity and Greek Eastern Christianity multiplied after the fall of the Roman Empire in the West. In 1054 these differences came to a head in a schism between the two churches that has never been repaired.

One of the greatest Byzantine cultural achievements was the transmission of their civilization to Russia and the eastern Slavs, who were converted to Byzantine (Orthodox) Christianity in the ninth and tenth centuries. Because

of its Byzantine heritage, Kievan Russia developed very differently from western Europe.

Byzantium preserved and transmitted the works of ancient Greece. Byzantine literature and art were of a high standard and were influential in the West.

Islam, a monotheistic religion, was founded in Arabia by Muhammad in the seventh century. Muhammad's teachings are collected in the Koran, the Islamic holy book. His followers are called Muslims. Their holy city is Mecca.

Muhammad converted and united most of Arabia. After his death in 632 the Muslims conquered all of the Near East, Egypt, North Africa, much of Spain, Persia, and northern India. This rapid conquest was the result of the Muslims' religious zeal, the weakness of the Byzantine and Persian empires, and the Arabs' need to expand to reduce the overpopulation of the Arabian peninsula.

In the eighth century the Arab empire split into several rival states, the chief of which was the caliphate of Baghdad.

Islamic civilization was based on religion and on the Arabic language. In government, literature, and philosophy, the Arabs borrowed extensively from the Greeks and Persians. In science, philosophy, and literature, the achievements of Arab civilization were very high.

7

Church and Society in the Medieval West

Until recently, twentieth-century historians tended to see medieval history as a period of "looking backward," well separated from a watershed such as the Renaissance, which seemed "forward looking" because of our ability to relate more closely to Renaissance figures. In recent years, however, new views of history have tended to lessen this emphasis on significant watersheds, to decrease the concern of identifying the "end of the Middle Ages" or "the beginning of modernity," and to argue that the past is one long continuum in which the Middle Ages are no less relevant to us today than times closer to us chronologically.

Our knowledge of all periods of history is changing rapidly, though not equally so. Perhaps four areas of knowledge have been transformed most in the past three decades: very early classical history, as a result of new archaeological finds and more sophisticated interpretation of old ones; the awareness of the richness of Byzantine and early Islamic history, which had been relatively dismissed by nineteenth-century historians who, for reasons of their own, sought their roots in the classical past; major debates and concepts about the Middle Ages; and social history in general, and the study of the family, women, ethnic communities, sexuality, and the management of disease in particular. All these subjects have influenced our view of the Middle Ages.

I   THE SOCIETY AND ITS ECONOMY

In Christian Europe at the beginning of the tenth century, as the monkish biographer of the Anglo-Saxon king Alfred wrote, society was made up of those who prayed (the clergy), those who fought (the nobility), and those who worked (everyone else). These three orders of society, defined in terms of their functional contributions, were generally an accurate reflection of economic and social reality through the tenth century, but the idea of these three orders continued long after society could be accurately described in such a way. By the early thirteenth century the idea was made part of royal ideology. Thus a conception of society that was once broadly true as a generalization was given renewed life as a conservative defense against competing models of social organization that had begun to threaten the security of orderly notions of society—whether in church or state—by the eleventh century. This three-orders view of society looked back to Augustine, Gregory the Great, and Greek ideas about the Philosopher-King. However, the monasteries, various heretical movements, and the rise of a growing commercial class that was aware of competing systems of ideas originating elsewhere challenged such a scheme of things.

One major theme in the history of the Middle Ages is the growth in authority of kings. Generally this authority depended less on internal or external struggles for power, on which court chroniclers most often focused, than on religious sanctions that would provide ultimate justification. Although kings might challenge the church on specific matters, they sought to use it, and were used by it; thus, anything that weakened the church ultimately weakened the source of authority to which the monarch would turn to defend "divine right." So kings, too, were interested in matters of theological dispute.

Kings governed their lands with the assistance of nobles, to whom authority was delegated and from whom obedience was expected. This created tension between central and local government that was never resolved, and since tension usually represents flux, any generalization about the relationship between central and local government is bound to be true only for a specific place and at a specific time. Yet the historian must generalize or historical narrative will become lost in detail. As authority in the name of people slowly became an alternative to authority in the name of the king, and the Crown was undermined, the language of authority began to differ more widely from place to place, so that "the state" means one thing in German history, another in Japanese history, yet another in American history. Still, historians must use terms in common, and this introduces another complexity into our understanding of, for example, the emergence of the idea of national identity at the end of the Middle Ages.

These observations are necessary if we are to understand why the medieval world appears so complex, so remote, so discontinuous to us, and why it is nonetheless so significant to our understanding of Western history. For the eleventh century proved to be a major turning point in the social and economic life of the West, even though no one at the time was fully conscious of this, and the sources therefore do not speak of it directly. As the raids of Muslims, Magyars, and Northmen tapered off, most of western Europe found itself secure against outside attack. By the end of the century, western Europeans took the offensive against Islam. During the eleventh century, the population of Europe grew rapidly, which may have reflected an increase in personal life expectancy. By modern standards, of course, people were still exposed every day to unpredictable dangers from diseases that no one could cure, from undernourishment and famine that no one could assuage, and often from violence that no one could combat or police.

This larger population needed more food and more land. Pioneers felled trees, drained swamps, opened up new areas for farming. When forests or marsh lay within a manor, a lord would often offer special inducements to his serfs to get them to undertake the extra heavy labor of clearing and farming it. Sometimes peasants would move into a new region that had lain empty before and would clear and farm it; if such uninhabited land belonged to a lord, he might invite peasants to

CLASSIFICATION IN HISTORY: THE DISAPPEARANCE OF THE WHEEL

To overcome problems of organization and argumentation, historians often turn to systems of classification to make knowledge appear systematic. The use of such systems is itself the product of assumptions about evolution, progress, orderliness, science. For example, agricultural history is extremely important to understanding the past, since over the ages most people have earned their living as tillers of the soil. Agriculture may be classified broadly into specific types: shifting agriculture, wet-rice cultivation, pastoral nomadism, Mediterranean agriculture, mixed farming, dairying, plantations, ranching, and large-scale grain production. Obviously the type of society dependent upon these types of food production will differ, but it does not follow that one type is inherently superior to another. Yet the act of classification leads some scholars to conclude that these types of agriculture represent phases, and that the phases are evolutionary, and that evolution represents progress toward some improved state. Immediately, a bias against an earlier state and the society dependent upon that form of agriculture is introduced, for that society is seen as one, three, or seven stages removed from the end of the process—that is, from "modernity."

Yet we now know that societies once possessed knowledge that was later lost: Greek science, Muslim scholarship, the wheel and the cart that disappeared from the region of their invention, the Middle East. Thus phases do not always represent a steady progression from a lower to a higher complexity, for complex knowledge and practice can be forgotten. This awareness may lead other scholars into the trap of a cyclical theory that assumes that history repeats itself. Such an assumption is most often used by those who wish to be able to predict the future, rather than by those who are studying the past for its own sake.

People have been concerned with certain questions virtually from the beginning of organized societies—questions about God, nature, human beings, society itself, and history. In contemplating these questions, philosophers sought a form of security; in acting upon their responses to these questions, rulers brought change, even as they attempted to assure continuity. Theologians who attempted to explain death, disease, sexuality, the need to labor, were contributing to the world as we know it today, for they were providing yet another set of answers to questions about God, nature, society, human beings, and the way these answers bear upon the past.

Thus all history is ultimately related to all other history, and any narrative, chronological, or classificatory system ultimately breaks down. All questions give rise to other questions. Consider the effort to explain the disappearance of the wheel and the cart from the Middle East for a thousand years, despite their diffusion around the world. To provide even a partial answer, the scholar must investigate the domestication of the camel, the invention of harnesses and saddles, the development of trade, the integration of the Arab nomads into imperial antiquity, the differing effectiveness of one-humped and two-humped camels, breeding, competing systems of commerce as discovered by the nomads, and a hundred other questions. Even then scholars are dependent upon the sources, and if these are not contemporary with the problem being investigated, they must also inquire into how the sources have been corrupted, used, abused, and manipulated over the centuries. The ultimate answer to the question about the wheel and the cart will be general at best and may contain much undoubted though sophisticated guesswork.

This example is drawn from a reading of Richard W. Bulliet, *The Camel and the Wheel* (Cambridge, Mass.: Harvard University Press, 1975).

Women played an increasingly important role in medieval Christianity. This mosaic, from the Basilica of St. Apollinaris the New, in Ravenna, shows four virgin martyrs. The left side of the basilica was reserved for women, the right side for men, and the mosaics reflect this division.
Scala/Art Resource

colonize it and offer them freedom from serfdom and the chance to pay a money rent instead of the usual services. This would bring profit to the lord and great advantages to the freed serfs.

New technology helped to improve the farmer's life. Farmers increasingly adopted devices that had been known earlier, such as the heavy wheeled plow with horses to draw it. Windmills made their first appearance on the European landscape in the twelfth century—possibly brought from Persia but more likely developed independently—especially in flat areas like Normandy and the Low Countries, where there was no falling water to run a watermill. Slowly the anonymous inventors of the Middle Ages perfected systems of gears that would turn the millstones faster and grind more grain in less time. The growth of Christianity, the decline of slavery, the extension of the profit motive, the incorporation of knowledge gained from military campaigns, the increased supply of paid labor from the rise in population, all contributed to the first revolution in power, whether supplied by water, wind, or animal (including human).

Trade and Town

As part of the same general development, trade began slowly to revive during the eleventh century. A bad harvest year left medieval farmers helpless, and plenty or scarcity varied widely from region to region. It seemed natural to bring surpluses into areas of famine and sell them at high prices to the hungry. The first new commercial centers arose in places such as Venice and the Low Countries, where local farms could not feed the increasing population, and which trading ships could easily reach. Even in the earlier Middle Ages such trade had never disappeared altogether, but now the incentives to increase its scale were pressing.

When the owner of a manor found that year after year he could make large sums by selling a certain crop, he began to plant more and more of that crop and used the money gained by its sale to buy the things he was no longer raising. Once he had more money than he needed for necessities, he began to think of how to spend it on something extra—a luxury. Such a demand quickly creates its supply; what was once a luxury becomes a necessity. Thus, for example, the people of Flanders, living in an area that was poor for growing grain but good for raising sheep, sold their raw wool, developed a woolen-manufacturing industry, and imported the food they needed.

The recovery of commerce and the beginnings of industries stimulated the growth of towns. Old Roman towns like London and Marseilles revived. Often, a new town grew around a castle (*bourg* in France, *burgh* in England, *burg* in Germany), especially if it was strategically located for trade as well as for defense. And so the resident *bourgeois, burgesses,* or *burghers* enter the language as castle-dwellers, but soon become recognizable as residents of towns, engaged in commerce. Protected by the lord of the castle or sometimes by the abbot of the local monastery, the townspeople built walls around their settlement and pursued their trades. They banded together into guilds to protect themselves from brigands on the roads and to bargain with the lord of the next castle, who might be showing unpleasant signs of confiscating their goods or charging indecently high tolls whenever they crossed his land. Grouped in a guild, merchants could often win concessions; if the lord they were bargaining with seemed unreasonable, they might threaten to take a route across the lands of some less greedy lord and receive a more moderate toll.

Mutual advantage soon led landowners, including kings, to grant privileges to the townspeople by issuing a charter. Although the contents of such documents vary, most of them guaranteed free status to the townspeople; even escaped serfs within the town would acquire freedom if they could avoid capture and function as townspeople for a year. The charter might also grant the townspeople the right to hold a perpetual market, to transfer property within the town walls, and to have their lawsuits tried in a town court by town custom, which slowly developed into a whole new kind of law—the *law merchant.* Slowly there began to develop a body of commercial law for merchants and their merchandise.

Industry followed commerce into the town. The merchant, with experience of distant markets, learned how to buy raw material, how to have workers do the manufacturing wherever it was cheapest, and how to sell the finished products wherever the best price might be found. Soon the workers also began to organize into craft guilds, which provided medical care and burial for members and often fixed minimum wages, the standards of quality of a product, and even the prices to be asked.

Enterprise was neither free nor private. It was highly regulated, which not only reduced outside competition but also reflected the ideas of the age. People believed that a "just price" for a pair of shoes included the cost of the leather and the thread, the amount needed to

sustain the shoemaker and family while making the shoes, and a bit more to pay the seller for time and trouble.

To "make money"—in the modern sense of charging all that the traffic will bear—was in theory to cheat the customer. If many medieval customers were in fact cheated in this sense, the ethics of the time condemned such action. Finance capitalism—the use of money to make money, the investment of funds at interest—was traditionally condemned as usury. But with the help of the church's own lawyers, pressure from business modified this strict view; in practice, after 1100 there were few obstacles to the advance of trade and moneylending.

Town and Countryside

In turn, the towns greatly affected the overwhelming mass of the population who remained in the countryside, who now had a place to sell their surplus and an incentive to produce it. Some peasants saved enough cash to buy their freedom; some fled to the town in the hope of acquiring freedom or at least in the hope that their children might acquire it. The very word "cash" suggests a most important development—the flourishing of a money economy instead of an economy of barter. Barter still continued, but as the magnates came

On the left, a fifteenth-century miniature showing an artisan at work, probably in Amiens. The second miniature provides rich detail for the social historian on the variety of workers involved in building a house.
Jean Masson Collection and Bibliotheque de l'Arsenal, Paris

59. BUILDING A HOUSE
Detail from a miniature, 15th century. Paris, Bibliothèque de l'Arsenal

to want more manufactured or imported or luxury items, they wanted cash rather than services. A serf's labors would produce grain, but not the money to buy armor, so the lord would let the peasant pay him cash and would forgive (commute) the serf's obligation to work on his land. More demand for money led to more money in circulation and an inflationary rise in wages and prices.

With the increase in demand for goods, large-scale fairs became a regular feature of medieval life. Some attracted traders and goods from all over Europe. In Champagne, in northeastern France, for example, there were several great fairs each year. The count of Champagne not only collected a fee from the towns for the privilege of holding the fair, but also received the revenues from a special court set up to try cases that arose there. As large-scale transactions grew more frequent, it became less practical for merchants to carry large amounts of cash, and during the thirteenth century they came to use a written promise to pay instead. Acceptance of these *bills of exchange*, a kind of primitive bank check, often made it unnecessary to transport money at all, since a Parisian creditor of a London merchant could call upon a Parisian debtor of the same merchant to pay the amount owed.

Historians continue to debate the causes and extent of the Western economic revival in the early Middle Ages. Many influences were at work. Muslim raids drove many people to take shelter in towns, the better to resist the invaders, and these towns created a more active economy; raids and settlement by Northmen had a similar effect in what was to become Germany. In the tenth century the economy, essentially in decline since classical times, began a slow though mostly steady growth; by the twelfth century the widespread use of instruments of credit had stimulated the economy even further. Climatic change at this time substantially altered the pattern of agriculture as far northern Europe became increasingly cold and unable to support grapes or some cereals. At the same time, the growth of more centralized monarchical states with different and evolving concepts of property rights in relation to feudal obligations led to a more efficient organization of society for production.

Population expansion, the commercial revival, agricultural growth, and the creation of a market system based on a money economy also changed the institutions of feudalism. The link between fiscal policy, property rights and new population pressures was especially significant in England and among the Dutch. Where an economic surplus existed, entire towns could specialize in producing one item for trade, tying themselves ever more closely to the market economy. From about 1500 the maritime expansion of western Europe would carry this economy overseas, while new products from overseas would further stimulate the European economy. Thus there was both a commercial revolution in the Middle Ages and a less heralded industrial revolution, in which agriculture, industry, construction, and mining

were revolutionized and the social and physical environment were utterly changed.

Yet despite the growth of towns and of trade, society in the West did not become predominantly urban. Its rulers generally preserved the attitudes of large country landowners, interested in the productivity of their estates, on which their wealth depended; regarding the great lords and their fellow landowners as sharing their interests, even when they quarreled with them; and respecting the clergy as men of education who were often useful in administering their affairs and who were indispensable to their salvation. They spent their money ostentatiously, but felt committed to give alms to the poor and to build churches. They remained part of the country, not the town. Warriors and priests continued to be the idealized types of the time, for those who worked—the third of the estates—lacked anyone to tell their stories.

The Changing Status of Women

The status of women also reflected this idealization. Ideas of courtly love emphasized feminine nobility, while the cult of the Virgin Mary emphasized the role of the mother or glorified virginity. Marriage remained an important social institution at all levels, since it was a sacrament and also provided access to property and inheritance. But the role of women was changing. The peasant's wife worked as a partner to her husband in the fields, while the lady of the castle did not. The wife of the peasant was recognized as rendering service, and daughters could inherit land; indeed, even among the nobility, maintaining the family bloodline was felt to be more important than male dominance of inheritance. In the early Middle Ages women of child-bearing age were in short supply, and this enhanced their value in marriage, so that they could demand a larger dowry from prospective husbands. Noble families, wealthy town dwellers, and the more prosperous peasants had more children than the poor did; they also married earlier and carefully registered the births of their children, since land passed through them. As infant mortality was high, large families were essential.

By the fourteenth century the male-female balance in population had been reversed. Aristotle had said that men outlived women, but there were more women than men in Italy by the thirteenth century. Women of that period also controlled more wealth, and they therefore needed to know how to read and to calculate, so their education was extended beyond handicrafts, especially among the rich merchant class. As upper-class women acquired more authority, they were also seen increasingly as a force for continuity. Many apparently disliked this role, for women were to be found expressing heretical views or showing strong antagonism toward the institutions that framed their lives. Still, heresy is not a test of the independence of women, since many appar-

WOMEN OF THE GENTLE CLASS

Robert of Blois, a thirteenth-century poet, wrote of the correct behavior for women "of the gentle class":

En route to church or elsewhere, a lady must walk straight and not trot or run, or idle either. She must salute even the poor.

She must let no one touch her on the breast except her husband. For that reason, she must not let anyone put a pin or a brooch on her bosom.

No one should kiss her on the mouth except her husband. If she disobeys this injunction, neither loyalty, faith nor noble birth will avert the consequences.

Women are criticized for the way they look at people, like a sparrowhawk ready to pounce on a swallow. Take care: glances are messengers of love; men are prompt to deceive themselves by them....

A lady does not accept gifts. For gifts which are given you in secret cost dear; one buys them with one's honor. There are, however, honest gifts which it is proper to thank people for.

Above all, a lady does not scold. Anger and high words are enough to distinguish a low woman from a lady. The man who injures you shames himself and not you; if it is a woman who scolds you, you will break her heart by refusing to answer her.

Women must not swear, drink too much or eat too much....

Ladies with pale complexions should dine early. Good wine colors the face. If your breath is bad, hold it in church when you receive the blessing....

Cut your fingernails frequently, down to the quick, for cleanliness' sake. Cleanliness is better than beauty.

From *Life in a Medieval City* by Joseph and Frances Gies. Copyright © 1969 by Joseph and Frances Gies. Reprinted by permission of Harper Collins Publishers.

---

ently followed their husbands into heresy, especially among the Albigensians (or Cathars, meaning "the pure"). Upper-class women were usually willing to play the roles assigned to them, however, since this would assure both salvation and inheritance.

Since Christianity associated nakedness with shame and sexual licentiousness, society developed strong dress signals to distinguish between the sexes at a glance. In the thirteenth century this need to obscure the body was combined with an aesthetic impulse to initiate through tailoring a concept of "fashion," which in turn became related to luxury. Though the role of women was ambivalent and changing, two developments brought the idea of womanhood into prominence. First was the rise of *Mariolatry* (the veneration of the Virgin Mary), which began in the ninth century and reached extraordinary heights by the twelfth century, when the Virgin was more likely to be the subject of an artist than was Jesus or the Apostles. Second was the celebration of courtly love and its accompanying forms of "manly combat" by the troubadours in France and Germany. Thus, as historians have noted, women greatly influenced two profoundly human activities—the making of love and the making of war.

Precisely when this first emancipation of women since the triumph of Christianity actually began is much debated by scholars. There is no doubt about the improved status of women by the fourteenth century. Because women participated in many significant ways in the spiritual movements (heretical as well as orthodox) of the twelfth century, their role was important within the medieval Christian tradition. However, it is also clear that in certain places—in Saxony, for example, where noblewomen founded many religious communities—women of the aristocracy were vigorously conducting affairs of state and church as early as the tenth century. Thus these four hundred years represent an inconsistent pattern of development, though by the end of the period women could aspire to substantial achievements within the models society had set for them and against the roles society had enforced upon men.

II THE MEDIEVAL CHURCH AS INSTITUTION

Down to 1500 society—both in western Europe and in Byzantium—was identical with the church. The separation of church and state, the existence indeed of several, even many, different churches, was simply unimaginable for any inhabitant of medieval Europe. Everyone except the Jews belonged to the church. And the church's laws protected the Jews from being killed or converted by force or having their worship impeded, although they often suffered social or financial disabilities and sometimes persecution or worse. But the Jews were the only exception; any others who sought to leave the church or departed from its teachings were outside the law, and it was the duty of society to exterminate them.

The Church Universal

The medieval church had many of the attributes of the modern state. Once baptized, everyone was subject to its laws, paid its taxes, and lived at its mercy. Yet while the rulers of the church—the popes—often strove to create the machinery that would make this absolutism work, they never fully succeeded. The story of their efforts, the degree of their success, the measure of their failure, the nature of the opposition to them are in some degree the political history of the Middle Ages in the West.

Having no armies of their own, the popes depended upon laymen—the kings and princes of Europe—to raise armies for the purposes of the church. Even a mighty secular ruler often bowed to the commands of a pope who seemed in every material respect far weaker than he. The pope had powerful spiritual weapons at his disposal: excommunication and interdict. *Excommunication* deprived the believer of the sacraments and threatened that person with hell fire if he or she died while excommunicated. This hell was a grim reality, and much attention was paid in the Middle Ages to working out the precise details of the "infernal journey." *Interdict* stopped all church services in a given area except baptism and the rites for the dying; none of the population could be married, take communion, confess and be absolved, or be buried with the assurance of salvation. A population under interdict sometimes became desperate, and its ruler often yielded.

As a superstate, the medieval church gradually saw its authority diminished by the growth of secular states. Yet even rulers of those secular states who challenged the popes took it for granted that they and all their subjects and the subjects of other kings and princes were automatically Christians. Holy relics were inserted into hollows built in the throne of Charlemagne, who often disagreed with the pope. The proudest possession of Otto the Great—who deposed one pope and installed another—was the holy lance, which, legend said, had been thrust into the side of Christ and had belonged to Constantine the Great. Such relics symbolized the total dependence of even the most powerful ruler in this world upon the will of God and served as a sign that he had God's favor. Coronation ceremonies both in the West and in the East emphasized the sacred character of the monarch being consecrated and were indispensable for public acceptance of the ruler.

But the economic expansion—it was almost an explosion—and the new drives of the eleventh century tended to diminish the sacred character of secular monarchy, as society grew more complex and more sophisticated and elaborate methods of government needed to be devised. As the king was perceived to be merely a human being doing a political job in this world and ceased to share an aura of sanctity with the churchmen, the churchmen alone, for a time, seemed to have a monopoly of spirituality. And since the secular rulers and their retainers were often unable to read and were almost always poorly educated, the tasks of secular government often fell to clerics, who performed them for both lay and ecclesiastical rulers. The western European church hierarchy of the eleventh to the fourteenth century has been well compared to a most efficient guild or labor union.

These centuries saw a sustained effort to build what has often been called a *papal monarchy*, to develop a system of ecclesiastical (canon) law, and to think through an overarching theological system. They also saw the expansion and proliferation of the monasteries as new orders of monks came into being, often with reform as their aim. In a sense, these centuries were the last great period of Western unity.

Theories of the Papal Monarchy

Those who use the term *papal monarchy* believe that the papacy strove steadily to dominate the temporal as well as the spiritual government. When secular states came into being, that in itself constituted a defeat of papal purposes. Others argue that Christian theorists had always understood that human affairs must be governed jointly by a secular and a religious authority and that, even when secular rulers came into severe conflict with the papacy, the popes, though voicing strong claims of supremacy, would never have wished to see secular rulers altogether powerless. A third group maintains that, at least in the heat of battle with secular authorities, the popes did in fact voice extreme claims to complete supremacy. In the controversies that marked the period between the eleventh and fourteenth centuries, both the papacy and secular rulers expressed many extreme views. It is often difficult to judge how far such statements were put forward with complete sincerity, how far as arguments to win adherents, or how far as expressions of extreme claims that might be used as bargaining positions, and from which some retreat was always envisioned.

Christ himself had cautioned the faithful to distinguish between the things that are Caesar's and the things that are God's (Luke 20:25), and to Peter he gave the keys of the kingdom of heaven and the power to "bind" and to "loose" both on earth and in heaven (Matthew 16:19). Paul cautioned all Christians that "the powers that be are ordained of God (Romans 13:1), so for Paul the secular powers were there to be obeyed. But at the time that Christ and Paul spoke, Christians were a tiny minority in the Roman world; the precepts became difficult to interpret later when the Christian church was supreme. As early as the fourth century, St. Ambrose, as bishop of Milan, excommunicated an emperor (Theodosius I) and forced him to do penance. Augustine had

THE GOOD WIFE

In the fourteenth century a source known to us as *The Goodman of Paris* recorded
what was expected of the good wife among the well-to-do burgher class:

You should be careful and thoughtful of your husband's person. Wherefore, fair sister, if you have another husband after me, know that you should think much of his person, for after that a woman has lost her first husband and marriage, she commonly findeth it hard to find a second to her liking, according to her estate, and she remaineth long while all lonely and disconsolate and the more so still if she lose the second. Wherefore love your husband's person carefully, and I pray you keep him in clean linen, for that is your business, and because the trouble and care of outside affairs lieth with men, so must husbands take heed, and go and come, and journey hither and thither, in rain and wind, in snow and hail, now drenched, now dry, now sweating, now shivering, ill-fed, ill-lodged, ill-warmed, and ill-bedded. And naught harmeth him, because he is upheld by the hope that he hath of the care which his wife will take care of him on his return, and of the ease, the joys, and the pleasures which she will do him, or cause to be done to him in her presence; to be unshod before a good fire, to have his feet washed and fresh shoes and hose, to be given good food and drink, to be well served and well looked after, well bedded in white sheets and nightcaps, well covered with good furs, and assuaged with other joys and desports, privities, loves, and secrets whereof I am silent. And the next day fresh shirts and garments. . . .

Wherefore, dear sister, I beseech you thus to bewitch and bewitch again your husband that shall be, and beware of roofless house and of smoky fire, and scold him not, but be unto him gentle and amiable and peaceable. . . . And in summer take heed that there be no fleas in your chamber, nor in your bed, the which you may do in six ways, as I have heard tell. [A long passage on how to deal with fleas and mosquitoes follows, after which the document turns to flies.]

And if you have a chamber or a passage where there is great resort of flies, take little sprigs of fern and tie them to threads like to tassels, and hang them up and all the flies will settle on them at eventide; then take down the tassels and throw them out . . . have whisks wherewith to slay them by hand . . . have little twigs covered with glue on a basin of water . . . have your windows shut full tight with oiled or other cloth . . . so tightly that no fly may enter. . . .

And thus shall you preserve and keep your husband from all discomforts and give him all the comforts whereof you can bethink you, and serve him and have him served in your house, and you shall look to him for outside things, for if he be good he will take even more pains and labour therein than you wish, and by doing what I have said, you will cause him ever to miss you and have his heart with you and your loving service and he will shun all other houses, all other women, all other services and households.

From *The Goodman of Paris,* trans. Eileen Power (London: Routledge & Kegan Paul Ltd., 1928), as excerpted in *The Portable Medieval Reader,* ed. James Bruce Ross and Mary Martin McLaughlin (New York: Viking Press, 1956), pp. 155–59.

conceded the necessity of a civil state with laws and police to enforce them, while cautioning true Christians to lift their eyes above the affairs of the mere earthly city. It was Pope Gelasius (r. 492–496), only two generations after Augustine, who wrote to the emperor at Constantinople that there were "two by which the world is ruled": the "sacred" authority (*auctoritas*) of priests and the royal power (*potestas*), and that the priests had the higher responsibility, since at the last judgment they would have to answer for the behavior of kings.

To this day scholars argue whether auctoritas meant "moral authority" or "the natural right to rule"; whether potestas meant "sovereign power" or only "a power delegated by a superior instructing church"; or even whether both words really meant essentially the same thing. Gelasius was surely thinking of the still more cryptic words of Luke 22:28, in which the apostles said to Christ, "Lord, behold, here are two swords," and Christ answered, "It is enough." This passage was constantly used in the Middle Ages to refer to the roles of the church and the state in human society.

Having broken with Byzantium and having been strengthened by the Frankish alliance and the protection of Pepin, Charlemagne, and their successors, the papacy in the tenth century sank into impotence, as the individual popes became instruments in the hands of rival Roman aristocratic families contesting for power in the city. Drunkenness, incest, arson, and murder were among the charges against the pope whom Otto deposed in 962. In such an atmosphere, the buying and selling of church offices (the sin of *simony*) was not uncommon, and immorality of other kinds—including the marriage or irregular union of priests or monks—was not curbed.

In medieval life, hell was real, specific, and very much to be feared. Historians are able to trace changing conceptions of sin and punishment from the way in which both high and low art depicted hell over the centuries. These scenes of hell from a wall painting at the Church of St. Peter and St. Paul in Surrey, England, date from about 1200. They show the weighing of souls, the tormenting of the wicked, the infernal cauldron, and the Bridge of Dread.
National Monuments Record, London

As early as the year 910, at Cluny, in eastern France, a Benedictine monastery was founded whose powerful abbots refused to tolerate, among their own flock or elsewhere, concubinage, the sale of church offices, and other abuses; they created a series of "daughter" monasteries all inspired with the same reforming principles. More than three hundred new monastic foundations were inspired by Cluny, which was probably the chief, though by no means the only, center of reforming currents in the church during the tenth and early eleventh centuries. Living in strict accordance with the ascetic rule of Benedict, the Cluniac monks acted as an organized pressure group to spread reform everywhere in the church.

Rome—home of the papacy and goal of pilgrims from all over western Europe, who believed it to be sanctified by the body of St. Peter himself in his church—remained the core of the church. Papal business continued to be conducted, even when the popes were viewed as unworthy. It was not until the mideleventh century that full-fledged reform came to the papacy itself. When it did so, the impulse was indeed partly Cluniac. But more important in papal reform, ironically enough, were the continued secular interests of the German monarchy. For this reason papal and German history became inextricably entwined.

III   THE INVESTITURE CONTROVERSY

As the Carolingian Empire gradually disintegrated in the late ninth and early tenth centuries, four duchies—Franconia, Saxony (of which Thuringia was a part), Swabia, and Bavaria—arose in the eastern Frankish lands of Germany. They were military units organized by the local Carolingians, who took the title of duke (army commander). When the Carolingian dynasty became extinct, they chose one of their own number—Conrad, duke of Franconia—as their king in 911, to protect their lands against Magyar invaders. But Conrad was a military failure and a newcomer. So the dukes for the first time asserted themselves as rivals to the Crown. They built their duchies into petty kingdoms, made themselves hereditary rulers, and took control over the church in their own duchies, dominating the local administrators of the king, the counts.

Saxon Administration and the German Church, 911–955

Conrad's successor, the duke of Saxony, became King Henry I (r. 919–936). He and his descendants—notably Otto the Great (r. 936–973) and Otto III (r. 983–1002)—successfully combated the ducal tendency to dominate the counts and to control the church; they made the counts serve under the Crown and regained the right to appoint bishops. In 939 the Crown obtained the duchy of Franconia; thenceforth the German kings, no matter what duchy they came from, would also have Franconia as the royal domain.

The Saxon dynasty established by Henry I relied on the church to perform much of the work of governing Germany, since bishops, unlike counts, could not pass on their offices to their sons, and bishops were better educated than laymen. The church welcomed the alliance because a strong central government was its best

Medieval Christianity

- Roman Catholic
- Orthodox Christian
- Muslims
- Pagan
- ◉ Seats of Patriarchs

The Empire, 962–1075

guarantee of stability; the papacy itself recognized the right of the German kings to appoint their own bishops. The Saxon monarchs gave church and abbey lands their special protection, exempting them from the authority of the counts and bringing them directly under the Crown. Like the former counts, the bishops obtained the right to administer justice within their own domain. In 1007, for instance, the bishops of the great sees of Bamberg and Würzburg were given all the rights that had formerly belonged to counts.

The church also supplied the German king with much of his revenue, and tenants of church lands furnished three-quarters of his army. The church participated in the German expansion to the east—the celebrated *Drang nach Osten*—in the defeat of the Magyars at Lechfeld (955), in the push into Slavic lands along the Elbe and Saale rivers, and in the advance into Silesia. New German bishoprics were set up, with Magdeburg as center, and subject sees were established east of the Elbe. Consequently, the church could impose Christianity upon the vanquished Slavs.

When King Otto took the title of emperor in 962, he created for his successors a set of problems that far transcended the local problems of Germany. In the Carolingian West, *emperor* had come to mean a ruler who controlled two or more kingdoms but who did not necessarily claim supremacy over the whole world, as had Rome. The kingdoms that the Western emperor was likely to control were Germany, Burgundy, and Italy. Burgundy had grown up under ambitious rulers in the region between the eastern and western Frankish lands. Italy, on the other hand, was weak, divided, and open to invasion. Thus the king of Germany had much to gain if he could secure the title of Emperor. And, if he did not make himself emperor, he faced a real danger that somebody else might.

Otto the Great's grandson, the brilliant young Otto III, used a seal with the words "Renewal of the Roman Empire." In Rome itself he strove to restore a Roman

German "Drang nach Osten"
Eastward Expansion, 800—1400

Areas of German Settlement

Boundary of the Empire
about 1200

■ Battle sites

Boundary between
Germans and Slavs
about 800

imperial palace, Roman titles, and Roman glory, possibly acting under the influence of his Byzantine mother and surely hoping to win the support of the Roman aristocracy. He also tried to make imperial power real in Italy by putting German officials on church lands to keep these lands out of the hands of the Italian nobility, and by appointing German bishops to Italian sees in an effort to build up the sort of government he had at home. Since Otto III did not ignore Germany but paid careful attention to relations between Germany and the Slavs, German contemporaries seem to have felt that his intervention in Italy was proper and legitimate. He was not trying to dominate the entire West but rather to establish himself as emperor in the new sense and to consolidate the rule of the Saxon dynasty.

German culture and trade benefited from the Italian connection. By the early eleventh century, the right of each new German king to be king of Italy and emperor was taken for granted; if a new king had not yet been crowned emperor by the pope, he called himself "king of the Romans, still to be promoted to emperor." Italy benefited as the long period of anarchy finally came to an end. The emperors raised the level of the papacy from the degradation it had reached in the tenth century. But as the emperors sponsored reform within the church, they set in motion forces that would make the papacy a world power and bring about their own eventual ruin.

A sense of German national unity was asserting itself, as shown by the general use of the term *teutonici* (Teutons, or Germans). When the Saxon dynasty died out in 1024, Conrad II (r. 1024–1039) was elected king. The new dynasty, which came from Franconia, produced activist administrators, notably Henry III (r. 1039–1056). Conrad began training members of the lower classes to serve as administrators. The church had long used such men to run its great estates, and now the kings used them to run the lands of the Crown. They often received lands as a reward, and their lands became hereditary. Thus these *ministeriales* depended directly on the Crown, had a status that could not be described as feudal, and remained as a class peculiar to Germany. Moreover, free men in Germany did not have to choose between becoming vassals of the dukes and destruction; both large and small estates continued to be owned outright by free men. Although the social distinction between the rich and poor was great, both were more often free of feudal ties than anywhere else in western Europe.

Though the class of free landholders had no feudal ties, it had no royal ties either. So when the attack came on the increasing centralization of the eleventh-century German monarchy, it came from these free landowners, a class that had no exact counterpart elsewhere in the West. They had strengthened their position by becoming the guardians or "advocates" (German *Vogt*) of monasteries, a process that was aided for a time by the Crown itself. In 973 there were 108 abbeys in Germany, probably all attached to the Crown; in 1075 there were more than seven hundred, and almost all the new ones were attached to members of the landowner class. Founding a new monastery in Germany was not solely a sign of the founder's piety, for monks colonized new lands, and the resulting revenues went to the founder of the house. To keep these valuable monasteries out of royal hands, the German nobles often made them the legal property of the pope, who was far away and could not interfere as readily as the king could. Thus, side by side with what may be termed the "royal" church and its bishops, there grew up in Germany a "noble" church based largely on monastic foundations.

Opposition to the royal church, to the power of the low-born ministeriales, and to the trend toward monarchical centralization led the German nobility to revolt. In 1073 the nobles rose in Saxony against the emperor Henry IV (r. 1056–1106); in 1075 Henry crushed the uprising. But only a few weeks later there began the open struggle with the papacy that gave the nobles new occasion to rebel. This was the Investiture Controversy, and it lasted half a century.

The Investiture Controversy, 1046–1122

The struggle originated in 1046, when the emperor Henry III found three rival popes simultaneously in office while mobs of their supporters rioted in the streets of Rome. He deposed all three. After two successive German appointees had died—perhaps by poison—Henry named a third German, Bishop Bruno of Toul, who became pope as Leo IX (r. 1049–1054). Leo was committed to the Cluniac program of monastic reform; the whole church hierarchy, he insisted, must be purged of secular influences, and over it all the pope must reign supreme. The emperor Henry III had thus put into power reformers whose chief target would be his own imperial system of government in Germany. Leo began to appoint *cardinals* (from the Latin *cardo*, a hinge), who now served as key advisers and administrators instead of merely ornamental dignitaries, which they had been. By 1059 the papacy had given these cardinals the power to elect new popes, depriving the German emperors of that role. And the Normans of southern Italy promised to give the cardinals military backing, so that they could do their job without fear of German intervention.

In 1073 the Italian monk Hildebrand became pope as Gregory VII (r. to 1085). He was determined to push ecclesiastical reform by ensuring the canonical (legal) election of all bishops and abbots. This would mean sweeping away the system of royal selection and appointment and its subsequent ceremony of lay investiture—that is, the conferring of the prelate's insignia of office (for bishops, a ring and a staff) by a layman, the

emperor. Yet the German royal administration largely depended on this royal appointment of prelates, which involved not only lay investiture but the granting of royal estates to bishops.

Gregory declared that the pope was subject to no human judgment; that the Roman church had never erred and never could err; that the pope alone could make new laws, create new bishoprics, depose bishops, and change his own mind; that all temporal princes should kiss his feet; that the imperial insignia were his alone to use; that he could absolve the subjects of a temporal prince from their allegiance and could depose emperors. By the merits of St. Peter, he declared, all popes were saints. Such claims were a new interpretation of Pope Gelasius's words of six centuries earlier.

In 1075 Gregory forbade lay investiture. Henry IV's bishops responded in 1076 by declaring Gregory deposed. Gregory then excommunicated Henry as a usurper, declared him deposed, absolved his subjects of loyalty to him, and deprived the bishops of their offices. The Saxon nobles, opponents of Henry, thereupon joined forces with the pope and made Henry promise to clear himself of the excommunication within four months, on pain of the loss of his crown; they also invited the pope to Germany.

To prevent this unwelcome visit, Henry secretly went to Italy in January of 1077 and appeared before the castle of Canossa, where Gregory was temporarily staying. Henry declared himself a penitent; Gregory kept him waiting outside the castle for three days, barefoot and in sackcloth. When he was finally admitted, Henry did penance and Gregory absolved him. The drama and symbolism of this famous episode have often led historians to marvel at the power of the pope. But it struck contemporaries the other way. By allowing himself to be publicly humiliated, Henry had forced Gregory's hand; the pope had been compelled to absolve him, and while in a state of being forgiven he could not be deposed.

Before Henry returned home, his German opponents had elected a new ruler, an "anti-king," Rudolf of Swabia. By refraining for three years from making a decision between the rival kings, Gregory VII did what he could deliberately to prolong the resulting civil war. When he did decide, it was against Henry, whom he deposed and excommunicated once more. But the pope's efforts failed; Rudolf was killed in battle, and a new anti-king commanded even less support. The German clergy again declared the pope deposed, and Henry marched to Italy, took Rome in 1084 after three years of bitter siege, and installed an "anti-pope," who proceeded to crown him emperor. Gregory's Norman vassals and allies did not arrive until after Henry had returned to Germany. They looted Rome and took Gregory with them to southern Italy, where he died; by 1091 the last vestige of the revolt against Henry in Germany had been stamped out.

No settlement of the Investiture Controversy could be reached until 1122. In the Concordat of Worms,

Henry IV at Canossa as traditionally
represented.
Art Resource

Henry V (1106–1125) renounced the practice of investing bishops with the clerical symbols of ring and staff. The pope permitted the emperor to continue investing bishops with the *regalia* (symbols of the worldly goods pertaining to the bishop's office). The investiture could take place before the bishop was consecrated, assuring the emperor of a previous oath of fealty from the bishop. Moreover, clerical elections in Germany were to be carried out in the presence of the emperor or his representatives, giving him an opportunity to exercise a strong influence over the decisions. In Italy and Burgundy the emperor retained less power; consecration was to take place before the regalia were conferred, and the emperor could not attend clerical elections. Thus the Concordat of Worms was a compromise that in effect ended the Investiture Controversy, despite its failure to settle many other issues.

But by 1122 Germany had become feudalized. During the years between 1076 and 1106 the princes and other nobles acted on the pretext that there was no king, since the pope had deposed him. They extended their powers and administered their lands without reference to the monarchy. Castles multiplied and became centers of administrative districts, laying the foundations for territorial principalities; free peasants fell into serfdom; the weakness of central authority drove lesser nobles to become dependent on greater nobles. In short, the familiar feudalizing process that had gone on in ninth- and tenth-century France now was operating in eleventh- and early twelfth-century Germany.

In Italy the Investiture Controversy had seen the further rise of the Norman kingdom of the south. The struggle had also been responsible for the growth of communes in the cities of the north. These communes had begun as sworn associations of lesser nobles who banded together to resist the power of the local bishops. In Lombardy, where they were favored by Gregory VII, the communes took advantage of his support to usurp the powers of municipal government. In Tuscany, where the ruling house was pro-papal, the communes allied themselves with the emperor, who granted them their liberties by charter. Thus, in Germany the Crown faced a newly entrenched aristocracy; in Italy it faced a new society of powerful urban communes.

The German nobles now controlled the election of the emperor. In 1138 they chose Conrad of Hohenstaufen, a Swabian prince, who became Emperor Conrad III (r. 1138–1152). In so doing, they passed over another claimant, Henry the Proud, duke of Bavaria and Saxony and marquis of Tuscany in Italy, a member of the powerful Welf family. Because of their ancestral estate, the Hohenstaufens were often known as Waiblings; in Italian, *Waibling* became *Ghibelline* and *Welf* became *Guelf*. Thus in the first half of the twelfth century, the Guelf-Ghibelline (or Welf-Waibling) feud—one of the most famous, lasting, and portentous in history—began. Henry the Proud, the Welf leader, refused homage to Conrad III; Conrad in turn deprived Henry of Saxony and Bavaria. Once more feudal warfare raged in Germany.

IV PAPACY AND EMPIRE, 1152–1273

With the revival of the study of Roman law during the twelfth century went a corresponding interest among churchmen in the systematization of canonical law. As the texts of Justinian's civil law became familiar to the students in the law schools—of which Bologna in Italy was the most important—the Bolognese monk Gratian about 1140 published the *Decretum*, a similar effort to codify for the first time past decrees of popes, enactments of church councils, and decisions of church fathers dating back a millennium. Gratian tried to reconcile apparently conflicting decisions and produced for church lawyers an indispensable tool that emphasized the papal role.

Investiture was replaced in the papal-imperial struggle by what we today call "the Italian question": How could an emperor be sovereign over Italy—including Rome—without trespassing on papal sovereignty? But if an emperor did not have effective sovereignty over Italy, did his title "Roman Emperor" become meaningless? Or was the pope in some sense the emperor's feudal overlord for his Italian possessions, and was the emperor therefore the pope's vassal? By the 1140s a mosaic picture in the papal palace of St. John Lateran showed the emperor kneeling at the pope's feet, and, as the inscription said, becoming his liege man and receiving the crown from him in return. This was not the sort of claim that a powerful or ambitious emperor would accept. And in 1152, when Frederick I Hohenstaufen (r. to 1190), nicknamed Barbarossa, "Redbeard," came to the throne of divided feudal Germany, the issue was joined.

Frederick Barbarossa and Henry VI, 1152–1192

In 1156 Frederick married the heiress to Burgundy, which had slipped out of imperial control during the Investiture Controversy. He made Switzerland the strategic center of his policy, for it controlled the Alpine passes into Italy. In Swabia he tried to build a compact, well-run royal domain, but he needed the loyalty of cooperative great vassals. And in Lombardy he also needed an alliance with the communes in the towns.

Frederick Barbarossa made six trips to Italy. He intervened first at Rome, where in 1143 a commune had risen up against papal rule. The leader of the commune, Arnold of Brescia, strongly favored the church's return to apostolic poverty and simplicity. Barbarossa won papal good will by offering the pope assistance not only against Arnold but also against the Normans and against the Byzantine threat to southern Italy. He was crowned emperor in Rome in 1155, after an argument over whether he would hold the pope's bridle and stirrup as well as kiss his foot. (Frederick lost.) At the pope's request, the emperor hanged and burned Arnold, whose death he is later said to have regretted. The pope, however, soon reached an accommodation with the Normans and quarreled with Frederick once more in 1157; the pope seemed to be claiming that Frederick held the empire for him as a *benefice*, a fief or a "concession."

The Milanese resisted Frederick, and when a vigorous pope Alexander III (r. 1159–1181) came to power, Frederick faced the pope, Milan, and Sicily united. They drove him back into Italy, and in 1176 their forces defeated his at Legnano. With the Peace of Constance in 1183, Frederick gave up his claims to direct imperial authority in the Lombard cities, though the Lombard League paid a special tax to support the imperial army. Frederick's claims as feudal suzerain were recognized, but the cities had gained independence over various matters.

To free himself for his Italian pursuits, Frederick Barbarossa made concessions to the German princes. His great Welf rival, Henry the Lion, who was Frederick's cousin, obtained the right to invest the bishops of several important sees; he also led a great wave of German eastward expansion into the Slavic lands across the Elbe. Henry married the daughter of Henry II of England. In 1176, when Henry tried to bargain with Frederick over troops needed for Italy, Frederick summoned him to his royal court. A refusal to come enabled the emperor to declare Henry a "contumacious" vassal and later to seize his property (1180).

The great territorial possessions of the Welf family were now broken up and divided among other smaller princes. Frederick could not hold on to his lands because he could not control his German vassals effectively. It was part of the price he paid for his Italian enterprises. In the same year (1180), Frederick recognized his immediate vassals as princes of the empire, giving formal recognition to the new feudal order in Germany by creating a new class jealous of its prerogatives.

Four years before he died, in 1186, Frederick arranged the marriage of his son, Henry, to Constance, the heiress of Norman Sicily—one of the most important dynastic marriages of the Middle Ages. The papal territories were squeezed between the heir to Germany and northern Italy and the heiress to southern Italy and Sicily. The marriage guaranteed a new round in the papal-imperial struggle.

When Henry VI (r. 1190–1197) married Constance, he acquired an extraordinary kingdom built up in less than two centuries by the descendants of the Norman adventurers. But the pope, the German Welfs, and King Richard I, the Lionhearted, of England jointly backed a rival of Henry for Sicily. Henry captured Richard and forced him to become his vassal and to break the alliance. By 1194 Henry was supreme at Palermo, the Sicilian capital, and he refused to do homage to the pope. Rather, Henry planned to acquire the Byzantine Empire, against which the Normans had waged intermittent warfare since the early eleventh century. He was building up a fleet to invade the eastern Mediterranean when he died suddenly in 1197. Henry had widened the concept of empire, but he had sacrificed such unity as he might have achieved in Germany to the imperial dreams of union with Sicily, by which the pope would remain encircled. To persuade the German princes to recognize the hereditary rights of his son, Frederick II, to succeed him, he offered each of them hereditary rights in his own fief.

Innocent III, 1198–1216

Three months after the death of Henry VI, when his infant son and heir, Frederick II, was only four years old, there came to the papal throne Innocent III (r. 1198–1216), the greatest of all the medieval popes and still one of the most controversial. His powerful intervention in the affairs of secular princes was by no means limited to the traditional papal-imperial struggle; Innocent played a major part in the politics of France, England, and the Byzantine Empire.

Innocent said that papal power was like the sun, and

Between 1296 and 1304 the artist Giotto di Bondone depicted the life of St. Francis in a great cycle of frescoes for the Upper Basilica of St. Francis in Assisi. Here Pope Innocent III is shown confirming the Rule of St. Francis.
Scala/Art Resource

kingly power like the moon, which derives its light from the sun. While he granted that his own position was "lower than God," he maintained that it was loftier than that of any other man. But he usually made such claims outside the context of any specific controversy; in such cases he usually found some explanation for his actions that did not depend on sweeping theoretical assertions. Yet occasionally he did seem to assert the right to act as supreme judge of any dispute in Christendom.

A professional lawyer, Innocent was a practical man of affairs, and he wanted to accomplish the ends he had in view. He held the loftiest conception of the role of the church in the world, and of the pope's role in the church. He legislated widely on matters quite unconnected with politics, and he favored reform of the church. However we evaluate his ambitions, he came closer than any pope before or after to making the papal monarchy a reality.

During the minority of Frederick II, who was the ward of the pope, Innocent determined to destroy the German-Sicilian combination. He backed a Welf educated in England, Otto of Brunswick, son of Henry the Lion, against Philip of Swabia, brother of Henry VI, who initially had the support of the German princes. Innocent revived the claim of Gregory VII that no emperor could rule without papal confirmation, while Philip argued that an emperor duly elected by the princes was emperor whether the pope approved or not. To assure himself of papal support, Otto promised to give up all rights with regard to investiture that the emperors had salvaged for themselves from the Investiture Controversy. The kings of England backed their Welf nephew, Otto, while their enemy, King Philip Augustus of France, naturally opposed the English-Welf coalition by backing Philip of Swabia. The fighting continued until 1208, when Philip of Swabia was assassinated.

The German princes elected Otto IV, and he was crowned by the pope in 1209. He undertook to conquer Sicily, the very thing Innocent III wanted most to prevent. So in 1210 the pope excommunicated Otto and turned to the young Frederick Hohenstaufen, son of Henry VI. Supported by the pope and given money by the French, Frederick reorganized the Hohenstaufen party in Germany. When Otto and the English were defeated at Bouvines by the French (1214), Frederick's position became more secure, especially after he promised Innocent III that he would never try to unite his German and Sicilian possessions into one imperial state.

In 1215 Innocent held a great council at the Church of St. John Lateran in Rome to pronounce not only on the sacraments but on church discipline. Annual confession, penance, and communion were required for all Christians; heresies were condemned; and a new holy war was proclaimed against the Muslims. Innocent seemed to have triumphed wholly. But he died the next year, and Frederick II soon gave the papacy more trouble than even Henry IV had.

Frederick II, 1212–1250

Frederick II is perhaps the most interesting medieval monarch. Intelligent and cultivated, he spoke Arabic and Greek, took a deep interest in scientific experiment, collected wild animals, and wrote poetry in Italian. He patronized the arts, wrote on the sport of falconry, and was a superb politician. He was cynical, tough, a sound diplomat, an able administrator, and a statesman with his father's vision of a Mediterranean empire. Furthermore, he felt at home in Sicily—the sophisticated society in which his mother had grown up—and greatly preferred it to Germany. Indeed, he spent only nine of his thirty-eight years as emperor in Germany.

In Sicily Frederick imposed his own completely centralized monarchical form of government upon his Italian subjects. Feudal custom was wiped out and trial by battle forbidden. At Naples Frederick founded a university, which became a state training school in which officials could be grounded in the Roman law. His army and navy were organized on a paid rather than a feudal basis. Finances were regularized and modernized, and an imperial bureaucracy collected taxes on incoming and outgoing merchandise. State monopolies like those at Byzantium controlled certain key industries, such as silk.

Germany, by contrast, suffered. The Germans felt that they had no stake in Frederick's empire. He could never extend to Germany the centralized administration that he built in Sicily. Indeed, when in 1220 he obtained for his son, Henry, election as king of Germany and a promise from the bishops and abbots that Henry would be the next emperor, he granted still more privileges to these ecclesiastical princes, who were already elected without imperial interference. Frederick abandoned his right to set up mints and customs stations in their territories, together with royal rights of justice. He promised to exclude from imperial cities any serfs who might run away from church lands to try their fortunes in the towns, and he agreed to build no new towns or fortresses on church lands. Thus he acted against the towns, failing to see that they were natural royal allies. In 1231 the secular German princes exacted similar privileges from Frederick. In Germany both the ecclesiastical and the secular princes had become virtually independent.

Yet the preoccupation of Frederick II's reign was his tremendous conflict with the papacy, beginning in the 1220s. His opponents were three successive popes—Honorius III (r. 1216–1227), Gregory IX (r. 1227–1241), and Innocent IV (r. 1243–1254)—who were not only consistently determined to prevent him from achieving his aims but were competent to fight him on even terms. Honorius did crown Frederick emperor in 1220, but before Honorius died, Frederick was already asserting himself in sensitive Lombard territory. During the emperor's absence from Italy on a crusade, Gregory IX's newly hired mercenary armies attacked his southern

Italian lands. When Frederick returned, he was able to make peace temporarily, but he soon created further trouble. After he had defeated the Lombard towns in 1237 for refusing to keep the terms of the Peace of Constance, he announced a new plan to extend imperial administration to all Italy, including Rome. So in 1239 the pope excommunicated him and war was resumed. Violent propaganda pamphlets were circulated by both sides. The pope called Frederick a heretic who was trying to found a new religion. Frederick called the pope a hypocrite and urged all monarchs in Europe to unite against the pretensions of the church. Hemmed in at Rome by the encroaching imperial system, the pope summoned a church council, presumably to depose Frederick. But Frederick's fleet captured the entire council of more than one hundred high churchmen. Just as Frederick was about to enter Rome itself, Pope Gregory IX died (1241). Frederick tried to install a new pope favorable to himself but failed. The new pope, Innocent IV, fled from Italy, summoned a council to Lyon (1245), and deposed Frederick. There followed five more years of struggle; but before the conflict had been settled Frederick died in 1250.

In its last phases, when he was locked in combat with Innocent IV, Frederick—who had hitherto always protested that he was a good Christian and had proper reverence for the papal office—wrote a letter to the princes of Europe furiously attacking the clergy for their greed. He himself, he said, would reform the church by confiscating all its wealth. Maybe a return to the poverty of the early Christian days would breed saints who would heal the sick and perform an occasional miracle rather than clergymen who stuck their noses into political affairs that were none of their business. Although his letter was obviously a cynical piece of propaganda that seems to have startled its recipients and won over no one, it foreshadowed the days, not far off, when powerful laymen would move vigorously against the organized church. In response, Innocent IV's propagandists had to fall back on a new interpretation of the Donation of Constantine, claiming that the popes had always had the right to make and unmake emperors.

After Frederick's death, the papacy pursued his descendants with fury. In 1266 a long-maturing papal plan succeeded. Charles of Anjou, the ruthless and able brother of Louis IX, king of France, was brought into Italy as the papal candidate for the southern territories. He defeated and killed Frederick's son and grandson and established himself as king in the south.

By 1268 the Hohenstaufen line was extinct. The Holy Roman Empire, given an Italian rather than a German base by Henry VI and Frederick II, had been destroyed by the papacy. Yet within only forty years of Charles of Anjou's entry into Italy as the instrument of papal vengeance, Charles's grandnephew, King Philip IV of France (Philip the Fair), would puncture the temporal claims of the papacy and carry it off to "captivity" in France.

Emperor Frederick II, on the ship on the left, watches his soldiers attack churchmen on their way to the council summoned by Gregory IX.
New York Public Library Collection

In Germany the imperial throne remained vacant from 1254 to 1273. The princes consolidated their power during this interregnum by taking advantage of the large grants made by rival candidates to the throne (all foreigners) in the hope of receiving their support. But the princes were pleased for a time not to have an emperor; their usurpation of rights that had formerly belonged to the monarchy was now well on its way to completion. Meanwhile, the old links with Italy were virtually broken, and the earlier form of the imperial idea vanished. Imperial preoccupation with Italy had ensured that the princes would emerge as the real rulers of Germany. Thereafter *particularism*, an intense localism, would dominate in Germany until the nineteenth century, while united nation-states were rising in the West. Ultimately, the monarchical papacy and the German kingdom would destroy each other.

V THE CHURCH IN SOCIETY

Frederick II's denunciation of the church was a partisan document issued for his own selfish purposes. Yet he was right in believing that the church needed reform. For example, Innocent IV, in fighting Frederick, had approved the appointment to a bishopric in German territory of an illiterate and dissolute young man of nineteen just because he was a member of a powerful anti-Hohenstaufen noble family; this bishop was forced to resign after twenty-five years, when the last Hohenstaufen was dead, but only because his public boasting about his fourteen bastards (some by abbesses and nuns), all of whom he had provided with ecclesiastical benefices, had become a scandal. Because the church had an efficient bureaucracy in each bishopric, it probably did not matter much if the bishop were incompetent or even wicked; in the end the papacy, which had installed him, removed him, in effect removing itself. The need for reform was constantly felt in the church itself, and successive waves of reforming zeal manifested themselves, especially in monastic movements. But reforming enthusiasm is difficult to sustain over a long period, especially after the particular abuses that arouse it begin to yield.

Cluny, within the Benedictine order, continued in its determination to rid the church of abuses; its centrally organized rule over daughter houses was its strength and its weakness. The effectiveness of centralized control depended on the personality of the abbot of the ruling house; a weak or selfish or cynical abbot would endanger the whole enterprise. Those who started out determined to leave the world and live in poverty and humility found themselves admired by the rich and

Medieval
Germany and Italy

At the Death of Frederick II, 1250

■   Battle sites

──   Boundary of the Holy Roman Empire

▨   Kingdom of the Two Sicilies

▨   Papal States

□   Claimed by papacy

▨   Venetian possessions

North Sea

PRUSSIA

Danzig

Lübeck
Hamburg
Bremen
Weser R.
Elbe R.
POMERANIA
Vistula R.

SAXONY
BRANDENBURG
Harz Mts.
Magdeburg
Goslar

POLAND

KINGDOM OF GERMANY
SILESIA
Oder R.

Meuse R.

Cologne
Aachen
THURINGIA
Elbe R.
Saale R.

LOWER
LORRAINE

Bouvines

Trier
Mainz
Worms
Frankfurt
Main R.
Würzburg
Bamberg
Prague
BOHEMIA
MORAVIA

UPPER
LORRAINE
PALATINATE
FRANCONIA

Ratisbon
AUSTRIA

F R A N C E

Danube R.
Augsburg
Strasbourg
Vienna

SWABIA
BAVARIA
STYRIA

Constance
Saône R.
KINGDOM OF BURGUNDY
(KINGDOM OF ARLES)

A L P S
CARINTHIA
TYROL
CARNIOLA
Trieste

Drava R.
Danube R.

Legnano
Brescia
Milan
Adige R.
Venice
LOMBARDY
Pavia
Po R.
Roncaglia
Ferrara
H U N G A R Y

Alessandria
Canossa
Genoa
Bologna
Ravenna
Zara
ROMAGNA

Rhône R.
KINGDOM
OF ITALY
Florence
Pisa
Ancona

S E R B I A

Avignon
Arles
Siena
Assisi
Ragusa

TUSCANY
Adriatic Sea

CORSICA
(to Pisa)

PAPAL
Rome ■ Tagliacozzo
STATES
Anagni
Bari

Melfi
APULIA
Naples
Amalfi Salerno
Taranto

SARDINIA
(to Pisa and Genoa)

KINGDOM
OF THE
TWO SICILIES
(Hohenstaufen, 1194)

CALABRIA

Palermo

SICILY
Syracuse

M e d i t e r r a n e a n S e a

0   100   200
Miles

199

often took gifts that in turn transformed them into worldly men of business all too concerned with the things of this life. Thus, by the late eleventh century, the Cluniac houses had become wealthy and their rule had relaxed.

Augustinians and Cistercians

One newly founded order broke with the rule of Benedict, finding its inspiration in a letter of Augustine that prescribed simply that monks share all their property, pray together at regular intervals, dress alike, and obey a superior. Some of the "Augustinians," as they called themselves, interpreted these general rules severely, living in silence, performing manual labor, eating and drinking sparingly, and singing psalms; others ate meat, conversed among themselves, and did not insist on manual labor. Beginning often as small informal foundations without large endowments, the Augustinians helped the sick and did useful, if humble, actions in the world, rather than leaving it altogether. They attracted modest donations from relatively modest donors. Unlike Cluny, with its vast collections of buildings crowned by a great and splendid church, the Augustinian foundations were simple and humble. The Augustinians wore neither splendid vestments nor hairshirts and ropes; but they preached, baptized, heard confessions, and helped the poor unobtrusively. They multiplied rapidly, and in the thirteenth century there were thousands of Augustinian houses in England and on the Continent.

Founded only a little later, the Cistercians abandoned the world instead of living in it. Their original house, Cîteaux (Cistercium) in Burgundy, lay in a dismal wasteland far from the distractions of the world and there they pioneered land reclamation and launched a period of agricultural expansion. By the twelfth century the Cistercians were looked to for their knowledge of how to make previously uncultivated lands, often swamps, productive. They considered themselves the only true Benedictines, aggressively declaring that the rule of Benedict, when lived purely, was identical with the message of the Gospels—life as Christ himself had lived it. Yet the self-denial, poverty, and wholly spiritual life in retirement that the Cistercians adopted was often seen by their contemporaries as arrogant, militant, worldly, and even greedy.

The most celebrated Cistercian leader was Bernard of Clairvaux (c. 1091–1153), who in 1115 led a small band of Cistercians to Clairvaux, a spot as unpromising as Cîteaux itself. From here the ostensibly unworldly Bernard influenced the affairs of the world to a degree almost beyond modern understanding. He not only upbraided clergymen for their laxity in observing ecclesiastical rules, but also helped to organize a Crusade to the Holy Land, advised the kings of France, and chastened even the greatest feudal nobles.

In the end, the Cistercians, too, changed. Display conquered austerity, and aristocratic traditions quenched humility. By the thirteenth century, great Cistercian monasteries—Fountains Abbey in Yorkshire, for instance—were wealthy centers of production. The expensive arts of architecture and sculpture—scorned initially by Bernard as devilish devices that took men's attention from worship—were lavished on their buildings. These Cistercian monasteries had become great corporations, thoroughly tied into the increasingly complex web of medieval economic life.

Friars: Dominicans and Franciscans

In the early thirteenth century, the reforming movement within the church took on new aspects. As town populations grew, the new urban masses—often neglected by the church and hostile to the rich and worldly clergy—were eager to "get religion" in a revivalist sense, and they were sometimes subject to waves of mass and unthinking emotional enthusiasms which could lead to heresy. These outbreaks and the fears that led to them were a cry for spiritual help. The mendicant orders, or begging orders, were, therefore, also meant to be a response to heresy. Two famous new orders of friars—Dominican and Franciscan—thus arose.

Dominic (1170–1221) was a Spanish Augustinian canon who saw richly dressed Cistercian abbots wholly failing in their mission to convert heretics in southern France in 1206. He revived the idea of apostolic simplicity that had given birth to the Augustinians, founded the "Order of Preachers" within the Augustinian rule, and until his death directed them in their work of preaching and living the life of simple, primitive Christians.

Francis (1182–1226), the son of a wealthy Italian merchant, gave his possessions to the poor in 1206, and with a few followers, who had also given up their property, obtained Pope Innocent III's approval of his new order of the Friars Minor (little brothers) in 1210. Poverty was not new, but the heavy emphasis that Francis placed upon it—the brothers were to be dependent for their daily bread upon alms from the charitable—was new. Much against his will, Francis was soon the head of a large, loosely structured organization.

Dominic subordinated all other duties to the obligation to preach, while Francis of Assisi led a truly grassroots urban movement of protest against wealth and show. They were rivals in a sense, and both orders were soon borrowing from each other's principles. The Franciscans adopted the more efficient organizing principles of the Dominicans; the Dominicans took over the Franciscan emphasis on poverty. From the first the Dominicans had emphasized the need of study as a fundamental duty; the Franciscans, who began by repudiating book learning, soon imitated the Dominicans, moved into the universities and became distinguished scholars. Both orders divided Europe into "provinces" and spread widely.

Scenes of student life in the Middle Ages.
Pierpont Morgan Library

Education

The church alone directed and conducted education in medieval Europe. Unless destined for the priesthood, young men of the upper classes had little formal schooling, though the family chaplain often taught them to read and write. Young women had no more and usually less education. But the monastic schools educated future monks and priests, and the Cluniac reform, with its increased demand for piety, stimulated study and the copying of manuscripts.

Medieval scholars divided knowledge into the seven liberal arts: the trivium (grammar, rhetoric, dialectic) and the quadrivium (arithmetic, geometry, astronomy, music). The first three included much of what we might call humanities today; the last four corresponded to the sciences. In the eleventh century only a few monastic schools taught all seven. In general monks sought to preserve rather than to advance knowledge.

The cathedral schools, on the other hand, whose teachers were often less timid about studying classical pagan writings, fostered a more inquiring spirit. In France during the eleventh century, at the cathedral schools of Paris, Chartres, Rheims, and other towns, distinguished teachers were often succeeded by men whom they themselves had trained, and distinguished pupils went on to join or found other schools. In Italy,

where the connection with cathedrals was less close, a medical school had existed at Salerno since the early Middle Ages. At Bologna law became the speciality, beginning as a branch of rhetoric and so within the trivium. Students were attracted to Bologna from other regions of Italy and even from northern Europe. In the early twelfth century, as education became fashionable for young men ambitious for advancement in the church or in the royal service, the number of students grew rapidly.

The student body at Bologna organized itself into two associations—students from Italy and students from beyond the Alps—and in the twelfth century the two incorporated as the whole body, the *universitas*, or university. As a corporate body they could protect themselves against being overcharged for food and lodging by threatening to leave town; having no property, they could readily have moved. They depended on their own work, or on their parents, to meet their fees:

> *Well-beloved father, I have not a penny, nor can I get any save through you, for all things at the University are so dear: nor can I study in my Code or my Digest, for they are all tattered. Moreover, I owe ten crowns in dues to the Provost, and can find no man to lend them to me: I send you word of greetings and money.**

* Quoted in G. G. Coulton, *Life in the Middle Ages* (Cambridge: Cambridge University Press, 1929), III. 113.

If the students did not like a professor, they simply stayed away from his lectures, and he starved or moved on, for he depended on their tuition fees for his living. Soon the students fixed the price of room and board in town and fined professors for absence or for lecturing too long. The professors organized, too, and admitted to their number only those who had passed an examination and so won a *license* to teach, remote ancestor of formal academic degrees.

In Paris and elsewhere in the north the cathedral schools were the forerunners of the universities. It was the teachers, not the students, who organized first, as a guild of those who taught the seven liberal arts and who got their licenses from the cathedral authorities. By the thirteenth century pious citizens had founded in Paris the first residence halls for poor students, who might eat and sleep free in these "colleges." The practice crossed the Channel to Oxford and Cambridge, where the schools' authorities stoutly resisted control by the secular powers. The friction of "town and gown" dates from medieval times, a friction to which the students contributed when they played, drank, sang, hazed new students, organized hoaxes and practical jokes, and rioted. Educational authorities passed many ordinances, usually in vain, against student sports and brawls.

The Question of Universals

Much of the study at that time consisted of mere memorizing by rote, since in the days before printing ready reference works were scarce. Though the formal rules of scholarly debate were fixed, there was, nonetheless, lively discussion available for those who worked to sharpen their minds, not just to load their memories. Discussion and teaching were particularly preoccupied with defining systems by which people could live faithfully within the expectations of Christendom.

At the turn of the eleventh century, Gerbert of Aurilac, who became Pope Sylvester II (r. 999–1003), stood out as the most learned man of his day; the smattering of mathematics and science that he had been able to pick up caused his contemporaries to suspect him of witchcraft. Because he was interested in logic, he turned to the work of Boethius. His probing mind delved into the portions of Aristotle that Boethius had translated and discovered in logic a systematic means of approaching the writings of the church fathers. By the end of the century, churchmen could debate whether it was proper to use human reason to consider a particular theological question (for example, was Christ actually present in the sacramental wafer and wine?), and in efforts to explain away inconsistencies in the Bible and in the writings of the church fathers. Even those who attacked the use of reason used it themselves in making new definitions that enabled them to argue that bread and wine could, in a certain way, become flesh and blood.

Once the new method became available, the dogmatists of the late eleventh and early twelfth centuries employed it in a celebrated controversy over the philosophical problem of *universals*. A universal encompasses a whole category of things; when we say "dog" or "table" or "person," we mean not any specific dog or table or person, but the idea of *all* dogs, tables, or people. The question that concerned medieval thinkers was whether universal categories exist: Is there such a thing as dogdom, tabledom, or humanity apart from the aggregate of individuals?

If you said no, you were a *nominalist*; that is, you thought dogdom, tabledom, humanity were merely *nomina*—names that people give to a general category from their experience of individual members of it. You experience dogs, tables, persons, and so you infer the existence of dogdom, tabledom, humanity because the individual members of the category have certain points of resemblance; but the category, the universal, has no existence in itself. If you said yes, you were a *realist*, that is, you thought that the general categories did exist. Many realists took this view a large step further and said that the individual dog, table, or person was far *less* real than the generalizing category or universal. Some said that the individual dog, table, or person was a mere reflection of one aspect of the category and existed only by virtue of belonging to the category: a person exists only by partaking of the nature of humanity, a dog because it partakes of the nature of dogdom.

If we transfer this question to politics and think of the state and the individual, we can see at once how great its practical importance may be. A pure nominalist would say that the state is just a name and exists only because the individuals who make it up are real. It could therefore be argued that the state must then serve its subjects, since after all it is only the sum of their individualities. A pure realist would say that the state is the only real thing, that its individual subjects exist only insofar as they partake of its general character, and that the state, by virtue of its existence, properly dominates the individual. In religion, an extreme nominalist, arguing that what we can perceive through our senses is alone real, might even have trouble believing in the existence of God. An extreme realist would tend to ignore, or even to deny, the existence of the physical world and its problems.

Moderate realists have to start with faith–to believe so that they may know, as Anselm (1033–1109) put it. A philosopher and theologian, Anselm was the archbishop of Canterbury, and likely to be listened to. He founded the approach to knowledge known as *Scholasticism*, which is based in part on his ontological proof for the existence of God. According to Anselm's proof, that which exists in reality *as well as* in the mind must be greater than that which exists in the mind alone, and since the mind can conceive the idea of a being greater than all else, it logically follows that this being *must exist in reality* as well as in the mind, or it is not in fact greater than anything else.

Peter Abelard (1079–1142), a popular lecturer at the University of Paris, tried to compromise the question. He argued that universals were not merely names, as the nominalists held, nor did they have a real existence, as the realists held. They were, he said, concepts in people's minds, and as such had a real existence of a special kind in the mind, which had created them out of its experience of particulars: humanity from individuals, dogdom from dogs, and so on. Abelard's compromise between nominalism and realism is called *conceptualism*.

Abelard insisted on the importance of understanding for true faith. He put reason first, and thus a person must understand in order to believe, instead of the other way around. His famous work *Sic et Non* (Yes and No), lists more than 150 theological statements and cites authorities both defending and attacking the truth of each. When Scripture and the fathers were inconsistent, he seems to argue, how could a person decide what to believe without logical thought? A rationalist and lover of argument, Abelard was nonetheless a deeply pious believer. However, by emphasizing the study of logic at Paris, Abelard took a step toward our modern universities, in which different disciplines apply methodologies specific to themselves in a logical manner in order to ask good questions. Bernard the Cistercian, who was a mystic and suspicious of reason, believed Abelard heretical and had his views condemned and denounced repeatedly.

Clearly, these various positions on universals were and are important, not only in the concept of the state or in a person's relationship to God but in terms of how abstract concepts govern daily life. Obviously, an idea such as "God is Love" takes a position in this debate; so, too, does any person's application of the idea of love to an individual circumstance.

Thomas Aquinas

By the time of Abelard's death, the Greek scientific writings of antiquity were starting to be recovered, often through translations from Arabic into Latin. In the second half of the century came the recovery of Aristotle's lost treatises on logic, which dealt with such subjects as how to build a *syllogism* (an expression of deductive reasoning), how to prove a point, and how to refute false conclusions. With these instruments, medieval thinkers for the first time could systematize and summarize their entire philosophical position.

Yet the recovery of Aristotle posed certain new problems. For example, the Muslim philosopher Averroës, whose comments accompanied the text of Aristotle's *Metaphysics*, stressed Aristotle's own view that the physical world was eternal; since the soul—a nonphysical thing—was essentially common to all humanity, no individual human soul could be saved by itself. Obviously, this ran counter to fundamental Christian teaching. Some scholars tried to say that both views could be true—Aristotle's in philosophy and the Christian in theology. But this led directly to heresy. Others simply tried to forbid the reading of Aristotle, though without success. It was the Dominican Albertus Magnus (1193–c. 1280), a Swabian, and his pupil Thomas Aquinas (1225–

1274), an Italian, who, in massive multivolume works produced over a lifetime, succeeded in reconciling the apparent differences between Aristotle's teachings and those of the Christian tradition. They were the greatest of the Schoolmen, exponents of Scholasticism.

Aquinas's best-known writings were the *Summa Theologica* and the *Summa contra Gentiles*. He discussed God, humans, and the universe, arranging his material in systematic topical order in the form of an inquiry into and discussion of each open question. First he cited the evidence on each side, then he gave his own answer, and finally he demonstrated the falsity of the other position. Although Aquinas always cited authority, he never failed to provide also his own logical analysis. For him, reason was a most valuable instrument, but only when it reasonably recognized its own limitations. When unaided reason could not comprehend an apparent contradiction with faith, it must yield to faith, since reason by itself could not understand the entire universe. Certain fundamentals must be accepted as unprovable axioms of faith, although, once they had been accepted, reason could show that they were probable. If a person put a series of arguments together and came out with a conclusion contrary to what orthodox Christians believed, the logic had been faulty, and the correct use of logic could readily show the error.

Thus the "Angelic Doctor," as Aquinas was called, worked out a systematic theology on rational principles, declaring that, since truth was indivisible, there was no contradiction between faith and reason, theology and science. In 1879 Pope Leo XIII would declare Thomism to be the official philosophy of Roman Catholicism.

Political Thought

In dealing with problems of human relations, medieval thinkers used a vocabulary that is different from ours, yet they came fairly close in many ways to modern democratic thinking. Except for extreme realism, medieval political thought was emphatically not autocratic. To the medieval thinker the perfection of the kingdom of heaven could not possibly exist on earth, where compromise and imperfection were inescapable.

Nor could full equality exist on earth. Medieval political thought accepted as its starting point an order of rank in human society. The twelfth-century *Policraticus* (Statesman's Book) of the English Scholastic philosopher John of Salisbury (c. 1115–1180) provided a complete statement of this social theory. The prince (or king) is the head of the body of the commonwealth; the senate (legislature) is the heart; the judges and governors of provinces are the eyes, ears, and tongue; the officials and soldiers are the hands; the financial officers are the stomach and intestines; and the peasants "correspond to the feet, which always cleave to the soil." This "organic" theory of society was a great favorite with those who opposed change, for obviously the foot does not try to become the brain, nor is the hand jealous of the eye. The whole body is at its best when each part

TRUTHS WHICH ARE ABOVE NATURE

Aquinas delighted in the game of inventing arguments against accepted beliefs, matching them with a set of even more ingenious arguments, and then reconciling the two with dazzling intellectual skill. Here is an example from a relatively unimportant part of the *Summa Theologica* which is fairly easy to follow; it brings out clearly how close to "common sense" Aquinas could be.

He is discussing the specific conditions of "man's first state"—the state of innocence before the Fall. He comes to the question of what children were like in the state of innocence. Were they born with such perfect strength of body that they had full use of their limbs at birth, or were they like human children now, helpless? In the Garden of Eden, we might think that any form of helplessness would detract from perfection, and that God might well have made the human infant strong and perfect, or might even have had men and women born adult. Aquinas did not think so; even Eden was as "natural" as he could make it:

By faith alone do we hold truths which are above nature, and what we believe rests on authority. Wherefore, in making any assertion, we must be guided by the nature of things, except in those things which are above nature, and are made known to us by Divine authority. Now it is clear that it is as natural as it is befitting to the principles of human nature that children should not have sufficient strength for the use of their limbs immediately after birth. Because in proportion to other animals man has naturally a larger brain. Wherefore it is natural, on account of the considerable humidity of the brain in children, that the sinews which are instruments of movement, should not be apt for moving the limbs. On the other hand, no Catholic doubts it possible for a child to have, by Divine power, the use of its limbs immediately after birth.

Now we have it on the authority of Scripture that *God made man right* (Ecclesiastes, 7: 30), which right-

ness, as Augustine says, consists in the perfect subjection of the body to the soul. As, therefore, in the primitive state it was impossible to find in the human limbs anything repugnant to man's well-ordered will, so was it impossible for those limbs to fail in executing the will's commands. Now the human will is well ordered when it tends to acts which are befitting to man. But the same acts are not befitting to man at every season of life. We must, therefore, conclude that children would not have had sufficient strength for the use of their limbs for the purpose of performing every kind of act; but only for the acts befitting the state of infancy, such as suckling, and the like.

The Summa Theologica of St. Thomas (Mission Hills, CA: Benzinger, 1947) Article 495, Quest. XCIX.

This apparently trivial passage contains much that is typical of *Thomism*, as the philosophy of Aquinas is termed. It reveals the supremacy that is granted to "truths which are above nature," which are held by faith and received through divine authority; the belief that God usually prefers to let nature run its course according to its laws; the belief that there is a "fitness" in human action conforming to these laws of nature; and, finally, the appeal to authority, in this case the Old Testament and Augustine. Notice also that Aquinas never even brings up the kinds of questions anticlerical rationalists were later to ask, such as: Just how were children procreated before the Fall? Or, were there any children, anyone but Adam and Eve, in Eden before the Fall? Such questions clearly fell outside the realm of faith on which the passage was posited. This passage, like Aquinas's famous "proofs," is representative of his thinking style.

does what nature meant it to do. The peasant, the blacksmith, the merchant, the lawyer, the wife, the priest, and the king had all been assigned a part of God's work on earth.

While medieval thought thus distinguished among vocations, it also insisted on the dignity and worth of

all vocations, even the humblest. It accepted the Christian doctrine of the equality of all souls before God, and held that no person could be a mere instrument of another. Even the humblest person on this earth could hope to enjoy bliss as full and eternal as any king's in the next world. Furthermore, medieval political theory by no means opposed all change on earth. Medieval thinkers were certainly not democratic in the sense of believing that the people had a right to, or could, "make" their own institutions. But they did not hold that, since God had arranged authority as it was in this world, humanity should preserve existing conditions, come what may. Bad conditions probably meant that good conditions had been perverted. The thing to do was to try to restore the original good conditions—"God's own plan."

Thomas Aquinas repudiated Augustine's views that the state was a necessary evil and the result of human sin. He concluded that kings were needed; good kings obviously were best; limited monarchy logically had the least chance of becoming a tyranny. Though the pope was at the peak of both temporal and spiritual power, he had "an indirect rather than a direct authority in temporal matters"—another example of Aquinas's moderation.

Later Marsiglio of Padua (c. 1290–1343), the author of *Defensor Pacis* (Defender of the Peace), found the only true source of authority in a commonwealth to be the *universitas civium*, the whole body of the citizens. Marsiglio probably did not mean to be as modern as this may seem. He still used medieval terms; the constitutionalism and popular sovereignty that have been attributed to him are a long way from any notion of counting votes to determine political decisions. But like many other medieval thinkers, Marsiglio believed that no one's place in the order of rank—even at the top—is such that those of lower rank must always and unquestioningly accept what is commanded of them. If worse came to worst, medieval political thinkers—even in autocratic Byzantium—were willing to approve tyrannicide. To the medieval mind, even to that of the lawyer, law was not made but found. Law for common everyday purposes was custom. But beyond custom lay the *law of nature*, or natural law—something like God's word translated into terms that made it usable by ordinary persons on earth. It was the ethical ideal, the "ought to be," that was discernible by those who were thinking rightly.

The medieval intellectual assumed that the universe was static; the modern intellectual assumes that it is dynamic. The one assumed that laws for right human action had been designed for all time by God in heaven, and that those laws were discoverable and clear to the good Christian. The other assumes that laws for right human action are worked out in the process of living, that no one can be sure of them in advance, and that new ones are constantly being created. The medieval thinker, if puzzled, tended to resolve problems by an appeal to authority—the best or the natural authority people had been trained to believe in, such as Aristotle or Aquinas or the customary law of the land. And medieval thinkers usually believed that no perfectly satisfactory solution to their problems would be available until they went to heaven. The modern thinker, if puzzled, tends at least to consult several different authorities and to compare them before deciding. Modern

thinkers may also try to experiment. If the inquiry is conducted in the right way, that could solve the difficulty. The right way for the medieval person already existed and had, at most, to be found; the right way for the modern person may have to be invented, created.

Mysticism

Although Scholasticism set faith above reason, it nevertheless held that the instrument of thought is a divine gift, and that it must be used and sharpened here on earth. Mystics who distrusted reason and intellect could never accept this view. There were many mystics in the Middle Ages. Bernard, mystic and activist, denounced Abelard, thinker and rationalist teacher. St. Francis also distrusted formal intellectual activity. For him, Christ was no philosopher; Christ's way was the way of submission, of subduing the mind as well as the flesh.

> *My brothers who are led by the curiosity of knowledge will find their hands empty in the day of tribulation. I would wish them rather to be strengthened by virtues, that when the time of tribulation comes they may have the Lord with them in their straits—for such a time will come when they will throw their good-for-nothing books into holes and corners.**

The quality of Francis's piety comes out in this fragment of a work which is almost certainly by his own hand, the *Canticle of the Brother Sun*:

> *Most High, omnipotent, good Lord, thine is the praise, the glory, the honour and every benediction.*
>
> *Praised be thou, my Lord, with all thy creatures, especially milord Brother Sun that dawns and lightens us.*
>
> *Be praised, my Lord, for Sister Moon and the stars that thou hast made bright and precious and beautiful.*
>
> *Be praised, my Lord, for Brother Wind, and for the air and cloud and the clear sky and for all weathers through which thou givest sustenance to thy creatures.*
>
> *Be praised, my Lord, for Sister Water, that is very useful and humble and precious and chaste.*
>
> *Be praised, my Lord, for Brother Fire, through whom thou dost illumine the night, and comely is he and glad and bold and strong.*
>
> *Be praised my Lord, for Sister, Our Mother Earth, that doth cherish and keep us and produces various fruits with coloured flowers and the grass.***

Aquinas's Franciscan contemporary Bonaventura (John of Fidanza, 1221–1274) preached to his students in Paris that the human mind, as an organ of Adam's sinful and unredeemed descendants, could understand only things of the physical world. Only by divine illumination could humans hope to gain cognition of the divine or supernatural. Prayer, not study; love and long-

---

* Quoted in H. O. Taylor, *The Mediaeval Mind* (Cambridge, Mass.: Harvard University Press, 1949), I, 444–45.
** Ibid, pp. 445–46.

ing for God, not reason—this was the answer of Bonaventura, as it always is for mystics. Yet Bonaventura was an accomplished philosopher, quite able to deal with rationalist opponents. In his *Voyage of the Mind to God* he echoes Augustine and the earlier Platonists: the grace of God helps the mind achieve the degree of love it needs to undergo the ultimate mystical experience of union with the divine.

The Arts

Medieval Romanesque and Gothic architecture expressed the Scholastics' perception of the world as a symbol of God and his creations. The Gothic style, in particular, with its soaring beauty, carried the eye of all of Western humanity upwards to the heavens, expressing the metaphysical views of the Augustinians. The arts changed throughout the period, aided by major new developments in architectural engineering, but it was the overriding sense of a developing Christian unity and not breakthroughs in technology that most fundamentally shaped the new-built environment.

The Romanesque style dominated church building in the eleventh and most of the twelfth centuries. The Gothic style, following it and developing from it, began in the late twelfth century and prevailed down to the fifteenth. Among the great Romanesque churches were those built at Mainz, Worms, and Speyer in western Germany by the emperors of the Salian line. Another great Romanesque monastery church, with its surrounding buildings, was the complex at Cluny, and yet another was the pilgrimage church of St. James (Santiago) at Compostela in northwestern Spain. To Compostela from all over western Europe, and especially from France, came crowds of pilgrims to worship at the shrine of the saint, since access to Jerusalem was perilous. In the twelfth century from 500,000 to 2 million pilgrims a year made their way to this site, using what may be the first "tourist guide" ever written, the Pilgrim Guide of 1130.

All art forms evolve, and beginning in the late eleventh century Romanesque structures began to change substantially. From being round, the arches now gradually rose to points at the peak. Similarly, the roofs also rose more and more steeply as the smooth flow of the arch was sharply broken and two loftier curves met instead at a point. This pointed arch and great windows to let in light were the chief features of the newer medieval architecture known as Gothic. It enabled the builder to carry his buildings to soaring heights. Pillars were used to take the place of a whole section of solid Romanesque wall, and the spaces between the pillars could be used for windows. Outside, too, increased lightness and soaring height were achieved by arched support, called "flying buttresses."

Into the new window spaces the craftsmen of the thirteenth century fitted a new form of art: windows in multicolored (stained) glass, glittering with gemlike colors in ruby, sapphire, and emerald, and showing biblical episodes or episodes from the life of the saint whose church they illuminated. The first were commissioned by Abbot Suger for the chapels of the choir of St. Denis and at Chartres cathedral in the midtwelfth century.

Gothic architecture flourished for at least two centuries everywhere in Europe. Its first and perhaps greatest moments came in northern France, between the 1190s and about 1269, with the building of the cathedrals of Chartres, Rheims, Amiens, Notre Dame of Paris, and other celebrated churches. Open and vast, solidly built, soaring upward according to carefully calculated mathematical architectural formulas, the Gothic cathedral terminated in aerial towers. Though its great windows let in the light, the stained glass kept the interior dim and awe inspiring. In the fourteenth and fifteenth centuries ornamentation grew richer, decoration became more intricate and flamelike (or *flamboyant*), and Gothic architecture on the Continent moved toward its

The abbey church of Cluny was begun in 1088 and completed in 1118. Much of the complex was demolished in 1811–1823, but the bell tower, shown here, survived. It is strongly representative of Romanesque architecture. *Giraudon/Art Resource*

A drawing of a model of the monastery of Cluny in 1157.

decline. In England, however, the later, richer Gothic produced such marvels as King's College Chapel in Cambridge and the Henry VII Chapel at Westminster Abbey in London.

Shortly before 1100 a revival of European sculpture began. The tradition had never been lost, as demonstrated by early medieval Irish and English crosses, but the finest surviving examples of the art of sculpture before the Romanesque revival were in ivory and metalwork. Now the stone of the churches began to blossom out with rosettes, palm leaf ornaments, and grapevines, and hiding behind the foliage would be mythical beasts, some of them illustrating the popular bestiaries of the time—collections of anecdotes about real and mythical animals, usually with a Christian allegorical explanation of the animals' fantastic characteristics. Scenes from the Bible also appeared on the capitals above the columns, now often interpreted individually by the artist.

In the years between 1180 and 1220, complex lifelike forms were rendered in exquisite sculpture that re-

vealed respect for architectural form, mastery of the craft of stonecutting, a high idealism, and a readiness to attempt realism. Physiques were not camouflaged or ignored but were studied; gestures developed an entirely new form of their own.

Gradually sculpture in the round became more common. Lifelike representation of drapery and the firm balance of the figures on their feet are principal characteristics of these new statues, occurring chiefly in northern France. Similar traits are seen elsewhere in metalwork and in manuscript illumination, rather than in monumental sculpture. The influences from outside that helped make the development possible came through Byzantine art, then undergoing a kind of classical renaissance, which became available to Western eyes through renewed and intensified contacts between East and West by pilgrims, travelers, and warriors during the period of the Crusades. Thus an artistic revival was launched as a result of matters of state as well as of religion. For most of those living in the West in the

Middle Ages, there were, however, no such distinctions; life was a whole, its customs and practices focused on the ideals and precepts of Christianity.

Perhaps no one figure can represent how art connected one conventionally named period—the Middle Ages—to another—the Renaissance. Still, the "rebirth" of the arts implied by the latter term was already in progress well before the dates normally assigned to the Renaissance, though not all the characteristics associated with Renaissance art were yet present. The career of the Florentine architect, sculptor, and painter Giotto di Bondone (c. 1266–1337) is particularly illustrative of how one stage of artistic development is father to the next. A friend of Dante, Giotto often followed the Byzantine models so popular in his day, but he also sought to make his paintings more lifelike and emotional. He learned from Italian sculptors who had studied the sculptures on the portals of Gothic cathedrals, especially at Chartres. Giotto executed similar forms in frescoes, creating the illusion of three dimensions by the use of foreshortening and perspective, in the chapel of Madonna dell'Arena in Padua, a great university and commercial center. Between 1304 and 1306 Giotto painted thirty-eight frescoes depicting the lives of the Virgin and of Christ. His scenes of the Kiss of Judas and of the Entombment became highly influential in the development of Renaissance art, as did that of Joachim and the Shepherds, which makes brilliant use of dramatic positioning of figures by forcing the viewer to "read" the picture from left to right and by employing *chiaroscuro*, the use of light and shade to enhance the effect.

Even before the Renaissance, Giotto exemplified the

Santiago de Compostela, goal of western European pilgrims. This drawing shows a restoration of the church to its medieval state.
The Medieval Academy of America and Mrs. Kenneth J. Conant

Renaissance artist's approach to his work—individualistic, intent upon fame and success, expecting lucrative commissions, and engaging in business activities (in this case as a debt-collector and a landlord to weavers) for

Variations on the typical Romanesque church can be found today throughout southwestern France. Domed roofs are representative of the style, sometimes with the domes in a row above the nave or, as shown left at St. Front of Perigueux, built 1120–1160, in a Greek (equal-armed) cross pattern.
Art Resource

The interior of the cathedral of Angouleme, above left, shows typical Romanesque barrel vaulting. It is massive, solid, and meant to be inspiring, but the eye does not soar to heaven, as the view is cut off by the essential elements of the structure. Durham Cathedral, in the north of England, above right, shows typical Norman Romanesque rib vaulting, which permits the eye a greater sense of spaciousness as one looks up the nave toward the east window. Romanesque had become an international style, for the same type of interior could also be found in Italy, in the cathedral of Pisa.
New York Public Library and the British Tourist Authority

further profit. The richest man in Padua had commissioned Giotto to decorate the Arena chapel on behalf of his father's soul, for Dante had placed him in Hell as a usurer. Thus money and art were wed through patronage, as when the great banking families of the Bardi and Peruzzi of Florence employed Giotto to apply his art to the Church of Santa Croce, later to be the resting place of Michelangelo, Machiavelli, and Galileo—symbols of the Renaissance to come.

Dante, Chaucer, Giotto, the soaring Gothic spire—all attested to the primacy of the Christian God. Each sought to show life as a pilgrimage, a search for salvation in an ever more complex world; each sought to draw the eye upward, literally to follow the Gothic tower toward heaven. Each was lively, energetic, fond of exquisite detail. The complexity of one of Chaucer's pilgrim's tales, the intricacy of an inner circle of Purgatory in Dante's vision of a netherworld, the carefully rendered individuality of one of Giotto's figures spoke to the desire to see the individual in relation to God. The Renaissance would place heavier emphasis on individualism, worldly success, the fascinating diversity of life. But the outward expression of the inward search for

glory, individually and collectively, for spiritual and physical adventure, would best be found in the several Crusades by which the Christian monarchs and their followers in the West sought to carry once again to the East, where the origins of Christianity lay, the authority of the church and of the states that supported that church.

For most of the medieval West the dominant authority remained the church, however clear the strains between the emerging state and the papacy might be. Few leaders in the area that was to become Germany thought that there could be a secular state, for all theory relating to governance derived from the church, which was an intermediary with God. Even architecture reflected this view. However, in the two areas that were becoming France and England, the contest between authorities was clearer. While no one anticipated a secular state, in both countries there were philosophers and statesmen who felt they could discern clear boundaries between temporal and spiritual matters. And in both countries science and literature were developing themes that, while Christian, nonetheless anticipated the rise of the secular domain.

These fine figures of Melchizedek, Abraham, and Moses from the north portal of the cathedral of Chartres, France, date from about 1238; they illustrate the movement toward sculpture in the round.
Bildarchiv Foto Marburg

The exterior of Chartres cathedral. On the left is the New Tower (which is the oldest, being from 1134), capped with a spire added in the sixteenth century. This contrasts with the simpler Old Tower to the right. Chartres became famous as the finest repository of stained glass on the Continent.
Photo Researchers, Inc.

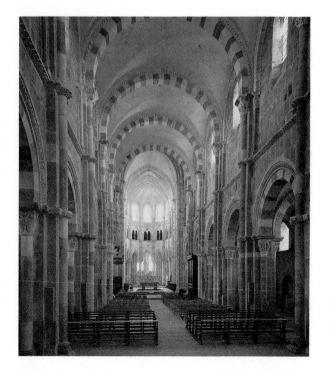

Romanesque Burgundy moved away from the Cluny style (of which Autun was an example) with the consecration of La Madeleine in Vezelay, France, in 1104. Here the barrel vault was replaced by a groined vault with transverse arches, creating a high, airy effect.
Giraudon/Art Resource

The Cathedral of Amiens, France, showing the nave (begun in 1220), a superb example of Gothic architecture.
Scala/Art Resource

King's College Chapel, in Cambridge, England, is perhaps the finest example of Gothic architecture in Britain. The fan vaulting is exceptionally intricate; it was completed between 1446 and 1515. The delicate windows and glass were calculated to give the sense of being open to air.
Bridgeman/Art Resource

A capital from the cathedral of Autun, France, about 1120, showing the Biblical scene of Judas hanging himself while winged demons pull on the rope.
Haeseler/Art Resource

Also at Autun, and sculpted between 1130 and 11'0, Christ is shown, enthroned, with the Virgin and saints nearby, while beneath them is a depiction of the Last Judgment. Such large-scale compositions gave the sculptor an opportunity to show his versatility and to portray more broadly the Christian conception of the universe.
Bulloz

Summary

Medieval Europe was in its most distinctive phase as a distinctively Western civilization, with many shared values that gave it some temporary intellectual unity and separated it from other civilizations. The European economy and population began to expand in the eleventh century. New technology such as the windmill and the heavy plow led to increased food production. Towns grew with increased trade and the growth of a money economy. The role of women improved, as more women came to be educated and to control property.

The church was the most important institution, political as well as religious, in society. Church reforms in the eleventh century strengthened the papacy in its relations with secular powers. Some historians believe that the medieval papacy sought to achieve a papal monarchy that would dominate the temporal as well as the spiritual government.

The Saxon emperors first sponsored church reform, but later clashed with the papacy over the investiture of bishops and the emperors' attempts to dominate Italy. The church emerged victorious from this struggle, but with diminished prestige and power.

The emperors failed to develop a strong government in either Germany or Italy, thus both areas were divided into petty, frequently quarrelsome, local states.

The need to reform was constantly felt in the medieval church. New religious orders—Augustinians, Cistercians, Dominicans, Franciscans—were founded to fill this need.

The church alone directed and conducted education. Medieval universities developed from schools attached to cathedrals.

Medieval thinkers sought to construct systems of thought that would have universal applicability. Nominalists opposed realists in the issue of whether universal categories could exist. The dominant approach to philosophy—Scholasticism—was primarily concerned with proving the existence of God. The leading Scholastic thinkers were Anselm, Albertus Magnus, and Thomas Aquinas. John of Salisbury's organic social theory adapted Scholastic thought to politics. Mystics distrusted human reason and relied on divine inspiration to achieve union with the divine.

The Romanesque style gave way to the Gothic in the twelfth century, and Gothic dominated down to the fifteenth. Among its greatest achievements are the cathedrals of Chartres, Notre Dame in Paris, Rheims, and Amiens. The Florentine architect, sculptor, and painter Giotto best bridges the styles of the late Middle Ages and the Renaissance that was to follow.

8

The Beginnings of the Secular State

In those lands that became France and England, a series of strong monarchs emerged to provide the state with a center of authority that could contest with the church for the loyalties of the people. While open conflict with the papacy was not yet contemplated, and no state in western Europe was secular in the sense of placing the monarch above the papacy, both France and England were experiencing a rise of collective identity that would lead to a succession of royal triumphs. Both would achieve unity as nation-states earlier than most other areas of Europe, in part because of the balance of force represented by the monarchies. In both an emerging tradition of scientific inquiry—not yet hostile to religion though not following overtly religious modes of thought—and the development of a lively, highly imaginative vernacular literary tradition would provide additional sources of controversy and discussion, sources which, though rooted in a churchly tradition, did not invariably support church policy.

I   THE DEVELOPMENT OF FRANCE: FROM HUGH CAPET TO PHILIP THE FAIR

The central thread of French history during the period between 987 and 1314 is royal success. The French monarchy grew in power and prestige from small beginnings until it dominated the machinery of government. France became the first large and unified state in the medieval West, a state built largely by the French monarchy.

The Capetians, 987–1226

When Hugh Capet (c. 938–996) came to the throne of France in 987, there was little to distinguish him from the last feeble Carolingians. Yet he was different, if only because he was the first of a male line that was to continue uninterrupted for almost 350 years. Like the Byzantine emperors, but with better luck, the Capetians had procured the election and coronation of the king's eldest son during his father's lifetime. When the father died, the son would already be king. After two centuries, when the king decided for reasons of his own not to follow this practice, the hereditary principle had become so well established that the succession was no longer questioned.

For a hundred years before the accession of Hugh Capet, his ancestors had been rivals of the Carolingians for the throne. As king of France, Hugh was recognized by all the feudal lords as their suzerain, but they were actually more powerful than he. Thus he might not be able to collect the aid (military service), the counsel,

and the feudal dues that his vassals in theory owed him. He was also, of course, lord of his own domain, the Ile de France. This was a piece of land including Paris and the area immediately adjacent, and extending south to Orléans on the Loire River. It was far smaller than the domain of any of the great feudal lords: the dukes of Normandy or Burgundy or Aquitaine, the counts of Flanders, Anjou, Champagne, Brittany, or Toulouse. It may indeed have been for this very reason that Hugh was chosen to be king; he seemed less likely to be a threat than any of the better-endowed lords. Yet the Capetian domain was compact and central, easy to govern and advantageously located. Unlike the Hohenstaufens, who were preoccupied with lands far afield, Hugh and his immediate successors concentrated on consolidating the administration of their center of power.

The Capetians also enjoyed the sanctity of kingship that came with coronation and unction (anointing) with holy oil, which tradition said a dove had brought down from heaven for Clovis at his baptism. In the eyes of the people, this ecclesiastical ceremony brought the king very close to God. He could work miracles, some believed. In this way the king was raised above all other feudal lords, however powerful.

Furthermore, the church was his partner. He defended it, according to his coronation oath, and it assisted him. In the great sees near Paris, the king could nominate successors to vacant bishoprics and archbishoprics, and he could collect the income of bishoprics during vacancies. As in Germany, these royal powers aroused the opposition of the papacy, but the French kings abandoned lay investiture without a prolonged struggle. The king retained his right of intervention in episcopal elections, and the bishops still took oaths of fealty to the king and accepted their regalia at his hands. This unbroken partnership with the church greatly strengthened the early Capetian kings.

The history of the Capetians during their first two centuries of rule in France is, on the surface, far less eventful than the contemporary history of several of their great vassals, such as the dukes of Normandy, who were conquering England, and whose vassals were establishing a great state in Sicily, or the dukes of Burgundy, whose relatives were taking over the throne in Portugal. The Capetian kings stayed at home, made good their authority within their own domain, and, piece by piece, added a little neighboring territory to it. Within the royal domain, the Capetians increased their control over the *curia regis* (king's court), which consisted of an enlargement of the royal household. The great offices at first tended to become hereditary, thus concentrating power in the hands of a few families. Under Louis VI (r. 1108–1137) one man held the key household offices of chancellor and *seneschal* (steward) as well as five important posts in the church. Louis VI, however, ousted this man and his relatives from their posts and made appointments of his own choosing. These new men were lesser nobles, lower churchmen, and members of the middle classes that were now emerging in the towns. Since they owed their careers to the Crown alone, they were loyal and trustworthy royal servants, not unlike the ministeriales in Germany. Most important among them was Suger (1081–1151), the abbé (abbot) of St. Denis, a man of humble origin and learned attainments who efficiently served both Louis VI and Louis VII (r. 1137–1180) for decades.

The most important single factor in the development of Capetian France, however, was the relationship of the kings with their most powerful vassals, the dukes of Normandy. By the mideleventh century, these dukes had centralized the administration of their own duchy, compelling their vassals to render military service, forbidding them to coin their own money, and curbing their rights of justice. The *viscounts*, agents of the ducal regime, exercised local control. After Duke William conquered England in 1066 and became its king, he and his successors were still vassals of the Capetians for Normandy. But they became so much more powerful than their overlords that they did not hesitate to conduct regular warfare against them. Norman power grew even greater during the early twelfth century, when an English queen, Matilda, married another great vassal of the French king, Geoffrey IV, count of Anjou. In the person of their son, King Henry II of England (r. 1154–1189), England was united with the French fiefs of Normandy, Anjou, Maine, and Touraine in what is sometimes called the Angevin, or English-French, Empire.

But this was not all. King Louis VII of France had married Eleanor, the heiress of Aquitaine, a great duchy in the southwest of France. When he had the marriage annulled (1152) for lack of a male heir, Eleanor lost no time in marrying Henry II and adding Aquitaine to his already substantial French holdings. So when Henry became king of England in 1154, he was also lord of more than half of France. He added Brittany and still other French territories. This Angevin threat was the greatest danger faced by the Capetian monarchs, and it was their greatest achievement that they overcame it.

The first round in the victorious struggle was the achievement of Philip II, or Philip Augustus (r. 1180–1223), who quadrupled the size of the French royal domain. Shrewd and calculating, Philip first supported Henry II's rebellious sons against him. Then, after Henry's death, Philip plotted with Henry's younger son, John, against John's older brother, Richard the Lionhearted—Philip's former companion on the Third Crusade and now (1192–1194) a captive in Austria. Philip married a Danish princess with the idea of using the Danish fleet against England and making himself heir to the Danish claims to the English throne. He later divorced her, but the mighty pope Innocent III, who had brought the church to its medieval high point, was able to force him to take her back in 1198. Even Innocent, however, could not force Philip to accept papal mediation in his English quarrel. When John succeeded Richard in 1199, Philip Augustus supported a rival claimant to the English throne—John's nephew, the young Arthur of Brittany.

Through legal use of his position as feudal suzerain, Philip managed to ruin John. In 1200 John married a girl who was betrothed to someone else. Her father, vassal of the king of France, complained in proper feudal style to Philip, his suzerain and John's. Since John would not come to answer the complaint, Philip declared John's fiefs forfeit and planned to conquer them with Arthur's supporters. John murdered Arthur and played right into Philip's hands. He lost his supporters on the Continent, and in 1204 he had to surrender Normandy, Brittany, Anjou, Maine, and Touraine to Philip Augustus.

Only Aquitaine was now left to the English, who had been expelled from France north of the Loire. In 1214, at the battle of Bouvines in Flanders, Philip Augustus, in alliance with Frederick II, now supported by the pope, defeated an army of Germans and English under the emperor Otto IV, John's ally. Unable to win back their French possessions, the English finally confirmed this territorial settlement by treaty in 1259. Though England's remaining possessions in France were to be the cause of much future fighting, John's great losses were now added to the French royal domain. The French kings had possession of the efficiently run duchy of Normandy, which they could use as a model for the rest of France.

The Winning of the South

The Capetians next moved to take over the rich Mediterranean south. Its people spoke a dialect different from that of the north of France, and many of them belonged to the heretical church of the Cathars, with its center at the town of Albi. Hence, they were called *Albigensians*. They believed that the history of the universe was one long struggle between the forces of light (good) and the forces of darkness (evil). The evil forces (Satan) created man and the earth, but Adam had some measure of goodness. Jesus was not born of a woman, nor was he crucified, because he was wholly good, wholly light. The Jehovah of the Old Testament was the god of evil. The Albigensians had an elite of their own ("the perfect"), who devoted themselves to pure living. Some of them forbade the veneration of the cross; others forbade infant baptism, the celebration of the Mass, or the holding of private property. Many of them denied the validity of one or more of the sacraments. Some even said the Catholic church itself was Satan's. Albigensians often had the support of nobles, and particularly women, who adopted their views to combat the church politically. The church proclaimed a Crusade against the Albigensians and a related heretical group, the followers of Peter Waldo (*Waldensians*), in 1208.

Philip Augustus did not at first participate in the expeditions of his nobles, who rushed south to plunder in the name of the Catholic church. Northern French nobles were soon staking out their claims to the lands of southern French nobles who embraced the heresy. By the year of Philip's death (1223), after the war had gone on intermittently for fourteen years, the territorial

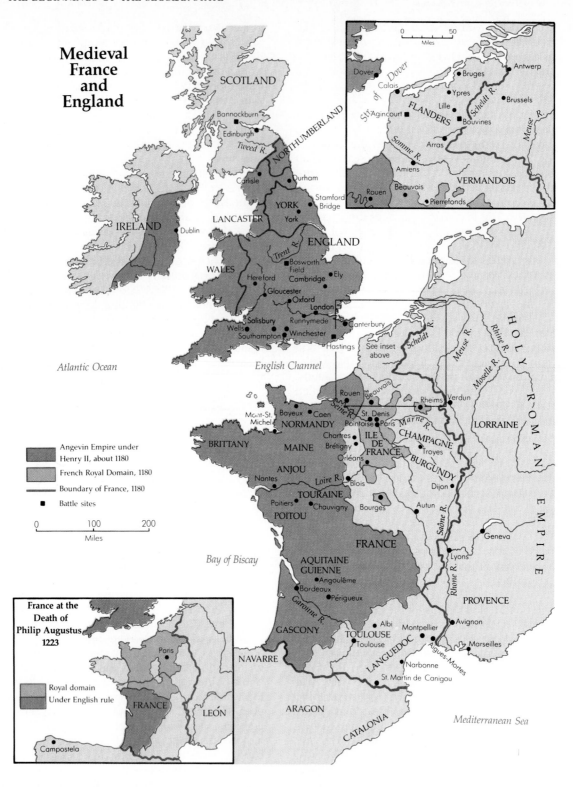

Medieval France and England

Angevin Empire under Henry II, about 1180

French Royal Domain, 1180

Boundary of France, 1180

■ Battle sites

0   100   200
Miles

France at the Death of Philip Augustus 1223

Royal domain

Under English rule

issue had become confounded with the religious one. So Philip sponsored an expedition led by his son, Louis VIII (r. 1223–1226). Assisted by a special clerical court called the *Inquisition*, which was first set up to root out this heresy, Louis VIII and his son Louis IX (r. 1226–1270) carried on the campaign, which by the 1240s had ferociously driven the heresy underground. The south was almost entirely taken over by the Crown, and it was arranged that the lands of the count of Toulouse, the greatest lord in the region, would come by marriage to the brother of the king of France when the last count died, as he did in 1249.

Royal Administration

Administrative advances kept pace with territorial gains. Indeed, it is doubtful if Philip Augustus and his successors could have added to the royal domain if they had not overcome many of the disruptive elements of feudalism, and if they had not asserted their authority effectively in financial, military, and judicial matters. Philip Augustus systematically collected detailed information on precisely what was owed to him from the different royal fiefs. He increased the number of his own vassals, and he reached over the heads of his vassals to their vassals, in an attempt to make the latter directly dependent on him. He exacted stringent guarantees—such as a promise that if a vassal did not perform his duties within a month, he would surrender his person as a prisoner until the situation was resolved. Moreover, if a vassal did not live up to this agreement, the church would lay an interdict upon his lands, which the people feared above all else.

Philip and his officials were alert to increase the royal power by purchasing new estates, by interfering as much as possible in the inheritance of fiefs upon the death of their holders, and by providing husbands of their own choosing for the great heiresses. A lady would sometimes outlast three or four husbands, inheriting from each; thus she became a more desirable prize each time and offered the king a chance to marry her off with profit to himself.

The local officials of the Crown, the *prévôts* (provosts), who administered justice and taxation, had regularly been rewarded by grants of land, which together with the office tended to become hereditary. The Crown lost income and power as well as popularity when a local provost imposed taxes on his own behalf. Early in his reign Philip Augustus held an investigation and heard the complaints to which the system had given rise. He appointed a new sort of official—not resident in the countryside, but tied to the court—who would travel about, enforcing the king's will in royal lands, rendering royal justice, and collecting moneys due to the king. This official received no fiefs to tie him to a given region; his office was not hereditary; he was a civil servant appointed by the king, who paid him a salary and could remove him at will. In the north, where this system was introduced, he was called a *bailli* (bailiff), and his territory a *baillage* (bailiwick). In the south, to which the new system was extended, he was called a *sénéchal* (not to be confused with the old officer of the household) and his district a *sénéchausée*.

Like any administrative system, this one had its drawbacks. A bailli or sénéchal far from Paris might become just as independent and unjust as the old prévôt had been, without the king's being aware of it. Louis IX had to limit the power of these officials. He made it easy for complaints against them to be brought to his personal attention, and he appointed a new kind of official to take care of the caretakers. These were the *enquêteurs* (investigators)—royal officials not unlike Charlemagne's *missi*. The enquêteurs had supervisory authority over the baillis and sénéchals and traveled about the country inspecting their work. This complex of new civil servants introduced in the late twelfth and thirteenth centuries meant that the king could interfere with almost all local and private transactions to collect what was due him and to supply royal justice at a price.

Naturally the curia regis was so swamped with new business that the old haphazard feudal way of attending to it could no longer be followed. The king's household slowly differentiated itself into departments, most of which had little to do with government. Rather, they attended to the needs of the king and the curia regis. This court consisted not only of retainers but of clerics and others who served as advisers on day-to-day problems. When a major policy question affecting the realm was up for decision or when a major legal case needed to be tried, the king was entitled to summon his vassals (both lay and clerical) for counsel, and those he summoned were obliged to come. They then joined the rest of the curia regis in a kind of enlarged royal entourage.

When the curia regis sat in judgment on a case, it came to be known as the *Parlement*—a high judicial tribunal. Naturally, as the laws grew more complex, trained lawyers had to handle more and more of the judicial business. At first they explained the law to the vassals sitting in judgment, and then, as time passed, they formed a court of justice and arrived at decisions themselves in the name of the king. By the fourteenth century this court of justice was called the *Parlement de Paris*, since Paris was its headquarters. When the curia regis sat in special session on financial matters, auditing the reports of income and expenditure, it acted as a kind of government accounting department. By the fourteenth century, this was called the *chamber of accounts*. Naturally enough, it engaged professional full-time employees, clerks, auditors, and the like.

Cash flowed to the Crown from the lands of the royal domain—from customs due and special tolls, from fees for government services, and from money paid by vassals in order to avoid rendering such outmoded feudal services as entertaining the king and his court. However, the king of France could not levy regular direct taxes on his subjects. During the twelfth century the regular collection of feudal aids had accustomed the nobles to paying money to the Crown. Then a special levy was imposed on those who stayed home from the Crusade that set out in 1147. In 1188 Philip Augustus collected one-tenth of the movable property and one-tenth of a year's income from all who failed to join in a Crusade. These extraordinary imposts, however, aroused a storm of protest.

St. Louis, 1226–1270

Further advances in royal power came with Louis IX, viewed as a perfect ruler, who stood in sharp contrast to his contemporary, Frederick II of Germany. Deeply pious, almost monastic in his personal life, Louis carried his high standards over into his role as king. He wore simple clothes, gave alms to beggars, washed the feet of lepers, built hospitals, and created in Paris the Sainte-Chapelle (Holy Chapel), a small church that is now a jewel-box of glowing stained glass, to hold a reliquary containing Christ's Crown of Thorns. The church made Louis a saint in 1297, less than thirty years after his death, for personally leading two Crusades against the Muslims.

St. Louis did not let his own devotion to the church stop him from defending royal prerogatives against every attempt of his own bishops or of the papacy to infringe upon them. For example, when the popes tried to enforce the theory that "all churches belong to the pope," and to assess the churches of France for money and men for papal military campaigns, the king declared that church property in France was "for the requirements of himself and his realm" and was not to be despoiled by Rome (1247). Yet when he himself became deeply interested in the crusading movement, he needed papal support to enable him to tax the French clergy. The clergy then complained to the pope about the king's demands for funds.

With the townspeople, too—those old allies of the Capetian dynasty—there were difficulties during Louis's reign. These difficulties arose in large measure out of internal conflicts between the small upper class of rich merchants, who kept city government a kind of oligarchy, and the lower class of tradespeople and artisans, who felt oppressed and excluded from their own government. When the Crown intervened, it was out of concern not so much for the poor and humble as for the maintenance of order and the continued flow of funds to the royal coffers. Louis began to send royal officials into the towns and in 1262 issued a decree requiring that the towns present their accounts annually.

This decree itself was a further instance of the king's assertion of royal prerogative. It was a new sort of enactment, an *ordonnance*, or royal command issued for all of France without the previous assent of all the vassals. Royal power and prestige had now so progressed that Louis did not feel the need to obtain all his vassals' consent each time he wished to govern their behavior; ordonnances signed by some vassals governed all. Examples of Louis's ordonnances were his prohibition of private warfare and his law providing that royal money was valid everywhere in France; both show his reformist views, as well as his determination to strengthen the power of the monarchy.

Royal justice had now become widely desired, and appeals flowed into the parlement from the lower feudal courts. The royal court of justice alone came to be recognized as competent to try cases of treason and of breaking the king's peace. The extension of royal justice to the towns was secured by bringing into the Parlement's deliberations representatives of the middle classes—the *bourgeois*. So fair and reasonable was the king's justice felt to be that his subjects often applied to him personally for it. He made himself available to them

In the middle of the Paris court of the devout St. Louis, connected to his apartments, was the Gothic Sainte-Chapelle, consecrated in 1248.
Scala/Art Resource

by sitting under an oak tree in the forest of Vincennes near Paris, and listening to the case of anyone, high or low, who wished to appeal to the king. He maintained no royal protocol on these occasions, and there were no intermediaries. His justice was prized not only in France but also abroad; he settled quarrels in Flanders, Navarre, Burgundy, Lorraine, and elsewhere. He reached a reasonable territorial settlement with England in 1259, and in 1264 was asked to judge a dispute between King Henry III of England and the English barons.

Louis was a remarkable and representative man of the thirteenth century. In his devotion to the crusading enterprise, for instance, he was wholeheartedly embracing the highest ideals of the period. But he never seemed to realize that the Holy Lands could not be won by more Crusades. Moreover, it cost France a great deal to have the king delayed abroad for years and to have him languish in captivity from which he was redeemed only at great expense. Yet for all his human failings, St. Louis typifies the medieval ideal that the divine law of God's revelation was mirrored in human law. As God ordered the universe, so human law established the proper relationships of individuals to one another in society. The king had his special role in society, and St. Louis, in his conception and enactment of that role, reached heights that had not been attained by other monarchs.

Philip the Fair, 1285–1314

After the death of St. Louis, the French monarchy experienced the same general change that was coming over the entire Western world in the thirteenth and fourteenth centuries, a trend towards centralization and consolidation of administrative functions. In the political history of France, this tendency began with the reign of St. Louis's grandson, Philip IV (r. 1285–1314). Called "the Fair" because he was handsome, Philip ruthlessly pushed the royal power and consolidated the royal hold; the towns, the nobles, and the church suffered further invasions of their rights by his agents. Against the excesses of Philip the Fair, the medieval checks against tyranny—which had been effective against many other aggressive kings—failed to operate. His humiliation of the papacy helped to end the idea of the Christian commonwealth. The vastly increased *gens du roi*, "the king's men," used propaganda, lies, and trickery to undermine all authority except that of the king. This undermining went on in a series of small engagements in local courts of justice, with the king's lawyers pushing his rights. Members of the parlement now traveled to the remotest regions of France, bringing royal justice to all parts of the king's own domain and more and more taking over the machinery of justice in the great lordships. The system of royal justice was thereby gradually swallowing up the system of feudal justice.

In the same period, the most intimate advisers of the king in the curia regis, whom he regularly consulted, became differentiated as the "narrow" or "secret," while the larger group of advisers, consisting of the remaining lords and high clerics, was called the "full council." In 1302, apparently for the first time, representatives of the towns attended a meeting of this larger council. When townspeople first participated, there began the long transition to a new kind of assembly, the Estates General (though the term would not be used in France for some time). An *estate* is a social class; traditionally, the clergy is considered the first estate, the nobility the second, and the townspeople the third. When all three estates are present, an assembly is therefore an *Estates General*. Though the clerics and nobles acted as individuals, the townspeople were a collective body representing the corporations of their municipalities.

War with England and Flanders kept Philip pressed for cash during much of his reign. He summoned the estates to explain his need for money and to obtain their approval for his proceeding to raise it. He usually asked for funds in a general way but did not fix the amount, since the groups he was asking to contribute had the right to bargain. Since medieval lords felt that no action was proper unless it was customary, whenever the king wanted to do anything new he had to try to make it seem like something old. A protest that such and such attempt to get money was an unheard-of exaction often was enough to frustrate the king's efforts. Philip tried all the known ways of getting money. One of the most effective was to demand military service of a man and then permit him to buy himself off. When protests arose, the king usually had to retreat to more orthodox methods. Still, requests for revenue that had hitherto been irregular were made regular. Forced loans, debasement of coinage, additional customs dues, and royal levies on commercial transactions also added to the royal income.

Although it was need for money for purely local problems that lay behind the most famous episode of Philip's reign—his fierce quarrel with the papacy—its importance and the significance of its outcome had a major impact on the medieval world. In his papal opponent, Boniface VIII (r. 1294–1303), Philip was tangling with a fit successor to Gregory VII and Innocent III. A Roman aristocrat and already an old man when elected pope, Boniface suffered from a malady that kept him in great pain and probably partly accounted for his undoubted bad temper and fierce language. During his fight with Philip, for instance, he said that he would rather be a dog than a Frenchman, whereupon Philip's pamphleteers charged Boniface with heresy for implying that Frenchmen, like dogs, had no souls.

Philip claimed the right to tax the clergy for the defense of France in his wars against England; the English monarch was taxing the clergy in his French possessions. Boniface issued an edict (known as a *bull* from the papal seal, or *bulla*, on it) declaring that kings lacked the right to tax clerics, and that clerics should disobey them, the bull *Clericis laicos* (1296). Philip the Fair answered not with theory but with action. He slapped an embargo on exports from France of precious metals, jewelry, and currency, which severely threatened the elaborate financial system of the papacy. Under pressure from his distressed bankers and from a hostile group of cardinals who were accusing him of heresy, simony, and even murder, the pope retreated, saying in 1297 that in an emergency the king of France could tax the clergy without papal consent, and that the king would decide when an emergency had arisen. Boniface also canonized Louis IX.

But a new quarrel arose in 1301. When Philip ordered Boniface's legate to Paris to be arrested, tried, and convicted of heresy and treason, he asked for papal approval of the sentence. But Boniface flatly refused and declared that when a ruler was wicked, the pope might take a hand in the temporal affairs of that realm. The meeting of the Estates General in 1302 backed Philip.

Boniface pushed his claims still further in the famous bull *Unam sanctam*, which declared that it was necessary for salvation for every person throughout the world to be subject to the pope. This was the single strongest statement made concerning the authority of the church over the state. When he also threatened to excommunicate the king, Philip issued a series of extreme charges against Boniface and sent a gang of thugs to kidnap him. They burst into the papal presence at the Italian town of Anagni and threatened the pope brutally, but did not dare put through their plan to seize him. Nonetheless, Boniface, who was over eighty, died not long after this humiliation.

ONE GOD, ONE CHURCH, ONE SOURCE OF SALVATION

According to Boniface VIII, there is but *one* church, and all Christ's sheep are committed to it:

That there is one Holy Catholic and Apostolic Church we are impelled by our faith to believe and to hold—this we do firmly believe and openly confess—and outside of this there is neither salvation or remission of sins.... The Church represents one mystic body and of this body Christ is the head; of Christ, indeed, God is the head. In it is one Lord, and one faith, and one baptism. In the time of the flood, there was one ark of Noah, prefiguring the one Church, finished in one cubit, having one Noah as steersman and commander. Outside of this, all things upon the face of the earth were, as we read, destroyed....

Therefore, in this one and only Church, there is one body and one head,—not two heads as if it were a monster—namely, Christ and Christ's Vicar, Peter and Peter's successor, for the Lord said to Peter himself, "Feed my sheep": *my* sheep, he said, using a general term and not designating these or those sheep, so that we must believe that all the sheep were committed to him.

"The Bull *Unam Sanction* of Boniface VIII," in *Translations and Reprints from the Original Sources of European History* (Philadelphia: The Department of History of the University of Pennsylvania, 1912), pp. 20–23. Courtesy of the Department of History of the University of Pennsylvania.

In 1305 Philip obtained the election of a French pope, Clement V (r. 1305–1314), who never went to Rome at all. Instead, in 1309 Clement went to Avignon, on the border between France and the Holy Roman Empire, and two years later made this city his permanent residence. Thus began the "Babylonian captivity" of the papacy at Avignon (1309–1377). Moreover, Clement issued bulls reversing Boniface's claims, lifted the sentence of excommunication from Boniface's attackers, and praised Philip the Fair for his piety.

The last installment of this long story—which had begun in 1046 when Henry III installed his reforming pope Clement II, whose successors fought the German emperors for two centuries—thus took the form of a quarrel between the pope and the king of France. The efforts of the papacy to use the spiritual authority of the church to govern the policies of national states had failed. Rather, for three-quarters of a century the papacy in Avignon was seen as a tool of the French monarchy.

In another notorious affair, Philip IV used the weakness of the papacy at Avignon to attack the Knights Templars, a crusading military order that had evolved into a rich banking house. He wanted their money and brought them to trial on a series of charges of vicious behavior, using as evidence against them confessions extorted by the increasingly brutal court of the Inquisition. The Templars were abolished, and Philip took over their funds, while a rival order was allowed to annex the Templars' lands. Philip also arrested the Jews, stripped them of their property, and expelled them from France in 1306. In 1311 he expelled the agents of Italian bankers. All debts owed to the Jews and Italians were collected by royal agents, and the Crown kept the money.

Just before Philip died in 1314, the towns joined with the lords in protest against the king's having raised money for a war in Flanders and then having made peace instead of fighting. Louis X (r. 1314–1316) calmed the unrest by revoking the aid, returning some of the money, and making scapegoats of the more unpopular bureaucrats. He also issued a series of charters to several of the great vassals that confirmed their liberties. The episode resembled in many ways the protest that had arisen in England a century earlier and had culminated there in one great charter, the Magna Carta.

But taxation was still thought of as inseparably connected with military service, and military service was an unquestioned feudal right of the king. So the king was still free to declare a military emergency, to summon his vassals to fight, and then to commute the service for money, just as Philip the Fair had done. For this reason the charters of Louis X did not effectively halt the advance of royal power, and there was no committee of barons (as there had been in England) to make sure that the king lived up to his promises. Because the French barons did not defend their corporate interests, the French monarch would continue to enjoy a position unique among the kings of western Europe.

II THE DEVELOPMENT OF ENGLAND

The England that for so long threatened the security of France had first become a major power as the result of the Norman Conquest of 1066. In that year William, duke

This large statue of Pope Boniface VIII (1294–1303), sculpted in 1300, bestows upon him the dignity appropriate to the person who issued the powerful papal bull *Unam sanctam*. *Scala/Art Resource*

of Normandy (c. 1027–1087), defeated the Anglo-Saxon forces at Hastings on the south coast of England. The Anglo-Saxon monarchy had, since the death of Canute in 1035, fallen prey to factions. Upon the death of Edward the Confessor (r. 1042–1066), a pious but ineffectual monarch who had been brought up at the Norman court speaking French, his brother-in-law Harold, half-Danish son of the powerful upstart Earl Godwin, had succeeded to the throne. But William of Normandy had an excellent competing claim to the English Crown.

The Norman Conquest, 1066

After a troubled minority, William had successfully asserted his rights in Normandy over the vigorous and tough Norman nobility. He allowed no castle to be built without his license, and insisted that, once built, each castle be put at his disposal on demand. Mideleventh-century Normandy was a unified duchy, overloaded with younger sons, even though many had gone off on the great south Italian adventure half a century earlier. The Norman cavalry was formidable and early perfected the technique of charging with the lance held couched, so

that all the force of horse and rider was concentrated in the point of the weapon at the moment of shock. Infantry and bowmen supported the charge. As a result of trade with Scandinavia and England, Normandy was prosperous even beyond the norms of the eleventh-century revival. It enjoyed a flourishing agriculture, growing towns, a flowering of monastic learning and church building under ducal patronage, and an effective fiscal administration. Moreover, because William put down private warfare and efficiently dispensed justice, there was peace and order.

While facing England across the Channel, Normandy had always maintained contact with the Scandinavian lands of Norman origin. After the Danish invasions of England all three regions were closely involved in commercial relations and often in strife. Emma, daughter of a Norman duke, married first the Anglo-Saxon king Ethelred II (r. 978–1016), by whom she was the mother of Edward the Confessor, and then married the Danish king Canute (r. 1016–1035), by whom she had a son, Harthacnut (r. 1040–1042). Wife of two English kings and mother of an English king by each of them, she apparently dominated all four. And she remained close to her Norman ducal relatives. William was her great-nephew. In the tangled English-Danish-Norman royal politics there were dark crimes, including the murder in 1036 of Edward the Confessor's older brother Alfred. Earl Godwin, Harold's father, was in part guilty, and the Normans at Hastings were in part revenging Godwin's act on his son Harold. It was Norman nobles, favorites of Edward the Confessor, who built the first castles in England shortly before the conquest. Edward gave important posts in the English church to Norman clerics, and as early as 1051 Edward had recognized William as his rightful heir.

In England pro- and anti-Normans intrigued and squabbled for two decades before 1066. Norman sources report that Harold went to Normandy, probably in 1064, and affirmed the promise of William's succession to the English throne, in exchange for a confirmation of Harold's English lands. If the sources are accurate, in taking the throne in 1066 Harold was breaking his oath. But some Anglo-Saxon sources say that on his deathbed Edward the Confessor had made Harold his heir after all; however, even if he did, it may have been under duress. And nothing can alter the fact that Harold, although his sister was married to Edward, was not of royal blood, English or Danish. Furthermore, there was a third claimant to the English throne: the king of Norway. Just before William's victory in 1066, the Norwegians landed and Harold defeated them at Stamford Bridge in Yorkshire.

William's invasion had the blessing of the papacy, which recognized his claim to the throne of England. His fleet had to be constructed in a single building season; he had to weld an army of seven thousand men, mostly Norman but including adventurers from many parts of France and from southern Italy, into a fighting unit; he then had to wait for favorable weather. William landed successfully and established two fortified beach-

William the Conqueror is shown here, in a thirteenth-century manuscript from the British Museum, as sharing up England among his followers. Feudal rights stemmed from the king, who in theory owned the entire kingdom. Here William is granting his nephew title to land.
British Museum

heads on the Sussex coast before Harold could get back from defeating the Norwegians. All was over in one hard day's fighting as Norman horsemen and bowmen slaughtered Harold's close-packed warriors, who were fighting on foot with battle-axes.

William was crowned on Christmas Day, 1066, by the archbishop of York. The joyous Norman accounts stress the new master's clemency. The Anglo-Saxon accounts echo the bitterness of defeat and of having to accept an alien master, who took vast quantities of loot from his victims to reward his triumphant Norman supporters. Yet William seems to have taken special pains to prevent disorders. *The Anglo-Saxon Chronicle*, a collection of contemporary vernacular histories, says of him:

> *Amongst other things the good security that he made in this country is not forgotten—so that any man could travel over his kingdom without injury, with his bosom full of gold; and no one dared strike another, however much wrong he had done him.**

* *The Anglo-Saxon Chronicle*, ed. Dorothy Whitelock, D. C. Douglas, and S. I. Tucker (London: Oxford University Press, 1961), p. 164.

This was after William had taken possession of the whole of England, which took two campaigns in the far southwest and expeditions to the north in which William punished pro-Danish English rebels by destroying the crops and causing widespread famine. The last uprising in England was crushed in 1071 on the Isle of Ely, and in 1072 the Conqueror won the submission of the king of Scotland, who became his vassal. There were political troubles even after this, but the conquest was essentially complete. Each state was marked by the building of new castles to hold the region and enforce order; the former ruling class of England was replaced by Norman and French nobles, perhaps a total of ten thousand newcomers in a population of not more than 1.5 million.

All of England belonged to William by right of conquest. He kept about one-sixth as royal domain, gave about half as fiefs to his great Norman barons, and returned to the church the quarter that it had held before. Although many of his barons subinfeudated their lands (gave part of them as fiefs to their own followers), these vassals owed military service only to William, and they swore primary allegiance to him in the Salisbury Oath of 1086, giving him authority that no French king would ever enjoy. The bishops and abbots also held of him and owed him feudal services. He alone claimed all castles, and none could be built without a license from him. He forbade private war and allowed only royal coinage. He continued to levy the *Danegeld*, to impose judicial fines, and to summon the *fyrd*, or national militia. He kept the Anglo-Saxon system of courts and bound local officials closely to the Crown by giving them wide local authority at the expense of bishop and earl. As on the Continent, Latin now became the language of administration.

The Conqueror thus maintained old English custom and law, while superimposing on it Norman feudal structure with its mounted knights and castles. The sheriffs provided continuity. The Norman curia regis superseded the Anglo-Saxon *witenagemot*; it met regularly three times a year, but could be summoned at any time to give counsel and try the cases of the great vassals. Its members also could be asked to perform special tasks in the *shires*—local administrative units that had been established in the early eleventh century and were divided into smaller units known as *hundreds*—for adjusting taxation, maintaining the peace, and settling local pleas.

In 1086 William ordered a careful survey of all landed property in England. The record of that survey is the Domesday Book, which included a full statement of ownership, past and present, for every piece of land, and a listing of all resources, so that the royal administration might learn whether and where more revenue could be obtained. Tenants, plows, forest land, fish ponds—all were listed in Domesday Book, which became an indispensable source for later historians. Contemporary accounts reveal the thoroughness of William's inquiry and the resentment it caused:

The Bayeux Tapestry is a work of art; it is also one of the most significant documents of early medieval history. Made only a few years after the event, the tapestry is rich in detail concerning the Norman Conquest. In this segment, showing the troops of William the Conqueror in battle with those of King Harold, William is on horseback.
Giraudon/Art Resource

So very narrowly did he have it investigated, that there was no single hide nor a yard of land, nor indeed (it is a shame to relate but it seemed no shame to him to do) one ox nor one cow nor one pig was there left out, and not put down on his record: and all these records were brought to him afterward. . . .

Other investigators followed the first; and men were sent into provinces which they did not know, and where they themselves were unknown, in order that they might be given the opportunity of checking the first survey and, if necessary, of denouncing its authors as guilty to the king. And the land was vexed with much violence arising from the collection of the royal taxes.*

Those who collected the information from the old Anglo-Saxon subdivisions of *regia villa* and hundred arranged it under the new Norman divisions of royal demesne and fiefs of the king's tenants-in-chief. The Domesday Book, then, was a formal written record attesting to the introduction of feudal landholding and law into England. No such monumental survey was ever compiled for any other country in the Middle Ages.

With the assistance of an able Italian, Lanfranc (d. 1089), whom he made archbishop of Canterbury, William established continental practices in the English church. Norman churchmen gradually replaced the English bishops. To commemorate the victory at Hastings, William founded Battle Abbey on the site of the battlefield; other monastic foundations followed, notably in the north. Norman abbots brought Latin books and learning from the Continent, and for a time vernacular writing in English ceased. William refused the pope's

* Ibid., and a note by the bishop of Hereford in *English Historical Documents 1042–1189*, ed. D. C. Douglas and G. W. Greenaway, (New York: Oxford University Press, 1953), II, 161, 851.

demand that feudal homage be done to him as overlord of England; rightly maintaining that none of his predecessors on the English throne had ever acknowledged papal suzerainty, he agreed only to pay the accustomed dues to the Church of Rome. The English church recognized no new pope without the king's approval and accepted no papal commands without his assent. When William died in 1087, the English monarchy was stronger than the French was to be for more than two hundred years.

Henry I and Henry II, 1100–1189

William's immediate successors extended his system. They made their administrators depend on the king alone by paying them fixed salaries, since payments in land (fiefs) often led the recipient to try to make his office hereditary, and since clerical administrators might feel the rival pull of papal authority. Household and curia regis grew in size, and special functions began to develop. Within the curia regis the king's immediate advisers became a "small council" and the full body met less often. The royal *chancery* (secretariat), also grew, since the king was also duke of Normandy and had much business on the Continent.

Henry I (r. 1100–1135) allowed his vassals to make payments (*scutage,* or "shield money") to buy themselves off from military service. He also exempted the royal towns or boroughs from Danegeld while collecting still heavier payments from them. To handle the increased income, the first specialized treasury department came into existence, the exchequer—so called because the long table on which the clerks rendered to the officers of the curia regis their semiannual audit of the royal accounts was covered with a cloth divided into checkerboard squares representing pounds, shillings, and pence.

Because Henry's only legitimate son drowned, the succession was disputed between Henry's daughter, Matilda, wife of Geoffrey IV of Anjou, and Henry's nephew, Stephen of Blois. A civil war (1135–1151) between their partisans produced virtual anarchy in England and did great harm to the prosperity of the realm. Yet when Henry II (r. 1154–1189), son of Matilda and Geoffrey, succeeded to the throne, he found the foundations of a powerful monarchy to add to the half of France under his rule.

Stormy and energetic, Henry II systematically cut at the roots of the anarchy; he had more than eleven hundred divisive, unlicensed castles destroyed. From the contemporary *Dialogue Concerning the Exchequer*, written by his treasurer, we learn how the money rolled in: from scutage plus special fees for the privilege of paying it, from fines, from aids, from tallage paid by the boroughs, and from a new tax collected from the knights who did not go on Crusades. Even more important than this reestablishment and strengthening of the financial institutions was Henry's contribution to the law of England, built on that of Henry I.

New law could not, in theory, be made at all. Law was what had always existed, and it was the job of the lawyers and government officials to discover what this was and to proclaim it. Henry I and Henry II therefore did not fill statute books with new enactments; instead Henry I asserted that he was ruling in accordance with the law of the Saxon king Edward the Confessor, and the law books issued in this period contain a mixture of Anglo-Saxon and other materials, including, for example, fixed schedules of money payments imposed as penalties for crime. It was not by issuing laws that Henry I and Henry II transformed the legal practices of England. Rather, by developing old instruments in new combinations, they created the new *common law*—law common to all of England because it was administered by the royal courts. Though hundred and shire courts had continued to exist, their jurisdiction had been diluted by competing courts, baronial and ecclesiastical; only the king could provide better ways of settling quarrels than the old trial by ordeal or trial by battle.

The chief royal instruments were writs, juries, and traveling justices. If, for example, someone seized a subject's property, by the middle of Henry II's reign the victim could buy a royal writ: an order from the king directing a royal official to give the plaintiff a hearing. The official would assemble a group of twelve neighbors who knew the facts in the case; they took an oath, and were therefore called a jury (from *jur,*, "man on oath"). They then told the truth as they knew it about whether dispossession had taken place, answering yes or no, and thus giving a verdict (from *veredictum*, "a thing spoken truly"). These early juries were not trial juries in the modern sense, but men who were presumed to be in the best position to know the facts already. By similar machinery of writ and jury, inheritances unjustly detained could be recovered, and a person unjustly held as a serf could be freed. Although the use of a jury or sworn inquest dated back to the ninth-century Carolingians and had come to England with the Conqueror, its application to civil cases between individuals was new, as was the flexibility permitted by the variety of writs. No matter who won, the royal exchequer profited, since the loser had to pay a fine. Also, judgments rendered by royal judges became new law without any legislation.

Building on the practice begun by Henry I, Henry II also regularly sent justices out to the shires. On their travels they were instructed to receive reports in each shire from the local officials and to try all cases pending in the shire court. Moreover, the sheriffs (or *shire reeves*, the king's chief executives in local government) had to bring before the justices from each hundred and township a group of sworn men to report under oath all crimes that had occurred since the last visit of the justices and to indicate whom they considered to be the probable criminal in each case. This was another use of the jury, the jury of *presentment*, since it "presented" the names of suspect criminals. (It is the ancestor of the modern grand jury—"grand" in the sense of large—consisting of more men than the twelve that took part in the petty juries.) Again the treasury profited, as the justices imposed heavy fines. Again blatant innovation was avoided, and refinements and combinations of existing instruments produced new legal conditions. Even so, the usual means of proof in a criminal trial under Henry II was still an ordeal by cold water. If the accused, with hands and feet tied, floated in a pool blessed by the church, he was guilty; if he sank, perhaps to drown, he was innocent.

Henry II, however, failed to limit the competing system of canon law. He had appointed his friend and chancellor Thomas à Becket (1118–1170) archbishop of Canterbury. But once he had become archbishop, Becket proved inflexibly determined not to yield any of the church's rights, but rather to add to them whenever he could. A great quarrel between the two broke out over the question of clerics convicted of crime. In publishing a collection of largely earlier customs relating to the church (Constitutions of Clarendon, 1164), Henry included a provision that clerics charged with crimes should be indicted in the royal court before being tried by the bishop's court, and then, if convicted, returned to the royal authorities for punishment. Becket refused to agree to this part of the document and appealed to the pope for support.

Although the issue was compromised after a dispute that lasted six years, Henry, in a fit of temper over Becket's Christmas Day excommunication of bishops who supported the king, asked whether no one would rid him of Becket. Four of his knights responded by murdering Becket in his own cathedral at Canterbury. Henry

An illuminated manuscript showing the murder of Archbishop Thomas à Becket in Canterbury cathedral on December 29, 1170. This version, dating from about 1200, is probably the earliest surviving representation.
British Museum

Richard I and John, 1189–1216

Henry II's son, Richard the Lionhearted (r. 1189–1199), spent less than six months of his ten-year reign in England, but thanks to Henry II, the bureaucracy functioned without the presence of the king. Indeed, it functioned all too well for the liking of the population, since Richard needed more money than had ever been needed before to pay for this Crusade, for his ransom from captivity, and for his wars against Philip Augustus of France. Heavy taxes were levied on income and on personal property; certain possessions, including silver plate, were simply confiscated; many charters were sold to cities. Thus it was that Richard's brother John (r. 1199–1216) succeeded to a throne whose resources had been squandered. John had the misfortune to face three adversaries who proved too strong for him: Philip Augustus, who expelled the English from France north of the Loire; the pope, Innocent III; and the outraged English barons.

In 1206 the election to the archbishopric of Canterbury was disputed between two candidates, one of whom was favored by John. The pope refused to accept either, and in 1207 procured the election of a third, Stephen Langton (c. 1155–1228), who was a learned English scholar at Paris. John exiled the monks of Canterbury and confiscated the property of the see. Innocent responded by putting England under an interdict and by excommunicating John. He threatened to depose John and thought of replacing him with a Capetian; he corresponded with Philip Augustus, who prepared to invade England. Fearing with good reason that such an invasion would strain the loyalty of his own vassals, John

A fourteenth-century manuscript illumination showing King John hunting deer.
British Museum

swore to the pope that he was innocent of complicity in the murder, but he had to undergo a humiliating penance and, more important, he had to yield on the issue. The church in England won the sole right to punish its clergy—*benefit of clergy*, the principle was called. Moreover, Henry had to accept the right of litigants in church courts to appeal to Rome directly, without royal intervention of any sort. This meant that the papacy had the ultimate say in an important area of English life. It was a severe defeat for Henry's program of extending royal justice. Yet the other clauses in the Constitutions of Clarendon were not challenged, and the king continued to prevent the pope from directly taxing the English clergy. Becket was made a saint only two years after his death, and pilgrimages to his tomb at Canterbury became an important scene in English life.

Henry's reign was also notable for the reorganization of the old Anglo-Saxon fyrd by the Assize of Arms in 1181, which made each free man responsible, according to his income, for maintaining suitable arms for the defense of the realm.

gave in (1213). Not only did he accept Langton as archbishop of Canterbury and promise to restore church property and to reinstate banished priests, but he also recognized England and Ireland as fiefs of the papacy and did homage to the pope for them. He also agreed to pay an annual tribute to Rome. Here was a startling papal victory. Thereafter Innocent sided with John in his quarrel with a large faction of the English barons—a quarrel that became acute after the French had won the battle of Bouvines.

Magna Carta, 1215

A quarrel with perhaps a third of the English barons arose from John's ruthlessness in raising money for the campaign in France and from his practice of punishing vassals without trial. At the moment of absolution by the pope in 1213, John had sworn to Stephen Langton that he would "restore the good laws of his predecessors." But he violated his oath. After Bouvines, the barons hostile to John renounced their homage to him and drew up a list of demands, most of which they forced him to accept on June 15, 1215, at a meadow called Runnymede on the banks of the Thames. The document that he agreed to send out under the royal seal to all the shires in England had sixty-three chapters, in the legal form of a feudal grant or conveyance, known as *Magna Carta*, the "Great Charter."

Magna Carta was a feudal document, a list of specific commissions drawn up in the interest of a group of barons at odds with their feudal lord, the king. The king promised reform in his exactions of scutage, aids, reliefs, and in certain other feudal practices. He made certain concessions to the peasantry, the tradespeople (uniform weights and measures, town liberties), and the church (free elections to bishoprics and maintenance of liberties).

This medieval special-interest document is often called the foundation stone of present liberties in Britain and North America largely because some of its provisions could be and were given new and expanded meanings in later centuries. For instance, the provision that "No scutage or aid, save the customary feudal ones, shall be levied, *except by the common consent of the realm*" in 1215 meant only that John would have to consult his great council (barons and bishops) before levying extraordinary feudal aids. Yet this could later be expanded into the doctrine that all taxation must be by consent, that taxation without representation was tyranny—which would have astonished everyone at Runnymede. Similarly, the provision that "No freeman shall be arrested or imprisoned, or dispossessed or outlawed or banished or in any way molested; nor will we set forth against him, nor send against him, unless by the lawful judgment of his peers and by the law of the land" in 1215 meant only that the barons did not want to be tried by anybody not their social equal, and they wished to curb the aggressions of royal justice. Yet it was later expanded into the doctrine of due process of law, that everyone is entitled to a trial by "his peers."

Although medieval kings of England reissued the charter with modifications some forty times, it was to be ignored under the Tudors in the sixteenth century, and it was not appealed to until the revolt against the Stuarts in the seventeenth century. By then the rebels against Stuart absolutism could read into the medieval clauses of Magna Carta many of the same modern meanings that we, just as inaccurately, see in them at first glance. Thus Magna Carta's lasting importance lies partly in what later interpreters were able to find in its original clauses. It also lies, perhaps even more, in two general principles underlying the whole document: that the king was subject to the law and that he might, if necessary, be forced to observe it. This is why this document—over seven and a half centuries old, dealing with a now obsolete social system—is still important for the twentieth century.

As soon as John had accepted the charter, he tried to break his promises. The pope declared the charter null and void, and Langton and the barons opposed to John now took the pope's former place as supporters of a French monarchy for England. Philip Augustus's son actually landed in England and occupied London briefly; but John died in 1216 and was succeeded by his nine-year-old son, Henry III (r. 1216–1272), to whose side the barons rallied. During Henry's minority, three figures in particular exercised effective power: William Marshal, as regent; Hubert de Burgh, the *justiciar*, or administrator of justice; and John's former captain Faulkes de Bréauté. The barons expelled the French from England, and it was not until 1258 that the king found himself again in an open clash with a faction of his own barons.

Henry reissued Magna Carta, formally ratifying it. Nonetheless, the barons felt that he did not fully adhere to it, and they were increasingly disturbed by his appointment of French administrative officials. The clash came to a head in 1258, a year of bad harvest, when Henry asked for one-third of the revenues of England as an extra grant for the pope. The barons came armed to the session of the great council and secured the appointment of a committee of twenty-four of their number, who then issued a document known as the Provisions of Oxford. This document, an effort to restore the charter, created a council of fifteen without whose advice the king could do nothing. The committee put its own men in the high offices of state, and it replaced the full great council with a baronial body of twelve. This provision clearly contained the seeds of a baronial tyranny as bad as the king's own.

But the barons could not agree among themselves, and Henry III resumed his personal rule. Open civil war broke out in 1263 between the king and the baronial party headed by Simon de Montfort (c. 1208–1265). When in the next year Louis IX was called in to arbitrate, he ruled in favor of the king and against the barons. Simon, however, would not accept the decision. He cap-

MAGNA CARTA

The Magna Carta reaffirmed traditional rights and personal liberties against royal authority. Many of its provisions became the basis for specific civil rights enjoyed in Western democracies today: In addition to early forms of the principle that there should be no taxation without representation, of the right of rebellion, and of the assertion that justice must be under law without restraint, the charter included:

20. A freeman shall be amerced [fined] for a small offence only according to the degree of the offence; and for a grave offence he shall be amerced according to the gravity of the offence, saving his contenement [property necessary for sustenance of his family and himself]. And a merchant shall be amerced in the same way, saving his merchandise; and a villein in the same way, saving his wainage [harvested crops needed for seed]—should they fall into our mercy. And none of the aforesaid amercements shall be imposed except by the oaths of good men from the neighbourhood....

28. No constable or other bailiff of ours shall take grain or other chattels of any one without immediate payment therefor in money, unless by the will of the seller he may secure postponement of that payment.

29. No constable shall distrain [require] any knight to pay money for castle-guard when he is willing to perform that service himself, or through another good man if for reasonable cause he is unable to perform it himself. And if we lead or send him on a military expedition, he shall be quit of castle-guard for so long a time as he shall be with the army at our command.

30. No sheriff or bailiff of ours, nor any other person, shall take the horses or carts of any freeman for carrying service, except by the will of that freeman.

31. Neither we nor our bailiffs will take some one else's wood for repairing castles or for doing any

other work of ours, except by the will of him to whom the wood belongs....

39. No freeman shall be captured or imprisoned or disseised [deprived] or outlawed or exiled or in any way destroyed, nor will we go against him or send against him, except by the lawful judgment of his peers or by the law of the land....

41. All merchants may safely and securely go away from England, come to England, stay in and go through England, by land or by water, for buying and selling under right and ancient customs and without any evil exactions, except in time of war if they are from the land at war with us. And if such persons are found in our land at the beginning of a war, they shall be arrested without injury to their bodies or goods until we or our chief justice can ascertain how the merchants of our land who may then be found in the land at war with us are to be treated. And if our men are to be safe, the others shall be safe in our land....

54. No one shall be arrested or imprisoned upon the appeal of a woman, for the death of any other than her husband.

From *Sources of English Constitutional History* edited by Carl Stephenson and Frederick George Marcham. Copyright 1937 by Harper and Row, Publishers, Inc., renewed 1964 by Frederick George Marcham, James Stephenson, and Richard Stephenson. Reprinted by permission of Harper Collins Publishers.

---

tured the king and set up a regime of his own, based on the restoration of the Provisions of Oxford. This regime lasted fifteen months. In 1265 Simon called an assembly of his supporters, which was a step in the evolution of Parliament. But the heir to the throne, Prince Edward, defeated and killed Simon and restored his father, Henry III, to the throne. For the last seven years of Henry's reign (1265–1272), as well as for the next thirty-five years of his own rule (1272–1307), Edward I was the true ruler of England.

The Origins of Parliament, 1258–1265

The revolts of the thirteenth century had given the barons experience in the practical work of government, and many of their reforms had been accepted by the

royal governments that followed. Still more important, during the struggle the local communities of England had emerged as significant elements in the central administration. Indeed, it is to these years under Henry III that historians turn for the earliest signs of the major contribution of the English Middle Ages to the West— the development of Parliament.

The word *parliament* comes from French and simply means a "talk" or "parley"—a conference of any kind. The French vernacular historian Geoffrey de Villehardouin (c. 1150–1212) refers to a discussion between the French and Venetian leaders in the Fourth Crusade (1204) as a *parlement*. Joinville, the biographer of St. Louis, refers to his hero's secret conversations with his wife on the palace staircase as *parlement*. And the word was applied in France to that part of the curia regis which acted as a court of justice. In England during the thirteenth century, the word often refers to the assemblies summoned by the king, especially those that were to hear petitions for legal redress. In short, a parliament in England in the thirteenth century was much like the parlement in France—a session of the king's large council acting as a court of justice.

The Anglo-Saxon witenagemot had been an assembly of the great churchmen and laymen of the kingdom who advised the king on taxation and on matters of policy, and who could also act as a supreme court in important cases. In these respects the great council of the Norman kings was not much different from the witenagemot. Feudal law simply reinforced the king's right to secure from his chief vassals both aid (that is, military service and money) and counsel (that is, advice on law and custom and a share in judicial decisions). The Norman kings made attendance at sessions of the great council compulsory; it was the king's privilege, not his duty, to receive counsel, and it was the vassal's duty, not his privilege, to offer it.

But by requiring the barons to help govern England, the kings unconsciously, and contrary to their own intentions, strengthened the assembly of vassals, the great council. The feeling gradually grew that the king must consult the council; this feeling is reflected in the scutage and aid provision of Magna Carta. Yet the kings generally consulted only the small council of their permanent advisers; the great council met only occasionally and when summoned by the king. The barons who sat on the great council thus developed a sense of being excluded from the work of government in which they felt entitled to participate. It was baronial discontent that led to the troubles under Henry III. When the barons took over the government in 1258, they determined that the great council should meet three times a year, and they called it a *parliament*. When Henry III regained power, he continued to summon the feudal magnates to the great council, to parliament.

The increasing prosperity of England in the thirteenth century had enriched many members of the landed gentry who were not necessarily the king's direct vassals. The inhabitants of the towns had also increased in number and importance with the growth of trade. Representatives of these newly important classes in country and town now began to attend parliament at the king's summons. They were the knights of the shire, two from each shire, and the burgesses of the towns. Accustomed since Anglo-Saxon times to compulsory participation in their local hundred and shire courts, the knights were landholders with local standing, and they were often rich men. By the time of Richard I, some were occasionally selected to bring court records to the judges. At royal command, the towns had chosen representatives to bring documents proving titles before the royal justices, either on circuit in the shires or in London. In 1254 knights of the shire were summoned for the first time to a meeting of the great council. Meanwhile, burgesses of townsmen were also being summoned by the king to appear before his justices, either on circuit in the shires or in London.

The Parliament of Edward I. This picture is one of the oldest views in existence of Parliament in session. To the right of Edward is Alexander III, king of the Scots, and to his left is Llewellyn, prince of Wales. In the center are members seated on the original woolsacks; on the left are the lords spiritual (archbishops, bishops, and abbots); and on the right are the lords temporal. In fact, neither Alexander nor Llewellyn was ever present, and the arrangement of the figures, probably painted about 1524, was meant to make a political point.
New York Public Library Picture Collection

Although controversy on the subject still rages, recent research has made it seem probable that the chief reason for the king's summons to the shire and town representatives was his need for money. By the thirteenth century the sources of royal income, both ordinary and extraordinary, were not enough to pay the king's ever-mounting bills. Thus he was obliged, according to feudal custom, to ask for "gracious aids" from his vassals. These aids were in the form of percentages of personal property, and the vassals had to assent to their collection. So large and so numerous were the aids that the king's immediate vassals naturally collected what they could from their vassals to help make up the sums. Since these subvassals would contribute such a goodly part of the aid, they, too, came to feel that they should consent to the levies. The first occasion for which there is clear evidence of the king summoning subvassals for this purpose was the meeting of the great council in 1254.

The towns also came to feel that they should be consulted on taxes, since in practice they could often negotiate with the royal authorities for a reduction in the levy imposed on them. Burgesses of some towns were included for the first time in Simon de Montfort's "Parliament" of 1265. Knights of the shire also attended this meeting because Simon apparently wanted to muster the widest possible support for his program. But only known supporters of Simon were invited to attend the Parliament.

This Parliament proved, in time, to be a precedent, for the presence of shire and town representatives made it the first true ancestor of the modern House of Commons. Not all subsequent parliaments had representatives from shire and town, and not all assemblies attended by knights and burgesses were parliaments. Knights and burgesses had no "right" to come to parliament; no doubt, they often felt it a nuisance and an expense to come, and not a privilege. But gradually they came to attend Parliament regularly.

Edward I, 1272–1307

By the late thirteenth century the earlier medieval belief that law is custom and that it cannot be made was fading, and Edward I enacted a great series of systematizing statutes, for which he is sometimes called "the English Justinian." Edward's statutes were framed by the experts of the small council, who elaborated and expanded the machinery of government, and under whose rule Parliament's function was more judicial than legislative or consultative. Each of the statutes was really a large bundle of different enactments. Taken together, they reflect a declining feudalism and show us an England in which the suzerain-vassal relationship was becoming a mere landlord-tenant relationship and in which the old duties of fighting were becoming less important than financial obligations. The second Statute of Westminster (1285), for example, was designed to assure the great landowner that an estate granted to a tenant could not be disposed of except by direct inheritance: this is what we could call *entail*. Similarly, the Statute of Mortmain (1279) prevented transfer of land to the church without the consent of the suzerain. The church placed a "dead hand" (*mortmain*) on land and could hold on forever to any land it received; lay landlords, therefore, found it highly unprofitable to see portions of their holdings transferred to clerical hands. Besides these statutes, which protected the interest of the landlord, Edward I, in a statute of 1290, commanded the barons to show by what authority (*quo warranto*) they held any privilege, such as the right to have their own court of justice. Some privileges (franchises) he revoked, but his chief aim was to assert the principle that all such franchises came from the king, and that what he had given he could take away.

Under Edward the business of royal justice increased steadily, and specialized courts began to appear, all offspring of the central curia regis. The Court of Common Pleas, which handled cases that arose between subjects, had begun to take shape earlier, but now it crystallized into a recognizable, separate body. The new Court of King's Bench handled criminal and Crown cases, and a special Court of Exchequer dealt with disputes about royal finance.

Edward I also regularized and improved existing financial and military practices. He made permanent the king's share in export duties on wool and leather, the burden of which fell mostly on foreigners, and in customs dues on foreign merchandise, which soon became the most important single source of royal income— eloquent testimony to the flourishing commerce of the period. At the request of Parliament, Edward did away with an important source of loans, expelling the Jews from England in 1290; they were not allowed to return until the midseventeenth century. After this expulsion, the Italians assumed the role of money lenders.

Edward I's Parliament of 1295 is traditionally called the Model Parliament because it included all classes of the kingdom—not only barons, higher clergy, knights of the shire, and burgesses, but also representatives of the lower clergy. In the royal summons of 1295 appeared a celebrated clause: "What touches all should be approved by all." This basic principle would be repeated two years later, even though the lower clergy soon turned to their own convocations and ceased attending.

Edward also required all freemen to equip themselves for military service. The less wealthy served as foot soldiers. But those with a certain minimum amount of property were compelled to become knights (this was called distraint of knighthood) and serve on horseback, in part for financial reasons: once they had achieved knight's status, the king could collect feudal dues from them.

Edward's vigorous extension of royal power aroused the same sort of opposition that had plagued John and undone Henry III. In 1297 both the clergy (under the influence of Pope Boniface VIII) and the barons refused to grant the aid that Edward wanted; they were able to make him confirm Magna Carta and promise not to make any nonfeudal levy without first obtaining consent. Unlike the French monarchs, the English kings had encountered a corporate baronial opposition, which by forcing consultation upon the king had begun to create new institutions.

In France, the Capetian kings, beginning as relatively powerless and insignificant local lords, had by 1300 extended their royal administration into the lands of their great vassals and created the institutions of a powerful centralized monarchy. The question of the English claims to large areas on the Continent remained to be settled in the grim struggle of the Hundred Years' War. In England, on the other hand, the Norman conquerors proved able to make the most of existing Anglo-Saxon institutions and to superimpose effective feudal monarchy, while they and their successors developed the common law, bringing not only money and power to the monarch but relative security to the subject.

Whereas in France the vassals were unaware of the danger to their position until it was too late, and were too divided among themselves to unite in opposition to the monarch's aggressions, in England the vassals early recognized the need for presenting a united opposition if they were to preserve their rights. Out of their opposition emerged the guarantees that limited the king: promises given in the first instance on behalf of the great vassals, though later subject to much broader interpretation. By the early fourteenth century, out of the king's need to obtain assent for taxation and out of the custom of consultation between king and subject, there was beginning to emerge a recognizable parliament that would have a major impact on the world. The English and French were launched upon contrasting historical paths.

III   SCIENCE AND LITERATURE IN THE WEST

There was throughout the West a growing interest in scientific inquiry that served to unite peoples. Science had always been international, since ideas cannot be restrained within the borders of a state, but technology—that is, the application of science to practical ends—may for a time be held within the confines of a single nation through legislation or restrictions on immigration. Thus England, France, and the German states, but most especially England, were cautiously setting themselves apart from the mainstream of ready acceptance of all logic as deriving from churchly authority. Literature, too, contributed to this sense of inquiry and artistic experimentation.

Science

The Middle Ages saw considerable achievement in natural science. Modern scholars have revised downward the reputation of the Oxford Franciscan Roger Bacon (c. 1214–1294) as a lone, heroic devotee of "true" experimental methods; but they have revised upward such reputations as those of Adelard of Bath (twelfth century), who was a pioneer in the study of Arab science; William of Conches (twelfth century), whose greatly improved cosmology was cited for its particularly elegant clarity; and Robert Grosseteste (c. 1175–1253) at Oxford, who clearly did employ experimental methods. No doubt much medieval theological and philosophical thought was concerned with forms of human experience that natural science is not concerned with, but in many ways even modern Western science goes back at least to the thirteenth century.

First, especially in the late Middle Ages, real progress took place in the technologies that underlie modern science—in agriculture, in mining and metallurgy, and in the industrial arts generally. Accurate clockwork, optical instruments, and the compass all emerged from the later Middle Ages. Even such sports as falconry and such dubious subjects as astrology and alchemy helped lay the foundations of modern science. The breeding and training of falcons taught close observation of the birds' behavior; astrology involved close observation of the heavens and complicated calculations; alchemy, though it was far short of modern chemistry, nevertheless brought the beginnings of identification and rough classification of elements and compounds. Second, mathematics was pursued throughout the period. Thanks in part to Arab influences, it had been fashioned into a tool ready for the use of early modern scientists. Through the Arabs, medieval Europeans learned Arabic numerals and the symbol for zero—a small thing, but one without which the modern world could hardly get along. Try doing long division with Roman numerals—dividing, say MCXXVI by LXI. The process is difficult and time-consuming.

Finally, and most important, the discipline of Scholasticism, antagonistic as it often was to experimental science, formed a trained scholarly community that was accustomed to a rigorous intellectual discipline. Natural science uses deduction as well as induction, and early modern science inherited from the deductive Scholasticism of the Middle Ages the meticulous care, patience, and logical rigor without which all the inductive accumulation of facts would be of little use to scientists. Without the Aristotelian revival of the thirteenth century, science could not have developed along the path it took.

Literature

In literature, as in science and in social and economic life, Latin continued to be the language of the church and of learned communication everywhere in western Europe. In fact, by the eleventh century it was written better than in the earlier Middle Ages. All the churchmen—John of Salisbury, Abelard, Bernard, Aquinas, and the rest—wrote Latin even when corresponding informally with their friends. Children began their schooling by learning it. It was also the language of the law and of politics; all documents, not only important ones like Magna Carta but private ones like a deed to a piece of property, were written in Latin. Sermons were delivered in Latin, and church hymns and popular songs were written and sung in it.

But if Latin was widely used for all learned purposes, the period after the eleventh century marks the gradual triumph of the vernacular languages all over Europe for the literature of entertainment, of *belles-lettres*. Whereas *Beowulf*, coming from a Britain never thoroughly Latinized, was the only important literary vernacular poem during the early Middle Ages, now such poems began to appear in ever greater numbers everywhere except Britain, where English was in temporary eclipse. A particularly celebrated one in Old French is *The Song of Roland*, whose earliest surviving manuscript probably dates from a little after the year 1100, and which survives in hundreds of versions, the variations of which can tell the scholar much about the culture from which the version originated.

The poem was known from oral tradition earlier, as

THE CONFESSION OF GOLIAS

Much verse was still written in Latin in the medieval West, even extremely colloquial or satirical verse, such as the famous student songs of the twelfth century still preserved in a single manuscript found in a German monastery.

These songs, all anonymous, are called *Goliardic* because the authors—mostly, we imagine, wild young renegade clerics wandering about Europe from one lecturer to another—claimed to be in the service of a certain Golias, a kind of satanic figure perhaps deriving originally from the Old Testament giant, Goliath, whom David slew with a stone from his sling. Their verses mocked the form and the values of the serious religious poetry of the time and satirized the clergy and the church and even the Bible. No doubt the Goliardic verses in praise of wine, women, and song shocked the virtuous, as they were intended to do.

Here is the way in which the Confession of Golias defined the highest good:

My intention is to die
In the tavern drinking;
Wine must be on hand, for I
Want it when I'm sinking.

Angels when they come shall cry
At my frailties winking:

"Spare this drunkard, God, he's high,
Absolutely stinking."

From George F. Whicher, *The Goliard Poets* (New York: New Directions, 1949). Copyright 1949 by George F. Whicher. Reprinted by permission of New Directions Publishing Corporation.

it was sung by William's men at Hastings in 1066. It deals with a historic episode far in the past, the defeat of Charlemagne's rear guard by the Muslims in 778 in the mountain pass of Roncevaux in the Pyrenees. In *The Song of Roland* human beings, not monsters, are the enemy; the landscape has brightened; a more intense Christian piety softens some of the worst violence; Roland sees to it that comrades slain by the infidel receive a Christian blessing. It is human treachery that brings tragedy down on the heroic forces of Charlemagne, leaving Roland and the king grief-stricken. The highest virtue in the poem is loyalty to one's lord—a quality that was the first necessity in a feudal society where, it

was felt, only the knight's loyalty to his suzerain saved all from anarchy. In Roland's deep loyalty to his lord, Charlemagne, there is something new—a patriotic note of love of country that was struck at about the earliest moment that we can speak of Europeans as having "a country."

As the knight was always defined as a mounted man, a man on a horse, so the unwritten but generally accepted code that came to govern his behavior—in elaborate detail—was called *chivalry*, from the French word *cheval*, a horse.

The literature of chivalry and courtly love developed with particular complexity at the court of Eleanor of

Popular interest in astronomy during the Middle Ages is demonstrated by the inclusion in the Bayeux Tapestry of Halley's Comet passing over Normandy in 1066.
Giraudon/Art Resource, with special authorization City of Bayeux

THE SONG OF ROLAND

Roland has died on the field of battle, and Charlemagne believes that he was betrayed by Ganelon, who with his men deserted the field at a crucial moment. Ganelon is found guilty by trial, but before he can be executed one of his followers, Pinabel, challenges one of the emperor's most devoted liege men to battle. The following passage describes that battle, revealing much about feudal attitudes, and captures the songlike rhythm of the poetry:

In a broad meadow   below Aix la Chapelle,
The barons meet;   their battle has begun.
Both are courageous,   both of them valiant lords,
And their war-horses   are spirited and swift
They spur them hard,   and loosening the reins,
They charge each other   and strike with all their might.
Both shields are shattered   —they're broken into bits—
The hauberks break,   the girths are split apart,
The saddles fall,   and with them both the knights.
A hundred thousand   are weeping at the sight.

Both chevaliers   have fallen to the ground.
Losing no time,   they're on their feet again.
Agile and swift   is Pinabel, and strong;
They face each other   —they have no horses now—
And raise their swords   whose hilts are made of gold
To strike and hew   each other's shining helms;
Those heavy blows   can cut right through the steel.
The French lament,   thinking their man must fail.
"O God," says Charles,   "now let the right prevail!"

Says Pinabel,   "Thierry, admit you've lost!
I'll be your vassal   in loyalty and love,
All I possess   shall be at your command—
But reconcile   the king and Ganelon."
Then Thierry answers,   "That's easy to decide!
I'll take no offer   unworthy of a knight!
Let God determine   which one of us is right!"

Says Pinabel,   "Almighty God forbid!
I stand here now   for all my family—
I won't surrender   to any man on earth!
Better to die   than live to merit blame."
So once again   they slash with their great swords,
Striking the helmets   brilliant with gold and jewels—
Great fiery sparks   fly out against the sky.
Now neither champion   will to the other yield
Until a dead man   is lying on the field.

The Song of Roland, trans. Patricia Terry (Indianapolis: Bobbs-Merrill, 1977), pp. 141–45.

Thierry, fighting for Charlemagne (here called Charles), is wounded but defeats Pinabel. Justice demands that Ganelon must die, together with all of his kinsmen. Ganelon's thirty followers are hanged and Ganelon, "there where a river across a meadow flows," is lashed to four horses which, as they bolt in different directions, tear him apart. "So Ganelon as a foul traitor died."

Aquitaine, who left Henry II of England in 1170 to live with her daughter Marie, countess of Champagne, at the court of Poitiers in western France, where the two became patrons of writers and poets. The hopes of aristocratic women were revealed through the tales of courtly love, and such tales were commentaries on the domestic life of the aristocracy under the strict tenets of feudal relations. The most distinguished court literature was the work of Marie de France, Chrétien de Troyes, and Andrew the Chaplain. De Troyes's *Chevalier de la Charette* expressed the doctrines of courtly love in their most developed form, and his work has been called "the perfect romance" for its presentation of a Lancelot who would cast aside all conventions for the love of Queen Guinevere. Marie wrote simpler tales

about the physical attraction exerted by youth and beauty, while Andrew wrote, in *De Amore,* a most extensive treatise on courtly, carnal, profane, and platonic love and the attitudes of the church toward the subject.

These stories, like *The Song of Roland,* were told, sung, and written in *cycles,* added to by troubadours (wandering minstrels) as they spread the tales to other lands, rewritten and glossed by subsequent generations. Perhaps the best-known were the stories that evolved in the same period around King Arthur of Britain, far more legendary than Charlemagne. The exploits of Arthur's knights (of whom Lancelot was one) became part of the vernacular literature in most of western Europe. Taken up in France, these stories were passed in the thirteenth century into Germany, where Wolfram von

A ROUNDEL BY CHRISTINE DE PISAN

A *roundel* was a popular form of poetry, written to a prescribed length and format and intended to be recited or sung. Christine de Pisan wrote the following one:

Laughing grey eyes, whose light in me I bear,
Deep in my heart's remembrance and delight,
Remembrance is so infinite delight
Of your brightness, O soft eyes that I fear.

Of love-sickness my life had perished here,
But you raise up my strength in death's respite,
Laughing grey eyes, whose light in me I bear.
Certes, by you my heart, I see full clear,

Shall of desire attain at last the height,
Even that my lady; through your sovereign might,
May-me continue in her service dear,
Laughing grey eyes, whose light in me I bear.

From *The Book of the Duke of True Lovers,* trans. Alice Kemp-Welch (London: Chatto & Windus, 1908), p. 36. Reprinted by permission of the author's Literary Estate and Chatto & Windus.

Eschenbach wrote a long poem about Arthur's knight Sir Percival, and thus gave new impetus to an old tradition that would not culminate perhaps until Richard Wagner's opera *Parsifal* in the nineteenth century. Writers of both elite and popular culture drew upon the Arthurian cycle, as did Alfred Lord Tennyson in nineteenth-century Britain and a host of moderns, including detective and science fiction writers (the *Star Trek* cycle of the late twentieth century may be the best known). Thus have the weavers of tales always been ready to retell a well-known story in a way that would speak afresh to the psychological attitudes of new generations.

The elaborate and artificial game that became courtly love flourished through lyric poetry. The Roman poet Ovid was rediscovered and misunderstood; he wrote of carnal appetites rewarded, while the code of *courtoisie* (courtly love, from which would develop modern concepts of "courtesy") required that the singer's lady almost always prove unattainable. The wife of another, made inaccessible by the obligations of feudal vassalage, the lady was to be worshiped from afar. The singer celebrated in ecstasy even the slightest kindness she might offer him. Her merest word was a command, and her devoted knight undertook without question even the most arduous mission she might propose to him, without hope of a reward. But a lady who failed to reward him, at least to some degree, was not playing by the rules of this elaborate and artificial game. The twelfth-century troubadours who sang in the southern French language (called Provençal after the large region of Provence, and quite a different dialect from that spoken in the north) were often half-humorous as they expressed their hopeless longings for the unattainable lady.

Needless to say, few medieval nobles behaved according to the code, and yet some of the ideals fostered by the troubadours did become part of the developing

Portrait of Dante, attributed to the school of Giotto, now in the Bargello Museum in Florence. The scene is meant to show Dante in the Paradise of his own making.
Bargello Museum, Florence

notions of chivalry. St. Louis was as close to a truly chivalrous figure as may have existed.

In Italy, the original home of Latin, a vernacular language was somewhat slower to develop. But here, too, at the sophisticated and cosmopolitan court of the emperor Frederick II in Palermo, some of Frederick's chief advisers began to write love poetry in what they themselves called the "sweet new style," and soon the fashion spread northward. It was not until somewhat later, with Dante Alighieri (1265–1321) of Florence, that the vernacular Italian tongue scored its definitive triumph. It is significant to note that Dante himself, among his other books, felt impelled to write (in Latin) a stirring defense of vernacular Italian: *De Vulgari Eloquentia* (Concerning the Speech of Every Day). For his own greatest work, *The Divine Comedy*, he chose Italian.

Among writers in the Western tradition, Dante belongs with Homer, Vergil, Shakespeare, and Goethe as a supreme master. As a towering intellectual figure, he heralds the new age of rebirth at least as loudly as he sounds the now-familiar medieval note. But *The Divine Comedy* was a medieval book, perhaps the most famous and in some ways the most typical of all medieval literary expressions.

Lost in a dark wood, in his thirty-fifth year, "halfway along the road of our human life," Dante encounters the Roman poet Vergil, who consents to act as his guide through two of the three great regions of the afterlife: Hell and Purgatory. Descending through the nine successive circles of Hell, where the eternally damned must remain forever, the two meet and converse with souls in torment, some of them historic persons like Judas or Brutus, others recently deceased Florentines of Dante's own acquaintance, with whose sins he was familiar. In Purgatory less sinful human beings are being punished before they can be saved. The souls of the great pagan figures, born too early to have become Christians, are neither in Hell nor in Purgatory, but in Limbo—a place of rest on the edge of Hell where Vergil himself must spend eternity. Here he introduces Dante to the shades not only of such ancients as Homer, Plato, and Socrates, but of characters in ancient myth and poetry such as Hector, Odysseus, and Aeneas. According to Dante, even the Muslim scholar Averroës and the Muslim hero Saladin are in Limbo, not in Hell.

When the poet comes to the gates of Paradise, Vergil cannot continue to escort him; so the guide to the final region of the afterlife is Beatrice, a Florentine girl with whom Dante had fallen desperately in love as a youth but whom he had worshiped only at a distance. Here Dante was consciously transforming one of the central experiences of his own life into literature in accordance with the traditions of the code of courtly love. In Paradise he finds the Christian worthies and the saints—Benedict, Bernard, Aquinas, and others—and at the climax of the poem he sees a vision of God himself.

This voyage through the afterlife is designed to show in new pictorial vividness a traditional Christian concept: that people's actions in this life determine their fate in the next. From the lost souls in Hell, who have brought themselves to their hopeless position ("Abandon Hope, All Ye Who Enter Here" reads the inscription over the gates of Hell), through those who despite their

A handsomely illuminated sheet from the Canterbury Tales.
The British Library

sufferings in Purgatory confidently expect to be saved, to those whose pure life on earth has won them eternal bliss, Dante shows the entire range of human behavior and its eternal consequences. It is a majestic summary of medieval Christian moral and ethical ideas, and it has often been compared in its completeness and its masterful subordination of detail to general vision with the philosophical work of Aquinas.

Another late medieval giant was Geoffrey Chaucer (1340–1400). By Chaucer's day the vernacular had long since recovered in England, and the Old English of the pre-Conquest period had evolved into a new form of the language usually called Middle English, recognizable today as an archaic version of the present language. Chaucer is the supreme poet of Middle English and surely the most brilliant English literary voice before Shakespeare. An experienced man of affairs who served his king at home and abroad, Chaucer left behind many literary works, including a long and moving poetic narrative love story, *Troilus and Criseyde*, deriving its characters from the Trojan War stories then fashionable in western Europe.

Chaucer's most celebrated work, however, is *The Canterbury Tales*—tales told by a group of pilgrims on their way to the tomb of Thomas à Becket, the sainted archbishop of Canterbury murdered under Henry II. The pilgrims come from all walks of English life except the high nobility and include a knight, a squire, a prioress, a clerk, a monk, a friar, a sailor, a miller, and others. On the way from London each tells at least one story, fully consonant with his or her personality and experience.

The knight tells a romantic story of chivalric love. Two cousins fall in love with a maiden whom they have barely glimpsed from the window of their prison cell. Deadly rivals thereafter, they cherish their mutual strife, in prison and out, without the lady's being aware of them. In the end, one kills the other and wins the lady

as his own—a story of courtly love. The miller tells a raw story of a young wife's deception of her elderly husband with a young lover—a barnyard anecdote full of liveliness and good humor. The prioress tells a saint's legend, the squire an unfinished story full of semi-scientific marvels, and so on. Chaucer does not hesitate to satirize his churchmen. The fourteenth century was a period of much discontent with the English church, and the poet was striking a note that was sure to be popular. The sophistication, delicacy, power, passion, and humor that Chaucer commands put him in the same class with Dante and with no other medieval writer in any country.

Summary

Between 987 and 1314 the French monarchy grew in power and prestige until it dominated the machinery of government. France became the first large, unified state in the medieval West.

The Capetian kings made good their authority over their own territory and piece by piece added to it. By 1214 at the battle of Bouvines they had overcome the Norman-Angevin threat; in the south under Louis IX (St. Louis) they drove the Albigensian heresy underground and took over Mediterranean lands. They increased their control over the curia regis, the king's court, and under Philip IV, the Fair, they consolidated the royal hold on power against the towns, the nobles, and the church.

After the Norman Conquest of England in 1066, English kings developed existing Anglo-Saxon institutions into a strong and unified state. Henry I and Henry II extended William the Conqueror's system of administration. The de-velopment of common law brought power to the monarch and security to the subject.

However, the united opposition of the English barons limited the royal power. The guarantees first given to the great vassals in Magna Carta were in time broadened to include most of the population. By the early fourteenth century a recognizable parliament began to emerge.

Progress took place in the technologies that underlie modern science, and the discipline of Scholasticism formed a trained scholarly community that was accustomed to a rigorous intellectual discipline.

Although Latin was still widely used, the vernacular languages were increasingly employed for the literature of entertainment, as in the French tales of chivalry, *The Song of Roland*, Dante's *Divine Comedy*, and Chaucer's *Canterbury Tales*.

9

The Late Middle Ages in Eastern Europe

In Spain the fighting of Christian against Muslim had been virtually continuous since the Muslim conquest in the eighth century. Just after the year 1000 the Cordovan caliphate weakened, and the Spanish Christian princes of the north won the support of the powerful French abbey at Cluny. Under prodding from Cluny, French nobles joined the Spaniards in warring on the Muslims. Soon the pope offered an indulgence to all who would fight for the Cross in Spain. In 1085 the Christians took the city of Toledo, though a new advance by Muslim Berbers from North Africa set them back for a time. The Christian movement continued into the twelfth century, recovering a large area of central Spain. It was itself a *Crusade*—a holy war against the infidel supported by the papacy. So, too, were the wars of the Normans against the Muslims of Sicily.

I   THE CRUSADES

Origins of the Crusades

From the third century on, Christians had visited the scenes of Christ's life. In Jerusalem Constantine's mother, St. Helena, had discovered what was believed to be the True Cross and other relics of Christ's Passion, and her son built the Church of the Holy Sepulcher there. Before the Muslim conquest in the seventh century, pilgrims came from Byzantium and the West, often seeking sacred relics for their churches at home. For a while after the Muslim conquest, pilgrimages were very dangerous and could be undertaken only by the hardiest pilgrims. During the reign of Charlemagne, conditions had improved for Western pilgrims, largely because of the excellent relations between Charlemagne and Caliph Harun al-Rashid. The caliph made Charlemagne a present of the actual recess in which Christ was believed to have been buried and allowed him to endow a hostel in Jerusalem for the use of pilgrims. So deep was Charlemagne's interest that there sprang up a legend that he had somehow acquired from Harun a "protectorate" over the Holy Land, and another that he had actually made a pilgrimage to the East in person. By the tenth century the belief had grown that pilgrimage would procure God's pardon for sins—a Western form of the Muslim *haj*. Santiago of Compostela in Spain, and of course Rome itself, had become favorite places of pilgrimage, but no place could compare in importance with the shrines of Palestine.

Obviously, stable conditions in both Muslim and Byzantine dominions were essential for the easy and safe continuance of pilgrimages. But in the early eleventh century the able though eccentric Egyptian ruler of Palestine, Hakim (r. 996–1021), abandoned the tolerant practices of his predecessors and began to persecute Christians and Jews and to make travel to the Holy Places unsafe. He destroyed the Church of the Holy Sepulcher and declared himself to be God incarnate. Moreover, with the death of the last ruler of the Macedonian house in 1057, an open struggle began at Byzantium between the civil servants of the court and the military led by the great landowners of Asia Minor. Simultaneously came Pecheneg invasions of the Balkans, Norman attacks on Byzantine southern Italy, and the rise in Asia of the Seljuk Turks.

By 1050 the Seljuks had created a state centering on Persia. In 1055 they entered Baghdad on the invitation of the Abbasid caliph and became the champions of Sunnite Islam against the Shi'ite rulers of Egypt. In the 1050s Seljuk forces raided deep into Anatolia, almost to the Aegean. Their advance culminated in the catastrophic Byzantine defeat at Manzikert in 1071, followed by the occupation of most of Asia Minor and the establishment of a new sultanate with its capital at Nicaea. Jerusalem fell in the year of Manzikert and became part of a new Seljuk state of Syria.

In 1081, amid disorder and palace intrigue, with the Empire reduced in territory and the capital in danger, Alexius I Comnenus, a general and a great landowner, came to the Byzantine throne (r. to 1118). He held off the Norman attack on the Dalmatian coast through an alliance with Venice, and he played one local Turkish potentate off against another, slowly reestablishing a Byzantine foothold in Asia Minor. Civil wars among the Turks and the multiplication of brigands on the highways in Anatolia and Syria made pilgrimage in the two decades after Manzikert ever more dangerous.

The schism between Eastern and Western churches provided the papacy with an additional incentive for intervention in the East. To the vigorous reforming popes of the later eleventh century, the disunity of Christendom was intolerable. In 1073 Pope Gregory VII sent an ambassador to Constantinople, who reported that the emperor was anxious for a reconciliation. Gregory VII planned to reunite the churches by extending the holy war from Spain to Asia. He would send the Byzantines an army of Western knights, which he would lead himself. It was only the quarrel over investiture with the German emperor that prevented the pope from carrying out this plan.

The First Crusade, 1095

Pope Urban II (r. 1088–1099) carried on the tradition of Gregory VII. To his Council of Piacenza in 1095 came envoys from Alexius, who asked for military help against the Turks. Turkish power was declining, and now would be a good time to strike. The Byzantine envoys also seem

Crusader's map of Jerusalem, with the principal Christian sites clearly marked.
New York Public Library Picture Collection

to have stressed the sufferings of the Christians in the East. Eight months later, at the Council of Clermont, Urban preached to a throng of the faithful. He emphasized the appeal received from the Eastern Christians, brothers in difficulty, and painted in dark colors the hardships that now faced pilgrims to Jerusalem. He summoned his listeners to form themselves, rich and poor alike, into an army, which God would assist. Killing each other at home would give way to fighting a holy war. Poverty at home would yield to the riches of the East (a theme especially important in view of the misery in which so many Europeans lived). If a man were killed doing this work of God, he would automatically be absolved of his sins and assured of salvation (a *plenary indulgence*). The audience greeted this moving oration with cries of "God wills it." Throngs of volunteers took a solemn oath, and sewed crosses of cloth onto their garments. Recruitment was under way. The First Crusade had been launched.

On the popular level, a certain Peter the Hermit, an unkempt, barefoot old man who lived on fish and wine and was a moving orator, proved the most effective preacher of the Crusade. Through France and Germany he recruited an undisciplined mob of ignorant peasants, including women and children, many of them serfs living wretched lives, suffering near-starvation as a result of crop failure. Often they believed that Peter was leading them straight to heaven, the New Jerusalem, flowing with milk and honey, which they confused with the Jerusalem on earth.

In two installments, they poured up the Rhine, across Hungary, where four thousand Hungarians were killed in a riot over the sale of a pair of shoes, and into Byzantine territory at Belgrade. The Byzantines, who had hoped for the loan of a few hundred well-trained knights, were appalled at the prospect of the enormous armies of human locusts about to descend on them from the West. They proceeded to arrange military escorts and to take all precautions against trouble. Despite their best efforts, the undisciplined crusaders burned houses and stole everything that was not chained down, including the lead from the roofs of churches.

Once in Constantinople, the crusaders were graciously received by Alexius Comnenus, who shipped them across the Straits as quickly as possible. In Asia Minor they quarreled among themselves, murdered the Christian inhabitants, scored no success against the Turks, and were eventually massacred. The trouble brought upon the Byzantines by this first mob of crusaders was a sample of future difficulties.

Meanwhile, at the upper levels of Western society, no kings had enlisted in the Crusade, but a considerable number of great lords had been recruited, including a brother of the king of France, the duke of Normandy, and the count of Flanders. The most celebrated, however, were Godfrey of Bouillon (duke of Lower Lorraine), and his brother Baldwin, Count Raymond of Toulouse, Count Stephen of Blois, and Bohemond, a Norman prince from southern Italy. Better-equipped and better-disciplined, the armies led by these lords now began to converge on Constantinople by different routes, arriving at intervals. Still, there was plenty of trouble for the people on the routes. "My lips are tight," wrote the distressed Byzantine archbishop of Bulgaria, through whose see so many of the crusaders passed. "The passage of the Franks, or their invasion, or whatever you want to call it, has upset and gripped us all. . . . As we have grown accustomed to their insults, we bear trouble more easily than we used to. Time can teach a person to get used to anything."*

The emperor Alexius was in a very difficult position. He was ready to have the Western commanders carve out principalities for themselves from Turkish-occupied territory. But he wanted to assure himself that Byzantine lands would be returned to his control and that whatever new states might be created would be dominated by him. He knew of the Western custom of vassalage and the importance attached to an oath taken to an overlord. So he decided to require each great Western lord

---

* From J. P. Migne, *Patrolgia census completus: Graeca* (Rome: Lutetiad Parisiorum, 1857–1903), CCXXVI, 324–25. Our translation.

POPE URBAN AT CLERMONT

Pope Urban proclaimed the First Crusade with these words:

The Turks, a race of Persians, who have penetrated within the boundaries of Romania even to the Mediterranean to that point which they call the Arm of Saint George, in occupying more and more of the lands of the Christians, have overcome them, have overthrown churches, and have laid waste God's kingdom. If you permit this supinely for very long, God's faithful ones will be still further subjected. . . .

I speak to those present, I send word to those not here; moreover, Christ commands it. Remission of sins will be granted for those going thither, if they end a shackled life either on land or in crossing the sea, or in struggling against the heathen. I, being vested with that gift from God, grant this to those who go.

O what a shame, if a people, so despised, degenerate, and enslaved by demons would thus overcome a people endowed with the trust of almighty God, and shining in the name of Christ! O how many evils will be imputed to you by the Lord Himself, if you do not help those who, like you, profess Christianity!

Let those who are accustomed to wage private wars wastefully even against Believers, go forth against the Infidels in a battle worthy to be undertaken now and to be finished in victory. Now, let those, who until recently existed as plunderers, be soldiers in Christ; now, let those, who formerly contended against brothers and relations, rightly fight barbarians; now, let those, who recently were hired for a few pieces of silver, win their eternal reward.

"The Chronicles of Fulcher of Chartres" trans. Martha E. McGinty, from *The First Crusade: The Chronicle of Fulcher of Chartres and Other Source Material*, ed. Edward Peters (Philadelphia: University of Philadelphia Press), 30–3.

to take an oath of liege homage to him on arrival. To obtain these oaths, Alexius had to resort to bribery with splendid gifts and to all sorts of pressure, including in some cases the withholding of food from the unruly crusading armies.

The armies were all ferried across the Straits. There was no supreme command, but the armies acted as a unit, following the orders of the leaders assembled in council. In June of 1097 at Nicaea, the Seljuk capital, the Turks surrendered at the last minute to Byzantine forces rather than suffer an assault from the crusader armies. This the crusaders bitterly resented, since they had not been informed of the negotiations for surrender, and had been looking forward to plundering the town. Crossing Asia Minor, the crusaders defeated the Turks in a battle at Dorylaeum, captured the Seljuk sultan's tent and treasure, and opened the road to further advance. Godfrey's brother Baldwin, leaving the main army, marched to Edessa, a splendid ancient imperial city near the Euphrates, strategically situated for the defense of Syria from attacks coming from the East. Here, after negotiations with the local Armenian rulers, he became count of Edessa—lord of the first crusader state to be established (1098).

The Crusader States, 1098–1109

Meanwhile, the main body of the army was besieging the great fortress city of Antioch, which finally was conquered by treachery after more than seven months. An-tioch became the center of the second crusader state under the Norman Bohemond. The other crusaders then took Jerusalem by assault in July 1099, followed by a slaughter of Muslims and Jews, men, women, and children.

The Lorrainer Godfrey of Bouillon was chosen, not king, for he would not consent to wear a royal crown in the city where Christ had worn the crown of thorns, but "defender of the Holy Sepulcher." The third crusader state had been founded. When Godfrey died not long afterward, his brother Baldwin of Edessa became first king of Jerusalem in 1100.

Venetian, Genoese, and Pisan fleets now assisted in the gradual conquest of the coastal cities, ensuring sea communications with the West and the vital flow of supplies and reinforcements. In 1109 the son of Raymond of Toulouse founded the fourth and last of the crusader states, centering around the seaport of Tripoli. The king of Jerusalem was the theoretical overlord of the other three states but was often unable to enforce his authority. The Byzantine emperors never relinquished the rights that had been secured to them by the oath that the crusaders had made to Alexius and were, especially in the case of Antioch, occasionally able to assert those rights successfully.

The holdings of the Westerners lay within a long narrow coastal strip extending from the Euphrates River to the borders of Egypt, more than five hundred miles long and seldom as much as fifty miles wide. From the Muslim cities of Aleppo, Hamah, Emesa (Homs), and Damascus, just inland from the strip, and from Egypt to

A fourteenth-century miniature illustrating a French account written in 1337 of the crusader assault on Jerusalem in 1099. Leading the assault is Godfrey of Bouillon; to the far left is Peter the Hermit.
The Granger Collection

the southwest, danger constantly threatened. The Westerners failed to take obvious measures for the common defense. The great lords built superb castles at strategic places but often fought with one another, sometimes in alliance with neighboring Muslims.

The Assizes of Jerusalem—not written down until the thirteenth century, when the Muslim reconquest was nearly complete—record the governmental practices of the crusader states. The great officers of the realm were the officers of the king's household: seneschal, constable, marshal, and the like. The high court of barons not only settled disputes but acted as council of state for the king's business. The lords had rights of justice on their own fiefs. Police and civil cases were under the direction of *viscounts*, royal officers in the towns, and there were special commercial and maritime courts. The Italian commercial cities, as colonial powers, had quarters of their own in the coastal cities, with privileged status. Revenues were raised by carefully collected customs dues, by monopolies on tanning and similar industries, by a poll tax on Muslims and Jews, and by a land tax on the native population. Yet money was scarce, and the kings raided Muslim caravans or married rich wives in an effort to bolster their shaky finances. Ecclesiastical organization was complex: the two Latin patriarchs of Jerusalem and Antioch each had a hierarchy of Roman Catholic archbishops and bishops

subject to them, but Greek, Syrian, and Armenian churches continued to exist, each with its own clergy, in addition to the Muslim and Jewish faiths.

The Military Orders, 1119–1798

Early in their occupation of the eastern Mediterranean, the Westerners founded the military orders of knighthood. The first of these were the Templars, started about 1119 by a Burgundian knight who sympathized with the hardships of the Christian pilgrims, and who banded together with several others to protect the helpless on their way to pray at the Holy Places. These knights took vows of poverty, chastity, and obedience, and were given headquarters near the ruins of the Temple of Solomon—hence the name Templars. St. Bernard himself inspired their rule, based on the rules for his own Cistercians and confirmed by the pope in 1128. A second order, founded shortly after, was attached to the ancient Hospital of St. John of Jerusalem, and was therefore called the Hospitalers. Made up of knights, chaplains, and serving brothers under the command of a grand master, with branches both in the East and in Europe, the two orders were the most effective fighting forces in the Holy Land. Each had a special uniform; the Templars wore red crosses on white, the Hospitalers white crosses on black. Later a third, purely German group became the order of the Teutonic Knights with headquarters at Acre; they wore black crosses on white.

The orders rapidly grew wealthy; they had fortresses and churches of their own in the Holy Land and villages from which they obtained produce. Moreover, Western monarchs endowed them richly with lands in Europe. Their original purposes were soon dimmed or lost sight of, and they became another element in the complicated political, military, and ecclesiastical tangle in the crusader states. They often allied themselves with Muslims and so completely forgot their original vows of poverty that they engaged in banking and large-scale financial operations. In the early fourteenth century the Templars were destroyed by Philip IV of France for political reasons of his own. The Teutonic Knights, most of whose fighting was done against the pagans of the eastern Baltic shore, transmitted some of their lands and much of their outlook toward the world to the modern state of Prussia. The Hospitalers moved first to Cyprus and then to Rhodes in the early fourteenth century; they were driven to Malta by the Turks in 1522 and continued there until Napoleon's seizure of the island in 1798.

The Muslim Reconquest and the Later Crusades, 1144–1291

Tormented as they were by the political disunity characteristic of feudal society at its height, it is a wonder that the crusader states lasted so long. It was not the castles or the military orders that preserved them so much as the disunion of their Muslim enemies. When the Muslims did achieve unity under a single powerful leader, the Christians suffered grave losses. Thus, beginning in the late 1120s, Zangi, governor of Mosul on the Tigris (the town that gives its name to our muslin cloth), succeeded in unifying the local Muslim rulers of the region. In 1144 he took Edessa, first of the crusader cities to fall. It was never to be recaptured. Two years later Zangi was assassinated, but the Muslim reconquest had begun.

As an answer to the loss of Edessa, St. Bernard himself preached the so-called Second Crusade in Europe. He aroused enormous enthusiasm, and for the first time Western monarchs—King Louis VII of France and King Conrad III of Germany—came to the East. But the Second Crusade proved a shattering failure. As the German and French armies passed through Constantinople, relations with the Byzantines were worse than ever. It is quite likely that the emperor, Manuel I Comnenus (r. 1143–1180), whose capital the crusaders seriously considered attacking, mixed chalk with the flour that he sold them before he managed to get them across the Straits and altogether possible that he was in touch with the Turks.

The Western armies were almost wiped out in Asia Minor. When the remnants reached the Holy Land, they found themselves in hopeless conflict with the local lords, who feared that the newcomers would take over the kingdom and who sabotaged what might otherwise have been a successful siege of the key Muslim city—Damascus. The crusaders' failure to take Damascus in 1149 brought its own punishment. In 1154 Zangi's son, Nureddin, took it, and Muslim Syria was united against the Latins. St. Bernard had boasted of his success in recruiting the Crusade: "Because of my preaching, towns and castles are empty of inhabitants. Seven women can scarcely find one man." He now lamented:

We have fallen on evil days, in which the Lord, provoked by our sins, has judged the world, with justice, indeed, but not with his wonted mercy.... The sons of the Church have been overthrown in the desert, slain with the sword, or destroyed by famine.... The judgments of the Lord are righteous, but this one is an abyss so deep that I must call him blessed who is not scandalized therein.*

The next act of the Muslim reconquest was carried out in Egypt by a general of Nureddin's who was sent to assist one of the quarreling factions in Cairo. This general became vizier of Egypt and died in 1169, leaving his office to his nephew, Saladin, celebrated in both history and legend, who became the greatest Muslim leader of the Crusade period. A vigorous and successful general, often moved by impulse, Saladin was also often chivalrous and humane.

Saladin brought the Muslim cities of Syria and Mesopotamia under his control and distributed them to faithful members of his own family. By 1183 his brother ruled Egypt, his sons ruled Damascus and Aleppo, and close relatives ruled all the other important centers. Internal decay in the kingdom of Jerusalem and a squabble over the throne gave Saladin his chance, and a violation of a truce by an unruly crusader lord gave him his excuse. In 1187 Jerusalem fell, and soon there was nothing of the kingdom left to the Christians except the port of Tyre and a few castles.

These events elicited the Third Crusade (1189–1192). The Holy Roman emperor, Frederick Barbarossa, led a German force through Byzantium, only to be drowned in Asia Minor (1190) before reaching the Holy Land. Some of his troops, however, continued to Palestine. There they were joined by Philip Augustus of France and Richard I, the Lionhearted, of England, deadly rivals in the West. Each was at least as interested in thwarting the other as he was in furthering any common cause. The main operation of the Third Crusade was a long siege of the seaport of Acre, which was finally captured in 1191. Jerusalem itself could not be taken, but Saladin signed a treaty with Richard allowing Christians to visit the city freely.

---

* Quoted in A. J. Toynbee, *Civilization on Trial* (New York: Oxford University Press, 1948), p. 171.

Crusader States

| | Kingdom of Jerusalem and its Fiefs, 1140 | | Latin Empire, 1204–1261 |
| | Venetian possessions after 1204 | | Other Latin states in Greece after 1204 |

◉ Capitals of Crusader States

When Saladin died in 1193 his dominions were divided among his relatives, and the Christians obtained a respite. Reinforcements from the West, however, had dwindled away to a small trickle. The failures in the East were partly balanced by successes in Spain, where, by the end of the thirteenth century, the Christians had restricted the Muslims to the kingdom of Granada in the southeastern corner of the peninsula; far to the northeast, the pagan Lithuanians and Slavs received the attention of the Teutonic Knights in the Baltic region.

Innocent III came to the papal throne in 1198 and called for a new Crusade, the Fourth. Several powerful lords responded and decided to proceed to their goal by sea. The Venetians agreed to furnish transportation and food—at a price that proved higher than the crusaders could pay—and also to contribute fifty armed warships on condition that they would share equally in all future conquests. The shrewd, blind old doge (duke) of Venice, Enrico Dandolo (c. 1108–1205) agreed to forgive the debt temporarily if the crusaders would help him reconquer Zara, a town on the eastern side of the Adriatic that had revolted against Venetian domination and had gone over to the king of Hungary. So the Fourth Crusade began with the sack and destruction of a Roman Catholic town in 1202. Angrily, the pope excommunicated the crusaders, who settled down to pass the winter

in Zara before pressing on. Their primary worry was finance; the leaders had badly overestimated the number who would join the crusade and had committed themselves to a larger contract to which the Venetians intended to hold them.

During the winter the crusaders turned their attention to a new goal: Constantinople. The German king, Philip of Swabia—who was Barbarossa's son and brother to the late emperor Henry VI, and who thus had a large following—proposed that the massed army escort Alexius, a young prince with a strong claim to the Byzantine throne, to Constantinople and enthrone him in the place of a usurper. If successful, Alexius would finance the subsequent expedition, whose goal was actually Egypt, though the organizers of the Crusade had hoped to keep this secret. The idea had much to recommend it, for it would serve to pay off the debt, would restore the unity of Christendom by bringing Byzantium under its rightful and friendly heir, and would most likely (as Dandolo knew) vastly expand Venice's power. Most of the knights agreed to this plan.

In the spring of 1203 a greatly augumented crusader fleet, with enthusiastic Venetian support, attacked Constantinople. Despite advance warning, the usurper, Alexius III, had done little to prepare the capital. After all, no one had successfully attacked Constantinople in nine

The *Krak des Chevaliers* (Castle of the Knights), a Crusader fortress built by the Hospitalers and taken by Saladin in 1188. Saladin later adapted its architecture to his own defenses.
Noboru Komine/Photo Researchers

hundred years. In the initial onslaught the attackers won a resounding naval victory, though the city held. A second attack on land and sea broke through the defenses, and Alexius III fled the city. The young Alexius was then crowned as Alexius IV. While he was away pursuing Alexius III, the city was badly damaged by the worst fire in its history, probably begun when a group of Franks set fire to a mosque in the Saracen quarter. Angry, Alexius IV declined to make the promised payment. Certain that he could neither bring peace with the increasingly impatient crusaders nor defeat them in battle, a group of senators, clergy and the populace deposed Alexius IV. He was murdered in prison by another usurper, who showed such qualities of leadership as to convince the crusaders that they must attack quickly before the city was fully prepared against them.

In March 1204 the crusaders and Venetians agreed to seize the city a second time, to elect a Latin emperor (who would receive a quarter of the empire and its booty), and to divide the other three-quarters equally between Venetians and non-Venetians. The second siege ended in a second capture and a systematic three-day sack of Constantinople, Byzantium's darkest hour.

The pope himself criticized the outrages committed by the crusaders. What was destroyed in the libraries of the capital is untold. Despite general destruction, the Venetians salvaged much of great value and beauty, shipping it all back to their city. The booty included the four

Twelfth-century Spanish Muslim warships, showing both decorative and technological details borrowed from the Normans and from the Byzantines. Each vessel had up to 130 galley slaves at the oars.
New York Public Library Picture Collection

great bronze horses that had been a symbol of the city since Constantine, a host of sacred relics the Greek emperors had been collecting (including a fragment of what was identified as the True Cross and a part of the head of St. John the Baptist), and hundreds of works of Byzantine art. The crusaders now paid their debt in full to the Venetians and chose not to continue on to their professed goal.

The zeal that had driven men toward the Holy Land was thoroughly tainted by the Fourth Crusade, which horrified Innocent III. Perhaps most of all, their zeal was diluted by the continuing worldly struggle between the papacy and its European opponents: first, the Albigensian heretics of southern France between 1208 and 1240; and second, the emperor Frederick II between 1220 and 1250. In these affairs the popes were offering those who would fight against a European and nominally Christian enemy the same indulgence they offered those who fought Muslims. All these developments brought disillusionment when combined with the spectacle of repeated military failure and internal Christian dissension in the Holy Land itself.

Perhaps the culmination of tragic futility was the so-called Children's Crusade in 1212, when throngs of French and German children went down to the Mediterranean, expecting that its waters would divide before them and open a path to the Holy Land along which they could march to a bloodless victory. When this failed to happen, several thousand pushed on to Marseilles and other seaports. There many were sold into slavery.

The rest was a history of short-term victory measured against long-term defeats. In the Fifth Crusade (1218–1221) the Christians attempted the conquest of Egypt, on the sound theory that this was the center of Muslim strength. They failed. Emperor Frederick II personally led the Sixth Crusade (1228–1229). The papacy excommunicated him once for not going on the Crusade and a second time for going on it. No fighting was involved, partly because the Syrian Christians would not support a ruler at odds with the pope, partly because Frederick was too sophisticated to fight when he could get what he wanted by diplomacy. Speaking Arabic and long familiar with the Muslims from his experience in Sicily, he secured more for the Christians by negotiation than any military commander since the First Crusade had secured by war. In 1229 he signed a treaty with Saladin's nephew that restored Jerusalem to the Latins again, except for the site of the Temple. Bethlehem and Nazareth were also handed over, and a ten-year truce was agreed upon. But the Egyptian ruler now took into his service several thousand Turks from central Asia who took Jerusalem in 1244 and shortly thereafter thoroughly defeated the Latins in battle at Gaza. Jerusalem remained in Muslim hands until 1917.

Now St. Louis, king of France, launched the first of his two Crusades, sometimes called the Seventh (1248–1254), aimed at Egypt. Louis himself was taken prisoner and had to pay a very heavy ransom. In 1250 the household troops of the Egyptian sultan (called Mamluks, or slaves) took power into their own hands in Egypt. Soon

after, the Mongols, fresh from their victories in Asia, where they had finally ended the Abbasid caliphate in Baghdad (1258), invaded Syria and were defeated in battle by the Mamluk general Baibars, who immediately made himself sultan. Baibars reduced the number of strongholds remaining to the crusaders, taking Antioch in 1268. He delayed his advance in fear of a new Crusade (the Eighth) by St. Louis in 1270, then resumed it when the king landed in Tunis and died there. The Muslims took Tripoli in 1289 and Acre in 1291, massacring sixty thousand Christians.

The century-long, partly secular sequel to the first hundred years of more pious crusading fervor was now over, and the Christian settlements were wiped out. They were not deeply mourned even in western Europe, from which so much blood and treasure had flowed for their establishment and defense. They had proved divisive, had distracted attention from the building of states in Europe, and had produced little of spiritual value. Thereafter the Christian states entertained no realistic hope of taking Jerusalem back.

There would be a final burst of crusading, launched by the papacy when located in Avignon, in southern France. Between 1305 and 1378, the Roman Catholic church sought not so much to recover Palestine as to protect its lands against non-Christian peoples. Crusaders fought from Alexandria to the Canary Islands, from Livonia to Greece, in defense of the Faith, while the Avignon papacy devoted enormous effort to planning, taxing, and campaigning, especially through naval warfare. The church also used economic sanctions against those who threatened it. Still, except for the capture of Smyrna and, for a time, Alexandria, these last crusades achieved little for Christianity, especially as crusaders' goals shifted to national purposes in service of a sovereign rather than to the benefit of the church.

The Impact of the Crusades on the West

The number of crusaders and pilgrims who went to the East and returned home was large. From Marseilles alone the ships of the Hospitalers and the Templars carried six thousand pilgrims a year—so many that the shipowners of the port sued the knightly orders for unfair competition. Ideas flowed back and forth with the people. Arabic words in Western languages testify to the concepts and products borrowed by the Westerners in commerce: *bazaar, tariff*, the French *douane* and the Italian *dogana* (a customs house, from the Arabic *diwan*, the sofa on which the officials sat); in foods: *sugar, saffron, rice, lemon, apricot, shallot, scallion, melon*, and *pistachio*; in manufactured goods: *cotton, muslin, damask* (from Damascus), and many others.

The new products stimulated the markets and fairs and the growing commercial life of the West. Venice and Genoa, the ports from which much of the produce of the East was funneled into Europe, prospered exceedingly. So did the cities of Flanders, whose own man-

THE SACK OF CONSTANTINOPLE

A contemporary Greek historian who was an eyewitness to the sack of Constantinople in 1204 described atrocities of which he had thought human beings incapable:

How shall I begin to tell of the deeds done by these wicked men? They trampled the images underfoot instead of adoring them. They threw the relics of the martyrs into filth. They spilt the body and blood of Christ on the ground, and threw it about. . . .

They broke into bits the sacred altar of Santa Sophia, and distributed it among the soldiers. When the sacred vessels and the silver and gold ornaments were to be carried off, they brought up mules and saddle horses inside the church itself and up to the sanctuary. When some of these slipped on the marble pavement and fell, they stabbed them where they lay and polluted the sacred pavement with blood and ordure. A harlot sat in the Patriarch's seat, singing an obscene song and dancing lewdly. They drew their daggers against anyone who opposed them at all. In the alleys and streets, in the temple, one could hear the weeping and lamentations, the groans of men and the shrieks of women, wounds, rape, captivity, separation of families. Nobles wandered about in shame, the aged in tears, the rich in poverty.

Nicetas Choniates, *Historia,* ed. Immanuel Bekker (Bonn, 1835), pp. 757 ff. Condensed; our translation.

---

ufacture of woolen goods was stimulated by the availability of Eastern luxuries for trade. Letters of credit and bills of exchange became a necessity in an ever more complex commercial and financial system, stimulated by the vast numbers traveling and making financial arrangements for a journey and a long absence from home. Italian banking houses sprang up with offices in the Holy Land. The orders of knighthood—especially the Templars—played their own role in the money trade.

Thus the Crusades contributed to the introduction of new products, first luxuries and then necessities, and helped create the conditions that led to modern methods of finance. In the long run, they probably also stimulated the movement of population from the country to the towns, which in turn permitted the smaller rural population to live better on their lands and perhaps to improve their methods of agriculture. Yet these changes, though surely speeded by the Crusades, were under way before they began, partly because of earlier contact with Islam in Spain and Sicily.

Historians can only speculate about the political and religious impact of the crusading experience upon Western society. Some believe that the Crusades helped to weaken and impoverish the feudal nobility and therefore benefited the monarchies. Certainly, kings could tax directly for the first time as a result of the need to raise money for expeditions to the Holy Land. The papacy was strengthened in its climb to leadership over all Western Christendom by sponsoring so vast an international movement. Yet this short-term gain may have been outweighed by a long-term loss. The religious motive was diluted more and more by worldly considerations. The spectacle of churchmen behaving like laymen, the misuse of the crusading indulgences for purely

European papal purposes, and the cumulative effect of failure and incompetence contributed to a disillusionment with the original concept of the Crusades. Moreover, the discovery that all Muslims were not savage beasts, that profit lay in trade with them, and that coexistence was possible, must have broadened the outlook of those who made the discovery and must have led them to question statements to the contrary, even when these statements came from Rome.

The fourteenth- and fifteenth-century Europeans who explored the coasts of Africa and Asia and crossed the Atlantic were the direct descendants of the crusaders. It is perhaps as a medieval colonization movement, inspired, like all else in the Middle Ages, largely by the church, that the Crusades are best understood. The Westerners called the crusader states in Syria *Outremer*, the "land beyond the sea." The failure of the Crusades meant that these eastern Mediterranean lands, once a significant part of Western history and self-awareness, were increasingly thrust away from the mainstream of European thought, until they were no longer seen as a natural part of the story of Western civilization.

II THE FALL OF BYZANTIUM, 1081–1453

During its last 372 years, the fate of the Byzantine Empire increasingly depended upon western Europe. The increasing economic power of the Italian merchants robbed the emperors of their independence on the sea. The flood of crusaders first made the Byzantines uneasy and ultimately destroyed them. From 1204 to 1261, while the Byzantine government was in exile from its own capital, its chief aim was to drive out the hated Latins. But even after the Byzantine leaders had recaptured Constantinople in 1261, they still could not shake off the West. The economic and military dominance of Westerners was such that twice (1274 and 1439) the Byzantine emperors actually concluded a formal "union" with the Church of Rome, only to have it repudiated by Greek public opinion.

The Western attitude is revealed in the crisp words of the great fourteenth-century Italian poet Petrarch:

> *I do not know whether it is worse to have lost Jerusalem or to possess Byzantium. In the former Christ is not recognized; in the latter he is neglected while being worshiped. The Turks are enemies but the schismatic Greeks are worse than enemies. The Turks openly attack our Empire [the Empire of the West]; the Greeks say that the Roman Church is their mother, to whom they are devoted sons; but they do not receive the commands of the Roman pontiff. The Turks hate us because they fear us less. The Greeks both hate and fear us deep in their bellies.**

The Greek attitude is revealed by a fifteenth-century Greek churchman who said that he would rather see the turban of the Turk in Constantinople than the red hat of a cardinal. Those who shared this opinion got their wish in 1453. One of the great ironies of history is that the fate of Eastern Christendom was settled by Western Christendom, and that the Muslim rule that the Latin West had sought to roll back was vastly extended by Western Christians.

Byzantine Decline, 1081–1204

The drama of Byzantium's last centuries was played out to the accompaniment of internal decay. "The powerful," in the person of Alexius I Comnenus, had captured the throne in 1081. Thereafter the imperial accumulation of lands and of tenants—who could serve as soldiers in the landlords' private armies—seems to have gone unchecked. With the weakening of the central government and the emergence of the local magnates, a form of feudalism became the characteristic way of life, as free peasants increasingly were forced by economic decline to sell their lands to the great landowners and sink into serfdom. Severe depopulation of the countryside followed, while in the cities imperial police officials or local garrison commanders acted as virtually independent rulers, while the peasant army disintegrated.

Economic ruin and social misery mounted steadily in the twelfth century. The tax collectors demanded food and lodging, presents and bribes. They would seize cattle on the pretext that they were needed for work on state projects, and then sell them back to the owners and keep the money for themselves. Irregular taxes for

defense gave further chances to oppress the population. With the decline of the navy, piracy became a major problem. The coasts of Greece and the Aegean islands became nests of raiders, preying not only on merchant shipping but upon the population on shore. Bands of wandering monks, at odds with the secular clergy, swarmed everywhere; with no means of support they also often acted like bandits.

In 1171 Emperor Manuel I Comnenus made a desperate effort to rid the capital of Venetian merchants by suddenly arresting all he could lay his hands on in one day; more than ten thousand were imprisoned. But the economic hold of Venice was too strong, and the emperor was soon forced to restore its privileges, though its rulers remained angry with the Byzantines. In 1182 a passionate wave of anti-Latin feeling led to a savage massacre by a Constantinople mob of thousands of Westerners living in the capital. In 1185 the Normans of Sicily, pursuing their century-old wars against the empire, avenged the Latins by sacking Thessalonica, second city of theByzantines. The last of the Comnenian dynasty, Andronicus I (r. 1182–1185), was tortured to death by the frantic citizens of Constantinople as the Norman forces approached the city walls. The weak dynasty of the Angeloi succeeded, and in 1204 Constantinople fell to the Latin West.

The Latin Empire, 1204–1261

After the sack of Constantinople, the Latins set about governing their conquest. They elected Baldwin of Flanders as the first Latin emperor (1204–1205), and the title continued in his family during the fifty-seven years of Latin occupation. The Venetians chose the first Latin patriarch and kept a monopoly on that rich office. The territories of the Empire were divided on paper, since most of them had not yet been conquered. The Venetians secured for themselves the long sea route from Venice by claiming the best coastal towns and strategic islands. A hybrid state was created in which the emperor's council consisted half of his own barons and half of Venetian merchants. Although in theory the Latin emperors were the successors of Constantine and Justinian, and although they wore the sacred purple boots, in practice they never commanded the loyalty of the Greek population and could not make important decisions without the counsel of their barons.

In Asia Minor Greek refugees from Constantinople, under Theodore Lascaris (d. 1222), son-in-law of the deposed Alexius III, set up a state in Nicaea and constantly threatened to recapture Constantinople. Outnumbered, incompetent as diplomats, slow to learn new military tactics, miserably poor after the treasures of Byzantium had been wasted, the Westerners could not maintain their Latin Empire, especially after its main sponsors ceased to assist it. When the popes became deeply involved in their quarrel with the Western emperor Frederick II, the Latin Empire was doomed. In

* From H. A. Gibbons, *Foundation of the Ottoman Empire* (New York: Century, 1916), p. 133.

1261 the Greeks of Nicaea seized Constantinople and reestablished the Byzantine Empire.

Meanwhile, however, the Latins had fanned out from Constantinople. Greece was divided into a series of feudal principalities, and French dukes of Athens worshiped in the Parthenon. The Peloponnesus became the principality of Achaia, with twelve feudal baronies and many minor lordships. Thessalonica became the capital of a new kingdom, which, however, fell to the Greeks in 1224. In the Aegean a Venetian adventurer established the duchy of Naxos, and other barons, mostly Italian, founded their own tiny lordships among the islands. The Venetians held Crete and yet other islands. These feudal states of Greece lasted for varying periods, but most of them were wiped out during the long process of Turkish conquest in the fifteenth century; none existed after the sixteenth.

Yet, despite catastrophic decline, Byzantium in the eleventh and twelfth centuries retained much vitality. Economic activity appears to have increased as government controls were relaxed. There was much artistic and architectural flowering, while literature, law, and scholarship flourished. Vernacular literature was popularized; heresy grew, and alien cultures were viewed with less suspicion. A class of professional intellectuals emerged, as did a new aristocracy. Such social changes did not necessarily enable Byzantium to retain its earlier sense of pride and relative coherence, however. Unlike the West, where provincial towns became centers of importance, Byzantine towns did not develop beyond an artisanal level. International trade was left to foreigners, especially to the Venetians. If not in absolute decline, Byzantium was clearly advancing far less rapidly, culturally and economically, than the West.

Byzantium after 1261

When the Greeks of Nicaea under Michael VIII Palaeologus (r. 1259–1282) recaptured Constantinople, they found it depopulated and badly damaged and the old territory of the Empire mostly in Latin hands. It was impossible for Michael and his successors to reconquer all of Greece or the islands, to push the frontier in Asia Minor east of the Seljuk capital of Konia, or to deal effectively with the Serbians in the Balkans. Therefore, Michael VIII's diplomacy was distinguished for its subtlety, even by Byzantine standards. He staved off the threat posed to his empire by Charles of Anjou, younger brother of St. Louis, to whom the popes had given the south Italian kingdom of the Normans and Hohenstaufens. Just as a new and powerful force seemed headed for Byzantium from Sicily in 1282, a revolt known as the Sicilian Vespers forestalled invasion. The French were massacred by the population, Charles of Anjou's plans had to be abandoned, and the way was open for the conquest of Sicily by the Aragonese from Spain.

So incompetent and frivolous were most of the successors of Michael VIII, however, that they contributed materially to the decline of their own beleaguered Empire. Wars among rival claimants for the throne tore the Empire apart internally just when the preservation of unity in the face of external enemies seemed of the utmost necessity. The social unrest characteristic of the period before the Latin conquest reappeared in even sharper form, as Thessalonica was torn by civil strife. The value of the currency was allowed to decline. New theological controversy, which barely concealed political disagreements, divided the clergy, already tormented by the choice between uniting with Rome or, it appeared, perishing.

In a theocentric empire, religious controversy continued to be important. From about 1330 a new movement was reviving monasticism throughout the whole of eastern Europe, a revival associated with *Hesychasm* (Greek *hesychia*, "quietude"). In the tenth century, monks of the Orthodox Eastern church had founded at Mount Athos, isolated in northern Greece, a remarkable monastery from which females, human or animal, were banned. Responsible directly to the patriarch of Constantinople, these monks preserved their independence of Byzantine emperors, Ottoman sultans, and contemporary Greek rulers alike, governing themselves and devoting their energies to self-sufficiency, to the preservation of an exceptional library of Byzantine illuminated manuscripts and icons, and to scholarship. From Mount Athos many monks founded other movements. One of these monks, St. Gregory of Sinai, set up a monastery in southeastern Bulgaria that emphasized the Hesychast goal: a mystical state of recollection and inner silence that would be achieved after man's victory over his passions. Only contemplative prayer could lead to God, though bodily exercises meant to aid spiritual concentration were also important. From Mount Athos and from Bulgaria cosmopolitan Hesychast monks covered all of eastern Europe.

In the early fourteenth century monastic churches within the walls of Constantinople were restored under the patronage of wealthy men. Byzantine churchmen took a renewed interest in scholarship, in the maintenance of libraries, and in the Greek heritage, preserving for future generations the knowledge of the past. Byzantine society recognized both the life of the world and the life of the spirit. Some monks emphasized Greek literature and philosophy, known as the "outer" wisdom, which prepared one for the truth; others, often illiterate, emphasized the "inner" knowledge that came from the "divine light" that illuminated the soul. This illumination was said to be the uncreated Light of the Transfiguration, the Metamorphosis. Humans were sanctified through this divine light, through a direct experience that involved the body and the soul. Obviously such teachings posed grave problems for the traditional views of the Orthodox church, and many commentators ridiculed the Hesychast movement. Nonetheless, the mystical movement, the growing and regenerated monasteries, and the heated discussion that arose initiated a renaissance of learning and spirituality in fourteenth-century Byzantium.

A view of the Piazza San Marco in Venice, looking toward St. Mark's Cathedral. Much of the cathedral dates from the eleventh century and was intended to house the remains of the apostle Mark. This painting by Canaletto (1697–1768) was completed about 1730.
Fogg Art Museum, Harvard University

The *Anastasis*, a fourteenth-century fresco in the Church of the Chora, a restored monastic church in Istanbul. Christ is shown raising Adam and Eve from the dead. Below are the locks, bolts, and hinges of the smashed gates of Hell.
The Granger Collection

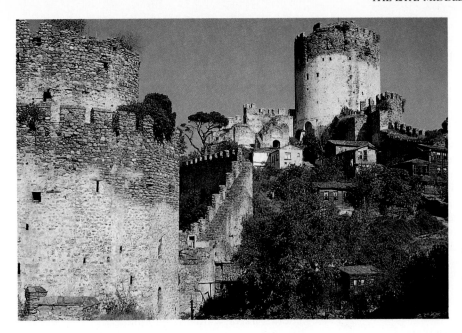

The walls of Constantinople now stand in ruins. Originally begun in the fifth century, these fortifications were added to until the fifteenth century.
Shostal/Super Stock

As the Turks pressed against Constantinople, pious Byzantines increasingly believed that their downfall at the hands of the infidels was the result of their sins; only repentance might save Byzantium from Turkish conquest. Long before the fall of Constantinople in 1453, the patriarchs had been preaching that the Second Coming of Christ was near. Science, superstition, and theology tended to merge; though able to foretell eclipses through scientific principles, astronomers nonetheless interpreted the eclipses as signs of future disasters. Much controversy took place over the approaching end to the world—over its nature, over who would be saved, over when it would occur. There came to be a reasonable consensus on the likely date of the event: 1492. Thus when the Turks poured into Constantinople, the patriarch could take comfort in the thought that the final victory would, in a few years, be his.

The Advance of the Ottoman Turks, 1354–1453

By the fourteenth century the Ottoman Turks had begun to press against the borders of Byzantine Asia Minor. Economic and political unrest led the discontented population of this region to prefer the Ottomans to the harsh and ineffectual Byzantine officials. Farmers willingly paid tribute to the Turks, and as time went on many of them were converted to Islam to avoid payment. They learned Turkish and taught the nomadic Turkish conquerors the arts of a settled agricultural life; the Turks, in turn, adopted Byzantine practices in government.

Having absorbed the Byzantine territories in Asia Minor, the Turks built a fleet and began raiding in the Sea of Marmora and the Aegean. In 1354 one of the rivals for the Byzantine throne allowed them to establish

themselves in Europe. Soon they had occupied much of Thrace. In 1363 they moved their capital to the city of Adrianople, well beyond the European side of the Straits. Constantinople was now surrounded by Turkish territory and could be reached from the West only by sea. To survive it all, the later emperors had to make humiliating arrangements with the Turkish rulers—in some cases becoming their vassals.

Although the Byzantine Empire lasted to 1453, its survival was no longer in its own hands. The Turks chose to attack much of the Balkan region first, conquering the Bulgarian and Serbian states in the 1370s and 1380s; the final defeat of the Serbs occurred at the battle of Kossovo in 1389. A French and German "crusade" against the Turks on behalf of the Hungarians was wiped out at Nicopolis on the Danube in 1396.

But further Turkish conquests were delayed for half a century when a new wave of Mongols under Timur the Lame (celebrated in literature as Tamerlane, c. 1336–1405) emerged from central Asia in 1402 and defeated the Ottoman armies at Ankara, the present-day capital of Turkey. Like most Mongol military efforts, this proved temporary, and the Ottoman armies and state recovered. In the 1420s and 1430s the Turks moved into Greece. The West, now thoroughly alarmed at the spread of Turkish power in Europe, tried to bolster the Byzantine defenses by proposing a union of the Eastern and Western churches in 1439 and by dispatching another "crusade," this time to Bulgaria in 1444. Both efforts proved futile.

With the accession of Muhammad II (also called Mehmed the Conqueror) to the Ottoman throne in 1451 (r. to 1481), the doom of Constantinople was sealed. New Turkish castles on the Bosporus prevented ships from delivering supplies to the city. In 1453 strong forces of troops and artillery were drawn up in siege array, and the Turks even dragged a fleet of small boats uphill on runners and slid them down the other side into the Golden Horn itself. As final defeat grew more and more certain, the Greeks and Latins inside the city took communion together in the Hagia Sophia for the last time, and the last emperor, Constantine XI (r. from 1448), died bravely defending the walls against the Turkish attack.

On May 29, 1453, with the walls breached and the emperor dead, the Turks took the city. Muhammad II gave thanks to Allah in Hagia Sophia and ground the altar of the sanctuary beneath his feet; thenceforth, it was to be a mosque. Shortly thereafter, he installed a new Greek patriarch and proclaimed himself protector of the Christian church. On the whole, during the centuries that followed the Orthodox church accepted the sultans as the secular successors to the Byzantine emperors.

III THE OTTOMAN EMPIRE, 1453–1699

Part of the Ottomans' inheritance no doubt came from their far-distant past in central Asia, when they had almost surely come under the influence of China and had lived like other nomads of the region. Their language, their capacity for war, and their rigid adherence to custom may go back to this early period. From the Persians and the Byzantines, the Turks seem to have derived their exaltation of the ruler, their tolerance of religious groups outside the state religion, and their practice of encouraging such groups to form independent, separate communities inside their state. Persian was always the literary language and the source of Turkish literature. From Islam, the Turks took the sacred law and their approach to legal problems, the Arabic alphabet in which they wrote their Turkish tongue, and the Arabic vocabulary of religious, philosophical, and other abstract terms. All the wellsprings of their inheritance—Asiatic, Persian, Byzantine, and Muslim—tended to make them highly traditional people.

The Ottoman System

Until the sixteenth century, the Ottomans showed tolerance to their infidel subjects, permitting Christians and Jews to serve the state and allowing the patriarch of Constantinople and the Grand Rabbi to act as leaders of their own religious communities, or *millets*. The religious leader not only represented his people in their dealings with the Ottoman state but also had civil authority over them in civil, judicial, and financial matters that affected them alone. Non-Muslims paid a head tax and lived in comparative peace. Thus, the patriarch of

Constantinople exercised far more power than he ever had under the Byzantines.

From 1280 to 1566 ten able sultans ruled the Ottomans. In theory, the sultan possessed the entire wealth of his dominions, and his object was to exploit it to the full. To do so he maintained an elaborate system of administrators whose lives and property belonged absolutely to him. All of them were considered his slaves (*kullar*) and at the same time members of the ruling class (Ottomans). To belong to the ruling class, a man had to be loyal to the sultan, a Muslim, and a true Ottoman—that is, he had to master the "Ottoman way" of speaking and behaving. Anyone who lacked one or more of these attributes was not a member of the ruling class but a subject (*raya*, literally "cattle"). Any raya could become an Ottoman by acquiring the necessary attributes. Beyond collecting, spending, and increasing the imperial revenues, and defending and adding to the imperial possessions, the Ottomans had no duties. Rayas could, in their own millets, take care of everything else of interest to the infidel communities.

The Ottoman ruling class included four subdivisions: the men of the emperor, the men of the sword, the men of the pen, and the sages. The first—the imperial class—comprised an inner service, embracing the sultan himself and his wives, sons, servants, private purse, and palace attendants, including the entire harem. In addition, there was an outer service, including the grand viziers and the other highest officers of the state, those who directed all the other branches of the service. A grand vizier presided over the council of state, and if the sultan trusted him might exercise great influence; but the sultan, too, could depose or kill him. As a slave, the vizier was completely subject to the sultan's whim.

In the early days of the Ottoman Empire the Turkish princely families from Anatolia virtually monopolized both the inner and the outer services of this imperial class. But by the fourteenth century the sultans had learned to balance their influence by recruiting new talent from among their Christian subjects. Some entered the system as prisoners of war; some the sultan bought or received as presents. But most he obtained through the regular levying of a tribute of male children between the ages of ten and twenty that took place every four years. The recruits had to accept Islam, and so these recruits, all originally Christian, competed with the older Turkish aristocratic families for the honor of staffing the imperial class.

The men of the sword included all those connected with the Ottoman armies. Besides the usual irregular troops and garrison forces, these were the cavalrymen who predominated in early Ottoman history. They received fiefs of land in exchange for service and could administer these fiefs as they wished, collecting taxes from their tenants and keeping order and justice among them. The infantrymen, at first far less important, received fixed salaries from the treasury. But with the introduction of gunpowder and the development of ar-

CONSTANTINOPLE FALLS TO THE TURKS

After seven weeks of siege, the sultan's armies took up positions along the land walls of Constantinople, and after ten days of preparation began a direct assault against the walls on April 18, 1453. After the city fell on May 29, a Turkish chronicler, Ashikpashazade, described the events in a straightforward manner:

For fifty days the battle went on by day and night. On the fifty-first day the Sultan ordered free plunder. They attacked. On the fifty-first day, a Tuesday, the fortress was captured. There were good booty and plunder. Gold and silver and jewels and fine stuffs were brought and stacked in the camp market. They began to sell them. They made the people of the city slaves and killed their emperor, and the *gazis* [frontier fighters] embraced their pretty girls....

A century later, when the passage of time had lessened the immediacy of the brutal events, a famous Ottoman historian, Sa'd ed-Din (1536–1599), described what had happened in more literary terms:

That wide region, that strong and lofty city ... from being the nest of the owl of error, was turned into the capital of glory and honor. Through the noble efforts of the Muhammadan sultan, for the evil-voiced clash of the bells of the shameless misbelievers was substituted the Muslim call to prayer, the sweet five-times repeated chant of the Faith of glorious rites, and the ears of the people of the Holy War were filled with the melody of the call to prayer. The churches which were within the city were emptied of their vile idols, and cleansed from their filthy and idolatrous impurities; and by the defacement of their images, and the erection of the Islamic prayer niches and pulpits, many monasteries and chapels became the envy of the Gardens of Paradise....

From *Istanbul and the Civilization of the Ottoman Empire*, by Bernard Lewis. Copyright © 1963 by the University of Oklahoma Press.

tillery and rifles, the Ottomans founded a special new corps to use these weapons, the *janissaries*. Most of the janissaries came from the recruits who were not selected for training for the imperial class. The janissaries lived in special barracks in the capital and enjoyed special privileges. They were both a source of strength and a constant potential danger to the state.

The men of the pen performed the other duties of government, striving to see that all land was tilled and that all trade was carried on as profitably as possible, so that the sultan might obtain his share in taxes. Once the money came in, these officials spent it on the necessary expenses of state, including salaries for troops and other employees. To keep an official honest and zealous, the Ottoman system often rewarded him by giving him in place of a salary a portion of the sultan's property as a kind of fief to exploit for himself. In the country every farm and village, in town every business and trade, in government every job thus became a kind of fief. As the Ottoman system declined in the seventeenth and eighteenth centuries, the transformation of these fiefs of land or money into private possessions without obligations signaled the loss by the sultan's administration of its former power to extract wealth from all its resources.

The sages (*ulema*) included all those connected with religion: the judges who applied Muslim law in the courts, the teachers in the schools, and the scholars of the Koran and the holy law (*Shariya*), the *muftis*. The muftis, or jurists, answered questions that arose from lawsuits and that were submitted to them by the judges. They applied the sacred law of Islam and usually gave short replies without explanation. The grand mufti in Istanbul, the former Constantinople, whom the sultan himself consulted, was known as *Sheikh-ul-Islam*, the ancient or elder of Islam, and outranked everyone except the grand vizier. Since he could speak the final word on the sacred law, he exercised a kind of check on the absolute power of the sultan himself. He alone could proclaim the beginning of war or denounce a sultan for transgressing the sacred law. The opinions of the muftis were collected as a body of interpretative law, lying between the changeless, age-old sacred law of Islam and the current enactments of the sultans. The general acceptance by all Muslims of the supremacy of the sacred law and the reluctance of the muftis to elab-

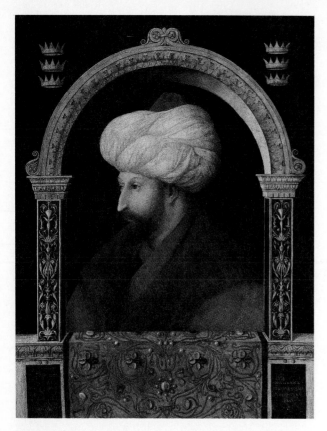

Sultan Muhammad II of Turkey, painted by Gentile Bellini (1429–1507). Muhammad ruled from 1451 to 1481; he is seen here shortly before his death. Most famous for painting Venetian ceremonial occasions with exceptional detail, Bellini lived in Constantinople from 1476 until 1481.
National Gallery, London

orate upon change were two of the factors that accounted for the failure of the Ottoman system to develop to meet the needs of the times. There were no "reformations" in Turkish history until the twentieth century.

Ottoman Expansion and Retraction, to 1699

By the end of the 1460s most of the Balkan peninsula was under Turkish rule. Thus the core of the new Ottoman state was Asia Minor and the Balkans—the same area around which the Byzantine Empire had been built. From this core, before the death of Muhammad II in 1481, the Turks expanded across the Danube into modern Romania and seized the Genoese outposts in the Crimea. They also fought the Venetians and landed forces in Italy. The limits of their expansion were marked by the great Hungarian fortress of Belgrade, key to a farther advance into central Europe, and the island fortress of Rhodes in the Aegean, stronghold of the Hospitalers and key to a farther naval advance westward.

Sultan Selim I, the Grim (1512–1520), nearly doubled the territories of the Empire in Asia at the expense of the Persians and in Africa at the expense of Egypt, which was annexed in 1517 and the rule of the Mamluks ended. From them the sultan inherited the duty of protecting the Muslim holy cities of Mecca and Medina. He also assumed the title of Caliph, with the sacred insignia of office. It is doubtful whether this alone greatly enhanced his prestige, since the title had for centuries been much abused. At one moment in his reign, Selim contemplated a general massacre of all his Christian subjects; only the refusal of the Sheikh-ul-Islam to grant consent saved the Christians. This episode vividly illustrates the insecurity of Christian life under the Turks. It also demonstrates that the character of the Ottoman state was substantially altered by the acquisition of so much territory. It was now no longer necessary to appease the Christians by generous treatment because most of the population was Muslim. Moreover, most of the newly acquired Muslims were Arabs, more intent upon enforcing widespread conversion to Islam than the Ottoman Turks had hitherto been.

Suleiman I, the Magnificent (1520–1566), resumed the advance into Europe. The Ottoman Empire thus became deeply involved in western European affairs. It participated in the wars between the Habsburgs and France and affected the Protestant Reformation in Germany by the threat of military invasion from the southeast. The newly consolidated national monarchies of the West had begun to be more of a danger to the Turks than the Venetians and Hungarians were.

Suleiman took Belgrade in 1521 and Rhodes in 1522, thus removing the two chief obstacles to westward advance. In 1526 at Mohács in Hungary, he defeated the Christian armies, and the Turks entered Buda, the Hungarian capital on the middle Danube. In September 1529 Suleiman besieged Vienna but had to abandon the siege after two weeks. In the years that followed, Suleiman acquired Algeria, which remained an Ottoman vassal state in the western Mediterranean until the nineteenth century. In Asia he defeated the Persians, annexed modern Iraq, including Baghdad, and secured an outlet on the Persian Gulf from which he fought naval wars against the Portuguese in the gulf and on the Indian Ocean.

In 1536 a formal treaty was concluded between France and the Ottoman Empire, the first of several so called "capitulations." It permitted the French to buy and sell throughout the Turkish dominions on the same basis as any Turk. In Turkish territory, the French were to enjoy complete religious liberty and were also granted a protectorate over the Holy Places, the old aim of the Crusades. This was a great advance in prestige for the Roman Catholic church.

These "capitulations" contributed to the wealth and prestige of France and gave it a better position in the Ottoman Empire than that of any other European power. They also brought the Turks into the diplomatic world of western Europe. And they are parallel to the Byzan-

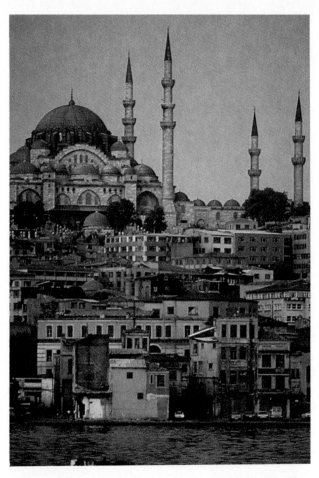

The sixteenth-century mosque of the emperor Suleiman the Magnificent, in Istanbul.
Louis Goldman, Photo Researchers

tine trade treaties with Venice and Genoa, which granted them virtually the same privileges beginning at the end of the eleventh century. In this respect, the Ottoman sultans were behaving as the successors of the Byzantine emperors.

After Suleiman the Ottoman system, already manifesting signs of weakness, deteriorated despite occasional successes. The Ottoman capture of Cyprus was preceded by the formation of a Western Holy League headed by the pope against the Turks, an enterprise as near to a crusade as the sixteenth century produced. In 1571 the League won a great naval battle (Lepanto) off the Greek coast, destroying the Ottoman fleet. However, the Spanish and Venetians failed to follow up the victory, and the Turks rebuilt their fleet.

In 1606 the Turks signed a peace treaty with the Habsburgs. Previously all treaties with Western states had been cast in the form of a truce granted as a divine favor from the sultan to a lesser potentate and had required the other party to pay tribute to the sultan. This time the Turks had to negotiate as equals; they gave the Habsburg emperor his proper title and were unable to demand tribute. Had western Europe not been preoccupied by the Thirty Years' War, the Ottoman Empire might have suffered even more severely in the first half of the seventeenth century than it did. As it was, internal anarchy disturbed the state; janissaries rebelled, troops rioted, and several sultans were deposed within a few years. The Persians recaptured Baghdad, and rebellion raged in the provinces.

Yet a firm sultan, Murad IV (r. 1623–1640), temporarily restored order through brutal means. He reduced the janissaries, initiated a new military system, reorganized military fiefs, and abolished tribute in Christian

This manuscript depicts Suleiman and his troops engaged against the Christians. From the Bibliothèque Arsenal, Paris.
Scala/Art Resource

Ottoman Empire to 1683

Ottoman Empire, 1481
Territory acquired 1481–1520
Territory acquired 1520–1566
Territory acquired 1566–1683
States tributary to Ottoman Empire
■ Battle sites

Map labels (selected): Caspian Sea, Persian Gulf, PERSIA, DAGHESTAN, GEORGIA, AZERBAIJAN, LURISTAN, Euphrates R., SHAHRZUR, Baghdad, Tigris R., MESOPOTAMIA (IRAQ), ARMENIA, ARABIA, Volga R., RUSSIA, Don R., KHANATE OF THE CRIMEA, Sea of Azov, CIRCASSIA, Dnieper R., CRIMEA, Black Sea, SYRIA, Cairo, Nile R., EGYPT, CYPRUS, ANATOLIA, Ankara, Iznik (Nicaea), BITHYNIA, Brusa, Istanbul (Byzantium), RHODES, Mediterranean Sea, CRETE, Aegean Sea, CHIOS, POLAND, PODOLIA, Dniester R., Pruth R., MOLDAVIA, Sambor, Grosswardein, TRANSYLVANIA, WALLACHIA, Danube, Nicopolis, BULGARIA, Andrianople, GALLIPOLI PEN., MACEDONIA, Monemvasia, Athens, Lepanto, PELOPONNESUS (Morea), Modon, Karlovitz, Belgrade, SERBIA, Kossovo, ALBANIA, Butrinto, Tisza R., Pest, Buda, Mohács, Sava R., BOSNIA, MONTE NEGRO, Ragusa, Antivari, HUNGARY, Agram (Zagreb), Vienna, THE EMPIRE, Danube R., Venice, Po R., Adriatic Sea, SICILY

Scale: 0–300 Miles

254

children. Despite renewed revolts after Murad's death, the revival continued under a family of viziers, the Köprülü of Albania. The first Köprülü executed thirty-six thousand people in five years (1656–1661), hanged the Greek patriarch for predicting in a private letter that Christianity would defeat Islam, rebuilt the army and navy, and suppressed revolt. Between 1661 and 1676 the second Köprülü took Crete from Venice and temporarily won large areas of the Ukraine from the Russians and Poles. In 1683 the Turks again penetrated the heart of Europe and besieged Vienna. All Europe anxiously awaited the outcome. But for the second time in two centuries the Turkish wave was broken, this time by a German and Polish army, and Europe began a great counteroffensive. The Turks remained fearsome warriors, but the Ottoman Empire was decaying from the center, for the Köprülü had been unable to effect the kinds of domestic reforms essential to future stability.

The Habsburgs drove the Turks out of Hungary, the Venetians seized the Peloponnesus, and the Russians appeared for the first time since the Tatar invasion on the shores of the Sea of Azov, which opens into the Black Sea. In 1699, after an international congress at Karlowitz on the Danube, most of the gains of the European counteroffensive were recognized by the Turks. The extensive territorial losses suffered by the Turks, the strengthening of the Habsburgs to the west, and the appearance of Russia as an important enemy of the Turks made this settlement a landmark. The western European powers could stop worrying about the Ottoman menace, which had preoccupied them since the fourteenth century and had replaced the Crusades as a great cause for which Christendom could occasionally be united. Thereafter, Turkey was a power in decline over whose possible disintegration and division the states of Europe began to squabble and negotiate. With Karlowitz, what is called the "Eastern question" in European diplomacy had begun.

IV RUSSIA FROM THE THIRTEENTH TO THE END OF THE SEVENTEENTH CENTURIES

Scholars conventionally refer to "the Russian question" as a means in invoking several historical concerns. What forces were at work to generate a Russian expansionism and consolidation of outlying territories? For how long would an enlarged or enlarging Russia remain stable? Would individual nationalities and languages reassert themselves despite Russian conquest? What role would Russia, a society of both the West and the East, play in European affairs, or in Near or Middle Eastern? Though these questions have been the focus of an enormous literature in the last two centuries, their origins lay in the fifteenth century, during a time when Russia was weak, dominated from eastern Europe, and largely manorial.

Western and Northern Lands, 1386–1478

The collapse of Kievan Russia about the year 1200 led to the formation of a series of virtually independent petty principalities. These states were too weak and disunited to resist the constant pressure from Poland and Lithuania. By the early fourteenth century, the grand duke of Lithuania, with his capital at Vilna, ruled nominally over most of western Russia. The Lithuanians, still mostly pagan, gradually took over the language and manners of their Russian vassals. But in 1386 the grand duke married the heiress to the Polish throne and became king of Poland. As a result, the Polish Roman Catholic church and the Polish nobility came to the fore in Lithuania.

Had it not been for the antagonism between Orthodox Russians and Catholic Poles and for the conflicting interests of the nobles of different religions and languages, the original Lithuanian-Russian combination might have proved to be the center around which Russia could reunite. Yet even before the connection with Poland, this region had become so feudal that its potential ability to unify Russia is doubtful. Even under the grand duke of Lithuania, most of the lands nominally affiliated with his duchy were ruled without interference by local nobles who were bound to him only by an oath of fealty and by their obligations to render military service. An assembly of nobles also limited the political authority of the grand duke. As in the West, the economic basis of society in western Russia was manorial, and restrictions were placed on the freedoms of the peasant farmer quite early.

In the north the town commonwealth of Novgorod came to rule over the vast, empty, infertile regions that were explored by armed merchants and pioneers in search of furs and other products. Even before the collapse of Kiev there grew up in Novgorod a tradition of municipal independence. The town council, or *veche*, became very strong. The lifeblood of the city was its trade with the Germans, who had their own quarter in Novgorod, which they maintained for centuries despite constant friction with the Russians.

Internally, Novgorod had a rigid class system. The representatives of the richer merchants came to control the veche, and a few powerful families concentrated the city's wealth in their hands and vied for political power. The gap between rich and poor grew wide. A man who could not pay his debts would be made a slave, and slaves frequently revolted and became brigands. Because the surrounding countryside had little good soil, the city depended upon the region to the southeast, around Moscow, for its grain. When in the fifteenth century the Polish-Lithuanian state and the state of Moscow were competing, the struggle inside Novgorod was reflected in the allegiances of the population. The upper classes favored the Poles and Lithuanians; the lower favored Moscow. In 1478 the ruler of Moscow conquered Novgorod and deported the upper classes to central Russia. While Novgorod may be compared with Venice

Medieval and Early Modern Russia

and other commercial patrician oligarchies in the West, its inability to solve internal problems deprived it of any chance to unify Russia.

The Tatars, 1223–1400

By the early thirteenth century Genghis Khan had consolidated under his command the Mongolian nomads of central Asia—Huns, Avars, and Polovtsky—who had repeatedly erupted into Europe. Having conquered northern China and Asia from Manchuria to the Caspian Sea, Genghis Khan led his Tatars across the Caucasus Mountains and into the steppes of southern Russia, defeating the Russians and dissident Polovtsky together near the Sea of Azov in 1223. He then retreated to Asia, where he died in 1227. Batu Khan (d. 1255) brought the Tatars back again in the 1230s, sacked Moscow in 1237 and Kiev in 1240, and moved into the western Russian regions and into Poland, Hungary, and Bohemia.

Tatar success seems to have been due largely to excellent military organization: unified command, general staff, clever intelligence service, and deceptive battle tactics. Though Batu defeated the Poles and the Germans in 1241, political affairs in Asia drew him eastward, and the Tatars never again appeared so far to the west. Batu retreated across Europe, and at Sarai, near the great bend of the Volga, he founded the capital of a new

state—the Golden Horde—which accepted the overlordship of the far-off central government of the Mongols in Peking.

Other Mongol leaders ended the Abbasid caliphate in 1258 and were defeated by the Mamluks in 1260. The enmity between Mongols and Muslims led the popes, St. Louis, and other leaders of western Europe to hope that they could convert the Mongol rulers to Christianity and ally with them against the Muslims. Several embassies were sent to Mongolia and China during the thirteenth and fourteenth centuries with this end in view. Nothing came of it except a great increase in geographical knowledge derived from the accounts of the European ambassadors, who were usually Franciscans or Dominicans.

The most lasting effect on Europe of the Tatar invasions was in Russia. Here the Tatars' main purpose was the efficient collection of tribute. Although they ravaged Russia while they were conquering it, after the conquest they shifted to a policy of exploitation. They took a survey of available resources and assessed tribute at the limit of what the traffic would bear. They did not disturb economic life as long as their authority was recognized. They did draft Russian recruits for their armies, but they made the local Russian princes responsible for the delivery of manpower and money, and they stayed out of Russian territory except to take censuses, survey property, and punish rebels. Each tributary Russian prince traveled to Sarai or to China on his election to do homage. Although no part of Russia was exempt from Tatar attacks during the conquest, the expensive burden of tribute and the humiliating sense of subservience fell most heavily upon Moscow.

Toward the end of the fourteenth century, as the Mongol Empire itself grew feebler, the Russians grew bolder. The first Russian victories over the Tatars, scored by a prince of Moscow in 1378 and 1380, were fiercely avenged. Yet they showed that the Tatars could be defeated. The Golden Horde did not disintegrate until the early fifteenth century, and even then the Tatars did not disappear from Russian life. Three separate *khanates*, or Tatar states, were formed from the debris of the Golden Horde: one at Kazan on the middle Volga, where it blocked the full use of the river for another century and a half to Russian trade; one at Astrakhan at the mouth of the Volga on the Caspian; and one in the Crimea, which became a vassal of the Ottoman sultan.

Historians have long debated the effect upon Russia of the "Tatar yoke." Some have argued that the experience was beneficial because it eventually enabled the centralizing influence of the prince of Moscow, successor of the Tatar khan, to prevail, and further, that trade with Asia helped Russia. They minimize the devastation wrought by the Tatar forces and emphasize that, except for an occasional punitive expedition, the Russian people never saw a Tatar after the conquest was over. Yet the Tatar conquest also had negative effects on Russia. As the great nineteenth-century Russian poet Alexander Pushkin remarked, the Tatars brought to the Russians "neither algebra nor Aristotle." By this he meant to contrast the cultural impact of the Tatars on Russia with that of the Muslims on, let us say, Spain.

There was no inherent reason why Russia in the late twelfth century should not have developed as a European state with characteristics of its own. After two centuries of Tatar domination, however, it had not advanced, as measured against the material progress of western Europe. Contemporaries felt that the Tatar yoke was a calamity, and historians have yet to prove otherwise. When the Tatar power was finally shattered in the fifteenth century, Russian civilization was far less complex than that of the West. To the retarding effect of Byzantine Christianity, there had been added the tremendous handicap of two centuries of cultural stagnation.

The Development of the Muscovite State

During these two centuries, the princes of Moscow assumed leadership. Moscow lay near the great watershed from which the Russian rivers, always the major routes for trade, flow north into the Baltic or south into the Black Sea. It was richer than the north, could provide enough food for its people, and had flourishing forest industries. Thus, when the Tatar grip relaxed and trade could begin again, Moscow was advantageously located. Moreover, Moscow was blessed with a line of remark-

ably able princes—shrewd administrators, anxious to increase their holdings and to consolidate their own authority within the steadily expanding borders of their principality. They married into powerful families, acquired land by purchase and by foreclosing mortgages, and inherited it through wills. Moreover, unlike the princes of Kiev, they did not divide their domain among their sons in each generation.

They also developed useful relations with their Tatar overlords. It was the princes of Moscow whom the Tatars chose to collect the tribute from other neighboring princes and deliver it to Sarai. Soon the princes could point to their success in excluding the Tatar agents from Russia, and could attract settlers to their lands. They scored the first victories over the Tatars and could truthfully claim to be the champions of Russia.

Finally, and very possibly most important, the princes of Moscow secured the support of the Russian church. In the early fourteenth century the metropolitan archbishop made Moscow the ecclesiastical capital of Russia. When the effective line of Muscovite princes temporarily faltered, it was the metropolitan who administered the principality loyally and effectively until the ruling house recovered. Thus the Russian church cast its lot with Moscow.

By the middle of the fifteenth century, Moscow was a self-conscious Russian national state that could undertake successful wars against both the Polish-Lithuanian kingdom and the Tatars. Ivan III (r. 1462–1505) put himself forward as the heir to the princes of Kiev and declared that he intended to regain the ancient Russian lands that had been lost to Poles and Tatars—a national appeal, although a purely dynastic one. Many nobles living in the western lands came over to him with their estates and renounced their loyalties to the Lithuanian-Polish state. In 1492 the prince of Lithuania was forced to recognize Ivan III as sovereign of "all the Russians." This new national appeal was fortified by a religious appeal, for Ivan was also the champion of Orthodoxy against the Catholic Poles and the now Muslimized Tatars.

In 1472 Ivan had married Zoe, niece of the last Byzantine emperor, Constantine XI, who had been killed fighting against the Turks in Constantinople in 1453. Ivan adopted the Byzantine title of Autocrat, used the Byzantine double eagle as his seal, and began to behave like a Byzantine emperor. He sometimes used the title *Czar* (Caesar) and no longer consulted his nobles, reaching decisions in solitude. Italian architects built him an enormous palace, the Kremlin (or fortress), a building set apart like the palace at Byzantium. When the Holy Roman emperor in the 1480s decided to make an alliance with Ivan III and to arrange for a dynastic marriage, Ivan responded that he already had unlimited power derived directly from God—a claim that a Byzantine emperor might have made.

When a rebellious noble fled Russia under the reign of Czar Ivan IV, the Terrible (1533–1584), he wrote the czar from abroad, denouncing him for failing to consult his nobles on important questions, as had been the cus-

Members of the Muscovite cavalry in the early sixteenth century. The cavalry formed the bulk of the army, but it performed badly in warfare and was generally ill equipped.
New York Public Library Picture Collection

tom in the days of Kievan Russia. Ivan replied that he was free to bestow favors on his slaves or inflict punishment on them as he chose; the czar thought of Russian nobles as his slaves. The first to formally take the title of czar, Ivan broke the power of the Tatars, conquered Kazan, Astrakhan, and Siberia, and systematically and brutally suppressed the most powerful nobles to establish a thoroughly autocratic government.

Part of the explanation for this rapid growth of autocratic theory is that Russia lived in a constant state of war or preparation for war; a national emergency prolonged over centuries may lead to a dictatorship. Perhaps more significant is that in Moscow, feudalism had not developed a united class of nobles who would fight against the rising monarchy for their privileges, as it had in the West. Instead of uniting against the pretensions of the monarch, the Muscovite nobility produced various factions with which the monarch could deal individually.

But most important of all was the ideology supplied by the church and taken over largely from Byzantium. In the West, the church itself was a part of feudal society and jealous of its prerogatives. In Russia it became the ally of the monarchy and something like a department of state. Russian churchmen were entirely familiar with Rome's claim to world empire and to Constantinople's centuries-long position as "new Rome." They knew many written Byzantine claims to world domination, and they were conscious of many historical legends that

could be useful to them. With the fall of Constantinople (Czargrad) to the Turks, they elaborated a theory that Moscow was the successor to the two former world capitals:

> *The Church of Old Rome fell because of its heresy; the gates of the Second Rome, Constantinople, have been hewn down by the axes of the infidel Turks; but the Church of Moscow, the Church of the New Rome, shines brighter than the Sun in the whole Universe. . . . Two Romes have fallen, but the Third stands fast; a fourth there cannot be.* *

Russian churchmen spread the story that Rurik, the first political organizer of Russia, was descended from the brother of Augustus. They claimed that the Russian czars had inherited certain insignia and regalia not only from the Byzantines but even from the Babylonians. All the czars down to the last, Nicholas II (r. 1894–1917), were crowned with a cap and clothed with a jacket that were of Byzantine manufacture, though of uncertain history. Thus the church supplied the state with justification for its acts. Imperial absolutism became one of the chief political features of modern Russia.

Nobles and Serfs

Between the accessions of Ivan III in 1462 and Peter the Great in 1689, the autocracy overcame the opposition of the old nobility. This was done in part by the virtual creation of a new class of military service gentry who owed everything to the czar. Their estates, at first granted only for life in exchange for service, eventually became hereditary, like the western European fief. The estates of the old nobility, which had always been hereditary but for which they had owed no service, became service estates, and thus like fiefs, too. By the end of the period the two types of nobles and the two types of estates had by a gradual process become almost identical: the hereditary nobles often owed service; the military service nobles often had hereditary land. Under Peter the Great (r. 1689–1725) this process was to be completed, and state service was to become universal. A central bureau in Moscow kept a census of the service gentry and of their obligations in time of war.

This important social process was accompanied by the growth of serfdom. Economic factors and political unrest in Russia had forced more and more peasants to ask large landowners for protection. The peasants would accept contracts that required payment of rent in produce and performance of service on the landlord's own land, in return for a money loan that had to be repaid over a period of years with interest or with extra services. By the early seventeenth century the peasant could not leave his plot until he paid off his debt; but since the debt was often too great for him to repay, he could in fact never leave.

The process was speeded up when the czars gave estates to the new military service gentry. An estate was

---

* Quoted in T. A. Archer and C. L. Kingsford, *The Crusades* (London: T. F. Unwin, 1919) p. 220.

not much good unless there was farm labor to work it. In the bitter agrarian and political crises of the sixteenth and seventeenth centuries, the government helped the service gentry to keep their farmers where they were. And since the peasants paid most of the taxes, it was easier for the government to collect its own revenues if it kept the peasants where they were. Gradually it was made harder for a tenant to leave his landlord, until by 1649 the avenues of escape were closed, and the serf was fixed to the soil. The landlord administered justice and had police rights on the estate; he collected the serfs' taxes; he could sell, exchange, or give away his serfs. The status of serf became hereditary; children of serfs were enrolled on the estate's census books as serfs like their fathers.

Russian serfs were not emancipated until 1861. Together with absolute autocracy, the institution of serfdom is the most dramatic feature of Russian society. It affected every Russian for the centuries it existed. Russian serfdom became a fixed custom much later in time than did western European serfdom; it was extended most widely during the eighteenth century, when the serfs in western Europe had long been on their way to complete liberation. Thus once again Russia went through the same processes as the West, but with greater intensity and at a later time.

The Reign of Ivan the Terrible, 1533–1584

Many of the disorders that characterized Russian history in the sixteenth and seventeenth centuries began in the long reign of Ivan IV, the Terrible. Pathologically unbalanced, Ivan succeeded to the throne as a small child. When strong enough in 1547 to throw off the tutelage of the nobles, he embarked upon a period of sound government and institutional reform. He regulated the greediness of the imperial administrators in the provinces, who had oppressed the population. He convoked the first *zemski sobor* (land assembly), a consultative body consisting of nobles, clerics, and representatives from the towns, to assist with imperial business, particularly with important questions of war and peace. Though comparable in social composition to the various assemblies of medieval western Europe, the zemski sobor under Ivan appears to have met only once and cannot be regarded as a parliamentary body.

When Ivan fell ill in 1553, the nobles refused to take an oath of allegiance to his son. This refusal apparently reawakened his anger. Upon his recovery he created a new institution—the *oprichnina*, or "separate realm"— to belong to him personally, while the rest of Russia continued to be administered as before. The men Ivan appointed to run the oprichnina (called *oprichniks*), dressed grimly in black and riding black horses, bore on their saddlebows a dog's head (for vigilance) and a broom (symbolizing a clean sweep). They were the forerunners of the secret police forces that have long characterized Russian society. They waged a fierce, re-

A contemporary icon portrait of Ivan the Terrible dating from 1500–1550. It now hangs in the National Museum of Denmark, in Copenhagen.
National Museum, Copenhagen

lentless war on the nobles, confiscating their estates, exiling them, killing them. The oprichniks took over the estates of the men they were destroying. By Ivan's death, many of the oprichniks themselves had been murdered at his orders, and Russian administration was close to chaos. Yet Ivan had extended Russian authority far to the east against the Kazan and Astrakhan Tatars, thus for the first time opening the whole Volga waterway to Russian commerce.

The Time of Troubles, 1598–1613

Though the territory was wide and the imperial rule absolute, ignorance, illiteracy, and inefficiency weakened Russian society. The few foreigners who knew the Russia of Ivan could foresee chaos ahead. Though the old nobility had been weakened, the new gentry had as yet no sense of corporate entity and therefore was not firmly in control of the machinery of government. Ivan's son and heir, Fëdor (r. 1584–1598), was an imbecile, and with his death the Moscow dynasty, descended from the rulers of Kiev, died out. Cliques of rival nobles intrigued for power. Fëdor's brother-in-law, Boris Godunov (r. 1598–1605), emerged as the dominant figure in the state.

Though Boris Godunov was probably a man of talent, he could not overcome his handicaps: Ivan's legacy of disorder, the intrigues of the nobility, and a famine and plague that began in 1601. Bandits roamed the countryside, and when in 1603 a pretender arose under the protection of the king of Poland and falsely declared that he was a son of Ivan the Terrible (thus he is known as "the false Dmitri"), he won the support of many of the discontented. Russia was launched on the decade known as the "Time of Troubles" (1598–1613).

After Godunov's death, the pretender ruled briefly as czar. But within a year he was murdered and was succeeded by a representative of the ancient aristocracy. New pretenders arose; the mobs of peasants and bandits were rallied once again; civil war continued, as Poles and Swedes intervened and Polish forces took Moscow. It soon appeared that the king of Poland intended to reign in Russia himself. It was this specter of foreign and Catholic domination that aroused the national sentiments of the Russians. In answer to a summons from the patriarch, there assembled a kind of national militia, drawn largely from prosperous free farmers of the middle Volga region. They were organized by a butcher named Kuzma Minin and led by a nobleman named Dmitri Pozharski, the national heroes of the Time of Troubles. Under their command the militia won the support of other rebellious elements and drove the Poles from Moscow in 1612–1613.

The Role of the Zemski Sobor, 1613–1653

The zemski sobor now elected as czar Michael Romanov, grand-nephew of Ivan IV. The Romanov dynasty reigned from the election of Michael in 1613 to the Russian Revolution of 1917. Michael succeeded with no limitations placed upon his power by the zemski sobor or by any other body; he was an elected autocrat. For the first ten years of his reign, the zemski sobor stayed in continual session. Since it had picked the new czar in the midst of a crisis, it had indeed performed a constitutional function. It even included some representatives of the free peasantry. It assisted the uncertain new dynasty to get under way by endorsing the policies of the czar and his advisers, thus lending them the semblance of popular support. But after 1623 the zemski sobor was summoned only to help declare war or make peace, to approve new taxation, and to sanction important new legislation. It endorsed the accession of Michael's son Alexis (r. 1645–1676), and in 1649 confirmed the issuance of a new law code. After 1653 Alexis did not summon it again, nor did his son and successor, Fëdor III (r. 1676–1682).

No law abolished the zemski sobor, and none had created it. The dynasty was entrenched and no longer needed it. Autocratic czardom was taken for granted. No czar needed to consult with any of his subjects unless he wanted to. No subject had the right to insist on being consulted, though all subjects had the duty to give advice when asked. The Romanovs no longer felt the need to consult anyone except their court favorites.

The Role of the Church

The church remained the partner of the autocracy. The czar controlled the election of the patriarch of Moscow, a rank to which the archbishop was elevated in 1589. In the seventeenth century there were two striking instances when a patriarch actually shared power with the czar. In 1619 the father of Czar Michael Romanov, Filaret, who had become a monk, became patriarch and was granted the additional title of "Great Sovereign." He assisted his son in all the affairs of state. In the next generation Czar Alexis appointed a cleric named Nikon to the patriarchal throne and gave him the same title and duties. Nikon proved so arrogant that he aroused protests from clergy as well as laity, especially when he revised Russian church ritual to bring it into line with Greek practice. (Those who thereupon seceded from the Russian church, taking the name of Old Believers, were condemned as schismatics.)

Nikon also argued that the authority of the patriarch in spiritual affairs exceeded that of the czar and that, since the spiritual realm was superior to the temporal, the patriarch was actually superior to the czar. This was a claim parallel to that made regularly in the West by the more powerful popes but seldom made in Byzantium or in Russia. In 1666 a church council deposed Nikon, who died a mere monk. These two experiments with two-man government (*dyarchy*, it was called, in contrast with *monarchy*) were never repeated. Thereafter, the church accepted that it depended upon the state. Peter the Great was to abolish the patriarchate itself, largely because he did not wish Nikon's claims ever to be repeated.

The church, almost alone, inspired the literature and art of the Muscovite period. History was written by monks in the form of chronicles. Travel literature took the form of accounts of pilgrimages to the Holy Land. Theological tracts attacked the Catholics and later also the Protestants, whose doctrines were known in the western regions. This literature is limited, and it was still dominated by the church several centuries after the West had begun to produce secular writing. Almost all of it was written in Old Church Slavonic, the language of the liturgy and not the language of everyday speech. Though stately and impressive, Old Church Slavonic was not an appropriate vehicle for innovation. There was almost no secular learning, no science, no flowering of vernacular literature, no philosophical debate, despite the presence of immensely rich monasteries that owned perhaps a third of the cultivable land.

The Expansion of Russia, to 1682

The sixteenth and seventeenth centuries saw tremendous physical expansion of the Russian domain. Russian pioneers, in search of furs to sell and new land to settle, led the way, and the government followed. Frontiersmen in Russia were known as Cossacks (*kazakh* is a Tatar word meaning "free adventurer")—Russians living on the frontiers organizing themselves for self-defense against the Tatars. Cossack communities gradually became more settled, and two Cossack republics, one on the Dnieper River, the other on the Don, were set up. These republics had a kind of primitive democracy relatively independent of Moscow. As time passed, more Cossack groups formed along the Volga River, in the Ural Mountains and elsewhere.

The frontier movement took the Russians eastward into the Urals and on across Siberia—one of the most dramatic chapters in the expansion of Europe. Far more slowly, because of Tatar, Turkish, and Polish opposition, the Russians also moved southeast toward the Caucasus and south toward the Black Sea. Repeated wars were fought with Poland over the Ukraine. Sometimes the Cossacks favored the Poles and sometimes the Russians. By 1682 the Poles were weakening and were soon to yield. On the European frontiers it was the Swedes, still controlling the Baltic coast, against whom Russia's future wars would be fought. There were also constant struggles with the Tatars of the Crimea. The Ottoman Turks, overlords of the Tatars, held the key fort of Azov and controlled the Black Sea. But in 1681 they abandoned most of their holdings in the Ukraine to the czars.

Russia and the West

A final development of these two centuries was to prove of the utmost importance for the future Russia. This was the slow and gradual penetration of foreigners and foreign ideas, a process welcomed—as in most societies—with mixed feelings by those who prized the technical and mechanical learning they could derive from the West while fearing Western influence on society and manners. This ambivalent attitude toward Westerners and Western ideas became characteristic of later Russians; they sought what the West could give, but they often feared the giver.

The first foreigners to come were the Italians, who helped build the Kremlin at the end of the fifteenth century. But they were not encouraged to teach the Russians their knowledge, and they failed to influence even the court of Ivan III in any significant way. The English, who arrived in the midsixteenth century as traders to the White Sea, were welcomed by Ivan the Terrible. He gave the English valuable privileges and encouraged them to trade their woolen cloth for Russian timber and

St. Basil's Cathedral in Red Square, Moscow, built 1555–1560.
George Holton/Photo Researchers

rope, pitch, and other naval supplies. These helped build the great Elizabethan fleets that sailed the seas and defeated the Spanish Armada. The English were the first foreigners to penetrate Russia in any numbers and the first to teach Russians Western industrial techniques. They got along well with the Russians and supplied many officers to the czar's armies. Toward the middle of the seventeenth century the Dutch were able to displace the English as the most important foreign group engaged in commerce and manufacturing, opening their own glass, paper, and textile plants in Russia.

After the accession of Michael Romanov in 1613, the foreign quarter of Moscow, always called "the German suburb," grew rapidly. Foreign technicians of all sorts—textile weavers, bronze founders, clockmakers—received enormous salaries from the state. Foreign merchants sold their goods, much to the distaste of the native Russians; foreign physicians and druggists became fashionable. By the end of the seventeenth century Western influence was fully apparent in the life of the court. A few nobles began to buy books and form libraries, to learn Latin, French, and German. The people, meanwhile, distrusted and hated the foreigners, looted their houses when they dared, and jeered at them in the streets.

Suspicion of foreign influences had divided the Russian church, cut the people off from sources of change, smothered the development of even modest represen-

tative institutions, assured the continuation of serfdom, and, together with the impact of the Ottoman Empire, kept the East under medieval conditions to the end of the seventeenth century—long after Renaissance and Reformation, exploration and discovery, and a commercial revolution had transformed society in the West. The Middle Ages came to have quite different dates in East and West, reflecting the different pace of development.

Summary

By the late eleventh century, instability in the Muslim and Byzantine empires and the expansion of the Seljuk Turks had made pilgrimages to Palestine unsafe for Christians. When Byzantine envoys asked Pope Urban II for military aid against the Seljuks, the pope responded by calling for a Crusade. Crusades, or holy wars supported by the papacy against the infidel, had been waged in Spain since the Muslim invasions of the eighth century.

People responded to the pope's call for both religious and secular motives. During the First Crusade, feudal lords established four crusader states: Edessa, Antioch, Jerusalem, and Tripoli. The Templars, Hospitalers, and Teutonic Knights, orders of military knights, were established to protect pilgrims traveling to Palestine, but as the orders grew in wealth and power, they were diverted from their original purpose.

During the Second and Third Crusades, monarchs of France, Germany, and England tried to repel Muslim advances in the East. The Fourth Crusade, which resulted in the sack of Constantinople, and other later Crusades showed how far the crusaders had strayed from the original crusading spirit.

Increased trade and travel during the Crusades resulted in the introduction of new products, ideas, and methods of finance. The Crusades also helped foster the explorations of the fourteenth and fifteenth centuries. The failure of the Crusades, however, meant the closing of the eastern Mediterranean to western Europe.

The Byzantine Empire had been in decline even before crusaders looted its palaces and churches in 1204. Official corruption had contributed to economic and social decay. Under the Latin emperors, the Byzantine Empire was divided into feudal states, but in 1261, the Greeks of Nicaea ousted the Latin emperors from Constantinople.

Rival claims to the throne, social unrest, and religious controversy led to further decay in the Empire. Thus weakened, the Byzantine Empire could not withstand the advance of the Ottoman Turks in the fourteenth century. In 1453, even the supposedly impregnable city of Constantinople fell to the invaders and was renamed Istanbul.

Ottoman rulers were generally tolerant of other religions, including Christianity. They organized their state based on a strong ruling class that included men of the emperor, men of the sword, men of the pen, and the sages. The Turks expanded their empire into Africa, Persia, and Europe. Twice, Ottoman armies besieged Vienna, but each time, they were turned back. By the seventeenth century, however, the Ottoman Empire entered a long decline.

In the thirteenth century, Genghis Khan and his successors invaded Russia. For two hundred years, Tatars collected tribute from the Russians although they allowed Russian princes to rule themselves. In the fourteenth and fifteenth centuries the princes of Moscow challenged Tatar rule and eventually, with the support of the church, established an absolute autocratic state.

Historians have debated the impact of Tatar rule on Russia, which resulted in Russia's falling behind the West. Not until the seventeenth century, after the accession of Michael Romanov, was Russia exposed to Western ideas and learning. During this period Russia expanded eastward to the Urals and into Siberia, south toward the Caucasus and Black Sea, north toward the Baltic Sea, and westward into territory ruled by Poland.

Suggested Readings

Lists of supplementary or additional readings are usually intended to offer the student guidance into fuller, more specialized or more advanced historical literature. These lists also include sources—that is, primary documentary materials—for students who want to enter into the spirit of the period under study by reading of that period in the words of contemporaries. Because footnotes have been used throughout the text to provide information on the origins of many quotations, the following list is not intended to serve as a formal bibliography of books used in preparing the text. No titles are included that author Robin Winks has not read, but titles are not supplied to support all potentially controversial statements made in the text. Rather, the purpose of these lists, which are broken down by chapter and general subject matter, is to provide the student with a way to learn more about the major subjects.

Information listed refers to the latest edition available at the time this text went to press. Obviously there are dozens, even hundreds, of books on any of the subjects discussed in the text. The criteria for selection, therefore, have had to be clear: books, preferably short, written in a manner likely to be of interest to students of history, and when possible, books that are in print and in paperback editions. Clarity, accuracy, and availability were the primary tests. The most recent book on a subject is not always the best, though many recent titles have been included if they met the criteria. The authors believe that this list of suggested readings is therefore both up-to-date and useful, and books that have been included should be available in any good college library.

THE VALUE OF HISTORY

Our first controversy was to define *civilization*, and this was done in the introductory chapter. Readers wishing to pursue this thorny problem further might best begin with Robert Redfield, *The Primitive World and Its Transformations* (Ithaca, N.Y.: Cornell University Press, 1953); move on to Lloyd Warner, *A Black Civilization*, rev. ed. (New York: Harper and Row, 1958); A. L. Kroeber, *The Nature of Culture* (Chicago: University of Chicago Press,

1952); and Arnold Toynbee, *Civilization on Trial* (Oxford: Oxford University Press, 1953), of which Kroeber was critical. Then explore Glyn Daniel, *The First Civilizations: The Archaeology of Their Origins* (New York: T. Y. Crowell, 1968) and *The Idea of Prehistory* (Cleveland: World Publishing Co., 1962).

CHAPTER 1: THE FIRST CIVILIZATIONS

General Accounts

William F. Albright, *From the Stone Age to Christianity*, 2d ed. (New York: Doubleday, 1957). Superb survey of a field that has been much altered by modern scholarship.
Rushton Coulborn, *The Origins of Civilized Societies* (Princeton, N.J.: Princeton University Press, 1959). A scholarly, readable, and stimulating study.
Alexander Marshack, *The Roots of Civilization* (New York: McGraw-Hill, 1972). Magnificently illustrated (and controversial) account of new research into the artifacts and mental processes of Paleolithic (Old Stone Age) people.
James Mellaart, *Çatal Hüyük* (London: Thames and Hudson, 1967). The discoverer's account of the Neolithic settlement of 6500 B.C. in southern Turkey.
Stuart Piggott, *Approach to Archaeology* (New York: McGraw-Hill, 1965). Short, up-to-date account of the problem of creating through archaeology time scales that can be used by historians.
Karl A. Wittfogel, *Oriental Despotism* (New York: Random House, 1981). Famous controversial statement of the thesis that hydraulic societies strive for total power.

The Near East

Geoffrey Bibby, *Four Thousand Years Ago* (New York: Knopf, 1962). A most readable account of the crucial millennium from 2000 to 1000 B.C.
James H. Breasted, *History of Egypt* (New York: Scribner's, 1979). By a celebrated Egyptologist of another generation; though dated, still a classic worth reading.
Christiane Desroches-Noblecourt, *Egyptian Wall Paintings from Tombs and Temples* (New York: Mentor, n.d.). An informative sampler.
Louis Finkelstein, ed., *The Jews: Their History, Culture and Religion*, 4th ed., 2 vols. (New York: Schocken Books, 1970). Comprehensive; popular in the best sense.
Henri Frankfort, *The Birth of Civilization in the Near East*, 5th ed. (New York: Barnes and Noble, 1968). A brief and stimulating essay by an expert in the area.
Henri Frankfort et al., *Before Philosophy* (Baltimore: Penguin, 1972). Admirable essays on the intellectual history of the ancient Near East.
Cyrus H. Gordon, *Forgotten Scripts*, rev. ed. (New York: Basic Books, 1982). Lively and up-to-date survey of the history of decipherment.
Oliver R. Gurney, *The Hittites*, 2d ed. (Baltimore: Penguin, 1972). Authoritative survey of a people rescued from almost total oblivion by archaeology.

William W. Hallo and William K. Simpson, *The Ancient Near East: A History* (New York: Harcourt, 1971). Up-to-date survey: not always easy to read.
Donald Harden, *The Phoenicians* (New York: Praeger, 1962). Clear summary.
Samuel N. Kramer, *History Begins at Sumer* (Philadelphia: University of Pennsylvania Press, 1981). Introduction by an expert.
J. Lassoe, *People of Ancient Assyria* (New York: Barnes and Noble, 1963). An attempt to show the Assyrians as more than mere militarists.
Sabatino Moscati, *The Face of the Ancient Orient: A Panorama of Near Eastern Civilization in Pre-Classical Times* (Garden City, N.Y.: Anchor, 1962). Good introductory survey.
Joan Oates, *Babylon* (London: Thames and Hudson, 1979). Outstanding introductory text.
H. M. Orlinsky, *The Ancient Jews*, 2d ed. (Ithaca, N.Y.: Cornell University Press, 1960). A good introductory manual.
Henry B. Parkes, *Gods and Men: The Origins of Western Culture* (New York: Knopf, 1959). Perceptive survey of early religions.
Reader's Digest Atlas of the Bible (New York: Reader's Digest Association, 1981). A popular and accurate history interspersed with useful maps.
Chester G. Starr, *Early Man* (New York: Oxford University Press, 1973). Well-illustrated, simple introduction.
John A. Wilson, *The Culture of Ancient Egypt* (Chicago: University of Chicago Press, 1956). One of the best single-volume studies of the subject.

Crete and Early Greece

C. W. Blegen, *Troy and the Trojans* (New York: Praeger, 1963); and Lord William Taylor, *Mycenaeans* (New York: Praeger, 1964). Volumes in the series Ancient Peoples and Places; clear, scholarly introductions.
John Chadwick, *The Decipherment of Linear B* (Cambridge: Cambridge University Press, 1970). By Michael Ventris's collaborator.
M. I. Finley, *Early Greece: The Bronze and Archaic Ages*, 2d ed. (New York: Norton, 1982). Authoritative, detailed survey.
Geoffrey S. Kirk, *Homer and the Epic* (Cambridge: Cambridge University Press, 1962). The most recent summary; nontechnical and authoritative.
Denys L. Page, *History and the Homeric Iliad* (Berkeley: University of California Press, 1959). Readable, scholarly set of lectures.

Leonard R. Palmer, *Mycenaeans and Minoans*, 2d ed. (Westport, Conn.: Greenwood, 1980). Controversial reassessment in the light of the Linear B tablets.

Leonard R. Palmer, *A New Guide to the Palace of Knossos* (London: Faber and Faber, 1969). A clear statement of our present knowledge.

Emily Vermeule, *Greece in the Bronze Age* (Chicago: University of Chicago Press, 1964). Excellent.

CHAPTER 2: THE GREEKS

General Accounts

M. M. Austin and P. Vidal-Naquet, *Economic and Social History of Ancient Greece* (Berkeley: University of California Press, 1978). Sober, thorough examination, with many extracts from and commentaries on sources.

John Boardman, Jasper Griffin, and Oswyn Murray, eds., *The Oxford History of the Classical World* (Oxford: Oxford University Press, 1986). Stimulating and up-to-date essays on the Greeks and Romans.

André Bonnard, *Greek Civilization*, 3 vols. (New York: Macmillan, 1957–1961). Stimulating chapters on many aspects of Greece by a European scholar.

J. B. Bury, *A History of Greece to the Death of Alexander the Great*, 4th ed. rev. (New York: St. Martin's, 1975). Another celebrated, somewhat idealized, older account; stresses war and politics.

Robert M. Cook, *The Greeks till Alexander* (London: Thames and Hudson, 1961). Well-illustrated survey stressing material accomplishments.

Eric R. Dodds, *The Greeks and the Irrational* (Berkeley: University of California Press, 1951). A fine balance to the tendency to overrationalize the Greeks.

M. I. Finley, *The Ancient Economy* (Berkeley: University of California Press, 1973). Brief, clear analysis; especially good on the difference between town and country.

M. I. Finley, *The Ancient Greeks* (New York: Penguin, 1977). Compact, up-to-date, and perceptive introduction to Greek life and thought.

M. I. Finley, *Economy and Society in Ancient Greece* (London: Penguin, 1983). Excellent on slavery, debt, inflation, and property.

M. I. Finley, *Studies in Ancient Society* (London: Routledge and Kegan Paul, 1978). Key essays on the Romans as well as the Greeks, demagogues, peasants, and Greek and Roman thought.

William G. Forrest, *The Emergence of Greek Democracy* (New York: McGraw-Hill, 1966). A clear, general account focusing on the years from 800 to 400 B.C.

William G. Forrest, *A History of Sparta, 950–192 B.C.* (New York: Norton, 1969). Best general history.

N.G.L. Hammond, *A History of Greece to 332 B.C.*, 2d ed. (Oxford: Clarendon Press, 1967). A good, up-to-date survey.

Donald Kagan, *The Archidamian War* (Ithaca, N.Y.: Cornell University Press, 1974). The fullest reconstruction.

Donald Kagan, *The Outbreak of the Peloponnesian War* (Ithaca, N.Y.: Cornell University Press, 1969). A rethinking of the evidence by a scholar interested in the causes of war.

H.D.F. Kitto, *The Greeks* (Chicago: Aldine Publishers, 1964). Lively, though opinionated, introduction.

M. I. Rostovtzeff, *Greece* (Oxford: Oxford University Press, 1963). A famous older account by a distinguished Russian scholar; now somewhat out-of-date on details.

Morton Smith, *The Ancient Greeks* (Ithaca, N.Y.: Cornell University Press, 1960). Very short summary of the generally accepted views.

Special Studies: The Polis

Antony Andrewes, *The Greek Tyrants* (New York: Humanities Press, 1956). Informative comparative survey of emerging Greek constitutions.

Victor Ehrenberg, *The Greek State*, 2d ed. (New York: Methuen, 1974). A solid scholarly introduction.

Kathleen Freeman, *Greek City-States* (New York: Norton, 1963). Excellent overview; focuses on interesting examples usually neglected in the concern for Athens and Sparta.

Gustave Glotz, *The Greek City and Its Institutions* (New York: Barnes and Noble, 1965). Celebrated study by a French scholar; now somewhat out-of-date.

A. H. M. Jones, *Athenian Democracy* (Oxford: Blackwell, 1969). An up-to-date interpretation.

Humfrey Michell, *Sparta* (Cambridge: Cambridge University Press, 1964). A comprehensive survey; somewhat more favorable in tone than most treatments of the subject.

A. G. Woodhead, *The Greeks in the West* (New York: Praeger, 1962); and John M. Cook, *The Greeks in Ionia and the East* (New York: Praeger, 1965). Volumes in the series Ancient Peoples and Places; highlight the often-neglected geographical outposts of the Greek world.

Special Studies: Greek Civilization

Cecil M. Bowra, *Classical Greece* (New York: Time-Life, 1965). A beautifully illustrated short history.

Cecil M. Bowra, *The Greek Experience* (New York: New American Library, 1961). Stresses interpretation rather than fact; by a literary scholar.

Emile Bréhier, *The Hellenic Age* (Chicago: University of Chicago Press, 1963). The first volume of a detailed history of philosophy by a French scholar.

Rhys Carpenter, *The Esthetic Basis of Greek Art* (Bloomington: Indiana University Press, 1959). Analysis by an expert.

Francis M. Cornford, *Before and After Socrates* (Cambridge: Cambridge University Press, n.d.). First-rate short introduction to Greek science and philosophy.

J. K. Davies, *Athenian Propertied Families* (Oxford: Oxford University Press, 1971). Covers the years from 600 to 300 B.C.

J. K. Davies, *Democracy and Classical Greece* (New York: Humanities Press, 1978). Clearest reexamination of the present state of our knowledge about democratic concepts in Athens and Sparta.

Aubrey de Sélincourt, *The World of Herodotus* (Berkeley: North Point Press, 1982). Loving, careful evocation of the Greece on which Herodotus reported.

G.E.M. de Ste. Croix, *The Class Struggle in the Ancient Greek World* (Ithaca, N.Y.: Cornell University Press, 1982). Controversial examination of labor in archaic Greece.

G. Lowes Dickinson, *The Greek View of Life* (Ann Arbor: University of Michigan Press, 1958). Greek culture appraised from an older point of view.

K. J. Dover, *Greek Homosexuality* (Cambridge, Mass.: Harvard University Press, 1978). Exploration of a generally neglected subject.

William K. Guthrie, *The Greeks and Their Gods* (Boston: Beacon, 1955). Detailed but stimulating study of the origins and the nature of Greek religion.

Moses Hadas, *A History of Greek Literature* (New York: Columbia University Press, 1950). Helpful survey.

Edith Hamilton, *The Greek Way to Western Civilization* (New York: Avon, 1973). Enthusiastic popular treatment by a great admirer of the Greeks.

Edith Hamilton, *Mythology* (New York: New American Library, 1971). Brief introduction, centered on Greek myths.

John Herington, *Aeschylus* (New Haven: Yale University Press, 1986). A fine introduction.

Werner Jaeger, *Paideia*, 3 vols. (Oxford: Oxford University Press, 1939–1944). (Volume I also in paperback.) An advanced study of Greek civilization and ideals.

H. I. Marrou, *A History of Education in Antiquity* (Madison: University of Wisconsin Press, 1982). Useful account; also treats the Romans and early Christians.

Martin P. Nilsson, *Greek Folk Religion* (Philadelphia: University of Pennsylvania Press, 1972). Informative lectures on popular beliefs and practices.

J. J. Pollitt, *Art and Experience in Classical Greece* (Cambridge: Cambridge University Press, 1972). A succinct reexamination of what we know about Greek art.

Special Studies: The Hellenistic World

Emile Bréhier, *The Hellenistic and Roman Age* (Chicago: University of Chicago Press, 1965). Another volume of the French scholar's history of philosophy.

Andrew R. Burn, *Alexander the Great and the Hellenistic World* (London: English Universities Press, 1964). Brief popular account.

Kurt Emmrich, *Alexander the Great* (London: Thames and Hudson, 1970). Beautiful pictures of the remains and scenery of Alexander's world.

Peter Green, *Alexander of Macedon, 356–323 B.C.*, rev. ed. (Hammonds-worth: Penguin, 1974). A generally critical examination of Alexander's record.

Moses Hadas, *Hellenistic Culture* (New York: Norton, 1972). Good evaluation.

Bernard M. Knox, *The Heroic Temper* (Berkeley: University of California Press, 1965). Focuses on Sophocles to examine the concept of tragic heroism.

Russell Meiggs, *The Athenian Empire* (Oxford: Oxford University Press, 1979). Excellent account of the rise and fall of the empire; a model of how to draw knowledge from ancient inscriptions.

M. I. Rostovtzeff, *The Social and Economic History of the Hellenistic World* (Oxford: Clarendon, 1941). Detailed study by a great historian.

W. W. Tarn, *Alexander the Great* (Boston: Beacon, 1956). A sympathetic (and not always convincing) study by one of the foremost experts on the subject.

W. W. Tarn, *Hellenistic Civilization*, rev. ed. (New York: New American Library, 1961). Comprehensive survey of civilization under Alexander's successors.

Sources

Note: The following list includes only the most famous works, many of which are available in other translations and editions.

The Works of Aristotle, ed. W. D. Ross (Oxford: Oxford University Press, 1908–1931). Selections by the same editor are also available (New York: Macmillan, 1976).

W. H. Auden, ed., *The Portable Greek Reader* (New York: Penguin, 1977). Excellent short anthology.

The Dialogues of Plato, trans. B. Jowett (New York: Random House, 1937). New edition of a famous (and controversial) old translation.

Herodotus, *The Histories*, trans. Aubrey de Sélincourt (New York: Penguin, 1954).

Homer, *The Iliad.* Two of many translations; that of Richard Lattimore (Chicago: University of Chicago Press, 1961) is a good poetic translation; that of W.H.D. Rouse (New York: New American Library, 1954) is in modern English prose.

Whitney J. Oates and Eugene O'Neill, Jr., eds., *The Complete Greek Drama* (New York: Random House, 1938). A selection of dramas by the same editors may be found in *Seven Famous Greek Plays* (New York: Random House, 1955).

Thucydides, *History of the Peloponnesian War* (New York: Oxford University Press, 1960). A standard translation by Richard Livingstone.

A. J. Toynbee, ed., *Greek Civilization and Character*, 2d ed. (Boston: Beacon, 1950), and *Greek Historical Thought* (New York: New American Library, 1964). Two volumes of excerpts from Greek writers that afford a kaleidoscopic view of Greek attitudes.

Xenophon, *Anabasis: The March Up Country*, trans. W.H.D. Rouse (Ann Arbor: University of Michigan Press, 1958). Very readable.

CHAPTER 3: THE ROMANS

General Accounts

Reginald H. Barrow, *The Romans* (London: Penguin, 1955). Sound popular introduction.

A.E.R. Beak and William G. Sinnigen, *A History of Rome to 565 A.D.*, 6th ed. (New York: Macmillan, 1977). A detailed study.

Tenney Frank, *A History of Rome* (Darby, Penn.: Darby Books, 1981). Useful, though opinionated, survey by an American scholar.

Michael Grant, *The World of Rome* (Chicago: World, 1960). General introduction to imperial Rome; handsomely illustrated.

M. I. Rostovtzeff, *Rome* (New York: Oxford University Press, 1960). Excellent survey by a famous scholar.

The Etruscan Background and the Roman Republic

Ernest Badian, *Roman Imperialism in the Late Republic*, 2d ed. (Ithaca, N.Y.: Cornell University Press, 1971). Readable, brief lectures on whether the Senate was for or against imperial expansion.

John P. Balsdon, *Roman Women: Their History and Habits* (Westport, Conn.: Greenwood, 1975). A relaxed, clear description.

Raymond Bloch, *The Etruscans* (London: Cresset, 1969), and *The Origins of Rome* (New York: Praeger, 1960). Two volumes in the series Ancient Peoples and Places. The first volume is a general introduction, generously illustrated; the second takes the story of Rome to the early fifth century B.C.

Michael Grant, *The Etruscans* (New York: Scribner's, 1981). Highly readable, up-to-date, popular history.

T.G.E. Powell, *The Celts* (London: Thames and Hudson, 1980). Informative survey.

Howard H. Scullard, *Roman Politics, 220–150 B.C.* (Westport, Conn.: Greenwood, 1982), and *From the Gracchi to Nero* (New York: Methuen, 1976). The first is a detailed study of the era when Rome began to dominate the Mediterranean world; the second, a clear, balanced history of the later republic and early empire.

A. N. Sherwin-White, *Racial Prejudice in Imperial Rome* (London: Cambridge University Press, 1970). Short, clear lectures on the rise of racial tension, especially between Romans and the "barbarians."

Richard E. Smith, *The Failure of the Roman Republic* (New York: Arno Press, 1975). A provocative essay critical of the Gracchi.

Lily R. Taylor, *Party Politics in the Age of Caesar* (Boston: Peter Smith, 1962). Analytic as well as descriptive study of the way in which Roman politics worked; learned and stimulating.

Malcolm Todd, *The Northern Barbarians, 100 B.C.–A.D. 300* (New York: Hutchinson, 1976). An excellent corrective to the biased impressions handed down from the time of Caesar.

Otto-Wilhelm von Vacano, *The Etruscans in the Ancient World* (New York: St. Martin's, 1960). Scholarly study carefully based on archaeological evidence.

The Roman Empire

John P. Balsdon, *Romans and Aliens* (Chapel Hill: University of North Carolina Press, 1980). Lively, often amusing look at how one could become a Roman.

P. A. Brunt, *Italian Manpower, 225 B.C.–A.D. 14* (Oxford: Clarendon Press, 1971). Authoritative, careful inquiry into all the issues relating to the supply of manpower for the fields, cities, and armies; makes excellent use of census figures.

J. H. d'Arms, *Commerce and Social Standing in Ancient Rome* (Cambridge, Mass.: Harvard University Press, 1981). The latest available information on trade and class.

Emilio Gabba, *Republican Rome, The Army and the Allies* (Berkeley: University of California Press, 1977). A series of essays on the professional army.

Michael Grant, *From Alexander to Cleopatra* (New York: Scribner's, 1982). Fine survey of the meaning of the Hellenistic world.

William V. Harris, *War and Imperialism in Republican Rome, 327–70 B.C.* (Oxford: Oxford University Press, 1979). A reexamination of Roman attitudes toward war and the controversial question of self-defense.

Keith Hopkins, *Conquerors and Slaves* (Cambridge: Cambridge University Press, 1981). Fine study of slavery in the Roman Empire.

A.H.M. Jones, *The Later Roman Empire*, 4 vols. (Oxford: Basil Blackwell, 1964). Magnificently detailed master work.

Ramsay MacMullen, *Roman Government's Response to Crisis, A.D. 235–337* (New Haven: Yale University Press, 1976). Thoughtful, balanced short account; especially good on the "perception of decline."

Ramsay MacMullen, *Roman Social Relations, 50 B.C. to A.D. 284* (New Haven: Yale University Press. 1981). Excellent short examination of rural and urban differences.

William H. McNeill, *Plagues and People* (Garden City, N.Y.: Doubleday, 1977). Brilliantly argued, controversial book on the relationship between disease and demography.

Fergus Millar, *The Emperor in the Roman World: 31 B.C.–A.D. 337* (Ithaca, N.Y.: Cornell University Press, 1977). Impressive, massive study of the scope and function of the emperor and his relations to his subjects.

Stewart Perowne, *Hadrian* (Westport, Conn.: Greenwood, 1976). Entertaining modern treatment.

Henry T. Rowell, *Rome in the Augustan Age* (Norman: University of Oklahoma Press, 1971). Sympathetic appraisal of Augustus and his work.

Ronald Syme, *The Roman Revolution* (London: Oxford University Press, 1939). Detailed study of the transformation of the Roman state and society under Caesar and Augustus.

K.D. White, *Roman Farming* (Ithaca, N.Y.: Cornell University Press, 1970). A book that has substantially revised previous views on the subject.

CHAPTER 4: JUDAISM AND CHRISTIANITY

General Accounts

Christopher H. Dawson, *Religion and the Rise of Western Culture* (New York: AMS Press, 1977). Excellent survey to the thirteenth century.

L.M.O. Duchesne, *Early History of the Christian Church*, 3 vols. (New York: Longmans, 1912–1924). A lengthy standard account; very readable.

Kenneth Latourette, *History of Christianity* (New York: Harper and Row, 1975). A short survey, balanced and sympathetic.

Hans Lietzmann, *The Beginnings of the Christian Church, The Founding of the Church Universal, From Constantine to Julian,* and *The Era of the Church Fathers,* trans. B. L. Woolf (Guildford: Butterworth, 1949–1951). A learned and well-written survey of the early church.

Arthur C. McGiffert, *A History of Christian Thought,* Vol. I (New York: Scribner's, 1932). A good, brief account from a Protestant position.

Henry B. Parkes, *Gods and Men: The Origins of Western Culture* (New York: Knopf, 1959). A clear and sympathetic account; includes a fine reading list.

Richard M. Pope, *The Church and Its Culture* (St. Louis: Bethany, 1965). A brief, sympathetic account; includes a full bibliography.

Special Studies

Peter R. L. Brown, *Augustine of Hippo* (Berkeley: University of California Press, 1967). A brilliant, learned, and well-written biography; takes all modern scholarship into account.

Peter R. L. Brown, *The World of Late Antiquity* (New York: Harcourt, 1971). A lively exploration of A.D. 150 to 750.

Rudolf Bultman, *Primitive Christianity in Its Contemporary Setting,* trans. R. H. Fuller (Philadelphia: Fortress, 1980). An up-to-date, scholarly treatment.

Millar M. Burrows, *The Dead Sea Scrolls* (Grand Rapids, Mich.: Baker Books, 1978). Of the many books on the subject this is perhaps the most useful for the student of general history.

Franz Cumont, *The Oriental Religions in Roman Paganism* (New York: Dover, 1911). A classic introduction to the general religious climate in which Christianity took root.

Jean Danielou, *The Theology of Jewish Christianity,* trans. and ed. John A. Baker (London: Darton, Longman and Todd, 1964). The fullest treatment of the subject by a great modern authority.

John Ferguson, *The Religions of the Roman Empire* (Ithaca, N.Y.: Cornell University Press, 1970). Up-to-date and comprehensive.

W. H. Frend, *Martyrdom and Persecution in the Early Church* (Grand Rapids, Mich.: Baker Books, 1981). A scholarly yet readable account; includes a full bibliography.

Maurice Goguel, *Jesus and the Origins of Christianity, The Birth of Christianity,* and *The Primitive Church,* trans. H. C. Snape (New York: Humanities Press, 1964). Highly scholarly studies of Christianity through the year A.D. 150.

Erwin R. Goodenough, *The Church in the Roman Empire* (Totowa, N.J.: Cooper Square, 1970). A brief, balanced account directed to the beginning student.

Michael Grant, *The Fall of the Roman Empire: A Reappraisal* (New York: Crown, 1976). An interesting exploration of the ways in which Christianity contributed to social disunity.

Michael Grant, *The Jews in the Roman World* (New York: Scribner's, 1973). A short, though full, account.

Timothy E. Gregory, *Vox Populi: Popular Opinion and Violence in the Religious Controversies of the Fifth Century* A.D. (Columbus: Ohio State University Press, 1979). An excellent analysis of the explosion of popular violence, especially over the councils of Ephesus and Chalcedon.

Richard S. Kirby et al., *Engineering in History* (New York: McGraw-Hill, 1956). An excellent survey, especially good on the Romans.

David Knowles, *Christian Monasticism* (New York: McGraw-Hill, 1969). The best general history; carries the story to the present.

J. H. Liebeschuetz, *Continuity and Change in Roman Religion* (New York: Oxford University Press, 1979). Largely about the late Roman republic and early empire; especially enlightening on cults, magic, and astrology.

Ramsay MacMullen, *Constantine* (New York: Dial Press, 1969). A readable, short biography that provides the most recent views on the various controversies.

Sigmund Mowinckel, *He That Cometh* (London: Oxford University Press, 1956). A study of the Jewish concept of the Son of man.

Arthur D. Nock, *Early Gentile Christianity and Its Hellenistic Background* (New York: Harper and Row, 1964). An important essay with two shorter studies, of which one, "Hellenistic Mysteries and Christian Sacraments," is also a landmark.

Arthur D. Nock, *St. Paul* (Oxford: Oxford University Press, 1955). A classic treatment; originally published in 1938.

Jaroslav Pelikan, *The Christian Tradition: A History of the Development of Doctrine* (Chicago: University of Chicago Press, 1977). The first two volumes of this massive study examine the growth of doctrinal argumentation to A.D. 600.

Jaroslav Pelikan, *Jesus through the Centuries: His Place in the History of Culture* (New Haven: Yale University Press, 1985). The best introduction to the subject.

Reader's Digest Atlas of the Bible (Pleasantville, N.Y.: Reader's Digest Association, 1981). Good maps and informative illustrations are combined with accurate popular histories of the events recounted in the Old and New Testaments.

A. J. Toynbee, ed., *The Crucible of Christianity* (New York: World, 1969). Learned essays by leading scholars, including the editor, on Judaism, Hellenism, and the historical background of Christianity; splendidly illustrated.

F. W. Walbank, *The Awful Revolution: The Decline of the Roman Empire in the West* (Toronto: University of Toronto Press, 1969). A controversial book that emphasizes slavery rather than political disunity, inflation, or religion as the engine of Rome's destruction.

Sources

The New Testament is the best source reading. The inquisitive reader may wish to compare several versions: the Authorized version (many editions) is also called the King James version; the Revised Standard version (Nelson, 1952) has received some unfavorable comment both from literary reviewers and from fundamentalist Protestants; a recent American edition of the Douay (Roman Catholic version) was published in 1950 (Catholic Book Publishing Company); finally, there is an American Protestant version by Smith and Goodspeed (University of Chicago, 1939).

Next to the New Testament may be ranked the writings of St. Augustine: his spiritual autobiography, *The Confessions,* trans. J. F. Sheed (New York: Sheed and Ward, 1947), and *The City of God,* trans. G. E. McCracken, 6 vols. (Cambridge, Mass.: Harvard University, Loeb Classical Library, n.d.).

H. S. Bettenson, ed., *Documents of the Christian Church,* 2d ed. (Oxford: Oxford University Press, 1963). An excellent collection, accompanied by enlightening summaries and editorial comments; useful not only for the early period but also for the whole history of Christianity.

P. R. Coleman-Norton, ed., *Roman State and Christian Church,* 3 vols. (London: S.P.C.K., 1966). Translations of the key legal documents through 535.

CHAPTER 5: THE EARLY MIDDLE AGES IN EUROPE

General Accounts

Maurice Barley, *Houses and History* (London: Faber and Faber, 1986). Why we live in the houses we do.

Geoffrey Barraclough, *The Medieval Papacy* (New York: Norton, 1979). Lively general survey.

Marc Bloch, *Slavery and Serfdom in the Middle Ages* (Berkeley: University of California Press, 1975). Corrects the long-maintained notion that the church systematically opposed slavery.

Christopher Dawson, *The Making of Europe* (New York: New American Library, 1956). A scholarly account.

Alfons Dopsch, *The Economic and Social Foundations of European Civilization* (New York: Gordon Press, 1969). An influential German work that emphasizes the continuity between the fifth and eleventh centuries rather than a specific beginning period for the "Middle Ages," as defined by others.

Georges Duby, *Rural Economy and Country Life in the Medieval West* (Columbia: University of South Carolina Press, 1968). Translation of Duby's work on the manorial economy by Cynthia Postan.

Lina Eckenstein, *Woman under Monasticism* (New York: Russell, 1963). Covers the years 500 to 1500 in detail.

Robert Folz, *The Concept of Empire in Western Europe from the Fifth to* the Fourteenth Century (Westport, Conn.: Greenwood, 1980). Especially informative on Charlemagne and the law.

Richard Hodges and David Whitehouse, Mohammed, Charlemagne and the Origins of Europe: Archaeology and the Pirenne Thesis (London: Duckworth, 1984). Fresh, very short reexamination of cultural contact.

Harold V. Livermore, The Origins of Spain and Portugal (London: Allen and Unwin, 1971). Covers the later Roman empire, the Hispano-Gothic kingdom of Toledo, and the Muslim invasions.

Robert S. Lopez, The Birth of Europe (New York: M. Evans, 1967). Fine, original summary.

Alexander Murray, Reason and Society in the Middle Ages (Oxford: Clarendon Press, 1978). Complex, fresh examination of theory and practice.

P. H. Sawyer, From Roman Britain to Norman England (New York: St. Martin's, 1979). Significantly alters earlier views on the Mercians and Vikings.

Norman Zacour, An Introduction to Medieval Institutions (Toronto: Macmillan, 1969). Concise survey.

Western Europe

The Cambridge Medieval History, 2d ed. (Cambridge: Cambridge University Press, 1964–1968). One of the few scholarly surveys of the whole period in a single volume.

Christopher Dawson, The Making of Europe (New York: New American Library, 1956). A scholarly account.

Deno J. Geanakoplos, Medieval Western Civilization and the Byzantine and Islamic Worlds (Lexington, Mass.: D. C. Heath, 1979). Perhaps the best general history on the interaction of the three cultures.

James Graham-Campbell and Adfydd Kidd, The Vikings (New York: Morrow, 1980). Well-illustrated; incorporates the most recent views.

Archibald R. Lewis, The Development of Southern French and Catalan Society, 718–1050 (New York: AMS Press, 1981). Excellent on the Carolingians.

Ferdinand Lot, The End of the Ancient World and the Beginnings of the Middle Ages (New York: Knopf, 1931). A balanced survey by a French historian.

Lucien Musset, The Germanic Invasions: The Making of Europe, A.D. 400–600 (University Park: Pennsylvania State University Press, 1975). A fine translation of a judicious French work.

Joseph F. O'Callaghan, A History of Medieval Spain (Ithaca N.Y.: Cornell University Press, 1975). Full and fine coverage from 415 to 1479.

E. A. Thompson, The Early Germans (Oxford: Clarendon Press, 1965). A brief, up-to-date general survey.

John M. Wallace-Hadrill, The Barbarian West: The Early Middle Ages, A.D. 400–1000 (New York: Harper and Row, 1967). Brief up-to-date account.

Special Studies

J. D. Bernal, Science in History, Vol. I: The Emergence of Science (London: C. A. Watts, 1969). Clear introductory account.

Peter H. Blair, Roman Britain and Early England, 55 B.C.–871 A.D. (New York: Norton, 1966). Supplements Stenton (see later entry) and is equally scholarly.

Marc Bloch, Feudal Society, 2 vols. (Chicago: University of Chicago Press, 1961–1964). The masterpeice of a great French scholar.

Ernest Brehaut, An Encyclopedist of the Dark Ages: Isidore of Seville (New York: B. Franklin, 1967). A revival of a long-neglected figure.

Christopher N. Brooke, The Saxon and Norman Kings (London: Batsford, 1963). The first nine (of thirteen) chapters relate the story of the kingship from the reign of Canute in authoritative, up-to-date, crisp prose.

Raymond W. Chambers, Beowulf: An Introduction to the Study of the Poem,

suppl. C. L. Wrenn, 3d ed. (Cambridge: Cambridge University Press, 1959). A full compendium of the scholarship on the poem.

J. H. Clapman and Eileen Power, eds., The Cambridge Economic History, Vol. I (Cambridge: Cambridge University Press, 1941). A scholarly study of agrarian life in the Middle Ages.

Lowrie J. Daly, Benedictine Monasticism: Its Formation and Development through the Twelfth Century (New York: Sheed and Ward, 1965). A general account of a major monastic order.

Samuel Dill, Roman Society in Gaul in the Merovingian Age (Totowa, N.J.: Rowman, 1970), and Roman Society in the Last Century of the Western Empire (Philadelphia: R. West, 1979). Useful older social and cultural accounts.

Jean Dunrabin, France in the Making, 843–1180 (Oxford: Oxford University Press, 1985). Complex analytical study.

Heinrich Fichtenau, The Carolingian Empire: The Age of Charlemagne (Toronto: University of Toronto Press, 1979). A competent study.

Charles H. Haskins, The Normans in European History (New York: Ungar, 1966). A readable and sympathetic introduction; largely covers the later period.

Edward James, Visigothic Spain: New Approaches (Oxford: Clarendon, 1980). Fascinating collection of essays; good on freedmen and on Isidore of Seville.

Gwyn Jones, The Norse Atlantic Saga (New York: Oxford University Press, 1964), and A History of the Vikings (Oxford: Oxford University Press, 1968). Two excellent studies.

David Knowles, Christian Monasticism (New York: McGraw-Hill, 1969). Readable short history.

Max L. Laistner and H. H. King, Thought and Letters in Western Europe, A.D. 500–900, 2d ed. (Ithaca, N.Y.: Cornell University Press, 1966). A good scholarly study.

K. J. Leyser, Rule and Conflict in an Early Medieval Society: Ottonian Saxony (Bloomington: Indiana University Press, 1980). An original, well-researched case study.

Otto J. Maenchen-Helfer, The World of the Huns (Berkeley: University of California Press, 1973). Scholarly, detailed, authoritative work.

Henri Pirenne, Mohammed and Charlemagne (New York: Barnes and Noble, 1968). Propounds and defends the highly controversial thesis that the Arab conquest of the Mediterranean harmed western Europe more than the German invasions had done.

Edward K. Rand, Founders of the Middle Ages (Cambridge, Mass.: Harvard University Press, 1928). Excellent essays on early medieval men of letters.

F. M. Stenton, Anglo-Saxon England (New York: Gordon Press, 1977). A standard account.

Carl Stephenson, Medieval Feudalism (Ithaca, N.Y.: Cornell University Press, 1967). A quite simple introductory manual.

Dorothy Whitelock, The Beginnings of English Society (London: Penguin, 1964). A briefer introduction to Anglo-Saxon England.

David M. Wilson, The Anglo-Saxons, rev. ed. (London: Penguin, 1971). An excellent summary account of Anglo-Saxon archaeology.

Richard Winston, Charlemagne: From the Hammer to the Cross (New York: Harper and Row, 1968). An excellent biography.

Sources

Bede, the Venerable, A History of the English Church and People, trans. Leo Sherley-Price (New York: Penguin, 1955). A readable new edition.

Beowulf, trans. Kevin Crossley-Holland (New York: Farrar, Straus and Giroux, 1968). A good new translation.

Arthur J. Grant, ed., Early Lives of Charlemagne (London: Chatto and Windus, 1922). Extracts.

Gregory of Tours, History of the Franks, ed. O. M. Dalton (Oxford: Clarendon Press, 1927). The account of a sixth-century historian.

Sidonius, Poems and Letters, trans. W. B. Anderson (Cambridge, Mass.: Harvard University Press, 1936). The observations of a fifth-century Roman aristocrat.

CHAPTER 6: BYZANTIUM AND ISLAM

General Accounts

Wilson B. Bishai, Humanities in the Arabic-Islamic World (Dubuque, Iowa: William C. Brown, 1973). Concise, learned, up-to-date.

The Cambridge Medieval History, Vol. IV: The Byzantine Empire. Part 1: Byzantium and Its Neighbours, ed. J. M. Hussey (Cambridge: Cambridge University Press, 1966). Collaborative work with contributions by many excellent scholars; includes full bibliographies.

Norman Daniel, The Arabs and Medieval Europe, 2d ed. (New York: Longmans, 1979). A fine survey of how the Latin West dealt with the Muslim world.

Michael T. Florinsky, Russia: A History and an Interpretation, Vol. 1 (New York: Macmillan, 1954). A good textbook, solid and accurate.

Hamilton A. Gibb, Mohammedanism: An Historical Survey (New York: Oxford University Press, 1953). An excellent, somewhat dated essay by a leading Western authority on the subject.

Alfred Guillame, *Islam* (London: Pelican, 1956). Very clear, balanced account; especially good on the Koran.

P. K. Hitti, *History of the Arabs from the Earliest Times to the Present*, 10th ed. (New York: St. Martin's, 1970). A detailed treatment; useful for reference.

Joan M. Hussey, *The Byzantine World* (Westport, Conn.: Greenwood, 1982). Useful shorter sketch.

V. O. Kluchevsky, *A History of Russia*, 5 vols. (London: Dent, 1911–1931). The greatest single work on Russian history; its usefulness is impaired, however, by a poor translation.

Bernard Lewis, *The Arabs in History*, 3d ed. (New York: Harper and Row, n.d.). A reliable, short treatment.

Harry J. Magoulias, *Byzantine Christianity: Emperor, Church, and the West* (Chicago: Rand McNally, 1970). Good, brief account of the religious aspects of Byzantine history.

John Julius Norwich, *A History of Venice* (New York: Knopf, 1982). Superb major reexamination.

Georgeije Ostrogorsky, *History of the Byzantine State*, rev. ed., trans. Joan M. Hussey (New Brunswick, N.J.: Rutgers University Press, 1969). A brilliant historical synthesis; includes a rich bibliography.

Fazlur Rahman, *Islam*, 2d ed. (Chicago: University of Chicago Press, 1979). Sound comprehensive introduction; excellent on religious disputes.

Alexander A. Vasiliev, *History of the Byzantine Empire, 324–1453*, 3 vols. (Madison: University of Wisconsin Press, 1952). A good, comprehensive work.

Gustave E. von Grunebaum, *Medieval Islam*, 2d ed. (Chicago: University of Chicago Press, 1961). A learned essay on Islamic culture; in part controversial.

W. Montgomery Watt, *Muhammad: Prophet and Statesman* (London: Oxford University Press, 1974). Clear and informative study.

T. Cuyler Young, ed., *Near Eastern Culture and Society* (Princeton, N.J.: Princeton University Press, 1966). Fine essays on Islamic literature, science, and religion.

Special Studies

Sigfus Blondal, *The Varangians of Byzantium*, trans. Benedikt S. Benedikt (New York: Cambridge University Press, 1979). The best account of the origins and functioning of the Varangian corps.

Peter R. L. Brown, *The Cult of the Saints: Its Rise and Function in Latin Christianity* (Chicago: University of Chicago Press, 1982). Fresh study.

Robert Browning, *Byzantium and Bulgaria: A Comparative Study across the Early Medieval Frontier* (Berkeley: University of California Press, 1975). A fine, fresh review of the "ethnic mosaic" that shaped the relationship.

J. B. Bury, *A History of the Later Roman Empire, 395–802*, 1st ed., 2 vols. (New York: Macmillan, 1889). This is the first edition of a work later revised only through 565. The second edition (New York: Dover, 1957) is one of the best works on the period from 395 to 565.

Charles Diehl, *Byzantine Portraits*, (New York: Knopf, 1927). A collection of excellent essays on important Byzantine personalities.

George Every, *The Byzantine Patriarchate, 451–1204*, 2d rev. ed. (New York: AMS Press, 1978). A good summary.

George P. Fedotov, *The Russian Religious Mind* (Woodside, N.Y.: Northland, 1976). A study of the Kievan period of Russian history from an unusual point of view.

Deno J. Geanakoplos, *Byzantine East and Latin West: Two Worlds of Christendom in Middle Ages and Renaissance* (New York: Harper and Row, 1966). Short, able restatement of the influences of Byzantine culture on the West.

Deno J. Geanakoplos, *Interaction of the "Sibling" Byzantine and Western Cultures in the Middle Ages and Italian Renaissance (330–1600)* (New Haven: Yale University Press, 1976). A well-written examination of cultural interaction which draws in part on sociology.

André Grabar, *Byzantine Painting* (New York: Rizzoli International, 1979). Superb reproductions of mosaics and frescoes.

Joan M. Hussey, *Church and Learning in the Byzantine Empire, 867–1185* (London: Oxford University Press, 1937). Good introduction to the subject.

R.J.H. Jenkins, *Byzantium: The Imperial Centuries, A.D. 610–1071* (New York: Random House, 1967). Reliable narrative.

A.H.M. Jones, *Constantine and the Conversion of Europe* (Toronto: University of Toronto Press, 1979). A sensible and helpful introduction.

Paul Lemerle, *Le premier humanisme Byzantin* (Paris: Presses Universitaires de France, 1971). Though not yet available in English, this is an exceptional reexamination of Byzantine humanism to the tenth century.

Guy Le Strange, *Baghdad during the Abbasid Caliphate* (New York: Barnes and Noble, 1972). A standard work.

Muhsin Mahdi, *Ibn Khaldun's Philosophy of History* (Chicago: University of Chicago Press, 1971). A fine study of the *Muqaddimah*, a pioneering work in sociology and the philosophy of history.

Roy P. Mottahedeh, *Loyalty and Leadership in Early Islamic Society* (Princeton, N.J.: Princeton University Press, 1980). Fine study of how the Hadith—the traditional sayings and actions of Muhammad as reconstructed by Islamic dogmatists—shaped early Islamic society.

Donald M. Nicol, *Church and Society in the Last Centuries of Byzantium* (Cambridge: Cambridge University Press, 1979). Fine, short study of the "inner" and "outer" wisdom in Byzantine religious thought.

Dimitri Obolensky, *The Byzantine Commonwealth: Eastern Europe, 500–1453* (New York: Praeger, 1971). Thorough, well-argued reconstruction of Balkan history.

David T. Rice, *The Art of Byzantium* (London: Thames and Hudson, 1959). A beautiful picture book.

Steven Runciman, *History of the First Bulgarian Empire* (New York: AMS Press, 1980). Lively and reliable.

George Vernadsky, *Kievan Russia* (New Haven: Yale University Press, 1973). Vol. 11 of the Yale History of Russia; authoritative and complete.

Sources

Charles M. Brand, *Icon and Minaret* (Englewood Cliffs, N.J.: Prentice-Hall, 1969). A well-chosen series of excerpts from Byzantine and medieval Islamic sources.

Digenes Akrites, trans. John Mavrogordato (Oxford: Clarendon Press, 1956). The first English translation of a Byzantine frontier epic; includes a good introduction.

Procopius, trans. H. B. Dewing, 7 vols. (Cambridge, Mass.: Harvard University Press, 1914–1940). The writings of a major historian who lived through the events he recounts. His work includes histories of Justinian's wars and of his activities as a builder, and also a scurrilous secret denunciation of Justinian. There is a one-volume Penguin abridgment of the *Secret History*.

Michael Psellus, *Chronographia*, trans. E.R.A. Sewter (New Haven: Yale University Press, 1953). A contemporary account of eleventh century history.

The Russian Primary Chronicle, Laurentian Text, ed. S. H. Cross and O. P. Sherbowitz-Wetzor (Cambridge, Mass.: Mediaeval Academy, 1953). The oldest source for early Russian history.

St. John Damascene, *Barlaam and Ioasaph*, trans. G. R. Woodward and H. Mattingly (Cambridge, Mass.: Harvard University Press, 1967). The transformed life of Buddha. The attribution to St. John of Damascus is no longer regarded as correct. See D. M. Jang's introduction and bibliography.

CHAPTER 7: THE MEDIEVAL WEST: THE CHURCH AND THE EMPIRE

Social and Economic Foundations

William J. Brandt, *The Shape of Medieval History: Studies in Modes of Perception* (New Haven: Yale University Press, 1966). On the aristocratic, clerical, and "scholarly" views of human nature.

The Cambridge Economic History, Vols. I and II (Cambridge: Cambridge University Press, 1944, 1952). Detailed investigations of the medieval European economy: includes chapters by scholarly specialists.

Georges Duby, *The Three Orders: Feudal Society Imagined*, trans. Arthur Goldhammer (Chicago: University of Chicago Press, 1980). A stunning examination of an intellectual problem.

Jean Gimpel, *The Medieval Machine: The Industrial Revolution of the Middle Ages* (New York: Penguin, 1980). Especially good on changing energy resources.

David Herlihy, *The Social History of Italy and Western Europe, 700–1500* (London: Variorum, 1980). A superb reassessment of a range of controversial social subjects.

Paul Hohenberg, *A Primer on the Economic History of Europe* (New York: University Press of America, 1981). A clear survey based on the idea of "the economic surplus."

C. Warren Hollister, *Medieval Europe: A Short History*, 5th ed. (New York: Wiley, 1982). Excellent general survey.

Robert S. Lopez, *The Birth of Europe* (New York: Evans, 1967). Basic work by a distinguished economic historian.

Robert S. Lopez, *The Commercial Revolution of the Middle Ages* (Cambridge: Cambridge University Press, 1976). Short summary presentation of a controversial argument that suggests steady growth from the tenth century.

Sidney Painter, *Mediaeval Society* (Westport, Conn.: Greenwood, 1982). Useful introduction.

Henri Pirenne, *Medieval Cities* (Princeton, N.J.: Princeton University Press, 1952). Classic essay by a notable scholar.

Lynn White, Jr., *Medieval Technology and Social Change* (New York: Oxford University Press, 1966). Scholarly, readable, and full of original insights.

The Church, the State, and the Medieval Empire

John W. Baldwin, *The Scholastic Culture of the Middle Ages, 1000–1300* (Lexington, Mass.: D. C. Heath, 1971). An excellent students' introduction.

Geoffrey Barraclough, *The Origins of Modern Germany* (Oxford: Blackwell, 1957). A good general treatment of medieval Germany.

Geoffrey Barraclough, ed., *Mediaeval Germany, 911–1250*, 2 vols. (New York: AMS Press, 1975). A series of scholarly essays by German historians, conveniently translated and commented upon.

James B. Bryce, *The Holy Roman Empire* (Darby, Penn.: Arden Library, 1978). A brilliant undergraduate essay whose conclusions have been much modified by recent investigation.

Ernst Kantorowicz, *Frederick the Second, 1194–1250* (New York: Ungar, 1957). Scholarly and imaginative treatment.

Richard W. Southern, *Western Society and the Church in the Middle Ages* (New York: Penguin, 1970). Volume II of the Pelican History of the Church, 1970. Authoritative, well written; a fine introduction to the subject.

Gerd Tellenbach, *Church, State, and Christian Society at the Time of the Investiture Controversy*, trans. R. F. Bennett (New York: Humanities Press, 1979). Useful and intelligent.

Walter Ullman, *Medieval Papalism: The Political Theories of the Medieval Canonists* (New York: Methuen, 1949). *The Growth of Papal Government in the Middle Ages*, 2d ed. (New York: Methuen, 1968). *Principles of Government and Politics in the Middle Ages* (New York: Barnes and Noble, 1961). *A History of Political Thought in the Middle Ages* (New York: Pelican, 1965). By one of the leading scholars in the field, whose views are highly controversial.

Church and Civilization

Frederick B. Artz, *The Mind of the Middle Ages, A.D. 200–1500.* 3d ed. (Chicago: University of Chicago Press, 1980). A useful survey.

M. D. Chenu, *Toward Understanding St. Thomas* (Chicago: Regnery, 1964). Standard work translated from the French.

A. C. Crombie, *Medieval and Early Modern Science*, 2d ed. (Cambridge, Mass.: Harvard University Press, 1963). Good introductory account.

Christopher H. Dawson, *Religion and the Rise of Western Culture* (New York: AMS Press, 1977). An admirably sympathetic but also realistic survey in terms of cultural history.

Maurice De Wulf, *Philosophy and Civilization in the Middle Ages* (Westport, Conn.: Greenwood, 1979). Popular lectures by a great medieval scholar of an older generation.

Etienne Gilson, *The Spirit of Medieval Philosophy* (New York: Scribner's, 1936), and *Reason and Revelation in the Middle Ages* (New York: Scribner's, 1968). By a distinguished French scholar, author of many other important works sympathetic to the Middle Ages.

Charles H. Haskins, *The Renaissance of the Twelfth Century* (Cambridge, Mass.: Harvard University Press, 1971). and *The Rise of Universities* (Ithaca, N.Y.: Cornell University Press, 1957). The first is an important work, stressing "modern" elements in medieval civilization; the second is a delightful series of short essays.

David Knowles, *The Evolution of Medieval Thought* (New York: Random House, 1964). Stresses the continuity between classical and scholastic thought.

K. J. Leyser, *Rules and Conflict in an Early Medieval Society* (Bloomington: Indiana University Press, 1980). Revised views on Ottonian Saxony.

D.D.R. Owen, *The Vision of Hell: Infernal Journeys in Medieval French Literature* (Edinburgh: Scottish Academic Press, 1970). A fascinating examination of how hell was depicted in medieval French literature.

Eileen Power, *Medieval People* (New York: Harper and Row, 1963). An admirable set of brief biographical sketches of a half-dozen people from various walks of medieval life.

Hastings Rashdall, *The Universities of Europe in the Middle Ages*, new ed., 3 vols. (Oxford: Clarendon Press, 1936). The classic account; full and readable.

Henry Daniel Rops, *Bernard of Clairvaux* (New York: Hawthorne, 1964). An excellent account translated from the French.

H. O. Taylor, *The Mediaeval Mind*, 2 vols. (Cambridge, Mass.: Harvard University Press, 1949). Sympathetic and objective in its treatment of the Middle Ages, but in some respects outdated.

Sources

B. J. Kidd, *Documents Illustrative of the History of the Early Church* (London: Macmillan, 1941). Multivolume, advanced collection.

Robert S. Lopez and Irving W. Raymond, eds., *Medieval Trade in the Mediterranean World* (New York: Columbia University Press, 1955). Basic collection.

J. M. Powell, ed., *Innocent III, Vicar of Christ or Lord of the World?* (Lexington, Mass.: D. C. Heath, 1963). Succinct collection of excerpts from original sources.

James Bruce Ross and Mary Martin McLaughlin, eds., *The Portable Medieval Reader* (New York: Viking Press, 1956). Broad coverage.

Brian Tierney, *The Crisis of Church and State, 1050–1300* (Englewood Cliffs, N.J.: Prentice-Hall, 1964). A valuable collection of excerpts from original sources; includes particularly authoritative commentary.

CHAPTER 8: THE BEGINNINGS OF THE SECULAR STATE

The Medieval West (see also Chapter 7)

Christopher Brooke, *The Twelfth Century Renaissance* (London: Thames and Hudson, 1969). Concise, clear general statement.

R.H.C. Davis, *A History of Medieval Europe: From Constantine to St. Louis* (London: Longmans, 1972). Clear, succinct, and up to date.

Joseph Gies and Francis Gies, *Life in a Medieval City* (New York: Harper and Row, 1981). Lively, humanizing account.

Special Studies: France

Marc Bloch, *French Rural History*, trans. Jane Sondheimer (Berkeley: University of California Press, 1966). A classic work.

Joan Evans, *Life in Medieval France*, 3d ed. (London: Phaedon, 1969). Good picture of French society.

Robert Fawtier, *The Capetian Kings of France* (New York: St. Martin's, 1960). An up-to-date account.

Amy R. Kelly, *Eleanor of Aquitaine and the Four Kings* (Cambridge, Mass.: Harvard University Press, 1966). A learned and lively treatment; one of the best in English.

Achille Luchaire, *Social France at the Time of Philip Augustus* (New York: Gordon Press, 1976). A well-written account, perhaps overemphasizing the seamy side of life.

Charles E. Petit-Dutaillis, *The Feudal Monarchy in France and England from the Tenth to the Thirteenth Century*, trans. E. D. Hunt (New York: AMS Press, 1980). A clear political analysis.

General Accounts: England

Helen M. Cam, *England before Elizabeth* (London: Hutchinson's University Library, 1950). Excellent overview.

A. R. Myers, *England in the Late Middle Ages* (New York: Penguin, 1952). A useful introduction at the popular level.

Austin L. Poole, *From Domesday Book to Magna Carta, 1087–1216* (London: Oxford University Press, 1955). Well written, sometimes criticized, general examination.

Frederick M. Powicke, *Mediaeval England, 1066–1485* (London: Home University Library, 1948), and *The Thirteenth Century, 1216–1307*, 2d ed. (Oxford: Oxford University Press, 1962). Though needing revision on significant matters of detail, still standard works.

Richard W. Southern, *Western Society and the Church in the Middle Ages* (Baltimore: Penguin, 1979). Superbly balanced, judgmental examination.

Doris M. Stenton, *English Society in the Early Middle Ages* (Baltimore: Penguin, 1952). A good, quite short history.

Special Studies: England

Frank Barlow, *William I and the Norman Conquest* (London: English Universities Press, 1965). Popular.

Reginald A. Brown, *The Normans and the Norman Conquest* (London: Constable, 1969). Well written, authoritative introduction to the subject; excellent for students.

David C. Douglas, *William the Conqueror: The Norman Impact upon England* (Berkeley: University of California Press, 1964). Scholarly.

George L. Haskins, *Growth of English Representative Government* (Boston: Peter Smith, 1948). A clear account of a most difficult and vital subject.

C. Warren Hollister, *Anglo-Saxon Military Institutions on the Eve of the Norman Conquest* (London: Oxford University Press, 1964), and *The Military Organization of Norman England* (London: Oxford University Press, 1965). Excellent scholarly monographs which settle many disputed questions.

James C. Holt, *Magna Carta* (Melbourne, Fla.: Krieger, 1982). The best shorter analysis; challenged on some points.

George C. Homans, *English Villagers of the Thirteenth Century* (New York: Norton, 1975). Interesting study of social organization and behavior.

Sydney K. Mitchell, *Taxation in Medieval England* (Hamden, Conn.: Shoe String, 1977). Discusses central organization and local machinery of taxation.

Sidney Painter, *French Chivalry* (Ithaca, N.Y.: Cornell University Press, 1957). Lively examination of courtly love.

Frederick M. Powicke, *King Henry III and the Lord Edward* (Oxford: Clarendon Press, 1947). Scholarly.

P. H. Sawyer, *From Roman Britain to Norman England* (New York: St. Martin's, 1979). Excellent review.

George O. Sayles, *The Medieval Foundations of England* (New York: A. S. Barnes, 1961). Excellent basic study. With H. G. Richardson, Sayles is coauthor of *The Governance of Medieval England from the Conquest to Magna Carta* (Edinburgh: Edinburgh University Press, 1963), a brilliant and provocative analysis.

John A. F. Thomson, *Popes and Princes, 1415–1517* (London: Allen and Unwin, 1980). The popes in politics in the late Middle Ages.

Bertie Wilkinson, *The Constitutional History of England, 1216–1399* (London: Longmans, 1952–1963). Uses the latest scholarly investigations of a much-debated subject.

Literature

C. S. Lewis, *The Discarded Image: An Introduction to Medieval and Renaissance Literature* (Cambridge: Cambridge University Press, 1968). Original and provocative.

Erwin Panofsky, *Gothic Architecture and Scholasticism* (New York: New American Library, 1957). Controversial and readable.

Helen Waddell, *The Wandering Scholars*, 7th rev. ed. (New York: Barnes and Noble, 1968). Lively account.

Sources

Andreas Capellanus, *The Art of Courtly Love*, trans. J. J. Parry (New York: Columbia University Press, 1941). Materials from Marie de Champagne.

The Chronicle of Jocelin of Brakelund, trans. H. E. Butler (London: Nelson, 1949). Medieval monastery life.

D. C. Douglas and G. W. Greenway, eds., *English Historical Documents, 1042–1189* (London: Oxford University Press, 1953). Volume II of a monumental series.

Joinville and Villehardouin: Chronicles of the Crusades, trans. M.R.B. Shaw. (Baltimore: Penguin, 1977). A fine translation.

The Song of Roland, trans. Patricia Terry (Indianapolis: Bobbs-Merrill, 1977). Captures the drumlike rhythm and the high spirits of the story.

CHAPTER 9: THE LATE MIDDLE AGES IN EASTERN EUROPE

General Accounts

E. S. Creasy, *History of the Ottoman Turks*, 2 vols. (1854–1856), new ed., intro. Z. Zeine (Beirut: Khayats, 1961). Despite its age, still a good general account in English; based on a ten-volume German work.

A History of the Crusades, Vol. I: *The First Hundred Years*, ed. M. W. Baldwin; Vol. II: *The Later Crusades, 1189–1311*, ed. R. L. Wolff and H. W. Hazard; 2d ed., K. M. Setton, general ed. (Madison: University of Wisconsin Press, 1969). Collaborative work with authoritative contributions by many scholars; includes good bibliographies.

Steven Runciman, *A History of the Crusades*, 3 vols. (Cambridge: Cambridge University Press, 1951–1954). The fullest treatment of the subject by a single scholar; goes well beyond the Crusades.

Special Studies

Aziz A. Atiya, *The Crusade in the Later Middle Ages* (Millwood, N.Y.: Kraus, 1965). A study of the propaganda and the expeditions that marked the decline of the crusading movement.

J. W. Barker, *Manuel II Palaeologus, 1391–1425* (New Brunswick, N.J.: Rutgers University Press, 1969). Good monograph on a late Byzantine emperor.

Charles M. Brand, *Byzantium Confronts the West, 1180–1204* (Cambridge, Mass.: Harvard University Press, 1968). Scholarly study of the diplomacy of an important period.

Claude Cahen, *Pre-Ottoman Turkey* (New York: Taplinger, 1968). The only recent survey work in English on the subject; by the leading authority on the period before 1330.

Anwar G. Chejne, *Muslim Spain: Its History and Culture* (Minneapolis: University of Minnesota Press, 1974). Full inquiry into Spain's political and cultural history; strong on Granada.

J. L. I. Fennell, *Ivan the Great of Moscow* (New York: Macmillan, 1961). Valuable monograph.

H.A.R. Gibb and Harold Bowen, *Islamic Society and the West*, Vol. I, Parts 1 and 2 (London: Oxford University Press, 1950, 1956). A useful survey of Ottoman institutions.

Herbert A. Gibbons, *The Foundation of the Ottoman Empire* (Totowa, N.J.: Biblio Distributors, 1968). An older work whose conclusions are again finding favor.

Halil Inalcik, *The Ottoman Empire: The Classical Age, 1300–1600* (London: Weidenfeld & Nicolson, 1973). Recent monograph by a distinguished Turkish scholar; lacks interpretation.

Norman Itzkowitz, *Ottoman Empire and Islamic Tradition* (Chicago: University of Chicago Press, 1980). Excellent brief introduction covering the period to the end of the eighteenth century.

Angus MacKay, *Spain in the Middle Ages: From Frontier to Empire, 1000–1500* (New York: St. Martin's, 1977). Excellent summary with fresh insights into the Inquisition.

Barnett Miller, *Beyond the Sublime Porte* (New Haven: Yale University Press, 1931), and *The Palace School of Mohammed the Conqueror* (Salem, N.H.: Arno, 1973). Studies of the Ottoman imperial palace and the Ottoman educational system, respectively.

Joshua Prawer, *The Crusaders' Kingdom* (New York: Praeger, 1972). A fine study of the Crusader states as European colonies.

Donald E. Queller, *The Fourth Crusade: The Conquest of Constantinople, 1201–1204* (Philadelphia: University of Pennsylvania Press, 1977). A fine, fresh look at the reasons for the crusaders' attack on the Byzantine capital.

D. M. Vaughan, *Europe and the Turk: A Pattern of Alliances, 1350–1700* (Liverpool: Liverpool University Press, 1954). Role of the Ottoman Empire in European diplomacy.

George Vernadsky, *The Mongols and Russia* (New Haven: Yale University Press, 1953). Volume III of the Yale History of Russia.

Speros Vryonis, *The Decline of Medieval Hellenism in Asia Minor and the Process of Islamization from the Eleventh through the Fifteenth Century* (Berkeley: University of California Press, 1971). The title describes well the subject of this massive, scholarly study.

Paul Wittek, *The Rise of the Ottoman Empire* (London: Royal Asiatic Society, 1938). A suggestive essay on the elements that helped to advance the Ottoman state.

Sources

An Arab-Syrian Gentleman and Warrior in the Period of the Crusades: Memoirs of Usamah ibn-Munquidh, trans. P. K. Hitti (New York: Columbia University Press, 1929).

Anna Comnena, *The Alexiad*, trans. E.A.S. Dawes (New York: AMS Press, 1976). The life and reign of Emperor Alexius Comnenus (from 1081 to 1118), by his daughter.

Foucher of Chartres, *Chronicle of the First Crusade*, trans. M. E. McGinty (Philadelphia: University of Pennsylvania Press, 1941). Readable.

William, Archbishop of Tyre, *A History of Deeds Done beyond the Sea*, trans. E. A. Babcock and A. C. Krey, 2 vols. (New York: Columbia University Press, 1943). The greatest contemporary account of the crusaders' Levant.

Index

Note: Pages in boldface locate substantial discussions of entries; pages followed by *m* locate maps.